The Nature of Truth

The Nature of Truth

Classic and Contemporary Perspectives

Edited by Michael P. Lynch, Jeremy Wyatt, Junyeol Kim, and Nathan Kellen

The MIT Press
Cambridge, Massachusetts
London, England

© 2021 Massachusetts Institute of Technology

All rights reserved. No part of this book may be reproduced in any form by any electronic or mechanical means (including photocopying, recording, or information storage and retrieval) without permission in writing from the publisher.

This book was set in Stone Serif and Stone Sans by Westchester Publishing Services, Danbury, CT. Printed and bound in the United States of America.

Library of Congress Cataloging-in-Publication Data

Names: Lynch, Michael P. (Michael Patrick), 1966- editor. | Wyatt, Jeremy, editor. | Kim, Junyeol, editor. | Kellen, Nathan, editor.
Title: The nature of truth : classic and contemporary perspectives / edited by Michael P. Lynch, Jeremy Wyatt, Junyeol Kim, and Nathan Kellen.
Other titles: Nature of truth (M.I.T. Press)
Description: Second edition. | Cambridge, Massachusetts : The MIT Press, 2021. | Includes bibliographical references and index.
Identifiers: LCCN 2020025462 | ISBN 9780262542067 (paperback)
Subjects: LCSH: Truth.
Classification: LCC BD171 .N35 2021 | DDC 121--dc23
LC record available at https://lccn.loc.gov/2020025462

10 9 8 7 6 5 4 3 2 1

Contents

Preface to the Second Edition: Truth in a Post-Truth Age

Michael P. Lynch

The truth, according to Oscar Wilde, is rarely pure and never simple. Given everything that has happened since the first edition of this book—from the wars in Iraq, to Brexit, to the recurring train wreck of US presidential politics—you could be excused for wondering if it exists at all. As more than one commentator has noted, we seem to be living in a "post-truth" society where lies are tolerated and facts are ignored.

So what *is* truth, anyway? That's the question to which this book is devoted. It is a question so philosophical it can seem rhetorical. But it is not, as today's political situation makes clear. If we want to understand why truth matters, we first need to understand what it is.

When we ask about the nature of truth, we are usually interested in what makes a belief or statement true (and others false). Unsurprisingly, philosophers (being, you know, *philosophers*) have been divided, and this collection of essays reflects that fact.

Historically speaking, two ideas, each organized around a central metaphor, stand out. The first idea is that true statements are like maps. The road map Google pulls up on your phone is accurate when it represents the roads as they are and inaccurate when it doesn't. In the same way, the thought goes, a statement is true when it corresponds to the facts as they are. Truth is found; it is a matter of correspondence to the world.

The correspondence theory is an old idea, going back to Aristotle. But it is not without problems. The prevailing objection echoes Wilde: the theory seems to make truth *too* plain and simple. It may be plausible when we are talking about physical things in our immediate environment: roads and bridges, roses and bees. But most of the statements we make are riddled with value judgments, and it is harder to see statements about values as maps. That's because statements like "Not paying your fair share of taxes is wrong" aren't empirically verifiable. Unlike a map, there seems to be no way of checking whether this statement is accurate—which is precisely what makes many folks think that political or moral truth is a philosophers' fantasy.

Elements of this preface first appeared in *The Skeptical Razor*, an online discussion of the value of truth published by Euromind.

Partly inspired by this problem, some philosophers—including Hegel, Brand Blanshard, and William James—have embraced variations of a second idea: that true statements are those that fit into a workable narrative, one that we can use to explain things to ourselves and others. One way to develop this idea is to suggest, as James does, that false statements are those that don't fit, that we can't use, that run up against the other things we believe. Another is to suggest, following Hegel and Blanshard, that truth is more like a coherent story.

There is something right about the coherence theory. Not all statements are like little maps. Statements about values and politics *are* more like stories; very messy, disorderly stories with which we weave the fabric of much of our lives. But the mere coherence of a story can't by itself make it true. You can make any story internally coherent as long as you are willing to say enough crazy stuff (talk to any conspiracy theorist, or just watch the last presidential debate). Mere coherence is too easy to achieve.

To be true, a story has to be more than internally coherent; it also must cohere with what else we know about the world. It has to be nailed down to the outside facts. White supremacists can (maybe) tell an internally coherent story about what they value, but their whole story isn't true because it contains assumptions like "Science tells us nonwhites aren't as intelligent as whites." And that sort of statement would have to correspond to certain measurable facts in the world were it true. (News flash: it doesn't.)

So neither metaphor seems to work across the board. One natural thought is that perhaps this is a sign that we asked a bad question. Maybe truth really doesn't have a nature. Perhaps to say that a statement like "Torture is wrong" is true is just another way of making that statement (that torture is wrong). If so, then it may be that the word "true" is merely a device or logical tool that gives us a way to talk about the world indirectly by talking about our statements. And as a tool, its "nature" *is* its function. No deeper story needed.

That this "deflationary" approach to truth came to dominate discussions of truth at the end of the twentieth century is perhaps not surprising. Philosophical theorizing, like anything else, tends to go through cycles, whether we are talking about the nature of morality, beauty, or identity. Theories are proposed and problems are found and then we start wondering what the fuss was all about in the first place.

Yet here in the twenty-first century, it is growing increasingly clear that the question of truth is not going away. Its persistence owes, in part, to the fact that despite living at a time when information is easier to acquire than ever before, understanding which information is accurate—when we are so often bombarded with conflicting opinions— seems more difficult than ever. At the same time, and partly as a result, a kind of cynicism about truth has become more widespread—as summarized by the presidential spokesperson who said recently that "truth isn't truth." To some, it now seems that the very distinction between what is true and what isn't, between reality and illusion, has little real value, particularly in the social and political realm.

The idea that truth doesn't matter has always been useful to tyrants, who wish that truth would be whatever they say it is. But that is precisely why, for those who wish to resist this thought, the question of truth has taken on a new urgency. And that is why, in my view, understanding the philosophical roots of truth, and our confusions about it, still matters, and matters more now than ever. Truth may be a complicated and distant target whose nature is difficult to discern, but there is value at aiming to understand it, and we must continue to do so while there are still arrows left in our quiver.

Acknowledgments

The editors would like to thank Phil Laughlin at MIT Press and all of the contributors for their work in putting this volume together.

Michael Lynch is particularly thankful to his coeditors for their patience and dedication, and to Terry Berthelot for the same. Jeremy Wyatt is grateful to his coeditors and to the many theorists of truth, both past and present, whose ideas have expanded our understanding of this topic. He is also very grateful to Sohyun Kim, whose encouragement and care have sustained him during the preparation of this volume. Junyeol Kim is thankful to his coeditors and to Mary Gregg. Nathan Kellen is eternally grateful to his coeditors and to Kelsey Pixler.

Original Sources

I Correspondence Theories

Austin, J. L. 1950. "Truth." *Proceedings of the Aristotelian Society*, suppl., 24: 111–128. Reprinted with permission of Oxford University Press.

Russell, Bertrand. 1912. "Truth and Falsehood." Chapter 12 of *The Problems of Philosophy*. Oxford: Oxford University Press.

Sher, Gila. 2004. "In Search of a Substantive Theory of Truth." *Journal of Philosophy* 101(1): 5–36. Reprinted by courtesy of the author and the editor of the *Journal of Philosophy*.

II Coherence Theories

Blanshard, Brand. 1939. "Coherence as the Nature of Truth." From *The Nature of Thought*, vol. 2, 260–279. London: G. Allen and Unwin. Reprinted with the permission of Taylor and Francis Books.

Walker, Ralph C. S. 1989. "The Coherence Theory." From *The Coherence Theory of Truth*, 1–6, 25–40. London: Routledge. Copyright 1989 by Routledge. Reprinted with the permission of Taylor and Francis Books. New material added by the author.

III Pragmatist and Verificationist Theories

Dummett, Michael. 1958–1959. "Truth." *Proceedings of the Aristotelian Society* 59(1): 141–162. Copyright 1958–1959. Reprinted with permission of Oxford University Press.

James, William. 1907. "Pragmatism's Conception of Truth." From *Pragmatism: A New Name for Some Old Ways of Thinking*, 197–236. New York: Longmans.

Misak, Cheryl. 1999. "Truth, Inquiry, and Experience: A Pragmatist Epistemology." Chapter 2 of *Truth, Politics, Morality: Pragmatism and Deliberation*. London: Routledge. Copyright 1999 by Cheryl Misak. Reprinted with permission of the author.

Peirce, Charles Sanders. 1878. "How to Make Our Ideas Clear." *Popular Science Monthly* 12: 286–302.

Putnam, Hilary. 1981. "Two Philosophical Perspectives." From *Reason, Truth, and History*, 49–56. Cambridge: Cambridge University Press. Copyright 1981 by Cambridge University Press. Reprinted with the permission of Cambridge University Press.

Rorty, Richard. 1995. "Is Truth a Goal of Inquiry? Donald Davidson versus Crispin Wright." *Philosophical Quarterly* 45: 281–300. Copyright 1995 by the editors of the *Philosophy Quarterly*. Reprinted with permission of Oxford University Press.

IV   Tarski's Theory and Its Importance

Field, Hartry. 1972. "Tarski's Theory of Truth." *Journal of Philosophy* 69(13): 347–375. Reprinted by courtesy of the author and the *Journal of Philosophy*.

Tarski, Alfred. 1944. "The Semantic Conception of Truth and the Foundations of Semantics." *Philosophy and Phenomenological Research* 4(3): 341–376. Reprinted with permission of Blackwell Publishing Ltd.

V   Deflationary Theories

Bar-On, Dorit, and Simmons, Keith. 2007. "The Use of Force against Deflationism: Assertion and Truth." In Dirk Greimann and Geo Siegwart, eds., *Truth and Speech Acts: Studies in the Philosophy of Language*, 61–89. London: Routledge. Reprinted with permission of the authors.

Hill, Christopher. 2014. "A Substitutional Theory of Truth, Reference, and Semantic Correspondence." Chapter 4 of *Meaning, Mind, and Knowledge*. Oxford: Oxford University Press. Reprinted with permission of the publisher.

Horwich, Paul. 2010. "A Defense of Minimalism." Chapter 3 of *Truth-Meaning-Reality*. Oxford: Oxford University Press. Reprinted by courtesy of the author and the publisher.

Quine, W. V. O. 1990. "Truth." From *Pursuit of Truth*, 77–88. Cambridge, MA: Harvard University Press. Copyright 1990, 1992, by the President and Fellows of Harvard College. Reprinted by permission of the publisher.

Ramsey, Frank Plumpton. 1990. "The Nature of Truth." *Episteme* 16: 6–16. Copyright 1990. Reprinted by permission of Springer Nature.

Strawson, P. F. 1949. "Truth." *Analysis* 9. Copyright 1949. Reprinted with permission of Oxford University Press.

Wyatt, Jeremy. 2016. "The Many (Yet Few) Faces of Deflationism." *Philosophical Quarterly* 66(263): 362–382. Reprinted with permission of Oxford University Press.

VI   Primitivist and Identity Theories

Davidson, Donald. 1996. "The Folly of Trying to Define Truth." *Journal of Philosophy* 93(6): 263–279. Copyright 1996 by Donald Davidson. Reprinted courtesy of the *Journal of Philosophy* on behalf of Dr. Marcia Cavell.

Hornsby, Jennifer. 1997. "Truth: The Identity Theory." *Proceedings of the Aristotelian Society* 97: 1–24. Reprinted with omissions from *Proceedings of the Aristotelian Society* 97. Copyright 1997. Reprinted with permission of Oxford University Press.

VII   Pluralist and Replacement Theories

Blackburn, Simon. 2013. "Deflationism, Pluralism, Expressivism, Pragmatism." Chapter 13 of Nikolaj Jang Lee Linding Pedersen and Cory Wright, eds., *Truth and Pluralism: Current Debates*. Oxford: Oxford University Press. Reprinted with permission of Oxford University Press.

Burgess, Alexis. 2013. "Keeping 'True': A Case Study in Conceptual Ethics." *Inquiry: An Interdisciplinary Journal of Philosophy* 57(5–6): 580–606. Reprinted with permission of Taylor & Francis Ltd.

Edwards, Douglas. 2013. "Truth, Winning, and Simple Determination Pluralism." Chapter 6 of Nikolaj Jang Lee Linding Pedersen and Cory Wright, eds., *Truth and Pluralism: Current Debates*. Oxford: Oxford University Press. Reprinted with permission of Oxford University Press

Lynch, Michael P. 2013. "Three Questions for Truth Pluralism." Chapter 2 of Nikolaj Jang Lee Linding Pedersen and Cory Wright, eds., *Truth and Pluralism: Current Debates*. Oxford: Oxford University Press. Reprinted with permission of Oxford University Press.

Introduction: The Metaphysics of Truth

Michael P. Lynch

> What is truth?
> —Pontius Pilate
>
> Humanly speaking, let us define truth, while waiting for a better definition, as a statement of the facts as they are.
> —Voltaire

In court, witnesses swear to tell the truth, the whole truth, and nothing but the truth. One is expected to know what this means, and in some sense, it is clear that we do. Yet at the same time, truth seems so stubbornly abstract that, like Pontius Pilate, we treat questions about its nature as rhetorical. We frequently avoid it, courageously pursue it, and lament its distortion, but when pressed to say what truth is, we find ourselves tongue-tied and frustrated. The nature of truth seems a mystery.

There are some obvious and not so obvious reasons for this fact. The most obvious is the ambiguity of the word. Even if we restrict ourselves to "true," one can speak of "true friends," "true north," "aiming true," and so on. The sense of the word that concerns philosophers, however, is the sense being assumed in the very first sentence of this introduction. In the courtroom, we want the witness to report what she believes to be true—that is, to express true propositions. This is the sense of the word that matters most in our everyday lives.

Limiting the scope of the question in this way helps somewhat, but not much. As Voltaire's droll remark illustrates, it may seem as if one can define truth only by platitudes, by saying, for example, that true propositions tell it as it is or correspond with the facts. This gets us somewhere, perhaps, but "Truth is correspondence with fact" will remain a platitude unless we can say what "correspondence" and "fact" mean in terms that don't already presuppose an understanding of truth.

A moment's reflection indicates how difficult that task is. One reason is that truth is an extremely basic concept. It is difficult to engage in any theoretical inquiry without employing it. You cannot even argue over a theory of truth without using the concept because to question a theory is to question its truth, and to endorse a theory is to endorse it as true. In comparison, we can easily discuss what it is to be a person, or the nature of justice, without employing those concepts while doing so. But we cannot get behind the concept of truth as we can with these other concepts.

It seems that few concepts are as tightly wound into our thought as truth. Truth, for instance, is deeply connected to belief: when the witness tells us what she believes, this implies that she is reporting what she believes to be true. It is similar with assertion or endorsement: when we assert, we present ourselves as speaking the truth. Truth is also connected to knowledge: one doesn't know that the butler did it unless it is really true that the butler did it. Truth is the central concept of logic as well: an argument is valid in classical logic just when it is impossible for its premises to be true and its conclusion false. And as our platitudes about truth tell us, truth is related to that other mysterious concept, reality. To speak the truth is to speak of reality as it is. The fact that truth is so tightly interconnected with so many other philosophically interesting concepts is another reason why truth seems deep, and why it seems important to understand what truth is.

This connection between truth and other issues often muddies the very philosophical waters we are attempting to measure. Philosophers are frequently interested in different subjects when they ask about truth, subjects that involve the connection between truth and other areas of philosophical interest. Thus, some philosophers who portray themselves as working on truth are actually interested in how we acquire truth, or in justification and knowledge; others are curious about the relation of truth to linguistic meaning; and still others wonder about the relation between truth and logic. These are all important issues, but none are the main focus of this book. For in each of the cases above, the issue is the explanatory role of truth rather than its nature. When inquiring about truth's explanatory role, it would seem that we must have prior knowledge of what truth is. Throughout this book, we will be investigating a diverse array of views about the latter issue.

But what does it mean to ask what truth is? In general, whenever we ask what something is, there are two questions we might be interested in. Suppose that I ask you what gold is. I might want to understand the concept of gold or what the word "gold" means. Alternatively, I might want to know about the underlying nature of the property of gold and the substantive facts about gold (e.g., that it is an element with atomic number 79). Of course, these projects needn't be completely distinct: my concept of gold presumably picks out many important and substantive facts about gold (e.g., that gold is a malleable yellow metal). Yet it also seems clear that I could have a good grasp on the concept of gold without knowing all the facts about its underlying nature.

When philosophers ask what truth is, they are interested sometimes in the concept, sometimes in the underlying nature of the property, and sometimes in both.

With regard to the concept, one might wonder whether "true"—even in its narrower usage noted above—actually expresses just one concept or whether there are various concepts we might have in mind. Moreover, it seems worthwhile to wonder whether the concept is even internally coherent. Philosophical concepts like those of identity, logical consequence, and, of course, truth generate puzzles and outright paradoxes. One of the most famous of these is the liar paradox. That paradox, which emerges when we consider a sentence such as "This very sentence is false" (which if true, is false, and if false, is true) has suggested to some that the very concept of truth needs revision or even replacement.

In the case of gold, giving an analysis of the concept (for instance, by supplying necessary and sufficient conditions for its application) needn't tell you everything about the nature of the property. But in the case of truth, it is somewhat trickier to say how theories of the concept and theories of the property relate. Unlike the case of gold, it would seem that we have no independent, empirical access to the property of truth itself except via reflecting on, or at least using, our concept of truth. Thus, disputes over the property of truth are frequently (but not always) fought on conceptual ground, over how we might best understand the concept of truth. On the one hand, according to this latter method, we learn about the property of truth by learning about the concept. On the other hand, we might hold that as in the case of gold, learning about the concept can tell us much about the property without necessarily telling us everything about that property.

Whichever methodological stance we take, there are two central questions one might ask about the underlying nature of the property of truth. First, does truth even have a nature, and second, if it does, what sort of nature does it have? These questions, respectively, serve as jumping-off points for two major debates about truth (see figure 1.1).

The more traditional of these two debates is the second, concerning what sort of property truth is. Theories that try to answer this question are often called substantive theories of truth since they assume that truth is an important property that requires a substantive and complex explanation. Those who engage in constructing such theories are motivated by questions such as the following: What sort of relationship, if any, do true propositions have to the world? Are all truths verifiable by sense experience? Could even our best theories turn out to be false? Is there such a thing as absolute truth, or is all truth in some way or other subjective or relative? And so on. Broadly speaking, these questions all concern the objectivity of truth. Thus, one of the key issues for substantive theories of truth is that of realism (see the introduction to part I for a more extensive discussion of this question).

While the realism debate continues to be of central importance, much contemporary work on truth concerns the question of whether truth even has a nature to explain. This is the other main debate that we cover in this volume. Since the beginning of the last century, *deflationists* have suspected that the so-called problem of truth was really a pseudo-problem. Driven by the seemingly intractable disputes over the nature of truth, as well as by a broadly empiricist epistemological attitude, deflationists hold that no

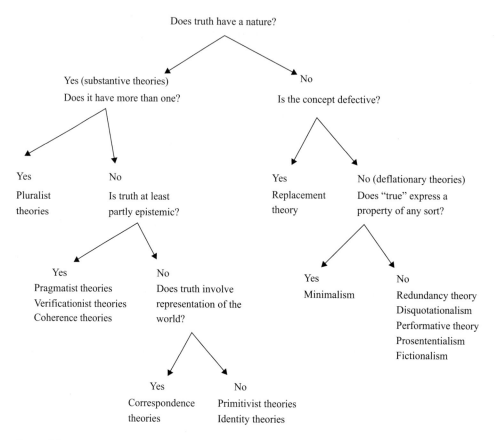

Figure 1.1

single, substantive property is shared by all of the propositions we take as true. Consequently, the word "true" should not be understood as expressing such a property but rather as fulfilling some other function. Put somewhat differently, substantive theorists argue that the various mysteries of truth require substantive metaphysical explanation, while deflationists believe that no such explanation is needed. In their view the alleged mysteries should not be explained but rather explained away.

Although distinguishing the realism debate from the deflationary debate is helpful, we must be careful not to oversimplify. A significant number of the authors in this volume are engaged in both debates. Further, there is a growing consensus among many philosophers that neither traditional, substantive theories nor completely deflationary theories are on the right track. For some, that means rethinking the traditional assumption that truth has only a single nature; for others it means accepting that truth can't be defined; and for others it means replacing the concept altogether. If any of these suggestions are right, we must find new ways to think about this old idea.

Further Reading

Armour-Garb, B. P., and Beall, Jc, eds. 2005. *Deflationary Truth*. Chicago: Open Court. A collection of papers on deflationary theories of truth that contains many of the central contributions to these debates.

Beall, Jc, Glanzberg, M., and Ripley, D. 2018. *Formal Theories of Truth*. Oxford: Oxford University Press. A detailed and user-friendly introduction to the truth-theoretic paradoxes and the formal theories of truth that attempt to address them.

Blackburn, S., and Simmons, K., eds. 1999. *Truth*. Oxford: Oxford University Press. A collection of papers concentrating on deflationism. The introduction by the editors is highly recommended.

Burgess, A., and Burgess, J. 2011. *Truth*. Princeton, NJ: Princeton University Press. A compact introduction to substantive, deflationary, and formal theories of truth.

Edwards, D. 2019. *Truth: A Contemporary Reader*. London: Bloomsbury Academic. A collection of many classic papers on truth organized by an emerging major scholar in the field.

Glanzberg, M., ed. 2018a. *The Oxford Handbook of Truth*. Oxford: Oxford University Press. A wide-ranging and thorough handbook covering many topics related to truth, including topics related to formal theories of truth.

Glanzberg, M. 2018b. "Truth." *Stanford Encyclopedia of Philosophy*. https://plato.stanford.edu/entries/truth/. An accessible and rigorous survey of major theories of truth.

Halbach, V. 2011. *Axiomatic Theories of Truth*. New York: Cambridge University Press. An authoritative study of axiomatic theories of truth.

Horwich, P., ed. 1994. *Theories of Truth*. Aldershot, UK: Dartmouth Publishing. A difficult-to-find but comprehensive collection of classic papers.

Kirkham, R. 1992. *Theories of Truth: A Critical Introduction*. Cambridge, MA: MIT Press. An influential introduction to both substantive and deflationary theories of truth.

Künne, W. 2003. *Conceptions of Truth*. Oxford: Clarendon Press. Arguably the most comprehensive and detailed history of the debates over the nature of truth.

Maffie, J., ed. 2001. *Social Epistemology* 15(4). A special issue containing a number of papers that investigate truth using the methods of comparative philosophy. The editorial introduction is very helpful.

McLeod, A. 2016. *Theories of Truth in Chinese Philosophy: A Comparative Approach*. London: Rowman and Littlefield. An excellent comparative study of thought about truth in early Chinese philosophy.

Medina, J., and Wood, D., eds. 2005. *Truth: Engagements across Philosophical Traditions*. Malden, MA: Blackwell. A unique volume that covers approaches to truth by both analytic and continental thinkers.

Wrenn, C. 2015. *Truth*. London: Polity Press. An excellent introduction to the literature, with special attention to the question of the value of truth.

Wright. C. D., and Pedersen, N. 2010. *New Waves in Truth*. New York: Palgrave Macmillan. An important collection of contemporary papers addressing a broad range of issues pertaining to truth.

I Correspondence Theories

Introduction

Michael P. Lynch, Jeremy Wyatt, and Junyeol Kim

The intuition behind *alethic realism* is that truth hinges not on us but on the world. A proposition is true in this sense when things in the world are as that proposition claims. Some aspect of reality must simply be a certain way—if it is, then the proposition is true; if not, the proposition is false. Minimally speaking, this implies that truth has a nature and that its nature is objective: whether a proposition is true does not depend on what anyone believes (unless, of course, the proposition is about what someone believes).

The most venerable realist view is certainly the *correspondence theory of truth*, the view that a proposition is true just when it corresponds to reality. This is often thought to be the view that Aristotle puts forward in his famous claim, "To say of what is that it is not, or of what is not that it is, is false, while to say of what is that it is, or of what is not that it is not, is true" (*Metaphysics* Γ.7, 1011b26–28, Ross trans.).

Of course, Aristotle's remark and the thought that truth is "correspondence with reality" are no more than platitudes that few would deny. To flesh these platitudes out into a full-blown theory of truth, correspondence theorists must spell out three implicit metaphysical aspects of their position: they must say something about the types of entities that are able to correspond to reality (the *truth-bearers*), the nature of the correspondence relation, and the nature of the "reality," or "parts of reality," to which true truth-bearers correspond (their *truthmaker(s)*).

In his classic essay, Bertrand Russell (chapter 1) argues that it is beliefs that are true or false and facts that make beliefs true. Believing, for Russell, always consists in a believer's relation to two or more objects (what he sometimes calls the *terms* of the belief), which are united by another relation. Thus, my belief that *A* loves *B* consists in my being related to *A*, *B*, and the relation *loving*. Objects related in this way form a *complex unity*; when the objects are related in the exact same order as they are in my belief, then "this complex unity is called the fact corresponding to the belief." A belief is true when it corresponds to a certain complex unity (a fact) and false when it does not.

Correspondence in Russell's theory consists in a structural isomorphism or the *congruence* between the parts of a belief and the parts of a fact. True beliefs fit facts as a hand fits a glove. Russell, however, pays a high price for this structural fit between true beliefs and facts: for the objects of any belief and the objects that compose a complex unity are the same. How then do we understand my (false) belief that *A* loves *B* when there is no such person as *B*? If there is no *B*, it seems that on Russell's theory I can't even have the belief that *A* loves *B*, since any such belief would involve a relation between myself and *B*. Furthermore, how exactly is it that *A*, *B*, and the relation of loving *combine* to form the particular "unity" or fact that *A* loves *B*, as opposed to the rather different fact that *B* loves *A*? We might wonder what, given Russell's theory, could distinguish these facts from one another.

Unlike Russell, J. L. Austin (chapter 2) takes correspondence to be a matter of *correlation* between whole statements, or "sentences as used by a certain person on a certain occasion" and whole facts, or "particular states of affairs." Correspondence here is not structural: states of affairs and statements don't "fit" one another because of the relations of their parts; they match up one to one. Further, Austin insists that correspondence is conventional. Our linguistic conventions determine whether the particular state of affairs I am referring to is of the appropriate type to make my statement true. In a highly influential response to Austin, P. F. Strawson (1950) points out that it is not altogether clear what facts or states of affairs actually are. To talk of the fact or state of affairs that the cat is on the mat seems just like another way of talking about the true statement that the cat is on the mat. As a consequence, Strawson argues, facts sound suspiciously like mere linguistic shadows of true propositions.

William P. Alston (chapter 3) takes a completely different tack. Alston argues that just as we distinguish between the concept of gold and the property of gold itself, so we should distinguish between the concept and property of truth. In Alston's view, we should be no more surprised that our ordinary concept of truth fails to reveal the nature of correspondence or representation than we are that our ordinary concept of gold fails to reveal that gold, in essence, is the element with atomic number 79. Reflection on our ordinary concept of truth tells us only that propositions are true when the world is as they say and that truth is a real property of propositions. Despite his rather minimal take on the concept of truth, Alston forcefully argues that his theory of truth qualifies as a form of alethic realism. First, while our concept of truth does not give us specific information about the underlying nature of truth, the concept does imply that truth has a nature. Second, the concept provides a constraint on how that nature can be understood: truth is objective in the sense that whether a proposition is true does not depend on whether anyone is justified in believing the proposition. Thus, on Alston's account, as on the correspondence accounts discussed above, truth is mind-independent in the sense that, to use Hilary Putnam's expression, it is "radically non-epistemic" (1978, 125).

Most realists about truth *extend* this mind-independence to the truthmakers as well. Facts, states of affairs, or propertied objects are taken to be as they are independently of human concepts or beliefs. The concept of independence here is often cashed out counterfactually: "Stars are mind-independent" means that if there were no minds, there would still be stars. This view of truthmakers, however, is best seen as a form of ontological realism: it is realism applied not to truth but to what exists in the world.

While ontological realism is often thought to entail a correspondence theory of truth and vice versa, it is worth noting that these views can be pried apart. Strictly speaking, one could believe that objects are partly or wholly constituted by their relations to concepts and still hold a correspondence or realist account of truth. For suppose that objects and facts were so constituted. Then, what true propositions correspond to would be mind-dependent. But that does not entail, without further argument, that whether or not propositions correspond to these mind-dependent entities depends on what we believe about those propositions. In this case, propositions would still be made true by, for example, the obtaining of a certain state of affairs; that this state of affairs is mind-dependent is irrelevant (see Lynch 1998).

As we've seen, one can attack particular correspondence theories by criticizing their candidates for truth-bearers, truthmakers, or the correspondence relation. Correspondence theories also face difficult objections in virtue of their alleged implicit commitment to realism about truth. Perhaps the oldest criticism of this type is that they entail a debilitating form of global skepticism. In its traditional form (see, e.g., Kant 1992, introduction, sec. VII), the objection is that since we cannot step outside of our beliefs, we cannot ever check to see if they correspond to the world or not. Therefore, we can never know whether our beliefs are true. A more contemporary way of putting this problem has been presented by Hilary Putnam (see chapter 12 in this volume). According to realism about truth, the truth of every proposition is completely independent of the justification we may or may not have for believing that proposition. If so, then it is possible that any and all of our beliefs could be false—no matter how well justified they are. Some philosophers believe that radical skepticism of this sort is either impossible to answer or absurd, and they therefore are suspicious of any view that entails it. (Those who subscribe to coherence or pragmatist theories of truth, for instance, often cite this worry as the reason they reject realism; see Parts II and III in this volume.[1]) Another general problem for correspondence theories of truth concerns their scope. Traditional correspondence theories take correspondence to be the nature of truth for every proposition. But propositions come in many varieties. Thus, whatever correspondence consists in, it must be a property that can be had by propositions as diverse as *Two and two make four*, *Sherlock Holmes is smarter than Watson*, and *Sexism is wrong*. What sort of relation could possibly have relata that include abstract objects like numbers, fictional characters like Holmes, and a property like sexism? Note that this is a particularly difficult problem for those attracted to a causal/referential variety of correspondence. Presumably, what makes it true that two and two make four is a certain fact involving the numbers two and four as well as the addition function. But numbers and functions are not physical objects and hence are unlikely to enter into any causal relations with anything (Benacerraf 1973). Yet surely mathematical propositions can be true. Further still, it can seem that any realist theory will have problems accounting for the truths of economics, law, and morality.

It is precisely this problem of scope that leads Gila Sher (chapter 5) to present an original version of the correspondence theory. Sher suggests that the problem of balancing unity and disunity is one that arises "for any theory of a broad, complex, and multi-faceted subject matter in any field of knowledge." It comes as no surprise, then, that we face this problem when attempting to construct a comprehensive theory of truth.

Sher attempts to capture the unity of truth by way of what she regards as substantive, universal principles regarding truth. She argues that one of these principles—the *immanence thesis*—entails that truth always consists in correspondence. Despite their importance, however, Sher contends that these principles can only make up part of our overall theory of truth. This is because they are rather general and as such, they fail to describe important differences in how truth behaves across different fields of knowledge (e.g., mathematics and physics). To capture these differences, and in turn the disunity of truth, Sher proposes that we think of correspondence as itself being governed by a "network of interconnected (sub-)principles," which serve to detail different types of correspondence relations. Because Sher aims to do justice to the disunity of truth while also taking truth to always consist in correspondence, she describes her view of truth as a "moderate" sort of truth pluralism. As we will see in part VII, other theorists, such as Michael P. Lynch (chapter 30) and Douglas Edwards (chapter 31), also aim to advance what are often described as moderate pluralist views of truth. By contrast, truth pluralists such as Filippo Ferrari, Sebastiano Moruzzi, and Nikolaj Jang Lee Linding Pedersen (chapter 32) advance a version of what is often called strong alethic pluralism.

In chapter 4, Ruth Garrett Millikan argues that in seeking to understand the truth-conditions of a sentence or a belief, we should investigate the proper function associated with the sentence or belief. Proper functions serve to explain why sentences or beliefs of a given sort have proliferated. Millikan contends that a sentence or belief's proper function determines its truth-conditions. She also contends that in seeking to understand the proper function of certain sentences and beliefs—namely, sentences and beliefs that purport to be about matters of empirical fact—it is helpful to appeal to *correspondence mapping rules* that relate these beliefs or sentences to what they represent. However, she is careful to grant that in attempting to understand the proper functions of other sorts of sentences and beliefs (e.g., sentences/beliefs about morality, mathematics, matters of taste, or religious issues), we may need explanations that are different in kind, insofar as they don't involve correspondence mapping rules. Additionally, she points out that if it proves to be necessary to appeal to facts about the members of a particular culture when explaining the proper function of a sentence (e.g., a moral sentence) that is used within that culture, then it may be necessary to relativize the sentence's truth-conditions to that culture. Millikan's proposal is thus distinctive not only because of her unique suggestions regarding the determinants of truth-conditions but also because of the room she leaves for both pluralist and relativist developments of her views.

Note

1. A related problem for realist theories of truth is noted by Michael Dummett (chapter 11 in this volume). It is common to hold that understanding a statement consists in knowing its truth conditions. To know the truth conditions of a statement is to know the conditions under which that statement is either true or false. But if by "true" the realist means "true independently of what we justifiably believe," then how we could come to know the conditions under which many of our statements are true seems mysterious.

Further Reading

Acton, H. B. 1934–1935. "The Correspondence Theory of Truth." *Proceedings of the Aristotelian Society* 35: 177–194.

Alston, W. 1996. *A Realist Conception of Truth*. Ithaca, NY: Cornell University Press.

Alston, W. 2002. "Truth: Concept and Property." In R. Schantz, ed., *What Is Truth?*, 11–26. New York/Berlin: de Gruyter.

Armstrong, D. M. 1997. *A World of States of Affairs*. Cambridge: Cambridge University Press.

Armstrong, D. M. 2004. *Truth and Truthmakers*. Cambridge: Cambridge University Press.

Austin, J. L. 1970. "Unfair to Facts." In J. O. Urmson and G. Warnock, eds., *Philosophical Papers*, 154–174. Oxford: Oxford University Press.

Barnard, R., and Horgan, T. 2013. "The Synthetic Unity of Truth." In N. J. L. L. Pedersen and C. D. Wright, eds., *Truth and Pluralism: Current Debates*, 180–196. New York: Oxford University Press.

Barnard, R., and Ulatowski, J. 2013. "Truth, Correspondence, and Gender." *Review of Philosophy and Psychology* 4(4): 621–638.

Bealer, G. 1982. *Quality and Concept*. Oxford: Oxford University Press.

Benacerraf, P. 1973. "Mathematical Truth." *Journal of Philosophy* 70: 661–679.

David, M. 1994. *Correspondence and Disquotation*. Oxford: Oxford University Press.

David, M. 2015. "The Correspondence Theory of Truth." *Stanford Encyclopedia of Philosophy*. https://plato.stanford.edu/entries/truth-correspondence/.

Davidson, D. 1984. "True to the Facts." In *Inquiries into Truth and Interpretation*, 37–54. New York: Oxford University Press.

Devitt, M. 1997. *Realism and Truth*. 2nd ed. Princeton, NJ: Princeton University Press.

Dummett, M. 1978. *Truth and Other Enigmas*. London: Duckworth.

Englebretsen, G. 2006. *Bare Facts and Naked Truths: A New Correspondence Theory of Truth*. Burlington, VT: Ashgate.

Field, H. 1974. "Quine and the Correspondence Theory." *Philosophical Review* 83: 200–228.

Forbes, G. 1986. "Truth, Correspondence, and Redundancy." In C. Wright and G. MacDonald, eds., *Fact, Science, and Morality*, 29–54. Oxford: Blackwell.

Fumerton, R. 2002. *Realism and the Correspondence Theory of Truth*. Oxford: Rowman and Littlefield.

Horgan, T., and Potrc, M. 2008. *Austere Realism*. Cambridge, MA: MIT Press.

Ingthorsson, R. 2019. "There's No Truth Theory like the Correspondence Theory." *Discusiones Filosóficas* 20(34): 15–41.

Kant, I. 1992 (1800). *The Jäsche Logic*. Part IV of *Lectures on Logic*. Translated and edited by J. Michael Young. Cambridge: Cambridge University Press.

Lynch, M. 1997. "Realistic Minimalism or Minimal Realism?" *Philosophical Quarterly* 47: 512–518.

Lynch, M. 1998. *Truth in Context*. Cambridge, MA: MIT Press.

Moore, G. E. 1953. "Propositions." In *Some Main Problems in Philosophy*, 52–71. New York: Macmillan.

Neale, S. 2001. *Facing Facts*. New York: Oxford University Press.

Newman, A. 2004. *The Correspondence Theory of Truth: An Essay on the Metaphysics of Predication*. Cambridge: Cambridge University Press.

Pendlebury, M. 1986. "Facts as Truthmakers." *Monist* 69: 177–188.

Putnam, H. 1978. *Meaning and the Moral Sciences*. Part 4. New York: Routledge and Kegan Paul.

Putnam, H. 1981. *Realism, Truth, and History*. Cambridge: Cambridge University Press.

Rasmussen, J. 2014. *Defending the Correspondence Theory of Truth*. Cambridge: Cambridge University Press.

Russell, B. 1906–1907. "On the Nature of Truth." *Proceedings of the Aristotelian Society* 7: 28–49.

Russell, B. 1940. *An Inquiry into Meaning and Truth*. London: George Allen and Unwin.

Sellars, W. 1963. "Truth and 'Correspondence.'" In *Science, Perception, and Reality*, 197–224. New York: Humanities Press.

Sher, G. 2016. *Epistemic Friction: An Essay on Knowledge, Truth, and Logic*. Oxford: Oxford University Press.

Sosa, E. 1993. "Epistemology, Realism, and Truth: The First *Philosophical Perspectives* Lecture." *Philosophical Perspectives* 7(1): 1–16.

Strawson, P. F. 1950. "Truth." *Proceedings of the Aristotelian Society*, suppl., 24: 129–156.

Van Inwagen, P. 1988. "On Always Being Wrong." *Midwest Studies in Philosophy* 12: 95–112.

Vision, G. 2004. *Veritas: The Correspondence Theory and Its Critics*. Cambridge, MA: MIT Press.

Wiggins, D. "What Would Be a Substantial Theory of Truth?" In Z. van Straaten, ed., *Philosophical Subjects*, 189–221. Oxford: Oxford University Press.

Wiredu, K. 1985. "The Concept of Truth in the Akan Language." In P. O. Bodunrin, ed., *Philosophy in Africa: Trends and Perspectives*, 43–54. Ile-Ife, Nigeria: University of Ife Press.

Wiredu, K. 1987. "Truth: The Correspondence Theory of Judgment." *African Philosophical Inquiry* 1(1): 19–30.

Wiredu, K. 2004. "Truth and an African language." In L. M. Brown, ed., *African Philosophy: New and Traditional Perspectives*, 35–50. Oxford: Oxford University Press.

Wittgenstein, L. 1922. *Tractatus Logico-philosophicus*. London: Routledge and Kegan Paul.

1 Truth and Falsehood

Bertrand Russell

Our knowledge of truths, unlike our knowledge of things, has an opposite, namely *error*. So far as things are concerned, we may know them or not know them, but there is no positive state of mind which can be described as erroneous knowledge of things, so long, at any rate, as we confine ourselves to knowledge by acquaintance. Whatever we are acquainted with must be something; we may draw wrong inferences from our acquaintance, but the acquaintance itself cannot be deceptive. Thus there is no dualism as regards acquaintance. But as regards knowledge of truths, there is a dualism. We may believe what is false as well as what is true. We know that on very many subjects different people hold different and incompatible opinions: hence some beliefs must be erroneous. Since erroneous beliefs are often held just as strongly as true beliefs, it becomes a difficult question how they are to be distinguished from true beliefs. How are we to know, in a given case, that our belief is not erroneous? This is a question of the very greatest difficulty, to which no completely satisfactory answer is possible. There is, however, a preliminary question which is rather less difficult, and that is: What do we *mean* by truth and falsehood? It is this preliminary question which is to be considered in this chapter.

In this chapter we are not asking how we can know whether a belief is true or false: we are asking what is meant by the question whether a belief is true or false. It is to be hoped that a clear answer to this question may help us to obtain an answer to the question what beliefs are true, but for the present we ask only "What is truth?" and "What is falsehood?," not "What beliefs are true?" and "What beliefs are false?" It is very important to keep these different questions entirely separate, since any confusion between them is sure to produce an answer which is not really applicable to either.

There are three points to observe in the attempt to discover the nature of truth, three requisites which any theory must fulfil.

1. Our theory of truth must be such as to admit of its opposite, falsehood. A good many philosophers have failed adequately to satisfy this condition: they have constructed theories according to which all our thinking ought to have been true, and

have then had the greatest difficulty in finding a place for falsehood. In this respect our theory of belief must differ from our theory of acquaintance, since in the case of acquaintance it was not necessary to take account of any opposite.

2. It seems fairly evident that if there were no beliefs there could be no falsehood, and no truth either, in the sense in which truth is correlative to falsehood. If we imagine a world of mere matter, there would be no room for falsehood in such a world, and although it would contain what may be called "facts," it would not contain any truths, in the sense in which truths are things of the same kind as falsehoods. In fact, truth and falsehood are properties of beliefs and statements: hence a world of mere matter, since it would contain no beliefs or statements, would also contain no truth or falsehood.

3. But, as against what we have just said, it is to be observed that the truth or falsehood of a belief always depends upon something which lies outside the belief itself. If I believe that Charles I died on the scaffold, I believe truly, not because of any intrinsic quality of my belief, which could be discovered by merely examining the belief, but because of an historical event which happened two and a half centuries ago. If I believe that Charles I died in his bed, I believe falsely: no degree of vividness in my belief, or of care in arriving at it, prevents it from being false, again because of what happened long ago, and not because of any intrinsic property of my belief. Hence, although truth and falsehood are properties of beliefs, they are properties dependent upon the relations of the beliefs to other things, not upon any internal quality of the beliefs.

The third of the above requisites leads us to adopt the view—which has on the whole been commonest among philosophers—that truth consists in some form of correspondence between belief and fact. It is, however, by no means an easy matter to discover a form of correspondence to which there are no irrefutable objections. By this partly— and partly by the feeling that, if truth consists in a correspondence of thought with something outside thought, thought can never know when truth has been attained— many philosophers have been led to try to find some definition of truth which shall not consist in relation to something wholly outside belief. The most important attempt at a definition of this sort is the theory that truth consists in *coherence*. It is said that the mark of falsehood is failure to cohere in the body of our beliefs, and that it is the essence of a truth to form part of the completely rounded system which is The Truth.

There is, however, a great difficulty in this view, or rather two great difficulties. The first is that there is no reason to suppose that only *one* coherent body of beliefs is possible. It may be that, with sufficient imagination, a novelist might invent a past for the world that would perfectly fit on to what we know, and yet be quite different from the real past. In more scientific matters, it is certain that there are often two or more hypotheses which account for all the known facts on some subject, and although, in such cases, men of science endeavour to find facts which will rule out all the hypotheses except one, there is no reason why they should always succeed.

In philosophy, again, it seems not uncommon for two rival hypotheses to be both able to account for all the facts. Thus, for example, it is possible that life is one long dream, and that the outer world has only that degree of reality that the objects of dreams have; but although such a view does not seem inconsistent with known facts, there is no reason to prefer it to the common-sense view, according to which other people and things do really exist. Thus coherence as the definition of truth fails because there is no proof that there can be only one coherent system.

The other objection to this definition of truth is that it assumes the meaning of "coherence" known, whereas, in fact, "coherence" presupposes the truth of the laws of logic. Two propositions are coherent when both may be true, and are incoherent when one at least must be false. Now in order to know whether two propositions can both be true, we must know such truths as the law of contradiction. For example, the two propositions, "this tree is a beech" and "this tree is not a beech" are not coherent, because of the law of contradiction. But if the law of contradiction itself were subjected to the test of coherence, we should find that, if we choose to suppose it false, nothing will any longer be incoherent with anything else. Thus the laws of logic supply the skeleton or framework within which the test of coherence applies, and they themselves cannot be established by this test.

For the above two reasons, coherence cannot be accepted as giving the *meaning* of truth, though it is often a most important *test* of truth after a certain amount of truth has become known.

Hence we are driven back to *correspondence with fact* as constituting the nature of truth. It remains to define precisely what we mean by "fact" and what is the nature of the correspondence which must subsist between belief and fact, in order that belief may be true.

In accordance with our three requisites, we have to seek a theory of truth which (1) allows truth to have an opposite, namely falsehood, (2) makes truth a property of beliefs, but (3) makes it a property wholly dependent upon the relation of the beliefs to outside things.

The necessity of allowing for falsehood makes it impossible to regard belief as a relation of the mind to a single object, which could be said to be what is believed. If belief were so regarded, we should find that, like acquaintance, it would not admit of the opposition of truth and falsehood, but would have to be always true. This may be made clear by examples. Othello believes falsely that Desdemona loves Cassio. We cannot say that this belief consists in a relation to a single object, "Desdemona's love for Cassio," for if there were such an object, the belief would be true. There is in fact no such object, and therefore Othello cannot have any relation to such an object. Hence his belief cannot possibly consist in a relation to this object.

It might be said that his belief is a relation to a different object, namely "that Desdemona loves Cassio," but it is almost as difficult to suppose that there is such an object as this, when Desdemona does not love Cassio, as it was to suppose that there is "Desdemona's love for Cassio." Hence it will be better to seek for a theory of belief which does not make it consist in a relation of the mind to a single object.

It is common to think of relations as though they always held between *two* terms, but in fact this is not always the case. Some relations demand three terms, some four, and so on. Take, for instance, the relation "between." So long as only two terms come in, the relation "between" is impossible: three terms are the smallest number that render it possible. York is between London and Edinburgh; but if London and Edinburgh were the only places in the world, there could be nothing which was between one place and another. Similarly, "jealousy" requires three people: there can be no such relation that does not involve three at least. Such a proposition as "*A* wishes *B* to promote *C*'s marriage with *D*" involves a relation of four terms; that is to say, *A* and *B* and *C* and *D* all come in, and the relation involved cannot be expressed otherwise than in a form involving all four. Instances might be multiplied indefinitely, but enough has been said to show that there are relations which require more than two terms before they can occur.

The relation involved in *judging* or *believing* must, if falsehood is to be duly allowed for, be taken to be a relation between several terms, not between two. When Othello believes that Desdemona loves Cassio, he must not have before his mind a single object, "Desdemona's love for Cassio," or "that Desdemona loves Cassio," for that would require that there should be objective falsehoods, which subsist independently of any minds; and this, though not logically refutable, is a theory to be avoided if possible. Thus it is easier to account for falsehood if we take judgement to be a relation in which the mind and the various objects concerned all occur severally; that is to say, Desdemona and loving and Cassio must all be terms in the relation which subsists when Othello believes that Desdemona loves Cassio. This relation, therefore, is a relation of four terms, since Othello also is one of the terms of the relation. When we say that it is a relation of four terms, we do not mean that Othello has a certain relation to Desdemona and has the same relation to loving and also to Cassio. This may be true of some other relation than believing; but believing, plainly, is not a relation which Othello has to *each* of the three terms concerned, but to *all* of them together: there is only one example of the relation of believing involved, but this one example knits together four terms. Thus the actual occurrence, at the moment when Othello is entertaining his belief, is that the relation called "believing" is knitting together into one complex whole the four terms Othello, Desdemona, loving, and Cassio. What is called belief or judgement, is nothing but this relation of believing or judging, which relates a mind to several things other than itself. An *act* of belief or of judgement is the occurrence between certain terms at some particular time, of the relation of believing or judging.

We are now in a position to understand what it is that distinguishes a true judgement from a false one. For this purpose we will adopt certain definitions. In every act of judgement there is a mind which judges, and there are terms concerning which it judges. We will call the mind the *subject* in the judgement, and the remaining terms the *objects*. Thus, when Othello judges that Desdemona loves Cassio, Othello is the subject, while the objects are Desdemona and loving and Cassio. The subject and the objects together are called the *constituents* of the judgement. It will be observed that the relation of judging has what is called a "sense" or "direction." We may say, metaphorically, that it puts its objects in a certain *order*, which we may indicate by means of the order of the words in the sentence. (In an inflected language, the same thing will be indicated by inflections, e.g. by the difference between nominative and accusative.) Othello's judgement that Cassio loves Desdemona differs from his judgement that Desdemona loves Cassio, in spite of the fact that it consists of the same constituents, because the relation of judging places the constituents in a different order in the two cases. Similarly, if Cassio judges that Desdemona loves Othello, the constituents of the judgement are still the same, but their order is different. This property of having a "sense" or "direction" is one which the relation of judging shares with all other relations. The "sense" of relations is the ultimate source of order and series and a host of mathematical concepts, but we need not concern ourselves further with this aspect.

We spoke of the relation called "judging" or "believing" as knitting together into one complex whole the subject and the objects. In this respect, judging is exactly like every other relation. Whenever a relation holds between two or more terms, it unites the terms into a complex whole. If Othello loves Desdemona, there is such a complex whole as "Othello's love for Desdemona." The terms united by the relation may be themselves complex, or may be simple, but the whole which results from their being united must be complex. Wherever there is a relation which relates certain terms, there is a complex object formed of the union of those terms; and conversely, wherever there is a complex object, there is a relation which relates its constituents. When an act of believing occurs, there is a complex, in which "believing" is the uniting relation, and subject and objects are arranged in a certain order by the "sense" of the relation of believing. Among the objects, as we saw in considering "Othello believes that Desdemona loves Cassio," one must be a relation—in this instance, the relation "loving." But this relation, as it occurs in the act of believing, is not the relation which creates the unity of the complex whole consisting of the subject and the objects. The relation "loving," as it occurs in the act of believing, is one of the objects—it is a brick in the structure, not the cement. The cement is the relation "believing." When the belief is *true*, there is another complex unity, in which the relation which was one of the objects of the belief relates the other objects. Thus, e.g., if Othello believes *truly* that Desdemona loves Cassio, then there is a complex unity, "Desdemona's love for Cassio," which is composed exclusively of the *objects* of the belief, in the same order as they had in the belief, with the relation which was one of the objects occurring now as the cement that binds together the other objects of the belief. On the other hand, when a belief is *false*, there is no such complex unity composed only of the objects of the belief. If Othello believes *falsely* that Desdemona loves Cassio, then there is no such complex unity as "Desdemona's love for Cassio."

Thus a belief is *true* when it *corresponds* to a certain associated complex, and *false* when it does not. Assuming, for the sake of definiteness, that the objects of the belief are two terms and a relation, the terms being put in a certain order by the "sense" of the believing, then if the two terms in that order are united by the relation into a complex, the belief is true; if not, it is false. This constitutes the definition of truth and falsehood that we were in search of. Judging or believing is a certain complex unity of which a mind is a constituent; if the remaining constituents, taken in the order which they have in the belief, form a complex unity, then the belief is true; if not, it is false.

Thus although truth and falsehood are properties of beliefs, yet they are in a sense extrinsic properties, for the condition of the truth of a belief is something not involving beliefs, or (in general) any mind at all, but only the *objects* of the belief. A mind, which believes, believes truly when there is a *corresponding* complex not involving the mind, but only its objects. This correspondence ensures truth, and its absence entails falsehood. Hence we account simultaneously for the two facts that beliefs (a) depend on minds for their *existence* and (b) do not depend on minds for their *truth*.

We may restate our theory as follows: If we take such a belief as "Othello believes that Desdemona loves Cassio," we will call Desdemona and Cassio the *object-terms* and loving the *object-relation*. If there is a complex unity "Desdemona's love for Cassio," consisting of the object-terms related by the object-relation in the same order as they have in the belief, then this complex unity is called the *fact corresponding to the belief*. Thus a belief is true when there is a corresponding fact, and is false when there is no corresponding fact.

It will be seen that minds do not *create* truth or falsehood. They create beliefs, but when once the beliefs are created, the mind cannot make them true or false, except in the special case where they concern future things which are within the power of the person believing, such as catching trains. What makes a belief true is a *fact*, and this fact does not (except in exceptional cases) in any way involve the mind of the person who has the belief.

2   Truth

J. L. Austin

1

"What is truth?" said jesting Pilate, and would not stay for an answer. Pilate was in advance of his time. For "truth" itself is an abstract noun, a camel, that is, of a logical construction, which cannot get past the eye even of a grammarian. We approach it cap and categories in hand: we ask ourselves whether Truth is a substance (the Truth, the Body of Knowledge), or a quality (something like the color red, inhering in truths), or a relation ("correspondence").[1] But philosophers should take something more nearly their own size to strain at. What needs discussing rather is the use, or certain uses, of the word "true." *In vino*, possibly, "*veritas*," but in a sober symposium "*verum*."

2

What is it that we say is true or is false? Or, how does the phrase "is true" occur in English sentences? The answers appear at first multifarious. We say (or are said to say) that beliefs are true, that descriptions or accounts are true, that propositions or assertions or statements are true, and that words or sentences are true: and this is to mention only a selection of the more obvious candidates. Again, we say (or are said to say) "It is true that the cat is on the mat," or "It is true to say that the cat is on the mat," or "'The cat is on the mat' is true." We also remark on occasion, when someone else has said something, "Very true" or "That's true" or "True enough."

Most (though not all) of these expressions, and others besides, certainly do occur naturally enough. But it seems reasonable to ask whether there is not some use of "is true" that is primary, or some generic name for that which at bottom we are always saying "is true." Which, if any, of these expressions is to be taken *au pied de la lettre*? To answer this will not take us long, nor, perhaps, far: but in philosophy the foot of the letter is the foot of the ladder.

I suggest that the following are the primary forms of expression:

It is true (to say) that the cat is on the mat.

That statement (of his, etc.) is true.

The statement that the cat is on the mat is true.

But first for the rival candidates.

a. Some say that "truth is primarily a property of beliefs." But it may be doubted whether the expression "a true belief" is at all common outside philosophy and theology: and it seems clear that a man is said to hold a true belief when and in the sense that he believes (in) *something which* is true, or believes that *something which* is true is true. Moreover if, as some also say, a belief is "of the nature of a picture," then it is of the nature of what cannot be true, though it may be, for example, faithful.[2]

b. True descriptions and true accounts are simply varieties of true statements or of collections of true statements, as are true answers and the like. The same applies to propositions too, in so far as they are genuinely said to be true (and not, as more commonly, sound, tenable and so on).[3] A proposition in law or in geometry is something portentous, usually a generalization, that we are invited to accept and that has to be recommended by argument: it cannot be a direct report on current observation—if you look and inform me that the cat is on the mat, that is not a proposition though it is a statement. In philosophy, indeed, "proposition" is sometimes used in a special way for "the meaning or sense of a sentence or family of sentences": but whether we think a lot or little of this usage, a proposition in this sense cannot, at any rate, be what we say is true or false. For we never say "The meaning (or sense) of this sentence (or of these words) is true": what we do say is what the judge or jury says, namely that "*The words* taken in this sense, or if we assign to them such and such a meaning, or so interpreted or understood, *are true.*"

c. Words and sentences are indeed said to be true, the former often, the latter rarely. But only in certain senses. Words as discussed by philologists, or by lexicographers, grammarians, linguists, phoneticians, printers, critics (stylistic or textual) and so on, are not true or false: they are wrongly formed, or ambiguous or defective or untranslatable or unpronounceable or misspelled or archaistic or corrupt or what not.[4] Sentences in similar contexts are elliptic or involved or alliterative or ungrammatical. We may, however, genuinely say "His closing words were very true" or "The third sentence on page 5 of his speech is quite false": but here "words" and "sentence" refer, as is shown by the demonstratives (possessive pronouns, temporal verbs, definite descriptions, etc.), which in this usage consistently accompany them, to the words or sentence *as used by a certain person on a certain occasion.* That is, they refer (as does "Many a true word spoken in jest") to *statements.*

A statement is made and its making is an historic event, the utterance by a certain speaker or writer of certain words (a sentence) to an audience with reference to an historic situation, event or what not.[5]

A sentence is made *up of* words, a statement is made *in* words. A sentence is not English or not good English, a statement is not in English or not in good English. Statements are made, words or sentences are used. We talk of *my* statement, but of *the English* sentence (if a sentence is mine, I coined it, but I do not coin statements). The *same* sentence is used in making *different* statements (I say "It is mine," you say "It is mine"): it may also be used on two occasions or by two persons in making the *same* statement, but for this the utterance must be made with reference to the same situation or event.[6] We speak of "the statement that S," but of "the sentence 'S,'" not of "the sentence that S."[7]

When I say that a statement is what is true, I have no wish to become wedded to one word. "Assertion," for example, will in most contexts do just as well, though perhaps it is slightly wider. Both words share the weakness of being rather solemn (much more so than the more general "what you said" or "your words")—though perhaps we are generally being a little solemn when we discuss the truth of anything. Both have the merit of clearly referring to the historic use of a sentence by an utterer, and of being therefore precisely not equivalent to "sentence." For it is a fashionable mistake to take as primary "(The sentence) 'S' is true (in the English language)." Here the addition of the words "in the English language" serves to emphasize that "sentence" is not being used as equivalent to "statement," so that it precisely is not what can be true or false (and moreover, "true in the English language" is a solecism, mismodeled presumably, and with deplorable effect, on expressions like "true in geometry").

3

When is a statement true? The temptation is to answer (at least if we confine ourselves to "straightforward" statements): "When it corresponds to the facts." And as a piece of standard English this can hardly be wrong. Indeed, I must confess I do not really think it is wrong at all: the theory of truth is a series of truisms. Still, it can at least be misleading.

If there is to be communication of the sort that we achieve by language at all, there must be a stock of symbols of some kind which a communicator ("the speaker") can produce "at will" and which a communicatee ("the audience") can observe: these may be called the "words," though, of course, they need not be anything very like what we should normally call words—they might be signal flags, etc. There must also be something other than the words, which the words are to be used to communicate about: this may be called the "world." There is no reason why the world should not include the words, in every sense except the sense of the actual statement itself which on any particular occasion is being made about the world. Further, the world must exhibit (we must observe) similarities and dissimilarities (there could not be the one without the other): if everything were either absolutely indistinguishable from anything else or completely unlike anything else, there would be nothing to say. And finally (for present purposes—of course there are other conditions to be satisfied too), there must be two sets of conventions:

> *Descriptive* conventions correlating the words (= sentences) with the *types* of situation, thing, event, etc., to be found in the world.

> *Demonstrative* conventions correlating the words (= statements) with the *historic* situations, etc., to be found in the world.[8]

A statement is said to be true when the historic state of affairs to which it is correlated by the demonstrative conventions (the one to which it "refers") is of a type[9] with which the sentence used in making it is correlated by the descriptive conventions.[10]

3a

Troubles arise from the use of the word "facts" for the historic situations, events, etc., and in general, for the world. For "fact" is regularly used in conjunction with "that" in the sentences "The fact is that S" or "It is a fact that S" and in the expression "the fact that S," all of which imply that it would be true to say that S.[11]

This may lead us to suppose that

> i. "fact" is only an alternative expression for "true statement." We note that when a detective says "Let's look at the facts" he does not crawl round the carpet, but proceeds to utter a string of statements: we even talk of "stating the facts";
>
> ii. for every true statement there exists "one" and its own precisely corresponding fact—for every cap the head it fits.

It is (i) which leads to some of the mistakes in "coherence" or formalist theories; (ii) to some of those in "correspondence" theories. Either we suppose that there is nothing there but the true statement itself, nothing to which it corresponds, or else we populate the world with linguistic *Doppelgänger* (and grossly overpopulate it—every nugget of "positive" fact overlaid by a massive concentration of "negative" facts, every tiny detailed fact larded with generous general facts, and so on).

When a statement is true, there is, *of course*, a state of affairs which makes it true and which is *toto mundo* distinct from the true statement about it: but equally of course, we can only *describe* that state of affairs *in words* (either the same or, with luck, others). I can only describe the situation in which it is true to say that I am feeling sick by saying that it is one in which I am feeling sick (or experiencing sensations of nausea):[12] yet between stating, however truly, that I am feeling sick and feeling sick there is a great gulf fixed.[13]

"Fact that" is a phrase designed for use in situations where the distinction between a true statement and the state of affairs about which it is a truth is neglected; as it often is with advantage in ordinary life, though seldom in philosophy—above all in discussing truth, where it is precisely our business to prise the words off the world and keep them off it. To ask "Is the fact that S the true statement that S or that which it is true of?"

may beget absurd answers. To take an analogy: although we may sensibly ask "Do we *ride* the word 'elephant' or the animal?" and equally sensibly "Do we *write* the word or the animal?" it is nonsense to ask "Do we *define* the word or the animal?" For defining an elephant (supposing we ever do this) is a compendious description of an operation involving both word and animal (do we focus the image or the battleship?); and so speaking about "the fact that" is a compendious way of speaking about a situation involving both words and world.[14]

3b

"Corresponds" also gives trouble, because it is commonly given too restricted or too colorful a meaning, or one which in this context it cannot bear. The only essential point is this: that the correlation between the words (= sentences) and the type of situation, event, etc. which is to be such that when a statement in those words is made with reference to an historic situation of that type the statement is then true, is *absolutely and purely* conventional. We are absolutely free to appoint *any* symbol to describe *any* type of situation, so far as merely being true goes. In a small one-spade language tst nuts might be true in exactly the same circumstances as the statement in English that the National Liberals are the people's choice.[15] There is no need whatsoever for the words used in making a true statement to "mirror" in any way, however indirect, any feature whatsoever of the situation or event; a statement no more needs, in order to be true, to reproduce the "multiplicity," say, or the "structure" or "form" of the reality, than a word needs to be echoic or writing pictographic. To suppose that it does, is to fall once again into the error of reading back into the world the features of language.

The more rudimentary a language, the more, very often, it will tend to have a "single" word for a highly "complex" type of situation: this has such disadvantages as that the language becomes elaborate to learn and is incapable of dealing with situations which are nonstandard, unforeseen, for which there may just be no word. When we go abroad equipped only with a phrase-book, we may spend long hours learning by heart—

A$^\text{i}$-moest-fa$^\text{i}$nd-$^\text{e}$tschâ$^\text{r}$woum$^\text{e}$n,
    Ma$^\text{i}$-hwîl-iz-wau$^\text{r}$pt (bènt),

and so on and so on, yet faced with the situation where we have the pen of our aunt, find ourselves quite unable to say so. The characteristics of a more developed language (articulation, morphology, syntax, abstractions, etc.) do not make statements in it any more capable of being true or capable of being any more true, they make it more adaptable, more learnable, more comprehensive, more precise, and so on; and *these* aims may no doubt be furthered by making the language (allowance made for the nature of the medium) "mirror" in conventional ways features descried in the world.

Yet even when a language does "mirror" such features very closely (and does it ever?) the truth of statements remains still a matter, as it was with the most rudimentary languages, of the words used being the ones *conventionally appointed* for situations of the type to which that referred to belongs. A picture, a copy, a replica, a photograph—these are *never* true in so far as they are reproductions, produced by natural or mechanical means: a reproduction can be accurate or lifelike (true *to* the original), as a gramophone recording or a transcription may be, but not true (*of*) as a record of proceedings can be. In the same way a (natural) sign *of* something can be infallible or unreliable but only an (artificial) sign *for* something can be right or wrong.[16]

There are many intermediate cases between a true account and a faithful picture, as here somewhat forcibly contrasted, and it is from the study of these (a lengthy matter) that we can get the clearest insight into the contrast. For example, maps: these may be called pictures, yet they are highly conventionalized pictures. If a map can be clear or accurate or misleading, like a statement, why can it not be true or exaggerated? How do the "symbols" used in mapmaking differ from those used in statementmaking? On the other hand, if an air-mosaic is not a map, why is it not? And when does a map become a diagram? These are the really illuminating questions.

4

Some have said that—

To say that an assertion is true is not to make any further assertion at all.

In all sentences of the form "*p* is true" the phrase "is true" is logically superfluous.

To say that a proposition is true is just to assert it, and to say that it is false is just to assert its contradictory.

But wrongly. TstS (except in parodoxical cases of forced and dubious manufacture) refers to the world or any part of it exclusive of tstS, i.e., of itself.[17] TstST refers to the world or any part of it *inclusive* of tstS, though once again exclusive of itself, i.e., of tstST. That is, tstST refers to something to which tstS cannot refer. TstST does not, certainly, include any statement referring to the world exclusive of tstS which is not included already in tstS—more, it seems doubtful whether it does include that statement about the world exclusive of tstS which is made when we state that S. (If I state that tstS is true, should we really agree that I have stated that S? Only "by implication.")[18] But all this does not go any way to show that tstST is not a statement different from tstS. If Mr. Q writes on a notice-board "Mr. W is a burglar," then a trial is held to decide whether Mr. Q's published statement that Mr. W is a burglar is a libel: finding "Mr. Q's statement was true (in substance and in fact)." Thereupon a second trial is held, to decide whether Mr. W is a burglar, in which Mr. Q's statement is no longer under consideration: verdict "Mr. W is a burglar." It is an arduous business to hold a second trial: why is it done if the verdict is the same as the previous finding?[19]

What is felt is that the evidence considered in arriving at the one verdict is the same as that considered in arriving at the other. This is not strictly correct. It is more nearly correct that whenever tstS is true then tstST is also true and conversely, and that whenever tstS is false tstST is also false and conversely.[20] And it is argued that the words "is true" are logically superfluous because it is believed that generally if any two statements are always true together and always false together then they must mean the same. Now whether this is in general a sound view may be doubted: but even if it is, why should it not break down in the case of so obviously "peculiar" a phrase as "is true"? Mistakes in philosophy notoriously arise through thinking that what holds of "ordinary" words like "red" or "growls" must also hold of extraordinary words like "real" or "exists." But that "true" is just such another extraordinary word is obvious.[21]

There is something peculiar about the "fact" which is described by tstST, something which may make us hesitate to call it a "fact" at all; namely, that the relation between tstS and the world which tstST asserts to obtain is a *purely conventional* relation (one which "thinking makes so"). For we are aware that this relation is one which we could alter at will, whereas we like to restrict the word "fact" to *hard* facts, facts which are natural and unalterable, or anyhow not alterable at will. Thus, to take an analogous case, we may not like calling it a fact that the word "elephant" means what it does, though we can be induced to call it a (soft) fact—and though, of course, we have no hesitation in calling it a fact that contemporary English speakers use the word as they do.

An important point about this view is that it confuses falsity with negation: for according to it, it is the same thing to say "He is not at home" as to say "It is false that he is at home." (But what if no one has said that he *is* at home? What if he is lying upstairs dead?) Too many philosophers maintain, when anxious to explain away negation, that a negation is just a second order affirmation (to the effect that a certain first order affirmation is false), yet, when anxious to explain away falsity, maintain that to assert that a statement is false is just to assert its negation (contradictory). It is impossible to deal with so fundamental a matter here.[22]

Let me assert the following merely. Affirmation and negation are exactly on a level, in this sense, that no language can exist which does not contain conventions for both and that both refer to the world equally directly, not to statements about the world: whereas a language can quite well exist without any device to do the work of "true" and "false." Any satisfactory theory of truth must be able to cope equally with falsity:[23] but "is false" can only be maintained to be logically superfluous by making this fundamental confusion.

5

There is another way of coming to see that the phrase "is true" is not logically superfluous, and to appreciate what sort of a statement it is to say that a certain statement is true. There are numerous other adjectives which are in the same class as "true" and "false," which are concerned, that is, with the relations between the words (as uttered with reference to an historic situation) and the world, and which nevertheless no one would dismiss as logically superfluous. We say, for example, that a certain statement is exaggerated or vague or bald, a description somewhat rough or misleading or not very good, an account rather general or too concise.

In cases like these it is pointless to insist on deciding in simple terms whether the statement is "true or false." Is it true or false that Belfast is north of London? That the galaxy is the shape of a fried egg? That Beethoven was a drunkard? That Wellington won the battle of Waterloo? There are various *degrees and dimensions* of success in making statements: the statements fit the facts always more or less loosely, in different ways on different occasions for different intents and purposes. What may score full marks in a general knowledge test may in other circumstances get a gamma. And even the most adroit of languages may fail to "work" in an abnormal situation or to cope, or cope reasonably simply, with novel discoveries: is it true or false that the dog goes round the cow?[24] What, moreover, of the large class of cases where a statement is not so much false (or true) as out of place, *inept* ("All the signs of bread" said when the bread is before us)?

We become obsessed with "truth" when discussing statements, just as we become obsessed with "freedom" when discussing conduct. So long as we think that what has always and alone to be decided is whether a certain action was done freely or was not, we get nowhere: but so soon as we turn instead to the numerous other adverbs used in the same connection ("accidentally," "unwillingly," "inadvertently," etc.), things become easier, and we come to see that no concluding inference of the form "Ergo, it was done freely (or not freely)" is required. Like freedom, truth is a bare minimum or an illusory ideal (the truth, the whole truth and nothing but the truth about, say, the battle of Waterloo or the *Primavera*).[25]

6

Not merely is it jejune to suppose that all a statement aims to be is "true," but it may further be questioned whether every "statement" does aim to be true at all. The principle of Logic, that "Every proposition must be true or false," has too long operated as the simplest, most persuasive and most pervasive form of the descriptive fallacy. Philosophers under its influence have forcibly interpreted all "propositions" on the model of the statement that a certain thing is red, as made when the thing concerned is currently under observation.

Recently, it has come to be realized that many utterances which have been taken to be statements (merely because they are not, on grounds of grammatical form, to be classed as commands, questions, etc.) are not in fact descriptive, nor susceptible of being true or false. When is a statement not a statement? When it is a formula in a calculus: when it is a performatory utterance: when it is a value-judgment: when it is a definition: when it is part of a work of fiction—there are many such suggested answers. It is simply not the business of such utterances to "correspond to the facts" (and even genuine statements have other businesses besides that of so corresponding).

It is a matter for decision how far we should continue to call such masqueraders "statements" at all, and how widely we should be prepared to extend the uses of "true" and "false" in "different senses." My own feeling is that it is better, when once a masquerader has been unmasked, *not* to call it a statement and *not* to say it is true or false. In ordinary life we should not call most of them statements at all, though philosophers and grammarians may have come to do so (or rather, have lumped them all together under the term of art "proposition"). We make a difference between "You said you promised" and "You stated that you promised": the former can mean that you said "I promise," whereas the latter must mean that you said "I promised": the latter, which we say you "stated," is something which is true or false, whereas for the former, which is not true or false, we use the wider verb to "say." Similarly, there is a difference between "You say this is (call this) a good picture" and "You state that this is a good picture." Moreover, it was only so long as the real nature of arithmetical formulas, say, or of geometrical axioms remained unrecognized, and they were thought to record information about the world, that it was reasonable to call them "true" (and perhaps even "statements"— though were they ever so called?): but, once their nature has been recognized, we no longer feel tempted to call them "true" or to dispute about their truth or falsity.

In the cases so far considered the model "This is red" breaks down because the "statements" assimilated to it are not of a nature to correspond to facts at all—the words are not descriptive words, and so on. But there is also another type of case where the words *are* descriptive words and the "proposition" does in a way have to correspond to facts, but precisely not in the way that "This is red" and similar statements setting up to be true have to do.

In the human predicament, for use in which our language is designed, we may wish to speak about states of affairs which have not been observed or are not currently under observation (the future, for example). And although we *can* state anything "as a fact" (which statement will then be true or false[26]) we need not do so: we need only say "The cat *may be* on the mat." This utterance is quite different from tstS—it is not a statement at all (it is not true or false; it is compatible with "The cat may *not* be on the mat"). In the same way, the situation in which we discuss whether and state that tstS is *true* is different from the situation in which we discuss whether it is *probable* that S. Tst it is probable that S is out of place, inept, in the situation where we can make tstST, and, I think, conversely. It is not our business here to discuss probability: but is worth observing that the phrases "It is true that" and "It is probable that" are in the same line of business,[27] and in so far incompatibles.

7

In a recent article in *Analysis*, Mr. Strawson has propounded a view of truth which it will be clear I do not accept. He rejects the "semantic" account of truth on the perfectly correct ground that the phrase "is true" is not used in talking about *sentences*, supporting this with an ingenious hypothesis as to how meaning may have come to be confused with truth: but this will not suffice to show what he wants—that "is true" is not used in talking about (or that "truth is not a property of") *anything*. For it *is* used in talking about *statements* (which in his article he does not distinguish clearly from sentences). Further, he supports the "logical superfluity" view to this extent, that he agrees that to say that ST is not to make any further assertion at all, beyond the assertion that S: but he disagrees with it in so far as he thinks that to say that ST *is* to *do* something more than just to assert that S—it is namely to *confirm* or to *grant* (or something of that kind) the assertion, made or taken as made already, that S. It will be clear that and why I do not accept the first part of this: but what of the second part? I agree that to say that ST "is" very often, and according to the all-important linguistic occasion, to confirm tstS or to grant it or what not; but this cannot show that to say that ST is not also and at the same time to make an assertion about tstS. To say that I believe you "is" on occasion to accept your statement; but it is also to make an assertion, which is not made by the strictly performatory utterance "I accept your statement." It is common for quite ordinary statements to have a performatory "aspect": to say that you are a cuckold may be to insult you, but it is also and at the same time to make a statement which is true or false. Mr. Strawson, moreover, seems to confine himself to the case where I *say* "Your statement is true" or something similar—but what of the case where you state that S and I *say* nothing but *"look and see"* that your statement is true? I do not see how this critical case, to which nothing analogous occurs with strictly performatory utterances, could be made to respond to Mr. Strawson's treatment.

One final point: if it is admitted (*if*) that the rather boring yet satisfactory relation between words and world which has here been discussed does genuinely occur, why should the phrase "is true" not be our way of describing it? And if it is not, what else is?

Notes

1. It is sufficiently obvious that "truth" is a substantive, "true" an adjective and "of" in "true of" a preposition.

2. A likeness is true *to* life, but not true *of* it. A *word* picture can be true, just because it is *not* a picture.

3. Predicates applicable also to "arguments," which we likewise do not say are true, but, for example, valid.

4. Peirce made a beginning by pointing out that there are two (or three) different senses of the word "word," and adumbrated a technique ("counting" words) for deciding what is a "different sense." But his two senses are not well defined, and there are many more—the "vocable" sense, the philologist's sense in which "grammar" is the same word as "glamour," the textual critic's sense in which the "the" in l. 254 has been written twice, and so on. With all his 66 divisions of signs, Peirce does not, I believe, distinguish between a sentence and a statement.

5. "Historic" does not, of course, mean that we cannot speak of future or possible statements. A "certain" speaker need not be any definite speaker. "Utterance" need not be public utterance—the audience may be the speaker himself.

6. "The same" does not always mean the same. In fact it has no meaning in the way that an "ordinary" word like "red" or "horse" has a meaning: it is a (the typical) device for establishing and distinguishing the meanings of ordinary words. Like "real," it is part of our apparatus *in* words for fixing and adjusting the semantics *of* words.

7. Inverted commas show that the words, though uttered (in writing), are not to be taken as a statement by the utterer. This covers two possible cases, (i) where what is to be discussed is the sentence, (ii) where what is to be discussed is a statement made elsewhen in the words "quoted." Only in case (i) is it correct to say simply that the token is doing duty for the type (and even here it is quite incorrect to say that "The cat is on the mat" is the *name* of an English sentence— though possibly *The Cat Is on the Mat* might be the title of a novel, or a bull might be known as *Catta est in matta*). Only in case (ii) is there something true or false, viz. (not the quotation but) the statement made in the words quoted.

8. Both sets of conventions may be included together under "semantics." But they differ greatly.

9. "Is of a type with which" means "is sufficiently like those standard states of affairs with which." Thus, for a statement to be true one state of affairs must be *like* certain others, which is a natural relation, but also *sufficiently* like to merit the same "description," which is no longer a purely natural relation. To say "This is red" is not the same as to say "This is like those," nor even as to say "This is like those which were called red." That things are *similar*, or even "exactly" similar, I may literally see, but that they are the *same* I cannot literally see—in calling them the same color a convention is involved additional to the conventional choice of the name to be given to the color which they are said to be.

10. The trouble is that sentences contain words or verbal devices to serve both descriptive and demonstrative purposes (not to mention other purposes), often both at once. In philosophy we mistake the descriptive for the demonstrative (theory of universals) or the demonstrative for the descriptive (theory of monads). A sentence as normally distinguished from a mere word or phrase is characterized by its containing a minimum of verbal demonstrative devices (Aristotle's "reference to time"); but many demonstrative conventions are nonverbal (pointing, etc.), and using these we can make a statement in a single word which is not a "sentence." Thus, "languages" like that of (traffic, etc.) *signs* use quite distinct media for their descriptive and demonstrative elements (the sign on the post, the site of the post). And however many verbal demonstrative

devices we use as auxiliaries, there must *always* be a nonverbal *origin* for these coordinates, which is the point of utterance of the statement.

11. I use the following *abbreviations*:

S for the cat is on the mat.
ST for it is true that the cat is on the mat.
tst for the statement that.

I take tstS as my example throughout and not, say, tst Julius Caesar was bald or tst all mules are sterile, because these latter are apt in their different ways to make us overlook the distinction between sentence and statement: we have, apparently, in the one case a sentence capable of being used to refer to only one historic situation, in the other a statement without reference to at least (or to any particular) one.

If space permitted other types of statement (existential, general, hypothetical, etc.) should be dealt with: these raise problems rather of meaning than of truth, though I feel uneasiness about hypotheticals.

12. If this is what was meant by "'It is raining' is true if and only if it is raining," so far so good.

13. It takes two to make a truth. Hence (obviously) there can be no criterion of truth in the sense of some feature detectable in the statement itself which will reveal whether it is true or false. Hence, too, a statement cannot without absurdity refer to itself.

14. "It is true that S" and "It is a fact that S" are applicable in the same circumstances; the cap fits when there is a head it fits. Other words can fill the same role as "fact": we say, e.g., "The situation is that S."

15. We could use "nuts" even now as a codeword: but a code, as a transformation of a language, is distinguished from a language, and a codeword dispatched is not (called) "true."

16. Berkeley confuses these two. There will not be books in the running brooks until the dawn of hydrosemantics.

17. A statement may refer to "itself" in the sense, for example, of the sentence used or the utterance uttered in making it ("statement" is not exempt from all ambiguity). But paradox does result if a statement purports to refer to itself in a more full-blooded sense, purports, that is, to state that it itself is true, or to state what it itself refers to ("This statement is about Cato").

18. And "by implication" tstST asserts something about the making of a statement which tstS certainly does not assert.

19. This is not quite fair: there are many legal and personal reasons for holding two trials—which, however, do not affect the point that the issue being tried is not the same.

20. Not *quite* correct, because tstST is only in place at all when tstS is envisaged as made and has been verified.

21. *Unum, verum, bonum*—the old favorites deserve their celebrity. There *is* something odd about each of them. Theoretical theology is a form of onomatolatry.

22. The following two sets of logical axioms are, as Aristotle (though not his successors) makes them, quite distinct:

(a) No statement can be both true and false.
No statement can be neither true nor false.
(b) Of two contradictory statements—
Both cannot be true.
Both cannot be false.

The second set demands a definition of contradictories, and is usually joined with an unconscious postulate that for every statement there is one and only one other statement such that the pair are contradictories. It is doubtful how far any language does or must contain contradictories, however defined, such as to satisfy both this postulate and the set of axioms (b).

Those of the so-called "logical paradoxes" (hardly a genuine class) which concern "true" and "false" are *not* to be reduced to cases of self-contradiction, any more than "S but I do not believe it" is. A statement to the effect that it is itself true is every bit as absurd as one to the effect that it is itself false. There are *other* types of sentences which offend against the fundamental conditions of all communication in ways *distinct from* the way in which "This is red and is not red" offends— e.g., "This does (I do) not exist," or equally absurd "This exists (I exist)." There are more deadly sins than one; nor does the way to salvation lie through any hierarchy.

23. To be false is (not, of course, to correspond to a nonfact, but) to miscorrespond with a fact. Some have not seen how, then, since the statement which is false does not describe the fact with which it miscorresponds (but misdescribes it), we know which fact to compare it with: this was because they thought of all linguistic conventions as descriptive—but it is the demonstrative conventions which fix which situation it is to which the statement refers. No statement can state what it itself refers to.

24. Here there is much sense in "coherence" (and pragmatist) theories of truth, despite their failure to appreciate the trite but central point that truth is a matter of the relation between words and world, and despite their wrongheaded *Gleichschaltung* of all varieties of statemental failure under the lone head of "partly true" (thereafter wrongly equated with "part of the truth"). "Correspondence" theorists too often talk as one would who held that every map is either accurate or inaccurate; that accuracy is a single and the sole virtue of a map; that every country can have but one accurate map; that a map on a larger scale or showing different features must be a map of a different country; and so on.

25. Austin pursues this line of thought further in *How to Do Things with Words* (Oxford: Clarendon Press, 1962), 139ff.—Eds.

26. Though it is not yet in place to call it either. For the same reason, one cannot lie or tell the truth about the future.

27. Compare the odd behaviors of "was" and "will be" when attached to "true" and to "probable."

3 A Realist Conception of Truth

William P. Alston

Introduction

In this essay I will set out what I call a realist conception of truth and defend it, insofar as that is required. The basic idea is a simple and familiar one. A statement, for example, is true if and only if (iff) what the statement is about is as the statement says it to be (or, more soberly, as the one making the statement says it to be). The statement that this room is lit is true iff what the statement is about, this room, is as it is said to be in making that statement, namely, lit. More succinctly, *the statement that this room is lit is true iff this room is lit*. The content of the statement, what it states to be the case, gives us everything we need to specify what it is for the statement to be true. That, in essence, is the conception of (propositional) truth I wish to defend.[1] It has many distinguished antecedents, reaching back at least as far as Aristotle, who said in a famous passage of the *Metaphysics*, "To say of what is that it is and of what is not that it is not is true" (IV, 6, 1001b, 28). But though the basic idea is very simple, it is not so easy to know how best to formulate it.

I will say something about that task in a moment, though not as much as in Alston (1996), but first I want to explain why I call this a *realist* conception. Though realism is more commonly used for one or another metaphysical position, I find it appropriate to call this conception of truth realist. The reason is this: What it takes to render a statement true is something that is objective vis-à-vis that statement, namely, a fact involving what the statement is about. The truth value of the statement depends on how it is with the world beyond the statement rather than on some feature of the statement itself. In particular, and looking forward to the main competitor of the realist conception, truth value does not depend on the epistemic status of the statement, whether it is justified, warranted, counts as an expression of knowledge, or coheres with some system or other. I will use the term *alethic realism* for the view that the realist conception of truth is the one that is ordinarily used in application to statements, beliefs, and propositions.

Now for more elaborated formulations. There are two things to determine: (1) What to take as truth-value (*T-value*) bearers—that is, what sort of thing is true or false;

(2) How do we say, in general, what, on this conception, it is for a T-value bearer to be true? I will take them in that order.

The Choice of Truth-Bearers

My brief introductory remarks were in terms of *statements*. But since by far the most popular choice for T-value bearers in recent English-speaking philosophy is *sentences*, I must say a word as to why I do not go along with this. First, we must distinguish between sentence types and tokens. A sentence type is the sort of entity that can be uttered and heard on many different occasions. For instance, you and I both utter *the sentence* "I'm hungry." I utter it, the same sentence, many times. Here we are speaking of a sentence type. Each of the utterances of the sentence is a different sentence token. Most discussions of the truth of sentences deal with types. When someone brings out the old chestnut, "Snow is white is true iff snow is white," she is not speaking of some particular utterance of that sentence but rather of what is common to all those utterances. But there are decisive reasons against attributing T-values to sentence types. The most serious one concerns the radical underdetermination of reference by meaning in natural languages. You and I both say, "The indicator on the dial is at 7," but it may be that what I say is true, and what you say is false. The dial I'm looking at reads 7, but you have misread the dial you are looking at. What are we to say of the sentence type "The indicator on the dial is at 7"? If we regard it as a bearer of T-values, we will have to say that it is sometimes true and sometimes false. And it's worse than that. Since many people utter this sentence at various times, the sentence type is constantly changing its T-value. But there are strong reasons against thinking of T-value bearers as so unstable. If I want to know whether it is true that the dial I was looking at reads 7, it is so that I can use that reading in the testing of some hypothesis. If the T-value of a T-value bearer with which I am concerned were constantly changing, or even occasionally changing, I could neither include it nor reject it as a bit of evidence. And the same is true of more practical matters. I am concerned with whether it is true that you are hungry. If it is the sentence type "I'm hungry" that is in question, *that* may well not retain the same T-value long enough for me to prepare food for you. These elementary points have been ignored by many philosophers in this century—primarily, I speculate, because of their preoccupation with artificial, formalized "languages," in which, since it is just stipulated what the referent of each singular term is, the kind of problem just mentioned does not arise.

Recently, such considerations have led many philosophers to switch to sentence tokens as T-value bearers. A particular token can be assigned a stable T-value *provided* the speaker has satisfied the requirements, referential and otherwise, for making a definite statement. An alternative is to continue to ascribe T-values to sentence types but relative to various contextual features that serve to pin down singular reference and other respects in which one token can differ in T-value from other tokens of the same type. So they think of the type "I'm hungry" as having one T-value relative to one speaker and time and another T-value relative to a different speaker and time. On both of these alternatives, things become much less clear cut than they were when sentence types were straightforwardly taken to be true or false. In both cases matters other than purely linguistic ones are brought into the T-value bearer: the speaker, time of utterance, contextual factors that determine the reference of an expression like "the chair," and so on.

However, the sentential choice faces a much more fundamental problem, one that points the way to a superior alternative. So far as I can see, there is no ordinary, non-technical practice of applying true and false either to sentence types or to sentence tokens. Ask someone innocent of Anglo-American philosophy whether the sentence *type* "The chair is broken" (not what someone is asserting by a particular utterance of that sentence) is true or false, and see if he can understand the question.

As for tokens, an utterance like "Is that sequence of sounds you just made with your vocal organs true or false?" has no natural interpretation available to each fluent speaker of the language by virtue of her linguistic competence. But there is a way of introducing such a practice, at least for sentence tokens, as well as for sentence types that do not vary in the ways I have been illustrating. For the token, we consider what statement was made in issuing that token and take the token to enjoy the T-value of that statement. For stable types, like "Snow is white," we consider what statement would normally be made by a standard use of that sentence. And that, in effect, is what people do who assign truth values to sentences. This was implicit in the account I gave above of how sentence types can be assigned T-values *relative to certain other factors*. We pick factors that will affect what *statement* would be made by a particular utterance of the sentence.

But note where this has brought us. To understand what it is for a sentence to be true, we have to use the notion of the truth of a statement. A sentence token is true iff the statement made by uttering that sentence is true. And so even if attributing T-values to sentences is a viable project, it is conceptually dependent on thinking of statements as T-value bearers. Hence statements are more fundamental bearers of T-values.

But in what sense of "statement"? "Statement" is ambiguous between the *act* of stating and *what is stated*, the *content* of the statement. Similarly, "belief," the term for another prominent T-value bearer, is ambiguous between the *psychological state* of believing something and *what is believed*, the *content* of the belief. It seems clear that in both cases it is in the content sense that "true" or "false" applies. When I wonder whether Smith's statement that Clinton will address the nation this evening is true, my interest is in whether it is true *that Clinton will address the nation this evening*, rather than in some feature peculiar to Smith's speech act. And the same holds of beliefs. You say that you believe that Clinton is innocent of the charges brought by Paula Jones, and I say "Do you really think that's true?" What is the referent of "that" here? Not your psychological state of belief, but *that Clinton is innocent of the charges*.

Now for the final step. The content of a belief or statement can be termed a *proposition*. The "that" clauses we use to specify those contents can also be used to individuate propositions. Just as we can speak of the statement that gold is malleable and the belief that gold is malleable, so we can refer to the proposition that gold is malleable by, so to say, detaching the proposition from its status as the content of a statement or belief (or hope, fear, doubt, wondering, or whatever) and hold it up for examination on its own. And just as statements or beliefs can be termed true or false, so can propositions— naturally, since when we engage in the former talk, it is *what is stated* or *what is believed* to which we attribute a T-value; that is, we attribute the T-value to the *proposition* that is the content of the act of stating or believing. Hence we can take *propositions* as the most fundamental bearers of truth values. Statements and beliefs have that status by virtue of the propositions that are their contents, and sentences have that status, if at all, by derivation from statements.

Talk of propositions often raises philosophical hackles, and if I were seriously to address issues concerning the ontological status of propositions, I would never get to my main concerns here. Propositions are variously construed as abstract entities with an independent (Platonic) mode of timeless existence, as sets of possible worlds, as states of affairs that might or might not obtain, as complexes with structures that mirror those of sentences, and so on. Insofar as I have a view on such matters, it is Aristotelian rather than Platonist in that I think that the basic ontological locus of propositions is the acts of stating and the "propositional" attitudes in which they figure as contents. But for present purposes I sidestep all such questions. I take it that if one knows how to use "that" clauses to specify statements, propositional psychological attitudes, and propositions, one has all the working grasp of the notion of propositions one needs to talk and think intelligibly of propositions as the basic bearers of T-values. The ontological chips may be left to fall where they may.

How to Formulate the Realist Conception of Truth

The next issue concerns how to give a general formulation of the realist conception of what it is for a proposition to be true. The initial rough formulation of the truth of a statement as dependent on *what the statement is about* seems less felicitous when applied to propositions as such. But the gut insight is the same. The proposition that this room is lit is true iff the room is lit. Underlying this, and any other formulation concerning a particular proposition, is a general schema, which I will call the T-schema.

(1) The proposition that *p* is true iff *p*.

The similarity to Tarski's famous *equivalence of the form (T)* will not have escaped your notice.

(2) X is true iff p.

But the differences are equally significant.

- Schema (2) is about sentences, while schema (1) is about propositions.
- Schema (2), unlike schema (1), is designed for use with artificial, formalized "languages."
- Schema (2) is to be read in terms of material equivalence. Schema (1) is to be so understood that any substitution instance of the schema is a necessary, conceptual, analytic truth.[2]

Now (1), being a schema rather than a definite proposition, does not amount to a thesis about what it is for a proposition to be true. Nevertheless, it contains the seed of such a thesis. The simplest way to develop the seed into a full-blown plant is to use substitutional quantification to give it a universal generalization.

(3) It is a necessary, conceptual, analytic truth that (p) the proposition that p is true iff p.

This is not objectual quantification, but not because propositions are not "objects." Even if they are, it still doesn't count as objectual quantification, because the variables cannot be replaced by singular referring expressions that pick out objects. They must be replaced by declarative sentences. (Some philosophers try to treat declarative sentences as referring expressions, but so much the worse for them.) And substitutional quantification makes many philosophers nervous. Since I am not among them, I have no objection to treating (3) as a general statement of the position. But for those who do find it objectionable, there are alternatives. We can convey the same conception of propositional truth by going metalinguistic as in schema (4):

(4) Any substitution instance of (1) is a necessary, conceptual, analytic truth.

Anyone who realizes the necessary, conceptual, analytic truth of any substitution instance of the T-schema has grasped the realist conception of truth.

Note that none of this can claim to be a definition of truth, in the sense of a synonym of "true" that can be substituted for "true" whenever it occurs as a predicate of propositions. Even the most explicit formulation, (3), is not even a contextual definition. For even though, as I take it, it is true just by virtue of the meaning of "true" that for any p, p's being the case is a necessary and sufficient condition for the truth of p, I am not willing to admit, as "deflationists" claim, that "It is true that gold is malleable" is synonymous with "Gold is malleable." For the former contains a concept lacking in the latter—namely, the concept of truth. And it seems clear to me that one could understand "Gold is malleable" (or at least simpler proposition-expressing sentences like "The dog is scratching itself") without possessing the concept of truth. What I claim for (3) and (4) is that they are effective ways of bringing out the concept of propositional truth, in that anyone who accepts them is thereby in possession of that concept.

A Defense of the Realist Conception of Truth

When I try to reflect on the question of why I accept this way of bringing out what it is for a proposition to be true, I find it difficult to know how to answer. For (3) and (4) seem to me to be miserable truisms, which no one who fully realized what he was saying would deny. If someone should say, "There is no doubt that oil is thicker than water," but it is not at all clear to me that it is true that oil is thicker than water, how should we respond? I would respond by saying that if the speaker had his mind on what he was saying and had no difficulty with the other terms of the utterance like "doubt" and "clear," then we must judge that he is deficient in his grasp of "true" and that he simply does not have the ordinary concept of propositional truth. It simply doesn't make sense to say, "Oil is thicker than water, but it is not true that oil is thicker than water."

But if this is so truistic, why should I have devoted a sizable book to laying it out and defending it? As for laying it out, the difficulty of identifying the best way of formulating it may be a sufficient reason. But as for defending it, the reason is that many contemporary thinkers deny it, or at least take positions that appear to be inconsistent with it. As Cicero once wrote, there is nothing so absurd that it may not be found in the books of the philosophers. And if it weren't for the fact that philosophers, especially the cleverest among them, are given to espousing and defending what seem to be obviously false positions, the more sensible among us might be at a loss as to how to spend our time. (Or perhaps we would find more useful pursuits!) Against that background I feel it is not a waste of time to exhibit clearly and defend the ordinary way of understanding propositional truth.

A word is in order concerning the relation of the realist conception of truth to various forms of metaphysical realism and anti-realism. Since metaphysical realism is a large and sprawling territory, I cannot properly enter into it in this essay. But I will just stick my toe in. My account of truth is neutral between the historically prominent metaphysical debates between realists and their opponents. The basic point can be put this way. The metaphysical realist and the metaphysical anti-realist differ as to *what* propositions are true or false, but they need not differ as to *what it is* for a proposition to be true or false. This is obvious with respect to what we might call "parochial" realisms and anti-realisms, realism with respect to a certain putative domain of reality: properties, propositions, and other "abstract objects"; physical objects; theoretical entities; moral properties; aesthetic values; God. The "realist" and the phenomenalist about physical objects can agree that their claims are true or false, depending on whether what they are talking about is as they say it to be. The same point can be made concerning realists and instrumentalists about theoretical entities, and concerning theists and atheists. I would even say that the more "objective" forms of idealism, typified by Berkeley, can accept a realist account of truth. On a Berkeleyan idealism, a certain physical fact—for example, that there is a spruce tree in my front yard—turns out to be a fact about the mind of God. But whether it is true that there is a spruce tree in my front yard depends on whether the mind of God is organized as that proposition (interpreted in a Berkeleyan way) would have it organized.

I am prepared to go further and hold that even an ontological relativism like that espoused by Putnam or Goodman is compatible with realism about truth. On these views, what seems to be a purely objective fact (say, about my spruce tree) obtains only relative to a certain conceptual scheme, one to which there are viable alternatives. But if we put the relativity into the content of propositions rather than in the concept of truth (something that Putnam sometimes denies), then we can say, in the spirit of the T-schema, that it is true that, relative to scheme C, there is a spruce tree in my front yard iff relative to scheme C there is a spruce tree in my front yard.[3]

To be sure, what a given philosopher calls *metaphysical realism* may include a commitment to a realist conception of truth, and when that philosopher opposes metaphysical realism, that opposition can be expected to include a rejection of the realist conception of truth. We find this exemplified in, for example, Putnam (1981). But from my point of view, in that book Putnam has linked together what I would regard as a distinctively metaphysical realism ("The world consists of some fixed totality of mind-independent objects") and a realist view of truth ("Truth involves some sort of correspondence relation between words or thought-signs and external things and sets of things") (1981, 49).[4] If we separate out the strictly metaphysical claim, we find that one can deny that without denying the realist conception of truth.

Does the Account Go Far Enough?

Even if one were prepared to admit that my account is accurate, as far as it goes, one might maintain that it does not go far enough. To bring out the basis for this reaction, I need to identify how my account is *minimal*. Its minimality consists in its undertaking the fewest commitments compatible with identifying the concept of truth. It is restricted to bringing out how the truth of a proposition depends, to vary the expression a bit, on whether its content is "actualized" or "realized" in the "world." In the terms I used above, it is confined to affirming the conceptual truth of all instantiations of the T-schema and anything equivalent to that. But traditionally, accounts of truth that are of a generally realist cast have been more ambitious. They have taken truth to consist in some kind of *correspondence* between a proposition and a fact. This is typically spelled out by specifying a kind of structural isomorphism that must hold between a proposition and a fact if the proposition is to be true. And my account is silent about all that. I take this to be a virtue, but the present objection deems it a vice. So which is it?

My answer is that it is both, and to sustain that answer I need to make a distinction. The distinction I need is one that, in other cases, has been prominent in philosophy lately: that between the *concept* of *P* and the *property* of *P*. To take a familiar example, the ordinary concept of water is something like *a stuff that is liquid (in certain temperature ranges), tasteless and colorless when pure, what falls in rain, what is in oceans, lakes, and streams, etc.* The ordinary, pretheoretic concept contains no specification of chemical composition, much less finer physical structure. But empirical investigation has revealed that the *property* of being (pure) water, the property of belonging to that *natural kind*, is *having the chemical constitution* H_2O. This is a feature of the kind that, while compatible with the features represented in the concept, goes beyond them to a significant extent. The same distinction can be made here. Even if the ordinary concept of truth is adequately picked out by my T-schema-based account, it may be that further investigation will reveal additional features of *what truth is*, what the property is whose possession makes a proposition true. To be sure, this case differs from the water case in that the investigation will not be empirical in the same way. It will consist, rather, of reflection on a proposition's being true and of an attempt to specify what is necessarily involved in that. I have just hinted at a direction such an investigation might take: exploring the structures of propositions and facts and spelling out what it takes for the right kind of "match." In these terms I deny that my account does not "go far enough" to identify the *concept*, but I agree that it does not go so far as to spell out features of the *property* that go beyond that. My position on the concept is not committed to the success of any such further characterization, but it is not committed to its failure either.

Moreover, my realist conception of truth is by no means neutral between different ideas as to what further features the property might have. As I will argue below, it sorts ill with accounts of the property of truth in terms of epistemic features of T-value bearers. On a more positive note, it seems clear that the T-schema suggests a correspondence theory of the property; indeed, such a theory seems to be implicit in the schema. The T-schema naturally gives rise to the idea that a proposition is made true by a fact. The dictum that *the proposition that lemons are sour is true iff lemons are sour* is naturally read as saying that the proposition is made true by the *fact* that lemons are sour (rather than that lemons are made sour by the truth of the proposition). We could embody that idea in what might be called a minimalist form of a correspondence theory.

(5) (*p*) the proposition that *p* is true iff it is a fact that *p*.

This is, at most, an inchoate form of correspondence theory because it does nothing to spell out how a fact has to be related to a proposition to make it true. But the T-schema does *exhibit* what it is about a particular fact that makes a particular proposition true; it does so by using the same "that" clause to specify both. We might put this by saying that it is an identity of content that makes that fact, rather than some other, the truth-maker for that proposition. And this talk of identity of content has brought us to the verge of a full-blown correspondence theory, which would go into what the content of propositions and of facts consists in—an attempt that would presumably lead to a specification of something like a structural isomorphism between a proposition and the truth-making fact.

Epistemological Objections to the Realist Conception

Now I want to consider a widespread kind of objection to a realist conception of truth, what I call an *epistemological* objection. By this I mean not an argument that an epistemic account of the concept is superior to a realist one, but rather an argument that is concerned with the epistemology *of* truth, with what it takes to tell whether a given proposition is true. The argument is that this is impossible on a realist conception of truth.

The argument exists in many versions. A prominent one depends on the assumption that determining that a proposition is true, on the realist conception, requires "comparing a proposition with a fact," and it is argued (or more frequently, just assumed) that this is impossible.[5]

Here are some dicta to that effect (in terms of statements or beliefs, rather than propositions, but we have seen to how to translate back and forth):

> Each statement may be combined or compared with other statements, e.g., in order to draw conclusions from the combined statements, or to see if they are compatible with each other or not. But statements are never compared with a "reality," with "facts." None of those who support a cleavage between statements and reality is able to give a precise account of how a comparison between statements and facts may possibly be accomplished, and how we may possibly ascertain the structure of facts. (Hempel 1935, 50–51)

> If meanings are given by objective truth conditions there is a question how we can know that the conditions are satisfied, for this would appear to require a confrontation between what we believe and reality; and the idea of such a confrontation is absurd. (Davidson 1986, 307)

> Justification is a matter of accommodating beliefs that are being questioned to a body of accepted beliefs. Justification always terminates with other *beliefs* and not with our confronting raw chunks of reality, for that idea is incoherent. (Williams 1977, 112)

Neither the claim that to tell that a proposition is true, on a realist account, requires comparing a proposition and a fact, nor the claim that this is impossible is supported by any argument here. And why should we suppose that I have to make any such comparison to discover that a proposition is realistically true? In reflecting on this question, we discover an important distinction between ways of understanding the requirement. It is susceptible of an innocuous interpretation in which whenever I recognize that it's true that this room is lit just by recognizing that this room is lit, I have carried out a comparison of proposition and fact. If *that's* all it amounts to, it is unsurprising that philosophers like those just quoted mount no argument for its impossibility. But presumably they have in mind something more ambitious and (allegedly) more difficult. Thus, it is sometimes made explicit that it is a maximally *direct* awareness of facts and their relation to propositions, along with the epistemic statuses of infallibility and indubitability customarily associated with direct awareness, that is said to be both required by the realist conception and to be impossible. This is suggested by Davidson's (1986) and Williams's (1977) use of the metaphor of *confrontation*. It is more explicit in Rorty's (1979) attack on a realist understanding of truth as presupposing an indefensible account of the mind as a "mirror of nature," as capable of unmediated, foolproof awarenesses of extramental fact.

But why suppose that even an explicit, conscious comparison of fact and proposition requires that one be *immediately* aware of the fact in question? Why wouldn't it be enough to have any sort of knowledge of fact, whether immediate, inductively derived, based on inference to the best explanation, or whatever? So long as we know that the fact obtains, why should it matter how we get that knowledge?

In any event, if we think of a kind of awareness that is properly termed *direct*, even if not infallible and indubitable, such as perception of the immediate environment as viewed by direct realists about perception, why isn't that possible, and why can't that be a basis for determining whether facts and propositions match? Here is a spirited defense of that possibility by Moritz Schlick, in response to the 1935 article by Hempel, from which I quoted above.

> I have been accused of maintaining that statements can be compared with facts. I plead guilty. I have maintained this. But I protest against my punishment. I have often compared propositions to facts; so I had no reason to say that it couldn't be done. I found, for instance, in my Baedeker the statement: "This cathedral has two spires," I was able to compare it with "reality" by looking at the cathedral, and this comparison convinced me that Baedeker's assertion was true. …
>
> Perhaps you say: "But if we analyze the process of verification of Baedeker's assertion we shall find that it amounts to a comparison of propositions." I answer: whatever the result of your analysis may be, at any rate we can distinguish between cases in which a written, printed or spoken sentence is compared with some other written, printed or spoken sentence, and cases like our example, where a sentence is compared with the thing of which it speaks. And it is this latter case which I took the liberty of describing as a "comparison of a proposition with a fact." …
>
> You insist that a statement cannot or must not be compared to anything but statements. But why? It is my humble opinion that we can compare anything to anything if we choose. Do you believe that propositions and facts are too far removed from each other? Too different? Is it a mysterious property of propositions that they cannot be compared with anything else? That would seem to be a rather mystical view. (Schlick, in Macdonald 1954, 232–235)

Against this eminently commonsensical protest by Schlick there is a serious argument from the nature of perceptual cognition, an argument that was prominent in absolute idealism and that has enjoyed a recent revival of influence. This argument picks up on Schlick's surmise that his opponent will claim that his perceptual verification amounts to a comparison between propositions. We find it, to pick one source out of a crowd, in Blanshard (1939). There, in responding to a claim like Schlick's, he writes as follows:

> It [the position Blanshard opposes] assumes that, corresponding to our judgment, there is some solid chunk of fact, directly presented to sense and beyond all question, to which thought must adjust itself. And this "solid fact" is a fiction. What the theory takes as fact and actually uses as such is another judgement or set of judgements, and what provides the verification is the coherence between the initial judgement and these. (Blanshard 1939, 2:228)

This is a form of the currently popular view that perceptual awareness of objects is conceptually structured and, in stronger forms like that of Blanshard's, propositionally structured in such a way as to involve judgments with the propositional content in question. Hence Blanshard takes it that one can't see a cardinal without judging it to be such and such (not necessarily to be a cardinal). And from that he draws the conclusion that the supposed external fact of the cardinal sitting on a branch is really itself a judgment (statement, proposition), rather than a fact correspondence with which could render the judgement true.

But, of course, even if all perceptual awareness is propositionally structured, and even if it all involves judgment (which I do not admit for a moment), it would *not* follow that there is nothing to the perceptual awareness of a cardinal but a judgment. Seeing a cardinal is obviously different from merely judging that a cardinal is there. And that difference reflects something in the perception that is in addition to judgment, some kind of distinctively perceptual awareness of what any judgment that may be involved is about. And so the thesis that perception has a pervasively propositional structure leaves open the possibility that this distinctively perceptual awareness of objects might constitute a presentation, even a direct presentation, of extrajudgmental fact. But though I don't think that the proponents of this objection to a realist conception of truth have closed off the possibility of a direct awareness of extramental facts, I don't want to rest my case on that highly controversial claim. Instead what I take to be my strongest point is the earlier one: that even if no such direct awareness is possible, one can compare proposition and fact, provided one has knowledge of each, whether that knowledge is direct or not.

Finally, I want to look at a more general epistemological argument against a realist conception of truth. This one is based on the supposition that it is essential to realism to construe truth value as determined by a reality that is external to our knowledge, not just in the sense of being other than our knowledge, but also in the sense of being *inaccessible* to it. There is a forthright statement of this position in Horwich (1982). There he characterizes "metaphysical realism" as the doctrine that "the concept of truth involves a primitive non-epistemic idea—for example, 'correspondence with reality.' ... Truth is held to be a genuine property of certain propositions ... and the goal that motivates our standards of justification and our verification procedures" (182). This is along the same lines as my alethic realism. Horwich goes on to say:

> The respect in which metaphysical realism is committed to autonomous facts is ... radical. It concerns the adequacy of the canons of justification implicit in scientific and ordinary

linguistic practice—what reason is there to suppose that they guide us towards the truth? This question, given metaphysical realism, is substantial and, I think, impossible to answer; and it is this gulf between truth and our ways of attempting to recognize it which constitutes the respect in which facts are radically autonomous. Assuming a grasp of propositions, and knowledge of *what it is* for them to have the property of metaphysical truth, it is far from clear how we could derive the ability to recognize *when* this property applies. Indeed, it is our total inability to see how this problem might be solved which should lead us to reject metaphysical realism. ... Thus metaphysical realism involves to an unacceptable, indeed fatal, degree the autonomy of facts: there is from that perspective no reason to suppose that scientific practice provides even the slightest clue to what is true. (1982, 185–186)

Needless to say, Horwich is free to define "metaphysical realism" in any way he pleases. What he is not free to do is first to define the view in terms of a nonepistemic concept of truth that takes it to be something like correspondence with fact, and then to attribute to the view so defined a representation of facts whereby we have no way of determining what the facts are, without giving any reasons for supposing that this view of truth is committed to the latter.[6] And he gives no reason for supposing that "metaphysical realism," as he defines it, is committed to taking the truth-making facts to be cognitively inaccessible. It is sheerly arbitrary to burden the view with such crippling consequences.

Another attempt to saddle realism about truth with the doctrine that facts are inaccessible is found in Rorty's essay "The World Well Lost" (in Rorty 1982), in which he presents this extreme conception as the only alternative to regarding "the world" as consisting of the beliefs we take to be firmly established and immune from doubt. Referring to the Davidsonian position that it is necessary that most of our beliefs are true, he writes:

> If one accepts the Davidson-Stroud position, then "the world" will just be the stars, the people, the tables, and the grass—all those things which nobody except the occasional "scientific realist" philosopher thinks might not exist. So in one sense of "world"—the sense in which (except for a few fringe cases like gods, neutrinos, and natural rights) we now know perfectly well what the world is like and could not possibly be wrong about it—there is no argument about the point that it is the world that determines truth. But this is, of course, not enough for the realist. What he wants is precisely what the Davidson-Stroud argument prevents him from having— the notion of a world *so* "independent of our knowledge" that it might, for all we know, prove to contain none of the things we have always thought we were talking about. This notion of the world must be the notion of something *completely* unspecified and unspecifiable—the thing in itself, in fact. To sum up the point, I want to claim that "the world" is either the purely vacuous notion of the ineffable cause of sense and goal of intellect, or else a name for the objects that inquiry at the moment is leaving alone: those planks in the boat which are at the moment not being moved about. (1982, 14–15)

Here Rorty, the master of caricature, is exercising his art. If you are not content to construe "the world," "reality," as consisting of beliefs that are taken as firmly established (or as needing no establishment), then the only alternative is a world of which we can know nothing. But as soon as this disjunction is formulated, it can be seen to be obviously not exhaustive. Why couldn't the world be made up of facts that are what they are, independent of our cognitive successes and failures, without all these facts being inaccessible to our knowledge? Why foist onto the realist, who takes the truth of p to depend solely on whether it is the case that p, the commitment to p's being unknowable? Isn't there room for the category of *might or might not be known*, as well as the categories of *known* and *unknowable*?

You will note that Rorty's argument attacks a form of metaphysical realism properly so called that takes the facts on which (many) propositions depend for their truth value to be what they are independent of our cognitive dealings with them. Rorty, like many philosophers, makes no sharp distinction between such metaphysical realism and realism about truth. (Indeed, Rorty associates the T-schema with his *alternative* to realism about truth!) By contrast, I have already dissociated my realism about truth from any commitment to such a metaphysical position, though the two positions do have an affinity for each other. Nevertheless, Rorty's line of argument can be turned against a realist construal of truth, and that is why I introduced it here. This is because Rorty presents the view of reality as cognitively inaccessible by us as the only alternative to a coherence theory of truth, and this leaves no room for a realist account of truth on which the facts that make propositions true are often accessible. Hence it is not irrelevant to the defense of my view to point out the defects in arguments that purport to show that any alternative to a coherence account of truth makes truth undiscoverable.

Epistemic Conceptions of Truth

The main alternatives to a realist conception of truth are *epistemic* conceptions, which identify truth with some positive epistemic status of T-value bearers. This positive epistemic status is variously identified with membership in a maximally comprehensive and coherent system (as with the absolute idealist views of truth as coherence that were prominent in the late 1800s and early 1900s), with what, in Peirce's well-known formulation, "is fated to be ultimately agreed to by all who investigate"; with what, in Dewey's phrase, is "instrumental to an active reorganization of the given environment, a removal of some specific trouble or perplexity"; and more recently in Putnam (1981), with being such that it "would be justified in epistemically ideal conditions." To give focus to this brief discussion, I will concentrate on Putnam's view, abbreviating his candidate for truth as *ideal justifiability* (IJ) and his view as the *ideal justifiability conception* (IJC).

Though epistemic conceptions of truth have been attractive to many, I believe that they are among the few widely held philosophical positions that can be definitively refuted. I will give brief presentations of four arguments against them.[7]

i

The first is an extensional argument to the effect that truth and IJ are not completely coextensive. That is the case if there are propositions that are true but not IJ, or IJ but not true. I will concentrate here on the former possibility. If I were to try to give particular examples, it could be objected that I can hardly be confident that a belief is true without supposing myself to be justified in accepting it and supposing that this justification would hold up no matter how improved my epistemic situation. Even if that is so, it would not follow that a belief could not *be* true without being IJ. But rather than continuing that argument, I prefer to proceed more indirectly. I will consider how plausible it is to hold that there are true propositions that would not be justifiable in an ideal epistemic situation.

The most extreme candidates would be propositions such that nothing that tells for or against their truth is cognitively accessible to human beings, even in principle. I need not restrict myself here to propositions we are able to envisage. May there not be states of affairs, or even entire realms or aspects of reality, that are totally inaccessible to human cognition? If so, propositions to the effect that such states of affairs obtain will be true, even though no beliefs or statements bearing those propositions as their content would be justifiable in an epistemically ideal situation.

But how plausible is it that there *are* realms or aspects of reality that are in principle inaccessible to human cognition? There are considerations that render it quite plausible. Think of the limitations of our cognitive powers—limitations on our storage and retrieval capacity, on the amount of data we can process simultaneously, on the considerations we can hold together in our minds at one moment, on the complexity of propositions we are capable of grasping. Isn't it highly likely that there are facts that will forever lie beyond us just because of these limitations? And it is not just our finitude; there is also what we might call our *particularity*. The cognitive design of human beings represents only one out of a large multitude of possible designs for cognitive subjects, even for embodied cognitive subjects as finite as we are, leaving out of account angels and God. It seems clear that there could be corporeal cognitive subjects with forms of sensory receptivity different from ours, with sensitivity to different forms of physical energy. There could be subjects with different innate cognitive tendencies, propensities, and hard-wired beliefs and concepts. There could be subjects who reason in patterns different from those we employ. All this strongly suggests that there are many facts accessible to cognizers with radically different hardware and software but totally inaccessible to us.

One possible response to this objection would be to make the IJC range over cognitive subjects generally. Truth would then be identified with justifiability for some cognitive subjects or other in situations that are the most ideal for those subjects. And if there are still true propositions unenvisageable by any actual subjects, we could make the conception range over possible subjects as well. These modifications would certainly take the sting out of the present objection. But they would also take much of the sting out of the IJC. If we survey the reasons that have been given for an epistemic definition of truth, we will see that they are heavily anthropocentric. Dummett's arguments for a verificationist conception of truth, for example, depend on considering what sorts of truth conditions *we* could learn to attach to sentences. James and Dewey are preoccupied with how *we* judge beliefs to be true or false and with the functions that beliefs we call true play for *us* in *our* lives. And Putnam (1981) writes: "A true statement is a statement that a rational being would accept on sufficient experience of the kind that is actually possible for beings *with our nature* to have" (64; emphasis added). And in any event, we would have to restrict consideration to finite cognitive subjects. If an omniscient deity were brought into the picture, the position would lack the anti-realist bite it is designed to have.[8] Realism should have no hesitation in recognizing that a necessary condition of the truth of a proposition is that it would be known (accepted, believed, etc.) by an omniscient cognitive subject. And with the restriction to finite subjects in place, we still have to take seriously the idea that some aspects of reality are inaccessible in principle to *any* subjects—actual or possible.

ii

Another objection is that we can't spell out ideal justifiability without making use of the concept of truth. Hence the explication cannot go the other way without circularity. Here are two ways of seeing this.

First, what is meant by one's being (epistemically) justified in holding a certain belief? Most epistemologists who address this issue take a *truth-conducivity* position, according to which a belief is justified iff it is formed and/or held so as to make the belief likely to be *true*. There are a variety of suggestions as to what confers this likelihood: being based on adequate evidence, grounds, or reasons; being formed by the operation of a reliable belief-forming mechanism; cohering in the right sort of system; etc. But in taking these to be justification-conferring conditions, one supposes them to render the belief likely to be true. And the basic reason for this is that otherwise justification would not have the value for our cognitive endeavors that we take it to have. Laurence BonJour (1985) puts the matter strongly:

> Why should we, as cognitive beings, *care* whether our beliefs are epistemically justified? Why is such justification something to be sought and valued? ... The following answer seems obviously correct. ... What makes us cognitive beings at all is our capacity for belief, and the goal of our distinctively cognitive endeavors is *truth*: we want our beliefs to correctly and accurately depict the world. ... The basic role of justification is that of a *means* to truth, a more directly attainable mediating link between our subjective starting point and our objective goal. ... *If our standards of epistemic justification are appropriately chosen*, bringing it about that our beliefs are epistemically justified will also tend to bring it about ... that they are true. If epistemic justification were not conducive to truth in this way, if finding epistemically justified beliefs did not

substantially increase the likelihood of finding true ones, then epistemic justification would be irrelevant to our main cognitive goal and of dubious worth. (BonJour 1985, 7–8)

But if that is the case—if epistemic justification is essentially truth-conducive—then unless "justification" is being used in some different sense that would need explanation, being justified in an ideal epistemic situation would differ from being justified by ordinary, everyday standards only in that it is even more strongly indicative of truth than the latter. Hence we can't explain what is meant by an ideal epistemic situation without employing the concept of truth.

This point can be driven home by considering some alternatives to a truth-conducivity conception of justification. Foley (1987) holds that a belief is "epistemically rational" iff the believer would, on sufficient reflection, take there to be a conclusive argument for it (where in limiting cases the argument can be from itself to itself). This makes justification independent of truth by carrying out a considerable subjectivization of the concept of justification. And this very feature makes justification, so construed, of doubtful cognitive value. If we allow an unrestrained variation in what a given individual would take, on considerable reflection, to be a conclusive argument for p, we may well wonder why anyone should be concerned to see to it that their beliefs are "epistemically rational."

A somewhat more widespread approach is to tie justification to the lack of any violation of intellectual obligations or duties. Just as I am justified in an action (e.g., resigning from my job with only two weeks' notice, provided I violate no rule, regulation, or commitment in doing so), on this view, I am justified in believing that there is intelligent life elsewhere in the universe, provided my believing this is not the result of failures to conduct my intellectual operations as I should. To be sure, whether this way of thinking of justification is opposed to a truth-conducivity conception depends on what intellectual obligations we have. If they include an obligation to do what we can to believe what is true and to avoid believing what is false, this is not sharply opposed to a truth-conducivity view. But if we think of these obligations in some other way, e.g., as looking carefully for pro and con considerations on the issue, then this may or may not be closely connected with a likelihood of truth for the belief in question. And if it isn't, the question again arises as to why we should take justification in this sense to be an important value for our cognitive lives.

So truth already enters into the very conception of epistemic justification. Another way in which truth is presupposed in the understanding of the IJC has to do with what makes an epistemic situation *ideal*. A natural understanding of this is in terms of the *ready availability of all relevant evidence* (reasons, considerations). Now to say that evidence is available is to say that one could come into possession of it. So the crucial notion is that of *possession* of evidence. The evidence itself will presumably consist of facts. What is it for the subject to *possess* those facts so as to make use of them in justifying a belief? The most obvious answer is that the subject comes to *know* them. But the notion of knowledge involves the notion of *truth*. (Knowledge is *true* belief that satisfies

certain further conditions.) To avoid this conclusion, we would have to construe possession of the facts in terms of belief without mentioning knowledge. But then we will
have to require the beliefs to be *true*. Otherwise, one is not in possession of genuine
evidence but only mistakenly supposes himself to be so. At this point the suggestion
might be that possession of evidence consists in having *justified* beliefs. But we have
already seen that the notion of justification involves the notion of truth. Moreover,
this involves a different circle. The justification involved here obviously can't be justification by everyday standards. For by those standards, a belief can be justified in one
situation and not in another, which means that there is no unique answer to what the
relevant evidence is for a given target belief. Hence these will have to be beliefs that
would be justified in *ideal epistemic circumstances*. But then we are in an even smaller
circle. We define ideal justifiability in terms of an ideal epistemic situation, but then we
have to define such a situation in terms of what beliefs would be justified in an ideal
epistemic situation!

I believe there are other points at which the concept of an ideal epistemic situation
rests on the concept of truth, but sufficient unto the day is the difficulty thereof.

iii

Next I would like to present an argument against the IJC that is based on the T-schema,
the heart of alethic realism. According to the T-schema, or a suitable generalization
thereof, the fact that sugar is sweet is conceptually both necessary and sufficient for its
being true that sugar is sweet. And that would seem to leave no room for any *epistemic*
necessary or sufficient conditions. Nothing more than *sugar's being sweet* is needed to
make the proposition true, and nothing less would suffice. How, then, can some epistemic condition be conceptually necessary and/or sufficient?

My opponent can complain that I am begging the question by basing the argument on what my position takes to be conceptually necessary and sufficient for truth.
But to see that the argument is free of special pleading, we only have to note that the
T-schema is almost universally endorsed by epistemic theorists (though many of them,
thinking in terms of sentences as T-value bearers, endorse the Tarskian version instead).
Thus Putnam (1978) writes, "We could … *keep* formal semantics (including 'Tarski-type'
truth-definitions) … and yet *shift* our notion of 'truth' over to something approximating 'warranted assertibility'" (29). Thus epistemic theorists are anxious to square their
position with the T-schema or its brethren. And that is not surprising if the T-schema is
as obviously true as I have been claiming. And so in arguing from that schema against
epistemic theorists' construal of the concept of truth, I rely on what is common ground
between us.

But, of course, there is a possible answer to my charge. An epistemic concept of truth
like the IJC may not be incompatible with the T-schema. It wouldn't be if the IJC were
conceptually equivalent with the realist necessary and sufficient condition for truth,

namely, the corresponding fact. If *the belief that sugar is sweet being ideally justifiable* is itself conceptually equivalent to *sugar's being sweet*, then, by the transitivity of conceptual equivalence, the former is likewise conceptually equivalent to its being true that sugar is sweet. I say this is a possible answer, but, so far as I can see, it is only abstractly conceivable. In particular, it is no epistemic possibility. What basis could there be for holding that the ideal justifiability of the belief that sugar is sweet is *conceptually* both necessary and sufficient for sugar's being sweet? Even if they were extensionally equivalent, which I do not admit, why suppose that the concepts involved guarantee the equivalence? On the basis of linguistic intuition, it seems clear that we can consistently conceive of a fact (if not sugar's being sweet, then some more recondite fact like the Big Bang's being preceded by a collapse of a previous universe into a point) without its being ideally justifiable that the fact obtains. The most I can see to be even minimally plausible along this line is the following. On one type of absolute idealism, anything I can think of that is external to my current thought is some fully realized development of my thought, an "all comprehensive and fully realized whole" of which Anglo-American absolute idealism spoke, or, in more Hegelian terms, the culmination of the Absolute Spirit's process of attaining full self-development. On such a view it would, if you like, be *metaphysically* impossible that sugar would be sweet without that judgment's figuring in an all-comprehensive and ideally coherent system of thought. But that would still not make that combination *conceptually* impossible. It would still not prevent us from consistently and intelligibly envisaging that sugar is sweet, although it is not ideally justifiable that it is. And so this suggested out for the epistemic theorist turns out to be a blind alley. And even if it weren't, I doubt very much that any contemporary advocate of an epistemic conception of truth would be willing to purchase acceptability for the view at the price of accepting absolute idealism.

iv

One final shot against the IJC. We have seen that a common objection against a realist conception of truth is that it makes it impossible to determine truth values. And correspondingly, a main attraction of epistemic conceptions is that they avoid this disability of their rival. But ironically enough, the tables are turned against epistemic accounts on just this point. As soon as we make the epistemic conception strong enough to be at all plausible as an account of truth, it turns out that on that conception, it is *much more* difficult to determine truth values than it is on the realist conception. If we could identify truth with, say, justification by ordinary standards, then it would be easier to determine truth values than on the realist conception. But any such account would be palpably inadequate. Clearly, some beliefs justified by ordinary standards are false. For an epistemic account of truth to have any plausibility at all, we have to identify truth with some highly idealized epistemic status: membership in a *maximally* comprehensive and coherent system or what would be justified in *ideal* epistemic conditions. And having inflated the conception to that extent, it becomes extremely problematic to determine whether a belief satisfies the condition. Who can say which of our present beliefs would still be justifiable if we had ready access to *all* relevant evidence? Whenever the topic is difficult or controversial, as with many issues in science, history, and philosophy, we are in no position to say with any assurance what position would be justified in the most ideal of circumstances. And where simpler matters are concerned, as with garden-variety perceptual judgments, we are in a much better position with a realist conception. Because of the severe problems of working out a determinate conception of ideal epistemic circumstances, it is much easier to determine that my computer is on now than it is to determine whether that belief would be justified in *ideal epistemic circumstances*. So the IJC doesn't deliver the goods for the sake of which it is sought. It makes truth values less accessible, not more.

Notes

This essay is mostly a condensation of material to be found in chapters 1, 3, and 7 of Alston (1996), with a few additional twists. A closer ancestor is two keynote lectures delivered at the 1997 Wheaton Philosophy Conference on Truth and Realism.

1. There are other senses of "true" in addition to the one I will be examining. We speak of a "true friend," a "true copy," "being true to one's word," and so on. My interest is in the sense of "true" that applies to beliefs, statements, propositions, and the like. When I want to emphasize this, I will use the term *propositional truth*, but even when I don't, this restriction should be understood.

2. Talk of *conceptual* or *analytic* truths is distasteful to those philosophers who deny that we can distinguish between what belongs to our *concept* of P and what is obviously true of Ps, or between what is true solely by virtue of the meanings of terms and what is true, at least in part, on other bases. I agree that it is often difficult, even impossible, to find a sharp line of division. But it also seems clear that there are many clear cases on both sides. The conceptual, analytic truth of instances of the T-schema is one of those clear cases.

3. See Alston (1996, 162–187) and Lynch (1998) on this point.

4. This correspondence view of truth goes beyond my "minimalist" version of a realist conception of truth, but as I will suggest below, it is in the direction pointed out by my account.

5. This argument is usually directed against a correspondence theory of truth, but we can take it to be directed against my minimalist realist conception of truth as well. For, as just pointed out, my position holds that a proposition must share a content with a fact if it is to be true. And so it may be argued that my position, as much as a full-blown correspondence theory, implies that I can tell that a proposition is true only by telling that it corresponds with a fact.

6. Actually, Horwich says both this and that on metaphysical realism we have no reason for supposing that satisfying *ordinary criteria of justification* is likely to get us closer to the truth, which is not equivalent to its being impossible to know the truth-makers.

7. The arguments are presented in more detail in Alston (1996, 188–230).

8. See Plantinga (1982). Putnam (1981) identifies metaphysical realism, which he opposes, with a "God's-eye point of view."

References

Alston, William P. 1996. *A Realist Conception of Truth.* Ithaca, NY: Cornell University Press.

Blanshard, Brand. 1939. *The Nature of Thought.* 2 vols. London: George Allen and Unwin.

BonJour, Laurence. 1985. *The Structure of Empirical Knowledge.* Cambridge, MA: Harvard University Press.

Davidson, Donald. 1986. "A Coherence Theory of Truth and Knowledge." In Ernest LePore, ed., *Truth and Interpretation: Perspectives on the Philosophy of Donald Davidson,* 307–319. New York: Blackwell.

Foley, Richard 1987. *The Theory of Epistemic Rationality.* Cambridge, MA: Harvard University Press.

Hempel, Carl G. 1935. "On the Logical Positivists' Theory of Truth." *Analysis* 2(4): 49–59.

Horwich, Paul. 1982. "Three Forms of Realism." *Synthese* 51: 181–201.

LePore, Ernest, ed. 1986. *Truth and Interpretation: Perspectives on the Philosophy of Donald Davidson.* New York: Blackwell.

Lynch, Michael. 1988. *Truth in Context.* Cambridge, MA: MIT Press.

Macdonald, Margaret, ed. 1954. *Philosophy and Analysis.* Oxford: Basil Blackwell.

Plantinga, A. 1982. "How to Be an Anti-realist." *Proceedings and Addresses of the American Philosophical Association* 56: 47–70.

Putnam, Hilary. 1978. *Meaning and the Moral Sciences.* London: Routledge and Kegan Paul.

Putnam, Hilary. 1981. *Reason, Truth, and History.* Cambridge: Cambridge University Press.

Rorty, Richard. 1979. *Philosophy and the Mirror of Nature.* Princeton, NJ: Princeton University Press.

Rorty, Richard. 1982. *Consequences of Pragmatism.* Minneapolis: University of Minnesota Press.

Williams, Michael. 1977. *Groundless Belief.* New Haven, CT: Yale University Press.

4 On Truth

Ruth Garrett Millikan

1 The Plan

The plan is to investigate the nature of truth by looking first for the central linguistic function or functions of the construction "is true" and then asking what this construction's contribution to truth conditions, if any, must be in order for it to serve this or these functions. Preliminarily, I will describe a perspective on natural language from which the centrality of questions about the functions of various linguistic constructions becomes evident. I will explain what I mean by the function of a construction or, more exactly, by the "proper" or "stabilizing" function of a construction. I will clarify my usage of *linguistic construction*, which diverges somewhat from tradition. As the essay proceeds, I will be illustrating stabilizing functions and their relation to truth conditions by offering preliminary descriptions of the stabilizing functions and contribution to truth conditions of various constructions that have puzzled linguists and philosophers.

Interpreting Wilfrid Sellars's analysis of "the translation rubric" in a reasonable way yields a promising proposal on the nature of truth conditions and the relation of truth conditions to function. According to this proposal, functions determine truth conditions, but truth conditions do not determine functions. That is why I will be looking for the stabilizing function of "is true" first, then for its truth conditions.

Sellars' proposal is, in part, that some sentences do not require that one think of or even understand their truth conditions in order to understand them. Some kinds of sentences have what I will call *submerged* truth conditions. I illustrate that although a given sentence, a given superimposition of constructions, may have a single stabilizing function and make a single contribution to truth conditions, there may be different ways of describing and hence thinking of that truth condition, many (sometimes all) of which are submerged. Given this, it turns out to be plausible that the truth conditions for some kinds of sentences—say, those that concern empirical matters of fact—can be described by reference to correspondence rules that govern their stabilizing uses. It also leaves open that truth conditions for many kinds of sentences—say, those concerning morality or aesthetics or mathematics—cannot be described this way. It leaves open that some kinds of sentences may not fit the dichotomy of true or false. Finally, this analysis does not rule out various kinds of truth relativism.

2   Stabilizing Functions and Constructions

Typically, linguistic forms are reproduced by speakers because in the speaker's experience they have, often enough, had effects of a kind that the speaker *purposes* to reproduce.[1] These effects have been produced with the cooperation of the hearers. Hearers cooperate because in their experience cooperation has, often enough, resulted in benefits to the hearer. When the speaker is successful, both the linguistic form and its effects, both the form and the function, are reproduced. Thus, a reproducing form-plus-function family is established, the members of which consist in the production of a certain *sign design* followed by a certain effect. To produce this effect is the *stabilizing function* of the family. It is what the family is doing that keeps it alive. Whether or not a given token actually produces this effect, to produce this effect is what I call the *proper function* of each sign-design token that is copied from this family. It is the function that accounts for the family's existence and hence also for the token's existence.

Linguistic sign-design tokens that are members of the same reproducing family are tokens of the same "construction," otherwise not. That the "bank" in "riverbank" and the "bank" in "piggy bank" do not have common ancestors is sufficient to render them *different* constructions. (Except for this added requirement of common ancestry, this parallels the common characterization of constructions as individuated by form and meaning.)

A natural language is a designed vehicle of what is called *mutualistic symbiosis* between speakers and hearers of the language. Speaker and hearer each benefit from its use often enough to motivate continued reproduction and hence stability of both speaker uses and hearer reactions to its forms. This symbiosis has been designed by an analog of natural selection, the failure to be reproduced by speakers/hearers corresponding to the failure of a phenotypic trait to be reproduced. Only tokens that serve speaker purposes by prompting hearer responses that also further purposes of the hearers will continue to be repeated/copied by speakers with the same purpose and followed through in the same way by hearers. Only tokens of this successful kind will help to proliferate a construction and to stabilize the function of its sign-design tokens to keep the construction alive.

Constructions may take the form of words or of conventionalized phrases ("by the way," "reach out to you," "beyond the pale"). They may take the form of syntactic structures or of multiword structures containing blanks for variables ("... put the [dress/coat/lipstick/gloves] on"—meaning on themselves, not on someone else). Any natural language form routinely reproduced (copied) whole by speakers rather than reinvented, rather than constructed anew by superimposition of prior simpler

constructions, is a construction. A natural language consists of a collection of constructions, tokens of which are combined and recombined by superimposition to form
new and more complex tokens combining the functions of their element constructions. Each constituent construction has a stabilizing function of its own, these fitting
together to compose a stabilizing function for the whole.

Looking at languages this way suggests that central to a detailed study of any particular language must be the question, for each of its constructions: What is its stabilizing
function? What does this construction do to keep itself alive? What response has this
construction been effecting in hearers or effecting through the responses of hearers that
speakers (i.e., their cognitive settings) typically purpose in its use and that has, often
enough, also accorded with hearer aims? A task, perhaps the primary task, of semantics
should surely be to uncover the stabilizing functions of various linguistic constructions
and to describe the ways that many of these constructions can be superimposed in
order to work together, composing more complicated linguistic forms with more complicated functions.[2]

3   Indicatives, Imperatives, and Interrogatives

We can start with functions of constructions that indicate grammatical moods. (Usually, these are syntactic structures.) I'll speculate on constructions that indicate indicative, imperative, and interrogative moods.

So what is it that sentences containing indicative constructions are accomplish-
ing often enough to keep these constructions alive and reproducing? A ready answer
might be that their job is to prompt the formation of beliefs in hearers, the contents of
these beliefs being determined by constructions filling variable slots in the indicative-
forming structure. More carefully, their job is either to produce new beliefs in hearers or
to remind hearers of, and hence to make occurrent, beliefs these hearers already possess
but were not currently considering. Call this the *occasioning* of a belief in the hearer.

This ready answer couldn't be right, however, unless simply occasioning beliefs were
in some way rewarding for hearers regardless of content and truth value. But only the
occasioning, specifically, of *true* beliefs would encourage hearers to continue to understand and believe indicative mood sentences as they do. If too high a proportion of
indicative sentence tokens heard were false, language could not even be learned. As for
speakers, the question of why they are motivated to occasion true beliefs in hearers has
diverse answers. Of central importance, undoubtedly, is that humans, unlike chimps,
seem to be *designed* to be cooperative (Tomasello 2009, 2014). In any event, it is clear
that speakers, for whatever reason, are often motivated to pass genuine information
on to hearers.

We can posit that the stabilizing function of imperative constructions is to prompt the
hearer to intend to perform the action represented—but further, to effect performance

of the represented action. If hearers never complied with imperatives, speakers would not try to use them. Hearers comply with imperatives for many reasons, including reliance on the cooperative nature of humans, which instills confidence that complying will be in their best interest; sanctions of many kinds; because they are following directions for doing what they want to do; and so forth. Why speakers are often motivated to prompt hearer actions of one kind or another is obvious.

The interrogative is often considered to be a kind of imperative. Accordingly, its function is, in part, to prompt the hearer to reply. And further, of course, to reply correctly. If hearers didn't reply and reply correctly enough of the time, speakers would no longer bother to ask questions, and the interrogative would disappear. Speakers want correct replies because believing correct replies supplies them with true beliefs, which are needed for action. The final result, then, that proliferates the interrogative is the acquisition of true speaker beliefs. Its stabilizing function is production of true beliefs in speakers.

4   Sellars and the Translation Rubric: "'___' (in L) Means …"

Central to the aim of Wilfrid Sellars's program in philosophy of language was to disabuse us of the traditional and natural view, for example, that the sentence "'Hund' (in German) means *dog*" ascribes a relation, the *denoting* or *standing for* relation, between the mentioned word "Hund" and dogs. He reminds us of uses of this rubric, such as "'Und' (in German) means *and*," where it is obvious that "und"s are not being claimed to denote or stand for *and*s or anything else. Instead of stating a fact about the relation of a mentioned linguistic expression to something for which it "stands," Sellars argues that the rubric "'___' (in L) means ___" has a "use" or function. In the sentence "'Und' (in German) means *and*," the English word "and" is neither used in the usual way (it is not a conjunction) nor mentioned. Rather, the speaker

> uses ["and"] … in a peculiar way, a way which is characteristic of *semantical* discourse. He presents us with an instance of the word itself, not a name of it, and, making use of the fact that we belong to the same language community, indicates to us that we have only to rehearse our use of "and" to appreciate the role of "und" on the other side of the Rhine. (Sellars 1963, 314–315)

> It is because the understanding of ["'Dreieckig' (in German) means triangular"] involves an imaginative rehearsal of the use of "triangular" that [it] differs from a simple statement to the effect that "dreieckig" is the German counterpart of the English word "triangular." The latter statement could be fully understood, as the former could not, by someone who did not have the English word "triangular" in his active vocabulary. (272)

Assume that the "use" of a construction is to effect its stabilizing function. Then we might give as our Sellarsian account that the stabilizing function of the translation rubric is, say, to bring it about that the hearer is able to understand and use the mentioned, the left-hand, linguistic construction in the same way as members of its home language community do. It would follow that for the translation rubric to serve its *own* stabilizing function (in the normal way), the right- and the left-hand constructions that appear in the rubric must have the same stabilizing function or, as Sellars puts it, must "play the same role" or "have the same use" in their respective languages.

Accordingly, Sellars tells us that "the essential feature of this use of ["means"] is that ... the translated expression and the expression into which it translates must have the same use" (1963, 110). And he tells us that "a statement of this form ['β means *B* (in L)'] is *true*, if and only if 'β' stands to 'B' as another embodiment of the same 'piece' [in the language game]" (355; emphasis in original). That "und" and "and" have the same "use" (for us, *stabilizing function*) in their respective languages is the *truth condition* for "'Und' means *and*."

Sellars is clear that the "use" of "'Und' means *and*" is not to produce a *belief* in its truth condition. Such a belief might be had by a person who understood neither the word "und" nor the word "and." Conversely, an English-speaking child might understand "'Und' means *and*" without having any idea that words have Sellarsian "uses" or "roles" (or stabilizing functions). Required for "'Und' (in German) means *and*" to play its conventional role is only that it should prompt the hearer, when using German, to begin understanding and using "und" in the same way she already uses the word "and" in English. And to be prompted in this way does not require the hearer to form beliefs about either words or their roles.

What Sellars is counting as the truth condition for his rubric is not something the hearer normally believes or thinks of. What then is it? I suggest this formulation and will use it in what follows, illustrating where it leads with various examples.

The truth condition of a sentence is a condition peculiar to the sentence (along with strictly synonymous sentences) that is required to be in place for the sentence to serve its stabilizing function (the superimposed stabilizing functions of its element constructions) in the (historically) normal way.

On this interpretation, stabilizing function determines truth conditions, but truth conditions do not determine stabilizing function. "'Und' (in German) means *and*" has the same truth condition as "'Und' has the same stabilizing function in German that 'and' has in English." But these constructions do not have the same stabilizing function. Knowing that "und" and "and" have the same stabilizing function in their respective languages would not help a monolingual Frenchman to use the word "und" as the Germans do.

Sellars's move here in prying truth conditions from functions is a fairly radical reconstruction of the notion of a truth condition. One important feature is the implication that constructions can have functions that do not require the truth conditions of sentences in which they are embedded to be understood. I will call the truth conditions of sentences containing such constructions *submerged truth conditions*. I will give more examples in the paragraphs that follow.

Notice, however, that in the most common cases this way of understanding what truth conditions are yields the same result as does the view that the truth condition for an indicative sentence s is just that *s*. The truth condition for "Grass is green" is that grass is green. And it is true, of course, that for "Grass is green" to serve its stabilizing function of occasioning a true belief (the contents of which are determined according to the superimposed stabilizing functions of its components), grass must be *green*. Further, this requirement is peculiar to the sentence "Grass is green" and its synonyms.

Let me continue trying to clarify the notion *stabilizing function*, and now also the notion *submerged truth condition*, by offering some suggestions about the stabilizing functions of several more constructions and the truth conditions of sentences containing them.

5   Strawson on Assertions of Identity; *LTOBC* on "Exists"

In *Subject and Predicate in Logic and Grammar*, Strawson (1974: 54–55) suggests that the use of an identity sentence "*A* is *B*" is to prompt the hearer to merge his concepts of *A* and of *B* to form just one concept. This concept is linked equally in his mind to each of the predicates, including *is called A* and *is called B*, that were formerly linked either to his *A* or to his *B* concept. Placating Frege, "*A* is *B*" states a fact about neither *A* nor *B* nor about the names *A* and *B*. But it is neither necessary nor helpful to introduce a third man, *sense*, to explain how an identity sentence works.

If Strawson is right, then although the truth of "*A* is *B*" depends on a truth about the *words* "A" and "B"—roughly, that they have the same extension—its function is not to induce a belief about words (or any other belief) in the hearer but only to effect a merging of the hearer's *A* and *B* concepts. Again, producing an understanding of truth conditions is not on the normal route to performance of the stabilizing function. Sentences of the form "*A* is *B*" have submerged truth conditions.

In *Language, Thought, and Other Biological Categories* (*LTOBC*), I claimed that "Unicorns do not exist" does not state a fact about either unicorns (and existence) or about the word "unicorn." Its function is to prompt the hearer either to remove the idea that he expresses with the word "unicorn" from his inner representational system or to disengage it from use in real-world contexts,[3] reserving it exclusively for pretend thought and talk. Necessary and sufficient for the truth of the sentence "Unicorns do not exist" is that the name "unicorn" has no extension. Sufficient for the truth of the sentence "Unicorns exist" would be that the term "unicorn" did have an extension. But thinking about or having ideas, either of words or of extensions, is not required for understanding or for believing either of these sentences. For these sentences to function normally, to fulfill their stabilizing functions normally, including being understood and believed, does not require that their truth conditions be thought of or even known by the hearer. Sentences of the form "Unicorns do not exist" have submerged truth conditions.

6 Some Puzzling Conjunctions

How to treat certain constructions such as "but," "therefore," "so," "accordingly," "moreover," "that is," and "anyway," which are used to link certain kinds of clauses, has puzzled linguists since Frege. An underlying assumption seems to be that because each of these constructions is appropriately used only when a particular relation holds between the states of affairs represented by the linked clauses, the functions of these constructions must involve informing the hearer about relations between the states of affairs represented by the linked clauses, but this information is communicated only in an indirect way. For example, "but" says that what comes after it contrasts with what came before. But what is the point of saying this only in an indirect way? And how is this indirect communication accomplished?

Also puzzling is the status of sentences containing these linking expressions wrongly or inappropriately: "She was utterly devastated but she cried." If the use of "but" were in part to convey to the hearer that crying is usually incompatible with being devastated, then such a sentence ought to be plain false. But it doesn't seem to be.

Let me add to the puzzle what has not, I think, been noticed—that the relations indicated by these linking expressions seem characteristically to be ones that are perfectly obvious without being mentioned, relations the hearer would see for himself if interested and would not need to be told about. Consider "He was frightened but unhurt." "He was unhurt" obviously contrasts with "He was frightened." The "but" in "He was frightened but unhurt" would be gratuitous if its function were to inform the hearer of a contrast. It would seem that the stabilizing function of "but" is not, primarily, informing the hearer of a contrast.

Instead, I suggest that what "but" does is to prepare the hearer to understand what is coming in the next clause by priming an *expectation* of contrast. Yes, that *is* what she means despite the seeming incompatibility. Being primed to expect and listen for a contrast facilitates comprehension. "But," "however," and "yet" prime for a contrast; "therefore" and "so" prime for a consequence; "moreover" and "and" prime for more of the same; "accordingly" primes for a natural sequel; and so forth. Priming of this sort facilitates understanding, especially, of the intent or point of what is being said.

To see this possibility, we have to allow that taking account of or being prepared for something need not involve a *belief* about that something. Being prepared for a contrast does not require occasioning a belief that there will be a contrast. Surely, the young child understands "but" before possessing the concept of contrast. Being prepared (psychologically) for the oncoming softball to pass on my left does not require me to have a belief that it will be on my left. There are many things in the mind other than beliefs (attitudes, nonpropositional attitudes).

What, then, are the truth conditions for "She was utterly devastated but she cried"? If the stabilizing function of "but" is to aid the hearer's understanding by preparing her for an upcoming contrast, then to serve its stabilizing function in the usual way it must be followed by a contrast. The presence of a contrast figures among the truth conditions for a sentence containing "but." It is a submerged part of the truth conditions. Understanding "She was utterly devastated but she cried" does not require thinking about a contrast.

An implication is that "She was utterly devastated but she cried" is not true. It doesn't follow, however, that it is false. More illuminating, I think, would be to say that it is not well formed. (So, of course, it is not true.) Without a contrast between p and q, "p but q" cannot be processed normally. If it cannot be processed normally, it is not well formed. The full meaningfulness of a "p but q" sentence requires that there be a contrast between p and q.[4]

7   Conditionals

In *Beyond Concepts* (2017), I offered suggestions about the stabilizing functions of a number of different kinds of conditionals. I described first what appears to be the root function of the conditional from which other uses are, plausibly, derived. Conditionals like other common expressions have, of course, acquired additional functions over time—some derived, in the case of conditionals, from salient analogies and some from dead implicatures. Conditionals divide, that is, into a number of separate related constructions, closely related but separate species. Here I discuss only what I take to be the root conditional. The root conditional has an indicative antecedent and an indicative, or an imperative, or an interrogative consequent:

1. If it rains, the field will be muddy.
2. If it rains, be sure to wear your boots!
3. If it rains, will they play anyway?

The stabilizing function of the root construction "If A then C" is not, I suggest, to effect acquisition of any kind of propositional attitude in either the hearer or the speaker. It is to effect acquisition of a *disposition*. In (1), where the consequent is indicative, it is to produce in the hearer a disposition upon acquiring a belief that A to complete the stabilizing function that belongs to C, namely, to acquire a true belief that the field will be muddy. In (2), where the consequent is imperative, the stabilizing function is to produce in the hearer a disposition upon occasioning a belief that A to complete the stabilizing function that belongs to C, namely, to acquire an intention, which is then executed, to wear boots. In (3), where the consequent is interrogative, the stabilizing function is to produce in the hearer a disposition upon occasioning a belief that A to further the stabilizing function that belongs to C, namely, to occasion in the speaker the belief either that they will or that they won't play.[5]

Returning to the relation of stabilizing functions to truth conditions, consider the root construction "If A then C," where C is indicative. A disposition to move from thinking that p to thinking that q clearly does not necessitate a disposition to move from thinking that *not-q* to thinking that *not-p*. Modus tollens is a valid inference, but a valid inference is not the same as one that is typically or even often performed. It seems unlikely that a resulting hearer use of modus tollens is required for conditionals to be useful enough to proliferate. Thus, the stabilizing function of "If A then C" is probably different from the stabilizing function of "If *not-C* then *not-A*." No one has suggested, however, that the truth conditions for "If A then C" and for "If *not-C* then *not-A*" might be different.

A considerable literature emerged in the twentieth century debating what the truth conditions are for various kinds of conditionals. All in all, if conditionals have truth conditions, it seems that these must be submerged.[6]

8   Stabilizing Functions and Truth Conditions for "That p Is True" and for "s Is True"

To understand how "is true" contributes to the truth conditions of a sentence in which it occurs would be, arguably, a way to understand what truth is. On the assumption that it is the functions of linguistic constructions that determine their contributions to truth conditions, in this section I will examine the function and look for the truth conditions of "is true" in sentences of the form

(1) That wolves eat mice is true.

In the next section, I will do this for sentences of the form

(2) "Wolves eat mice" is true.

That the hearer should occasion or acquire the belief that wolves eat mice is surely at least part of the stabilizing function of (1). Unsurprisingly, then, that wolves eat mice must at least be part of the truth condition for (1).

Strawson (1949, 1950) and others have noted that this use of "is true" also has speech act functions. The following, at least, would seem to be functions that help to proliferate sentences like (1).

(a) Explicitly endorsing what's inside the "that" clause

(b) Confirming or granting what someone else has said

These are speech acts of a kind that have no truth conditions. There are speech acts that do have truth conditions, such as the act performed in saying "I now pronounce you man and wife," which is, I suppose, false if the speaker has no authority to marry people. Conditions are not then right for it to be able to serve its stabilizing function in a normal way. But endorsing and acknowledging and confirming and granting are not like that.

Common to all uses of the frame "that ___ is true" seems to be that it serves to mark off the content inside the frame as a part of the whole of the content that one is concerned, specifically, to endorse, or to acknowledge, or that might be in question, and so forth. Saying "That wolves eat mice is true" seems to be exactly like saying "Wolves eat mice. Yes," which surely adds nothing to the truth conditions of "Wolves eat mice."

In sum, what "is true" contributes to the truth conditions of "That wolves eat mice is true" seems to be nothing whatsoever. "True" is a word that has a function in the context "That ___ is true," but no special conditions are required for it to serve that function beyond conditions already required for "___." Asking for "the nature" of this kind of truth would be as misguided as asking for the nature of "andness" or "ofness" would be. There is no such thing as "truth" of this kind. Certainly, it is not a property.

9   The Function of "*s* Is True"

What about sentences of kind (2): "'Wolves eat mice' is true"? Spoken language has no quotation marks. Rather than "'Wolves eat mice' is true," in spoken language you have to say "The *sentence* 'Wolves eat mice' is true," strongly suggesting that in both of these cases "is true" is being predicated of a sentence. It appears to be metalinguistic, assigning a property, truth, to a sentence. Moreover, "is true" can follow a quoted sentence in a language that is known to neither speaker or hearer. Sentences can be talked about without understanding them: "'Her şeyin bir rengi var' is true, they say, in Turkish, but I don't know what it means."

If we consider how a sentence like "'Wolves eat mice' is true" might actually be used, its appearance would be extremely odd outside of a context in which sentences or other bits of language were under discussion. Sudden injection of the sentence "'Wolves eat mice' is true" in place of plain "Wolves eat mice" in a conversation strictly about the diets of mammals would be highly anomalous, eliciting, perhaps, "I thought we were talking about mammals, not sentences." The "Wolves eat mice" in "'Wolves eat mice' is true" certainly appears to be mentioned rather than used. "That he prevaricated is true" and "That he lied is true" have the same truth condition. "'He prevaricated' is true" and "'He lied' is true" have different truth conditions.

If that is right, the function of (written) "'Wolves eat mice' is true" would seem to be to prompt the occasioning of a hearer belief about the sentence "Wolves eat mice." What kind of a belief? What was the child thinking about "Her şeyin bir rengi var" when she said it was true? Was she thinking that its truth condition (whatever it might be) holds? But, surely, the child, along with the usual speaker of English, has no idea of a truth condition. Maybe that if you understood it you should believe it?

We have seen that understanding and believing its truth conditions is not always required for understanding and believing a sentence. Some truth conditions are submerged.

Understanding and accepting a translation-rubric sentence requires only acquiring a certain disposition, not belief in its truth condition. Many have held that sentences expressing moral opinions or opinions about aesthetic properties and so forth have as their functions to produce in hearers not beliefs about what the world is like but other kinds of attitudes or dispositions. What the truth conditions of a particular sentence are, however, is an empirical matter of fact resting on the actual histories of the constructions of which it is composed and the mechanisms by which their functions have normally been performed. If sentences expressing moral opinions or opinions about aesthetic properties impart only nonpropositional attitudes to hearers, their truth conditions, granted they have definite truth conditions, must be submerged. It could be that the truth conditions of a very large portion of sentences are submerged.

I suspect that the stabilizing function of the form "*S* is true" is merely to implant in the hearer a disposition to process the sentence *S* normally, that is, to believe it. The stabilizing function of "'Wolves eat mice' is true" is to dispose the hearer to process "Wolves eat mice" in the normal way. Whether this requires awareness of truth conditions depends on whether understanding *S* requires awareness of its truth conditions.

10   Truth Conditions for "*s* Is True"

There is another sense in which truth conditions can be submerged in which almost all of them *are* submerged.

If *S1* is a sentence stating a certain condition and *S2* is logically equivalent to *S1*, then *S2* is a way of stating that same condition. If the condition of compliance is that she bring along a dozen apples, it is also a condition of compliance that she bring seven plus five. There is only one criterion for her compliance, but there are multiple ways of understanding that criterion. This also holds, of course, for the *truth* condition of "She brought a dozen apples." If she is young, she may believe that she has 12 apples without believing she has seven plus five. Responding even to a purely fact-stating sentence in the normal way is not just responding by believing its truth condition. It is responding by believing its truth condition under the description articulated by the sentence.

Nor is only logical equivalence relevant here. Besides logical equivalence, there is natural equivalence, equivalence in the natural world. Talk of stabilizing functions and of conditions required for their performance is, implicitly, talk about causal processes and natural-world conditions. Language is designed for talking about this world, not about logically possible worlds. Conditions in logically possible worlds have nothing to do with the reasons for proliferation of constructions in this world. The condition expressed by "It's raining" is naturally equivalent to the condition expressed by "Molecules of H_2O in the upper atmosphere are coalescing to form liquid droplets that are falling to the earth around here." If one of these conditions is the truth condition for "It's raining," then so is the other. But believing that it is raining does not require believing anything about molecules. Nor does believing the above about molecules require believing that it is raining. That molecules of H_2O in the upper atmosphere are coalescing to form liquid droplets that are falling to the earth around here is, however, a submerged truth condition of "It's raining."

Suppose a child who asks what "Es regnet" means in German is told that it means it's raining. "And what," she perversely asks, "is *raining*?" "Well, you know, drops of water fall down from the sky." "How does that happen? I want to know *exactly* what it is that would make 'Es regnet' true." You now try to explain to the child as a scientist would, but the tiresome child persists: "But what is it that makes *that* what 'Es regnet' means?"

So, as a good correspondence theorist, you now try to explain the relevant rules of German that, you take it, map true sentences of German onto states of affairs in the world, allowing fluent Germans to be guided by these sentences such that their activities will fit or use or take account of these states of affairs in productive ways. The most fundamental, but submerged, truth condition of "Es regnet" (the correspondence theorist holds) is that its pattern must map onto a real state of affairs in accordance with such-and-such correspondence rules. You offer an account of how true German sentences map onto the world. You offer an account of the most fundamental submerged truth condition for "Es regnet."

11   Truth Conditions for Sentences in Different Modalities

Questions about the truth conditions for a sentence or kind of sentence are empirical questions. The answers depend on the history of the language and on some of the detailed workings of human cognition. Empirical questions of this sort are typically pursued by forming hypotheses and then sorting through evidence for or against. In the case of strictly empirical fact-stating language, a common hypothesis has been that the way this kind of language works requires some kind of mapping between sentence structures in the world and their truth conditions. I have spoken for the reasonableness of this correspondence view in Millikan (1984, 2017) and elsewhere. But if a sentence concerns morality, or aesthetics, or politeness, or logic, or mathematics and so forth, in each of these cases an unquestionably respectable tradition or traditions can be found arguing that no kind of correspondence can determine truth conditions for this kind of sentence.

Not much is known, or even much speculated, about the functions of language other than empirical fact-stating language. We know little about these functions or about how they are performed and hence about what conditions in the world might have to be in place for them to perform these functions in their normal way. We don't know if there are any special world conditions specific to individual sentences of certain kinds that are required for them to serve their functions normally. Some kinds of sentences might not fit the dichotomy *true or false* at all. Some have thought that certain sentences from religious texts are like that.

Performance of what kinds of stabilizing functions keep various types of sentences alive and reproducing—and hence what deeper descriptions of their truth conditions may be—matches the traditional philosophers' question about the nature of various kinds of truth: empirical truth, moral truth, aesthetic truth, logical truth, mathematical truth, religious truth, and so forth. What is the function of moral language, of the language of aesthetics, of the language of manners or of mathematics? How do they work? What keeps them alive? What do they accomplish that accounts for their proliferation, for their continued use by speakers, and for the continued reproduction of the responses they induce in hearers? What do beliefs about religion *do*? Beliefs about mathematics? Beliefs about morals? By what mechanisms do they perform these functions?[7]

One absorbing question concerns whether some kinds of truth depend in part or whole on the culture in which a language is used. What promotes proliferation of a certain kind of language might sometimes depend on peculiarities of the culture that its speakers and hearers share. Suppose, for example, that the moral language used in a culture helps to maintain certain structures and uniformities of a kind that help to maintain that community. The deep reason this language continues to proliferate is that it is helping to maintain the community that uses it. And suppose that exactly what structures and what uniformities are combining to do this job varies from one culture or community to another so that moral attitudes that are appropriate in one community may not be appropriate in another. The truth conditions for moral assertions would depend then on how the rest of a culture was structured so that moral truths in one community might differ from moral truths in another. Relativist answers to some of our questions about truth are not ruled out in advance.

Notes

1. I use the unfamiliar verb "purpose" rather than "intend" because intenders may be thought of as being aware of what they intend, whereas I want to include purposing and purposes of a much more primitive kind—for example, the purpose of the reflex eyeblink, the purpose of putting one's left foot forward when walking, and the purpose of shouting when angry.

2. The next few sections consist in part of abbreviated versions of suggestions on the stabilizing functions of traditionally problematic linguistic forms from Millikan (2018). These suggestions are experimental, initial suggestions, but they should give a sense of what I mean by *stabilizing function*. I will give examples of rather different kinds, hoping to prepare the reader for the variety of things that linguistic constructions may accomplish.

3. In *LTOBC* I followed Strawson, who thinks of ideas as "concepts." Now I would express this by saying "remove the unicept connected with the name 'unicorn.'" See Millikan (2017), where I argue for replacing the theoretical entity concept with the theoretical entity unicept.

4. Comment: among the "rules" of language are rules about how certain conventional linguistic forms have to be *embedded in the world* if they are to figure in the construction of complete and well-formed sentences (compare indexicals and demonstratives).

5. Compare (of course) Ryle (1950) on *inference licenses*.

6. In Millikan (2018), I argue that counerfactual conditionals do not have truth conditions.

7. What spurs reproduction is not always a benefit to the reproducer. That a certain kind of language has a function, that it is causing itself to be reproduced, does not necessarily mean that it is doing something that benefits us, its users. Compare memes.

References

Dennett, D. 2017. *From Bacteria to Bach and Back: The Evolution of Minds*. New York: W. W. Norton.

Horn, L. 1985. "Metalinguistic Negation and Pragmatic Ambiguity." *Language* 61: 121–174.

Horn, L. 1989. *A Natural History of Negation*. Chicago: University of Chicago Press.

Millikan, R. 1984. *Language, Thought, and Other Biological Categories*. Cambridge, MA: MIT Press.

Millikan, R. 2005. *Language: A Biological Model*. Oxford: Oxford University Press.

Millikan, R. 2017. *Beyond Concepts: Unicepts, Language, and Natural Information*. Oxford: Oxford University Press.

Millikan, R. 2018. "Biosemantics and Words That Don't Represent." *Theoria* 84: 229–241.

Ryle, G. 1950. "'If,' 'So,' and 'Because.'" In Max Black, ed., *Philosophical Analysis*, 323–340. Ithaca, NY: Cornell University Press.

Sellars, W. 1963. *Science, Perception and Reality*. New York: Humanities Press.

Strawson, P. F. 1949. "Truth." *Analysis* 9: 83–97.

Strawson, P. F. 1950. "Truth." *Proceedings of the Artistotelian Society*, suppl., 24: 129–156.

Strawson, P. F. 1971. *Logico-linguistic Papers*. London: Methuen.

Strawson, P. F. 1974. *Subject and Predicate in Logic and Grammar*. London: Methuen.

Tomasello, M. 2009. *Why We Cooperate*. Cambridge, MA: MIT Press.

Tomasello, M. 2014. *A Natural History of Human Thinking*. Cambridge, MA: Harvard University Press.

Wittgenstein, L. 1922. *Tractatus Logico-philosophicus*. London: Kegan Paul.

5   In Search of a Substantive Theory of Truth

Gila Sher

> The layman ... expects philosophers to answer deep questions of great import for an under-
> standing of the world. ... And the layman is quite right. ... Yet he finds most writings by
> philosophers of the analytical school disconcertingly remote from these concerns. ... The
> complaint ... is understandable. ... Analytical philosophy passed, comparatively recently,
> through a destructive phase. ... During that phase, it appeared as though demolition was the
> principal legitimate task of philosophy. Now most of us believe once more that philosophy has
> a constructive task; but, so thoroughly was the demolition accomplished, that the rebuilding
> is of necessity slow.
>
> —Michael Dummett, *The Logical Basis of Metaphysics*

Is a substantive theory of truth feasible? What would be the scope, structure, and content of such a theory? My idea of "a substantive theory" has the everyday connotation
of "a theory that provides an explanatory, constructive, and systematic account of a
rich, significant, and fundamental subject-matter." "A substantive theory of truth" in
this sense contrasts with "a deflationist theory of truth." Where deflationists say that
"truth is entirely captured by the ... triviality ... that each proposition specifies its own
condition for being true,"[1] advocates of a substantive theory of truth (henceforth, *substantivists*) say that truth is not entirely captured by this triviality; where deflationists
say that "the truth predicate exists solely for the sake of a certain logical need"[2] (that
is, indirect reference to, and generalization over, propositions), substantivists say that
it exists for other needs as well; where deflationists say that truth is not a deep notion,
substantivists say it is; and where deflationists say that a theory of truth cannot be, or
need not be, genuinely explanatory, substantivists say it can and should be. Substantivists accept the deflationist claim that truth is not mysterious, but they believe truth
yields itself to substantive inquiry. My notion of a substantive theory of truth is close
to what some call an "inflationary theory,"[3] but "substantive," in its everyday usage,
better captures the ordinary, common-sense considerations that motivate me. Like
Michael Dummett, I believe that philosophy should take on important "questions ...

for … understanding … the world," and, like the early Hartry Field, I think that "we'd be crazy to give … up in [philosophy] … a methodology [of substantive theorizing] that has proved extremely fruitful in science."[4]

The attempts to construct a substantive theory of truth, however, have come upon great difficulties, and many philosophers have given up hope of ever producing such a theory. Field, for example, has renounced his plan for a substantive theory of truth (based on a causal account of reference), and today he, along with many adherents of his original plan, is an avid champion of deflationism. Not all contemporary philosophers, however, are satisfied with the prevalent trend. Donald Davidson, Michael Devitt, Anil Gupta, Michael Lynch, Hilary Putnam, Crispin Wright, and others (including me in an earlier essay) have dissented, to a greater or lesser extent, from mainstream deflationism.[5]

Here I will further pursue the attempt to construct a substantive theory of truth by investigating some of the challenges facing it and offering a few ideas about how to meet them. In particular, I will connect the methodological challenges facing the theorist of truth with those facing the natural (and social) scientist. This will enable me to place the debate on truth in a new, broader perspective, and point to new ways of approaching the issues. I will concentrate on two complementary challenges: the challenge of *disunity*, and the challenge of *unity*. In the case of truth, these are the challenges of (i) recognizing the diversity, complexity and multidimensionality of truth, and (ii) uncovering its unifying principles.

This essay is divided into two sections: (I) "The Disunity of Truth" and (II) "The Unity of Truth." Section I presents two disunity challenges: a radical challenge, conducive to deflationism, and a moderate challenge, compatible with a substantive theory. I argue that the radical challenge is unsound but the moderate challenge is a genuine challenge, confronting any theory of a broad and diverse subject matter. To meet this challenge, I propose a few commonsensical guidelines, and I note a few similarities and differences between my approach and that of earlier philosophers (specifically Kant, James, and Wittgenstein).

One ramification of the disunity challenge is moderate pluralism. Moderate pluralism with respect to truth has recently been advanced by Wright and Lynch. Wright, for example, raises the possibility that truth in physics is based on correspondence while truth in mathematics is based on coherence. My own analysis suggests a different kind of pluralism: pluralism within the bounds of correspondence. The idea is that truth both in physics and in mathematics is based on correspondence, but since physics and mathematics involve different aspects of language and the world, their correspondence principles differ. This kind of pluralism brings us closer to the ideal of a balanced theory: a theory balancing the demands of unity with those of diversity. Two problems for any pluralist conception of truth are: (i) In what sense are diverse principles of truth principles of the same thing, namely, truth? and (ii) How can logical inference transmit truth from sentences governed by one type of truth to sentences governed by another? Solutions to both problems are offered in section II.

Section II: The debate on unity and diversity in science sometimes gives the impression that recognition of diversity and a search for unity are incompatible. Like many philosophers, I believe that unity and diversity complement rather than exclude each other, and neither has priority over the other. Wright, too, accepts this view, but his conception of the unifying principles differs from mine. While Wright's conception is minimalistic (the unifying principles are mere "platitudes"), I believe the unifying principles can and should be substantive. Unity is linked to substantiveness through its role in explanation, and the question is not whether substantive unification is possible, but what kind(s) of substantive unifiers are available in our field. I point out two types of such unifiers, *core unifier* and *specialized unifier*, and I formulate two theses exemplifying these types of unifier, the *Immanence Thesis* and the *Logicality Thesis*. The first thesis has implications for correspondence and skepticism; the second yields a new solution to the problem of logical inference across types of truth.

I The Disunity of Truth[6]

I.A Radical Disunity Challenge

A well-known argument against the feasibility of a substantive theory of truth says that since every thought (proposition, belief, cognition, judgment, sentence of a given language) has its own unique truth condition, a general and substantive account of truth is impossible. I will call this argument "the radical disunity argument." One formulation of this argument is:

> Compare "is true" ... with a genuine target of philosophical analysis. ... We know *individually* what makes ["is true"] applicable to the judgements or sentences of an understood language. "Penguins waddle" is a sentence true, in English, if and only if penguins waddle. It is true that snow is white if and only if snow is white. The reason the first sentence deserves the predicate is that penguins waddle, and the reason why the judgement that snow is white deserves the predicate is that snow *is* white. But these reasons are entirely different. There is no single account, or even little family of accounts, in virtue of which each deserves the predicate, for deciding whether penguins waddle has nothing much in common with deciding whether snow is white. There are *as* many different things to do, to decide whether the predicate applies, as there are judgements to make. So how *can* there be a unified, common account of the "property" which these quite different decision procedures supposedly determine?[7]

The theoretical principle underlying the radical disunity argument is clearly expressed by Kant in the introduction to "Transcendental Logic" of the *Critique of Pure Reason*. Inquiring whether it is possible to go beyond a minimalist characterization (literally, name clarification) of truth as agreement of a cognition with its object and provide a criterion that determines the precise conditions under which each cognition is true, Kant reasons:

> If truth consists in the agreement of a cognition with its object, then this object must thereby be distinguished from others; for a cognition is false if it does not agree with the object to which it is related even if it contains something that could well be valid of other objects. Now a general criterion of truth would be that which was valid of all cognitions without any distinction among their objects. But it is clear that since with such a criterion one abstracts from all content of cognition (relation to its object), yet truth concerns precisely this content, it would be completely impossible and absurd to ask for a mark of the truth of this content of cognition, and thus it is clear that a sufficient and yet at the same time general sign [Kennzeichen] of truth cannot possibly be provided. Since above we have called the content of cognition its matter, one must therefore say that no general sign of the truth of the matter of cognition can be demanded, because it is self-contradictory.[8]

A somewhat different formulation of this line of reasoning appears in Kant's logic lectures:

> A universal material criterion of truth is not possible; it is even self-contradictory. For as a *universal* criterion, valid for all objects in general, it would have to abstract fully from all difference among objects, and yet at the same time, as a material criterion, it would have to deal with just this difference, in order to be able to determine whether a cognition agrees with just that object to which it is related and not just with any object in general, in which case nothing would really be said. ... It is absurd to demand a universal material criterion of truth, which should abstract and at the same time not abstract from all difference among objects.[9]

The point is that a general and substantive criterion of truth would give rise to an irresoluble conflict between generality and particularity. Using "theory of truth" for "theory that provides a criterion of truth," we may express the radical disunity argument as follows:

(a) Truth consists in the particular agreement of a thought with its unique object.

(b) A general theory of truth must, in order to be general, abstract from the particularity of this relation.

(c) But a substantive theory of truth cannot (if it is to be substantive) abstract from its particularity. Hence:

(d) A general and substantive theory of truth is impossible.[10]

Now, on some level, this argument is persuasive. Not only is it formally valid, but its conclusion is, in some sense, correct: it is absurd to think that the theorist of truth could come up with a general and substantive criterion (or necessary and sufficient condition) that would determine, all by itself, the truth value of each and every truth bearer. But in a deeper and more important way the radical disunity argument is unsound. The argument assumes an altogether unreasonable conception of a substantive theory of truth as consisting of, or offering, a Kantian criterion of truth. There is no reason that a theory aiming at a philosophical explanation of truth be interested in, or be required to provide, such a criterion. Achieving a genuine understanding of truth does not mean detecting all the minute differences between any distinct truths, or determining what exactly has to be done in order to find out whether such sentences as "Penguins waddle" and "Snow is white" are true. There is a whole array of intermediate projects between the minimalist (deflationist) project of name clarification of truth and the maximalist project of providing a Kantian criterion of truth. And a substantive theory of truth aims at (some of) the intermediate projects. A comparison with the theory of knowledge might help. No one, least of all Kant, would require a substantive theory of knowledge to provide a full and detailed criterion of knowledge—a criterion determining, all by itself, with respect to each and every judgment, whether it should be included in our corpus of knowledge. Why should the theory of truth be required to provide such a detailed criterion of truth? One might answer that truth is special: the truth of a thought *is* dependent on its specific content and object. But does not the same hold for knowledge? (Are not the knowledge conditions of "Penguins waddle" and "Snow is white" just as particular and just as diverse as their truth conditions?) Should we conclude, then, that a substantive theory of knowledge is also impossible?[11]

The radical disunity argument is, in my view, best interpreted as a *reductio ad absurdum* of the criterial, maximalist view of a substantive theory of truth. Substantive theories are, in general, selective; they abstract from, that is, overlook, some aspects, features, and differences of objects in their domain.[12] The choice is not between a deflationist theory and a criterion of truth; the choice is between the former and a substantive account of the *major principles* and *facets* of truth.

It is not clear whether Kant himself drew a false dilemma between (what we call today) a deflationist theory and a criterion of truth. On the one hand, in introducing his argument he does appear to contrast the mere "name clarification" of truth (his conception of a deflationist theory) with a criterion of truth.[13] On the other hand, elsewhere he repeatedly affirms the existence of substantive accounts of various facets of truth and makes substantive claims about truth. For example, he declares that general logic provides a universal negative criterion of truth; he characterizes Transcendental Analytic as "a logic of truth" (saying it sets negative but not narrowly logical conditions on the possibility of truth); he claims that "transcendental truth, which precedes all empirical truth and makes it possible, consists in the general relation [of cognitions to the entirety of all possible experience]"; he suggests that an account of "the formal conditions of empirical truth" is possible; he proclaims that the principle of causality is a condition of empirical truth; he argues that the possibility of experience is a necessary condition for truth; he implies that a "sufficient mark of empirical truth" is possible; and he contends that his own theory, unlike Berkeley's, is capable of providing a "certain criterion for distinguishing truth from illusion" (in a more reasonable sense of "criterion" than in the introduction to "Transcendental Logic").[14] Be that as it may, the dilemma raised by the radical disunity argument is a false dilemma. The radical disunity argument rejects the possibility of a substantive theory of truth by arguing against an absurd conception of such a theory.

Furthermore, the radical disunity argument assumes that the theory of truth has only one goal: account for the truth conditions of sentences (cognitions, and so forth). But the theory of truth has other goals as well: explain the normativity of truth, determine its applicability to various fields of discourse, adjudicate between different conceptions of truth (correspondence, coherence, and so forth), elucidate the relation between truth and other topics of philosophical investigation, and so on. The radical disunity argument does not question the feasibility of any of these goals.[15]

But while the radical disunity challenge is a false challenge, the tensions between generality and particularity, unity and diversity, abstraction and detailed investigation, to which it directs our attention, do pose a genuine, if not insurmountable, challenge to knowledge. This challenge was taken up by Kant (in another section of the *Critique of Pure Reason*), James, and Wittgenstein, but I prefer to approach it through a more contemporary venue—the ongoing debate on disunity in science. It seems to me that many of the issues raised in this debate pertain to substantive theories in general, and the challenge facing the theorist of truth would be better understood by a judicious comparison with the one facing the scientist.

I.B Moderate Disunity Challenge

Challenges to substantive theories of truth may be of three kinds: (a) challenges to substantive theories *in general*, (b) challenges to substantive *philosophical* theories, and (c) challenges to substantive theories of *truth*. The moderate disunity challenge falls under the first category, and to discuss it I will turn to the literature on disunity in science.[16]

The disunity of science is commonly conceived either as a disunity of theories or as a disunity of their subject matter, namely, nature. These two types of disunity are interconnected, but the former places a greater emphasis on conceptual differences, the latter on "the disorder of things" (to borrow the title of John Dupré's book). The disunity of theories challenges the unification of science on three levels: (i) total unification (that is, construction of a "theory of everything"), (ii) intertheoretic unification (for example, reduction of psychology to biology), and (iii) intratheoretic unification (for example, elimination of the particle-wave duality in physics). The disunity of nature challenges the ability of science to systematize its subject matter. It is an open question how much order there is in nature and, as a result, whether nature can be subsumed under general laws. Now, it seems to me that both challenges can be generalized to other fields of knowledge, including philosophy with its broad, diverse, and highly complex subject matters—knowledge, ontology, meaning, and truth. Among the more general considerations raised by scientists and philosophers of science are:[17]

(1) *The complexity of the world*:

    (a) The world exhibits different complexities and interdependencies on different levels, and at each level of complexity entirely new properties appear (P. W. Anderson).

    (b) There are both higher and lower organizing principles, and in the course of investigation we sometimes have to add new levels of basic entities, concepts, and principles (Dupré, R. B. Laughlin and David Pines, Laughlin et al.).

    (c) The behavior of objects and properties is sensitive to a multiplicity of factors governed by multiple principles (Dupré, Nancy Cartwright).

(2) *The limitations of our cognitive powers*:

The great complexity of the world on the one hand, and our cognitive limitations on the other, limit our ability to comprehend it by a single, unified principle or theory (Comte[18]).

(3) *The partiality of knowledge*:

Human knowledge is, by its nature, partial: (i) universal principles and explanations are, due to their high level of abstraction and idealization, inherently partial, covering certain aspects of the phenomena under discussion while leaving others uncovered; (ii) as concepts and knowledge are extended, universal principles become partial, so that what was thought, at one point, to be complete, turns out, later on, to be unfinished (Patrick Suppes, Noam Chomsky,[19] Ian Hacking, Stephen Hawking,[20] Laughlin and Pines).

(4) *Richness of interests, multiplicity of perspectives, human creativity*:

There are many legitimate ways of dividing things into units and many advantageous points of view on things; these, given our creativity, give rise to a multiplicity of theories, a multiplicity which enriches our understanding rather than impedes it (Jerry Fodor, Suppes, Dupré).

(5) *Other methodological considerations*:

    (a) In any field of knowledge we are continuously confronted with new situations and new problems; as new problems arise, new theories and new methods of investigation are often required (Suppes, Hacking).[21]

    (b) There can be many unifiers, of different interest, in any field of knowledge; hence, there may be room for more than one unifying theory (Hacking).

    (c) Generality is not always a guide to a better theory. A small collection of simple principles is preferable to a single, highly complex, universal principle (Hacking).

None of these considerations has to do with the specific features of science, and all are either directly applicable or easily extendable to philosophy. In the field of truth, they have the potential of changing our perspective on existent theories, suggesting further developments, and pointing to new solutions to old problems. I will not be able to work out the details of these influences here, but a few examples might indicate the direction of change.

Consider the equivalence schema. Deflationists claim that the equivalence schema (or something like it) exhausts the topic of truth. But from the present perspective the equivalence schema describes only one, high-level, principle of truth, and as such it provides a *partial* account of truth, to be complemented by other accounts, centering on other principles of various levels of generality.

One example of a lower-level account of truth is given by Alfred Tarski's theory.[22] While the equivalence schema treats all sentences on a par, Tarski's theory distinguishes them along a given parameter—logical structure. Sentences exhibiting distinct logical structures have different Tarskian truth conditions, whereas those exhibiting the same logical structure have essentially the same truth condition. From the present perspective, Tarski's theory provides an account of a special factor of truth—the *logical factor*—and as such it is a mid- (or low-) level theory.[23] Most importantly, Tarski's theory, like the equivalence schema, offers a *partial* account of truth (logical structure is not the only thing that determines the truth value of sentences), and a "complete" account of truth must go beyond it.

One way of going beyond Tarski's theory was suggested by Field.[24] While Tarski's theory does not distinguish the truth conditions of atomic sentences in any informative manner, Field envisions an informative account of their truth conditions. The realization of Field's vision has, however, come upon great difficulties, and these are commonly attributed to a special feature of his approach, namely, its physicalistic orientation. (Field wants to base the account of atomic truth on a physicalistic theory of reference, application, and fulfillment—in short, satisfaction—for our nonlogical vocabulary.) The disunity perspective points to a different explanation. The problem, from our perspective, lies in an implicit assumption of Field's project, independent of physicalism, namely, that the satisfaction conditions of the entire vocabulary of human thought (minus a small part of this vocabulary—the logical vocabulary) are based on one and the same principle, or kind of principle. From our perspective this assumption is unwarranted: the totality of extralogical expressions exhibits an enormous diversity, and one cannot take it for granted that physical and moral expressions, biological and philosophical expressions, psychological and mathematical expressions, expressions pertaining to religion and expressions pertaining to technology, are all governed by the same satisfaction principle, or the same kind of principle.

Field's reaction to the difficulties faced by his project was a retreat to deflationism. But the right lesson from our perspective is not deflationism, minimalism, or quietism. A more productive lesson is openness and flexibility in devising our methodology. The theorist of truth, like the scientist, must adjust his methodology to the peculiarities of his subject matter, and to do so effectively he should take a cue from his fellow theorists and follow such straightforward, commonsensical, and workable guidelines as:

(A) In constructing a theory of truth, do not legislate in advance the form the theory shall take. Whether the study of truth will lead to the discovery of a single, universal principle (definition, schema, necessary and sufficient condition), or to a number of partial principles, is an open question, the answer to which largely depends on features of our subject matter, that is, on things that will emerge in the course of, not prior to, investigation. The answer also depends on our resources and capacities, but they, too, cannot always be determined at the outset of inquiry.

(B) Do not think of the study of truth as focused on a single problem. Truth is a broad, complex, and diversified topic, and as such it poses a plethora of problems rather than a single problem. Today, it is common to center the study of truth on the subject of truth conditions, but although this undoubtably is a central subject, it does not exhaust, or even come close to exhausting the topic of truth. Other subjects include the normativity of truth, the role of truth in knowledge, the relation between truth and correspondence, skepticism and relativism with respect to truth, the interplay between mind and world in creating a standard of truth, and so on.

(C) In developing a theory of truth, aim at a fruitful balance between universality and particularity, similarity and diversity, abstraction and attention to detail, systematicity and applicability. Freeman Dyson's dictum that "every theory needs for its healthy growth a creative balance between unifiers and disunifiers"[25] applies not only to scientific but also to philosophical theories.

(D) Think of the development of a theory of truth as a dynamic process, in the course of which the theory is likely to expand, contract, undergo revision, change direction, stall, make leaps of progress, yield unexpected results, and so forth. The question is not whether the theory of truth *is* (atemporally or eternally) a unified or a disunified theory; the question is what steps can we take to increase its unity without sacrificing its substantiveness.

These guidelines suggest that we need not conceive the theory of truth as either a Tarski-style definition, or an equivalence-like schema, or a Kantian criterion. Tarski's characterization of truth with its emphasis on logical structure is extremely fruitful in logic, where it is incorporated in the definition of logical consequence and, through it, makes an invaluable contribution to logical semantics. But it is not clear that to understand whether, why, and how truth applies to, say, ethics we need a Tarskian definition of truth for moral discourse. A similar point applies to correspondence. Obviously, if we start with the usual paradigms of correspondence associated with simple observational statements ("Snow is white," "Grass is green," "The cat is on the mat"), we are likely to conclude that correspondence is out of the question in ethics. But if we investigate the moral domain without prejudice, if we take it by its own measure, we open up the possibility of new insights into correspondence, insights that would liberate us from the naive, simple-minded view of true thought as a *mirror of* (or as *isomorphic to*) reality.

The disunity challenge, as a challenge to knowledge in general and/or to philosophy in particular, was discussed by a number of philosophers. To further clarify my view, I will indicate a few points of similarity and difference with the views of three of these: Kant, James, and Wittgenstein.

Kant   In "On the Regulative Use of the Ideas of Pure Reason" (first *Critique*), Kant says:

> To the logical principle of genera which postulates identity there is opposed another, namely that of *species*, which needs manifoldness and variety in things despite their agreement under the same genus, and prescribes to the understanding that it be no less attentive to variety than to agreement. This principle (of discrimination, or of the faculty of distinguishing) severely limits the rashness of the first principle (of wit [an innate talent of the mind for comparing and assimilating things that are superficially different]); and here reason shows two interests that conflict with each other: on the one side, an interest in the *domain* (universality) in regard to genera, on the other an interest in *content* (determinacy) in respect of the manifoldness of species.
>
> Reason thus prepares the field for the understanding: 1. by a principle of *sameness of kind* in the manifold under higher genera, 2. by a principle of the *variety* of what is same in kind under lower species. ... We can call these the principles of the *homogeneity* [and] *specification* of forms.
>
> The first law ... guards against excess in the manifold variety of original genera, and recommends sameness of kind; the second, on the contrary, limits in turn this inclination to unanimity, and demands that one distinguish subspecies before one turns to the individuals with one's universal concepts.[26]

Like Kant, I regard the disunity problem as a problem of balance, but Kant's construal of the problem strikes me as too narrow. Kant tries to fit the disunity problem into a neat and orderly picture of our system of knowledge as a hierarchical, species-genera structure, but the tension between unity and diversity, as I see it, is more complex, intricate, and multidimensional than the species-genera picture suggests. Accordingly, I regard our system of knowledge as a polymorphic structure rather than a regular tree-structure, as envisaged by Kant.

James   In his lectures on pragmatism, James subsumes the disunity problem under the classical puzzle of "the one and the many":

> If ... we talk in general of our intellect and its needs, we quickly see that unity is only one of them. ... What our intellect really aims at is neither variety nor unity taken singly, but *totality*. In this, acquaintance with reality's diversities is as important as understanding their connexion.
>
> The ... point is to notice that the oneness and the manyness are absolutely co-ordinate here. Neither is primordial or more essential or excellent than the other.[27]

While James, too, regards the disunity problem as a problem of balance, his solution to the problem is fundamentally unbalanced. James recommends a shift toward radical pragmatism, a pragmatism that requires, at least in philosophy, rejecting the rational, the abstract, and the theoretical in favor of the experiential, the concrete, and the practical. I agree with James that balancing the demands of unity and diversity requires a certain amount of pragmatic "juggling." But I see no reason why this should conflict with rational, abstract, and theoretical reasoning. The disunity challenge is a challenge to the *design* of theories, not to theorizing itself; it necessitates the introduction of pragmatic considerations into philosophy, not the elimination of theoretical, rational, and abstract considerations from philosophy.[28]

Wittgenstein Wittgenstein's disunity challenge is expressed in his "family resemblance" remarks. Wittgenstein objects to what I have elsewhere called "the myth of the common denominator," namely, the view that to understand a concept is to identify the common denominator of all objects falling under it, or to formulate a necessary and sufficient condition for falling under it (*op. cit.*). Many concepts, according to Wittgenstein, have no single defining characteristic (or a small set of such characteristics); instead, they exhibit "a complicated network of similarities overlapping and criss-crossing: sometimes overall similarities, sometimes similarities of detail."[29] This is the case, in particular, with concepts representing the traditional subject matters of philosophy: language, thought, number, and, significantly, truth.[30]

I share many of Wittgenstein's views: that philosophy tends to produce "network" rather than "one characteristic" concepts, that its theories face a serious disunity challenge, that its vulnerability to disunity is due to the breadth, complexity, and multidimensionality of the problems it seeks to resolve, and so forth. I also support Wittgenstein's conclusion that philosophers should increase the element of "looking" in their investigations: "Do not say: 'There *must* be something common, or they would not be called ["truths"]'—but *look and see* whether there is anything common to all." "Do not think, but look!" (*op. cit.*, §66). Wittgenstein, however, goes too far. Like James he concludes that philosophy "may not advance any kind of theory," that it "must do away with all *explanation*" (*op. cit.*, §109),[31] and that it should abandon any aspirations to systematicity. These conclusions, I believe, are *nonsequitur*. It is an open question how much disunity there is in various branches of philosophy; whether this disunity rules out the existence of structure, hence of theory and explanation; and how resourceful philosophers will be in facing this disunity.[32] The tensions between unity and plurality, generality and particularity, abstraction and attention to detail challenge philosophy but need not stifle it. In fact, they create a fertile ground for theory construction, since what is it to construct a theory but to systematically connect elements that, prior to the construction, are disparate, varied, disorderly, and disconnected? Just as important, there is no real conflict between looking and thinking. Much of thinking is looking, and in many fields (for example, meta-logic) looking is abstract (for example, looking at a proof system to see whether it is complete). Philosophers ought to increase the element of "looking" in their methodology: carefully examine the objects of their inquiry, be open-minded and nondogmatic, aim at correctness, provide justification, be mindful of counter-evidence, and so forth. But this does not conflict with theory and explanation.

The idea that truth might be based on multiple principles suggests a *moderate pluralism* with respect to truth. The idea is that the theory of truth may profitably be constructed as a *family* of theories, rather than a single theory. Each theory in the family would investigate some area, aspect, or factor of truth, and together these theories would produce (in the ideal limit) a comprehensive account of truth. This pluralism is moderate since, on the one hand, it does not rule out the possibility that a single, exhaustive, and substantive theory of truth can, in principle, be constructed; on the other hand, it holds that such a theory (though desirable) is not a *sine qua non* for a thorough and genuine (that is, substantive) understanding of truth.

Moderate pluralism has recently been advocated by a number of philosophers, for example, Wright and Lynch.[33] Wright, like me, argues that universal principles might not exhaust the topic of truth and if they do not, they may be complemented by other, more specific, principles. But for Wright this means that different fields of discourse (physics, mathematics, ethics, the comic, and so forth) might be governed by altogether different types of truth, say, physical discourse by correspondence truth and mathematical discourse by coherence truth. This is a rather radical division, and it is important to note that pluralism may come in more moderate versions. First, the plurality of truth may lie within the bounds of a single type of truth, say, correspondence. In that case, truth in all areas of discourse would be based on correspondence, but the principles underlying correspondence in physics would differ from those underlying correspondence in, say, mathematics. (Later on, I will argue that truth is in fact based on correspondence, and the potential multiplicity of principles of truth is indeed a multiplicity of correspondence principles). Second, the plurality of truth need not center on "fields" of truth; it might center on "factors" of truth. The point is that truth might be based on a multiplicity of factors, but the same factor may operate in diverse fields of truth. Thus consider the "moral" sentence "All humans are good," and the "biological" sentence "All humans are two-legged." The truth values of these sentences are determined by (at least) three factors—the logical factor (which is reflected in the satisfaction conditions of the universal quantifier and the conditional), the biological or physical factor (which is reflected in the satisfaction conditions of "is human" and "is two-legged"), and the moral factor (which is reflected in the satisfaction conditions of "is (morally) good"). Two of these factors are relevant to the truth value of both the moral and the biological sentence, and only one distinguishes between them. A pluralism based on factors of truth is finer and more nuanced than one based on fields of truth, yet it recognizes (and can account for) differences among truths in different areas of discourse.

Two objections to pluralist conceptions of truth naturally arise:

(1) If truth is based on multiple principles, in what sense are these principles of the same thing, namely, truth?

(2) If two statements are governed by different types of truth (or their truth is determined by different factors) how can logical inference transmit truth from one to the other? For example, how can a comical conclusion follow logically from a physical premise (or from a set of premises which essentially contains a physical premise)?[34]

Solutions to both problems will be offered in section II.

II   The Unity of Truth

II.A   Unity Challenge

The unity challenge is the challenge of finding as significant, as comprehensive, as informative, and as enlightening unities as possible. Unity, as many philosophers have pointed out, is a condition as well as a goal of knowledge. One aspect of unity, namely, its contribution to the explanatory power of theories (a major mark of substantive theories), is especially relevant to the present inquiry. The connection between unity and explanation has been emphasized by several philosophers of science (Carl Hempel, Michael Friedman, Philip Kitcher, and others[35]), and much of what they say about the role, forms, and problems of unity applies to philosophy as well: philosophical unification, like scientific unification, may be local or global (unification of disparate elements of a single philosophical field, unification of hitherto distinct philosophical fields, unification of all fields of philosophy, and unification of philosophy with other fields of knowledge). It may center on elements of different kinds: laws and principles, theories, arguments, concepts, methods of inquiry, justification procedures, and so forth. Its goals, like those of scientific unification, may vary: decreasing the overall number of tenets and principles, creating reliable styles (patterns) of argumentation, harmoniously integrating disparate elements, and so forth. Philosophical unification may be stricter or looser: reduction versus supervenience, supervenience versus (mere) integration, hierarchical integration versus holistic integration, and so forth. Among the reductionist projects in philosophy are idealism, materialism, physicalism, logicism, the *Aufbau* project, the "linguistic turn," and extreme naturalism; all major philosophical systems and movements—rationalism, empiricism, transcendental idealism, moderate naturalism, and so on—aim at harmonious integration of some issues, principles, problems, and/or methods.

Two well-known pitfalls of scientific unification are *spurious* unification and *exclusionary* unification. Spurious unification trivially reduces multiple laws to fewer laws without gain in understanding. One example (due to Hempel and Paul Oppenheim[36]) is conjunction: unifying *A* and *B* by constructing their conjunction, *A&B*. In the field of truth, deflationists often define truth by an infinite list, or an infinite conjunction, of T-sentences (instances of the disquotational schema). Such a definition arguably provides a spurious unification of diverse truth conditions. Field's criticism of Tarski's theory is also one of spurious unification, directed at Tarski's list-like specification of the truth conditions of atomic sentences.

Exclusionary unification is a flaw in attitude: to think that the success of, say, string theory would leave no worthwhile scientific questions unanswered, or would rule out the usefulness of all other unifiers, is to yield to this pitfall. Disquotationalism arguably suffers from this flaw as well. It is not uncommon for a disquotationalist to say that *all* there is to truth is disquotation, meaning *all* worthwhile philosophical questions about truth are answerable by the disquotational schema, and the *only* genuine unifier of truth is this schema.

The connection between unity and explanation in science has been recently challenged by Margaret Morrison.[37] Morrison argues that the highest degree of unification is achieved by structural explanations, but the best scientific explanations are causal rather than structural. I will not get into the issue of structural versus causal explanation here. The claims that structural explanations are not the only unifying explanations, that different kinds of explanation are unifying in different ways, and that the most general explanations do not automatically impart the greatest degree of understanding, I find congenial. But the implicit suggestion that science admits only one type of effective explanation (namely, causal explanation), and the sweeping declaration that "general principles fail to be explanatory in any substantive sense" (ibid., 33), I regard as unfounded. The latter, in fact, is refuted by Morrison herself, since many of her causal principles are in fact highly general. The search for a substantive theory, as I understand it, is first and foremost a search for explanatory unifiers, on various levels of generality.

The view that in spite of its diversity truth can be unified by general principles is supported by Wright.[38] Wright proposes a series of universal principles of truth, including:

(P1) To assert is to present as true.

(P2) Any truth-apt content has a significant negation which is likewise truth apt.

(P3) To be true is to correspond to the facts.

(P4) A statement may be justified without being true, and vice versa.[39]

My own conception of the universal principles differs from Wright's in one respect. While Wright regards the universal principles as "platitudes," and as such as minimalistic, that is, deflationist, I see no reason why the universal principles could not be substantive (informative, explanatory, and so forth). The key to a balance between unity and diversity is, in my view, not platitudiness (with its implication of triviality), but *partiality*. The universal principles are partial in the sense of not exhausting the topic of truth, that is, leaving room for other principles, on various levels of generality.[40]

Below I will propose two substantive and universal principles of truth: *Immanence* and *Logicality*. The former is related to Wright's (P1) and (P3); the latter is somewhat related to his (P2).

II.B Substantive Unifiers of Truth

1. Two types of universal and substantive unifiers. Consider a broad and multidimensional concept, *C*, that (due to its breadth and multidimensionality) cannot be fully captured by either a single definition or a necessary-and-sufficient condition. This situation leaves open at least two possibilities for (substantive) universal unifiers of *C*: (i) a "core" unifier—a unifier that traces the roots of *C* to some general principle(s) of human thought and/or the world (without purporting to exhaust *C*), and (ii) a "specialized" unifier—a unifier centering on a particular factor of *C* (one among many) that, due to its special features, applies to all instances of *C* (or to many instances of *C* in every area to which *C* applies). Below I will delineate two universal and substantive unifiers of truth: a core unifier, *Immanence*, described by the *Immanence Thesis*, and a specialized unifier, *Logicality*, described by the *Logicality Thesis*.

2. Immanence Thesis. The Immanence Thesis (upper-case "I") traces the roots of our concept of truth to three basic principles of human thought: *immanence* (lower-case "i"), *transcendence*, and *normativity*.

A. Immanence. The immanence principle says that one basic mode of human thought is the *immanent* mode. By "immanence" I understand something akin to, but more general than, W. V. Quine's notion of immanence.[41] Quine says that to speak immanently is to speak from within a theory, where speaking from within a theory is speaking literally and assertively, that is, declaring that a certain object or *n*-tuple of objects (mentioned in a sentence) possesses a certain property (also mentioned in it), or more generally that things are (literally) thus and so. For me, an immanent thought is not necessarily assertive or literal. A thought is immanent if it attributes some property to some object(s) or says (assertively or unassertively) that things are one way or another. In other words, any thought attachable to Frege's content stroke is immanent in my sense.

The Immanence Thesis says that truth is immanent in three ways: (i) truth is a property of immanent thoughts, (ii) the question of truth arises for all immanent thoughts, and (iii) truth statements—that is, statements of the form "*X* is true/false" (or "It is true/false that *X*")—are immanent. Thus: (i) If truth is a property of *X*, *X* is a thought that attributes some property to some object, or says how things are. ("Snow is white," for example, of which truth is a property, is a thought—a sentence—and it attributes some property [the property of being white] to some object [the stuff snow].) (ii) If *X* is an immanent thought, the question of truth, that is, the question "Is *X* true?," arises with respect to *X*. (The question "Is it true?" arises with respect to "Snow is white," "Coal is green," and so forth.) (iii) If *X* is a truth statement (for example, the statement

"'Snow is white' is true"), then X attributes some property (namely, the property of being true) to some object (in our example, the sentence "Snow is white").

The range of immanent thoughts is vast and diverse: immanent thoughts may take the form of a sentence or a theory, they may be realistic or fictional, contingent or law-like, directed at objects and properties of one kind or another (physical, mathematical, philosophical, moral), syntactically simple or syntactically complex (logical compounds, modal compounds, subjunctive conditionals), and so on. The vastness, diversity, and inner complexity of the immanent domain partly explain the breadth, complexity, and diversity of our concept of truth.

B. Transcendence. The principle of transcendence is a generalization of Tarski's principle of meta-linguistic predication. This principle says that a second basic mode of human thought is the transcendent mode: we transcend a given thought, or domain of thoughts, in order to *reflect* upon it. "Transcendence" has fallen into disrepute lately. To say that truth is transcendent is (so it is claimed) tantamount to saying that we have a "God's eye view" on the world, that we have access to "things in themselves," and so forth. *Transcendence, as I use this term here, has neither of these connotations.* What I mean by "transcending" is casting a reflective look at a thought, or at a region of thought, from a standpoint external to it, yet within the domain of (human) thought. Transcendence does not rule out immanence. On the contrary, most transcendent thoughts are immanent: they attribute properties to thoughts, draw relations between thoughts, say this is how things are with respect to thoughts.[42] The Immanence Thesis says that truth is a transcendent property of thoughts and that truth statements are (immanent) transcendent statements.

C. Normativity. The principle of normativity says that a third basic mode of human thought is the normative mode, a mode closely related to the human proclivity for critical reflection. This is how Christine Korsgaard (who studies normativity in the moral domain, but draws analogies to other domains as well) explains it:

> Normative concepts exist because human beings have normative problems. And we have normative problems because we are self-conscious rational animals, capable of reflection about what we ought to believe and do. That is why the normative question can be raised in the first place: because even when we are inclined to believe that something is right and to some extent feel ourselves moved to do it we can still *always* ask: But is this really true? And must I really do this? ... It is ... because we are normative animals who can question our experience, that normative concepts exists. ... It is always possible for us to call our beliefs and motives into question.[43]

In the present case, it is our disposition to question whether things are as our thoughts say they are, that leads to the concept of truth. The critical question is: "Is it so as a given thought says it is?" and truth is a *standard* for a positive answer to this question. The question "Is it so?" is an especially broad and basic question: it applies to any immanent thought, and is included in other critical questions (for example, critical questions concerning knowledge). The Immanence Thesis says that the concept of truth is a normative concept, and its breadth is associated with the universality of the critical question "Is it so?" in the (vast) domain of immanent thought.

D. Immanence Thesis. Truth, according to the Immanence Thesis, lies at the juncture of three basic principles of human thought: immanence, transcendence, and normativity. Given an immanent thought, *t*, the critical, transcendent question "Is it so as *t* says it is?" arises with respect to *t*, and truth is a standard for a positive answer to this question, a standard for *it being so as t says it is*: object *o* has the property *P*, objects $o_1, \ldots, o_n$ stand in the relation *R*, and so forth. Truth, of course, is not the only standard for immanent thoughts; other standards (associated with other critical questions) include coherence, justification, empirical verification, explanatory value, utility, and so forth. But the critical question "Is it so?" is one of the more basic questions of human thought, and truth, therefore, is a fundamental standard of thought. A theory of truth explains this standard, specifies its principles, and works out its connections to other standards of human thought.

In developing a theory of truth it is important to recognize that the domain of immanent thought is an ever expanding, ever changing domain. The dynamic nature of this domain is connected to our tendency to create new concepts, acquire new interests, develop new perspectives, raise new problems, revise our concepts and theories, devise new cognitive tools, and so on. One task of the theory of truth is to study how changes in the domain of immanent thought affect our concept of truth. Other tasks are to determine whether the concept of truth actually applies to a given domain of thought, how it applies to it (for example, directly or indirectly), and so forth. Expressivists, for example, argue that truth does not apply to ethics; Russell argues that truth applies to sentences containing definite descriptions indirectly, through sentences that do not contain such descriptions; physicalists argue that truth conditions for any statements must be reformulated in physicalistic terms; and so on. Much more remains to be said about the Immanence of truth and the three principles underlying it, but the main idea should be clear: truth is a transcendent standard, or a family of standards, for immanent thoughts—a standard for a positive answer to the critical question "Is it so?" directed at such thoughts.

The Immanence Thesis is rich in consequences. Two of its consequences concern (a) correspondence, and (b) skepticism and relativism with respect to truth.

(a) *Correspondence.* Truth, according to the Immanence Thesis, is a standard for a positive answer to the question "Is it so, as a given immanent thought says it is?" Given the content of this question, a positive answer carries us outside the given thought into things external to it, things it is about—"the world" in a broad sense of the word. The question is whether the objects the thought is about have the properties it attributes to them or, more generally, whether the world is as it says it is. This, of course, is a correspondence question, and in this way the Immanence Thesis implies a correspondence view of truth—the view that for an immanent thought to be true there must be some positive correlation between what it says (literally or nonliterally) and how things are. But while the Immanence Thesis affirms correspondence, the view it affirms does not suffer from the rigidity, simplism, and dogmatism that correspondence views are often charged with. The reason is that, as we have seen above, the thesis is sensitive to expansions, changes, and variations in the domain of thought, both internal and transcendent, and this sensitivity protects it from commitment to an overly simplistic, one-dimensional view of correspondence.

Correspondence, from the standpoint of the Immanence Thesis, is a *research program* rather than a *dogma*. Among the questions raised by this program are: What correspondence principles govern truth in logic? Mathematics? Physics? Psychology? (Or what are the logical, mathematical, physical, and psychological factors of correspondence?) What are their similarities and differences? Is there correspondence in ethics? What kind of correspondence? (Are we misled by the surface structure of ethical thoughts?) All these are open questions, and a judicious response to them requires an understanding not just of correspondence per se, but of the specific field of knowledge in which it is realized (to which its various factors belong). Below I will offer an account, or rather an outline of an account, of one type (aspect, factor) of correspondence, the *logical* one, based on prior investigations of logic.[44]

(b) *Skepticism with respect to truth.* Skepticism is often divided into two kinds: *local skepticism* and *global skepticism*. Local skepticism with respect to truth questions the existence of a standard of truth in a specific area; global skepticism questions the existence of a standard of truth in any area. Local skeptical challenges are part and parcel of a critical approach to knowledge; global skepticism is a barrier to knowledge. The Immanence Thesis affirms the legitimacy of skepticism, leaving the success of local skepticism (in particular cases) an open question, and posing counterchallenges to global skepticism.

Skepticism is sanctioned by the same principles that sanction truth itself: immanence, transcendence, and normativity. Given a "truth thought," *t*, that is, a thought that attributes truth/falsity to some thought (or truth aptness to some domain of thought), the critical transcendent question "Is it so?" arises with respect to *t*, and one possible answer to this question is the skeptical answer: there is no way to determine whether things are as *t* says they are; there is no standard of truth for *t*.

Local skepticism. Consider the following local skeptical statements, expressing three degrees of skepticism with respect to *moral* truth:[45]

(1) Moral statements have a standard of truth, but this standard is a standard of psychological truth, not of *sui generis* moral truth. Explanation: although the surface structure of moral statements is "*X* has moral property *Y*," their deep structure is "Speaker *Z* has attitude *Y** toward *X*," where "*Y**" stands for a psychological attitude, mental state, or feeling correlated with *Y* (for example, "*Y*" stands for "good"

and "$Y*$" for "approbation"). The standard by which the truth of moral statements is measured is, therefore, a standard of psychological truth.

(2) Moral statements have a standard of truth (either a standard of *sui generis* moral truth or a standard of some other kind of truth), but this standard is not their primary standard of success. Explanation: while moral statements do attribute properties to objects (actions, intentions, and so forth), their main goal is to express, support, or arouse feelings or attitudes. Their primary success standard is therefore a standard of persuasiveness or expressivity, not a standard of truth.

(3) Moral statements have no standard of truth whatsoever, either primary or secondary. Explanation: moral statements are not immanent. They do not attribute any properties to any objects or purport to say how things are. They *merely* express attitudes or feelings, and expressions of feelings are not subject to a standard of truth.

The Immanence Thesis is compatible with all three degrees of moral skepticism, leaving their correctness an open question. That is, from the point of view of the Immanence Thesis it is an open question whether moral statements are literal, whether truth is their main standard of success, and whether they are immanent.

Global skepticism. Global skepticism says that there is no standard of truth for any thought whatsoever. The Immanence Thesis challenges the global skeptic to defend his view by showing either (1) that there are no immanent thoughts, or (2) that the critical transcendent question "Is it so as *t* says it is?" does not apply to any immanent thought *t*, or (3) that there are no standards for a positive answer to this question with respect to any *t*. These challenges are not easy to meet. All of them involve negative existential claims which, especially in philosophy, are notoriously difficult to establish. Furthermore, each of them poses a special difficulty: to meet (1) the skeptic has to show that the skeptical statement itself is not immanent, and do so without using any other immanent statement—a self-defeating task according to many philosophers, for example, Thomas Nagel.[46] To meet (2) the skeptic has to explain how the question "Is it so?" cannot apply to a thought that says that things *are* thus and so—something that goes against both grammar and semantics. And to meet (3) the skeptic has to establish not just that a certain truth standard does not apply to any thought, but that no truth standard at all (either one that has already been considered or one that might someday be considered) does—a formidable task indeed.

While the Immanence Thesis answers the first critical question posed at the end of section I—What makes the (potentially) diverse principles of truth principles of the same thing, namely truth?—in a traditional manner, that is, by pointing to a *core* principle underlying all truths, the Logicality Thesis offers a nontraditional answer to this question. The Logicality Thesis identifies a *highly specialized* factor of truth and shows that it is due to its specialty that it is universally applicable in the domain of truth. (Its specialty renders it so abstract that it overlooks all, or most, differences between fields of truth.)

3. Logicality Thesis. The Logicality Thesis says that one central factor of truth is *the logical factor*, a factor having to do with the role played by *logical structure* in rendering sentences true (false). The logical factor applies to truths and falsehoods in all areas of discourse and all fields of knowledge; at the same time, it is just one among a whole array of factors of truth, and its contribution to truth is specific and sharply delimited. The logical factor is, thus, an example of a factor of truth that, while substantive and universal, is partial and highly specialized—an example, in fact, of a factor whose substantiveness and universality are closely related to its partiality and specialization.

A comprehensive discussion of the logical factor in truth is beyond the scope of the present essay.[47] Briefly, however, and without going into detail, my conception of the logical factor is the following:

The distinctive characteristic of the logical factor is its *formality*, which is most clearly expressed in the semantics of the logical constants. Logical constants are *formal* in the sense of *not distinguishing between objects (properties, relations) that are structurally the same*, or more precisely, not distinguishing between *argument structures* (see below) that are structurally the same. To see what this amounts to, consider three logical constants: identity ("="), the universal quantifier ("$\forall$"), and conjunction ("&"). An argument structure for "=" is a pair, $<A, <b,c>>$, where A is a universe (that is, a nonempty set of individuals, either actual or possible) and b,c are individuals in A; an argument structure for "$\forall$" is a pair, $<A,B>$, where A is as above, and B is a subset of A; and an argument structure for "&" is a pair $<A, <X,Y>>$, where either A is as above and X,Y are subsets of A, or A is a universe of propositions (with a truth value) and X,Y are members of A. (The former is the case when "&" functions as an operator on predicates (open formulas); the latter is the case when "&" functions as an operator on propositions.) Let us call an argument structure whose universe is a set of individuals "an objectual argument structure" and an argument structure whose universe is a set of propositions "a propositional argument structure." Say that (i) two objectual argument structures for a given constant are *structurally the same* if and only if they are *isomorphic*, that is, if and only if each is obtainable from the other by a 1–1 replacement of the members of their universes[48]; (ii) two propositional argument structures for a given constant are structurally the same if and only if they are "*T-isomorphic*," that is, their corresponding elements have the same truth values.[49] Now, "=" does not distinguish between isomorphic argument structures in the sense that if $<A_1,<b_1,c_1>>$ and $<A_2,<b_2,c_2>>$ are isomorphic, $<b_1,c_1>$ satisfies "=" in A_1 if and only if $<b_2,c_2>$ satisfies it in A_2. "$\forall$" does not distinguish between isomorphic argument structures in the sense that if $<A_1,B_1>$ and $<A_2,B_2>$ are isomorphic, B_1 satisfies "$\forall$" in A_1 if and only if B_2 satisfies it in A_2. And similarly for "&." Since formality is preserved under combinations of logical constants, logical structures in general are formal.

The formality of the logical constants explains their universality, that is, their applicability in any field of discourse. If a logical constant, C, applies to an argument structure $<A,\alpha>$, where A is a universe of objects/propositions of any type (physical, psychological, cultural, mathematical, and so forth), then it applies to any isomorphic image, $<B,\beta>$, of $<A,\alpha>$, no matter what type the objects/propositions in B are. That is, if C applies to one type of object/proposition, it applies to all types of object/proposition. Moreover, the satisfaction conditions of C do not change from one type of object/proposition to another; that is, if $<A,\alpha>$, is isomorphic to $<B,\beta>$, the conditions under which α satisfies C in A are exactly the same as those under which β satisfies it in B. In short, C abstracts from all (nonformal) differences between domains of objects/propositions.

Now, generally the logical factor does not determine, all by itself, the truth value of sentences, but it combines with other factors to determine their truth value. For example, the truth value of "Wet cats are funny,"[50] formulated (in order to display its logical structure) as:

(1) $(\forall x)[(\text{Wet } x \text{ \& Cat } x)] \supset \text{Funny } x]$,

is determined by three factors—the physical factor, P, reflected in the satisfaction conditions of "Wet" and "Cat," the comical factor, C, reflected in the satisfaction conditions of "Funny," and the logical factor, L, reflected in the satisfaction conditions of "$\forall$," "&," and "$\supset$."[51]

While the L-factor plays only a partial role in determining the truth value of (1), it determines, all by itself, the truth value of

(2) $(\forall x)(\text{Cat } x \lor \sim\text{Cat } x)$.

And in general, the L-factor is the only relevant factor in the truth (falsity) of logical truths (falsehoods). When we turn to logical inferences, the L-factor is the only relevant factor for their *validity* but not for their *soundness*. Consider, for example, the logically valid and, let us assume, sound inference,

(I)   (1) $(\forall x)[(\text{Wet } x \text{ \& Cat } x) \supset \text{Funny } x]$

     (3) $(\exists x)(\text{Wet } x \text{ \& Cat } x)$

     (4) $(\exists x) (\text{Cat } x \text{ \& Funny } x)$.

The validity of (I) is guaranteed by the L-factor alone, but the soundness of (I) is guaranteed by the L-factor *together with* the P- and C-factors.

We can now answer the second critical question raised at the end in section I: How can logical inference transmit truth across fields of discourse? For example: How can logical inference transmit truth from the physical domain to the domain of the comic?

The answer is: the logical factor plays a role in determining the truth value of sentences in all areas of discourse, including the physical and the comical, and this common role enables it to transmit truth from sentences in one area to sentences in another. More specifically:

(a) The truth value of sentences is generally determined by a multiplicity of factors, including factors that are not distinctive of the field of discourse to which these sentences belong.

(b) Due to its strong invariance property the logical factor can operate in all areas of discourse, that is, combine with all sorts of other factors in determining the truth conditions of sentences.

(c) The logical factor sets formal conditions on the truth of logically-structured sentences, and these conditions interact with other conditions, set by other factors, in determining the truth conditions of these sentences. For example, (3) is true if and only if the formal condition of nonemptiness is satisfied by the formal structure of intersection, applied to two collections of objects satisfying the physical conditions of being a cat and being wet, respectively.

(d) Due to connections between the formal elements of the truth conditions of sentences, the satisfaction of one constellation of formal conditions—that applicable to the premises of a given argument—may guarantee the satisfaction of another constellation of formal conditions—that applicable to the conclusion of this argument and, in so doing, tie the truth of the premises to that of the conclusion.

(e) In the case of (I), the logical factor guarantees that for any predicates, Φ, Ψ, Ω, and any factors, X, Y, Z, dominant in their satisfaction, the occurrence of the formal patterns

All objects which X-satisfy Φ and Y-satisfy Ψ also Z-satisfy Ω

and

Some object X-satisfies Φ and Y-satisfies Ψ

is always accompanied by occurrence of the formal pattern

Some object Y-satisfies Ψ and Z-satisfies Ω.

And it is this guarantee that enables us to infer the truth of the comic (yet logically structured) sentence (4) from the truth of the comic and physical (yet also logically structured) sentences (1) and (3).

Logical Correspondence. The Immanence Thesis implies that truth, in general, is based on correspondence. In what sense is logical truth (and logical consequence) based on correspondence? Our analysis suggests the following explanation: truth has to do with how things are in the world, and things in the world have formal properties in addition to physical, comical, and other kinds of properties. The two main principles of logical correspondence are: (i) Logical constants are denoting constants: they denote formal objects (properties, relations, functions) in the sense of formality explained above. (For example, "=" denotes the identity relation in any universe, "∃" denotes the second level property of nonemptiness [of 1st-level properties] in any universe, and "&," applied to predicates, denotes the operation of intersection, or more generally Cartesian product, in any universe.) (ii) Logical truth and consequence are based on formal laws governing and connecting structures of objects, the structures of objects (properties, relations) delineated by the sentences involved.[52] We can represent the workings of logical correspondence in the logical truth (2) and the logical inference (I) by the following diagrams:

Language:	*Logically True* '$(\forall x)[Cx \vee \sim Cx]$'
(2*)	$\Uparrow$ $\downarrow$
World (*formal law*):	*Universal* $C \cup \overline{C}$

Language: *True* '$(\forall x)[(Wx\&Cx) \supset Fx]$'; *True* '$(\exists x)$ $[Wx\&Cx]$'—> *True* '$(\exists x)$ $[Cx\&Fx]$'	
(I*) $\downarrow$ $\downarrow$ $\Uparrow$ $\uparrow$	
World (*formal law*): $W \cap C \subseteq F$; *Non-empty* $W \cap C \rightarrow\rightarrow\rightarrow\rightarrow$ *Non-empty* $C \cap F$	

The truth of (2) is based on correspondence in the following way: (2) is true because (a) it attributes the property of being universal to the union of the set of cats and its complement (in the given universe of discourse), and (b) the union of these sets is in fact universal (in that universe). But (2) is not simply true, it is logically true. And its logical truth is due to the fact that the correspondence responsible for its truth is of a special kind, connecting the *logical structure* of (2) with a *law* governing the *formal* behavior of the properties denoted by its predicates.

The transmission of truth in (I)—assuming the premises to be true—is based on correspondence in the following way:

(A) Materially, the transmission of truth is due to the fact that: (a) the truth of (1) guarantees that the intersection of the set of cats and the set of wet things is (in fact) included in the set of funny things; (b) the truth of (3) guarantees that the intersection of the set of cats and the set of wet things is (in fact) not empty; (c) it is a regularity (that holds in the actual world) that whenever a nonempty intersection of a set of cats and a set of wet things is included in a set of funny things, the intersection of the set of cats and the set of funny things is not empty; (d) the nonemptiness of the intersection of the set of cats and the set of funny things (materially) guarantees the truth of (4).

(B) But the transmission of truth in (I) is not just materially, but also logically guaranteed. And its logical guarantee is due to the fact that the regularity mentioned in

(c) is not accidental, but an instance of a *formal law*: the law that whenever a nonempty intersection of two sets is included in a third set, the intersection of the second and third sets is not empty.

It is in this way that the truth of (2) and the validity of (I) are based on correspondence, not physical or comical correspondence, but logical, or formal, correspondence: a systematic connection between the logical structure of linguistic entities on the one hand and patterns of objects-possessing-properties-and-standing-in-relations that constitute formal laws on the other.[53]

III   Conclusion

In this essay, I have examined the prospects of a substantive theory of truth and some of its challenges. Those who deny the feasibility of such a theory tend to construe its problems as relatively narrow, that is, as problems specific to the theory of truth (or at least to philosophy). My countersuggestion is that the problems facing the theory of truth are, in the first place, general methodological problems, problems arising for any theory of a broad, complex, and multi-faceted subject matter in any field of knowledge, and that it is important to realize the universality of these problems in order to deal with them effectively.

I have concentrated on two interrelated problems facing the theorist of truth: unity and disunity. The challenge facing the theorist of truth, like that facing the scientist, is finding a fruitful balance between the unity and diversity of his subject matter—truth. That is, the theorist of truth must balance recognition of the multiplicity of principles of truth (the variety of ways truth is realized in different fields of knowledge) with a search for order, common principles, and systematic interconnections. The key to a balanced theory is, I suggested, partiality. We may think of the theory of truth as a family of theories, each investigating one central aspect or factor of truth, and all being connected by a network of unifying principles, on various levels of generality. The theory of truth, on this conception, is not a deflationist theory. Like other theories in other branches of knowledge it aims at a genuine and deep understanding of its subject matter, and this it tries to achieve by renouncing unhelpful preconceptions (for example, that of capturing the whole topic of truth by a single definition or schema) and by committing itself to an open-minded and undogmatic investigation. My approach to a substantive theory of truth involves a new, moderate version of pluralism. This pluralism subsumes all truths under the correspondence principle, but correspondence itself it construes as a network of interconnected (sub-)principles.

Turning to unity, I have emphasized the importance of unity for substantiveness (through explanation) and I distinguished two types of substantive unifiers: *core unifiers* and *specialized unifiers*. The first type is exemplified by the Immanence Thesis, the second by the Logicality Thesis. The Immanence Thesis identifies a common source of our concept of truth in a combination of three basic principles of human thought: immanence, transcendence, and normativity. The Logicality Thesis identifies a special unifying factor of truth—the logical factor—a factor that, due to its unique features, partakes in the determination of truth in all areas of discourse regardless of their differences. Together, the Immanence and Logicality theses provide an answer to the two critical questions: (i) What is common to all truths? (ii) How is logical inference across diverse fields of truth possible?

Much work remains, of course, to be done. But I hope the general lessons from science, the idea of a moderate pluralism of correspondence principles, and the steps toward unraveling the substantive unifiers of truth, demonstrate (or make some progress toward demonstrating) the feasibility of a substantive philosophical theory of truth.

Notes

I would like to thank Roberta Ballarin, Yemima Ben Menachem, Charles Parsons, Carl Posy, Oron Shagrir, Peter Sher, Mark Steiner, Cory Wright, and the participants in my recent graduate seminar on truth for very helpful comments and conversation.

1. P. Horwich, *Truth* (Cambridge: Blackwell, 1990), xi.

2. Horwich, *Truth*, 2. (A compilation of two sentences in inverted order.)

3. See, for example, H. Field, "Deflationist Views of Meaning and Content," *Mind* 103 (1994): 249–284.

4. H. Field, "Tarski's Theory of Truth," *Journal of Philosophy* 69, no. 13 (July 13, 1972): 347–375, citation from p. 363. The full sentence is: "This is a methodology that has proved extremely fruitful in science, and I think we'd be crazy to give it up in linguistics." Field treats the theory of truth as part of linguistics, but what he says is directed to whatever discipline the theory of truth belongs to, that is, on our demarcation, philosophy. He specifically refers to reductionist theories which, he says, are pointless unless substantive. I think it is reasonable to presume that he extends this point to scientific theories in general. Note: some philosophers identify *substantive theory of truth* with *correspondence theory of truth*; I prefer to distinguish between the two. Although I will eventually advocate a substantive correspondence theory of truth, I do not want to rule out in advance the possibility of either a substantive noncorrespondence theory of truth or a nonsubstantive correspondence theory.

5. See Davidson, "The Structure and Content of Truth," *Journal of Philosophy* 87, no. 6 (June 1990): 279–328, and "The Folly of Trying to Define Truth," *Journal of Philosophy* 93, no. 6 (June 1996): 263–278; Devitt, *Realism and Truth*, 1st/2nd ed. (Cambridge: Blackwell, 1984/1991); Gupta, "Minimalism," *Philosophical Perspectives* 7 (1993): 359–369, and "A Critique of Deflationism," *Philosophical Topics* 21, no. 2 (1993): 57–81; Lynch, *Truth in Context* (Cambridge, MA: MIT Press, 1998); Putnam, *Reason, Truth, and History* (New York: Cambridge University Press, 1981), and *The Many Faces of Realism* (La Salle, IL: Open Court, 1987); Wright, *Truth and Objectivity* (Cambridge, MA: Harvard University Press, 1992), and "Truth: A Traditional Debate Reviewed," in S. Blackburn and

K. Simmons, eds., *Truth* (New York: Oxford University Press, 1999), 203–238; G. Sher, "On the Possibility of a Substantive Theory of Truth," *Synthese* 117 (1998–1999): 133–172.

6. This part of the essay continues my earlier discussion of the disunity of truth in "On the Possibility of a Substantive Theory of Truth." It is, however, self-sufficient.

7. S. Blackburn, *Spreading the Word* (New York: Oxford University Press, 1984), 230. This argument may also be interpreted as an argument against the existence of a *property* of truth, but here I am interested in it as an argument against the possibility of a substantive account of truth. Blackburn, it should be noted, does not endorse this argument.

8. *Critique of Pure Reason*, 1st/2nd ed. (1781/1787; repr., New York: Cambridge University Press, 1998), A58–A59/B83.

9. *Lectures on Logic*, "The Jäsche Logic" (1800; repr., New York: Cambridge University Press, 1992), 558.

10. My reading of Kant's argument is different from James Van Cleve's in his *Problems from Kant* (New York: Oxford University Press, 1999), chap. 13. Van Cleve regards Kant's argument as a version of the *diallelon*, an ancient argument which, based on circularity considerations, says that one cannot determine whether a cognition agrees with its object; one can only determine whether it agrees with another cognition of that object. While Kant's argument does appear in a section whose opening sentence mentions circularity—"The old and famous question with which the logicians were to be driven into a corner and brought to such a pass that they must either fall into a miserable circle [in the second edition, *Dialexis*, in the first, *Dialele*, that is, reasoning in a circle—Eds.] or else confess their ignorance, hence the vanity of their entire art, is this: What is truth?" [A57–A58/B82]—attention to the *content* of his argument shows that it makes an altogether different point from the *diallelon*. I should indicate that I agree with other aspects of Van Cleve's analysis, for example, his claim (contra Putnam and Norman Kemp Smith) that this argument does not signal Kant's withdrawal from the correspondence view of truth.

11. Note that for a while analytic philosophers did expect the theory of knowledge to provide something akin to a full and detailed definition, namely a necessary and sufficient condition of "*x* knows that *P*." But this is no longer the goal of (most) current epistemologists, nor was it Kant's goal. Note, too, that the chaotic results of the search for a necessary and sufficient condition of knowledge (reflected in the incessant stream of counter- and counter-counterexamples) undermined many philosophers' confidence in the possibility of a substantive analytic epistemology.

12. One exception might be mathematics, whose objects are already abstract and incomplete (in Alexius Meinong's sense).

13. See *Critique of Pure Reason*, A58/B82.

14. See *Critique of Pure Reason*, A59–A60/B83–B84, and *Lectures on Logic*, 280–281, 455–456, 558–560; *Critique*, A62/B87; A131/B170; A146/B185; A191/B236; A202/B247; A489/B517; and A651/B679; and *Prolegomena to Any Future Metaphysics* (1783; repr., New York: Macmillan, 1950), 124.

15. For further criticisms of the radical disunity argument, see Wright, "Truth: A Traditional Debate Reviewed," and Sher, "On the Possibility of a Substantive Theory of Truth."

16. See, for example, P. W. Anderson, "More Is Different," *Science* 177 (1972): 393–396; J. Fodor, "Special Sciences," *Synthese* 28 (1974): 77–115; P. Suppes, "The Plurality of Science," *Philosophy of Science* 2 (1978): 3–16; J. Dupré, *The Disorder of Things* (Cambridge, MA: Harvard University Press, 1993); I. Hacking, "The Disunities of the Sciences," in P. Galison and D. Stump, eds., *The Disunity of Science* (Stanford, CA: Stanford University Press, 1996), 37–74; N. Cartwright, *The Dappled World* (New York: Cambridge University Press, 1999); R. B. Laughlin and D. Pines, "The Theory of Everything," *Proceedings of the National Academy of Sciences of the USA* 97 (2000): 28–31; Laughlin et al., "The Middle Way," *Proceedings of the National Academy of Sciences of the USA* 97 (2000): 32–37.

17. The points listed below constitute a pastiche of multiple ideas by multiple authors. At the end of each point I will indicate some of its sources. For fuller references, see note 16 and the following notes.

18. See Hacking, "The Disunities of the Sciences," 38–39.

19. "Language and Interpretation: Philosophical Reflections and Empirical Inquiry" (1988), in J. Earman, ed., *Inferenre, Explanation, and Other Frustrations* (Berkeley: University of California Press, 1992), 99–128.

20. See Hacking, "The Disunities of the Sciences," 54.

21. Partly a citation from Suppes, "The Plurality of Science," 14–15.

22. "The Concept of Truth in Formalized Languages" (1933), in *Logic, Semantics, Metamathematics* (Indianapolis: Hackett, 1983), 152–278.

23. For a relevant discussion of Tarski's theory, see Sher, "On the Possibility of a Substantive Theory of Truth."

24. "Tarski's Theory of Truth."

25. *Infinite in All Directions* (New York: Harper and Row, 1988), 47.

26. A654/B682 (explanation in square brackets based on editors' footnote 117, p. 749), A657–A658/B685–B686, A660/B688; emphasis added.

27. "Pragmatism" (1907), in *Pragmatism and Other Writings* (New York: Penguin, 2000), 1–132, citations from pp. 59 and 62.

28. A similar point was made by Robert Brandom with respect to Putnam's pragmatism—"Hilary Putnam: *Renewing Philosophy*," *Journal of Philosophy* 91, no. 3 (March 1994): 140–143. It should be noted that not all interpreters view James's pragmatism as constricting in the way I described (see, for example, Y. Ben Menachem, "Pragmatism and Revisionism: James's Conception of Truth," *International Journal of Philosophical Studies* 3 [1995]: 270–289). But the tendency to associate pragmatism with a negative attitude towards abstract, rational theorizing is sufficiently prevalent to make it worthwhile to point out that an adequate solution to the disunity problem does not require such an attitude.

29. *Philosophical Investigations*, 3rd ed. (New York: Macmillan, 1953), §66.

30. See J. Floyd, "On Saying What You Really Want to Say: Wittgenstein, Gödel, and the Trisection of the Angle," in J. Hintikka, ed., *Essays on the Development of the Foundations of Mathematics* (Boston: Kluwer Academic Publishers, 1995), 373–425.

31. See also §126: "Philosophy simply puts everything before us, and neither explains nor deduces anything."

32. This point was also made by G. P. Baker and P. M. S. Hacker, *Wittgenstein: Understanding and Meaning* (New York: Blackwell, 1980), 327.

33. Other contemporary philosophers who consider pluralism with respect to truth (or cognate subject matters) are Davidson, Dummett, Resnik, Devitt, and Putnam, to name but a few. See Davidson, "Reality without Reference," *Dialectica* 31 (1977): 247–253; Dummett, "Realism," in *Truth and Other Enigmas* (Cambridge, MA: Harvard University Press, 1978), 145–165; M. Resnik, "Immanent Truth," *Mind* 99 (1990): 405–424; Devitt, *Realism and Truth*; Putnam, "Sense, Nonsense, and the Senses: An Inquiry into the Powers of the Human Mind," *Journal of Philosophy* 91, no. 9 (September 1994): 445–517.

34. See, for example, C. Tappolet, "Mixed Inferences: A Problem for Pluralism about Truth Predicates," *Analysis* 57 (1997): 209–210, and "Truth Pluralism and Many-Valued Logics: A Reply to Beall," *Philosophical Quarterly* 50 (2000): 382–385. A similar question was raised by C. Diamond, "Unfolding Truth and Reading Wittgenstein" (unpublished manuscript, 1999), with respect to the view that truth is relative to language games.

35. Hempel, *Aspects of Scientific Explanation* (New York: Free Press, 1965), and *Philosophy of Natural Science* (Englewood Cliffs, NJ: Prentice-Hall, 1966); Friedman, "Explanation and Scientific Understanding," *Journal of Philosophy* 71, no. 1 (January 17, 1974): 5–19; P. Kitcher, "Explanatory Unification," *Philosophy of Science* 48 (1981): 507–531, and "Explanatory Unification and the Causal Structure of the World," in P. Kitcher and W. Salmon, eds., *Scientific Explanation* (Minneapolis: University of Minnesota Press, 1989), 410–505.

36. "Studies in the Logic of Explanation," *Philosophy of Science* 15 (1948): 98–115.

37. *Unifying Scientific Theories* (New York: Cambridge University Press, 2000).

38. Wright, *Truth and Objectivity*, and "Truth: A Traditional Debate Reviewed."

39. Wright, *Truth and Objectivity*, 34 (almost verbatim).

40. It should be noted that Wright's claim that the unifying principles are minimal is made in a particular context, namely that of showing that truth aptness does not carry a commitment to a full-fledged realism. Construing the unifying principles as minimalistic is one way of showing this. It should also be noted that Wright does not rule out the possibility of substantive unifying principles. Thus he says, concerning the assertibility platitude: "On reflection … it is not necessary to insist that there is *no* suitable notion of deep assertoric content. It suffices that there is, at any rate, at least a more superficial one, carried by surface syntactic features; and that a minimal truth predicate is definable on any surface-assertoric discourse." *Truth and Objectivity*, 29.

41. "Ontological Relativity," in *Ontological Relativity and Other Essays* (New York: Columbia University Press, 1969), 26–68.

42. For an earlier articulation of the notion of immanent transcendence, see Sher, "Is There a Place for Philosophy in Quine's Theory?," *Journal of Philosophy* 96, no. 10 (October 1999): 491–524, 523.

43. *The Sources of Normativity* (New York: Cambridge University Press, 1996), 46–49.

44. See Sher, *The Bounds of Logic* (Cambridge, MA: MIT Press, 1991); "Semantics and Logic," in S. Lappin, ed., *Handbook of Contemporary Semantic Theory* (Cambridge: Blackwell, 1996), 509–535; "Did Tarski Commit 'Tarski's Fallacy'?," *Journal of Symbolic Logic* 61 (1996): 653–686; "Is Logic a Theory of the Obvious?," *European Review of Philosophy* 4 (1999): 207–238; "The Formal-Structural View of Logical Consequence," *Philosophical Review* 110 (2001): 242–261; and "Logical Consequence: An Epistemic Outlook," *Monist* 85 (2002): 555–579.

45. These statements are loosely based on discussions of moral expressivism in contemporary literature—see, for example, A. Gibbard, *Wise Choices, Apt Feelings* (Cambridge, MA: Harvard University Press, 1990).

46. *The Last Word* (New York: Oxford University Press, 1997).

47. For further discussion, see Sher, "On the Possibility of a Substantive Theory of Truth."

48. Formally, the structures $<A,\alpha>$ and $<B,\beta>$ are isomorphic if and only if there is a bijection f from A onto B such that β is the image of α under f. For the origins of this criterion, see Sher, *The Bounds of Logic*, 61–65.

49. Formally, the propositional structures $<A,\alpha>$ and $<B,\beta>$, where $A=B$, are T-isomorphic if and only if β is the image of α under some truth-preserving bijection f from A onto B (that is, a bijection f that assigns to every a in A a proposition b in B with the same truth value).

50. Tappolet, "Mixed Inferences," 209.

51. I use "satisfaction" here as a generic term for "application" and "fulfilment," which apply to predicates, including quantifiers (second-level predicates) and functions, respectively.

52. As I use the term "law" here, laws contrast with accidental generalizations: a biological law holds in all biologically possible structures of objects, a physical law holds in all physically possible structures of objects, … , and a formal law holds in all formally possible structures of objects. Formal laws apply to all structures of objects, regardless of their nonformal properties.

53. For further discussion, see the works mentioned in note 44.

II Coherence Theories

Introduction

Michael P. Lynch, Jeremy Wyatt, and Junyeol Kim

Coherence theories of truth rose to prominence at the end of the nineteenth century under the influence of the neo-Hegelian absolute idealists H. H. Joachim and F. H. Bradley. In contrast to the correspondence theory of truth, the absolute idealists denied that a belief is true because it represents the intrinsic features of reality. Truth is not a relation between a proposition and an independent realm of objects but, in Joachim's words, "the systematic coherence which characterizes a significant whole" (1906, 78).

The core of absolute idealism, which received its most crisp and comprehensive presentation in the hands of the American philosopher Brand Blanshard (chapter 6), is a particular way of looking at the relationship of thought to reality. Rejecting the traditional distinction between subject and object, Blanshard holds instead that "to think of a thing is to get that thing itself in some degree within the mind" (1921, 261–262). In the idealist view, a thought and its object do not differ in kind but *in degree of realization*; the purpose of thought is to become more developed and coherent until it literally is identical to, or "one with," reality. Hence, reality *just is* the realization of a fully articulated and maximally coherent system of judgments (a "significant whole"), and a particular judgment is true just when it belongs to such a system. In short, a judgment is true when and only when it is a member of an ideally coherent system of judgments.

There are several points to note about this theory. First, by "coherence" Blanshard has in mind not simply consistency but a much richer notion. At the ideal, a coherent system is (a) one that is comprehensive, or including all "known facts," and (b) one where the support between judgments is such that "every judgement entailed, and was entailed by, the rest of the system." Of course, our human belief systems are rarely ideal. But coherence is a matter of degree, and even if a belief isn't absolutely true unless it is part of an ideal system, it can be partly true to the extent that it is a member of a fairly coherent system.

Because the coherence theory stresses that truth consists in the coherence, or mutual support, of our beliefs, it is common to label the coherence theory as an *epistemic* conception of truth. Yet unlike some of his predecessors, Blanshard acknowledges that a coherence theory of justification (what Blanshard would call a theory of the test for truth) is logically distinct from a coherence theory of truth itself. But while Blanshard acknowledges that coherence theories of truth and of justification are distinct, he argues that "coherence is a pertinacious concept, and, like the well-known camel, if one lets it get its nose under the edge of the tent, it will shortly walk off with the whole" (1921, 267).

A common objection to any sort of coherence theory, first raised by Bertrand Russell (see chapter 1 in this volume), is that it allows any proposition to be true since any proposition can be a member of some coherent set or other. This seems counterintuitive in the extreme, for it implies that clearly false propositions, such as the proposition that Boston is the capital of Mississippi, may be true. In chapter 7, Ralph C. S. Walker defends the coherence theory of truth against this and several other common objections. In particular, Walker points out that the above objection misses the point, since coherence theorists hold that truth consists in the coherence of *some specific set of beliefs that actually are or would be held*, not in the coherence of propositions considered in the abstract. Thus it is irrelevant that the proposition that Boston is the capital of Mississippi coheres with some set of propositions.

Yet Walker ultimately argues that the very feature of coherence theories that makes them immune to Russell's objection proves to be their ultimate undoing. For consider the belief *that belief* b *is actually held*. The truth of this belief will consist in its coherence within the system of beliefs. Thus, whether belief *b* is true depends in part on whether *b* is an actual belief, and (for any belief whatsoever) whether it is an actual belief depends only on whether *the belief that* b *is an actual belief* is true (or coheres with the system). Thus it would seem that there is no way to ground or restrict membership in a coherent system. There is no independent way, outside of coherence, of determining which beliefs are actual beliefs and therefore which beliefs are true. So it seems that the worry behind Russell's objection remains.

Further Reading

Alcoff, L. 1995. *Real Knowing: New Versions of the Coherence Theory*. Ithaca, NY: Cornell University Press.

Alcoff, L. 1997. "Reply to Critics." *Social Epistemology* 12(3): 265–285.

Blanshard, B. 1921. *The Nature of Thought*. Vol. 2, chaps. 25–27. London: George Allen and Unwin.

Bonjour, L. 1985. *The Structure of Empirical Knowledge*. Cambridge, MA: Harvard University Press.

Bradley, F. H. 1897. *Appearance and Reality*. 2nd ed. Oxford: Clarendon Press.

Bradley, F. H. 1914. *Essays on Truth and Reality*. Oxford: Clarendon Press.

Candlish, S. 1989. "The Truth about F. H. Bradley." *Mind* 98: 331–348.

Candlish, S. 1990. "Critical Notice on Walker, *The Coherence Theory of Truth: Realism, Anti-realism, Idealism.*" *Mind* 99: 467–472.

Damnjanovic, N., and Candlish, S. 2013. "The Myth of the Coherence Theory of Truth." In M. Textor, ed., *Judgement and Truth in Early Analytic Philosophy and Phenomenology*, 157–182. New York: Palgrave Macmillan.

Dauer, F. 1974. "In Defense of the Coherence Theory of Truth." *Journal of Philosophy* 71: 791–811.

Davidson, D. 1986. "A Coherence Theory of Truth and Knowledge." In E. LePore, ed., *Truth and Interpretation*, 307–319. Oxford: Blackwell.

Dorsey, D. 2006. "A Coherence Theory of Truth in Ethics." *Philosophical Studies* 127: 493–523.

Joachim, H. H. 1906. *The Nature of Truth*. Oxford: Clarendon Press.

Lehrer, K. 1990. *Theory of Knowledge*. Boulder, CO: Westview Press.

Lynch, M. 2009. *Truth as One and Many*. New York: Oxford University Press. See esp. chap. 8, "Applying the View: Moral Truth."

Neurath, O. 1931. "Soziologie im Physikalismus." *Erkenntnis* 2: 393–431. Translated as "Sociology and Physicalism," in A. J. Ayer, ed., *Logical Positivism*, 282–317. Glencoe, IL: Free Press, 1959. Also translated as "Sociology in the Framework of Physicalism," in Neurath, *Philosophical Papers 1913–46*, 58–90. Dordrecht: Reidel, 1983.

Rescher, N. 1973. *The Coherence Theory of Truth*. Oxford: Oxford University Press.

Russell, B. 1966. "The Monistic Theory of Truth." In *Philosophical Essays*. New York: Simon and Schuster.

Walker, R. 1989. *The Coherence Theory of Truth: Realism, Anti-realism, Idealism*. London: Routledge.

Wright, C. 1995. "Critical Study of Walker, *The Coherence Theory of Truth: Realism, Anti-realism, Idealism.*" *Synthese* 103: 279–302.

Wright, C. 1998. "Truth: A Traditional Debate Reviewed." In C. Misak, ed., "Pragmatism," special issue, *Canadian Journal of Philosophy* 28, suppl. 1: 31–74. Reprinted in S. Blackburn and K. Simmons, eds., *Truth*, 203–238. Oxford: Oxford University Press. 1999.

6 Coherence as the Nature of Truth

Brand Blanshard

1

It has been contended in the last chapter [chapter 25 of *The Nature of Thought*, vol. 2] that coherence is in the end our sole criterion of truth. We have now to face the question whether it also gives us the nature of truth. We should be clear at the beginning that these are different questions, and that one may reject coherence as the definition of truth while accepting it as the test. It is conceivable that one thing should be an accurate index of another and still be extremely different from it. There have been philosophers who held that pleasure was an accurate gauge of the amount of good in experience, but that to confuse good with pleasure was a gross blunder. There have been a great many philosophers who held that for every change in consciousness there was a change in the nervous system and that the two corresponded so closely that if we knew the laws connecting them we could infallibly predict one from the other; yet it takes all the hardihood of a behaviourist to say that the two are the same. Similarly it has been held that though coherence supplies an infallible measure of truth, it would be a very grave mistake to identify it with truth.

2

The view that truth *is* coherence rests on a theory of the relation of thought to reality, and since this is the central problem of the theory of knowledge, to begin one's discussion by assuming the answer to it or by trying to make one out of whole cloth would be somewhat ridiculous. But as this was our main problem in the long discussions of Book II [of *The Nature of Thought*, vol. 1] we may be pardoned here for brevity. First we shall state in *résumé* the relation of thought to reality that we were there driven to accept, and sketch the theory of truth implicit in it. We shall then take up one by one the objections to this theory and ask if they can pass muster.

To think is to seek understanding. And to seek understanding is an activity of mind that is marked off from all other activities by a highly distinctive aim. This aim, as we saw in our chapter on the general nature of understanding [chapter 18 of *The Nature of Thought*, vol. 2] is to achieve systematic vision, so to apprehend what is now unknown to us as to relate it, and relate it necessarily, to what we know already. We think to solve problems; and our method of solving problems is to build a bridge of intelligible relation from the continent of our knowledge to the island we wish to include in it. Sometimes this bridge is causal, as when we try to explain a disease; sometimes teleological, as when we try to fathom the move of an opponent over the chessboard; sometimes geometrical, as in Euclid. But it is always systematic; thought in its very nature is the attempt to bring something unknown or imperfectly known into a sub-system of knowledge, and thus also into that larger system that forms the world of accepted beliefs. That is what explanation is. *Why* is it that thought desires this ordered vision? Why should such a vision give satisfaction when it comes? To these questions there is no answer, and if there were, it would be an answer only because it had succeeded in supplying the characteristic satisfaction to this unique desire.

But may it not be that what satisfies thought fails to conform to the real world? Where is the guarantee that when I have brought my ideas into the form my ideal requires, they should be *true*? Here we come round again to the tortured problem of Book II. In our long struggle with the relation of thought to reality we saw that if thought and things are conceived as related only externally, then knowledge is luck; there is no necessity whatever that what satisfies intelligence should coincide with what really is. It may do so, or it may not; on the principle that there are many misses to one bull's-eye, it more probably does not. But if we get rid of the misleading analogies through which this relation has been conceived, of copy and original, stimulus and organism, lantern and screen, and go to thought itself with the question what reference to an object means, we get a different and more hopeful answer. To think of a thing is to get that thing itself in some degree within the mind. To think of a colour or an emotion is to have that within us which if it *were developed and completed*, would identify itself with the object. In short, if we accept its own report, thought is related to reality as the partial to the perfect fulfilment of a purpose. The more adequate its grasp the more nearly does it approximate, the more fully does it realize in itself, the nature and relations of its objects.

3

Thought thus appears to have two ends, one immanent, one transcendent. On the one hand it seeks fulfilment in a special kind of satisfaction, the satisfaction of systematic vision. On the other hand it seeks fulfilment in its object. Now it was the chief contention of our second book that these ends are one. Indeed unless they are accepted as one, we could see no alternative to scepticism. If the pursuit of thought's own ideal were merely an elaborate self-indulgence that brought us no nearer to reality, or if the apprehension of reality did not lie in the line of thought's interest, or still more if both of these held at once, the hope of knowledge would be vain. Of course it may really be vain. If anyone cares to doubt whether the framework of human logic has any bearing on the nature of things, he may be silenced perhaps, but he cannot be conclusively answered. One may point out to him that the doubt itself is framed in accordance with that logic, but he can reply that thus we are taking advantage of his logico-centric predicament; further, that any argument we can offer accords equally well with his hypothesis and with ours, with the view that we are merely flies caught in a logical net and the view that knowledge reveals reality. And what accords equally well with both hypotheses does not support either to the exclusion of the other. But while such doubt is beyond reach by argument, neither is there anything in its favour.[1] It is a mere suspicion which is, and by its nature must remain, without any positive ground; and as such it can hardly be discussed. Such suspicions aside, we can throw into the scale for our theory the impressive fact of the advance of knowledge. It has been the steadfast assumption of science whenever it came to an unsolved problem that there was a key to it to be found, that if things happened thus rather than otherwise they did so for a cause or reason, and that if this were not forthcoming it was never because it was lacking, but always because of a passing blindness in ourselves. Reflection has assumed that pursuit of its own immanent end is not only satisfying but revealing, that so far as the immanent end is achieved we are making progress toward the transcendent end as well. Indeed, that these ends coincide is the assumption of every act of thinking whatever. To think is to raise a question; to raise a question is to seek an explanation; to seek an explanation is to assume that one may be had; so to assume is to take for granted that nature in that region is intelligible. Certainly the story of advancing knowledge unwinds as if self-realization in thought meant also a coming nearer to reality.

4

That these processes are really one is the metaphysical base on which our belief in coherence is founded. If one admits that the pursuit of a coherent system has actually carried us to what everyone would agree to call knowledge, why not take this ideal as a guide that will conduct us farther? What better key can one ask to the structure of the real? Our own conviction is that we should take this immanent end of thought in all seriousness as the clue to the nature of things. We admit that it may prove deceptive, that somewhere thought may end its pilgrimage in frustration and futility before some blank wall of the unintelligible. There are even those who evince their superior insight by taking this as a foregone conclusion and regarding the faith that the real is rational as the wishful thinking of the "tender-minded." Their attitude appears to us a compound made up of one part timidity, in the form of a refusal to hope lest they be disillusioned; one part muddled persuasion that to be sceptical is to be sophisticated;

one part honest dullness in failing to estimate rightly the weight of the combined postulate and success of knowledge; one part genuine insight into the possibility of surds in nature. But whatever its motives, it is a view that goes less well with the evidence than the opposite and brighter view. That view is that reality is a system, completely ordered and fully intelligible, with which thought in its advance is more and more identifying itself. We may look at the growth of knowledge, individual or social, either as an attempt by our own minds to return to union with things as they are in their ordered wholeness, or the affirmation through our minds of the ordered whole itself. And if we take this view, our notion of truth is marked out for us. Truth is the approximation of thought to reality. It is thought on its way home. Its measure is the distance thought has travelled, under guidance of its inner compass, toward that intelligible system which unites its ultimate object with its ultimate end. Hence at any given time the degree of truth in our experience as a whole is the degree of system it has achieved. The degree of truth of a particular proposition is to be judged in the first instance by its coherence with experience as a whole, ultimately by its coherence with that further whole, all-comprehensive and fully articulated, in which thought can come to rest.

5

But it is time we defined more explicitly what coherence means. To be sure, no fully satisfactory definition can be given; and as Dr. Ewing says, "It is wrong to tie down the advocates of the coherence theory to a precise definition. What they are doing is to describe an ideal that has never yet been completely clarified but is none the less immanent in all our thinking."[2] Certainly this ideal goes far beyond mere consistency. Fully coherent knowledge would be knowledge in which every judgement entailed, and was entailed by, the rest of the system. Probably we never find in fact a system where there is so much of interdependence. What it means may be clearer if we take a number of familiar systems and arrange them in a series tending to such coherence as a limit. At the bottom would be a junk-heap, where we could know every item but one and still be without any clue as to what that remaining item was. Above this would come a stone-pile, for here you could at least infer that what you would find next would be a stone. A machine would be higher again, since from the remaining parts one could deduce not only the general character of a missing part, but also its special form and function. This is a high degree of coherence, but it is very far short of the highest. You could remove the engine from a motor-car while leaving the other parts intact, and replace it with any one of thousands of other engines, but the thought of such an interchange among human heads or hearts shows at once that the interdependence in a machine is far below that of the body. Do we find then in organic bodies the highest conceivable coherence? Clearly not. Though a human hand, as Aristotle said, would hardly be a hand when detached from the body, still it would be something definite enough;

and we can conceive systems in which even this something would be gone. Abstract a number from the number series and it would be a mere unrecognizable *x*; similarly, the very thought of a straight line involves the thought of the Euclidean space in which it falls. It is perhaps in such systems as Euclidean geometry that we get the most perfect examples of coherence that have been constructed. If any proposition were lacking, it could be supplied from the rest; if any were altered, the repercussions would be felt through the length and breadth of the system. Yet even such a system as this falls short of ideal system. Its postulates are unproved; they are independent of each other, in the sense that none of them could be derived from any other or even from all the others together; its clear necessity is bought by an abstractness so extreme as to have left out nearly everything that belongs to the character of actual things. A completely satisfactory system would have none of these defects. No proposition would be arbitrary, every proposition would be entailed by the others jointly and even singly,[3] no proposition would stand outside the system. The integration would be so complete that no part could be seen for what it was without seeing its relation to the whole, and the whole itself could be understood only through the contribution of every part.

6

It may be granted at once that in common life we are satisfied with far less than this. We accept the demonstrations of the geometer as complete, and do not think of reproaching him because he begins with postulates and leaves us at the end with a system that is a skeleton at the best. In physics, in biology, above all in the social sciences, we are satisfied with less still. We test judgements by the amount of coherence which in that particular subject-matter it seems reasonable to expect. We apply, perhaps unconsciously, the advice of Aristotle, and refrain from asking demonstration in the physical sciences, while in mathematics we refuse to accept less. And such facts may be thought to show that we make no actual use of the ideal standard just described. But however much this standard may be relaxed within the limits of a particular science, its influence is evident in the grading of the sciences generally. It is precisely in those sciences that approach most nearly to system as here defined that we achieve the greatest certainty, and precisely in those that are most remote from such system that our doubt is greatest whether we have achieved scientific truth at all. Our immediate exactions shift with the subject-matter; our ultimate standard is unvarying.

7

Now if we accept coherence as the test of truth, does that commit us to any conclusions about the *nature* of truth or reality? I think it does, though more clearly about reality than about truth. It is past belief that the fidelity of our thought to reality should be rightly measured by coherence if reality itself were not coherent. To say that the nature of things may be *in*coherent, but we shall approach the truth about it precisely so far as our thoughts become coherent, sounds very much like nonsense. And providing we retained coherence as the test, it would still be nonsense even if truth were conceived as correspondence. On this supposition we should have truth when, our thought having achieved coherence, the correspondence was complete between that thought and its object. But complete correspondence between a coherent thought and an incoherent object seems meaningless. It is hard to see, then, how anyone could consistently take coherence as the test of truth unless he took it also as a character of reality.

8

Does acceptance of coherence as a test commit us not only to a view about the structure of reality but also to a view about the nature of truth? This is a more difficult question. As we saw at the beginning of the chapter, there have been some highly reputable philosophers who have held that the answer to "What is the test of truth?" is "Coherence," while the answer to "What is the nature or meaning of truth?" is "Correspondence." These questions are plainly distinct. Nor does there seem to be any direct path from the acceptance of coherence as the test of truth to its acceptance as the nature of truth. Nevertheless there is an indirect path. If we accept coherence as our test, we must use it everywhere. We must therefore use it to test the suggestion that truth *is* other than coherence. But if we do, we shall find that we must reject the suggestion as leading to *in*coherence. Coherence is a pertinacious concept and, like the well-known camel, if one lets it get its nose under the edge of the tent, it will shortly walk off with the whole.

Suppose that, accepting coherence as the test, one rejects it as the nature of truth in favour of some alternative; and let us assume, for example, that this alternative is correspondence. This, we have said, is incoherent; why? Because if one holds that truth is correspondence, one cannot intelligibly hold either that it is tested by coherence or that there is any dependable test at all. Consider the first point. Suppose that we construe experience into the most coherent picture possible, remembering that among the elements included will be such secondary qualities as colours, odours, and sounds. Would the mere fact that such elements as these are coherently arranged prove that anything precisely corresponding to them exists "out there"? I cannot see that it would, even if we knew that the two arrangements had closely corresponding patterns. If on one side you have a series of elements a, b, c ... , and on the other a series of elements $\alpha, \beta, \gamma \dots$, arranged in patterns that correspond, you have no proof as yet that the *natures* of these elements correspond. It is therefore impossible to argue from a high degree of coherence within experience to its correspondence in the same degree with anything outside. And this difficulty is typical. If you place the nature of truth in one sort of character and its test in something quite different, you are pretty certain, sooner or later, to find the two falling apart. In the end, the only test of truth that is not misleading is the special nature or character that is itself constitutive of truth.

Feeling that this is so, the adherents of correspondence sometimes insist that correspondence shall be its own test. But then the second difficulty arises. If truth does consist in correspondence, no test can be sufficient. For in order to know that experience corresponds to fact, we must be able to get at that fact, unadulterated with idea, and compare the two sides with each other. And we have seen in the last chapter [chapter 25 of *The Nature of Thought*, vol. 2] that such fact is not accessible. When we try to lay hold of it, what we find in our hands is a judgement which is obviously not itself the indubitable fact we are seeking, and which must be checked by some fact beyond it. To this process there is no end. And even if we did get at the fact directly, rather than through the veil of our ideas, that would be no less fatal to correspondence. This direct seizure of fact presumably gives us truth, but since that truth no longer consists in correspondence of idea with fact, the main theory has been abandoned. In short, if we can know fact only through the medium of our own ideas, the original forever eludes us; if we can get at the facts directly, we have knowledge whose truth is not correspondence. The theory is forced to choose between scepticism and self-contradiction.[4]

Thus the attempt to combine coherence as the test of truth with correspondence as the nature of truth will not pass muster by its own test. The result is *in*coherence. We believe that an application of the test to other theories of truth would lead to a like result. The argument is: assume coherence as the test, and you will be driven by the incoherence of your alternatives to the conclusion that it is also the nature of truth.

The theory that truth *consists* in coherence must now be developed more specifically. The theory has been widely attacked, and the average reader will not improbably come to it with numerous and dark suspicions. In presenting the theory we shall therefore follow a somewhat unusual procedure. We shall go down the line of these suspicions and objections, trying to deal with them in roughly the order in which they naturally arise, and seeking in our answers to bring the nature and implications of the theory gradually to light.

9

(1)

It is objected, first, that the view entails scepticism. What is it that our judgements must cohere with in order to be true? It is a system of knowledge complete and all-inclusive. But obviously that is beyond us—very probably forever beyond us. If to know anything as true, which means simply to know it, requires that we should see its relation to the total of possible knowledge, then we neither do nor can know anything.

The answer lies partly in an admission, partly in an explanation. The admission is that the theory does involve a degree of scepticism regarding our present knowledge and probably all future knowledge. In all likelihood there will never be a proposition of which we can say, "This that I am asserting, with precisely the meaning I now attach to it, is absolutely true." Such a conclusion may bring disappointment, but disappointment is not discredit. And in the light of the history of science, this refusal to claim absoluteness for our knowledge appears even as a merit. For the road of history is so thick with discarded certainties as to suggest that any theory which distributes absolute guarantees is touched with charlatanism. Those who would define truth as correspondence or self-evidence commonly believe that in certain judgements these characters can be found to the full and hence that the judgements are true absolutely. But it is easy to point to past judgements which, in the best opinion of the time, satisfied both definitions at once—judgements for example about the flatness of the earth or the rising of the sun—which nevertheless turned out false. In the light of such facts, theories that give patents of absoluteness to any of our present truths have antecedent probability against them. It may be answered that if judgements seeming to be true have turned out false, this does not show that truth has been wrongly defined but only that men have made a mistake as to whether its defining character was present. But the answer is obvious. The objection now before us is that, in contrast with other theories, coherence leads to scepticism. If it is now admitted that the other theories themselves are so difficult to apply that one can have no certainty, even in leading cases, whether the character they define as truth is present or not, then these theories are sceptical also.

We may reply, secondly, with an explanation, which comes essentially to this, that the coherence theory, like other theories, needs to be applied with some common sense. While the truth of a judgement does consist in the last resort in its relations to a completed system, no sensible person would claim to know these in detail, or deny the judgement *any* truth till he did know them, any more than he would deny some beauty to a picture because it failed of beauty absolute. The system we actually work with is always less than *the* whole; at the best it is the mass of scientific knowledge bearing on the point in question; on the average it is a cloudy congeries of memories, suggestions and inferences, ill-organized in the extreme, and yet capable of subconscious mobilization and use. And for all of us, except in rare moments, the interest in truth is satisfied by exercise within these limits. Even the scientist is commonly satisfied if his theory receives the *imprimatur* of the organized knowledge of his time, and he would think it fantastic to attack him on the ground that organized knowledge has been known to change, that it may do so again, and hence that his theory may have to change with it. This last he would no doubt admit, adding however that to allow one's pursuit of science, or one's confidence in it, to be practically affected by this is merely silly. We agree. For all the ordinary purposes of life, coherence does not mean coherence with some inaccessible absolute, but with the system of present knowledge; and since this is by no means beyond determining, to describe the theory as simply sceptical is misleading. In practice it is not sceptical at all; in theory it upholds the scepticism that is a mainspring of progress. It justifies our acceptance of beliefs scientifically tested, while providing a salutary warning that science itself may become a fetish. While supporting the belief in scientific advance, it refuses to believe that this advance has reached the end of the road. It is absolutistic without dogmatism, and relativistic without countenancing despair.

10

(2)

This answers by implication another objection to the theory. It is said that a truth once true must be always true, whereas on the coherence theory what *was* true may now be false, and what is now true may become false with expanding knowledge. That which coheres with the knowledge of an earlier time may conflict with the knowledge of a later time. Thus propositions may put on truth or falsity, and take them off again, with changing scientific fashions; which is absurd.

But the objection is baseless. The measure of truth, which, judged by the ultimate standard, belongs to the proposition "*x* is *y*" is quite unalterable, for the coherence theory as for its critics. But as just admitted, we cannot in practice make use of that ultimate standard, and are compelled to fall back on a second best. What the ultimate standard means *in practice* is the system of present knowledge as apprehended by a particular mind. That system changes; hence what coheres with it at one time may not cohere with it at another; thus in practice we shall be justified in accepting at one time what later we must reject. This is all true, but where is the inconsistency? We have neither said nor implied that truth itself changes. What we have said is that while truth as measured by the ultimate standard is unchanging, our knowledge of that truth does change—which is a very different thing. Our system of knowledge fluctuates; it is not now, for example, what it was in the Dark Ages, or even in the middle of the last century; and if we use as our standard this variable measuring-rod we shall naturally get varying results. But these varying results are in our knowledge, or in truth-as-revealed-in-our-knowledge, not in truth objective and complete. Between a truth that is itself invariant and varying degrees of manifestation of this truth, there is no sort of inconsistency.

11

(3)

This answer suggests a third objection. We have held that while the truth of any particular proposition must be tested by its coherence with present knowledge, the truth of this knowledge as a whole could be measured only by its approximation to an absolute system. But it has been charged that "approximation" covers a surrender to correspondence.[5] For do we not really mean by this that our present system is true so far as it *corresponds* to the further reality, and false so far as it fails of this?

We may call the relation "correspondence" if we wish. Indeed some of the most uncompromising advocates of coherence have used the language of correspondence in their discussions of this point; Bradley, for example, speaks of our judgements as "representatives" of reality which are true "just so far as they agree with, and do not diverge from," the real.[6] Again, "truth, to be true, must be true of something, and this something itself is not truth. This obvious view I endorse."[7] But he adds, "To ascertain its proper meaning is not easy." And what he arrives at as the "proper meaning" is certainly very far from correspondence as meant by its advocates. It is neither copying, nor a one-to-one relation, nor an indefinable "accordance"; "I mean," he writes of judgements, "that less or more they actually possess the character and type of absolute truth and reality. They can take the place of the Real to varying extents, because containing in themselves less or more of its nature. They are its representatives, worse or better, in proportion as they present us with truth affected by greater or less derangement." "We may put it otherwise by saying that truths are true, according as it would take less or more to convert them into reality."[8] Or, if we may put in our own terms a meaning that is certainly not far from Bradley's, the relation is one between a purpose partially fulfilled and a purpose fulfilled completely. Thought, we have insisted, *is* its object realized imperfectly, and a system of thought is true just so far as it succeeds in embodying that end which thought in its very essence is seeking to embody. If we want analogies for the relation of our thought to the system that forms its end, we should leave aside such things as mirrors and number systems and their ways of conforming to objects, and think of the relation between seed and flower, or between the sapling and the tree. Does the sapling *correspond* to the tree that emerges from it? If you say it does, we shall agree that a system of thought may correspond to reality. If, as seems far more likely, you say it does not, and that to use "correspondence" of such a relation is confusing, then you are at one with us in considering "correspondence" a misdescription of the relation we have in mind.

12

(4)

Just as certain critics have attempted to reduce coherence to correspondence, certain others have attempted to reduce it to self-evidence. They say: "When we grasp the coherence of a proposition with a system, we are seeing that it necessitates and is necessitated by the other elements in the whole; and what we mean by necessary relations is relations logically self-evident."

Again we must answer by defining terms. When anyone says he believes in self-evidence, he is commonly taken to mean that he believes in self-evident *propositions*, that is, in propositions whose truth can be seen without considering how they are related to the systems they belong to. Thus Descartes believed in self-evidence because he believed that there were certain "simple propositions" which, however fertile of consequences when the mind reflected on them, could be seen to be true by themselves before any such consequences were deduced. This is a useful way of conceiving self-evidence, and as it is also the commonest way, it seems wisest to conform to it. But if we do, it is plain at once that to reduce coherence to self-evidence is out of the question, since the two theories contradict each other on an essential point. The self-evidence theory says the truth of some propositions at least can be seen in isolation; the coherence theory says that the truth of *no* proposition can be seen in isolation.

However, the defender of self-evidence may reject the proposed definition; he may insist that what he means by self-evidence is something attaching equally to propositions in isolation and to the coherence of these with a system. This is a distinct view and demands a distinct answer. That answer is not difficult, and it is to our mind decisive against any form of self-evidence that may be offered as an account of truth. Self-evidence, in its essence, contains a reference to being seen; if a truth were too complicated and difficult for any human apprehension, no one would call it self-evident. And if not self-evident, then on the theory it could not be a truth at all. Now this is a violent paradox. It involves the conclusion that if the best human brains cannot *see* a proposition to be true, then it cannot *be* true. It suggests that when Newton, having hit on the law of gravitation, laid this aside for a while because his calculations failed to confirm it, the law was really not true, since it possessed self-evidence for no one. It is surely more natural to believe that there are numberless truths too recondite and elaborately conditioned for human wit. So long as self-evidence is offered merely as a criterion of truth, there is some plausibility in it, as we have seen; but when offered as the nature of truth, the plausibility vanishes.

13

(5)

We come now to an objection more frequently made than any we have been considering. Granting that propositions, to be true, must be coherent with each other, may they not be coherent without being true? Are there not many systems of high unity and inclusiveness, which nevertheless are false? We have seen, for example, that there are various systems of geometry each of which seems to be as coherent internally as the others. Since they are mutually inconsistent, not more than one of them can be true, and there are many mathematicians who would say that *none* of them are true; yet if truth lies merely in coherence, are we not compelled to take all of them as true? Again, a novel, or a succession of novels such as Galsworthy's *Forsyte Saga*, may create a special world of characters and events which is at once extremely complex and internally consistent; does that make it the less fictitious? To say that it does would imply that if we could only dream constantly enough and consistently enough our dreams would literally come true.

(i) This objection, like so many other annihilating criticisms, would have more point if anyone had ever held the theory it demolishes. But if intended to represent the coherence theory as responsibly advocated, it is a gross misunderstanding. That theory does not hold that any and every system is true, no matter how abstract and limited; it holds that one system only is true, namely the system in which everything real and possible is coherently included. How one can find in this the notion that a system would still give truth if, like some arbitrary geometry, it disregarded experience completely, it is not easy to see.

14

(ii) The objection gains point, however, when it goes on to inquire whether all that is actual might not be embraced in more than one system. When a murder is committed, there may be two theories of the crime which do complete and equal justice to all the known facts and yet are inconsistent with each other. Is it not conceivable similarly that there should be two perfect but conflicting systems in which all known and knowable facts should fall into place? If so, our standard would require us to say that both were true; yet since they conflict, this would be absurd. Now we might reply that such a contingency, though possible, is highly improbable. In the case of the murder, every new bit of evidence narrows the range of available hypotheses, and it does not even occur to us that if we knew *all* the relevant facts we might find ourselves at the end with conflicting theories. If such an issue is improbable where the facts are so few, is it not far more improbable where the facts are infinitely many?

Still, this answer seems inadequate, since a theory that leaves it even possible that in the ultimate nature of truth there should be inconsistency ought to be met, we feel, with some decisive disproof. Can it be shown that such an issue is not only improbable, but impossible? I think it can. There are to be two systems, each including all facts known or knowable, but differing in internal structure. Now if the first system is constructed according to plan A, and the second according to plan B, then the possession by the first of plan A is not a fact that is included in the second, and the possession of plan B by the second is not a fact included in the first. The two systems are thus *not*, as they are supposed to be, each inclusive of all the known facts. To put it otherwise, if the systems differ neither in facts nor in structure, they are not two systems but one. If, with the same facts, they are to differ at all, they must differ in structure, but then there will be at least one fact that each of them must omit, namely, the fact that the other possesses the particular structure it does. Thus that all actual and possible facts should be embraced in conflicting systems is unthinkable.

On the other hand, if the objector lowers his claim and says only that the facts *as so far known* may be ordered in different systems, he is saying nothing against our theory. For this certainly does not show that if all the facts were known these rivals would still stand as rivals; it shows only that with the facts now available we should not on our view be justified in making a choice. And this really confirms our view, through bringing it into line with science. Such suspension of judgement is precisely what is enjoined by scientific practice, which holds that so long as two rival hypotheses equally cover the facts, neither is to be preferred to the other, but that as soon as there appears an *instantia crucis* which one hypothesis can assimilate and the other not, we are justified in adopting the first.[9]

15

(iii) Suppose, however, that no crucial instance ever did arise. Suppose (to put an extreme but conceivable case) that we spent from twelve midnight to twelve noon of every day in dreaming, that our dreams were as vivid and orderly as our waking life, and that when we resumed them every night we did so at exactly the point at which we left off the day before. Would there then be any difference between sleep and waking? Would there be any sense in saying that one world was real and the other unreal, that in the one our perceptions and beliefs were true and in the other delusions merely? I think not. And our inability to make any choice in such a conjuncture confirms our theory. The argument runs: if truth did lie in coherence, then, confronted with two worlds equally coherent, we should be unable to select one as truer than the other; on reflection we can see that such inability is just what we should find; hence the equation of truth with coherence is so far verified.

16

(iv) It is further verified by our way of choosing between systems which in the above sense are *not* equal. There are various cases. Consider (a) how we recognize dreams or delusions for what they are. When we are suddenly roused from a vivid dream, we may be momentarily dazed, not knowing the dream from the actuality. How do we establish which is which? Mere vividness does not decide the matter; the dream may be of nightmare intensity while the perception of our familiar surroundings may be comparatively dim. The deciding factor in the battle is what may be called the mass and integration of the household troops. The bureau and windows of our familiar bedroom and the sound of a familiar voice throw out innumerable lines of connection that bring our everyday world around us again in irresistible volume. Against the great bulk of this world, and without any lodgement in it, the figures of our dream appear unsubstantial and fugitive, quickly dissolving for want of support; and it is just the recognition that what we have been experiencing will not fit into our common-sense world that we mean when we say we wake from dream. The power to measure such fancies and phantasms against the ordered mass of experience is the logical meaning of sanity; its disappearance is insanity. There may be organic differences between the man who thinks himself

Napoleon, the man who is sure he has committed the unpardonable sin, and the man who is persuaded that there is a universal conspiracy to keep him down; but intellectually they are alike; there are certain beliefs which resist appraisal by the mass of their general experience, and stand in the midst of it like solid capsules impervious to outer influences. In these cases that is what insanity means.[10]

Notes

1. See further, chap. 30, sec. 15 of *The Nature of Thought*, vol. 2 (London: George Allen and Unwin, 1921).

2. *Idealism: A Critical Survey* (London: Methuen and Co., 1934), 231.

3. Coherence can be defined without this point, which, as Dr. Ewing remarks (*Idealism*, 231), makes the case harder to establish. In no mathematical system, for example, would anyone dream of trying to deduce all the other propositions from any proposition taken singly. But when we are describing an ideal, such a fact is not decisive, and I follow Joachim in holding that in a perfectly coherent system every proposition would entail all others, if only for the reason that its meaning could never be fully understood without apprehension of the system in its entirety.

4. Cf. the criticism of the copy theory above, chap. 7, sec. 9 of *The Nature of Thought*, vol. 1 (London: George Allen and Unwin, 1921). And see the appendix to the present chapter for comment on a current defence of correspondence.

5. As, for example, by Schiller, *Studies in Humanism* (London: Macmillan and Co., 1907), 122.

6. *Appearance and Reality* (London: Swan Sonnenschein, 1893), 362–363.

7. *Essays on Truth and Reality* (Oxford: Clarendon Press, 1914), 325; and cf. "If my idea is to work it must correspond to a determinate being it cannot be said to make."

8. *Appearance and Reality*, 362–363.

9. It may be said that the truth is not established until *all* rivals have been eliminated. But this is not the view on which the natural sciences actually proceed. Of course in formal logic an argument from the affirmation of the consequent is fallacious, and when this is carried over into science it is often said to provide verification without proof; the proof is attained only when it is shown that from no other antecedent could these consequences have sprung. But it will be evident that in the ordinary work of science proof of this kind is seldom if ever practicable; one cannot be sure that *all possible* alternatives have been excluded. "The character of relativity and non-finality, which attaches to mere verification and causes it to be called the fallacy of the consequent, is really inevitable in the pursuit of truth."—Bosanquet, *Implication and Linear Inference* (London: Macmillan and Company, 1920), 102.

10. Much evidence could be adduced for the above suggestions as to the nature of sanity and of aberrations from it. See, e.g., McDougall's account of relative dissociation as explaining the lack of normal inhibition in hypnosis. *Abnormal Psychology* (New York: Charles Scribner's Sons, 1926), 110ff.

7 The Coherence Theory

Ralph C. S. Walker

I

The coherence theory of truth deserves better treatment than it has usually been given in the past fifty years or so. The stock dismissals of it—by Russell, by Schlick, and by many others who ought to have known better[1]—dispose only of a crude caricature. But they have been widely accepted as exhibiting the theory as a foolish aberration, suited only to the occasional muddled verificationist and to the Idealists of the last century (a time when, as we like to think, philosophical standards were so much lower that the most palpable absurdities escaped attention).

That these dismissals were unduly hasty is suggested by the theory's recent revival in the hands of such hard-headed philosophers as Quine, Davidson and Putnam; on a plausible interpretation of Wittgenstein it can be ascribed also to him. There are, of course, substantial differences between these contemporary philosophers and the coherence theorists of the last century, and also among these contemporary philosophers themselves. The differences are great enough to suggest that it might be better to speak of coherence theories, in the plural, rather than of "the coherence theory" of truth. Nevertheless I think these various views have enough in common to justify the traditional usage. The motivations for them—motivations which are powerful and hard to resist—are very similar; they run into parallel difficulties; and above all they share the same general character, the same radical conception of the kind of thing that truth is. I shall therefore continue to speak (when it is not misleading to do so) of "the coherence theory of truth" in the singular.

The first thing to be clear about is what this coherence theory is. It is a theory about the nature of truth. When Rescher wrote his book *The Coherence Theory of Truth* it seemed to him (because he accepted the stock objections) that no one could seriously have meant it in that way, and so he concerns himself instead with the view that coherence provides the *criterion* for truth—the way of finding out what is true.[2] That is itself an interesting view, but I shall not be considering it here, except incidentally. One can consistently hold (as Rescher himself does) that coherence provides the criterion of truth, but that the nature of truth consists in something different, a correspondence of some kind. One can also indeed combine the thesis that the nature of truth is coherence with the claim that we need some different way of finding out what is true; that is a consistent combination, but it is not so attractive a position, for reasons which will appear shortly.

The coherence theorist holds that for a proposition[3] to be true is for it to cohere with a certain system of beliefs. It is not just that it is true if and only if it coheres with that system; it is that the coherence, and nothing else, is what its truth consists in. In particular, truth does not consist in the holding of some correspondence between the proposition and some reality which obtains independent of anything that may be believed about it.

This is a radical thesis. It conflicts with what most of us naturally think. But it is important to notice that the coherence theorist does not depart so far from common sense as to have to deny such truisms as "true propositions correspond with the facts." It is common to treat the coherence and correspondence theories of truth as though they were rivals, and so they are, if the correspondence theory is also a theory about the nature of truth: a theory to the effect that truth *does* consist in some sort of correspondence between a proposition on the one hand, and on the other a real world whose nature and existence are quite independent of what may be believed about it. But although that is a very natural theory, one does not commit oneself to it just by saying things like "true propositions correspond with the facts." Coherence theorists can make such remarks quite freely; they just will not regard them as expressing the nature of truth, nor will they take "the facts" to belong to a metaphysically independent reality; on the contrary, on their view the facts are themselves determined by the coherent system of beliefs. But "corresponds with the facts" is so standardly used as a long-winded equivalent of "is true" that it would seem highly perverse to deny that in some sense true propositions do correspond with the facts. What is open to controversy is how informative a remark it is, and this will much depend on how we construe the correspondence relation, and what status we accord to "the facts." I shall return to this, and to how the coherence theory relates to the traditional discussions about truth and correspondence, in the next chapter [of Walker 1989]. In what follows, unless I indicate otherwise I shall mean by "the correspondence theory" the theory that truth consists in some kind of correspondence with a reality independent of what may be believed about it—the view that the coherence theorist is out to reject. (It would not do to characterize it as the theory that truth consists in correspondence with a reality independent of what may be believed, and leave it at that, because there are truths about beliefs, and truths about beliefs can hardly be independent of the beliefs that make them true. They may however be independent of anything that may be believed about those beliefs themselves, and that is what the correspondence theory holds. One's beliefs about what beliefs are held may very often be correct, especially if it is one's own beliefs that are in question, but there is an important distinction between believing that *p* and believing that it is believed that *p*.)

Before we can go any further, though, something more positive needs to be said about what the coherence theory of truth is. To start with, it is important to emphasize that what is to be cohered with is a set of *beliefs*, and some specific set of beliefs at that. One of the standard objections to the coherence theory, made for instance by Russell,[4] is that (on any plausible understanding of "coherence") virtually any proposition can be fitted into some coherent set. The proposition "Bishop Stubbs was hanged for murder" is in fact false, but one can imagine a world no less coherent than our own in which it is true; there is thus a coherent set of propositions to which it belongs, including perhaps such propositions as "All bishops are murderers" and "Bishops are generally hanged," just as there is a coherent set of propositions to which (the truth) "Bishop Stubbs died in his bed" belongs. But the objection misses the point, because it is not being suggested that truth consists in cohering with any arbitrary set of propositions. No coherence theorist would ever be tempted to think that the coherence relation held simply amongst propositions in the abstract, regardless of whether anyone believed them or ever would believe them, for propositions in the abstract are hardly to be distinguished from the facts that the correspondence theorist invokes. Instead coherence theorists maintain that truth consists in coherence with a set of beliefs, and some specific set of beliefs at that—though as we shall see in a moment they do not necessarily consider that these must be beliefs that are held either by ourselves or by anyone alive today. This answer to Russell's objection raises further problems, which we shall have to return to in due course; but at least the coherence theory is not eliminated straight away by so simple a criticism.

What, though, is understood by "coherence," and what system of beliefs is intended? Since coherence theorists are a varied lot, very different answers to these questions have been offered. Often the system of beliefs has been envisaged as being, broadly speaking, our own, though since most people's beliefs are inconsistent it cannot include all the things we believe. What many coherence theorists have in mind, therefore, is some subset of our beliefs; perhaps the largest subset that is in accord internally, perhaps some subset that is particularly fundamental, or indispensable, to our thinking (including no doubt the laws of logic and the principles of inference that we use in testing hypotheses and constructing theories). Others, conscious of the radical changes and developments that have taken place in human thought, have considered it wrong to tie truth to anything that we believe at present, and have taken it to be coherence with the system of beliefs that human beings will hold at the ultimate stage of their historical development. Others, more distrustful still of human fallibility, have regarded truth as coherence with the system of beliefs held by God or the Absolute; a view which must be carefully distinguished from that of a traditional theologian who is no coherence theorist but still maintains that God knows all the truths, and has no false beliefs. For the traditional theologian God's beliefs, unlike ours, invariably correspond with the relevant facts; these facts are independent of God's beliefs about them (though they may not be independent of His creative will). For the coherence theorist on the other hand truth consists in coherence, and if the coherence is coherence with God's beliefs then it is His beliefs that determine what the facts are.

Opinions have differed too about what is to be meant by "coherence." Sometimes it has been taken to be simply consistency with the basic principles that characterize the system of beliefs. Sometimes, at the other extreme, it has been held to require mutual entailment by all the propositions in question: p will cohere with q and r only if p, q and r all entail one another. Sometimes, again, it has been left thoroughly vague what coherence is supposed to amount to. Actually we cannot really decide what is to constitute coherence until we decide which system of beliefs is appropriate, for the two questions go together. Generally the system will itself determine what coherence with it amounts to. If for example it includes the laws of logic, a set of principles of scientific inference sufficient to determine a single theory as correct when enough evidence is in, and a further set of principles adequate to determine what counts as admissible evidence, then there is no further problem as to what constitutes coherence (at least within the domain of science): propositions describing admissible evidence will cohere, as will those stating theories determined as correct by the principles of inference. A view of very much this kind is quite often held by contemporary coherence theorists, particularly those influenced by Quine. Another commonly held view makes coherence simply a matter of agreement with the considered and long-term judgement of the community—a view often, and plausibly, ascribed to Wittgenstein. It should certainly *not* be taken for granted that any coherence theory worthy of the name must necessarily incorporate the standards of coherence that at first sight seem most natural to us, or even that it must incorporate those laws that we commonly regard as the laws of logic; Hegel's, for instance, works on a very different basis. There is no reason to place any limitation on what can count as coherence: we can consider someone to hold a coherence theory of truth if they hold that truth consists in some relationship within a set of beliefs, whatever that relationship may be. Of course, coherence theorists with particularly absurd ideas as to what it might be can be particularly easily dismissed. But most real-life coherence theorists are not in that category, even if at first sight they may appear to be.

Thus what makes something a coherence theory of truth (in the broad sense in which I am using the expression) is not that it is built round some specific concept of coherence. What makes it a coherence theory is that it is a theory about the nature of truth, to the effect that for a proposition to be true is for it to fit in with some designated set of beliefs; but which set of beliefs is designated will vary from one version of the theory to another, as will the kind of fit required. There need be no suggestion in this that every truth is the content of a belief that either is or ever will be actually held, but if coherence theorists intend their account to cover truths of all kinds they will claim that every truth is the content of a belief that *would* be held if the system of beliefs were fully worked out so as to include all those that cohere. By contrast I have described the correspondence theory of truth as claiming that truth consists in correspondence with a reality that is independent of anything that may be believed about it. Putting it in that fashion brings out that the correspondence and coherence theories are exclusive alternatives, provided that they are both intended to apply to *all* truths. But they are not quite exhaustive. For one thing there is the possibility of rejecting altogether any theory of the nature of truth, on the ground that general questions about what truth consists in are too broad to be intelligible. We shall return to this idea; it is less worth taking seriously than it may seem. And there is also the possibility of a theory which combines coherence and correspondence by giving a coherence account of some kinds of truth and a correspondence account of others. On such a mixed view—which I shall call an *impure* coherence theory—the nature of reality might be determined *partly* by the system of coherent beliefs and *partly* by something else independent of it. At first sight the idea of an impure coherence theory may seem rather peculiar, but we shall find in due course that certain theories which have historically been described as coherence theories of truth are in fact impure coherence theories. An example might be a theory which offered a correspondence account of the truth of statements about our experiences, but a coherence account of the truth of the more theoretical statements which we construct on the basis of them. Another example might be a theory which gave a correspondence account of straightforward "factual" truths about the world around us, but a coherence account of evaluative truths, or of truths about possibilities and necessities.[5]

II

Since the coherence theory is so often dismissed out of hand, we ought to consider the reasons which are standardly adduced for rejecting it. There are five of these. At least as they stand they are all worthless. This is not to say that it may not be possible to develop more serious difficulties for the theory out of them, and that is a matter to which we shall have to return. But it is a serious mistake to think they provide grounds for the instant dismissal the theory has so commonly received. Besides these five I shall consider two further objections of a rather more subtle kind; these are equally ineffective against the theory, but by considering them we shall be able to clarify one or two remaining points about what exactly the theory claims.

One of the five standard objections we have met already. It is the objection that the coherence theory is unable to distinguish between truth and falsity because virtually every proposition (including "Bishop Stubbs was hanged for murder") belongs to some coherent set. As we saw, this misses the point. Coherence theorists do not say that membership of any arbitrary coherent set of propositions is sufficient for truth. What they say is that truth is coherence with a certain particular set of beliefs.

The second standard objection is that the theory cannot take account of experience. Coherence theorists are not likely to be much impressed with this. They consider that they can, and do, take account of experience, and indeed they often spend a lot of time emphasizing the importance of experience in the construction of our knowledge of the world. What they reject is only the idea that taking account of it means bringing it about that our experiential beliefs match something that is given or presented to us in such a fashion that its nature is independent of beliefs about it, and the rejection of *that* picture is something they share with many philosophers who do not subscribe to the coherence theory of truth. They share it with the proponents of the coherence theory of knowledge; they share it also with those who hold that although experiential beliefs provide a foundation for our knowledge, the structure of our beliefs in general determines the character of experience. I dealt with this elsewhere.[6]

According to the coherence theory of truth, we have a great many beliefs about the content of our experience, but as with any other beliefs their truth can only consist in their coherence within the system; and if that means that the system must be a rich and elaborate system, well and good. This is not incompatible with the ordinary view that their truth depends on their being caused in us in the right sort of way, by the operation of things outside us upon our sense-organs; coherence theorists have no more difficulty in accepting that than anyone else does, for they will take the appropriate causal truths to belong to the coherent system. Admittedly, *whatever* theory one holds about truth there are going to be philosophical problems to be dealt with over the way experience bears upon our knowledge; but there is no special difficulty for the coherence theory here, and no simple refutation of it is to be achieved in this fashion.

The third of the standard objections is than the theory cannot accommodate its own truth, because it must claim more for itself that just that it coheres; it must claim to be actually *true*. But this seems quite unfair. Coherence theorists hold that truth consists in coherence, and are quite prepared to say that the truth of their own theory consists in its coherence with the relevant set of beliefs. They mean nothing more than that by calling it true, but that is quite enough, for coherence is what truth is.

Someone might seek to take this objection a stage further by asking what would happen if the coherence theory did not itself belong to the coherent system of beliefs, and the correspondence theory of the nature of truth did so instead. But this again creates no serious difficulty for the coherence theorist. If it were the correspondence theory, and not the coherence theory, that cohered with the system, it would not follow that the correspondence theory was true, but it would follow that truth cannot consist in coherence; for the coherence theory cannot be true unless it is true by its own standard. That, however, is not the position, according to coherence theorists, for the coherence theory *does* cohere with the system. And there is no reason for them to worry about what *would* have been the case if the system had been different in this respect, any more than there is reason for them to worry about what the position would have been if the system had been, for example, internally inconsistent. It is not.

A similar misunderstanding gives rise to the fourth objection, to the effect that the coherence theory makes truth relative. Of course in one sense this is perfectly true, for it does make truth depend upon the coherent system of beliefs. In exactly the same way the correspondence theory could be said to make truth "relative to" the independently existing facts. But in neither case is there any suggestion that some alternative standard would yield some alternative and equally good kind of truth. The coherence theorist might, it is true, admit that other people or other societies might operate with a different system of beliefs which they thought of as determining the truth; the coherence theorist might go so far as to hold that it was impossible in principle for us to convince them of the error of their ways. Nevertheless their ways are in error, and it is as important to the coherence theorist as to the correspondence theorist that this is so. Truth consists in coherence not just with any system of beliefs but with a certain specific one, and anything else, any alternative system however neat and self-contained, simply is not truth.

The fifth objection that is often made, and perhaps even more frequently felt than expressed, is that the theory does so much violence to our ordinary ways of thinking and talking as to be simply absurd—or perhaps even nonsensical, because it seeks to give our ordinary words a meaning they cannot carry. Truth is not a function of what is believed but a matter of matching external reality. The existence of trees and of dinosaurs is quite independent of anyone's beliefs; there were dinosaurs around even when there was nobody to have thoughts about them, and the fact that there are trees nowadays is not dependent on there being people.

Like the others this objection fails, but some care is necessary in order to be quite clear why it fails. It misses the point because it caricatures what coherence theorists are saying. To a very large extent they are happy to speak with the vulgar. As we have seen they are quite prepared to say that true propositions are those that correspond with the facts; though they hold that it is the coherent system of beliefs that determines what the facts are. In the same way they can talk of the world as objectively real, and as independent of my beliefs about it. Clearly (since I can be mistaken) the set of beliefs that determines the truth is not to be identified with the set of beliefs that I have at present, and to recognize that is to recognize a contrast which the coherence theorist will describe as the contrast between how things seem to me and how they really, or objectively, are. What he does maintain is that the nature of this objective reality is itself determined by the coherent system of beliefs. That certainly conflicts with our common-sense view of things, but not in a way that renders it evidently absurd.

The coherence theorist has no difficulty either over the existence of dinosaurs before there were thoughts about them. That there were dinosaurs before there were people is a familiar scientific fact, and like all scientific facts it is true (on his view) because it coheres with the system. Muddle can be caused here, as so often, by letting meta-phor run away with us: the coherence theorist is sometimes thought of as saying that the facts, and hence the world and its dinosaurs, are *created* by the system of beliefs, and the conclusion is drawn that they could not have existed before any beliefs did. But this is confused. The coherent system of beliefs determines as true all sorts of state-ments about the remote past, including the statement that there were dinosaurs before there were people; and being determined as true, they are true, for such is the nature of truth. It has sometimes been claimed that at least the coherence theory must be in difficulty over all sorts of *specific* truths about dinosaurs which we shall never be able to verify and which no one will ever believe: there must be some number *n*, for example, for which it is true that the total number of dinosaurs that ever existed was *n*.[7] But this objection too is misplaced, at any rate against many forms of the theory, for the coher-ence theorist is under no obligation to regard as true only what we shall someday be able to verify (although admittedly *some* coherence theorists may take this line). Setting aside the possibility of saying that the coherent system of beliefs is the system of *God's* beliefs (a possibility which, as we shall see, does have its disadvantages), it is open to the coherence theorist to hold that the truth is what one *would* get to *if* one made the best possible use of certain principles of reasoning and scientific inference; and these might suffice to determine the number of dinosaurs, even if none of us will ever determine it.

Furthermore, and for similar reasons, the coherence theorist can accept the truth of counterfactuals like "If there had been no people there would still have been trees"—a point that has been well made by Blackburn.[8] In the ordinary way of taking it, the counterfactual is supported by a fact of everyday science, to the effect that the exis-tence of trees does not depend on that of people. It will therefore come out true for the coherence theorist just as much as for anyone else, because it coheres with the body of beliefs that determines the truth. That body of beliefs is a set of propositions *p*, *q*, *r*, ... ; the truth is whatever coheres with *p*, *q*, *r*, ... ; and whatever *p*, *q*, *r*, ... may be in detail, we can expect the generalizations of ordinary science to cohere with them, and if they do, so must also the counterfactual conditionals they support.

What can cause confusion here is the thought that *p*, *q*, *r*, ... determine the truth only because they are believed; and beliefs require people to have them (or at any rate believers of some kind). That consideration is sufficient, given the coherence theory, to establish that there *are* people (or at any rate believers of some kind). That there are, no one of course disputes; what is being asked is what things would have been like if there had not been. Now counterfactual conditionals are tricky, because the assessment of them depends on just what features of the actual world are assumed to be held constant in the circumstance envisaged—not all features of the actual world can be, since the conditional's antecedent is in fact false. Thus we feel a sort of puzzlement if someone produces out of the blue the statement "If Bizet and Verdi had been compatriots Bizet would have been Italian"; we do not know how to assess it because nothing in the context or in the antecedent tells us whether Bizet's nationality should be held constant (in which case the conditional is false) or Verdi's (in which case it is true). In the *normal* way of understanding the conditional "If there had been no people there would still have been trees," it is clear enough that the supposition is being made within the context of our ordinary theory of the world; the proper way to assess the claim is therefore to ask what that theory, or so much of it as we can combine with the truth of the antecedent, tells us, and it is easy to see (as we did above) that the conditional thus comes out true. In the highly *abnormal* context of a discussion of the coherence theory of truth, however, things can look differently. For here it is possible to view the supposition, *not* as taking for granted our ordinary theory of the world, but as putting it in question. This gives us an alternative (though except in this special context highly unnatural) way of taking the conditional. On this alternative reading, what is assumed to be held constant is the coherence theory of truth itself: the theory that truth consists in coherence with a certain set of beliefs. This licenses the conclusion that if there were no beliefs there would be no truth at all (and thus in particular that it could not be true that there were still trees). Assuming that if there were no people there could be no beliefs, we get the result that on this interpretation "If there were no people there would still have been trees" is *false*.

Blackburn has rightly put a great deal of emphasis on the coherence theorist's ability to admit as true statements that at first seem to express the conception of truth and reality which he in fact rejects. Calling the correspondence view that he rejects "realism," Blackburn is able to show that coherence theorists can and should adopt a position of "quasi-realism," which allows them "to mimic the intellectual practices supposedly definitive of realism" without weakening in their repudiation of realism itself.[9] The question arises of how far this can go. Blackburn sometimes seems to be suggesting that there is *no difference* between the realist and the coherence theorist in their assignment of truth-values to statements, but this must be too strong, or it would be impossible to express the difference between the two positions. At other times he seems to be suggesting, more plausibly, that there is no difference between them in their assignment of truth-values to the things that ordinary people, as opposed to philosophers, are likely to say. This is certainly not far from the truth. But it would be wrong to suggest (as Blackburn sometimes appears to and others clearly would) that the coherence theory itself cannot be stated by using words with their ordinary *senses* and in a perfectly ordinary fashion. For it can.

It is easy to slip into the mistake of thinking that when the correspondence theory affirms, and the coherence theory denies, that truth consists in matching a reality that is independent of what may be believed about it, they are using "independent" in a special way—giving it a peculiarly philosophical or "transcendental" usage which must be distinguished from its everyday or "empirical" usage. If this were the case, there would be room for serious doubt whether any clear sense had been assigned or could be assigned to the word in its alleged transcendental usage; it would be utterly unclear which features of the ordinary sense were being retained and which abandoned. The idea that this is what is going on encourages the thought that the coherence theory may be strictly unintelligible. But fortunately that is not a difficulty we have to face. What is meant by "independent" is just what we all normally mean by it. It may be natural to take it for granted that the facts are independent (in the ordinary sense) of any beliefs about them, but it is exactly this that coherence theorists are denying— though they are not, of course, obliged to deny that the facts are independent of *my* beliefs about them. To suppose that it is the coherent system of beliefs that determines what the facts are may be unusual, but it is not absurd or self-evidently wrong. To suppose that the facts are determined by what I happen to believe at the moment, or by the current opinions of the British people, *would* be self-evidently wrong, but no sane coherence theorist is likely to think any such thing. On the contrary, he will agree that we hold a great many beliefs that are false. What makes them false is that they fail to cohere with that set of beliefs that determines the truth.

It should be admitted that the coherence theorist's view of truth *is* unusual, and contrary to common sense, though not therefore absurd. It thus cannot be quite true to say that the ordinary person and the coherence theorist will not differ in their assign-ments of truth-values, for they will differ over the statement of the coherence theory. At the same time, the ordinary person is not likely to have occasion to formulate this statement or its denial, so that Blackburn may be right to claim that there is no difference between the realist and the coherence theorist in their assignment of truth-values to the things ordinary people are likely to say.

An objection to this claim may be raised from a different quarter. For surely, it may be said, the realist—i.e. the correspondence theorist—will accept the principle of bivalence, which says that every statement is either true or false, whereas his opponent will not. The coherence theorist will reject it because he cannot rule out the possibility that there are statements such that neither they nor their negations cohere with the system. But that is not quite right: things are not so simple.

To start with it is a mistake to suppose that realists are necessarily committed to biva-lence. What they are committed to is that the nature of reality is independent of any beliefs about it, but that is compatible with the possibility that reality itself may admit of three or more truth-values. Hence there may be statements which are neither true nor false, just because of the nature of things. Dummett, who recognizes this point, claims that although realists are not necessarily committed to the view that every state-ment is either true or false, they *are* committed to the view that "any sentence on which a fully specific sense has been conferred has a determinate truth-value independently of our actual capacity to decide what that truth-value is";[10] but this again is wrong. It is correct to say that on the realist view a statement's truth-value is independent of our capacity to find out about it, our beliefs about it, and indeed anyone's beliefs about it.

But a realist might hold that the world was intrinsically vague in such a way as to make some quite specific claims (as for example the claim that so-and-so is not yet an adult) neither determinately true, nor determinately false, nor determinately anything else—not even determinately vague if the case is sufficiently borderline.

It is also not quite correct to say that the coherence theorist is committed to rejecting bivalence. For one thing he might draw up his theory in such a way that the coherent system of beliefs was adequate to determine every statement as true or as false. He could do this either by making sure that the coherent system was large enough—equating it, for instance, with the system of *God's* beliefs—or alternatively by restricting what is to count as a statement so as to admit nothing that is not determined as true or as false by the coherent system. This latter would be the position of certain verificationists. What *is* true, though, is that unless he takes one of these steps he will not be entitled to assert that the principle of bivalence is true. Nothing within the coherent system will warrant the denial of the possibility that there are statements such that neither they nor their negations are determined as true by the system. Admittedly, as Blackburn points out, there might be some practical value in his deciding to treat the principle of bivalence *as though* it were true; deciding, that is, to treat every statement *as though* it must be either true or false, rather as a judge may decide that every putative contract must be treated as though the legal system determined it either as valid or as invalid. But this is not the same as holding the principle of bivalence to be true literally.[11]

If he is not entitled to assert that the principle of bivalence is true, it does not follow that he is entitled to conclude that it is false. This will only follow if it is assumed that the totality of truths is determinate, in the sense that for any statement it is a determinate matter whether it belongs to the totality or not. Given that assumption, if the system allows for statements such that neither they nor their negations belong to it, these statements will be determinately neither true nor false, and consequently the principle of bivalence will itself be false. But it would be possible to deny the assumption, and some coherence theorists do: in their view the propositions that cohere with the system do *not* form a determinate totality. It would be natural to think that the totality of truths was indeterminate if one thought there was nothing more to truth than what we can recognize as true, and if one regarded it as somehow open-ended what we can recognize as true: as something that cannot be firmly delimited in advance of investigation. This is the line of thought taken by those who call themselves anti-realists, and as we shall see it was also taken by Kant.

Thus in fact there are three possibilities. (1) The coherent set may be such as to contain either p or not-p, for every value of p; the resultant system would be bivalent. (2) The coherent set may be such as to contain a specification, for each value of p, as to whether p, or not-p, or neither p nor not-p; then the principle of bivalence would be false of this system. But (3) the coherent set may not form a determinate totality, so that for some values of p the status of p may be indeterminate. This possibility subdivides further.

(3a) It may be that there are certain values of *p* to which the system determinately assigns the status "neither true nor false"; in that case, again, the principle of bivalence would be false of the system. This, as I shall argue in the next chapter [of Walker 1989], is the position of Kant: although admittedly he does not use this terminology, in effect he regards the totality of truths about the world of appearances as being indeterminate, but also considers that so far as the world of appearances is concerned the principle of bivalence is determinately false. (3b) On the other hand it may be that there are *no* propositions to which the system determinately assigns the status "neither true nor false." In that case the principle of bivalence would not be determinately false of the system, but it would not be determinately true of it either. This is the position that Dummett and others call anti-realism. Anti-realists equate something's being determinately true, in virtue of the coherent system, with our being able to recognize its truth, and they equate something's being determinately false with our being able to recognize the truth of its negation; but they also do not think it possible to find any statement which is determinately neither true nor false. Dummett puts this by saying that the anti-realist accepts the principle *tertium non datur*—the principle "that there can be no circumstances in which a statement can be recognised as being, irrevocably, neither true nor false."[12]

It may seem less than obvious that anti-realism is a form of coherence theory of truth. Anti-realism is essentially a theory about meaning and understanding: it holds that to understand the meaning of a sentence is to understand the conditions under which it is warrantedly assertible. These conditions may not be such as to ensure its truth, and indeed there are various types of statement—statements about the past, for example, or about other people's mental states—for which conclusive verification is never available. This naturally gives rise to the thought that these statements must *have* truth-values independently of our verification, and that just because our verification can never be conclusive, there must be some truth of the matter lying forever beyond our reach. But it is exactly this that the anti-realist most firmly denies. To say that the verification is never conclusive is to say that though our assertion of such a statement may be well warranted in the circumstances, our warrant for it is always defeasible; more evidence could always turn up which could render the assertion unjustifiable after all. There is no determinate totality of evidence which could settle the matter conclusively. The statement *has* no truth-conditions independent of our capacity to recognize it as true. To put it another way, he holds that there is nothing to its being true over and above its being recognizable as true by us.[13]

Anti-realists hold this because of their views about meaning. They consider that we can learn how to use words in assertoric sentences only by learning in what circumstances these sentences can justifiably be asserted, and it is only through the appropriate use of such sentences in such circumstances that our understanding of them can be exhibited. Since meanings can be learned and can be exhibited, to understand a sentence can be nothing more than to know the circumstances under which it can be justifiably asserted. Truth-conditions which we could never know about cannot enter into our understanding of a sentence, because there is no way in which we could either learn or manifest an understanding of them. Since the sentence is a sentence of our language it can therefore make no sense to suppose that it has truth-conditions of that kind at all, or that the statements we can use it to make possess a truth-value independently of what we can discover. It is the realist view, to which anti-realism is opposed, that whenever a sentence is used to make a specific statement, that statement is true, or false, or enjoys whatever intermediate status there may be, regardless of whether we can know that. According to the anti-realist this idea of verification-transcendent truth is a myth. The idea of verification-transcendent truth is just the idea of truth that the correspondence theory makes use of. In rejecting it, the anti-realist adopts the alternative view, that truth is not independent of our capacity to find out about it, or in other words to have beliefs about it—beliefs that are warranted in their context.[14]

What does it mean to say that a belief is warranted in its context? The context may consist of other beliefs which support it, or of perceptual circumstances, or both. With many beliefs, like the belief that it is cold or that there is a table before me, it is natural to feel that it is the perceptual circumstances that warrant them. But for the anti-realist the fact that such-and-such perceptual circumstances obtain cannot itself be independent of our recognition of it, any more than any other fact can be independent of our recognition. Hence even where a belief is warranted by something perceptual, it is still in effect another belief that warrants it; and this means that we have on our hands a pure form of the coherence theory of truth. Beliefs must fit in appropriately with other beliefs which are themselves warranted in the same fashion, through coherence; and so far as it makes sense to talk of truth at all, truth is a matter of what we can in this fashion recognize as true.

Where anti-realists differ from many other coherence theorists is in not thinking of the set of truths as a determinate totality—as was observed above. "What we can recognize as true" is indeterminate and open-ended. But their theory is none the less a coherence theory, in the sense explained. For what counts as true is determined by what we are able to discover. It may be objected that the anti-realist's talk of discovery and recognition implies that there is something there to be discovered or recognized, independently of our discovering or recognizing it, and that would seem incompatible with the coherence theory. But care is required here. It is open to anti-realists to hold that there are plenty of truths which we have not yet recognized, provided they acknowledge that what makes them truths is that we are capable of recognizing them;[15] in this they are in the same position as many other coherence theorists, who hold that in order to be true a statement does not have actually to be believed but only to fit with the system in the appropriate way. If, however, the suggestion is that there must be truths there to be discovered or recognized independently of our *capacity* to discover them or recognize them, then it is something anti-realists repudiate firmly, for as we have seen their account of meaning gives them no way to understand any such idea of truth.

Anti-realists may well say that they are not offering a theory of truth at all, but only a theory of warranted assertibility. If they do, however, we must ask what point they are seeking to make in saying it. If their point is that there is no determinate totality of truths, or that the principle of bivalence does not hold, then there is no need to disagree with them: if a "theory of truth" is committed to bivalence and to there being a determinate totality of truths, then certainly their theory is not a theory of truth. But it remains the case that they are committing themselves to a "theory of the nature of truth" in the sense in which I have been using these words, and to holding in particular that its nature consists in coherence. They might, perhaps, attempt to deny that any such claims about the nature of truth are warrantedly assertible, on the grounds that they are too general and abstract. But if they consider themselves entitled to assert that no statement can have verification-transcendent truth-conditions, and if they also recognize that the aim of warranted assertion is to describe how things are, they should regard themselves as equally entitled to assert that how things are is not independent of how we can discover them to be.

In the last chapter [of Walker 1989] I claimed that it was an attraction of certain forms of the coherence theory of truth that they could offer an answer to the extreme form of scepticism, by allowing us to rule out the possibility that our beliefs were radically false. In so far as the anti-realist regards our warranted assertions as being open-endedly defeasible, anti-realism cannot quite claim this advantage, because we can never be confident that circumstances will not arise which will defeat the ascriptions of truth-value that we have so far made. Typically, however, anti-realists do not regard *all* our assertions as being defeasible in this way; they hold that there are also types of statement that are susceptible of conclusive verification, and which we may therefore be able to know (indefeasibly) to be true because we have verified them. They could therefore resist extreme scepticism over the truth of these statements: not even the *malin génie* could make them false, since it is in our recognition of it that their truth consists.[16]

Moreover, and perhaps more importantly, the anti-realist has a reply to the sceptic even where statements of the defeasible type are concerned. For although we have no assurance that our judgements in this area will not be defeated, we do have an assurance that they are justified, provided we can recognize that the circumstances obtain which warrant their assertion. It is part of what we learn when we learn the meanings of the words involved that such-and-such a statement is warrantedly assertible—and therefore justified, although defeasibly—in such-and-such circumstances. And here again the *malin génie* could not be deceiving us; there is no possibility that this notion of justification is merely our notion, and matches nothing in reality. The reality of the matter is determined by how we think.

At any rate, it is clear that anti-realism is a version of the coherence theory of truth. I said I would conclude this chapter by looking at the relations between the coherence theory and idealism, so it is natural to start by asking whether anti-realism is a form of idealism. Here, of course, a lot depends on what idealism is. Like many "-ism" words the term is variously used. In one sense idealism is the theory that material-object statements are reducible without loss of meaning to statements about mental states or Berkeleian ideas; clearly the anti-realist is not committed to idealism in that sense. In another sense idealism is sometimes said to be the theory that our minds create the world; but this graphic metaphor is more likely to be misleading than to be helpful. Dummett himself makes use of a different metaphor when he associates anti-realism with the picture "of objects springing into being in response to our probing," and says: "We do not *make* the objects but must accept them as we find them ... but they were not already there for our statements to be true or false of before we carried out the investigations which brought them into being."[17] If that is not misleading it is only because it is obscure where it leads. To speak of us as creating the world suggests we have some choice in the matter, and that we make it in something like the same sense in which we make machines or write novels; these suggestions are fairly obviously false, and neither anti-realism nor any other coherence theory is committed to them. Dummett's own metaphor suggests that before we investigate there is nothing there, hardly a welcome thesis and one that anti-realists are in any case not committed to, since like any sensible coherence theorists they regard a statement like "There were dinosaurs before there were people" as making a well-warranted scientific claim. Dummett's metaphor also suggests that when we do investigate, the *nature* of what we find is independent of our cognitive capacities—a conclusion which as we have just seen the anti-realist is bound to repudiate.

In this area of philosophy (as in a number of others) metaphors are very tempting, but also dangerous; one should use them only when one is clear how they can be cashed out. If idealism is taken to be the thesis, not that minds or our minds create nature, but that how things are depends wholly upon some mind or minds, we have a more seriously discussable thesis; though it needs to be made clear that the dependence envisaged is logical and not causal, or the traditional account of the physical world as caused by an act of God's will would have to count as an idealist theory. If idealism is thought of in that way, its affinities with anti-realism, and with coherence theories of truth in general, become clear.

It seems clear, in fact, that not just anti-realists but any coherence theorists must be idealists in this sense. For they hold that truth consists in coherence with some system of beliefs; in the anti-realist version, that how things are is determined by our capacities to recognize them as such, i.e. to come to the belief that they are, in a context in which that belief is warranted (by its relation to our other warranted beliefs). In that case the character of reality is logically determined by certain beliefs. And it would not do, of course, to say that these beliefs might be the beliefs of no mind, for then they could not be distinguished from mind-independent facts about the world, logically independent of what is thought about them, and that is just what the coherence theorist rejects.

Must every idealist be a coherence theorist? One suggestion might be that the ideal-ist could hold that truth consists in some relationship between beliefs, but claim that the relationship was something other than *coherence*. As I have said, though, the term "coherence" is used in various different ways in different versions of the theory, and it might not seem unreasonable to count any truth-constituting relationship between beliefs as a form of coherence. If this suggestion is ruled out it might appear that ideal-ists do have to hold a coherence theory of truth; but in fact they do not, for there is another possibility. For one might hold that although the nature of the world entirely depends upon mind, it depends upon some other aspect of mind than the proposi-tions it accepts. On this view what would determine the truth would not be beliefs, but mental states of some other kind or kinds. They might include, for example, perceptual presentations; Berkeley's account of the material world is idealistic in the sense we are concerned with, but his "ideas" would seem to be perceptual presentations, or copies of them, rather than beliefs. F. H. Bradley, moreover, who is often described as a coherence theorist—and who often writes like one—is in the last resort not one, because what determines reality for him is ultimately not belief but feeling.[18]

Thus not every idealist need be a coherence theorist, but every coherence theorist must (if he is to be consistent) be an idealist. It may seem a surprising conclusion that every coherence theorist must be an idealist. The coherence theorist may be verifica-tionistically minded, as indeed anti-realists are: and verificationistically minded people have often expressed doubts about the meaningfulness of metaphysical theses like ide-alism, on the grounds that they cannot be verified or falsified. However, the conclu-sion does hold, though only because "idealism" is being interpreted in a comparatively harmless way. It is in fact formulated in such a way as to be entailed by the coherence theory, given that beliefs depend on the mind or minds that have them. Hence anyone prepared to subscribe to the coherence theory must be prepared to subscribe to ideal-ism as so formulated; the coherence theory could not be verifiable without idealism being verifiable also. It may be thought to be perverse to formulate idealism in this fashion. Certainly, as I have said, the term is often used in other ways. But it represents a radical enough thesis in this form, and as I hope will become clear in what follows it is in essentially this way that many of those who have called themselves idealists—such as Kant, Fichte, and Bradley—have understood their own positions.

III

So the coherence theory of truth does not fall to the standard objections, and whether it is ultimately defensible is an important question. If it is not, anti-realism fails, and so do a collection of metaphysical theories that can be called idealist. To assess whether the coherence theory is defensible, we must bear in mind that the coherence theory is a theory of the nature of truth, and we must be clear about what that entails. Truth is a property of beliefs or propositions, and an account of the nature of truth tells us what that property consists in, just as an account of the nature of heat tells us what that property, heat, consists in. It does not just tell us that something is true *if and only if* certain circumstances obtain—if and only if it has some other concomitant property, for example. Nor does it just tell us that something is true *necessarily if and only if* certain circumstances obtain. It tells us what truth is. If there is a necessary equivalence between something's being hot and its having a certain mean molecular kinetic energy, that doesn't show that this is what heat consists in, for it may be necessarily the case that something has a size if and only if it has a shape, yet having a size doesn't consist in having a shape (or vice versa). Likewise, it may turn out to be necessarily the case that a certain type of mental event coincides with the occurrence of a certain type of physical event, but it remains a further question whether the mental state consists in the occurrence of the physical one.

We saw earlier that the traditional contrast between correspondence and coherence theories depends on this. The kind of correspondence theory that properly contrasts with the coherence theory is one that offers a rival account of the nature of truth. There is no problem for a coherence theorist in agreeing that a proposition is true if and only if it corresponds with the facts, and for the same reason there is no problem for a correspondence theorist in agreeing that a proposition is true if and only if it meets certain standards of coherence. Some people have gone further and held that reality must *necessarily* exhibit some high degree of coherence, perhaps the maximum degree, if that makes sense. That still does not make them adherents of a coherence theory of truth, unless their grounds for holding this are that truth itself consists in coherence. And the grounds have sometimes been quite different. For instance, people have thought for metaphysical or theological reasons that there is an independent reality that has to be intrinsically coherent, and that what makes a proposition true is its correspondence with that coherent reality. F. H. Bradley, for instance, often seems to hold this. To the extent that he does, he subscribes not to a coherence theory of truth but to a kind of correspondence theory (Bradley 1893, 135–161; Walker 1998, 98–108). As the example of Bradley illustrates, though, one needs to be particularly careful here, because some writers commonly said to hold a coherence theory of truth have either not really done so at all or else been unclear in their own minds whether truth consists in coherence or rather in matching a reality that is necessarily coherent.

As theories of the nature of truth, the coherence theory holds that truth consists in coherence with some set of beliefs, while the correspondence theory holds it consists in matching a reality that is independent of anything that may be believed about it. Some versions of the correspondence theory make strong claims about the nature of the match, seeking to give informative accounts of the correspondence relation and of the ontology of facts. Austin's theory is of this kind, as is Wittgenstein's in the *Tractatus*. But one can be a correspondence theorist without making claims of that sort. Mackie's theory of "simple truth," recently defended by Alston, holds just that for a proposition to be true is for things to be as it says they are, and this is a correspondence theory provided it is understood that things are as they are independently of anything that may be believed about them. (Mackie and Alston both do understand it in this way: Mackie 1973, 17–63; Alston 1996, 5–64.) Just as it seems rather obvious that a true proposition (or belief or judgement) is distinct from whatever it is that makes it true, so it seems clear that there must be some relationship in virtue of which it is true. The correspondence theory says it is a relationship between the proposition and a reality independent of beliefs about it, while the point of the coherence theory is to hold that it is a relationship between the proposition and a reality determined by a coherent system of beliefs.

One could try avoiding either theory by saying that something is wrong with such a broad question about the nature of truth; all that one can properly do is to talk about the conditions for the truth, or the warranted assertibility, of particular propositions. Now it may be that the question is too broad, or too basic, to be susceptible of any very exciting answer, and that the best we can do is to say, "For a proposition to be true is for independent reality to be as it says," or something of the sort. That, though, is still an answer, even if not a very surprising one. Some would say it is unintelligible, on the grounds that such matters transcend verification. But we have seen that to adopt this anti-realist approach is to commit oneself to the coherence theory, and therefore to holding that the unexciting answer just offered is not unintelligible at all, but false. Others would concede that it is intelligible, and that its coherence rival is intelligible also, but they would say that the only way to cast light on the notion of truth is to provide a set of specific conditions for each proposition, or for each individual assertoric sentence of the language, along the lines of "'Snow is white' is true if and only if snow is white." This line of thought leads to what are called semantic and deflationary theories of truth. That need not, however, concern us here. We have seen that coherence and correspondence theorists must both accept that there is a harmless sense in which true propositions are those that "correspond with the facts." Equally, coherence and correspondence theorists can both debate the merits of the deflationary approach. This is because the deflationists and their opponents are trying to answer a different kind of question about truth from the question that is at issue between coherence and correspondence theorists. It is not a question about the nature of truth but a question about how to characterize the meaning of the predicate "is true" so as to exhibit the relation between "Snow is white" on the one hand and snow's being white on the other.

In effect, then, if truth does not consist in coherence, it will have to consist in correspondence. However, we must also recall the distinction drawn earlier between pure and impure coherence theories. Both are theories about the nature of truth. But pure coherence theories are theories about the nature of all truths: they hold that truth consists in coherence with some set of beliefs. Impure coherence theories hold that there are some truths that consist in coherence, but also that there are others that do not: some things just are the case independently of the coherent system; some truths consist in correspondence.

Pure coherence theories are not ultimately defensible. They collapse into incoherence, as I shall show in a moment. But impure coherence theories can escape this difficulty quite easily. Two problems remain for impure coherence theories, but opinions will differ as to how serious these problems are. One has to do with the concept of truth itself. The concept appears to be univocal. Can it really be that there are two kinds of truth, one consisting in coherence and applicable within a limited field, and the other not consisting in coherence? The other problem has to do with the reasons for adopting coherence theories in the first place. These are often reasons that would seem to apply globally if they apply at all. People are worried about what sort of match there could be between beliefs on the one hand and on the other a reality wholly independent of our beliefs and our ways of thinking about it. They are worried too about how we could ever *know* what such an independent reality is like or how we could ever succeed in making our words apply to it—a worry recently sharpened for us by Putnam (1983) but very clear in the work of idealists like Joachim (1906) as well as in the verificationists. If truth is cut loose from verification, scepticism seems to threaten, and perhaps meaninglessness. Such concerns do appear to apply quite generally, and not to one kind of truth rather than another.

Why Pure Coherence Theories Fail

Coherence theories maintain not that truth consists in coherence with some set of propositions in the abstract but in coherence with some set of beliefs that are held, or perhaps some set of beliefs that would be held, in specifiable circumstances. It is this point that generates the difficulty for pure coherence theories. They are unavoidably committed to it. To suggest that truth consists in coherence with some set of propositions in the abstract would immediately open the theories to Russell's Bishop Stubbs objection. There are plenty of different sets of abstract propositions that can determine standards of coherence that a given proposition conforms to, and plenty of them no doubt include the proposition that Bishop Stubbs was hanged for murder. But by saying instead that truth consists in coherence with some set of beliefs that are or would be held, the pure form of coherence theory runs into a difficulty of its own. This is because it cannot accommodate the factuality of the claim that a particular belief is held, or would be held under the appropriate circumstances.

According to the pure coherence theory, the truth that belief *b* is actually held must itself consist in its own coherence within the system of beliefs. It cannot be a fact, independent of that system, that *b* is held. If it were, the truth that *b* is held would be a truth that did not consist in coherence, and we should no longer have a pure coherence theory. The same applies if instead of the truth that *b* is actually held, we consider the truth that b would be held under the appropriate circumstances. From now on I shall just talk about the truth that "b is held," but what I say can be applied equally to "b is actually held," "b would be held under circumstances c," or any other variant that the pure coherence theorist might adopt.

The truth that b is held, then, must consist in its coherence within the system, on any pure coherence theory. We now have two questions: what is the system, and what is it for b to cohere within that system? These questions are not distinct, for we saw that what determines the system is not a set of propositions in the abstract but a set of beliefs that are held, and this set must include beliefs about what constitutes coherence if it is to provide any standard of coherence. However the answers might be spelt out in detail, the truth that b coheres within the system clearly consists in the coherence with the system of "b coheres with the system." This promises a regress. But it is not there that the problem lies, for the regress is not fatal. It is just a version of the regress one will get on any theory of truth: if it is true that p, it is true that it is true that p, and it is true that it is true that it is true that p. The problem arises because the system itself is determined not by reference to a set of propositions in the abstract but by reference to beliefs that *are held*.

If we are not pure coherence theorists, there is no difficulty for us here. We can just recognize it as a fact that these beliefs are held—a fact that obtains in its own right. To the pure coherence theorist, this course is not open. It is a fact that b is held, no doubt, but what makes it a fact is the coherence of "b is held" with the system. That means, in effect, the coherence of "b is held" with the various beliefs that determine the system. We might call them x, y, z. These beliefs can determine the system only because they are themselves held. But what determines that they are held is just the coherence of "x is held," "y is held," "z is held" with the system itself.

This gives us a new and decisive objection, more sophisticated than the Bishop Stubbs objection, though in some ways like it. There may not be room for as many coherent systems as Russell envisaged, but there will be room for a great many. There will be room for a system that includes most of our usual standards of coherence but that also requires coherence with the belief that Bishop Stubbs was hanged for murder. We can no longer repudiate this by saying that we have here only an arbitrary set of propositions, and not a belief that is held by the appropriate person or group. For "Bishop Stubbs was hanged for murder" will be an actual belief provided that "It is believed that Bishop Stubbs was hanged for murder" also belongs to the coherent set, since this is all that is required to make it a truth that the belief is held. The same point applies not just to beliefs about bishops but quite generally to whatever beliefs determine the standards of coherence and define the coherent system that supposedly constitutes the truth. This just means that there is nothing that determines truth. We sought to determine truth by reference to actual beliefs, beliefs that are held, but what beliefs are actual beliefs depends on whether "b is an actual belief" coheres with the system. So which beliefs are actual turns out to depend on the coherent system, which can itself be determined only by reference to some given set of actual beliefs.

Equally, of course, if someone puts forward a pure coherence theory according to which what matters is not just that these beliefs be held but that they be beliefs of type *t* and held by the members of group *g*, then the fact that these beliefs *are* of type *t* and held by the members of *g* will just consist in the *belief* that they are cohering with the other members of the set.

For this reason, no pure coherence theory is tenable. A tenable coherence theory will have to leave room for certain truths whose nature does not consist in coherence. These will *have* to include truths about the beliefs that define the system and determine coherence. Otherwise, the theory cannot get going.

Correspondence Theories Survive Frege's Objection

This objection to pure coherence theories may look similar to an objection Frege once made against any attempt to define truth, and which, if it worked, would equally be an objection against any attempt to say what truth consists in. A correspondence theory, for example, will say that truth consists in correspondence with facts. In that case, for *p* to be true is for *p* to correspond with the facts. But whether *p* corresponds with the facts or not is a question of whether it is *true* that *p* corresponds with the facts. So we attempted to give an account of what truth consists in only to find ourselves making use of the concept of truth again, so that "what is defined must itself be presupposed" (Frege 1969, 139–140).

But Frege's objection is not a good one. If truth consists in correspondence with the facts, then the truth of *p* will consist in its correspondence with the facts. If it does correspond with them, then evidently it will be true that it corresponds with them. But its correspondence with the facts does not consist in this. According to the correspondence theorist, its correspondence with the facts is just basic and does not consist in anything else. According to the correspondence theorist, the facts constitute an independent reality, and whether a proposition matches that reality is itself a factual matter. If *p* does match that reality, then equally "*p* corresponds with the facts" matches that reality, and thus so does "'*p* corresponds with the facts' corresponds with the facts." But that is simply, once again, a regress that may be interesting but is hardly vicious. The pure coherence theorist, on the other hand, is unable to make the analogous move, which would be to say that *p*'s coherence with the system is just basic and does not consist in anything else. For the pure coherence theorist is committed to a general account of reality in coherence terms. To treat it as basic that *p* coheres with the system would be to deny that the truth of "*p* coheres with the system" itself consists in coherence. The truth of "*p* coheres with the system" would consist in its simply being the case that *p* coheres with the system. It might be the case that "*p* coheres with the system" does also cohere with the system itself, but it would not be this that made it true.

The correspondence theorist, who treats it as basic that p corresponds with the facts, does not have to deny that the truth of "p corresponds with the facts" consists in its correspondence with the facts. There would be a problem with that only if some new and different set of facts had to be involved, and some new correspondence. But no new set of facts is involved. In the independently real world, p is the case—its being the case is a feature of that world. That by itself is enough to make the proposition "p" true, and it is what that proposition's truth consists in. In making it true that p, it also makes it true that "p" corresponds with the facts, that "'p' corresponds with the facts" corresponds with the facts, and so on. (The thought that a new set of facts might be needed at each stage perhaps arises through confusing propositions with sentences. The sentences "p" and "'p' corresponds with the facts" are certainly quite different, and one might think their relations to other things must also be different. But they express equivalent propositions.)

Correspondence theories may say less than people would like. If a correspondence theorist says just that for a proposition to be true is for things to be as it says they are in a reality that is independent of our beliefs about it, we may feel we are hardly being offered a *theory*. Yet we are at least being offered something substantive, for it constitutes a rejection of the coherence theory and involves a commitment to a reality that is independent of what we believe about it. We have already seen that it is right to reject pure coherence theories. What about impure coherence theories?

Impure Coherence Theories

Coherence theorists have often been rather unclear about whether their coherence theories are intended to cover the nature of *all* truth or whether there may be some truths to which the coherence account does not apply. They are often quite ambivalent, for example, as to how experience is to be handled. Some, like Neurath (1931, 1932–1933), are clear that judgements reporting the immediate content of experience owe their truth to their coherence with the overall system of beliefs, and this is what any pure coherence theorist is committed to (as Neurath was well aware). Others, however, have been uneasy about going so far and have been inclined to give such judgements a special status. This special status is sometimes extended to all judgements reporting on one's conscious mental content, which may be taken to include judgements about what beliefs one has. Someone who goes this far can certainly avoid the objection to pure coherence theories, for the resulting theory allows that there are truths about what we believe that do not consist in coherence.

That may well leave it unclear, however, that the theory still has the advantages that made the coherence theory seem desirable in the first place. If the point is to overcome the gap between our beliefs on the one hand and the world they are supposed to describe on the other, the theory can now help only if the judgements in this special class are *incorrigible*, in the sense that they cannot be falsely subscribed to. Many philosophers have indeed thought some or all such judgements to be incorrigible, though it is far from clear that they were right to. If the point is to avoid a problem about knowledge—how we can know about an independent reality—it may still be plausible to say that this problem is removed by a coherence theory of this type, provided we think that what judgements of the special class report is epistemologically secure in a special way so that no such problem arises over them. Then we can say that truths about other matters are epistemologically reachable because they do not concern a reality independent of our beliefs but instead consist in coherence. Judgements of the special class could have that epistemological security through being incorrigible, but there might be other and more plausible ways, though again it is far from clear that they actually are as secure epistemologically as they have often been claimed to be. Again, if the motivation for a coherence theory is semantic, because meaning is taken to be tied to the method of verification, we get the same result: it may be felt that judgements in this special class are verifiable in a particularly immediate way, so that unlike other judgements, they do not have to be explicated in terms of coherence. But as before, this is certainly contestable.

Actually, coherence theorists have sometimes gone further than this without being very clear about it, for they have sometimes been prepared to give a special status to principles like the law of noncontradiction, and perhaps to basic principles of inference generally. They have taken these to be definitive of "coherence," in that (for example) they have assumed it to be incoherent to hold both p and not p. In doing this, they have apparently taken such principles to be objectively right, so that their own truth seems to consist in matching some independent reality of a presumably rather Platonic kind. But nobody putting forward a global coherence theory of truth ought to be saying things of this kind, and those who have made these assumptions have not, I think, been conscious that this is what they were doing. There is a long and regrettable tradition in philosophy of taking such principles for granted without asking about their status and how they are known. What a pure coherence theorist ought to say, of course, is that it is the system itself that determines what counts as coherence. If it is a feature of the system that it requires coherence with a set of beliefs that include the law of noncontradiction and our other basic principles of inference, then that system will rule out holding p and not p together, and that's all there is to it. The same thing can and should be said in the sort of coherence theory we have just been considering, which is not entirely pure but remains as inclusive as is possible compatibly with avoiding the objection to which all pure coherence theories fall.

The main problem with a theory that seeks to be as inclusive as that is the one already noticed: that its plausibility may be weakened to the extent that the judgements in the special class turn out to be just as problematic as any others, in whatever way it was that inclined us to sympathy with coherence theories in the first place. There is another problem too, though perhaps not a very serious one. An impure theory, even an only slightly impure theory like this, has to give two different accounts of what truth consists in: one that applies to judgements in the special class and one that applies to other judgements. For other judgements, truth consists in coherence; for those in the special class, it does not. It seems odd to be suggesting that truth bifurcates in this way. There would then be two different kinds of truth, and it would appear misleading to use the same word for both of them.

When I wrote the book from which the above extracts came, I thought this second problem was quite serious. However, if one had good reason to adopt the kind of impure coherence theory we have been talking about, by the same token one would have reason to dismiss our intuitions about the univocity of "truth" and "true." Moreover, if we consider impure coherence theories that are less global—impure coherence theories that offer an account of truth as coherence that is intended to apply only to some much more restricted range of judgements—it is far from clear that our intuitions do not actually support the conclusion that two different kinds of truth are involved. People sometimes put forward coherence theories of mathematical, moral, or modal truth, for example. It seems rather natural to think that there might be some difference in kind between mathematical truths and ordinary truths about the world. Many will think the same about moral truths and modal truths. No doubt different people will have different intuitions about matters like this, but that should only caution us against putting very much weight on intuitions (or on the ordinary usage that encapsulates and expresses them).

The real problem about coherence theories is whether there are good grounds for holding them. It often seems to people that there must be something incoherent about the idea of a coherence theory of truth, and we have seen that the idea of a *pure* coherence theory is indeed incoherent. There is, however, no reason to think there is anything incoherent about an impure coherence theory, and an impure coherence theory confined to a limited area may be quite plausible. What generally makes coherence theories plausible is a worry about how our judgements can correspond to a reality that is independent of us and of our ways of thinking. Someone who thinks that there is no particular difficulty about this in the case of ordinary matter-of-fact judgements may think that the difficulty is acute in mathematics, in morals, or in dealing with counterfactual conditionals. In fields such as these, then, impure coherence theories may be attractive. How attractive they are will largely depend on how good the arguments may be for thinking that there is more of a problem in these fields than elsewhere with construing truth as correspondence, but here we are on familiar ground. It is important, of course, to bear in mind that what is needed is to show that there is something *special* about these areas that warrants providing for them a special account of truth. Some of the arguments put forward here for regarding truth as coherence are simply variants of arguments for regarding truth as coherence in general. If it is argued, for example, that the notion of correspondence is problematic here, or that truth in these fields would transcend possible verification unless it consisted in coherence, we need to be particularly cautious, because, taken in their general form, such arguments would apply to truth quite generally and lead us to a pure coherence theory of truth. And that theory is incoherent. So it is important to be clear what it is that differentiates the field within which truth is said to be coherence.

Impure coherence theories may or may not prove helpful in dealing with certain problematic areas. But because they are impure, they require us to recognize that there are at least some propositions for which truth consists in correspondence. The advantage of a pure coherence theory was that it promised to remove the problems over correspondence. No pure coherence theory is tenable. To show that is not to make those problems disappear. We have to recognize that there really are difficulties with the idea of correspondence with fact and over how we can succeed in knowing about a reality that is wholly independent of us and of our ways of thinking about it, and that there really are difficulties in seeing how we can refer to or meaningfully talk about such a reality. These difficulties cannot be conjured away. They constitute a serious philosophical problem that we cannot avoid. There is a good reason for being disappointed in a correspondence theory that says no more than that truth consists in correspondence with an independent reality, and it is that it leaves these problems untouched. It may serve to remind us, rightly, that correspondence theories do not need to saddle us with an ontology of facts or to provide us with a complete analysis of the correspondence relation. But how can we succeed in saying anything about a reality that is genuinely independent of us and of our ways of thinking about it? And how can we have beliefs about that independent reality that so regularly and reliably reflect how that reality is, since that reality is independent of us in this radical way? What can ensure that our beliefs match a genuine reality and not the illusions of Descartes's *malin génie*? Perhaps these classic questions are too large and too fundamental for most philosophers to expect them to be answered by a "theory of truth." They therefore turn aside to deal with problems that appear more tractable. But these are questions to which any serious thinking about truth inevitably leads us.[19]

Notes

1. B. Russell, "On the Nature of Truth," *Proceedings of the Aristotelian Society* 7 (1906–1907), mostly reprinted as "The Monistic Theory of Truth," in his *Philosophical Essays* (London: Longmans, Green, 1910); and M. Schlick, "The Foundation of Knowledge," in A. J. Ayer, ed., *Logical Positivism* (Glencoe, IL: Free Press, 1959). Cf. also A. J. Ayer, "Truth," in *The Concept of a Person* (London: Macmillan, 1963).

2. N. Rescher, *The Coherence Theory of Truth* (Oxford: Oxford University Press, 1973), chaps. 1 and 2.

3. There has been much discussion, most of it rather confused, as to what the bearers of truth and falsehood are. In what follows I shall take it for granted that they are propositions or statements, and I shall use these two terms equivalently unless the context indicates otherwise. They form the objects of belief, and the content of an unambiguous assertoric utterance on a particular

occasion of utterance; two utterances express the same statement or proposition if they have the same sense and the same reference. A particular *sentence* may thus be used on different occasions to express different propositions, though a sentence as uttered assertorically by a given speaker at a given time will express one specific proposition unless it is in some way ambiguous. As I use the terms, therefore, the possibility of a proposition's being neither true nor false is not ruled out by stipulation.

4. Russell, "On the Nature of Truth," 32ff., =156ff. of his *Philosophical Essays*. L. J. Cohen ("The Coherence Theory of Truth," *Philosophical Studies* 34 [1978]) has pointed out that this will not in fact be true if the requirement for coherence is made as strong as mutual entailment, and the system is also powerful enough to contain every proposition or its negation as a member of the coherent set; there can be at most one coherent system that meets those constraints. But the constraints are so strong that we must wonder whether any theory that demanded such stringent conditions for coherence could be of much interest. The systems of Bradley and Blanshard, which Cohen has in mind, are certainly said to be such that every true proposition entails every other, but it is not clear that they mean quite what we normally do by "entails"; nor is it at all clear that they satisfy the other requirement, by containing either p or not-p within the coherent set, for all values of p. But see also Walker (1989), the end of chap. 5, on Hegel, 100.

5. Cf. S. W. Blackburn, *Spreading the Word* (Oxford: Oxford University Press, 1984), chaps. 6 and 7.

6. See chapter 9 of Walker (1989).

7. H. Field, "Realism and Relativism," *Journal of Philosophy* 79 (1982): 556; cf. Blackburn, *Spreading the Word*, 246.

8. Blackburn, *Spreading the Word*, chap. 6, sec. 6.

9. S. W. Blackburn, "Truth, Realism, and the Regulation of Theory," *Midwest Studies in Philosophy* 5 (1980): 353.

10. M. A. E. Dummett, *Frege: Philosophy of Language* (London: Duckworth, 1973), 466.

11. Blackburn, "Truth, Realism, and the Regulation of Theory," sec. 3; Blackburn, *Spreading the Word*, chap. 6, sec. 4. It might be suggested that in the cases Blackburn considers the principle of bivalence is "warrantedly assertible" on practical grounds, and it would therefore have to be considered true by an anti-realist (see below); for anti-realists call true whatever is warrantedly assertible (though they admit that such judgments may be defeasible). But this exploits an ambiguity in "warrantedly assertible." The warrant for asserting the principle is a practical warrant, a warrant for treating it *as if* it were true, and it is not this kind of warranted assertibility that the anti-realist regards as truth.

12. M. A. E. Dummett, *Truth and Other Enigmas* (London: Duckworth, 1978), xxx.

13. Dummett, "Truth," with postscript, in *Truth and Other Enigmas*; see also the preface to *Truth and Other Enigmas*, esp. xxii–xxiii.

14. Ibid. See also M. A. E. Dummett, *Elements of Intuitionism* (Oxford: Oxford University Press, 1977), chap. 7.1, and his "What Is a Theory of Meaning? (ii)," in G. Evans and J. McDowell, eds., *Truth and Meaning* (Oxford: Oxford University Press, 1976).

15. How they fill out "capable of recognizing" may vary from theorist to theorist. The problems with it, of course, are similar to the problems of the verificationists in determining what is to be meant by "verifiable in principle."

16. Cf. Blackburn, *Spreading the Word*, 249–259.

17. Dummett, "Wittgenstein's Philosophy of Mathematics," in *Truth and Other Enigmas*, 185; cf. "Truth," in ibid., 18. For a proper discussion of the inadequacy of the metaphor, see C. Wright, *Wittgenstein on the Foundations of Mathematics* (London: Duckworth, 1980), chap. 11.

18. As I argue in later sections of Walker (1989) and in Walker (1998), what Bradley really thinks is that the world is a coherent whole, and he holds a correspondence theory of the nature of truth, which nonetheless (because of the coherence of the world) allows him to use coherence as a very effective test of correspondence. As well as R. Wollheim's book *F. H. Bradley* (Harmondsworth: Penguin, 1959), I have found very useful the collection of articles by A. Manser and G. Stock, eds., *The Philosophy of F. H. Bradley* (Oxford: Oxford University Press, 1984) and in this context particularly those by D. Holdcroft and J. Bradley.

19. Sections I and II of this chapter are excerpted from Walker (1989).

References

Alston, W. P. 1996. *A Realist Conception of Truth*. Ithaca, NY: Cornell University Press.

Bradley, F. H. 1893. *Appearance and Reality*. London: Swan Sonnenschein.

Frege, G. 1969. *Nachgelassene Schriften*. Edited by H. Hermes, F. Kambartel, and F. Kaulbach. Hamburg: Felix Meiner. Translated by P. Long and R. White as *Frege: Posthumous Writings*. Oxford: Blackwell, 1979.

Joachim, H. H. 1906. *The Nature of Truth*. Oxford: Oxford University Press.

Mackie, J. L. 1973. *Truth, Probability, and Paradox*. Oxford: Oxford University Press.

Neurath, O. 1931. "Soziologie im Physikalismus." *Erkenntnis* 2: 393–431. Translated as "Sociology and Physicalism," in A. J. Ayer, ed., *Logical Positivism*, 282–317. Glencoe, IL: Free Press, 1959. Also translated as "Sociology in the Framework of Physicalism," in Neurath, *Philosophical Papers 1913–46*, 58–90. Dordrecht: Reidel, 1983.

Neurath, O. 1932–1933. "Protokolsätze." *Erkenntnis* 3: 204–214. Translated as "Protocol Sentences," in A. J. Ayer, ed., *Logical Positivism*, 191–208. Glencoe, IL: Free Press, 1959. Also translated as "Protocol Statements," in Neurath, *Philosophical Papers 1913–46*, 91–99. Dordrecht: Reidel, 1983.

Putnam, H. 1983. *Realism and Reason*. Cambridge: Cambridge University Press.

Walker, R. C. 1989. *The Coherence Theory of Truth*. London: Routledge Press.

Walker, R. C. 1998. "Bradley's Theory of Truth." In G. Stock, ed., *Appearance versus Reality*, 93–110. Oxford: Oxford University Press.

III Pragmatist and Verificationist Theories

Introduction

Michael P. Lynch, Nathan Kellen, and Jeremy Wyatt

Classical Pragmatism: Peirce, James, and Misak

Pragmatism is the most influential and important American contribution to philosophy. Through its most famous advocates—Charles Sanders Peirce, William James, and John Dewey—pragmatist ideas have affected every aspect of American life, from psychology to education to the arts. And central to pragmatism is a particular conception of truth, one that sees a close link between truth and human experience.

In the classic essay included here, the founder of the pragmatist movement, Charles Sanders Peirce (chapter 8), introduces what William James would later identify as the key pragmatic maxim. In Peirce's view, if we wish to know the meaning of our ideas, we should "consider what effects, which might conceivably have practical bearings, we conceive the object of our conception to have. Then, our conception of these effects is the whole of our conception of the object." By "practical bearings," Peirce means those effects of the idea that have a bearing on our practice, our action. The meaning of an idea, in short, consists in its practical effects on human experience.

Peirce's principle has a number of dramatic effects itself. For example, if two ideas have the same practical consequences, they have the same meaning, while ideas without practical consequences are meaningless. Most importantly, it suggests to Peirce a particular definition of truth, namely "the opinion which is fated to be ultimately agreed to by all who investigate." This definition is epistemic; rather than saying that truth is a matter of agreement with reality, Peirce suggests that truth is determined by agreement among ourselves. But not merely any consensus will do; it must be consensus at the end of exhaustive empirical investigation—scientific inquiry when *complete*. In short, Peirce's view seems to be that a judgment is true if and only if it is justified at the end of scientific inquiry.

The great psychologist William James (chapter 9) often credited Peirce for his own ideas about truth. But their positions differ significantly (indeed, Peirce ultimately disavowed James's version of pragmatism). While James explicitly accepts Peirce's view of meaning and therefore accepts that truth has much to do with practical experience,

James stresses that what is of practical relevance is in part a matter of our interests and attitudes. For James, more than Peirce, the "trail of the human serpent is over all." Yet James also insists that the pragmatist can concur with the correspondence intuition that true ideas agree with reality. The pragmatist, according to James, is not denying this platitude; rather, he is trying to explain the nature of this "agreement."

James seems to give several different explanations of "agreement" and truth. In a Peircean vein, he claims that an empirical judgment is true just when it is verifiable. He also says that a true idea leads or guides us in our dealings with reality and that a true judgment is what is expedient to believe. If there is an overriding idea here, it seems to be that a judgment is true just when it continues to be useful over time in our interactions with reality. The truth of a judgment therefore consists in its continuous practical usefulness in our lives—but what this practical usefulness consists in, James seems to suggest, depends in part on the judgment in question. In this sense, James's conception of truth seems pluralist in design (for more on pluralist theories of truth, see the essays in part VII of this volume).

James's and Peirce's epistemic theories of truth have traditionally encountered stiff opposition. An important charge against James is that he is committed to a form of relativism.[1] If the truth of a judgment consists in its practical usefulness over the long run, then we might wonder whether there are any objective facts that determine whether a judgment is useful in this way. After all, isn't it the case that any particular judgment might be practically useful to one person, given their interests and attitudes, but not practically useful to another person who has different interests and attitudes?

With his more straightforward identification of "practical bearings" with what is empirically verifiable, Peirce seems to escape this charge of relativism. But Peirce's theory faces its own difficulties. First, his theory looks to assume that there is such a thing as a complete investigation and, thus, that such an idea makes sense. Second, it seems intuitive to think that there could be judgments that are true (or false) even though they are never discovered to be so by any scientific investigation whatsoever. Indeed, as we'll see, this intuition proves troubling for any pragmatist or verificationist theory of truth.

In chapter 10, Cheryl Misak takes up the mantle of Peirce's pragmatism and draws a distinction between traditional, "unhelpful" ways of understanding the pragmatist conception of truth and her preferred understanding. Misak argues that a pragmatist theory of truth shouldn't be understood as defining truth in terms of a hypothesized end of inquiry. Rather, she suggests that the core of such a theory is the thought that a true belief is "one that would withstand doubt, were we to inquire as far as we fruitfully could on the matter."[2] Understanding truth in this way, Misak maintains, makes truth a regulative ideal—a guide as to how we should conduct our inquiries, rather than a predicted terminus of those inquiries.

If the pragmatist frames their theory along these lines, then it would seem that they can overcome some of the standard concerns for pragmatist theories. Regarding the charge of relativism, Misak points out that according to her formulation of pragmatism,

"Truth is connected to human inquiry (it is the best that inquiry could do), but it goes beyond any particular inquiry (it is not simply the upshot of our current best attempts)." In light of this, it would seem that the Misak-style pragmatist isn't committed to relativism—or at least not to the sort of relativism—that James must apparently endorse. Moreover, given that Misak doesn't rely upon the notion of a hypothetical end of inquiry, she would seem to escape the difficulty of specifying what the conclusion of human inquiry would look like. Lastly, if truth amounts to the ability to withstand doubt, no matter how far human inquiry is pursued, then it would seem that we can allow for the possibility that some true (or false) beliefs are never discovered to be true (false) by human inquirers. Thus, although there is certainly more to say about Misak-style pragmatism, her formulation of the pragmatist theory of truth is a contemporary take on the tradition that enjoys undoubted importance.

Dummett and Verificationist Anti-realism

It is difficult to overestimate the impact of Michael Dummett's essay "Truth" (chapter 11) on subsequent work on the topic. The early part of the century saw an explosion of interest in theories, like those of the pragmatists in America or the positivists of the Vienna Circle in Europe, which linked truth to verification. But by the middle of the century, interest in these theories had flagged, stemming in part from the increasing popularity of the deflationary outlook. Originally written in 1958–1959, Dummett's essay served not only to revive the idea that truth may consist in verification but also to introduce his influential idea that the debate over realism is at heart a debate over the proper way to analyze the concepts of truth and meaning. Indeed, Hilary Putnam would later credit Dummett for waking him from the dogmatic slumber of his metaphysical realism.

Dummett compares the concept of truth to the concept of winning a game. Just as it is part of the concept of winning a game that one plays a game to win, so it is part of our concept of truth that we aim to make true statements. Dummett parlays this insight into an objection against deflationary views of truth. A deflationary view, Dummett suggests, tells us when our statements are true by telling us that a statement "p" is true if and only if p. But it says nothing about the fact that we aim at making true statements—that we value the truth, in short.[3]

Dummett claims that realism is characterized by the belief that there is something in virtue of which statements are definitely true or false. That is, a realist about a certain type of statement—for example, statements about the distant past—takes them to be either true or false, even if we lack evidence one way or the other. Realists thus believe that truth is possibly evidence-transcendent, while anti-realists deny that truth can transcend what a speaker can verify. In Dummett's view, realism is faced with a formidable problem. If truth does transcend what we can verify, then we won't necessarily be able to recognize when a statement has that property. And if we can't recognize when a statement has the property of truth, then it is difficult to say whether we actually understand the word "truth" at all. In short, realism makes our understanding of the concept of truth mysterious. And since understanding and truth are closely interlinked, realism makes understanding, or meaning, mysterious as well.

Dummett suggests that anti-realism provides a genuine alternative to the realist picture of the world. But he admits that it has quite radical consequences. Among others, anti-realism may force us to reject the Law of Excluded Middle and the Principle of Bivalence.[4] It implies that many statements, including those about the distant past or the far side of the universe, literally do not have truth values, for they can be neither verified nor falsified. To many philosophers, this seems counterintuitive. According to our ordinary understanding, statements such as "Caesar stubbed his toe when crossing the Rubicon" do have truth values.

Contemporary Pragmatism: Putnam and Rorty

In more recent years, Hilary Putnam and Richard Rorty were two of the most influential philosophers to wear the pragmatist label. But while Putnam takes his inspiration from James and is concerned to reconcile pragmatist insights with realism, Rorty looks to Dewey and urges us to leave behind our realist intuitions.

In chapter 12, Putnam contrasts two overall pictures of reality. Metaphysical realism is the tripartite view that truth is correspondence with reality, that there is a fixed totality of mind-independent objects, and that there is just one true description of the world. The implication is that there is a wide gap between mind and world. Thus, no matter how diligently we may try to believe truly, we can always be wrong. Of course, on this general theoretical picture, there must be some explanation of how thought relates to the world. Yet metaphysical realism, Putnam argues, can't give such an account—that is, a coherent account of truth and reference—that does not end up being decidedly unnatural in its metaphysical commitments.

Putnam calls his own view internal (and later *pragmatic*) realism. Unlike the metaphysical realist, the internal realist believes that the totality of objects is not fixed because objects themselves exist only relative to conceptual schemes. In Putnam's eyes, this is the consequence of rejecting metaphysical realism. According to Putnam's alternative account of truth, *a proposition is true just when that proposition would be rationally acceptable in ideal epistemic conditions.*

By framing his conception of truth subjunctively and in terms of "ideal" conditions, Putnam overcomes some of the standard objections to other epistemic theories. First, the theory is able to distinguish between propositions that we merely have good reason to believe and propositions that are true. For not all propositions that now pass for true would be rationally accepted were we to have all the relevant facts at hand. Second, Putnam can allow that propositions might have or lack the property of being ideally rationally acceptable even if ideal conditions never actually obtain, since ideal epistemic conditions, like frictionless planes, are just that: ideal. Finally, Putnam's notion of ideal conditions is a fairly broad one: unlike Peirce (on the standard interpretation), he is not claiming that the only truth is what is revealed at the end of scientific inquiry.

While Putnam's position clearly has many strengths that other epistemic theories lack, it still faces an extension of a by-now-familiar problem. Some propositions, such as the proposition that the number of stars in the universe at this moment is even, seem incapable of being rationally acceptable or unacceptable, even in ideal conditions. Creatures like us are just not capable of having evidence for such a proposition one way or the other, yet it seems that this proposition is either true or false. Further, one might worry whether Putnam's account can be informative. For how can we understand what it means to say that a proposition is rationally justified without at some point invoking a prior concept of truth? For a detailed discussion of these and other important objections to Putnam's position, see the essays by Crispin Wright (chapter 29) and William P. Alston (chapter 3).

Richard Rorty (chapter 13) begins by admitting that pragmatists like himself vacillate between defining truth in terms of justification (ideal or otherwise) and dismissing the problem of truth altogether as a pseudo-problem. This is because the pragmatist can see little practical difference between truth and justification. When we engage in inquiry, we aim at forming true beliefs, but we can do so only by trying to form justified beliefs. Anything we believe to be true we also believe to be justified, and anything we believe to be justified we also believe to be true. While there may not be much practical difference between truth and justification, Rorty agrees that a distinction can be made. The word "true" has what he calls its "cautionary use." By distinguishing between justification and truth, we remind ourselves that what is justified now may not be justified later. There is also something of a normative difference between the concepts: unlike justification, truth, Rorty thinks, requires a project of "metaphysical activism" that tries to say how the mind reflects reality.

Rorty opposes metaphysical activism with quietism, a position that he sees in the writings of James and Dewey as well as in the contemporary work of Donald Davidson (chapter 26). Rorty's quietism takes an essentially deflationist stance toward truth and related concepts like objectivity. Truth, on this account, does no real explanatory work distinct from that done by justification. Thus, Rorty argues against Wright, arguing that we don't need to think of truth as a distinct aim of inquiry.

After a discussion of Wright's reason for embracing a metaphysically active position on these issues, Rorty concedes that positions that leave room for a substantive and important concept of truth are bound to feel more intuitive than his own version of pragmatism. Thus, Rorty's position is ultimately normative: in his view, contemporary pragmatists are like atheists in overwhelmingly religious cultures. They must admit that their view is bound to seem strange, since it runs contrary to the mass of public opinion. To make their case, they cannot appeal to that opinion but rather must rely on pointing out what they take to be its unfortunate consequences. They must argue for their position on pragmatic grounds.

Notes

1. See, for instance, Gale (2005, 101–102), and for a response, see Hu (2016). See also Russell (2004, 861).

2. Compare the notion of superassertibility that Crispin Wright details in section 4 of chapter 29 in this volume.

3. In chapter 31, Douglas Edwards draws on Dummett's analogy between truth and winning in developing a distinctive pluralist view of truth.

4. Note that Misak also discusses Bivalence and the Law of Excluded Middle at length.

Further Reading

Ayer, A. J. 1968. *The Origins of Pragmatism*. London: Macmillan.

Brandom, R., ed. 2000. *Rorty and His Critics*. Oxford: Blackwell.

Brandom, R. 2008. *Between Saying and Doing: Towards an Analytic Pragmatism*. Oxford: Oxford University Press.

Brandom, R. 2011. *Perspectives on Pragmatism: Classical, Recent, and Contemporary*. Cambridge, MA: Harvard University Press.

Burch, R. 2014. "Charles Sanders Peirce." *Stanford Encyclopedia of Philosophy*. https://plato.stanford.edu/entries/peirce/#prag.

Capps, J. 2019. "The Pragmatic Theory of Truth." *Stanford Encyclopedia of Philosophy*. https://plato.stanford.edu/entries/truth-pragmatic/.

Capps, J. Forthcoming. "A Common-Sense Pragmatic Theory of Truth." *Philosophia*.

Dewey, J. 1981–1991. *John Dewey: The Later Works, 1925–1953*. 17 vols. Edited by Jo Ann Boydston et al. Carbondale: Southern Illinois University Press.

Dewey, J. 1999. *The Essential Dewey*. Edited by L. A. Hickman and T. M. Alexander. Bloomington: Indiana University Press.

Dummett, M. 1978. *Truth and Other Enigmas*. Cambridge, MA: Harvard University Press.

Dummett, M. 1981. *Frege: Philosophy of Language*. 2nd ed. Cambridge, MA: Harvard University Press.

Dummett, M. 1983. *The Seas of Language*. Oxford: Oxford University Press.

Gale, R. M. 2005. *The Philosophy of William James: An Introduction*. Cambridge: Cambridge University Press.

Goodman, N. 1978. *Ways of Worldmaking*. Indianapolis: Hackett.

Haack, S. 1976. "The Pragmatist Theory of Truth." *British Journal for the Philosophy of Science* 27(3): 231–249.

Haack, S. 1984. "Can James's Theory of Truth Be Made More Satisfactory?" *Transactions of the Charles S. Peirce Society* 20(3): 269–278.

Hookway, C. 2002. *Truth, Rationality and Pragmatism: Themes from Peirce*. New York: Oxford University Press.

Howat, A. 2014. "Prospects for Peircean Truth." *Canadian Journal of Philosophy* 44(3–4): 365–387.

Hu, X. 2016. "A Few Puzzles about William James' Theory of Truth." *Kriterion: Revista de Filosofia* 57(135): 803–821.

James, W. (1907, 1909) 1975. *Pragmatism and the Meaning of Truth*. Cambridge, MA: Harvard University Press.

Johnston, M. 1993. "Objectivity Refigured: Pragmatism without Verificationism." In J. Haldane and C. Wright, eds., *Reality, Representation, and Projection*, 85–130. Oxford: Oxford University Press.

Legg, C. 2014. "Charles Peirce's Limit Concept of Truth." *Philosophy Compass* 9(3): 204–213.

Legg, C., and Hookway, C. 2019. "Pragmatism." *Stanford Encyclopedia of Philosophy*. https://plato.stanford.edu/entries/pragmatism/.

Liu, JeeLoo. 2003. "The Daoist Conception of Truth: Lao Zi's Metaphysical Realism vs. Zhuang Zi's Internal Realism." In B. Mou, ed., *Comparative Approaches to Chinese Philosophy*, 278–293. Aldershot, UK: Ashgate.

Misak, C. J. 1999a. *Pragmatism*. Calgary: University of Calgary Press.

Misak, C. J. 1999b. *Truth, Politics, Morality: Pragmatism and Deliberation*. London: Routledge.

Misak, C. J., ed. 2004. *The Cambridge Companion to Peirce*. Cambridge: Cambridge University Press.

Misak, C. J., ed. 2007. *New Pragmatists*. Oxford: Oxford University Press.

Misak, C. J., ed. 2013. *The American Pragmatists*. Oxford: Oxford University Press.

Misak, C. J. 2015. "Pragmatism and the Function of Truth." In S. Gross, N. Tebben, and M. Williams, eds., *Meaning without Representation: Essays on Truth, Expression, Normativity, and Naturalism*, 262–278. New York: Oxford University Press.

Misak, C. J. 2018. *Cambridge Pragmatism: From Peirce and James to Ramsey and Wittgenstein*. Oxford: Oxford University Press.

Omar, M. 1999. "James's Theory of Truth." In J. Peregrin, ed., *Truth and Its Nature (If Any)*, 37–50. Dordrecht: Springer.

Peirce, C. S. 1905. "What Pragmatism Is." *Monist* 15: 161–181.

Peirce, C. S. 1931–1958. *Collected Papers of Charles Sanders Peirce*. 8 vols. Vols. 1–6, edited by C. Hartshorne and P. Weiss. Cambridge, MA: Harvard University Press, 1931–1935. Vols. 7–8, edited by A. Burks. Cambridge, MA: Harvard University Press, 1958.

Plantinga, A. 1982. "How to Be an Anti-realist." *Proceedings and Addresses of the American Philosophical Association* 56: 47–70.

Price, H. 2013. *Expressivism, Pragmatism, and Representationalism*. Cambridge: Cambridge University Press.

Putnam, H. 1981. *Reason, Truth, and History*. Cambridge: Cambridge University Press.

Putnam, H. 1990. *Realism with a Human Face*. Cambridge, MA: Harvard University Press.

Putnam, H. 1994. "Sense, Nonsense, and the Senses: An Inquiry into the Powers of the Human Mind." *Journal of Philosophy* 91(9): 445–517.

Putnam, H. 1995. *Pragmatism: An Open Question*. Cambridge: Blackwell.

Putnam, H., and Putnam, R. A. 2017. *Pragmatism as a Way of Life: The Lasting Legacy of William James and John Dewey*. Cambridge, MA: Harvard University Press.

Putnam, R. A., ed. 1997. *The Cambridge Companion to William James*. Cambridge: Cambridge University Press.

Ramberg, B. 2007. "Richard Rorty." *Stanford Encyclopedia of Philosophy*. https://plato.stanford.edu/entries/rorty/.

Rorty, R. 1979. *Philosophy and the Mirror of Nature*. Princeton, NJ: Princeton University Press.

Rorty, R. 1982. *Consequences of Pragmatism*. Minneapolis: University of Minnesota Press.

Rorty, R. 1991. *Objectivity, Relativism, and Truth: Philosophical Papers*. Vol. 1. Cambridge: Cambridge University Press.

Rorty, R. 1993. "Putnam and the Relativist Menace." *Journal of Philosophy* 90(9): 443–461.

Rorty, R. 1998. *Truth and Progress: Philosophical Papers*. Vol. 3. Cambridge: Cambridge University Press.

Russell, B. 1910. *Philosophical Essays*. Chaps. 4 and 5. London: Longmans, Green.

Russell, B. (1946) 2004. *History of Western Philosophy*. London: Routledge.

Siderits, M. 1979. "A Note on the Early Buddhist Theory of Truth." *Philosophy East and West* 29(4): 491–499.

Sosa, E. 1993. "Putnam's Pragmatic Realism." *Journal of Philosophy* 90(12): 605–626.

Ulatowski, J. 2017. *Commonsense Pluralism about Truth: An Empirical Defence*. Sec. 4.4. Cham, Switzerland: Palgrave Macmillan.

Wright, C. 1992. *Truth and Objectivity*. Chap. 2. Cambridge, MA: Harvard University Press.

Wright, C. 1993. *Realism, Meaning, and Truth*. 2nd ed. Oxford: Basil Blackwell.

Wright, C. 2000. "Truth as Sort of Epistemic: Putnam's Peregrinations." *Journal of Philosophy* 97(6): 335–364.

8   How to Make Our Ideas Clear

Charles Sanders Peirce

I

Whoever has looked into a modern treatise on logic of the common sort, will doubtless remember the two distinctions between *clear* and *obscure* conceptions, and between *distinct* and *confused* conceptions. They have lain in the books now for nigh two centuries, unimproved and unmodified, and are generally reckoned by logicians as among the gems of their doctrine.

A clear idea is defined as one which is so apprehended that it will be recognized wherever it is met with, and so that no other will be mistaken for it. If it fails of this clearness, it is said to be obscure.

This is rather a neat bit of philosophical terminology; yet, since it is clearness that they were defining, I wish the logicians had made their definition a little more plain. Never to fail to recognize an idea, and under no circumstances to mistake another for it, let it come in how recondite a form it may, would indeed imply such prodigious force and clearness of intellect as is seldom met with in this world. On the other hand, merely to have such an acquaintance with the idea as to have become familiar with it, and to have lost all hesitancy in recognizing it in ordinary cases, hardly seems to deserve the name of clearness of apprehension, since after all it only amounts to a subjective feeling of mastery which may be entirely mistaken. I take it, however, that when the logicians speak of clearness, they mean nothing more than such a familiarity with an idea, since they regard the quality as but a small merit, which needs to be supplemented by another, which they call *distinctness*.

A distinct idea is defined as one which contains nothing which is not clear. This is technical language; by the *contents* of an idea logicians understand whatever is contained in its definition. So that an idea is *distinctly* apprehended, according to them, when we can give a precise definition of it, in abstract terms. Here the professional logicians leave the subject; and I would not have troubled the reader with what they have to say, if it were not such a striking example of how they have been slumbering through ages of intellectual activity, listlessly disregarding the enginery of modern thought, and never dreaming of applying its lessons to the improvement of logic. It is easy to show that the doctrine that familiar use and abstract distinctness make the perfection of apprehension has its only true place in philosophies which have long been extinct; and it is now time to formulate the method of attaining to a more perfect clearness of thought, such as we see and admire in the thinkers of our own time.

When Descartes set about the reconstruction of philosophy, his first step was to (theoretically) permit skepticism and to discard the practice of the schoolmen of looking to authority as the ultimate source of truth. That done, he sought a more natural fountain of true principles, and professed to find it in the human mind; thus passing, in the directest way, from the method of authority to that of apriority, as described in my first paper.[1] Self-consciousness was to furnish us with our fundamental truths, and to decide what was agreeable to reason. But since, evidently, not all ideas are true, he was led to note, as the first condition of infallibility, that they must be clear. The distinction between an idea *seeming* clear and really being so, never occurred to him. Trusting to introspection, as he did, even a knowledge of external things, why should he question its testimony in respect to the contents of our own minds? But then, I suppose, seeing men, who seemed to be quite clear and positive, holding opposite opinions upon fundamental principles, he was further led to say that clearness of ideas is not sufficient, but that they need also to be distinct, i.e., to have nothing unclear about them. What he probably meant by this (for he did not explain himself with precision) was, that they must sustain the test of dialectical examination; that they must not only seem clear at the outset, but that discussion must never be able to bring to light points of obscurity connected with them.

Such was the distinction of Descartes, and one sees that it was precisely on the level of his philosophy. It was somewhat developed by Leibnitz. This great and singular genius was as remarkable for what he failed to see as for what he saw. That a piece of mechanism could not do work perpetually without being fed with power in some form, was a thing perfectly apparent to him; yet he did not understand that the machinery of the mind can only transform knowledge, but never originate it, unless it be fed with facts of observation. He thus missed the most essential point of the Cartesian philosophy, which is, that to accept propositions which seem perfectly evident to us is a thing which, whether it be logical or illogical, we cannot help doing. Instead of regarding the matter in this way, he sought to reduce the first principles of science to formulas which cannot be denied without self-contradiction, and was apparently unaware of the great difference between his position and that of Descartes. So he reverted to the old formalities of logic, and, above all, abstract definitions played a great part in his philosophy. It was quite natural, therefore, that on observing that the method of Descartes labored under the difficulty that we may seem to ourselves to have clear apprehensions of ideas which in truth are very hazy, no better remedy occurred to him than to require an abstract definition of every important term. Accordingly, in adopting the distinction of *clear* and *distinct* notions, he described the latter quality as the clear apprehension of everything contained in the definition; and the books have ever since copied his words. There is no danger that his chimerical scheme will ever again be overvalued. Nothing new can ever be learned by analyzing definitions. Nevertheless, our existing beliefs can be set in order by this process, and order is an essential element of intellectual economy, as of every other. It may be acknowledged, therefore, that the books are right in making familiarity with a notion the first step toward clearness of apprehension, and the defining of it the second. But in omitting all mention of any higher perspicuity of thought, they simply mirror a philosophy which was exploded a hundred years ago. That much-admired "ornament of logic"—the doctrine of clearness and distinctness— may be pretty enough, but it is high time to relegate to our cabinet of curiosities the antique *bijou*, and to wear about us something better adapted to modern uses.

The very first lesson that we have a right to demand that logic shall teach us is, how to make our ideas clear; and a most important one it is, depreciated only by minds who stand in need of it. To know what we think, to be masters of our own meaning, will make a solid foundation for great and weighty thought. It is most easily learned by those whose ideas are meagre and restricted; and far happier they than such as wallow helplessly in a rich mud of conceptions. A nation, it is true, may, in the course of gen- erations, overcome the disadvantage of an excessive wealth of language and its natu- ral concomitant, a vast, unfathomable deep of ideas. We may see it in history, slowly perfecting its literary forms, sloughing at length its metaphysics, and, by virtue of the untirable patience which is often a compensation, attaining great excellence in every branch of mental acquirement. The page of history is not yet unrolled which is to tell us whether such a people will or will not in the long run prevail over one whose ideas (like the words of their language) are few, but which possesses a wonderful mastery over those which it has. For an individual, however, there can be no question that a few clear ideas are worth more than many confused ones. A young man would hardly be persuaded to sacrifice the greater part of his thoughts to save the rest; and the muddled head is the least apt to see the necessity of such a sacrifice. Him we can usually only commiserate, as a person with a congenital defect. Time will help him, but intellectual maturity with regard to clearness comes rather late, an unfortunate arrangement of Nature, inasmuch as clearness is of less use to a man settled in life, whose errors have in great measure had their effect, than it would be to one whose path lies before him. It is terrible to see how a single unclear idea, a single formula without meaning, lurking in a young man's head, will sometimes act like an obstruction of inert matter in an artery, hindering the nutrition of the brain, and condemning its victim to pine away in the fullness of his intellectual vigor and in the midst of intellectual plenty. Many a man has cherished for years as his hobby some vague shadow of an idea, too meaningless to be positively false; he has, nevertheless, passionately loved it, has made it his compan- ion by day and by night, and has given to it his strength and his life, leaving all other occupations for its sake, and in short has lived with it and for it, until it has become, as it were, flesh of his flesh and bone of his bone; and then he has waked up some bright morning to find it gone, clean vanished away like the beautiful Melusina of the fable, and the essence of his life gone with it. I have myself known such a man; and who can tell how many histories of circle-squarers, metaphysicians, astrologers, and what not, may not be told in the old German story?

II

The principles set forth in the first of these papers lead, at once, to a method of reaching a clearness of thought of a far higher grade than the "distinctness" of the logicians. We have there found that the action of thought is excited by the irritation of doubt, and ceases when belief is attained; so that the production of belief is the sole function of thought. All these words, however, are too strong for my purpose. It is as if I had described the phenomena as they appear under a mental microscope. Doubt and Belief, as the words are commonly employed, relate to religious or other grave discussions. But here I use them to designate the starting of any question, no matter how small or how great, and the resolution of it. If, for instance, in a horse-car, I pull out my purse and find a five-cent nickel and five coppers, I decide, while my hand is going to the purse, in which way I will pay my fare. To call such a question Doubt, and my decision Belief, is certainly to use words very disproportionate to the occasion. To speak of such a doubt as causing an irritation which needs to be appeased, suggests a temper which is uncomfortable to the verge of insanity. Yet, looking at the matter minutely, it must be admitted that, if there is the least hesitation as to whether I shall pay the five coppers or the nickel (as there will be sure to be, unless I act from some previously contracted habit in the matter), though irritation is too strong a word, yet I am excited to such small mental activities as may be necessary to deciding how I shall act. Most frequently doubts arise from some indecision, however momentary, in our action. Sometimes it is not so. I have, for example, to wait in a railway station, and to pass the time I read the advertisements on the walls, I compare the advantages of different trains and different routes which I never expect to take, merely fancying myself to be in a state of hesitancy, because I am bored with having nothing to trouble me. Feigned hesitancy, whether feigned for mere amusement or with a lofty purpose, plays a great part in the production of scientific inquiry. However the doubt may originate, it stimulates the mind to an activity which may be slight or energetic, calm or turbulent. Images pass rapidly through consciousness, one incessantly melting into another, until at last, when all is over—it may be in a fraction of a second, in an hour, or after long years—we find ourselves decided as to how we should act under such circumstances as those which occasioned our hesitation. In other words, we have attained belief.

In this process we observe two sorts of elements of consciousness, the distinction between which may best be made clear by means of an illustration. In a piece of music there are the separate notes, and there is the air. A single tone may be prolonged for an hour or a day, and it exists as perfectly in each second of that time as in the whole taken together; so that, as long as it is sounding, it might be present to a sense from which everything in the past was as completely absent as the future itself. But it is different with the air, the performance of which occupies a certain time, during the portions of which only portions of it are played. It consists in an orderliness in the succession of sounds which strike the ear at different times; and to perceive it there must be some continuity of consciousness which makes the events of a lapse of time present to us. We certainly only perceive the air by hearing the separate notes; yet we cannot be said to directly hear it, for we hear only what is present at the instant, and an orderliness of succession cannot exist in an instant. These two sorts of objects, what we are *immediately* conscious of and what we are *mediately* conscious of, are found in all consciousness. Some elements (the sensations) are completely present at every instant so long as they last, while others (like thought) are actions having beginning, middle, and end, and consist in a congruence in the succession of sensations which flow through the mind. They cannot be immediately present to us, but must cover some portion of the past or future. Thought is a thread of melody running through the succession of our sensations.

We may add that just as a piece of music may be written in parts, each part having its own air, so various systems of relationship of succession subsist together between the same sensations. These different systems are distinguished by having different motives, ideas, or functions. Thought is only one such system, for its sole motive, idea, and function, is to produce belief, and whatever does not concern that purpose belongs to some other system of relations. The action of thinking may incidentally have other results; it may serve to amuse us, for example, and among *dilettanti* it is not rare to find those who have so perverted thought to the purposes of pleasure that it seems to vex them to think that the questions upon which they delight to exercise it may ever get finally settled; and a positive discovery which takes a favorite subject out of the arena of literary debate is met with ill-concealed dislike. This disposition is the very debauchery of thought. But the soul and meaning of thought, abstracted from the other elements which accompany it, though it may be voluntarily thwarted, can never be made to direct itself toward anything but the production of belief. Thought in action has for its only possible motive the attainment of thought at rest; and whatever does not refer to belief is no part of the thought itself.

And what, then, is belief? It is the demi-cadence which closes a musical phrase in the symphony of our intellectual life. We have seen that it has just three properties: First, it is something that we are aware of; second, it appeases the irritation of doubt; and, third, it involves the establishment in our nature of a rule of action, or, say for short, a *habit*. As it appeases the irritation of doubt, which is the motive for thinking, thought relaxes, and comes to rest for a moment when belief is reached. But, since belief is a rule for action, the application of which involves further doubt and further thought, at the

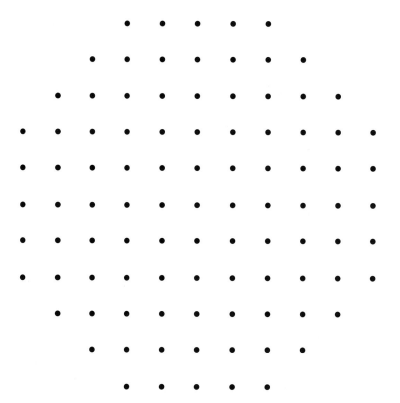

Fig. 1

same time that it is a stopping-place, it is also a new starting place for thought. That is why I have permitted myself to call it thought at rest, although thought is essentially an action. The *final* upshot of thinking is the exercise of volition, and of this thought no longer forms a part; but belief is only a stadium of mental action, an effect upon our nature due to thought, which will influence future thinking.

The essence of belief is the establishment of a habit, and different beliefs are distinguished by the different modes of action to which they give rise. If beliefs do not differ in this respect, if they appease the same doubt by producing the same rule of action, then no mere differences in the manner of consciousness of them can make them different beliefs, any more than playing a tune in different keys is playing different tunes. Imaginary distinctions are often drawn between beliefs which differ only in their mode of expression—the wrangling which ensues is real enough, however. To believe that any objects are arranged as in Fig. 1, and to believe that they are arranged in Fig. 2, are one and the same belief; yet it is conceivable that a man should assert one proposition and deny the other. Such false distinctions do as much harm as the confusion of beliefs

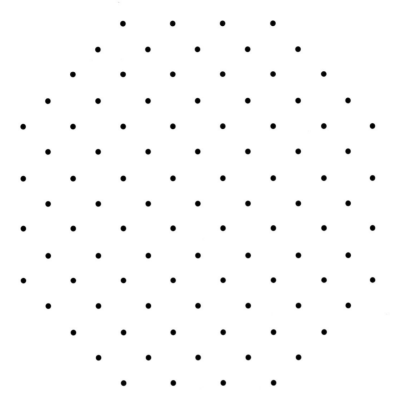

Fig. 2

really different, and are among the pitfalls of which we ought constantly to beware, especially when we are upon metaphysical ground. One singular deception of this sort, which often occurs, is to mistake the sensation produced by our own unclearness of thought for a character of the object we are thinking. Instead of perceiving that the obscurity is purely subjective, we fancy that we contemplate a quality of the object which is essentially mysterious; and if our conception be afterward presented to us in a clear form we do not recognize it as the same, owing to the absence of the feeling of unintelligibility. So long as this deception lasts, it obviously puts an impassable barrier in the way of perspicuous thinking; so that it equally interests the opponents of rational thought to perpetuate it, and its adherents to guard against it.

Another such deception is to mistake a mere difference in the grammatical construction of two words for a distinction between the ideas they express. In this pedantic age, when the general mob of writers attend so much more to words than to things, this error is common enough. When I just said that thought is an action, and that it consists in a relation, although a person performs an action but not a relation, which can only be the result of an action, yet there was no inconsistency in what I said, but only a grammatical vagueness.

From all these sophisms we shall be perfectly safe so long as we reflect that the whole function of thought is to produce habits of action; and that whatever there is connected with a thought, but irrelevant to its purpose, is an accretion to it, but no part of it. If there be a unity among our sensations which has no reference to how we shall act on a given occasion, as when we listen to a piece of music, why we do not call that thinking. To develop its meaning, we have, therefore, simply to determine what habits it produces, for what a thing means is simply what habits it involves. Now, the identity of a habit depends on how it might lead us to act, not merely under such circumstances as are likely to arise, but under such as might possibly occur, no matter how improbable they may be. What the habit is depends on when and *how* it causes us to act. As for the *when*, every stimulus to action is derived from perception; as for the *how*, every purpose of action is to produce some sensible result. Thus, we come down to what is tangible and practical, as the root of every real distinction of thought, no matter how subtle it may be; and there is no distinction of meaning so fine as to consist in anything but a possible difference of practice.

To see what this principle leads to, consider in the light of it such a doctrine as that of transubstantiation. The Protestant churches generally hold that the elements of the sacrament are flesh and blood only in a tropical sense; they nourish our souls as meat and the juice of it would our bodies. But the Catholics maintain that they are literally just that; although they possess all the sensible qualities of wafer-cakes and diluted wine. But we can have no conception of wine except what may enter into a belief, either—

1. That this, that, or the other, is wine; or,

2. That wine possesses certain properties.

Such beliefs are nothing but self-notifications that we should, upon occasion, act in regard to such things as we believe to be wine according to the qualities which we believe wine to possess. The occasion of such action would be some sensible perception, the motive of it to produce some sensible result. Thus our action has exclusive reference to what affects the senses, our habit has the same bearing as our action, our belief the same as our habit, our conception the same as our belief; and we can consequently mean nothing by wine but what has certain effects, direct or indirect, upon our senses; and to talk of something as having all the sensible characters of wine, yet being in reality blood, is senseless jargon. Now, it is not my object to pursue the theological question; and having used it as a logical example I drop it, without caring to anticipate the theologian's reply. I only desire to point out how impossible it is that we should have an idea in our minds which relates to anything but conceived sensible effects of things. Our idea of anything is our idea of its sensible effects; and if we fancy that we have any other we deceive ourselves, and mistake a mere sensation accompanying the thought for a part of the thought itself. It is absurd to say that thought has any meaning unrelated to its only function. It is foolish for Catholics and Protestants to fancy themselves in disagreement about the elements of the sacrament, if they agree in regard to all their sensible effects, here or hereafter.

It appears, then, that the rule for attaining the third grade of clearness of apprehension is as follows: Consider what effects, which might conceivably have practical bearings, we conceive the object of our conception to have. Then, our conception of these effects is the whole of our conception of the object.

III

Let us illustrate this rule by some examples; and, to begin with the simplest one possible, let us ask what we mean by calling a thing *hard*. Evidently that it will not be scratched by many other substances. The whole conception of this quality, as of every other, lies in its conceived effects. There is absolutely no difference between a hard thing and a soft thing so long as they are not brought to the test. Suppose, then, that a diamond could be crystallized in the midst of a cushion of soft cotton, and should remain there until it was finally burned up. Would it be false to say that that diamond was soft? This seems a foolish question, and would be so, in fact, except in the realm of logic. There such questions are often of the greatest utility as serving to bring logical principles into sharper relief than real discussions ever could. In studying logic we must not put them aside with hasty answers, but must consider them with attentive care, in order to make out the principles involved. We may, in the present ease, modify our question, and ask what prevents us from saying that all hard bodies remain perfectly soft until they are touched, when their hardness increases with the pressure until they are scratched. Reflection will show that the reply is this: there would be no *falsity* in such modes of speech. They would involve a modification of our present usage of speech with regard to the words "hard" and "soft," but not of their meanings. For they represent no fact to be different from what it is; only they involve arrangements of facts which would be exceedingly maladroit. This leads us to remark that the question of what would occur under circumstances which do not actually arise is not a question of fact, but only of the most perspicuous arrangement of them. For example, the question of free-will and fate in its simplest form, stripped of verbiage, is something like this: I have done something of which I am ashamed; could I, by an effort of the will, have resisted the temptation, and done otherwise? The philosophical reply is, that this is not a question of fact, but only of the arrangement of facts. Arranging them so as to exhibit what is particularly pertinent to my question—namely, that I ought to blame myself for having done wrong—it is perfectly true to say that, if I had willed to do otherwise than I did, I should have done otherwise. On the other hand, arranging the facts so as to exhibit another important consideration, it is equally true that, when a temptation has once been allowed to work, it will, if it has a certain force, produce its effect, let me struggle how I may. There is no objection to a contradiction in what would result from a false supposition. The *reductio ad absurdum* consists in showing that contradictory results would follow from a hypothesis which is consequently judged to be false. Many questions are involved in the free-will discussion, and I am far from desiring to say that both sides are equally right. On the contrary, I am of the opinion that one side denies important facts, and that the other does not. But what I do say is, that the above single question was the origin of the whole doubt; that, had it not been for this question, the controversy would never have arisen; and that this question is perfectly solved in the manner which I have indicated.

IV

Let us now approach the subject of logic, and consider a conception which particularly concerns it, that of *reality*. Taking clearness in the sense of familiarity, no idea could be clearer than this. Every child uses it with perfect confidence, never dreaming that he does not understand it. As for clearness in its second grade, however, it would probably puzzle most men, even among those of a reflective turn of mind, to give an abstract definition of the real. Yet such a definition may perhaps be reached by considering the points of difference between reality and its opposite, fiction. A figment is a product of somebody's imagination; it has such characters as his thought impresses upon it. That those characters are independent of how you or I think is an external reality. There are, however, phenomena within our own minds, dependent upon our thought, which are at the same time real in the sense that we really think them. But though their characters depend on how we think, they do not depend on what we think those characters to be. Thus, a dream has a real existence as a mental phenomenon, if somebody has really dreamt it; that he dreamt so and so, does not depend on what anybody thinks was dreamt, but is completely independent of all opinion on the subject. On the other hand, considering, not the fact of dreaming, but the thing dreamt, it retains its peculiarities by virtue of no other fact than that it was dreamt to possess them. Thus we may define the real as that whose characters are independent of what anybody may think them to be.

But, however satisfactory such a definition may be found, it would be a great mistake to suppose that it makes the idea of reality perfectly clear. Here, then, let us apply our rules. According to them, reality, like every other quality, consists in the peculiar sensible effects which things partaking of it produce. The only effect which real things have is to cause belief, for all the sensations which they excite emerge into consciousness in the form of beliefs. The question therefore is, how is true belief (or belief in the real) distinguished from false belief (or belief in fiction). Now, as we have seen in the former paper, the ideas of truth and falsehood, in their full development, appertain exclusively to the scientific method of settling opinion. A person who arbitrarily chooses the propositions which he will adopt can use the word "truth" only to emphasize the expression of his determination to hold on to his choice. Of course, the method of tenacity never prevailed exclusively; reason is too natural to men for that. But in the literature of the dark ages we find some fine examples of it. When Scotus Erigena is commenting upon a poetical passage in which hellebore is spoken of as having caused the death of Socrates, he does not hesitate to inform the inquiring reader that Helleborus and Socrates were two eminent Greek philosophers, and that the latter having been overcome in argument by the former took the matter to heart and died of it! What sort of an idea of truth could a man have who could adopt and teach, without the qualification of a perhaps, and opinion taken so entirely at random? The real spirit of Socrates, who I hope would have been delighted to have been overcome in argument, because he would have learned something by it, is in curious contrast with the naive idea of the glossist, for whom discussion would seem to have been simply a struggle. When philosophy began to awake from its long slumber, and before theology completely dominated it, the practice seems to have been for each professor to seize upon any philosophical position he found unoccupied and which seemed a strong one, to intrench himself in it, and to sally forth from time to time to give battle to the others. Thus, even the scanty records we possess of those disputes enable us to make out a dozen or more opinions held by different teachers at one time concerning the question of nominalism and realism. Read the opening part of the *Historia Calamitatum* of Abelard, who was certainly as philosophical as any of his contemporaries, and see the spirit of combat which it breathes. For him, the truth is simply his particular stronghold. When the method of authority prevailed, the truth meant little more than the Catholic faith. All the efforts of the scholastic doctors are directed toward harmonizing their faith in Aristotle and their faith in the Church, and one may search their ponderous folios through without finding an argument which goes any further. It is noticeable that where different faiths flourish side by side, renegades are looked upon with contempt even by the party whose belief they adopt; so completely has the idea of loyalty replaced that of truth-seeking. Since the time of Descartes, the defect in the conception of truth has been less apparent. Still, it will sometimes strike a scientific man that the philosophers have been less intent on finding out what the facts are, than on inquiring what belief is most in harmony with their system. It is hard to convince a follower of the *a priori* method by adducing facts; but show him that an opinion he is defending is inconsistent with what he has laid down elsewhere, and he will be very apt to retract it. These minds do not seem to believe that disputation is ever to cease; they seem to think that the opinion which is natural for one man is not so for another, and that belief will, consequently, never be settled. In contenting themselves with fixing their own opinions by a method which would lead another man to a different result, they betray their feeble hold of the conception of what truth is.

On the other hand, all the followers of science are fully persuaded that the processes of investigation, if only pushed far enough, will give one certain solution to every question to which they can be applied. One man may investigate the velocity of light

by studying the transits of Venus and the aberration of the stars; another by the oppositions of Mars and the eclipses of Jupiter's satellites; a third by the method of Fizeau;
a fourth by that of Foucault; a fifth by the motions of the curves of Lissajoux; a sixth,
a seventh, an eighth, and a ninth, may follow the different methods of comparing the
measures of statical and dynamical electricity. They may at first obtain different results,
but, as each perfects his method and his processes, the results will move steadily together
toward a destined centre. So with all scientific research. Different minds may set out with
the most antagonistic views, but the progress of investigation carries them by a force
outside of themselves to one and the same conclusion. This activity of thought by which
we are carried, not where we wish, but to a foreordained goal, is like the operation of
destiny. No modification of the point of view taken, no selection of other facts for study,
no natural bent of mind even, can enable a man to escape the predestinate opinion. This
great law is embodied in the conception of truth and reality. The opinion which is fated[2]
to be ultimately agreed to by all who investigate, is what we mean by the truth, and the
object represented in this opinion is the real. That is the way I would explain reality.

But it may be said that this view is directly opposed to the abstract definition which
we have given of reality, inasmuch as it makes the characters of the real to depend on
what is ultimately thought about them. But the answer to this is that, on the one hand,
reality is independent, not necessarily of thought in general, but only of what you or I
or any finite number of men may think about it; and that, on the other hand, though
the object of the final opinion depends on what that opinion is, yet what that opinion
is does not depend on what you or I or any man thinks. Our perversity and that of others
may indefinitely postpone the settlement of opinion; it might even conceivably cause an
arbitrary proposition to be universally accepted as long as the human race should last.
Yet even that would not change the nature of the belief, which alone could be the result
of investigation carried sufficiently far; and if, after the extinction of our race, another
should arise with faculties and disposition for investigation, that true opinion must be the
one which they would ultimately come to. Truth crushed to earth shall rise again, and the
opinion which would finally result from investigation does not depend on how anybody
may actually think. But the reality of that which is real does depend on the real fact that
investigation is destined to lead, at last, if continued long enough, to a belief in it.

But I may be asked what I have to say to all the minute facts of history, forgotten
never to be recovered, to the lost books of the ancients, to the buried secrets.

> Full many a gem of purest ray serene
>   The dark, unfathomed caves of ocean bear;
> Full many a flower is born to blush unseen,
>   And waste its sweetness on the desert air.

Do these things not really exist because they are hopelessly beyond the reach of our
knowledge? And then, after the universe is dead (according to the prediction of some

scientists), and all life has ceased forever, will not the shock of atoms continue though there will be no mind to know it? To this I reply that, though in no possible state of knowledge can any number be great enough to express the relation between the amount of what rests unknown to the amount of the known, yet it is unphilosophical to suppose that, with regard to any given question (which has any clear meaning), investigation would not bring forth a solution of it, if it were carried far enough. Who would have said, a few years ago, that we could ever know of what substances stars are made whose light may have been longer in reaching us than the human race has existed? Who can be sure of what we shall not know in a few hundred years? Who can guess what would be the result of continuing the pursuit of science for ten thousand years, with the activity of the last hundred? And if it were to go on for a million, or a billion, or any number of years you please, how is it possible to say that there is any question which might not ultimately be solved?

But it may be objected, Why make so much of these remote considerations, especially when it is your principle that only practical distinctions have a meaning? Well, I must confess that it makes very little difference whether we say that a stone on the bottom of the ocean, in complete darkness, is brilliant or not—that is to say, that it *probably* makes no difference, remembering always that that stone *may* be fished up to-morrow. But that there are gems at the bottom of the sea, flowers in the untraveled desert, etc., are propositions which, like that about a diamond being hard when it is not pressed, concern much more the arrangement of our language than they do the meaning of our ideas.

It seems to me, however, that we have, by the application of our rule, reached so clear an apprehension of what we mean by reality, and of the fact which the idea rests on, that we should not, perhaps, be making a pretension so presumptuous as it would be singular, if we were to offer a metaphysical theory of existence for universal acceptance among those who employ the scientific method of fixing belief. However, as metaphysics is a subject much more curious than useful, the knowledge of which, like that of a sunken reef, serves chiefly to enable us to keep clear of it, I will not trouble the reader with any more Ontology at this moment. I have already been led much further into that path than I should have desired; and I have given the reader such a dose of mathematics, psychology, and all that is most abstruse, that I fear he may already have left me, and that what I am now writing is for the compositor and proof-reader exclusively. I trusted to the importance of the subject. There is no royal road to logic, and really valuable ideas can only be had at the price of close attention. But I know that in the matter of ideas the public prefer the cheap and nasty; and in my next paper I am going to return to the easily intelligible, and not wander from it again. The reader who has been at the pains of wading through this month's paper, shall be rewarded in the next one by seeing how beautifully what has been developed in this tedious way can be applied to the ascertainment of the rules of scientific reasoning.

We have, hitherto, not crossed the threshold of scientific logic. It is certainly important to know how to make our ideas clear, but they may be ever so clear without being true. How to make them so, we have next to study. How to give birth to those vital and procreative ideas which multiply into a thousand forms and diffuse themselves everywhere, advancing civilization and making the dignity of man, is an art not yet reduced to rules, but of the secret of which the history of science affords some hints.

Notes

1. Peirce published "The Fixation of Belief" in *Popular Science Monthly* in 1877, a year before "How to Make Our Ideas Clear." See the *Collected Papers of Charles Sanders Peirce*, vol. 5, ed. C. Hartshorne and P. Weiss (Cambridge, MA: Harvard University Press, 1965), 223–247.—Eds.

2. Fate means merely that which is sure to come true, and can nohow be avoided. It is a superstition to suppose that a certain sort of events are ever fated, and it is another to suppose that the word "fate" can never be freed from its superstitious taint. We are all fated to die.

9 Pragmatism's Conception of Truth

William James

When Clerk-Maxwell was a child it is written that he had a mania for having every-thing explained to him, and that when people put him off with vague verbal accounts of any phenomenon he would interrupt them impatiently by saying, "Yes; but I want you to tell me the *particular go* of it!" Had his question been about truth, only a prag-matist could have told him the particular go of it. I believe that our contemporary pragmatists, especially Messrs. Schiller and Dewey, have given the only tenable account of this subject. It is a very ticklish subject, sending subtle rootlets into all kinds of cran-nies, and hard to treat in the sketchy way that alone befits a public lecture. But the Schiller-Dewey view of truth has been so ferociously attacked by rationalistic philoso-phers, and so abominably misunderstood, that here, if anywhere, is the point where a clear and simple statement should be made.

I fully expect to see the pragmatist view of truth run through the classic stages of a the-ory's career. First, you know, a new theory is attacked as absurd; then it is admitted to be true, but obvious and insignificant; finally it is seen to be so important that its adversaries claim that they themselves discovered it. Our doctrine of truth is at present in the first of these three stages, with symptoms of the second stage having begun in certain quarters. I wish that this lecture might help it beyond the first stage in the eyes of many of you.

Truth, as any dictionary will tell you, is a property of certain of our ideas. It means their "agreement," as falsity means their disagreement, with "reality." Pragmatists and intellec-tualists both accept this definition as a matter of course. They begin to quarrel only after the question is raised as to what may precisely be meant by the term "agreement," and what by the term "reality," when reality is taken as something for our ideas to agree with.

In answering these questions the pragmatists are more analytic and painstaking, the intellectualists more offhand and irreflective. The popular notion is that a true idea must copy its reality. Like other popular views, this one follows the analogy of the most usual experience. Our true ideas of sensible things do indeed copy them. Shut your eyes and think of yonder clock on the wall, and you get just such a true picture or copy of its dial. But your idea of its "works" (unless you are a clockmaker) is much less of a copy, yet it passes muster, for it in no way clashes with the reality. Even though it should shrink to the mere word "works," that word still serves you truly; and when you speak of the "time-keeping function" of the clock, or of its spring's "elasticity," it is hard to see exactly what your ideas can copy.

You perceive that there is a problem here. Where our ideas cannot copy definitely their object, what does agreement with that object mean? Some idealists seem to say that they are true whenever they are what God means that we ought to think about that object. Others hold the copyview all through, and speak as if our ideas possessed truth just in proportion as they approach to being copies of the Absolute's eternal way of thinking.

These views, you see, invite pragmatistic discussion. But the great assumption of the intellectualists is that truth means essentially an inert static relation. When you've got your true idea of anything, there's an end of the matter. You're in possession; you *know*; you have fulfilled your thinking destiny. You are where you ought to be mentally; you have obeyed your categorical imperative; and nothing more need follow on that climax of your rational destiny. Epistemologically you are in stable equilibrium.

Pragmatism, on the other hand, asks its usual question. "Grant an idea or belief to be true," it says, "what concrete difference will its being true make in any one's actual life? How will the truth be realized? What experiences will be different from those which would obtain if the belief were false? What, in short, is the truth's cash-value in experiential terms?" The moment pragmatism asks this question, it sees the answer: *True ideas are those that we can assimilate, validate, corroborate and verify. False ideas are those that we can not.* That is the practical difference it makes to us to have true ideas; that, therefore, is the meaning of truth, for it is all that truth is known as.

This thesis is what I have to defend. The truth of an idea is not a stagnant property inherent in it. Truth *happens* to an idea. It *becomes* true, is *made* true by events. Its verity *is* in fact an event, a process: the process namely of its verifying itself, its veri-*fication*. Its validity is the process of its valid-*ation*.

But what do the words "verification" and "validation" themselves pragmatically mean? They again signify certain practical consequences of the verified and validated idea. It is hard to find any one phrase that characterizes these consequences better than the ordinary agreement-formula—just such consequences being what we have in mind whenever we say that our ideas "agree" with reality. They lead us, namely, through the acts and other ideas which they instigate, into or up to, or towards, other parts of experience with which we feel all the while—such feeling being among our potentialities—that the original ideas remain in agreement. The connexions and transitions come to us from point to point as being progressive, harmonious, satisfactory. This function of agreeable leading is what we mean by an idea's verification. Such an account is vague and it sounds at first quite trivial, but it has results which it will take the rest of my hour to explain.

Let me begin by reminding you of the fact that the possession of true thoughts means everywhere the possession of invaluable instruments of action; and that our duty to gain truth, so far from being a blank command from out of the blue, or a "stunt" self-imposed by our intellect, can account for itself by excellent practical reasons.

The importance to human life of having true beliefs about matters of fact is a thing too notorious. We live in a world of realities that can be infinitely useful or infinitely harmful. Ideas that tell us which of them to expect count as the true ideas in all this primary sphere of verification, and the pursuit of such ideas is a primary human duty. The possession of truth, so far from being here an end in itself, is only a preliminary means towards other vital satisfactions. If I am lost in the woods and starved, and find what looks like a cow-path, it is of the utmost importance that I should think of a human habitation at the end of it, for if I do so and follow it, I save myself. The true thought is useful here because the house which is its object is useful. The practical value of true ideas is thus primarily derived from the practical importance of their objects to us. Their objects are, indeed, not important at all times. I may on another occasion have no use for the house; and then my idea of it, however verifiable, will be practically irrelevant, and had better remain latent. Yet since almost any object may some day become temporarily important, the advantage of having a general stock of *extra* truths, of ideas that shall be true of merely possible situations, is obvious. We store such extra truths away in our memories, and with the overflow we fill our books of reference. Whenever such an extra truth becomes practically relevant to one of our emergencies, it passes from cold-storage to do work in the world and our belief in it grows active. You can say of it then either that "it is useful because it is true" or that "it is true because it is useful." Both these phrases mean exactly the same thing, namely that here is an idea that gets fulfilled and can be verified. True is the name for whatever idea starts the verification-process, useful is the name for its completed function in experience. True ideas would never have been singled out as such, would never have acquired a class-name, least of all a name suggesting value, unless they had been useful from the outset in this way.

From this simple cue pragmatism gets her general notion of truth as something essentially bound up with the way in which one moment in our experience may lead us towards other moments which it will be worth while to have been led to. Primarily, and on the common-sense level, the truth of a state of mind means this function of a *leading that is worth while*. When a moment in our experience, of any kind whatever, inspires us with a thought that is true, that means that sooner or later we dip by that thought's guidance into the particulars of experience again and make advantageous connexion with them. This is a vague enough statement, but I beg you to retain it, for it is essential.

Our experience meanwhile is all shot through with regularities. One bit of it can warn us to get ready for another bit, can "intend" or be "significant of" that remoter object. The object's advent is the significance's verification. Truth, in these cases, meaning nothing but eventual verification, is manifestly incompatible with waywardness on our part. Woe to him whose beliefs play fast and loose with the order which realities follow in his experience; they will lead him nowhere or else make false connexions.

By "realities" or "objects" here, we mean either things of common sense, sensibly present, or else common-sense relations, such as dates, places, distances, kinds, activities. Following our mental image of a house along the cow-path, we actually come to see the house; we get the image's full verification. *Such simply and fully verified leadings are certainly the originals and prototypes of the truth-process*. Experience offers indeed other forms of truth-process, but they are all conceivable as being primary verifications arrested, multiplied or substituted one for another.

Take, for instance, yonder object on the wall. You and I consider it to be a "clock," although no one of us has seen the hidden works that make it one. We let our notion pass for true without attempting to verify. If truths mean verification-process essentially, ought we then to call such unverified truths as this abortive? No, for they form the overwhelmingly large number of the truths we live by. Indirect as well as direct verifications pass muster. Where circumstantial evidence is sufficient, we can go without eyewitnessing. Just as we here assume Japan to exist without ever having been there, because it *works* to do so, everything we know conspiring with the belief, and nothing interfering, so we assume that thing to be a clock. We *use* it as a clock, regulating the length of our lecture by it. The verification of the assumption here means its leading to no frustration or contradiction. *Verifiability* of wheels and weights and pendulum is as good as verification. For one truth-process completed there are a million in our lives that function in this state of nascency. They turn us *towards* direct verification; lead us into the *surroundings* of the objects they envisage; and then, if everything runs on harmoniously, we are so sure that verification is possible that we omit it, and are usually justified by all that happens.

Truth lives, in fact, for the most part on a credit system. Our thoughts and beliefs "pass," so long as nothing challenges them, just as banknotes pass so long as nobody refuses them. But this all points to direct face-to-face verifications somewhere, without which the fabric of truth collapses like a financial system with no cash-basis whatever. You accept my verification of one thing, I yours of another. We trade on each other's truth. But beliefs verified concretely by *somebody* are the posts of the whole superstructure.

Another great reason—beside economy of time—for waiving complete verification in the usual business of life is that all things exist in kinds and not singly. Our world is found once for all to have that peculiarity. So that when we have once directly verified our ideas about one specimen of a kind, we consider ourselves free to apply them to other specimens without verification. A mind that habitually discerns the kind of thing before it, and acts by the law of the kind immediately, without pausing to verify, will be a "true" mind in ninety-nine out of a hundred emergencies, proved so by its conduct fitting everything it meets, and getting no refutation.

Indirectly or only potentially verifying processes may thus be true as well as full verification-processes. They work as true processes would work, give us the same advantages, and claim our recognition for the same reasons. All this on the common-sense level of matters of fact, which we are alone considering.

But matters of fact are not our only stock in trade. *Relations among purely mental ideas* form another sphere where true and false beliefs obtain, and here the beliefs are absolute, or unconditional. When they are true they bear the name either of definitions or of principles. It is either a principle or a definition that 1 and 1 make 2, that 2 and 1 make 3, and so on; that white differs less from grey than it does from black; that when the cause begins to act the effect also commences. Such propositions hold of all possible "ones," of all conceivable "whites" and "greys" and "causes." The objects here are mental objects. Their relations are perceptually obvious at a glance, and no sense-verification is necessary. Moreover, once true, always true, of those same mental objects. Truth here has an "eternal" character. If you can find a concrete thing anywhere that is "one" or "white" or "grey" or an "effect," then your principles will everlastingly apply to it. It is but a case of ascertaining the kind, and then applying the law of its kind to the particular object. You are sure to get truth if you can but name the kind rightly, for your mental relations hold good of everything of that kind without exception. If you then, nevertheless, failed to get truth concretely, you would say that you had classed your real objects wrongly.

In this realm of mental relations, truth again is an affair of leading. We relate one abstract idea with another, framing in the end great systems of logical and mathematical truth, under the respective terms of which the sensible facts of experience eventually arrange themselves, so that our eternal truths hold good of realities also. This marriage of fact and theory is endlessly fertile. What we say is here already true in advance of special verification, *if we have subsumed our objects rightly*. Our ready-made ideal framework for all sorts of possible objects follows from the very structure of our thinking. We can no more play fast and loose with these abstract relations than we can do so with our sense-experiences. They coerce us; we must treat them consistently, whether or not we like the results. The rules of addition apply to our debts as rigorously as to our assets. The hundredth decimal of n, the ratio of the circumference to its diameter, is predetermined ideally now, though no one may have computed it. If we should ever need the figure in our dealings with an actual circle we should need to have it given rightly, calculated by the usual rules; for it is the same kind of truth that those rules elsewhere calculate.

Between the coercions of the sensible order and those of the ideal order, our mind is thus wedged tightly. Our ideas must agree with realities, be such realities concrete or abstract, be they facts or be they principles, under penalty of endless inconsistency and frustration.

So far, intellectualists can raise no protest. They can only say that we have barely touched the skin of the matter.

Realities mean, then, either concrete facts, or abstract kinds of things and relations perceived intuitively between them. They furthermore and thirdly mean, as things that new ideas of ours must no less take account of, the whole body of other truths already in our possession. But what now does "agreement" with such threefold realities mean?—to use again the definition that is current.

Here it is that pragmatism and intellectualism begin to part company. Primarily, no doubt, to agree means to copy, but we saw that the mere word "clock" would do instead of a mental picture of its works, and that of many realities our ideas can only be symbols and not copies. "Past time," "power," "spontaneity"—how can our mind copy such realities?

To "agree" in the widest sense with a reality *can only mean to be guided either straight up to it or into its surroundings, or to be put into such working touch with it as to handle either it or something connected with it better than if we disagreed.* Better either intellectually or practically! And often agreement will only mean the negative fact that nothing contradictory from the quarter of that reality comes to interfere with the way in which our ideas guide us elsewhere. To copy a reality is, indeed, one very important way of agreeing with it, but it is far from being essential. The essential thing is the process of being guided. Any idea that helps us to *deal*, whether practically or intellectually, with either the reality or its belongings, that doesn't entangle our progress in frustrations, that *fits*, in fact, and adapts our life to the reality's whole setting, will agree sufficiently to meet the requirement. It will hold true of that reality.

Thus, *names* are just as "true" or "false" as definite mental pictures are. They set up similar verification-processes, and lead to fully equivalent practical results.

All human thinking gets discursified; we exchange ideas; we lend and borrow verifications, get them from one another by means of social intercourse. All truth thus gets verbally built out, stored up, and made available for everyone. Hence, we must *talk* consistently just as we must *think* consistently: for both in talk and thought we deal with kinds. Names are arbitrary, but once understood they must be kept to. We mustn't now call Abel "Cain" or Cain "Abel." If we do, we ungear ourselves from the whole book of Genesis, and from all its connexions with the universe of speech and fact down to the present time. We throw ourselves out of whatever truth that entire system of speech and fact may embody.

The overwhelming majority of our true ideas admit of no direct or face-to-face verification—those of past history, for example, as of Cain and Abel. The stream of time can be remounted only verbally, or verified indirectly by the present prolongations or effects of what the past harbored. Yet if they agree with these verbalities and effects, we can know that our ideas of the past are true. *As true as past time itself was*, so true was Julius Caesar, so true were antediluvian monsters, all in their proper dates and settings. That past time itself was, is guaranteed by its coherence with everything that's present. True as the present *is*, the past *was* also.

Agreement thus turns out to be essentially an affair of leading—leading that is useful because it is into quarters that contain objects that are important. True ideas lead us into useful verbal and conceptual quarters as well as directly up to useful sensible termini. They lead to consistency, stability and flowing human intercourse. They lead away from eccentricity and isolation, from foiled and barren thinking. The untrammelled flowing of the leading-process, its general freedom from clash and contradiction, passes for its indirect verification; but all roads lead to Rome, and in the end and eventually, all true processes must lead to the face of directly verifying sensible experiences *somewhere*, which somebody's ideas have copied.

Such is the large loose way in which the pragmatist interprets the word agreement. He treats it altogether practically. He lets it cover any process of conduction from a present idea to a future terminus, provided only it run prosperously. It is only thus that "scientific" ideas, flying as they do beyond common sense, can be said to agree with their realities. It is, as I have already said, *as if* reality were made of ether, atoms or electrons, but we mustn't think so literally. The term "energy" doesn't even pretend to stand for anything "objective." It is only a way of measuring the surface of phenomena so as to string their changes on a simple formula.

Yet in the choice of these man-made formulas we can not be capricious with impunity any more than we can be capricious on the common-sense practical level. We must find a theory that will *work*; and that means something extremely difficult; for our theory must mediate between all previous truths and certain new experiences. It must derange common sense and previous belief as little as possible, and it must lead to some sensible terminus or other that can be verified exactly. To "work" means both these things; and the squeeze is so tight that there is little loose play for any hypothesis. Our theories are wedged and controlled as nothing else is. Yet sometimes alternative theoretic formulas are equally compatible with all the truths we know, and then we choose between them for subjective reasons. We choose the kind of theory to which we are already partial; we follow "elegance" or "economy." Clerk-Maxwell somewhere says it would be "poor scientific taste" to choose the more complicated of two equally well-evidenced conceptions; and you will all agree with him. Truth in science is what gives us the maximum possible sum of satisfactions, taste included, but consistency both with previous truth and with novel fact is always the most imperious claimant.

I have led you through a very sandy desert. But now, if I may be allowed so vulgar an expression, we begin to taste the milk in the coconut. Our rationalist critics here discharge their batteries upon us, and to reply to them will take us out from all this dryness into full sight of a momentous philosophical alternative.

Our account of truth is an account of truths in the plural, of processes of leading, realized *in rebus*, and having only this quality in common, that they *pay*. They pay by guiding us into or towards some part of a system that dips at numerous points into sense-percepts, which we may copy mentally or not, but with which at any rate we are now in the kind of commerce vaguely designated as verification. Truth for us is simply a collective name for verification-processes, just as health, wealth, strength, etc., are names for other processes connected with life, and also pursued because it pays to pursue them. Truth is *made*, just as health, wealth, and strength are made, in the course of experience.

Here rationalism is instantaneously up in arms against us. I can imagine a rationalist to talk as follows:

"Truth is not made," he will say; "it absolutely obtains, being a unique relation that does not wait upon any process, but shoots straight over the head of experience, and hits its reality every time. Our belief that yon thing on the wall is a clock is true already, although no one in the whole history of the world should verify it. The bare quality of standing in that transcendent relation is what makes any thought true that possesses it, whether or not there be verification. You pragmatists put the cart before the horse in making truth's being reside in verification-processes. These are merely signs of its being, merely our lame ways of ascertaining after the fact, which of our ideas already has possessed the wondrous quality. The quality itself is timeless, like all essences and natures. Thoughts partake of it directly, as they partake of falsity or of irrelevancy. It can't be analysed away into pragmatic consequences."

The whole plausibility of this rationalist tirade is due to the fact to which we have already paid so much attention. In our world, namely, abounding as it does in things of similar kinds and similarly associated, one verification serves for others of its kind, and one great use of knowing things is to be led not so much to them as to their associates, especially to human talk about them. The quality of truth, obtaining *ante rem*, pragmatically means, then, the fact that in such a world innumerable ideas work better by their indirect or possible than by their direct and actual verification. Truth *ante rem* means only verifiability, then; or else it is a case of the stock rationalist trick of treating the *name* of a concrete phenomenal reality as an independent prior entity, and placing it behind the reality as its explanation. Professor Mach quotes somewhere an epigram of Lessing's:

Sagt Hänschen Schlau zu Vetter Fritz,
"Wie kommt es, Vetter Fritzen,
Dass grad' die Reichsten in der Welt,
Das meiste Geld besitzen?"

Hänschen Schlau here treats the principle "wealth" as something distinct from the facts denoted by the man's being rich. It antedates them; the facts become only a sort of secondary coincidence with the rich man's essential nature.

In the case of "wealth" we all see the fallacy. We know that wealth is but a name for concrete processes that certain men's lives play a part in, and not a natural excellence found in Messrs. Rockefeller and Carnegie, but not in the rest of us.

Like wealth, health also lives *in rebus*. It is a name for processes, and digestion, circulation, sleep, etc., that go on happily, though in this instance we are more inclined to think of it as a principle and to say the man digests and sleeps so well *because* he is so healthy.

With "strength" we are, I think, more rationalistic still, and decidedly inclined to treat it as an excellence pre-existing in the man and explanatory of the herculean performances of his muscles.

With "truth" most people go over the border entirely, and treat the rationalistic account as self-evident. But really all these words in *th* are exactly similar. Truth exists *ante rem* just as much and as little as the other things do.

The scholastics, following Aristotle, made much of the distinction between habit and act. Health *in actu* means, among other things, good sleeping and digesting. But a healthy man need not always be sleeping, or always digesting, any more than a wealthy man need be always handing money, or a strong man always lifting weights. All such qualities sink to the status of "habits" between their times of exercise; and similarly truth becomes a habit of certain of our ideas and beliefs in their intervals of rest from their verifying activities. But those activities are the root of the whole matter, and the condition of there being any habit to exist in the intervals.

"The true," to put it very briefly, is only the expedient in the way of our thinking, just as "the right" is only the expedient in the way of our behaving. Expedient in almost any fashion; and expedient in the long run and on the whole of course; for what meets expediently all the experience in sight won't necessarily meet all farther experiences equally satisfactorily. Experience, as we know, has ways of *boiling over*, and making us correct our present formulas.

The "absolutely" true, meaning what no further experience will ever alter, is that ideal vanishing-point towards which we imagine that all our temporary truths will some day converge. It runs on all fours with the perfectly wise man, and with the absolutely complete experience; and, if these ideals are ever realized, they will all be realized together. Meanwhile we have to live today by what truth we can get today, and be ready tomorrow to call it falsehood. Ptolemaic astronomy, Euclidean space, Aristotelian logic, scholastic metaphysics, were expedient for centuries, but human experience has boiled over those limits, and we now call these things only relatively true, or true within those borders of experience. "Absolutely" they are false; for we know that those limits were casual, and might have been transcended by past theorists just as they are by present thinkers.

When new experiences lead to retrospective judgements, using the past tense, what these judgements utter *was* true, even though no past thinker had been led there. We live forwards, a Danish thinker has said, but we understand backwards. The present sheds a backward light on the world's previous processes. They may have been truth-processes for the actors in them. They are not so for one who knows the later revelations of the story.

This regulative notion of a potential better truth to be established later, possibly to be established some day absolutely, and having powers of retroactive legislation, turns its face, like all pragmatist notions, towards concreteness of fact, and towards the future. Like the half-truths, the absolute truth will have to be *made*, made as a relation incidental to the growth of a mass of verification-experience, to which the half-true ideas are all along contributing their quota.

I have already insisted on the fact that truth is made largely out of previous truths. Men's beliefs at any time are so much experience *funded*. But the beliefs are themselves parts of the sum total of the world's experience, and become matter, therefore, for the next day's funding operations. So far as reality means experienceable reality, both it and the truths men gain about it are everlastingly in process of mutation—mutation towards a definite goal, it may be—but still mutation.

Mathematicians can solve problems with two variables. On the Newtonian theory, for instance, acceleration varies with distance, but distance also varies with acceleration. In the realm of truth-processes facts come independently and determine our beliefs provisionally. But these beliefs make us act, and as fast as they do so, they bring into sight or into existence new facts which redetermine the beliefs accordingly. So the whole coil and ball of truth, as it rolls up, is the product of a double influence. Truths emerge from facts; but they dip forward into facts again and add to them; which facts again create or reveal new truth (the word is indifferent) and so on indefinitely. The "facts" themselves meanwhile are not *true*. They simply *are*. Truth is the function of the beliefs that start and terminate among them.

The case is like a snowball's growth, due as it is to the distribution of the snow on the one hand, and to the successive pushes of the boys on the other, with these factors co-determining each other incessantly.

The most fateful point of difference between being a rationalist and being a pragmatist is now fully in sight. Experience is in mutation, and our psychological ascertainments of truth are in mutation—so much rationalism will allow; but never that either reality itself or truth itself is mutable. Reality stands complete and ready-made from all eternity, rationalism insists, and the agreement of our ideas with it is that unique unanalyzable virtue in them of which she has already told us. As that intrinsic excellence, their truth has nothing to do with our experiences. It adds nothing to the content of experience. It makes no difference to reality itself; it is supervenient, inert, static, a reflexion merely. It doesn't *exist*, it *holds* or *obtains*, it belongs to another dimension from that of either facts or fact-relations, belongs, in short, to the epistemological dimension—and with that big word rationalism closes the discussion.

Thus, just as pragmatism faces forward to the future, so does rationalism here again face backward to a past eternity. True to her inveterate habit, rationalism reverts to "principles," and thinks that when an abstraction once is named, we own an oracular solution.

The tremendous pregnancy in the way of consequences for life of this radical difference of outlook will only become apparent in my later lectures. I wish meanwhile to close this lecture by showing that rationalism's sublimity does not save it from inanity.

When, namely, you ask rationalists, instead of accusing pragmatism of desecrating the notion of truth, to define it themselves by saying exactly what *they* understand by it, the only positive attempts I can think of are these two:

1. "Truth is the system of propositions which have an unconditional claim to be recognized as valid."[1]

2. Truth is a name for all those judgements which we find ourselves under obligation to make by a kind of imperative duty.[2]

The first thing that strikes one in such definitions is their unutterable triviality. They are absolutely true, of course, but absolutely insignificant until you handle them pragmatically. What do you mean by "claim" here, and what do you mean by "duty"? As summary names for the concrete reasons why thinking in true ways is overwhelmingly expedient and good for mortal men, it is all right to talk of claims on reality's part to be agreed with, and of obligations on our part to agree. We feel both the claims and the obligations, and we feel them for just those reasons.

But the rationalists who talk of claim and obligation *expressly say that they have nothing to do with our practical interests or personal reasons*. Our reasons for agreeing are psychological facts, they say, relative to each thinker, and to the accidents of his life. They are his evidence merely, they are no part of the life of truth itself. That life transacts itself in a purely logical or epistemological, as distinguished from a psychological, dimension, and its claims antedate and exceed all personal motivations whatsoever. Though neither man nor God should ever ascertain truth, the word would still have to be defined as that which *ought* to be ascertained and recognized.

There never was a more exquisite example of an idea abstracted from the concretes of experience and then used to oppose and negate what it was abstracted from.

Philosophy and common life abound in similar instances. The "sentimentalist fallacy" is to shed tears over abstract justice and generosity, beauty, etc., and never to know these qualities when you meet them in the street, because the circumstances make them vulgar. Thus I read in the privately printed biography of an eminently rationalistic mind: "It was strange that with such admiration for beauty in the abstract, my brother had no enthusiasm for fine architecture, for beautiful painting, or for flowers." And in almost the last philosophic work I have read, I find such passages as the following: "Justice is ideal, solely ideal. Reason conceives that it ought to exist, but experience shows that it can not. ... Truth, which ought to be, can not be. ... Reason is deformed by experience. As soon as reason enters experience it becomes contrary to reason."

The rationalist's fallacy here is exactly like the sentimentalist's. Both extract a quality from the muddy particulars of experience, and find it so pure when extracted that they contrast it with each and all its muddy instances as an opposite and higher nature. All the while it is *their* nature. It is the nature of truths to be validated, verified. It pays

for our ideas to be validated. Our obligation to seek truth is part of our general obligation to do what pays. The payments true ideas bring are the sole why of our duty to
follow them. Identical whys exist in the case of wealth and health.

Truth makes no other kind of claim and imposes no other kind of ought than health
and wealth do. All these claims are conditional; the concrete benefits we gain are what
we mean by calling the pursuit a duty. In the case of truth, untrue beliefs work as
perniciously in the long run as true beliefs work beneficially. Talking abstractly, the
quality "true" may thus be said to grow absolutely precious and the quality "untrue"
absolutely damnable: the one may be called good, the other bad, unconditionally. We
ought to think the true, we ought to shun the false, imperatively.

But if we treat all this abstraction literally and oppose it to its mother soil in experience, see what a preposterous position we work ourselves into.

We cannot then take a step forward in our actual thinking. When shall I acknowledge this truth and when that? Shall the acknowledgment be loud?—or silent? If sometimes loud, sometimes silent, which *now*? When may a truth go into cold-storage in
the encyclopedia? and when shall it come out for battle? Must I constantly be repeating the truth "twice two are four" because of its eternal claim on recognition? or is it
sometimes irrelevant? Must my thoughts dwell night and day on my personal sins and
blemishes, because I truly have them?—or may I sink and ignore them in order to be a
decent social unit, and not a mass of morbid melancholy and apology?

It is quite evident that our obligation to acknowledge truth, so far from being unconditional, is tremendously conditioned. Truth with a big T, and in the singular, claims
abstractly to be recognized, of course; but concrete truths in the plural need be recognized only when their recognition is expedient. A truth must always be preferred to a
falsehood when both relate to the situation; but when neither does, truth is as little of
a duty as falsehood. If you ask me what o'clock it is and I tell you that I live at 95 Irving
Street, my answer may indeed be true, but you don't see why it is my duty to give it. A
false address would be as much to the purpose.

With this admission that there are conditions that limit the application of the abstract
imperative, *the pragmatistic treatment of truth sweeps back upon us in its fulness*. Our duty
to agree with reality is seen to be grounded in a perfect jungle of concrete expediencies.

When Berkeley had explained what people meant by matter, people thought that he
denied matter's existence. When Messrs. Schiller and Dewey now explain what people
mean by truth, they are accused of denying *its* existence. These pragmatists destroy all
objective standards, critics say, and put foolishness and wisdom on one level. A favou-
rite formula for describing Mr. Schiller's doctrines and mine is that we are persons who
think that by saying whatever you find it pleasant to say and calling it truth you fulfil
every pragmatistic requirement.

I leave it to you to judge whether this be not an impudent slander. Pent in, as
the pragmatist more than anyone else sees himself to be, between the whole body of

funded truths squeezed from the past and the coercions of the world of sense about him, who so well as he feels the immense pressure of objective control under which our minds perform their operations? If anyone imagines that this law is lax, let him keep its commandment one day, says Emerson. We have heard much of late of the uses of the imagination in science. It is high time to urge the use of a little imagination in philosophy. The unwillingness of some of our critics to read any but the silliest of possible meanings into our statements is as discreditable to their imaginations as anything I know in recent philosophic history. Schiller says the true is that which "works." Thereupon he is treated as one who limits verification to the lowest material utilities. Dewey says truth is what gives "satisfaction." He is treated as one who believes in calling everything true which, if it were true, would be pleasant.

Our critics certainly need more imagination of realities. I have honestly tried to stretch my own imagination and to read the best possible meaning into the rationalist conception, but I have to confess that it still completely baffles me. The notion of a reality calling on us to "agree" with it, and that for no reasons, but simply because its claim is "unconditional" or "transcendent," is one that I can make neither head nor tail of. I try to imagine myself as the sole reality in the world, and then to imagine what more I would "claim" if I were allowed to. If you suggest the possibility of my claiming that a mind should come into being from out of the void inane and stand and *copy* me, I can indeed imagine what the copying might mean, but I can conjure up no motive. What good it would do me to be copied, or what good it would do that mind to copy me, if further consequences are expressly and in principle ruled out as motives for the claim (as they are by our rationalist authorities) I can not fathom. When the Irishman's admirers ran him along to the place of banquet in a sedan chair with no bottom, he said, "Faith, if it wasn't for the honour of the thing, I might as well have come on foot." So here: but for the honour of the thing, I might as well have remained uncopied. Copying is one genuine mode of knowing (which for some strange reason our contemporary transcendentalists seem to be tumbling over each other to repudiate); but when we get beyond copying, and fall back on unnamed forms of agreeing that are expressly denied to be either copyings or leadings or fittings, or any other processes pragmatically definable, the *what* of the "agreement" claimed becomes as unintelligible as the why of it. Neither content nor motive can be imagined for it. It is an absolutely meaningless abstraction.[3]

Surely in this field of truth it is the pragmatists and not the rationalists who are the more genuine defenders of the universe's rationality.

Notes

1. A. E. Taylor, "Truth and Practice." *Philosophical Review* 14, no. 3 (1905): 288.

2. H. Rickert, "Die Urtheilsnothwendigkeit," in *Der Gegenstand der Erkenntniss: Einfuhrung in die tranzendentale philosophie* (Tübingen, 1904).

3. I am not forgetting that Professor Rickert long ago gave up the whole notion of truth being founded on agreement with reality. Reality according to him, is whatever agrees with truth, and truth is founded solely on our primal duty. This fantastic flight, together with Mr. Joachim's candid confession of failure in his book *The Nature of Truth* (Oxford: Clarendon Press, 1906), seems to me to mark the bankruptcy of rationalism when dealing with this subject. Rickert deals with part of the pragmatistic position under the head of what he calls "Relativismus." I cannot discuss his text here. Suffice it to say that his argumentation in that chapter is so feeble as to seem almost incredible in so generally able a writer.

10 Truth, Inquiry, and Experience: A Pragmatist Epistemology

Cheryl Misak

Peirce, Truth, and the End of Inquiry

The pragmatism I shall articulate and defend has its pedigree in the work of the founder of pragmatism and one of the brightest intellectual lights of the turn of the century—C. S. Peirce. His orneriness and the poor judgement of Harvard and Johns Hopkins universities combined to thwart his attempts to obtain a permanent post. He died a hungry oddity on the fringes of academia, leaving piles of manuscripts and fragments on a wide range of topics. Some of the thoughts one finds there are in tension with each other and many must be rejected. But there is a strand in Peirce's work that I think presents a sustainable view of truth and objectivity, not bettered by any subsequent pragmatist.

[...]

The core of the pragmatist conception of truth is that a true belief would be the best belief, were we to inquire as far as we could on the matter. We shall see that "best" here amounts to "best fits with all experience and argument," not the kind of "best" that other pragmatists, James and Rorty, for instance, have flirted with—consoling, best for our lives, or most comfortable. A true belief, rather, is a belief that could not be improved upon, a belief that would forever meet the challenges of reasons, argument, and evidence.

Pragmatists sometimes put this idea in the following unhelpful way: a true belief is one which would be agreed upon at the hypothetical end of inquiry. But a better characterisation is that a true belief is one that would withstand doubt, were we to inquire as far as we fruitfully could on the matter. A true belief is such that, no matter how much further we were to investigate and debate, that belief would not be overturned by recalcitrant experience and argument.

Like the unhelpful formulation, this one captures what is important in pragmatism— the idea that a true belief is one which could not be improved upon. But the new formulation is much better.[1]

First, it does not run up against the possibility that inquiry might end prematurely, with, say, the destruction of life on earth. On the unhelpful formulation, it looks as if the beliefs which would be held then must be true, which is a crazy thing for a philosopher to suggest.

Second, the new formulation does not require the pragmatist to attempt the doomed task of saying just what is meant by the hypothetical end of inquiry, cognitively ideal conditions, or perfect evidence, whatever these might be. Any attempt at articulating such notions will have to face the objection that it is a mere glorification of what we presently take to be good.[2]

And, finally, the new formulation does not mislead one into thinking that the pragmatist is a contractarian or a certain kind of deliberative democrat—someone who thinks that what is important is *agreement*, rather than being the best a belief could be.

When the new formulation is unpacked, we shall see that there is a version of pragmatism on which truth is not as fickle as Rorty supposes. A belief is not true for one culture and false for another; and a belief is not true at one time and false at another. Beliefs do not, as William James suggested, "become" true and then "become" false, as the evidence for or against them comes to light.[3]

But truth, on the best version of pragmatism, is also not quite as objective as the correspondence theorist supposes. It is not, for instance, a property that holds regardless of the possibilities for human inquiry. Since philosophy is concerned with understanding our place in the world and with understanding the status of our beliefs, this seems to me an unobjectionable feature of pragmatism. But, of course, to properly argue for this picture of philosophy would be a large undertaking in itself. Some of the points in its favour will come out below, but the reader will have to turn to Misak (1991, 1995) for more sustained arguments.

[...]

Philosophy, Practice, and Correspondence

The central thought of pragmatism is that our philosophical theories must be connected to experience and practice. A belief, hypothesis, or theory which pretends to be above experience, which thinks so well of itself that it pretends to be immune from recalcitrant experience, is spurious. I have tried elsewhere to elucidate both the semantic and the epistemological arguments in this thought's favour,[4] and here I will briefly rehearse some of the reasons why we might think that a belief must be linked to experience. For this requirement will shape our theory of truth, objectivity, and morality.

One point is about the demands of inquiry. Hypotheses, Peirce argued, ought not to block the path of inquiry. A hypothesis that had no consequences, that was severed from experience, that provided nothing on to which to latch, would be useless for inquiry. It would be, as Wittgenstein put it, a cog upon which nothing turned.

Investigation into such hypotheses is bound to be barren and to direct attention away from worthwhile pursuits.

Another is a point about belief, a point made nicely by David Wiggins. A belief aims at truth[5]—if I believe p, I believe it to be true. But if this is right, then the belief that p must be sensitive to something—something must be able to speak for or against it. If beliefs need not be sensitive to something,

> then we could not interpret beliefs by asking: How do things have to be for *this* state of mind to succeed in its aim or be correct? What does this state of mind have, *qua* the belief it is, to be differentially sensitive to?[6]

If there was nothing a belief had to be sensitive to, then we could not individuate it; we could not tell it from another. A belief has a distinguishable content only if we can "envisage finding the right sort of licence to project upon subjects" (Wiggins 1991, 151). I can interpret or come to understand a sentence which is initially unintelligible to me only by coming to see what it is responsive to. Again, the requirement which presses itself upon the theorist is that a belief must be linked to something which we can experience.

We shall see that we can accept the idea that a belief is constitutively responsive to experience without committing ourselves to anything as strong as the verificationism of the logical positivists, for the kind of experiential consequences required of various beliefs will turn out to be very broad indeed. We do not need to say, with the positivists, that only scientific beliefs meet the standard. Nonetheless, certain hypotheses will be declared spurious.

The extreme form of the inverted spectrum hypothesis, for instance, would be declared spurious on our broad criterion. The thought that my colour spectrum might be inverted from yours, so that whenever you see black, I see white, etc., is such that, no matter how much evidence we gathered and argument we engaged in, we could never tell whether the hypothesis had anything going for it. The hypothesis is such that no evidence could be relevant to it. We shall see that this is not to say that we cannot understand it at all, but just that inquiry into it would be misplaced.

I suggested at the outset of Misak (2000) that moral deliberation has many marks of objectivity—the distinction between thinking that one (or one's culture) is right and being right, the use of moral beliefs in inferences, the thought that we can discover that something is right or wrong and improve our views, and the thought that it is appropriate, or even required, that we give reasons and arguments for our beliefs, to name a few.

One additional mark of objectivity is that the practice of moral deliberation is responsive to experience, reason, argument, and thought experiments where we, for instance, place ourselves in another's shoes. Such responsiveness is part of what it is to make a moral decision and part of what it is to try to live a moral life. It wouldn't be a moral life—it would not be engaged with the complexities of moral requirements—if we simply made our decisions about how to treat others by following an oracle, or an astrologer, or the toss of the dice. Such responsiveness meets the requirement set out above—an objective area of inquiry must be such that its beliefs are sensitive to something that can speak for or against them.

Our practice of justifying moral belief speaks against the non-cognitivist. It speaks against those who do not think there is good reason to see moral belief as being objective—those who think that the best explanation of a person's moral judgements is always a story about the person's cultural background or upbringing. A reason for trying to see morals as objective is that it is part of the phenomenology of inquiry that we are obliged to take seriously.

Here we are taken back to the thought articulated in the introduction to Misak (2000)—to the idea that our philosophical theory must take seriously the picture various inquiries have of themselves. In this case, it must take account of the way in which our moral judgements are responsive to reasons. For that is a central feature of the phenomenon it wants to study—moral judgement.

Of course we must be prepared for the possibility that, as Bernard Williams thinks, "ethical thought has no chance of being everything it seems" (1985, 135). But the commitment to keeping philosophy in touch with experience and practice is such that we should not be too quick to jump to this conclusion. We shall see that we needn't reject the part of the phenomenology of moral inquiry which has us aiming at truth or at getting things right, where "right" does not merely mean "right by the lights of my group."

One point I want to draw out from the requirement that theory be connected to practice is that, on the pragmatist view, a belief requires a justification when, and only when, it has been thrown into doubt by actual inquiry. Those issues which perplex are the issues which call for justification—science's search for an effective anti-malarial drug or for a further subatomic particle, society's struggle with the question of euthanasia or abortion, etc.

Peirce argued that an inquiry begins with the irritation of doubt and ends with a stable, doubt-resistant belief. If we were to have a belief which would always be immune to doubt—which would forever fit with experience, argument, and the rest of our theories—then Peirce holds that the belief is true. But since we can never know that a belief is like that, he will tell the philosopher not to ask whether this or that belief is true, but to focus on inquiry and on getting the best answers we can to the questions that have arisen. We cannot follow Descartes and try to bring into doubt all beliefs for which error is conceivable. Such doubts would be, as Peirce argued, "paper" or "tin"— not the genuine article:[7]

> There is but one state of mind from which you can "set out," namely, the very state of mind in which you actually find yourself at the time you do "set out"—a state in which you are laden

with an immense mass of cognition already formed, of which you cannot divest yourself if you would. ... Do you call it doubting to write down on a piece of paper that you doubt? If so, doubt has nothing to do with any serious business. (CP 5.416)

This leads to a second point. The key to avoiding an unthinking preservation of the status quo cannot be to begin again. Progress-jamming conservatism, in any area of inquiry, can be avoided only by recognising it as a possibility and then by trying to stay well away from it by listening to challenges to deeply held beliefs and practices. Those challenges can come from within, when my own judgements or principles conflict and I feel a pull towards revising them. And they can come from without, when I see that the judgements and principles of others, from within my circle or from afar, conflict with my own judgements and I feel a pull towards reconsidering them. I can then revise some of those beliefs and practices while holding enough unchanged against which the revision can take place.

So on the pragmatist epistemology, justification requires a fallible background of belief which is not in fact in doubt. Only against such a background can a belief be put into doubt and a new, better, belief be adopted. All our beliefs are fallible but they come into doubt in a piecemeal fashion. Those that inquiry has not thrown into doubt are stable and warrant our belief. What this means for epistemologists is that we have no choice but to begin our theory about truth and objectivity from where we find ourselves, laden with thoughts about what counts as evidence, about what truth and objectivity are, about where agreement is difficult to purchase, etc.

The Peircean model of inquiry, as Charles Larmore has pointed out, thus gives us the wherewithal to explain how our beliefs are rooted in our history and our practices, but nonetheless can be justified. This kind of epistemology, although it is entirely general, looks especially attractive with respect to our moral judgements. Moral theory should not be seen as "a guide to eternity," whatever that might be, but as "a code for problem-solving" (Larmore 1996, 60). We can carefully set out what we think are the principles of morality, and we can put these principles to use in our lives and in our policies, but they might well undergo revision as new experience and argument comes to light.

It is important to pause here to ensure that the thought that "inquiry aims at truth" is not mischaracterised. We have in our various inquiries and deliberations a multiplicity of aims—empirical adequacy, coherence with other beliefs, simplicity, explanatory power, getting a reliable guide to action, fruitfulness for other research, greater understanding of others, increased maturity, and the like. What the pragmatist argues is that when we say that we aim at the truth, what we mean is that, if a belief really were to satisfy all of our aims in inquiry, then that belief would be true. There is nothing over and above the fulfilment of those aims, nothing metaphysical, to which we aspire. So when we say "truth is our aim in inquiry," this is a way of expressing the thought that a belief is true if it is, and would continue to be, everything we want it to be. That is what we aim at in inquiry—getting the best beliefs we can. Truth is not some transcendental, mystical thing that we aim at for its own sake. It is not the be all and end all.

Science, some will want to interject here, aspires to truth and, whereas it makes sense to have that aspiration in science, it makes no sense at all in morals and politics. But I suggest that it would be a mistake, a begging of the question, to draw a hard distinction, at the outset, between science and morals. Similarly, it would be a mistake to draw an immediate analogy between science and morals so that the results of both are lumped into the undifferentiated domain of "fact." My suggestion is that we rather look to the aspirations of our inquiries in both morals and science, and see whether and how often those aspirations might be met. We shall see that the case for aiming at truth is indeed easier to make in science, but that matters are not quite so hopeless in morals. As Dewey says:

> To frame a theory of knowledge which makes it necessary to deny the validity of moral ideas, or else to refer them to some other and separate kind of universe from that of common sense and science, is both provincial and arbitrary. The pragmatist has at least tried to face, and not to dodge, the question of how it is that moral and scientific "knowledge" can both hold of one and the same world.[8]

The final point that I want to make about the connection between philosophy and practice is that the very conception of truth which the pragmatist holds is a product of that connection. The pragmatist's view of truth keeps inquiry at the centre; it refuses to sever the link between truth and inquiry. A true belief is the best that inquiry could do; it is what we would find survives the test of experience at the end of a well-pursued inquiry.

Those views which would like to make truth something more absolute, something less concerned with the human business of inquiry, unlink the philosophical theory of truth from the practice of inquiry. They hold that truth transcends or goes beyond inquiry. Truth, says the correspondence theorist, is a relationship between a proposition[9] and the believer-independent world. And this is a relationship that holds or fails to hold whatever human beings find worthy to believe. No matter how good a belief might appear to us, no matter if it were to be as good as it could be by way of accounting for the evidence, fitting with our other beliefs, etc., it could still be false. It might fail to get right that independent reality and there might be no way we could ever have an inkling of the failure.

That, I suggest, is a spurious thought. Like the inverted spectrum hypothesis, the correspondence theory runs afoul of the requirement that theory be connected to experience. The possibility it envisions—that "p fails to correspond to reality, despite its being the best that a belief could be"—is such that nothing could speak for or against it.

A set of explanatory failures, related to its empirical emptiness, presses upon the correspondence theory as well. First, the correspondence theorist is at a loss to tell us just what it is that a true proposition is supposed to correspond to. For any attempt at articulating it involves our concepts, our sense of what is important, our background beliefs. Any attempt at articulating what the mind-independent world is like takes us away from that world.

Second, the correspondence theorist seems to lose her grip on why we should aim to get beliefs which are consistent, account for the data, have explanatory power, etc. For these desiderata are not linked—appear irrelevant—to our aim of getting beliefs which correspond to the mind-independent world. Indeed, the correspondence theorist has trouble saying that we aim at the truth. For on her view, we cannot have any access to it, cannot know when we might have it, and cannot even know when we are on the right track. In what sense, then, can we aim at it?

Peirce sums up the problems with the idea of correspondence to an unknowable "thing-in-itself":

> You only puzzle yourself by talking of this metaphysical "truth" and metaphysical "falsity" that you know nothing about. All you have any dealings with are your doubts and beliefs ... If your terms "truth" and "falsity" are taken in such senses as to be definable in terms of doubt and belief and the course of experience, well and good: in that case you are only talking about doubt and belief. But if by truth and falsity you mean something not definable in terms of doubt and belief in any way, then you are talking of entities of whose existence you can know nothing and which Ockham's razor would clean shave off. Your problems would be greatly simplified, if, instead of saying that you want to know the "Truth," you were simply to say that you want to attain a state of belief unassailable by doubt. (CP 5.416; see also 5.572)

Here we have an early statement of the now-popular thought that we must deflate the notion of truth. The metaphysician has lost sight of the connection between truth and the less glamorous notions of experience, inquiry and assertion. Quine puts the point thus:

> What on the part of true sentences is meant to correspond to what on the part of reality? If we seek a correspondence word by word, we find ourselves eking reality out with a complement of abstract objects fabricated for the sake of the correspondence. Or perhaps we settle for a correspondence of whole sentences with *facts*: a sentence is true if it reports a fact. But here again we have fabricated substance for an empty doctrine. The world is full of things, variously related, but what, in addition to that, are facts? (1987, 213)

There are those who, in the face of the difficulties for the correspondence conception of truth, advise us to deflate truth so severely that we drop the notion altogether. We shall look in some detail at such a suggestion in the next section [omitted—Eds.]. We shall see that the trouble with this view is the trouble we encountered in Rorty's position. It deprives us of the substantial notion of truth we need in order to make some rather critical distinctions in inquiry. We will thus be taken back to the thought that inquiry requires truth, but not truth as the correspondence theorist sees it. And pragmatism, I shall argue, fits the bill.

Peirce insisted that we need a conception of truth which "can and ought to be used as a guide for conduct" (MS 684, 11). We need a conception of truth which can guide inquiry and deliberation. With this in mind, he asked what we would expect of a true belief. We would expect a true belief to be consistent with other well-grounded beliefs, to fit with the data, to have explanatory power, etc. We would expect, that is, that the belief would survive the trials of inquiry; if inquiry relevant to the issue were pursued diligently, we would never want to revise that belief in light of further evidence, argument and other considerations.

The first way pragmatism delivers a notion of truth which can be used in inquiry is to give us a conception of rational belief. It closes the gap between truth and inquiry and explains why some of our current beliefs are considered rational, or more likely to be true, than other beliefs, even if we cannot know that they are true. If truth is the belief which would best fit with the evidence, were we to have so much by way of good evidence that no further evidence would overturn the belief, then a rational belief is the belief which best fits with the evidence that we currently have. If truth is what would be justified by the principles of inquiry, were inquiry to be pursued as far as it could fruitfully go, then a rational belief is one which is justified by the current principles of inquiry. There is no gap between what we take, after careful consideration, to be rational and what is rational. Although we are never in a position to judge whether a belief is true or not, we will often be in a position to judge whether it is the best belief given the current state of inquiry.

Second, unlike the correspondence theorist, the pragmatist can make sense of the fact that we aim at the truth or at the objectively correct answer. For such a belief would lie at the end of the process of inquiry of which the inquirer is a part. Truth is in principle not beyond investigation; it is in principle accessible.

It is also objective. For one thing, truth is what *would* be thought best to believe, and so it is independent, as Peirce said, of whatever "you, I, or any number of men" think; it is independent of "the vagaries of you and me."[10] Truth is connected to human inquiry (it is the best that inquiry could do), but it goes beyond any particular inquiry (it is not simply the upshot of our current best attempts).

And finally, the pragmatic view of truth can justify a methodology, thereby guiding the inquirer in her deliberations. If truth were to be the belief which would best fit with experience and argument, then if we want true beliefs, we should expose them to experience and argument which might overturn them. Better to find out now that a belief is defeated by evidence against it, rather than down the line.

So the pragmatic conception of truth is a good one for the inquirer. It makes sense of and guides practice. We must think of truth in the down-to-earth terms of what it is to assert something properly—we must think of the relationship between truth and doubt, belief, experience, and perceptual disappointment.

[...]

Bivalence

One of the most pressing difficulties for those who take the very idea of truth to be linked to evidence, or to reasons we might have for a belief, concerns the status of bivalence and the corresponding law of excluded middle. Does the pragmatist not have to say that if inquiry would not decide upon a question, then it has no answer, that "*p* is true or *p* is false" fails to hold of the candidate answers? What about the statement that Churchill sneezed exactly 45 times in 1945, a statement for which the evidence has vanished? What about Goldbach's conjecture that any even number greater than four is the sum of two primes, a conjecture which cannot be confirmed and which may never be refuted?

[...]

I have said elsewhere (1991, 1995) that [the pragmatist] should not follow those who counterfactually spruce up inquirers so that they have superhuman abilities to, say, go back in time to answer questions about the remote past. (So the statement about Churchill's sneezes is bivalent—it is true if, were we to send someone back to 1945, he would count 45 sneezes, false if he would count some other number.) If the pragmatist does that, she loses the motivation for her view; she gives up on the idea that truth must be linked to *our* practices of inquiry, belief, and assertion, were they the best they could be.

It is also important to see that the pragmatist should not connect truth to inquiry with an indicative conditional, but rather, with a subjunctive conditional. It is not that a true belief is one which *will* fit the evidence and which *will* measure up to the standards of inquiry as we now know them. Rather, a true belief is one which *would* fit with the evidence and which *would* measure up to the standards of inquiry *were* inquiry to be pursued so far that no recalcitrant experience and no revisions in the standards of inquiry would be called for. Only then will pragmatism preserve the kind of objectivity that might suffice to attract those philosophers and inquirers who insist that truth is more than what we happen to think correct.

Peirce, who struggled long and hard with the issue of bivalence, ended up with the thought that bivalence is a regulative assumption of inquiry.[11] We must, for any given question, assume that there would be an upshot to our investigations, that it would emerge either that *p* is true or that it is false. Otherwise, we simply could not explain why we inquire into the issue. Such an assumption is one which we have to make in order to make sense of our practices of deliberation, investigation, and belief. The assumption of bivalence is our practice—it is part of inquiry.

Nothing, however, about the need to assume bivalence makes it true. Peirce argued that "the only assumption upon which [we] can act rationally is the hope of success" (CE 2, 272). But he did not mean to imply that in fact there will be an upshot to our inquiries, for his point is a point about what inquirers must *hope* for if they are to make sense of their practice of inquiry. He is very clear that we are "obliged to suppose" but we "need not assert" that there are determinate answers to all our questions. The fact that an assumption is indispensable should not convince us of its truth. Unlike Habermas and Apel, Peirce sees that a necessary assumption is not a necessary truth. He compared the matter with the need to make the assumption that he has money in his account, if he is to write cheques on it. The indispensability never affected his balance in the least (CP 2.113).

He thus turned his back on the opportunity to elevate the principle of bivalence into a necessary truth:

> Logic requires us, with reference to each question we have in hand, to hope some definite answer to it may be true. That *hope* with reference to *each* case as it comes up is, by a *saltus*, stated by logicians as a law concerning *all cases,* namely the law of excluded middle. (NE iv: xiii; a saltus is a leap in argument)

We must make assumptions about inquiry "for the same reason that a general who has to capture a position or see his country ruined, must go on the hypothesis that there is some way in which he can and shall capture it" (CP 7.219).

So refusing to assume the principle of bivalence is to impede the path of inquiry and that, Peirce argues, is something we should be loath to do (CP 1.135, 7.480). The principle is necessary only in the sense that it is required if we are to make sense of doing what we do by way of inquiry and deliberation.

In the light of this thought, the pragmatist will want to make a number of points about bivalence. First, she will not deny it of any statement which is the subject of a live deliberation. Any matter which we are seriously wondering about will be such that we think there is (or might be) a truth-value to be discovered there. As Hookway (2002, chap. 5) puts it, so long as we are aware of the dangers, we can use classical logic as a tool in our inquiries, for the propositions we make use of will generally be ones for which we believe bivalence holds.

Second, the pragmatist will not require the prospect of *proof* of a statement before sense can be made of its having a truth-value. We have reason to believe that Goldbach's conjecture is true, for, hard as we try, we have not been able to refute it. If a powerful computer program were to be run on Goldbach's conjecture and were it never to turn up an even number that was not the sum of two primes, then we would have a kind of inductive support for the conjecture. Just as the fact that we can never conclusively confirm a universal generalisation does not require the pragmatist to deny that it is bivalent, the fact that we do not have proof of Goldbach's conjecture need not have us deny that it is bivalent.

Third, even in the face of the strongest claim that we will have no evidence at all for or against a statement, we can still think that bivalence holds. For questions regarding the remote past, for instance, the fact that the evidence has dried up does not alter the truth-value of the following conditional: had we been able to pursue inquiry, were we to have the relevant evidence before us, we would believe p or we would believe $-p$.[12] As Blackburn (1989) has noted, we know what would count as having evidence for or against such statements; we know that they are the sort of statement for or against which evidence can speak. Or as Migotti (1998) puts it, we know that sentences about the remote past are instances of a general kind—and that kind of sentence is verifiable.

The pragmatist thus has a number of reasons for thinking that bivalence holds of those statements for which it seems that it must hold. But, nonetheless, bivalence must not be supposed to be a principle which governs every statement. There might well be underdetermination: some matters might not be governed by the principle of bivalence and the corresponding "law" of logic, excluded middle: $(p \vee -p)$.

Perhaps there are whole discourses for which our practice is not, or should not be, assumed to be bivalent.[13] A discourse such as that about the objective tastiness of recognisably edible foodstuffs might be a domain where we think that bivalence fails to hold, where it is reasonable to think that there is only underdetermination. For any statement "x tastes good," where x is something that some human beings are known to eat, and where the asserter refuses to qualify the statement with "to me" or "to so-and-so," we cannot say that the statement is either true or false.[14] The realist, not being able to avail himself of any hidden indexicality, will not want to say it, thinking that there is no fact that makes it true. The pragmatist will not want to say it, thinking that no amount of inquiry would settle on the right answer.

Perhaps there are also cases of genuine underdetermination in discourses where bivalence can be generally assumed to hold. Perhaps the question about whether light is a wave or a particle is such that there would be no univocal right answer.

Vagueness too interferes with the smooth holding of bivalence: "Cheryl Misak is a junior faculty member" might seem neither true nor false, as "junior" is a vague concept. So too may bivalence seem to fail of those statements which are such that by their very nature they are insulated from evidence. Statements such as "being nothings nothing," "the world and everything in it, including fossils and memories, was created five minutes ago," and "my colour spectrum is an exact inversion of yours" are such that nothing *could* speak for or against them.

[...]

Convergence and the End of Inquiry

It is supposed to be a pillar of the pragmatist position that our beliefs would converge in some kind of ideal limit of inquiry. We have seen that we can quiet some worries about that ideal limit by reformulating the pragmatic maxim in terms of beliefs that could not be improved, rather than beliefs we would converge upon under certain conditions. But even when that is cleared up, the idea of convergence can be responsible for much misunderstanding and subsequent dismissal of pragmatism. Quine has suggested, for instance, that Peircean pragmatism takes the notion of successive approximation, which is defined for numbers, and hopelessly tries to apply it to theories (1960, 23; 1981, 31). I want to make it clear, by running interference on some confusions, just what ought to be meant by the claim that a true belief is one which we would agree upon.

The pragmatist takes correct judgement not to be a matter for the individual, even though it is the individual who does the judging, but as a matter for the community of inquirers. Peirce was adamant that the "Cartesian Criterion"—"Whatever I am clearly convinced of is true"—makes individuals judges of truth, which is "most pernicious" (CE 2, 212). But this is not supposed to be the thought that the community is the epistemic agent—that it is the community which does the knowing or which has the beliefs, so to speak. Individuals are the possessors of belief, but whether or not a person's belief is correct is a matter of what the community would determine. What fits with *my* experience is not of paramount importance as far as truth is concerned. What is important is what fits with all the experience that would be available, what the community of inquirers would converge upon. A hallucination, Peirce says, is a compulsion which does "not fit into the general mass of experience" (CP 7.647).

One misconception about this community-based view of truth arises with respect to how the force of experience is supposed to encourage convergence. It might be right to say the following kinds of things. If we find that a person feels nothing for the plight of battered women, then taking him to a shelter for women where he can see for himself, as it were, how women experience battering, is something which we think ought to compel him to think differently. And we think that someone who is unmoved by the suffering of those under her employ in, say, apartheid South Africa is missing a moral cog—her failure to be compelled by the experience of others speaks against her.

But we should not leap from these thoughts to the idea that we will in fact be compelled so frequently by the experience of others that we will converge in our opinions. That is not what is meant by experience being compelling. We will often improve our views by taking into account what other people find compelling. But this does not entail that there is one set of beliefs to which we will all gravitate.

There is also a clutch of misconceptions which begin with a failure to notice that it is *only* the methodology that we ought to take seriously the experience of others (the democratic methodology, if you like), which is justified at the level of theory. The pragmatist should not be interested in setting out a list of standards for inquiry, standards which will make convergence likely. The pragmatist, at this level of abstraction, must remain agnostic about the details as to how inquiry (of any kind) should go. She will say that inquirers must expose themselves to new evidence, argument, and perspectives. For if truth is that which would best fit with the evidence and argument, were inquiry to have proceeded as far as it could fruitfully go, then the best way to inquire about the truth is to take in as much and as varied evidence and argument as one can.

Beyond that general principle, the methodological principles and standards of rationality which are best are those standards which would evolve, were inquiry to be diligently pursued. Those standards might turn out to be very different from what now gets counted as rational.[15] In science the standards will be set by scientists and those few historians and philosophers of science who have an impact on actual inquiry. In morals, the standards will be set by those engaged in moral inquiry. This does not mean only, or even mainly, philosophers, "experts" who sit on ethics boards in hospitals, and those novelists and essayists who engage particular issues. As feminists have stressed, we must not underestimate the value of listening to ordinary people's own *stories*— their accounts of how injustice, for instance, has played a part in their lives.

Perhaps this is the flip side of the fact that there is so much underdetermination in ethics. Moral deliberation displays a kind of epistemological democracy. We are all involved in moral discussion and in experiments in living, to borrow a phrase from Mill. Moral judgement is inextricably bound up with our relations to others and anyone who stands in such relationships has plenty of engagement in moral deliberation. Truth requires us to listen to others, and anyone might be an expert.

This, of course, does not mean that everyone is equally good at seeing when something is kind, unjust, or phoney. It just means that anyone, whatever their formal training, might be very good at it. One suspects that good novelists[16] are amongst the best, but so might the man on the Clapham omnibus.

Indeed, there is some reason to be suspicious of experts in morals and politics. As Dewey said, experts may well become "so removed from common interests as to become a class with private interests" themselves and not at all good at arriving at the best judgements in social matters (1976, 245). Ian Shapiro adds to this that purported knowledge about politics is regularly undermined by events and usually the experts turn out to be on somebody's side after all (1996, 128–129).

The point that only the general democratic methodological principle can be justified by a philosophical argument is important. Failure to attend to it can put the radical democratic core of pragmatism at risk. This is what is wrong, I think, with a certain interpretation of Hilary Putnam's pragmatism. Putnam, in *Reason, Truth and History*, argued that truth is what would be believed by an ideally rational inquirer. Brian Ellis, taking this ball and running with it, argues that we need the concept of an ideally rational being not only in order to "define how people would think if they were ideally rational," but also to serve as a "regulative ideal ... to tell us how we ought rationally to think." We may never realise the ideal, but nonetheless, we are somehow to construct the ideal out of what we currently take to be rational. For in arriving at a model of rationality, the "ideal of rationality ... should appeal to the normal intellect as a rational ideal" (1990, 235).

But there is too much emphasis here on what seems natural, or normal. If we earmark certain (fallible) claims about what is good by way of belief and glorify them by making them part of the ideal, the danger is that we will confirm our prejudices and block the path of inquiry. We must not take for granted the system of epistemic value which is now taken to be the best. The open-endedness of inquiry and the commitment to taking other perspectives seriously must be preserved if we are to have any hope of reaching beliefs which really do account for all experiences and argument. For surely what strikes the "normal" intellect, or the scientific intellect, or even the best intellect around, as epistemically valuable is not guaranteed to be valuable.

So the pragmatist must be careful not to suggest that the way in which we are converging on the truth is that we are getting closer and closer to some specified ideal. In suggesting that, he seems sure to get the ideal wrong. Pragmatism is not a view about the standards of our present human practices. We must not identify an ideally rational person with what we now take to be a good inquirer. Nor must we identify an ideally rational person with the scientist. Not only has science often failed to live up to its own ideals, but we do not know that those ideals will remain the same. Our standards even there evolve and we can never reach a point where we can say that they are fully evolved.

Indeed after the moral horrors of this century, surely no one will even want to say that we are marching forward in this domain—that we are getting closer to the truth. This should not prevent us from thinking that here and there we have made improvements, corrections, and progress, as opposed to changes in whim or fashion.

Of course, in making judgements about what is rational to believe, we cannot help but use the standards we presently think best. But again, we must be prepared for the possibility of a revision of those standards. The pragmatist, being a fallibilist, will leave room for radical revision of our methodological principles and this room will be made by paying attention to the views of those outside the mainstream. If there are standards and values that are characteristic of some group or other, they must be a part of this dialectic. It is not just the participants of a practice who must be heard. Those who would like to participate, but are barred, those affected directly or indirectly by the practice, and those who simply react to what they perceive in a distant practice also have something to say. We must be open to learning from them.

We also should not think that one set of standards will certainly emerge as best. As Ian Hacking (1982) has gone so far to show, there are different styles of reasoning and it might be agreed that various styles are suitable for various inquiries. We might even be prepared for the possibility that some styles of inquiry are most prominent in a certain kind of inquirer. It has been suggested, for instance, by some feminists, that women and men have different ways of approaching a problem.

So on the pragmatist view, we will not turn to the notion of an ideally rational inquirer to settle our debates. The view of truth offered here is not a version of the ideal spectator position, on which the truth is what a certain kind of ideal spectator, in ideal circumstances, would take to be true. For we have seen that we cannot fill in the details about what an ideal spectator would be like (impartial, sympathetic, utilitarian, interested in simplicity, or whatever) and then settle our debates by asking how such a spectator would settle them.

We must be careful with the Peircean notion of the end of inquiry. It is not some God's-eye view, where, if we could only guess what God (or whoever else occupies the view) would see, we would have the truth and a foundation for knowledge. Rather it is the down-to-earth view which involves the outcome of our actual human practices, if they were to be informed the best they could by evidence and argument. Sensitivity to context and situations will be a primary feature of moral inquiry. We must settle our debates the best we know how, paying careful attention to the particulars of situations, with the assumption that, were inquiry to be pursued as far as it could fruitfully go, there would be a best answer which would make itself apparent.

That "would" is of crucial importance. We have to pay special attention to Peirce's insistence that the expectations of a true belief be expressed with a subjunctive, not an indicative, conditional. We expect that a true belief is one which *would be* right to believe, were inquiry to have progressed (by way of evidence, argument, and standards) as far as it could fruitfully go. A true belief is not one that *is* now agreed to be best. If this point is missed, pragmatism turns into something that no one should want to hold.[17]

Despite the emphasis on this subjunctive, the end of inquiry is not to be pictured as some point in the future, where we would find ourselves with perfect and complete evidence. Neither is it to be pictured as a body of statements that constitutes the complete truth, a body where every statement is assigned a determinate truth-value. Truth is a regulative ideal of inquiry, and as Dorothy Emmet puts it, a regulative ideal differs significantly from an utopian blueprint (1994, 47ff). A blueprint, such as Marxism, is thought to be in principle realisable, but in fact unrealised. A regulative ideal, on the other hand, is not thought to be realisable. Its role is to set a direction and provide a focus of criticism for actual arrangements.

This brings me to the last thing that I want to say about convergence and the end of inquiry. Although all moral judgements may aspire to truth, not all will attain it. This does not entail that truth and falsity fail to apply to moral discourse; it does not entail that moral discourse is not truth-apt. Our deliberations in morals and politics are, I want to argue, regulated or governed by standards of correct and incorrect assertion—standards of when we have got something right and when we have made a mistake. It is important to see, however, that our discourse can measure itself by such standards, can be disciplined, without every case admitting of a right answer.

Again, the pragmatist must keep a cool head about convergence. A statement's being true is not a matter of its being such that every person would come to believe it under the right circumstances. And a discourse or an area of inquiry admits of truth not when we can expect convergence about every statement in that discourse. Rather, convergence enters into the pragmatist's account of truth as a way to mark the thought that a belief is true if it would be found to be the belief which would forever best account for all the experience and argument. The pragmatist says, loosely, that we would agree upon, or converge upon, the best belief. But the pragmatic account of truth is very tolerant of disagreement. It does not suggest that the reasons offered in the deliberative process must be ultimately acceptable or convincing to all.[18]

We can turn much of the current talk of convergence on its head. The expectation of convergence is a regulative assumption of inquiry—it, like its more formal partner, the principle of bivalence, has, in Simon Blackburn's phrase, imperative force (1993, 25). It tells us what to look for, what to hope for, of our practice. It requires us to keep looking for reasons, despite the fact that we might expect, in a discourse such as that of morals and politics, that there would be countless underdetermined beliefs.

As Joe Heath (1998) argues, we should not think of ourselves as examining a given discourse to see whether it is objective; to see whether it is about the world; to see whether the world here produces convergence of belief. Rather, the expectation of convergence is a normative presupposition of inquiry, differing in strength as our needs for convergence differ. The assumption, that is, presses itself on our practice more in some cases and less in others.

Heath suggests that one discourse which imposes a strong convergence constraint on participants is discourse about physical or natural events. We need to expect convergence here, we work hard in order to align our beliefs, because that is required if we are to interact or coordinate our actions with others. If we are going to have reasonable beliefs about how others will behave, we need to expect that we all assign pretty much the same probability to events.

In legal argument, too, the belief in an objective physical reality is maintained in the face of evidence to the contrary—contradictory accounts of what happened, for instance.[19] The assumption made by a traffic court that there is a single correct story about what caused a traffic accident is an assumption which here exerts a firm regulative grip on practice. It is taken to be unfalsifiable and the failure to maintain it is subject to various forms of social control. We wonder about the sanity of someone who thinks that contradictory descriptions of an accident are both in fact correct. That is just not how we think of "what happened."

We are not talking here of a case where two narratives can be correct in a "duck-rabbit" kind of way, where if you look at the picture one way you see it as a duck and if you look at it another way, you see it as a rabbit. When two narratives conflict about whether or not the car jumped the curb, we assume that only one can be correct. Because of the expectation that we can converge on a correct answer to our question, we pursue the inquiry. The expectation comes first and is in part responsible for the degree of convergence that follows.

Beliefs about moral requirements also command a high expectation of convergence. Heath points out that with migration and increased communication and transport, we find pressure for standardisation or convergence of our practices. In order for social interaction to go smoothly, it will often be important to share values (such as respect for persons).

With respect to desire, there is less call for agreement. We must share a vocabulary of what it is to have a motive, intention, and the like, but our actual motives and intentions can diverge without presenting too many difficulties. And where agreement is less important, where the norm of convergence is less a presupposition, we can happily agree to disagree.

We have seen, in our discussion of Habermas and Apel [in Misak (2000)], that this kind of point must be kept in its place. The expectation of convergence—the expectation that there is a truth of the matter—might be necessary to maintain a particular practice of inquiry, but it is not for that reason necessarily right. A practice might be entirely wrongheaded. Or we might find that we have an *unreasonable* expectation of convergence—we might find that our hopes are dashed with respect to a domain of inquiry and we have to revise our expectations and our practice. Preserving our regulative assumptions, preserving those thoughts without which we could not go on, does not entail that they are true. That we cannot imagine circumstances under which the need for them might disappear is not decisive. Even our methodological assumptions can be up for grabs, as can the best belief at any stage in inquiry.

The pragmatist, however, is set on exploring the other option—on making the best case for our expectation that moral inquiry is disciplined and properly aimed at truth. My attempt at an epistemology that respects the aspirations of morals has been as follows. We engage in the practice of scientific, mathematical, and moral inquiry. Each has its evolving standards of criticism and evaluation and each has a kind of experience most relevant to it. This experience, and the possibility of clashes with other sorts of judgements, constitutes a domain of evidence that could be for or against a hypothesis. The fact that the branch of inquiry in question is responsive to experience in part justifies our belief that it aims at the truth.

There are differences, to be sure, between the three inquiries and the prospect of judgements in some inquiries commanding consensus differ from those of others. But this should not lead us to think that science, say, is the sort of thing that might achieve a correspondence with an independent reality, for no thing is that sort of thing. Scientific hypotheses are laden with our concepts and theories—they are part of our attempt to make sense of what impinges upon us. The same holds for moral beliefs. We are in both cases adrift on Neurath's boat. We have our practices and their standards of success. To borrow an apt phrase from Wiggins, in prosecuting those practices, "we shall reach wherever we reach, for such reasons as seem good and appropriate" ([1987] 1991, 207). And if we were to reach a stage where we could no longer improve upon a belief, there is no point in withholding the title "true" from it.

In addition, and against Rorty, there is a point in thinking that we aim at true beliefs. For, as Peirce argues, an assumption of inquiry into any matter is that there is a hope of reaching the truth. Without the hope that there is an answer to the question at hand, there would be no point in debate or investigation. If we are to leave the path of inquiry unobstructed, we must assume that there is a truth of the matter with respect to the issue we are investigating. Those contemporary pragmatists who would replace the notion of truth with that of warranted assertion betray their commitment to taking seriously the practices of inquirers, who take their business to be that of trying to reach true beliefs.

Notes

1. Sometimes in Misak (1991), I expressed the pragmatic account of truth in the unhelpful way. This was partly because I was trying to address the standard objections to pragmatism and partly because I did not see just how resolutely one should stick to the better formulation.

2. For an extended argument along these lines, see Misak (1992).

3. See James ([1907] 1992, 100) and Misak (1994) for discussion.

4. Misak (1995), especially pp. 97–127, 152–162, and 171–178.

5. For the idea that belief involves the commitment to fact, reality and truth, see Wiggins (1998). See also Haack (1995, 199ff.; 1998). There will of course be nuances here—for instance we aim at interesting truth, not at trivial truth.

6. Wiggins (1991, 148); see Peacocke (1992, 203) for a similar thought.

7. MS 329, 12.

8. Dewey ([1908] 1977, 131–132). Dewey sometimes argued that we should carry out the method of science in other areas of inquiry but, as Richardson (1998) argues, Dewey wavered on this point.

9. Or a sentence or a statement. I take the bearers of truth-values to be the contents of beliefs or claims, but will sometimes drop "the belief that" or "the claim that." And, given the holistic nature of justification, inquiry into p will involve inquiry into many other issues.

10. CE 2, 239. This is not unlike McDowell's (1985) account of objectivity, where to be objective is to be independent of any particular experience, but not independent of all experience. Values are values to a sensibility like ours.

11. Blackburn (1989) also makes this suggestion. We have seen, and shall continue to see, that moral knowledge need not take as its model scientific inquiry—it need not see itself as always trying to ascertain whether a hypothesis is true or false. In morals, we may want—as a part of getting the best belief about what is right or wrong, just or unjust—greater self-understanding, greater maturity, etc. Because these aims are a part of seeking the best belief, bivalence still holds as a regulative assumption. It is still assumed that there is a belief which would be best.

12. Similarly, where the evidence is misleading or is caused in the wrong way, we can invoke the above conditional to make sense of the thought that the true belief is not the one we happen to get stuck with, but the one which would be best, were inquiry to proceed smoothly. This way of

coping with statements about the remote past is an improvement on my treatment in (1991), where I focused exclusively on the idea of bivalence being a regulative assumption.

13. Given the connection between bivalence and the law of excluded middle, we must then say that logic here is not classical. However, it would be more than a little odd to try to suggest that, for these discourses, excluded middle is not a logical law, while in others it is. Perhaps the pragmatist here can reject, *tout court*, excluded middle as a logical law (and adopt an intuitionist logic), but then reinstate it in most discourses as a theorem. So in most areas of inquiry—in most of our inferences—we could use excluded middle. With respect to conditionals with antecedents from one discourse and consequents from another, we could not use it. Joe Heath suggested this line of argument to me.

14. That refusal is important, for if it is not made, the disquotationalist has plenty of resources with which to render "*x* tastes good" bivalent. Notice also that the pragmatist might think that a discourse about the objective tastiness of non-edible stuff has sufficient discipline to be truth-apt. "Petrol tastes good" might well have a truth-value.

15. Railton (1996, 74) argues, in a spirit similar to that of the view I set out here, that a moral judgement is true if it would be approved by people in general under conditions of full information, impartiality and the like. "Full information" and "impartiality," he says, are vague and indeterminate—under one resolution *p* would be true, under another, *p* would be false. Railton sees no great problem here, for vagueness and indeterminacy are features of all our beliefs. "There is milk in the fridge" is true if you count the old spill, false if you do not.

16. Of course, good novelists and good novels needn't be moral. But even when a character or a theme in a novel exemplifies an evil, it can get us thinking—it can prompt moral reflection.

17. The point also deals with objections which ask what the pragmatist says about the possibility of a nuclear holocaust or mass hypnosis, freezing, as it were, a set of beliefs. Are those beliefs true just because they in fact will not be improved upon? The pragmatist says that, in such cases, the antecedent of the subjunctive conditional "were inquiry to be pursued as far as it could fruitfully go, *p* would be agreed upon" would not be fulfilled. That makes no difference to the truth-value of the conditional.

18. See the papers in Bohman and Rehg (1997) for how this thought is often present in contemporary deliberative democracy theorists.

19. Heath takes this point from Melvin Pollner's (1987) study of legal argument. Pollner also suggests that whether or not a person is guilty is assumed to be an objective matter.

References

Blackburn, S. 1989. "Manifesting Realism." In P. French et al., eds., *Midwest Studies in Philosophy* 14(1): 29–47. Minneapolis: University of Minnesota Press.

Blackburn, S. 1993. "Truth, Realism and the Regulation of Theory." In *Essays in Quasi-realism*, 15–34. Oxford: Oxford University Press.

Bohman, J., and Rehg, W., eds. 1997. *Deliberative Democracy: Essays on Reason and Politics*. Cambridge, MA: MIT Press.

Dewey, J. 1976. *The Moral Writings of John Dewey*. Edited by J. Gouinlock. New York: Macmillan.

Dewey, J. (1908) 1977. "Does Reality Possess Practical Character?" In J. A. Boydston, ed., *John Dewey: The Middle Works, 1899–1924*, vol. 4. Carbondale: Southern Illinois University Press.

Ellis, B. 1990. *Truth and Objectivity*. Oxford: Blackwell.

Emmet, D. 1994. *The Role of the Unrealisable*. London: Macmillan.

Haack, S. 1995. *Evidence and Inquiry: Towards Reconstruction in Epistemology*. Oxford: Blackwell.

Haack, S. 1998. "Confessions of an Old-Fashioned Prig." In *Manifesto of a Passionate Moderate: Unfashionable Essays*, 7–30. Chicago: University of Chicago Press.

Hacking, I. 1982. "Language, Truth and Reason." In M. Hollis and S. Lukes, eds., *Rationality and Relativism*, 48–66. Oxford: Basil Blackwell.

Heath, J. 1998. "A Pragmatist Theory of Convergence." In C. Misak, ed., "Pragmatism," special issue, *Canadian Journal of Philosophy* 28, suppl. 1: 149–175.

Hookway, C. 2002. *Truth, Rationality and Pragmatism: Themes from Peirce*. Oxford: Oxford University Press.

James, W. (1907) 1992. "Pragmatism: A New Name for some Old Ways of Thinking." In D. Olin, ed., *William James: Pragmatism in Focus*, 13–142. London: Routledge.

Larmore, C. 1996. *The Morals of Modernity*. Cambridge: Cambridge University Press.

McDowell, J. 1985. "Values and Secondary Qualities." In T. Honderich, ed., *Morality and Objectivity: A Tribute to John Mackie*, 110–129. London: Routledge and Kegan Paul.

Migotti, M. 1998. "Peirce's Double-Aspect Theory of Truth." In C. Misak, ed., "Pragmatism," special issue, *Canadian Journal of Philosophy* 28, suppl. 1: 75–108.

Misak, C. 1991. *Truth and the End of Inquiry: A Peircean Account of Truth*. Oxford: Clarendon Press.

Misak, C. 1992. "Critical Notice of B. Ellis: *Truth and Objectivity*." *Canadian Journal of Philosophy* 22: 3.

Misak, C. 1994. "Pragmatism in Focus." *Studies in the History and Philosophy of Science* 25: 1.

Misak, C. 1995. *Verificationism: Its History and Prospects*. London: Routledge.

Misak, C. 2000. *Truth, Politics, Morality: Pragmatism and Deliberation*. London: Routledge.

Peacocke, C. 1992. *A Study of Concepts*. Cambridge, MA: MIT Press.

Peirce, C. S. 1931–1958. [CP]. *Collected Papers of Charles Sanders Peirce*. 8 vols. Vols. 1–6, edited by C. Hartshorne and P. Weiss. Cambridge, MA: Harvard University Press, 1931–1935. Vols. 7–8, edited by A. Burks. Cambridge, MA: Harvard University Press, 1958.

Peirce, C. S. 1963. [MS]. The Charles S. Peirce Papers. 30 reels of microfilm. The Houghton Library, Harvard University Library Microreproduction Service, Harvard University, Cambridge, MA.

Peirce, C. S. 1976. [NE]. *The New Elements of Mathematics*. Edited by C. Eislie. The Hague: Mouton.

Peirce, C. S. 1982–1986. [CE]. *Writings of Charles S. Peirce: A Chronological Edition*. 4 vols. Vol. 1, edited by M. H. Fish et al. Bloomington: Indiana University Press, 1982. Vol. 2, edited by E. C. Moore et al. Bloomington: Indiana University Press, 1982. Vols. 3 and 4, edited by C. J. W. Kloesel. Bloomington: Indiana University Press, 1986.

Pollner, M. 1987. *Mundane Reason*. Cambridge: Cambridge University Press.

Quine, W. V. O. 1960. *Word and Object*. Cambridge, MA: MIT Press.

Quine, W. V. O. 1981. "The Pragmatist's Place in Empiricism." In R. Mulvaney and P. Zeltner, eds., *Pragmatism: Its Sources and Prospects*, 21–39. Columbia: University of South Carolina Press.

Quine, W. V. O. 1987. *Quiddities: An Intermittently Philosophical Dictionary*. Cambridge, MA: Harvard University Press.

Railton, P. 1996. "Moral Realism: Prospects and Problems." In W. Sinnott-Armstrong and M. Timmons, eds., *Moral Knowledge? New Readings in Moral Epistemology*, 49–81. Oxford: Oxford University Press.

Richardson, H. 1998. "Truth and Ends in Dewey's Pragmatism." In C. Misak, ed., "Pragmatism," special issue, *Canadian Journal of Philosophy* 28, suppl. 1: 109–147.

Shapiro, I. 1996. *Democracy's Place*, Ithaca, NY: Cornell University Press.

Wiggins, D. (1987) 1991. "A Sensible Subjectivism?" In *Needs, Values, Truth*, 2nd ed., 185–214. Oxford: Basil Blackwell.

Wiggins, D. 1991. "Truth, and Truth as Predicated of Moral Judgements." In *Needs, Values, Truth*, 2nd ed., 139–184. Oxford: Basil Blackwell.

Wiggins, D. 1998. "C. S. Peirce: Belief, Truth, and Going from the Known to the Unknown." In C. Misak, ed., "Pragmatism," special issue, *Canadian Journal of Philosophy* 28, suppl. 1: 9–29.

Williams, B. 1985. *Ethics and the Limits of Philosophy*. Cambridge, MA: Harvard University Press.

11 Truth

Michael Dummett

Frege held that truth and falsity are the references of sentences. Sentences cannot stand for propositions (what Frege calls thoughts), since the reference of a complex expression depends only on the reference of its parts; whereas if we substitute for a singular term occurring in a sentence another singular term with the same reference but a different sense, the sense of the whole sentence, i.e., the thought which it expresses, changes. The only thing which it appears *must* in these circumstances remain unchanged is the truth-value of the sentence. The expressions is true and is false look like predicates applying to propositions, and one might suppose that truth and falsity were properties of propositions; but it now appears that the relation between a proposition and its truth-value is not like that between a table and its shape, but rather like that between the sense of a definite description and the actual object for which it stands.

To the objection that there are non-truth-functional occurrences of sentences as parts of complex sentences, e.g., clauses in indirect speech, Frege replies that in such contexts we must take ordinary singular terms as standing, not for their customary reference, but for their sense, and hence we may say that in such a context, and only then, a sentence stands for the proposition it usually expresses.

If someone asks, "But what kind of entities are these truth-values supposed to be?" we may reply that there is no more difficulty in seeing what the truth-value of a sentence may be than there is in seeing what the direction of a line may be; we have been told when two sentences have the same truth-value—when they are materially equivalent—just as we know when two lines have the same direction—when they are parallel.

Nor need we waste time on the objection raised by Max Black that on Frege's theory certain sentences become meaningful which we should not normally regard as such, e.g., "If oysters are inedible, then the False." If sentences stand for truth-values, but there are also expressions standing for truth-values which are not sentences, then the objection to allowing expressions of the latter kind to stand wherever sentences can stand and vice versa is grammatical, not logical. We often use the word "thing" to provide a noun where grammar demands one and we have only an adjective, e.g., in "That was a disgraceful thing to do"; and we could introduce a verb, say "trues," to fulfil the purely grammatical function of converting a noun standing for a truth-value into a sentence standing for the same truth-value. It may be said that Frege has proved that a sentence does not ordinarily stand for a proposition, and has given a plausible argument that *if* sentences have references, they stand for truth-values, but that he has done nothing to show that sentences do have references at all. This is incorrect; Frege's demonstration that the notions of a concept (property) and a relation can be explained as special cases of the notion of a function provides a plausible argument for saying that sentences have a reference.

What *is* questionable is Frege's use of the words "truth" and "falsity" as names of the references of sentences; for by using these words rather than invented words of his own he gives the impression that by taking sentences to have a reference, with material equivalence as the criterion of identity, he has given an account of the notions of truth and falsity which we are accustomed to employ. Let us compare truth and falsity with the winning and losing of a board game. For a particular game we may imagine first formulating the rules by specifying the initial position and the permissible moves; the game comes to an end when there is no permissible move. We may then distinguish between two (or three) kinds of final positions, which we call Win (meaning that the player to make the first move wins), Lose (similarly), and, possibly, "Draw." Unless we tacitly appeal to the usual meanings of the words "win," "lose" and "draw," this description leaves out one vital point—that it is the object of a player to win. It is part of the concept of winning a game that a player plays to win, and this part of the concept is not conveyed by a classification of the end positions into winning ones and losing ones. We can imagine a variant of chess in which it is the object of each player to be checkmated, and this would be an entirely different game; but the formal description we imagined would coincide with the formal description of chess. The whole theory of chess could be formulated with reference only to the formal description; but which theorems of this theory interested us would depend upon whether we wished to play chess or the variant game. Likewise, it is part of the concept of truth that we aim at making true statements; and Frege's theory of truth and falsity as the references of sentences leaves this feature of the concept of truth quite out of account. Frege indeed tried to bring it in afterwards, in his theory of assertion—but too late; for the sense of the sentence is not given in advance of our going in for the activity of asserting, since otherwise there could be people who expressed the same thoughts but went in instead for denying them.

A similar criticism applies to many accounts of truth and falsity or of the meanings of certain sentences in terms of truth and falsity. We cannot in general suppose that we give a proper account of a concept by describing those circumstances in which we do, and those in which we do not, make use of the relevant word, by describing the *usage* of that word; we must also give an account of the *point* of the concept, explain what we use the word *for*. Classifications do not exist in the void, but are connected always with some interest which we have, so that to assign something to one class or another will have consequences connected with this interest. A clear example is the problem of justifying a form of argument, deductive or inductive. Classification of arguments into (deductively or inductively) valid and invalid ones is not a game played merely for its own sake, although it *could* be taught without reference to any purpose or interest, say as a school exercise. Hence there is really a problem of showing that the criteria we employ for recognizing valid arguments do in fact serve the purpose we intend them to serve: the problem is not to be dismissed—as it has long been fashionable to do—by saying that we use the criteria we use.

We cannot assume that a classification effected by means of a predicate in use in a language will always have just *one* point. It may be that the classification of statements into true ones, false ones, and, perhaps, those that are neither true nor false, has one principal point, but that other subsidiary ends are served by it which make the use of the words "true" and "false" more complex than it would otherwise be. At one time it was usual to say that we do not call ethical statements true or false, and from this many consequences for ethics were held to flow. But the question is not whether these words are in practice applied to ethical statements, but whether, if they were so applied, the point of doing so would be the same as the point of applying them to statements of other kinds, and, if not, in what ways it would be different. Again, to be told that we say of a statement containing a singular term which lacks reference that it is neither true nor false is so far only to be informed of a point of usage; no philosophical consequences can yet be drawn. Rather, we need to ask whether describing such a statement as neither true nor false accords better with the general point of classifying statements as true or false than to describe it as false. Suppose that we learn that in a particular language such statements are described as "false": how are we to tell whether this shows that they use such statements differently from ourselves or merely that "false" is not an exact translation of their word? To say that we use singular statements in such a way that they are neither true nor false when the subject has no reference is meant to characterize our use of singular statements; hence it ought to be possible to describe when in a language not containing words for "true" and "false" singular statements would be used in the same way as we use them, and when they would be used so as to be false when the subject had no reference. Until we have an account of the general point of the classification into true and false we do not know what interest attaches to saying of certain statements that they are neither true nor false; and until we have an account of how the truth-conditions of a statement determine its meaning the description of the meaning by stating the truth-conditions is valueless.

A popular account of the meaning of the word "true," also driving from Frege, is that ⌜It is true that P⌝ has the same sense as the sentence P. If we then ask why it is any use to have the word "true" in the language, the answer is that we often refer to propositions indirectly, i.e., without expressing them, as when we say "Goldbach's conjecture" or "what the witness said." We also generalize about propositions without referring to any particular one, e.g., in "Everything he says is true." This explanation cannot rank as a definition in the strict sense, since it permits elimination of is true only when it occurs attached to a "that"-clause, and not when attached to any other expression standing for a proposition or to a variable; but, since every proposition can be expressed by a sentence, this does not refute its claim to be considered as determining uniquely the sense of is true. It might be compared with the recursive definition of "+," which enables us to eliminate the sign "+" only when it occurs in front of a numeral, and not when it occurs in front of any other expression for a number or in front of a variable; yet there is a clear mathematical sense in which it specifies uniquely what operation+is to signify. Similarly, our explanation of is true determines uniquely the sense, or at least the application, of this predicate: for any given proposition there is a sentence expressing that proposition, and that sentence states the conditions under which the proposition is true.

If, as Frege thought, there exist sentences which express propositions but are neither true nor false, then this explanation appears incorrect. Suppose that P contains a singular term which has a sense but no reference: then, according to Frege, P expresses a proposition which has no truth-value. This proposition is therefore not true, and hence the statement ⌜It is true that P⌝ will be *false*. P will therefore not have the same sense as ⌜It is true that P⌝, since the latter is false while the former is not. It is not possible to plead that ⌜It is true that P⌝ is itself neither true nor false when the singular term occurring in P lacks a reference, since the *oratio obliqua* clause ⌜that P⌝ stands for the proposition expressed by P, and it is admitted that P does have a sense and express a proposition; the singular term occurring in P has in ⌜It is true that P⌝ its indirect reference, namely its sense, and we assumed that it did have a sense. In general, it will always be inconsistent to maintain the truth of every instance of "It is true that *p* if and only if *p*" while allowing that there is a type of sentence which under certain conditions is neither true nor false. It would be possible to evade this objection by claiming that the "that"-clause in a sentence beginning "It is true that" is not an instance of *oratio obliqua*; that the word "that" here serves the purely grammatical function of transforming a sentence into a nounclause without altering either its sense or its reference. We should then have to take phrases like "Goldbach's conjecture" and "what the witness said" as standing not for propositions but for truth-values. The expression "is true" would then be exactly like the verb "trues" which we imagined earlier; it would simply convert a noun-phrase standing for a truth-value into a sentence without altering its sense or its reference. It might be objected that this variant of Frege's account tallies badly with his saying that it is the *thought* (proposition) which is what is true or false; but we can express this point of Frege's by saying that it is the *thought*, rather than the *sentence*, which primarily stands for a truth-value. A stronger objection to the variant account is that it leans heavily on the theory of truth-values as references of sentences, while the original version depends only on the more plausible view that clauses in indirect speech stand for propositions. In any case, if there are meaningful sentences which say nothing which is true or false, then there must be *a* use of the word true which applies to propositions; for if we say ⌜It is neither true nor false that P⌝, the clause ⌜that P⌝ must here be in *oratio obliqua*, otherwise the whole sentence would lack a truth-value.

Even if we do not wish to say of certain statements that they are neither true nor false, this account cannot give the *whole* meaning of the word true. If we are to give an explanation of the word false parallel to our explanation of true we shall have to say that ⌜It is false that P⌝ has the same sense as the negation of P. In logical symbolism there exists a sign which, put in front of a sentence, forms the negation of that sentence; but in natural languages we do not have such a sign. We have to think to realize that the negation of "No-one is here" is not "No-one is not here" but "Someone is here"; there is no one rule for forming the negation of a given sentence. Now according to what principle do we recognize one sentence as the negation of another? It is natural to answer: The negation of a sentence P is that sentence which is true if and only if P is false and false if and only if P is true. But this explanation is ruled out if we want to use the notion of the negation of a sentence in order to explain the sense of the word "false." It would not solve the difficulty if we did have a general sign of negation analogous to the logical symbol, for the question would then be: How in general do we determine the sense of the negation, given the sense of the original sentence?

We encounter the same difficulty over the connective "or." We can give an account of the meaning of "and" by saying that we are in a position to assert ⌜P and Q⌝ when and only when we are in a position to assert P and in a position to assert Q. (This is not circular: one could train a dog to bark only when a bell rang *and* a light shone without presupposing that it possessed the concept of conjunction.) But, if we accept a two-valued logic, we cannot give a similar explanation of the meaning of "or." We often assert ⌜P or Q⌝ when we are not either in a position to assert P or in a position to assert Q. I use the word "we" here, meaning mankind, advisedly. If the history master gives the schoolboy a hint, saying, "It was either James I or Charles I who was beheaded," then the schoolboy is in a position to assert, "Either James I or Charles I was beheaded" without (perhaps) being in a position to assert either limb of the disjunction; but it is not this sort of case which causes the difficulty. The *ultimate* source of the schoolboy's knowledge derives from something which justifies the assertion that Charles I was beheaded; and this is all that would be required for the proposed explanation of the word or to be adequate. Likewise, the explanation is not impugned by cases like that in which I remember that I was talking either to Jean or to Alice, but cannot remember which. My knowledge that I was talking either to Jean or to Alice derives ultimately from the knowledge that I had at the time that I was talking to (say) Jean; the fact that the incomplete knowledge is all that survives is beside the point. Rather, the difficulty arises because we often make statements of the form ⌜P or Q⌝ when the ultimate evidence for making them, in the sense indicated, is neither evidence for the truth of P nor evidence for the truth of Q. The most striking instance of this is the fact that we are prepared to assert *any* statement of the form ⌜P or not P⌝, even though we may have no evidence either for the truth of P or for the truth of ⌜Not P⌝.

In order to justify asserting ⌜P or not P⌝, we appeal to the truth-table explanation of the meaning of "or." But if the whole explanation of the meanings of "true" and "false" is given by "It is true that *p* if and only if *p*" and "It is false that *p* if and only if not *p*," this appeal fails. The truth-table tells us, e.g., that from P we may infer ⌜P or Q⌝ (in particular, ⌜P or not P⌝); but *that* much we already knew from the explanation of "or" which we have rejected as insufficient. The truth-table does not show us that we are entitled to assert ⌜P or not P⌝ in every possible case, since this is to assume that every statement is either true or false; but, if our explanation of "true" and "false" is all the explanation that can be given, to say that every statement is either true or false is just to say that we are always justified in saying ⌜P or not P⌝.

We naturally think of truth-tables as giving the explanation of the sense which we attach to the sign of negation and to the connectives, an explanation which will show that we are justified in regarding certain forms of statement as logically true. It now appears that if we accept the redundancy theory of "true" and "false"—the theory that our explanation gives the whole meaning of these words—the truth-table explanation is quite unsatisfactory. More generally, we must abandon the idea which we naturally have that the notions of truth and falsity play an essential role in any account either of the meaning of statements in general or of the meaning of a particular statement. The conception pervades the thought of Frege that the general form of explanation of the sense of a statement consists in laying down the conditions under which it is true and those under which it is false (or better: saying that it is false under all other conditions); this same conception is expressed in the *Tractatus* in the words, "In order to be able to say that '*p*' is true (or false), I must have determined under what conditions I call '*p*' true, and this is how I determine the sense of the sentence" (4.063). But in order that someone should gain from the explanation that P is true in such-and-such circumstances an understanding of the sense of P, he must already know what it means to say of P that it is true. If when he inquires into this he is told that the only explanation is that to say that P is true is the same as to assert P, it will follow that in order to understand what is meant by saying that P is true, he must already know the sense of asserting P, which was precisely what was supposed to be being explained to him.

We thus have either to supplement the redundancy theory or to give up many of our preconceptions about truth and falsity. It has become a commonplace to say that there cannot be a criterion of truth. The argument is that we determine the sense of a sentence by laying down the conditions under which it is true, so that we could not first know the sense of a sentence and then apply some criterion to decide in what circumstances it was true. In the same sense there could not be a criterion for what constitutes the winning of a game, since learning what constitutes winning it is an essential part of learning what the game is. This does not mean that there may not be in any sense a theory of truth. For a particular bounded language, if it is free of ambiguity and inconsistency, it must be possible to characterize the true sentences of the language; somewhat as, for a given game, we can say which moves are winning moves. (A language is bounded if we may not introduce into it new words or new senses for old words.) Such a characterization would be recursive, defining truth first for the simplest possible sentences, and then for sentences built out of others by the logical operations employed in the language; this is what is done for formalized languages by a truth-definition. The redundancy theory gives the general form of such a truth-definition, though in particular cases more informative definitions might be given.

Now we have seen that to say for each particular game what winning it consists in is not to give a satisfactory account of the concept of winning a game. What makes us use the same term "winning" for each of these various activities is that the point of every game is that each player tries to do what for that game constitutes winning; i.e., what constitutes winning always plays the same part in determining what playing the game consists in. Similarly, what the truth of a statement consists in always plays the same role in determining the sense of that statement, and a theory of truth must be possible in the sense of an account of what that role is. I shall not now attempt such an account; I claim, however, that such an account would justify the following. A statement, so long as it is not ambiguous or vague, divides all possible states of affairs into just *two* classes. For a given state of affairs, either the statement is used in such a way that a man who asserted it but envisaged that state of affairs as a possibility would be held to have spoken misleadingly, or the assertion of the statement would not be taken as expressing the speaker's exclusion of that possibility. If a state of affairs of the first kind obtains, the statement is false; if all actual states of affairs are of the second kind, it is true. It is thus *prima facie* senseless to say of any statement that in such-and-such a state of affairs it would be neither true nor false.

The sense of a statement is determined by knowing in what circumstances it is true and in what false. Likewise the sense of a command is determined by knowing what constitutes obedience to it and what disobedience; and the sense of a bet by knowing when the bet is won and when it is lost. Now there may be a gap between the winning of a bet and the losing of it, as with a conditional bet; can there be a similar gap between obedience and disobedience to a command, or between the truth and falsity of a statement? There is a distinction between a conditional bet and a bet on the truth of a material conditional; if the antecedent is unfulfilled, in the first case the bet is off—it is just as if no bet had been made—but in the second case the bet is won. A conditional command where the antecedent is in the power of the person given the order (e.g., a mother says to a child, "If you go out, wear your coat") is always like a bet on the material conditional; it is equivalent to the command to ensure the truth of the material conditional, viz., "Do not go out without your coat." We cannot say that if the child does not go out, it is just as if no command had been given, since it may be that, unable to find his coat, he stayed in in order to comply with the command.

Can a distinction parallel to that for bets be drawn for conditional commands where the antecedent is not in the person's power? I contend that the distinction which looks as if it could be drawn is in fact void of significance. There are two distinct kinds of consequence of making a bet, winning it and losing; to determine what is to involve one of these is not yet to determine completely what is to involve the other. But there is only one kind of consequence of giving a command, namely that, provided one had the right to give it in the first place, one acquires a right to punish or at least reprobate disobedience. It might be though that punishment and reward were distinct consequences of a command in the same sense that paying money and receiving it are distinct consequences of a bet; but this does not tally with the role of commands in our society. The right to a reward is not taken to be an automatic consequence of obedience to a command, as the *right* to reproach is an automatic consequence of disobedience; if a reward is given, this is an act of grace, just as it is an act of grace if the punishment or reproach is withheld. Moreover, any action deliberately taken in order to comply with the command (to avoid disobedience to it) has the same claim to be rewarded as any other; hence to determine what constitutes disobedience to the command is thereby to determine what sort of behavior might be rewarded, without the need for any further decision. If the child stays in because he cannot find his coat, this behavior is as meritorious as if he goes out remembering to wear it; and if he forgets all about the order, but wears his coat for some other reason, this behavior no more deserves commendation than if he chooses, for selfish reasons, to remain indoors. Where the antecedent is not in the person's power, it is indeed possible to regard the conditional command as analogous to the conditional bet; but since obedience to a command has no consequence of its own other than that of avoiding the punishment due for disobedience, there is not for such commands any significant distinction parallel to that between conditional bets and bets about a material conditional. If we regarded obedience to a command as giving a right to a reward, we could then introduce such a distinction for commands whose antecedent was in the person's power. Thus the mother might use the form, "If you go out, wear your coat," as involving that if the child went out with his coat he would be rewarded, if he went out without it he would be punished, and if he stayed indoors—even in order to comply with the command—he would be neither punished nor rewarded; while the form, "Do not go out without your coat," would involve his being rewarded if he stayed indoors.

Statements are like commands (as we use them) and not like bets; the making of a statement has, as it were, only one kind of consequence. To see this, let us imagine a language which contains conditional statements but has no counterfactual form (counterfactuals would introduce irrelevant complications). Two alternative accounts are suggested of the way in which conditionals are used in this language: one, that they are used to make statements conditionally; the other, that they represent the material conditional. On the first interpretation, a conditional statement is like a conditional bet: if the antecedent is fulfilled, then the statement is treated as if it had been an unconditional assertion of the consequent, and is said to be true or false accordingly; if the antecedent is not fulfilled, then it is just as if no statement, true or false, had been made at all. On the second interpretation, if the antecedent is not fulfilled, then the statement is said to be true. How are we to settle which of these two accounts is the correct one? If statements are really like bets and not like commands; if there are two distinct kinds of consequence which may follow the making of a statement, those that go with calling the statement "true" and those that go with calling it "false," so that there may be a gap between these two kinds of consequence; then we ought to be able to find something which decides between the two accounts as definite as the financial transaction which distinguishes a bet on the truth of the material conditional from a conditional bet. It is no use asking whether these people *say* that the man who has made a conditional statement whose antecedent turns out false said something true or that he said nothing true or false: they may have no words corresponding to "true" and "false"; and if they do, how could we be sure that the correspondence was exact? If their using the words "true" and "false" is to have the slightest significance, there must be some difference in their behavior which goes with their saying true or neither "true" nor "false" in this case.

It is evident on reflection that there is nothing in what they do which could distinguish between the two alternative accounts; the distinction between them is as empty as the analogous distinction for conditional commands whose antecedent is not in the person's power. In order to fix the sense of an utterance, we do not need to make two separate decisions—when to say that a true statement has been made and when to say that a false statement has been made; rather, any situation in which nothing obtains which is taken as a case of its being false may be regarded as a case of its being true, just as someone who behaves so as not to disobey a command may be regarded as having obeyed it. The point becomes clearer when we look at it in the following way. If it makes sense in general to suppose that a certain form of statement is so used that in certain circumstances it is true, in others false, and in yet others nothing has been said true or false, then we can imagine that a form of conditional was used in this way (von Wright actually holds that *we* use conditionals in this way). If P turns out true, then ⌐If P, then Q⌐ is said to be true or false according as Q is true or false, while if P turns out false we say that nothing was said true or false. Let us contrast this with what Frege and Strawson say about the use in our language of statements containing a singular term. If there is an object for which the singular term stands, then the statement is true or false according as the predicate does or does not apply to that object, but if there is no such object, then we have not said anything true or false. Now do these accounts tell us the sense of sentences of these two kinds?—that is, do they tell us how these statements are used, what is *done* by making statements of these forms? Not at all, for an essential feature of their use has not yet been laid down. Someone uttering a conditional statement of the kind described may very well have no opinion as to whether the antecedent was going to turn out true or false; that is, he is not taken as having misused the statement or misled his hearers if he envisages it as a possibility that that case will arise in which he is said not to have made a statement true or false. All that he conveys by uttering the conditional statement is that he excludes the possibility that the case will arise in which he is said to have said something false, namely that antecedent is true and consequent false. With the case of a singular statement it is quite different. Here someone is definitely either misusing the form of statement or misleading his hearers if he envisages it as a possibility that that case will arise in which what he said will be said to be neither true nor false, namely that the singular term has no reference. He conveys more by making the statement than just that he excludes the possibility of its being false; he commits himself to its being true.

Are we then to say that laying down the truth-conditions for a sentence is not sufficient to determine its sense, that something further will have to be stipulated as well? Rather than say this we should abandon the notions of truth and falsity altogether. In order to characterize the sense of expressions of our two forms, only a twofold classification of possible relevant circumstances is necessary. We need to distinguish those states of affairs such that if the speaker envisaged them as possibilities he would be held to be either misusing the statement or misleading his hearers, and those of which this is not the case: and *one* way of using the words "true" and "false" would be to call states of affairs of the former kind those in which the statement was false and the others those in which the statement was true. For our conditional statements, the distinction would be between those states of affairs in which the statement was said to be false and those in which we said that it would either be true or else neither true nor false. For singular statements, the distinction would be between those states of affairs in which we said that the statement would either be false or else neither true nor false, and those in which it was true. To grasp the sense or use of these forms of statement, the twofold classification is quite sufficient; the threefold classification with which we started is entirely beside the point. Thus, on *one* way of using the words "true" and "false," we should, instead of distinguishing between the conditional statement's being true and its being neither true nor false, have distinguished between two different ways in which it could be true; and instead of distinguishing between the singular statement's being false and its being neither true nor false, we should have distinguished between two different ways in which it could be false.

This gives us a hint at a way of explaining the role played by truth and falsity in determining the sense of a statement. We have not yet seen what point there may be in distinguishing between different ways in which a statement may be true or between different ways in which it may be false, or, as we might say, between degrees of truth and falsity. The point of such distinctions does not lie in anything to do with the sense of the statement itself, but has to do with the way in which it enters into complex statements. Let us imagine that in the language of which the conditional statements we considered form a part there exists a sign of negation, i.e., a word which, placed in front of a statement, forms another statement; I call it a sign of negation because in most cases it forms a statement which we should regard as being used as the contradictory of the original statement. Let us suppose, however, that when placed in front of a conditional statement ⌜If P, then Q⌝, it forms a statement which is used in the same way as the statement ⌜If P, then not Q⌝. Then if we describe the use of the conditionals by reference to a twofold classification only, i.e., in the same way as we describe a material conditional, we shall be unable to give a truth-functional account of the behavior of their sign "not." That is, we should have the tables:

P	Q	⌜If P, then Q⌝	⌜Not: if P, then Q⌝
T	T	T	F
T	F	F	T
F	T	T	T
F	F	T	T

in which the truth-value of ⌜Not: if P, then Q⌝ is not determined by the truth-value of ⌜If P, then Q⌝. If, on the other hand, we revert to our original threefold classification, marking the case in which we said that no statement true or false had been made by "X," then we have the tables:

P	Q	⌜If P, then Q⌝	⌜Not: if P, then Q⌝
T	T	T	F
T	F	F	T
F	T	X	X
F	F	X	X

which can be quite satisfactorily accounted for by giving the table for "not":

R	⌜Not R⌝
T	F
X	X
F	T

(I have assumed that the statements P and Q take only the values T and F.) It now becomes quite natural to think of "T" as representing true, "F" "false" and "X" "neither true nor false." Then we can say that their symbol not really is a sign of negation, since ⌜Not P⌝ is true when and only when P is false and false when and only when P is true. We must not forget, however, that the justification for distinguishing between the cases in which a conditional was said to have the value T and the cases in which it was said to have the value X was simply the possibility, created by this distinction, of treating "not" truth-functionally. In the same way if we have in a language an expression which normally functions as a sign of negation, but the effect of prefacing a singular statement with this expression is to produce a statement whose utterance still commits the speaker to there being an object for which the singular term stands, it is very natural to distinguish between two kinds of falsity a singular statement may have: that when the singular term has a reference, but the predicate does not apply to it, and that when the singular term lacks a reference. Let us represent the case in which the singular term has no reference by the symbol Y, and let us suppose S to be a singular statement. Then we have the table:

S	⌜Not S⌝
T	F
Y	Y
F	T

Here again it is natural to think of "T" as representing "true," "F" "false" and "Y" "neither true nor false."

There is no necessity to use the words "true" and "false" as suggested above, so that we have to interpret X as a kind of truth and Y as a kind of falsity. Logicians who study many-valued logics have a term which can be employed here: they would say that T and X are "designated" truth-values and F and Y "undesignated" ones. (In a many-valued logic those formulas are considered valid which have a designated value for every assignment of values to their sentence-letters.) The points to observe are just these: (i) The sense of a sentence is determined wholly by knowing the case in which it has a designated value and the cases in which it has an undesignated one. (ii) Finer distinctions between different designated values or different undesignated ones, however naturally they come to us, are justified only if they are needed in order to give a truth-functional account of the formation of complex statements by means of operators. (iii) In *most* philosophical discussions of "truth" and "falsity," what we really have in mind is the distinction between a designated and an undesignated value, and hence choosing the names truth and falsity for particular designated and undesignated values respectively will only obscure the issue. (iv) Saying that in certain circumstances a statement is neither true nor false does not determine whether the statement is in that case to count as having an undesignated or a designated value, i.e., whether someone who asserts the statement is or is not taken as excluding the possibility that that case obtains.

Baffled by the attempt to describe in general the relation between language and reality, we have nowadays abandoned the correspondence theory of truth, and justify our doing so on the score that it was an attempt to state a *criterion* of truth in the sense in which this cannot be done. Nevertheless, the correspondence theory expresses one important feature of the concept of truth which is not expressed by the law "It is true that *p* if and only if *p*" and which we have so far left quite out of account: that a statement is true only if there is something in the world *in virtue of which* it is true. Although we no longer accept the correspondence theory, we remain realists *au fond*; we retain in our thinking a fundamentally realist conception of truth. Realism consists in the belief that for any statement there must be something in virtue of which either it or its negation is true: it is only on the basis of this belief that we can justify the idea that truth and falsity play an essential role in the notion of the meaning of a statement, that the general form of an explanation of meaning is a statement of the truth-conditions.

To see the importance of this feature of the concept of truth, let us envisage a dispute over the logical validity of the statement "Either Jones was brave or he was not." A imagines Jones to be a man, now dead, who never encountered danger in his life. B retorts that it could still be true that Jones was brave, namely, if it is true that if Jones *had* encountered danger, he would have acted bravely. A agrees with this, but still maintains that it does not need to be the case that either "Jones was brave" = "If Jones had encountered danger, he would have acted bravely" nor "Jones was not brave" = "If Jones had encountered danger, he would not have acted bravely" is true. For, he argues, it might be the case that however many facts we knew of the kind which we should normally regard as grounds for asserting such counterfactual conditionals, we should still know nothing which would be a ground for asserting either. It is clear that B cannot agree that this is a possibility and yet continue to insist that all the same either "Jones was brave" or "Jones was not brave" is true; for he would then be committed to holding that a statement may be true even though there is nothing whatever such that, if we knew of it, we should count it as evidence or as a ground for the truth of the statement, and this is absurd. (It may be objected that there are assertions for which it would be out of place to ask one who made them for his evidence or grounds; but for *such* assertions the speaker must always either be in a position to make or in a position to deny them.) If B still wishes to maintain the necessity of "Either Jones was brave or he was not," he will have to hold either that there must be some fact of the sort to which we usually appeal in discussing counterfactuals which, if we knew it, would decide us in favor either of the one counterfactual or of the other; or else that there is some fact of an extraordinary kind, perhaps known only to God. In the latter case he imagines a kind of spiritual mechanism—Jones' character—which determines how he acts in each situation that arises; his acting in such-and-such a way reveals to us the state of this spiritual mechanism, which was however already in place before its observable effects were displayed in his behavior. B would then argue thus: If Jones *had* encountered danger, he would either have acted bravely or have acted like a coward. Suppose he had acted bravely. This would then have shown us that he was brave; but he would *already* have been brave before his courage was revealed by his behavior. That is, either his character included the quality of courage or it did not, and his character determines his behavior. We know his character only indirectly, through its effects on his behavior; but each character-trait must be *there* within him independently of whether it reveals itself to us or not.

Anyone of a sufficient degree of sophistication will reject B's belief in a spiritual mechanism; either he will be a materialist and substitute for it an equally blind belief in a physiological mechanism, or he will accept A's conclusion that "Either Jones was brave or he was not" is not logically necessary. His ground for rejecting B's argument is that if such a statement as "Jones was brave" is true, it must be true in virtue of the sort of fact we have been taught to regard as justifying us in asserting it. It cannot be true in virtue of a fact of some quite different sort of which we can have no direct knowledge, for otherwise the statement "Jones was brave" would not have the meaning that *we* have given it. In accepting A's position he makes a small retreat from realism; he abandons a realist view of character.

In order, then, to decide whether a realist account of truth can be given for statements of some particular kind, we have to ask whether for such a statement P it must be the case that if we knew sufficiently many facts of the kind we normally treat as justifying us in asserting P, we should be in a position either to assert P or to assert ⌜Not P⌝: if so, then it can truly be said that there must either be something in virtue of which P is true or something in virtue of which it is false. It is easy to overlook the force of the phrase "sufficiently many." Consider the statement "A city will never be built on this spot." Even if we have an oracle which can answer every question of the kind, "Will there be a city here in 1990?" "In 2100?" etc., we might never be in a position either to declare the statement true or to declare it false. Someone may say: That is only because you are assuming the knowledge of only finitely many answers of the oracle; but if you knew the oracle's answers to *all* these questions, you would be able to decide the truth-value of the statement. But what would it mean to know infinitely many facts? It could mean that the oracle gave a direct answer "No" to the question, "Will a city ever be built here?": but to assume this is just like B's assumption of the existence of a hidden spiritual mechanism. It might mean that we had an argument to show the falsity of ⌜A city will be built here in the year N⌝ irrespective of the value of N, e.g., if "here" is the North Pole: but no one would suggest that it must be the case that either the oracle will give an affirmative answer to some question of the form "Will there be a city here in the year …?" or we can find a general argument for a negative answer. Finally, it could mean that we were *able* to answer every question of the form, "Will there be a city here in the year …?": but having infinite knowledge in *this* sense will place us in no better position than when we had the oracle.

We thus arrive at the following position. We are entitled to say that a statement P must be either true or false, that there must be something in virtue of which either it is true or it is false, only when P is a statement of such a kind that we could in a finite time bring ourselves into a position in which we were justified either in asserting or in denying P; that is, when P is an effectively decidable statement. This limitation is not trivial: there is an immense range of statements which, like "Jones was brave," are concealed conditionals, or which, like "A city will never be built here," contain—explicitly or implicitly—an unlimited generality, and which therefore fail the test.

What I have done here is to transfer to ordinary statements what the intuitionists say about mathematical statements. The sense of e.g., the existential quantifier is determined by considering what sort of fact makes an existential statement true, and this means: the sort of fact which we have been taught to regard as justifying us in asserting an existential statement. What would make the statement that there exists an odd perfect number true would be some particular number's being both odd and perfect; hence the assertion of the existential statement must be taken as a claim to be able to assert some one of the singular statements. We are thus justified in asserting that there is a number with a certain property only if we have a method for finding a particular number with that property. Likewise, the sense of a universal statement is given by the sort of consideration we regard as justifying us in asserting it: namely we can assert that every number has a certain property if we have a general method for showing, for any arbitrary number, that it has that property. Now what if someone insists that either the statement "There is an odd perfect number" is true, or else every perfect number is even? He is justified if he knows of a procedure which will lead him in a finite time either to the determination of a particular odd perfect number or to a general proof that a number assumed to be perfect is even. But if he knows of no such procedure, then he is trying to attach to the statement "Every perfect number is even" a meaning which lies *beyond* that provided by the training we are given in the use of universal statements; he wants to say, as B said of "Jones was brave," that its truth may lie in a region directly accessible only to God, which human beings can never survey.

We learn the sense of the logical operators by being trained to *use* statements containing them, i.e., to assert such statements under certain conditions. Thus we learn to assert ⌜P and Q⌝ when we can assert P and can assert Q; to assert ⌜P or Q⌝ when we can assert P or can assert Q; to assert ⌜For some n, F(n)⌝ when we can assert ⌜F(0)⌝ or can assert ⌜F(1)⌝ or. ... We learn to assert ⌜For every n, F(n)⌝ when we can assert ⌜F(0)⌝ and ⌜F(1)⌝ and ...; and to say that we can assert all of these means that we have a general method for establishing ⌜F(x)⌝ irrespective of the value of x. Here we have abandoned altogether the attempt to explain the meaning of a statement by laying down its truth-conditions. *We no longer explain the sense of a statement by stipulating its truth-value in terms of the truth-values of its constituents, but by stipulating when it may be asserted in terms of the conditions under which its constituents may be asserted.* The justification for this change is that this is how we in fact learn to use these statements: furthermore, the notions of truth and falsity cannot be satisfactorily explained so as to form a basis for an account of meaning once we leave the realm of effectively decidable statements. One result of this shift in our account of meaning is that, unless we are dealing only with effectively decidable statements, certain formulas which appeared in the two-valued logic to be logical laws no longer rank as such, in particular the law of excluded middle: this is rejected, not on the ground that there is a middle truth-value, but because meaning, and hence validity, is no longer to be explained in terms of truth-values.

Intuitionists speak of mathematics in a highly antirealist (antiplatonist) way: for them it is *we* who construct mathematics; it is not already *there* waiting for us to discover. An extreme form of such constructivism is found in Wittgenstein's *Remarks on the Foundations of Mathematics*. This makes it appear as though the intuitionist rejection of an account of the meaning of mathematical statements in terms of truth and falsity could not be generalized for other regions of discourse, since even if there is no independent mathematical reality answering to our mathematical statements, there is an independent reality answering to statements of other kinds. On the other hand the exposition of intuitionism I have just given was not based on a rejection of the Fregean notion of a mathematical reality waiting to be discovered, but only on considerations about meaning. Now certainly someone who accepts the intuitionist standpoint in mathematics will not be inclined to adopt the platonist picture. Must he then go to the other extreme, and have the picture of our creating mathematics as we go along? To adopt this picture involves thinking with Wittgenstein that we are *free* in mathematics at every point; no step we take has been forced on us by a necessity external to us, but has been freely chosen. This picture is not the only alternative. If we think that mathematical results are in some sense imposed on us from without, we could have instead the picture of a mathematical reality not already in existence but as it were coming into being as we probe. Our investigations bring into existence what was not there before, but what they bring into existence is not of our own making.

Whether this picture is right or wrong for mathematics, it is available for other regions of reality as an alternative to the realist conception of the world. This shows how it is possible to hold that the intuitionist substitution of an account of the *use* of a statement for an account of its truth-conditions as the general form of explanation of meaning should be applied to all realms of discourse without thinking that we create the world; we can abandon realism without falling into subjective idealism. This substitution does not, of course, involve dropping the words "true" and "false," since for most ordinary contexts the account of these words embodied in the laws "It is true that p if and only if p" and "It is false that p if and only if not p" is quite sufficient: but it means facing the consequences of admitting that this is the *whole* explanation of the sense of these words, and this involves dethroning truth and falsity from their central place in philosophy and in particular in the theory of meaning. Of course the doctrine that meaning is to be explained in terms of use is the cardinal doctrine of the later Wittgenstein; but I do not think the point of this doctrine has so far been generally understood.

12 Two Philosophical Perspectives

Hilary Putnam

The problems we have been discussing naturally give rise to two philosophical points of view (or two philosophical temperaments, as I called them in the Introduction) [to *Reason, Truth, and History*, 1981]. It is with these points of view, and with their consequences for just about every issue in philosophy that I shall be concerned: the question of "Brains in a Vat" would not be of interest, except as a sort of logical paradox, if it were not for the sharp way in which it brings out the difference between these philosophical perspectives.

One of these perspectives is the perspective of metaphysical realism. On this perspective, the world consists of some fixed totality of mind-independent objects. There is exactly one true and complete description of "the way the world is." Truth involves some sort of correspondence relation between words or thought-signs and external things and sets of things. I shall call this perspective the *externalist* perspective, because its favorite point of view is a God's Eye point of view.

The perspective I shall defend has no unambiguous name. It is a late arrival in the history of philosophy, and even today it keeps being confused with other points of view of a quite different sort. I shall refer to it as the *internalist* perspective, because it is characteristic of this view to hold that *what objects does the world consist of?* is a question that it only makes sense to ask *within* a theory or description. Many "internalist" philosophers, though not all, hold further that there is more than one "true" theory or description of the world. "Truth," in an internalist view, is some sort of (idealized) rational acceptability—some sort of ideal coherence of our beliefs with each other and with our experiences *as those experiences are themselves represented in our belief system*— and not correspondence with mind-independent or discourse-independent "states of affairs." There is no God's Eye point of view that we can know or usefully imagine; there are only the various points of view of actual persons reflecting various interests and purposes that their descriptions and theories subserve. ("Coherence theory of truth"; "Non-realism"; "Verificationism"; "Pluralism"; "Pragmatism"; are all terms that have been applied to the internalist perspective; but every one of these terms has connotations that are unacceptable because of their other historic applications.)

Internalist philosophers dismiss the "Brain in a Vat" hypothesis. For us, the "Brain in a Vat World" is only a *story*, a mere linguistic construction, and not a possible world at all. The idea that this story might be true in some universe, some Parallel Reality, assumes a God's Eye point of view from the start, as is easily seen. For *from whose point of view is the story being told?* Evidently *not* from the point of view of any of the sentient creatures *in* the world. Nor from the point of view of any observer in another world who interacts with this world; for a "world" by definition includes everything that interacts in any way with the things it contains. If *you*, for example, were the one observer who was *not* a Brain in a Vat, spying on the Brains in a Vat, then the world would not be one in which *all* sentient beings were Brains in a Vat. So the supposition that there could be a world in which *all* sentient beings are Brains in a Vat presupposes from the outset a God's Eye view of truth, or, more accurately, a No Eye view of truth— truth as independent of observers altogether.

For the externalist philosopher, on the other hand, the hypothesis that we are all Brains in a Vat cannot be dismissed so simply. For the truth of a theory does not consist in its fitting the world as the world presents itself to some observer or observers (truth is not "relational" in this sense), but in its corresponding to the world as it is in itself. And the problem that I posed for the externalist philosopher is that the very relation of correspondence on which truth and reference depend (on his view) cannot logically be available to him if he *is* a Brain in a Vat. So, if we *are* Brains in a Vat, we cannot *think* that we are, except in the bracketed sense [we are Brains in a Vat]; and this bracketed thought does not have reference conditions that would make it *true*. So it is not possible after all that we are Brains in a Vat.

Suppose we assume a "magical theory of reference." For example, we might assume that some occult rays—call them "noetic rays"[1]—connect words and thought-signs to their referents. Then there is no problem. The Brain in a Vat can think the *words*, "I am a brain in a vat," and when he does the word "vat" corresponds (with the aid of the noetic rays) to real external vats and the word "in" corresponds (with the aid of the noetic rays) to the relation of real spatial containment. But such a view is obviously untenable. No present day philosopher would espouse such a view. It is because the modern realist wishes to have a correspondence theory of truth *without* believing in "noetic rays" (or, believing in Self-Identifying Objects[2]—objects that intrinsically correspond to one word or thought-sign rather than another) that the Brain in a Vat case is a puzzler for him.

As we have seen, the problem is this: there are these objects out there. Here is the mind/ brain, carrying on its thinking/computing. How do the thinker's symbols (or those of his mind/brain) get into a unique correspondence with objects and sets of objects out there?

The reply popular among externalists today is that while indeed no sign *necessarily* corresponds to one set of things rather than another, *contextual* connections between signs and external things (in particular, causal connections) will enable one to explicate the nature of reference. But this doesn't work. For example, the dominant cause of my beliefs about electrons is probably various *textbooks*. But the occurrences of the word "electron" I produce, though having in this sense a strong connection to textbooks, do not *refer* to textbooks. The objects which are the dominant cause of my beliefs containing a certain sign may not be the referents of that sign.

The externalist will now reply that the word "electron" is not connected to textbooks by a causal chain *of the appropriate type*. (But how can we have intentions which determine which causal chains are "of the appropriate type" unless we are *already* able to *refer*?)

For an internalist like myself, the situation is quite different. In an internalist view also, signs do not intrinsically correspond to objects, independently of how those signs are employed and by whom. But a sign that is actually employed in a particular way by a particular community of users can correspond to particular objects *within the conceptual scheme of those users*. "Objects" do not exist independently of conceptual schemes. *We* cut up the world into objects when we introduce one or another scheme of description. Since the objects *and* the signs are alike *internal* to the scheme of description, it is possible to say what matches what.

Indeed, it is trivial to say what any word refers to *within* the language the word belongs to, by using the word itself. What does "rabbit" refer to? Why, to rabbits, of course! What does "extraterrestrial" refer to? To extraterrestrials (if there are any).

Of course the externalist agrees that the extension of "rabbit" is the set of rabbits and the extension of "extraterrestrial" is the set of extraterrestrials. But he does not regard such statements as telling us what reference *is*. For him finding out what reference *is*, i.e. what the *nature* of the "correspondence" between words and things is, is a pressing problem. (*How* pressing, we saw in the previous chapter [of *Reason, Truth, and History*].) For me there is little to say about what reference is within a conceptual system other than these tautologies. The idea that causal connection is necessary is refuted by the fact that "extraterrestrial" certainly refers to extraterrestrials whether we have ever causally interacted with any extraterrestrials or not!

The externalist philosopher would reply, however, that we can refer to extraterrestrials even though we have never interacted with any (as far as we know) because we have interacted with *terrestrials* and we have experienced instances of the relation "not from the same planet as" and instances of the property "intelligent being." And we can *define* an extraterrestrial as an intelligent being that is not from the same planet as terrestrials. Also, "not from the same planet as" can be analyzed in terms of "not from the same place as" and "planet" (which can be further analyzed). Thus the externalist gives up the requirement that we have some "real" connection (e.g. causal connection) with *everything* we are able to refer to, and requires only that the *basic* terms refer to kinds of things (and relations) that we have some real connection to. Using the basic terms in complex combinations we can then, he says, build up descriptive expressions which refer to kinds of things we have no real connection to, and that may not even exist (e.g. extraterrestrials).

In fact, already with a simple word like "horse" or "rabbit" he might have observed that the extension includes many things we have *not* causally interacted with (e.g. *future* horses and rabbits, or horses and rabbits that never interacted with any human being). When we use the word "horse" we refer not only to the horses we have a real connection to, but also to all other things *of the same kind*.

At this point, however, we must observe that "of the same kind" makes no sense apart from a categorial system which says what properties do and what properties do not count as similarities. In *some* ways, after all, anything is "of the same kind" as anything else. This whole complicated story about how we refer to some things by virtue of the fact that they are connected with us by "causal chains of the appropriate kind," and to yet other things by virtue of the fact that they are "of the same kind" as things connected with us by causal chains of the appropriate kind, and to still other things "by description," is not so much false as otiose. What makes horses with which I have not interacted "of the same kind" as horses with which I *have* interacted is that fact that the former as well as the latter are *horses*. The metaphysical realist formulation of the problem once again makes it seem as if there are to begin with all these objects in themselves, and then I get some kind of a lasso over a few of these objects (the horses with which I have a "real" connection, via a "causal chain of the appropriate kind"), and then I have the problem of getting my word ("horse") to cover not only the ones I have "lassoed" but also the ones I can't lasso, because they are too far away in space and time, or whatever. And the "solution" to this pseudo-problem, as I consider it to be—the metaphysical realist "solution"—is to say that the word *automatically* covers not just the objects I lassoed, but also the objects which are *of the same kind*—of the same kind *in themselves*. But then the world is, after all, being claimed to contain Self-Identifying Objects, for this is just what it means to say that the *world*, and not thinkers, sorts things into kinds.

In a sense, I would say, the world *does* consist of "Self-Identifying Objects"—but not a sense available to an externalist. If, as I maintain, "objects" themselves are as much made as discovered, as much products of our conceptual invention as of the "objective" factor in experience, the factor independent of our will, then of course objects intrinsically belong under certain labels; because those labels are the tools we used to construct a version of the world with such objects in the first place. But *this* kind of "Self-Identifying Object" is not mind-independent; and the externalist wants to think of the world as consisting of objects that are *at one and the same time* mind-independent and Self-Identifying. This is what one cannot do.

Internalism and Relativism

Internalism is not a facile relativism that says, "Anything goes." Denying that it makes sense to ask whether our concepts "match" something totally uncontaminated by conceptualization is one thing; but to hold that every conceptual system is therefore just as good as every other would be something else. If anyone really believed that, and if they were foolish enough to pick a conceptual system that told them they could fly and to act upon it by jumping out of a window, they would, if they were lucky enough to survive, see the weakness of the latter view at once. Internalism does not deny that there are experiential *inputs* to knowledge; knowledge is not a story with no constraints except *internal* coherence; but it does deny that there are any inputs *which are not themselves to some extent shaped by our concepts,* by the vocabulary we use to report and describe them, or any inputs *which admit of only one description, independent of all conceptual choices.* Even our description of our own sensations, so dear as a starting point for knowledge to generations of epistemologists, is heavily affected (as are the sensations themselves, for that matter) by a host of conceptual choices. The very inputs upon which our knowledge is based are conceptually contaminated; but contaminated inputs are better than none. If contaminated inputs are all we have, still all we have has proved to be quite a bit.

What makes a statement, or a whole system of statements—a theory or conceptual scheme—rationally acceptable is, in large part, its coherence and fit; coherence of "theoretical" or less experiential beliefs with one another and with more experiential beliefs, and also coherence of experiential beliefs with theoretical beliefs. Our conceptions of coherence and acceptability are, on the view I shall develop, deeply interwoven with our psychology. They depend upon our biology and our culture; they are by no means "value free." But they *are* our conceptions, and they are conceptions of something real. They define a kind of objectivity, *objectivity for us,* even if it is not the metaphysical objectivity of the God's Eye view. Objectivity and rationality humanly speaking are what we have; they are better than nothing.

To reject the idea that there is a coherent "external" perspective, a theory which is simply true "in itself," apart from all possible observers, is not to *identify* truth with rational acceptability. Truth cannot simply *be* rational acceptability for one fundamental reason; truth is supposed to be a property of a statement that cannot be lost, whereas justification can be lost. The statement "The earth is flat" was, very likely, rationally acceptable 3,000 years ago; but it is not rationally acceptable today. Yet it would be wrong to say that "the earth is flat" was *true* 3,000 years ago; for that would mean that the earth has changed its shape. In fact, rational acceptability is both tensed and relative to a person. In addition, rational acceptability is a matter of degree; truth is sometimes spoken of as a matter of degree (e.g., we sometimes say, *"the earth is a sphere" is approximately true*); but the "degree" here is the *accuracy* of the statement, and not its degree of acceptability or justification.

What this shows, in my opinion, is not that the externalist view is right after all, but that truth is an *idealization* of rational acceptability. We speak as if there were such things as epistemically ideal conditions, and we call a statement "true" if it would be justified under such conditions. "Epistemically ideal conditions," of course, are like "frictionless planes": we cannot really attain epistemically ideal conditions, or even be absolutely certain that we have come sufficiently close to them. But frictionless planes cannot really be attained either, and yet talk of frictionless planes has "cash value" because we can approximate them to a very high degree of approximation.

Perhaps it will seem that explaining truth in terms of justification under ideal conditions is explaining a clear notion in terms of a vague one. But "true" is *not* so clear when we move away from such stock examples as "Snow is white." And in any case, I am not trying to give a formal *definition* of truth, but an informal elucidation of the notion.

The simile of frictionless planes aside, the two key ideas of the idealization theory of truth are (1) that truth is independent of justification here and now, but not independent of *all* justification. To claim a statement is true is to claim it could be justified; (2) truth is expected to be stable or "convergent"; if both a statement and its negation could be "justified," even if conditions were as ideal as one could hope to make them, there is no sense in thinking of the statement as *having* a truth-value.

Notes

1. "Noetic rays" was suggested to me by Zemach.

2. The term "Self Identifying Object" is from *Substance and Sameness* by D. Wiggins (Cambridge: Blackwell, 1980).

13 Is Truth a Goal of Inquiry? Donald Davidson versus Crispin Wright

Richard Rorty

Pragmatists think that if something makes no difference to practice, it should make no difference to philosophy. This conviction makes them suspicious of the distinction between justification and truth, for that difference makes no difference to my decisions about what to do. If I have concrete, specific doubts about whether one of my beliefs is true, I can resolve those doubts only by asking whether it is adequately justified—by finding and assessing additional reasons pro and con. I cannot bypass justification and confine my attention to truth: assessment of truth and assessment of justification are, when the question is about what I should believe now, the same activity.[1] If, on the other hand, my doubts are as unspecific and abstract as Descartes's—are such that I can do nothing to resolve them—they should be dismissed, with Peirce, as "make-believe." Philosophy should ignore them.

This line of thought suggests to pragmatists that, although there is obviously a lot to be said about justification of various sorts of beliefs, there may be little to say about truth.[2] The sort of thing philosophers typically have said—that truth is some sort of correspondence to, or accurate representation of, reality—seemed empty and pointless to many[3] nineteenth-century idealists, and also to Dewey. The early pragmatists agreed with their idealist opponents that doubts about correspondence to reality can be settled only by assessing the coherence of the dubious belief with other beliefs. To both, the difference between true beliefs considered as useful nonrepresentational mental states, and as accurate (and *therefore* useful) representations of reality, seemed a difference that could make no difference to practice. No one profits from insisting on the distinction, both concluded, except for those who enjoy entertaining make-believe doubts.

Since the pragmatists, unlike the idealists, took Darwin and biology seriously, they had an additional reason for distrusting the idea that true beliefs are accurate representations. For representation, as opposed to increasingly complex adaptive behavior, is hard to integrate into an evolutionary story. Within such a story, it is easy to think of beliefs, with Bain and Peirce, as habits of action, patterns of complex behavior. But it is hard to imagine that, at a certain point in the evolutionary process, somewhere between the squids and the apes, these patterns began to be determined by inner representations, having previously been determined by mere neurological configurations. Even if one chooses to treat sufficiently complex neurological configurations *as* representations, the question of their accuracy seems to collapse immediately into that of their utility. So, once again, we seem to have a difference that makes no practical difference.[4]

William James said, "'The true' ... is only the expedient in the way of our thinking, just as 'the right' is only the expedient in the way of our behaving."[5] Elsewhere he said, "The true is the name of whatever proves itself to be good in the way of belief, and good, too, for definite, assignable reasons."[6] His point in analogizing truth to rightness and to goodness was that once you understand all about the justification of actions, including the justification of assertions, you understand all there *is* to understand about goodness, rightness, and truth.[7]

Philosophers who, like myself, find this Jamesian suggestion persuasive, swing back and forth between trying to reduce truth to justification and propounding some form of minimalism about truth. In reductionist moods we have offered such definitions of truth as "warranted assertibility," "ideal assertibility," and "assertibility at the end of inquiry." But such definitions always fall victim, sooner or later, to what Putnam has called the "naturalistic fallacy" argument—the argument that a given belief might meet any such conditions but still not be true. Faced with this argument, we pragmatists have often fallen back on minimalism and have suggested that Tarski's breezy disquotationalism may exhaust the topic of truth.[8]

In an article on Donald Davidson published in 1986, I suggested that we interpret Davidson both as a sort of pragmatist and as a sort of minimalist—as someone who, like James, thought that there was less to say about truth than philosophers had usually believed.[9] More specifically, I interpreted Davidson as saying that the word "true" had no explanatory use, but merely a disquotational use, a commending use, and what I called a "cautionary" use. The latter is its use in such expressions as "fully justified, but perhaps not true." The reason there is less to be said about truth than one might think, I suggested, is that terms used to commend or caution—terms such as "good!" "right!" "true!" "false!" "way to go!" and "watch it!"—do not need much philosophical definition or explication.

My underlying idea in that 1986 article was that the entire force of the cautionary use of "true" is to point out that justification is relative to an audience and that we can never exclude the possibility that some better audience might exist, or come to exist, to whom a belief that is justifiable to us would not be justifiable. But, as Putnam's "naturalistic fallacy" argument shows, there can be no such thing as an "ideal audience" before which justification would be sufficient to ensure truth, any more than there can be a largest integer. For any audience, one can imagine a better-informed audience and also a more imaginative one—an audience that has thought up hitherto-undreamt-of alternatives to the proposed belief. The limits of justification would be the limits of language, but language (like imagination) has no limits.

In an article of 1990, Davidson partially repudiated my interpretation.[10] He said that he should be considered neither a deflationist nor a disquotationalist. He defined "deflationism" as the view that "Tarski's work embraces all of truth's essential features" and said that I was mistaken in attributing this view to him on the basis of his eschewal of attempts to define "true" for variable L as opposed to defining "true-in-L" for particular values of L.[11] He went on to say that

> Tarski's definitions [of the term "true-in-L" for various values of L] give us no idea of how to apply the concept [of truth] to a new case. ... [T]hey depend on giving the extension or references of the basic predicates or names by enumerating cases; a definition given in this way can provide no clue for the next or general case.[12]

Davidson concluded that "[t]he concept of truth has essential connections with the concepts of belief and meaning, but these connections are untouched by Tarski's work."[13] He summed up by saying:

> What Tarski has done for us is to show in detail how to describe the kind of pattern truth must make. What we need to do now is to say how to identify the presence of such a pattern or structure in the behavior of people.[14]

The way we identify this pattern, Davidson tells us, is to gather information "about what episodes and situations in the world cause an agent to prefer that one rather than another sentence be true."[15] This information can be gleaned without knowing what the agent's sentences mean. But once we have enough such evidence we can, Davidson says, "make the crucial step from the nonpropositional to the propositional,"[16] from the nonintensional to the intensional. For the use of intensional terms to describe human behavior marks the emergence of the pattern that truth makes—the pattern that links those episodes and situations in the world with the noises and marks made by the agent. They are linked into the behavior we call "using a language." Detection of that pattern is what makes the adoption of what Dennett calls "the intentional stance" both possible and useful in our dealings with the agent. There is, Davidson says, "a fundamentally rational pattern that must, in general outline, be shared by all rational creatures."[17] This pattern that rationality makes is the same pattern truth makes, and the same pattern meaning makes. You cannot have language without rationality, or either without truth.[18]

It is important to realize that what Davidson adds to Tarski, when he displays the connections between the concept of truth and those of meaning and belief, has nothing whatever to do with the question of whether, or how, we can tell when a belief is true. Although Davidson describes himself as, in his Dewey Lectures, filling in the missing "content" of the "concept" of truth, all this filling-in amounts to is instructions for constructing an empirical theory for explaining and predicting behavior—a theory of truth for one or more speakers. "A theory of truth," as he says, "is an empirical theory about the truth conditions of every sentence in some corpus of sentences."[19]

Philosophers who discuss truth have often hoped to underwrite our assumption that, the more justification we offer of a belief, the likelier it is that that belief is true. The most familiar attempt at such ratification begins by saying that, at least in some areas of culture, and at the very least when we are concerned with observable physical objects, our predictions succeed insofar as our beliefs fit reality. It then goes on to say that each successive substitution of a better-justified for a worse-justified belief is an improvement in degree of fit. Such talk of "fit" interprets an increase in the coherence of nonobservational sentences with observation sentences as a sign of closer fit between the former sentences and the things observed.

Davidson, however, has no sympathy for this line of thought. His criticisms of the notion of "fitting reality," in "On the Very Idea of a Conceptual Scheme," parallel James's and Dewey's. In his Dewey Lectures he says:

> I have argued that certain familiar attempts to characterize truth which go beyond giving empirical content to a structure of the sort Tarski taught us how to describe are empty, false, or confused. We should not say that truth is correspondence, coherence, warranted assertibility, ideally justified assertability, what is accepted in the conversation of the right people, what science will end up maintaining, what explains the convergence on single theories in science, or the success of our ordinary beliefs. To the extent that realism or antirealism depend [sic] on one or another of these views of truth we should refuse to endorse either.[20]

Passages such as this suggest that Davidson would categorically repudiate the suggestion that philosophers need to explain why an increase in justification leads to an increased likelihood of truth, as opposed to acceptability to more and more audiences. For Davidson seems to think that philosophers have done *all* they need to do with the concept of truth once they have shown how to detect a certain pattern of behavior—the pattern exhibited in the truth theory for a language. It is hard to see how such detection could help to underwrite or improve our practices of justification, and Davidson gives no reason to think that it could or should.[21] This is, presumably, why he calls truth a "nonepistemic" concept.

I suspect that the only epistemological comfort that Davidson has to offer is his notorious thesis that most of our beliefs—most of *anybody's* beliefs—must be true. This thesis is, however, both less bracing and less provocative than it may seem at first. For when we remember that Davidson will have no truck with the idea that truth consists in correspondence to, or accurate representation of,[22] reality, we realize that he is not saying that our minds are, thanks to God's or Evolution's contrivance, well suited to the task of getting reality right. He can perfectly well agree with Goodman, Putnam, and Kuhn that there is no such task, because there is no Way the World Is. He is, rather, saying that most of anybody's beliefs must coincide with most of *our* beliefs (because to ascribe beliefs in the first place one must invoke the Principle of Charity) and that to reject that mass of shared beliefs (as perhaps not corresponding to reality) is to bring back a tangle of uncashable and useless metaphors—those used to state the scheme-content distinction. To say, as Davidson does, that "belief is in its nature veridi-cal" is not to celebrate the happy congruence of subject and object but rather to say that the pattern truth makes is the pattern that *justification to us* makes.[23]

Without charity, we cannot detect the pattern truth makes. But charity entails see-ing most of what the natives say as justified. If there is no justification of the sort that strikes us as reasonable, there will be no coherent set of inferential relationships to be detected between the various strings of marks and noises produced by speakers, and therefore no rationality—no pattern of the requisite sort. This seems to me the *sole* force of Davidson's claim that the guiding principles used in detecting this pattern "derive from normative considerations"[24] and of his reference to "the norms that govern our theories of intensional attribution."[25] The need to justify our beliefs and desires to ourselves and to our fellow agents subjects us to norms, and obedience to these norms produces a behavioral pattern that we must detect in others before confidently attribut-ing beliefs to them. But there seems no occasion to look for obedience to an *additional* norm—the commandment to seek the truth. For—to return to the pragmatist doubt with which I began—obedience to that commandment will produce no behavior not produced by the need to offer justification.

So far I have been sketching the sort of minimalism about truth that I would still wish to attribute to Davidson, even after accepting his repudiation of deflationism. But this minimalism is very different from certain other philosophical accounts of truth that have been called by that name. To highlight these differences, I turn now from Davidson to Crispin Wright.

Wright cares deeply about the topics of realism and antirealism, and sees insouci-ance about such issues as undesirable "quietism," defined as the view that "significant metaphysical debate is impossible."[26] James's and Dewey's pragmatism was, among other things, an attempt to shut off such debate—not by showing it to be impossible or senseless, but by showing it to be pointless. So Wright's *Truth and Objectivity* is a good example of contemporary opposition to pragmatism. If the argument of that book is on the right track, then pragmatism is merely an unhappy attempt to evade questions that are absolutely central to philosophical reflection.

Like Davidson, Wright distrusts deflationism. But his reasons are very different. For Davidson, Tarski failed to show us how to detect in nature the pattern his truth theo-ries for specific languages exhibit. But for Wright what Tarski failed to give us is a *norm*. Wright thinks our statement-making practices are regulated by two distinct norms: war-ranted assertibility and truth. These two are, Wright says, "distinct in the precise sense that although aiming at one is, necessarily, aiming at the other, success in the one aim need not be success in the other."[27] From Wright's point of view, the trouble with defla-tionism is not that it does not tell you how to work up a truth theory for a given natural language, but that it does not even mention your duty to attain the truth. It leaves you thinking that you have done enough if you have done all the justifying you can.

That, of course, is just what pragmatists want you to think. Here, it seems to me, Davidson can happily concur with the pragmatists. For, as I have already suggested, I see no way to fit the idea of truth as a goal of inquiry into Davidson's account of what we need to say about truth. So in order to widen still further the gulf that yawns between Davidson's quietism and the metaphysical activism urged by Wright, I shall stress the entanglement of Wright's claim that truth is a distinct norm with his unpragmatic and anti-Davidsonian attempt to keep the notions of "correspondence" and "representation" alive.

Wright says that "deflationism … is committed to the idea that warranted assertibility is the *only* norm operating over assertoric discourse."[28] But, he says, even the deflationist has to admit that "while 'is T' and 'is warrantedly assertible' are normatively coincident, satisfaction of the one norm need not entail satisfaction of the other."[29] So, Wright concludes, "deflationism reinflates." But this argument seems insufficient. The fact that beliefs can be justified without being true does not entail that two norms are being invoked. Analogously, the fact that an action can be fully justified to a given audience and still not be the right thing to do does not show that we have two duties— one to justify our actions to each other and another to do the right thing. It merely shows that what can be justified to some audiences cannot be justified to others.

Wright, however, has a more detailed argument for his claim that "deflationism is an inherently unstable view."[30] He takes the deflationist to say that the content of the truth predicate is "wholly fixed" by what he calls the Disquotationalist Schema:

"*P*" is true if and only if *P*.

Then he says that there is an "explanatory biconditional link effected by the Disquotational Schema between the claim that a sentence is T and its proper assertoric use."[31] He defines a predicate as "(positively) descriptively normative" just in case "participants' selection, endorsement, and so on of a move is as a matter of fact guided by whether or not they judge that move is F."[32] This enables him to conclude that

"T" is descriptively normative in the sense that the practices of those for whom warranted assertibility is a descriptive norm are exactly as they would be if they consciously selected the assertoric moves which they were prepared to make or allow in the light of whether or not the sentences involved were T.

He sums up by saying that "any actual assertoric practice will be just as it would be if T were a self-conscious goal."[33] Although the behavior of those selecting for warranted assertibility will be the same as that of those selecting for truth, Wright thinks that we can distinguish two selections by asking whether they are "as a matter of fact guided" by one consideration rather than another.

But is it enough for there to be a fact of such guidance that the agent thinks there is such a fact?[34] Consider an analogy: I am trying to decide whether to prosecute my father for impiety. In the course of doing so I sometimes describe myself as trying to do what

I am justified in thinking pious and sometimes as trying to obey the will of the gods. Socrates has pointed out to me that although the two criteria are normatively coincident, satisfaction of the first criterion does not entail satisfaction of the second—for my community, the one that has given me my sense of what counts as satisfactory justification, may be out of touch with the gods. Still, my hope of satisfying both criteria persists.

An atheist, however, may tell me that I am "as a matter of fact" guided by only one norm and have only one self-conscious goal—that only one process of conscious selection is at work in my decision making. Since there are no gods, he says, there is no such thing as their will, and I cannot, even if I want to, obey the norm of conformity to that will. But I, of course, shall rejoin that this line of thought is reductionist and that my belief in the gods is enough to enable me to attempt to obey this norm. What norms one obeys, after all, is a matter of what norms one thinks one is obeying.[35]

I do not think that Wright should be happy with this line of defense against the atheist. For the force of his term "as a matter of fact guided by" disappears once one grants that a belief in guidance is proof of guidance. An imaginative agent who proliferates goals, and thus lights by which to perform the self-conscious selection of moves, will soon have more guidance systems going than we can shake a stick at. He will, for example, be trying to hit every bull's-eye he aims at, to win all the archery competitions, to become known as a superb archer, to become world archery champion, to please the goddess Diana, and to find a sympathetic defender in the councils of the gods. He will see all of these as prescriptively coincident—they all lead him to perform exactly the same actions—while acknowledging that achievement of the last two goals may not be extensionally coincident with achievement of the first four. For he has heard rumors that Diana has long since lost interest in archery and is now into karate.

Wright must either concede that a goal is "descriptively normative" for an action if the agent thinks it is, or else give us a further criterion for detecting *real* descriptive normativity. I am not sure what such a criterion could look like. But if he cannot specify one, he may have to admit that, just as "deflationism reinflates," so atheism retheologizes.

My own view is that attaining divine favor was indeed a goal distinct from hitting the target for religious archers and that attaining truth as distinct from making justified statements *is* a goal for metaphysically active inquirers. We metaphysical quietists deplore the fact that most people in our culture can be incited to this sort of activity. They still, alas, take seriously such bad, unpragmatic questions as "subjective or objective?" "made or found?" "*ad nos* or *in se*?" "socially constructed or for real?" But just as religious archers can be (and to some extent have been) replaced by atheist archers, so we pragmatists hope our culture will eventually replace itself with the culture that James and Dewey foresaw. In that culture, the question "Are you trying to attain truth as well as to form justified beliefs?" would be greeted with the same puzzlement with which "Are you seeking divine favor?" is greeted by atheist archers.[36]

I shall return to the topic of cultural change at the end of this essay, but first I want to direct attention to Wright's motive for emphasizing the difference between deflationism, which does not recognize that truth is a distinct norm, and his own brand of minimalism, which does. Wright has two aims in his book. The first is to give deflationism its due by admitting that "truth is not intrinsically a metaphysically heavyweight notion."[37] This puts Wright in a position to rebuff "error-theorists" like John Mackie, who think it a mistake to apply the word "true" to moral judgments. For, as Wright rightly says, "the minimalist proposal is conservative of our ordinary style of thought and talk about the comic, the revolting and the delightful, the good, and the valuable, which finds no solecism in the description of contents concerning such matters as 'true.'"[38] Defeating philosophers like Mackie is Wright's first aim, and Davidson and Dewey would both applaud this project.

His second aim, however, is to make clear that "we do not, in going minimalist about assertoric content and truth, set ourselves on a fast track to quietism about traditional philosophical controversy concerning realism and objectivity."[39] Wright thinks that

> talk of "representation of the facts" is not just admissible phrasing, a harmless gloss on talk of truth, but incorporates a philosophically correct—as we might say, *seriously dyadic*—perspective on the truth predicate (at least for discourses where realism is appropriate).

His deflationist opponent, he goes on to say, will insist that such talk "is additional metaphysical theory, foisted onto phrases which, while characteristic of the idea of truth, can be saved by a deflationary account and merit no such metaphysical interpretation."[40]

Dewey or Davidson could hardly have expressed his quietistic antipathy to the notions of correspondence and representation with better words than those that Wright here puts in the deflationist's mouth. James's and Dewey's post-Darwinian attempt to naturalize our self-image by dissolving the traditional oppositions between mind and nature and between subject and object, as well as Davidson's later assault on the scheme-content distinction, are both nicely epitomized in the claim that our perspective on the truth predicate should *not* be "seriously dyadic."

One of the great merits of Wright's very dense and argument-packed book is that he sees the need to say more than Dummett does about the pragmatic cash value of the ideas of "realism," "representation," and "correspondence." He sees that the logical terminology made current by Dummett—in his explications of "realism" with the aid of notions like bivalence and failure of excluded middle—does not adequately capture the motives for traditional debates. He notes that David Wiggins attempted to remedy this defect by suggesting that a tendency toward convergence is a sufficient criterion for the applicability of such notions. But Wright criticizes Wiggins's suggestion on the ground that the presence of such a tendency would, for example, make judgments about the comic representational if, for some accidental sociohistorical reason, there was steady convergence toward consensus on the comic.

Wright is surely right that the idea of representationality, and thus of realism, needs to be explicated with the help of a notion that is neither merely logical nor merely sociological. But his choice of a candidate for such an intermediate notion is very revealing. He says that what lies behind the intuitive association of representationality with convergence is "the Convergence/Representation Platitude," namely:

> If two devices each function to produce representations, then if conditions are suitable, and they function properly, they will produce divergent output if and only if presented with divergent input.[41]

This so-called platitude is supposed to flesh out the intuitive difference between the cognitive and the noncognitive, and thus between discourses (e.g., physics) for which realism is appropriate and others (e.g., argument about what's funny) for which it is not. Wright says that in the latter example "the base—the sense of humor—may blamelessly vary from person to person." But when it comes to reporting on the colors and shapes of middle-sized pieces of dry goods, or to astronomical theory, we can blame people for not getting them right, not representing accurately, not living up to their cognitive responsibilities, not corresponding to reality.

One might think, however, that blamability itself might blamelessly vary for contingent sociohistorical reasons. Wright sees this point and grasps the nettle. Metaphysical questions, such as those about the cognitive status of a discourse, can, he says, be settled only a priori. He boldly offers the following definition:

> A discourse exhibits Cognitive Command if and only if it is a priori that differences of opinion arising within it can be satisfactorily explained only in terms of "divergent input"; that is, the disputant's working on the basis of different information (and hence guilty of ignorance or error, depending on the status of that information) or "unsuitable conditions" (resulting in inattention or distraction and so in inferential error, or oversight of data and so on) or "malfunction" (for example, prejudicial assessment of data, upwards or downwards, or dogma, or failing in other categories already listed).[42]

One might paraphrase this definition by saying that you are under Cognitive Command if you are functioning as a well-oiled representation machine. The picture Wright is using is the one used by all epistemologists who think of "prejudice" and "superstition" as sand in the wheels, the sort of foreign ingredient that causes malfunctions. Such philosophers share a picture of human beings as machines constructed (by God or Evolution) to, among other things, get things right. Pragmatists want our culture to get rid of that self image and to replace it with a picture of machines that continually adjust to each other's behavior, and to their environment, by developing novel kinds of behavior. These machines have no fixed program or function; they continually reprogram themselves so as to serve hitherto undreamt-of functions.

Wright's so-called platitude suggests that pragmatists should do to him what he did to Wiggins. We should say that representation drops out for the same reasons convergence did. When we drop both notions, what we are left with is their common cash value: the claim that it is a demarcating mark of the appropriateness of realism for a given discourse that a certain picture be applicable to that discourse: the picture of truth as the output of a well-functioning machine that incarnates an a priori knowable input-output function. Notice that it is not enough for Wright's purposes if we merely know a priori that some input-output function or other is at work and that failure of the machine to operate in accord with this function is a malfunction. That requirement will be uninterestingly satisfied by indefinitely many functions, and equally uninterestingly unsatisfied by equally many others. What Wright requires is that we should know a priori which of these functions is the *right* one—that our knowledge of the *content* of the output (for example, the comic, the geometric, the valuable) should pick out a particular function.[43]

I shall return to this last point later, when I take up Wright's response to McDowell's argument for quietism. For the time being, however, I simply note that pragmatists, particularly after reading Kuhn, discard the terms "prejudice" and "dogma," as well as the idea that before the New Science came along, with its prejudice-detecting rationality and superstition-dissolving rigor, our cognitive machinery malfunctioned.[44] Pragmatists doubt that cognitivity amounts to more than historically contingent consensus about what shall count as proper justification for a belief. They see such consensus as what distinguishes what Kuhn calls "normal science" from what he calls "revolutionary science." Whereas Wright thinks that philosophers can look at the "content" of a discourse[45] and decide the a priori question of whether it is apt for Cognitive Command, pragmatists see the aptness or inaptness of Wright's "representation machine" terminology as up for historicosociological grabs—as much up for such grabs as the aptness or inaptness of religious language for describing the human situation.

Pragmatists think that Wright's "Consensus/Representation Platitude" can be made plausible only if one specifies that the two devices in question were machines for representing something *according to the same conventions*. For wildly different outputs can count as representations of the same input, depending on the purpose that the representational machinery serves. A videotape, an audiotape, and a typed transcript represent the same press conference. Anything, indeed, can count as a representation of anything, if there is enough antecedent agreement that it will count as such. More generally, representationality, and thus cognitivity, is something we can create, if not exactly at will, at least by agreement.

Content, pragmatists say on the basis of this argument, counts for vanishingly little in determining cognitivity, and de facto agreement on conventions for everything. That is why pragmatists think cognitivity a purely empirical, historicosociological notion. But if conventions of representation can vary as blamelessly as sense of humor—or, more to the point, if the only relevant sort of blame is the sort that attaches to those who are insufficiently cooperative in achieving shared practical goals—then representationality, like convergence, is a broken reed. It is of no help in pinning down the nature of cognitivity or in offering a seriously dyadic account of truth.

How destructive to his overall program is this objection to Wright's putative platitude? I think the best way to find out is to turn to the only place in his book where Wright explicitly argues against quietism—his final chapter. For there he discusses a notion, "meaning," which is close kin to that of "convention of representation." The only argument in favor of quietism that he discusses is Wittgenstein's "rule-following argument."

Wright agrees with Gareth Evans that this argument is a "metaphysical wet blanket," to be tossed off if at all possible. For Wright, the *only* concession to the quietist that need be made is the one made in his first chapter: that truth and falsity can be had even where realism is out of the question (as it certainly is in the case of comedy and may be in the case of morals).[46] He considers two brands of wet Wittgensteinian blanket: McDowell's and Kripke's. For McDowell, Wright says, the moral noncognivitist is "driven by a misbegotten construal of *ethical* fact and objectivity"; like her Platonist, moral realist opponent, she labors

> under the misapprehension that anything worth regarding as moral cognitivism has to make out how the relevant subject matter is *there*, so to speak, for any enquiring agent, independently of an evaluative "point of view." Since, as Wittgenstein teaches us, no subject matter is ever "there" in that kind of way, no disadvantageous comparison remains to be made. The appreciation of moral fact requires, to be sure, a moral point of view. But then, the appreciation of *any* fact requires a point of view.[47]

Wright rejects this attempt to undermine "realist/anti-realist debate in general."[48] He thinks that one great advantage of his notion of Cognitive Command is that it involves no "hyper-objectified conception of fact" of the sort Wittgenstein and McDowell criticize. For "the question whether it is a priori that differences of opinion formulable within a particular discourse will, prescinding from vagueness, always involve something worth regarding as a cognitive shortcoming" is to be settled "by reference to what we conceive as the range of possible sources of such differences."[49]

This, however, is not a sufficient reply to McDowell. For to have a conception of the range of possible sources of such differences, we first need to specify an input-output function; without that, we will not be able to distinguish the smooth functioning of a representation machine from its malfunction. But many input-output functions will describe the machine, and not all these functions will range over the same inputs. There are many ways to classify the flux of causal interactions in which the statement maker is involved, and each will offer a new candidate for "input." The problem of whether Wittgenstein has in fact shown that the relevant subject matter is never "there" in the relevant sense is the problem of whether there is a way to isolate input without reference to what Wright calls "an evaluative point of view." This is the sixty-four-dollar question: whether we can (as Dewey and Davidson insist we cannot) separate out "the world's" contribution to the judgment-forming process from our own.

Wright has no doubts about the existence of isolable truth makers. At one point, for example, he says that

> the world's making such statements [those that are what he calls "superassertible"] likely is something conceptually quite independent of our standards of appraisal—something, as it were, which is wholly between the statement and its truth maker, and on which we impinge only in an (at most) detective role.[50]

But how are we supposed to separate out these truth makers from the flux of causal interactions in which the statement maker is involved? One of Davidson's reasons for having no truck with the idea of "truth makers"[51] is his hunch that only completely artificial objects called "facts"—what Strawson sneeringly called "sentence-shaped objects"—can meet Wright's needs. The problem is not with funny, Platonic, "hyper-objectivized" facts, but with *any* sentence-shaped nonsentence, any putatively (in McDowell's words) "nonconceptualized configurations of things in themselves." Insofar as they are nonconceptualized, they are not isolable as input. But insofar as they are conceptualized, they have been tailored to the needs of a *particular* input-output function, a *particular* convention of representation.[52]

That any causal transaction can exemplify many different input-output functions was, of course, Wittgenstein's point when he remarked that all my previous additions could be seen as satisfying indefinitely many different rules for the use of "plus." But it is only when Wright turns from McDowell's Wittgenstein to Kripke's that he takes up this sort of difficulty explicitly. In discussing Kripke's, he considers the possibility that "the thesis that there are no 'facts of the matter' as far as rules and meanings are concerned … must necessarily inflate … into a *global* irrealism: the thesis that there are no facts of the matter anywhere." For

> if there are no substantial facts about what sentences say, there are no substantial facts about whether or not they are true. Thus, irrealism about meaning must enjoin an irrealism about truth, wherever the notion is applied. And irrealism about truth, wherever the notion is applied, is irrealism about all assertoric discourse.[53]

On this account of what Wittgenstein was up to, the problem is not, as with McDowell's Wittgenstein, that the indefinite plurality of rules (or conventions of representations, or input-output functions) makes it impossible to draw an interesting representational-nonrepresentational line between discourses, but that we have (by some criterion of nonrepresentationality that remains obscure) discovered that there is no such thing as getting meanings right, no such thing as representing meanings accurately.

Wright has an answer to this suggestion, one that I found very hard to follow and will not try to summarize.[54] But it seems clear that this suggestion is not the interesting one. For the interesting question about quietism, the one to which Wright's final chapter is devoted, is whether the whole terminology of "getting right" and "representing accurately" is a useful way of separating off discourses from one another. This question, raised by McDowell's Wittgenstein, is begged by Kripke's.

Wright seems to recognize this point, for in the penultimate paragraph of his book, he grants that there is a "residual concern" to which he has not spoken. The following is his final formulation of this concern:

> Whether, even if the key distinctions [between representational, cognitive, substantive truth, and the other, merely minimalist sort of truth] can be formulated in ways that allow the status of a discourse to be determined independently of the rule-following dialectic, their serviceability as vehicles for the expression of realist intuition may not be so severely compromised by a proper understanding of that dialectic that there is no longer any *point* to the taxonomy which they might enable us to construct?[55]

Raising this doubt—a doubt about whether there was a point to the book we have just finished reading—on the book's last page seems to me a very honest, and rather brave, thing to do.

Wright's response to this doubt, in his final paragraph, is that though there may be a case to be made for the view that there is no point, his book has helped set the terms for debating any such case by giving us "a more pluralistic and fine-grained conception of the realist/anti-realist debates than has been commonplace."[56] It has indeed given us such a conception, but the increased fineness of grain may not serve the purpose Wright suggests. For what looks like desirable fineness of grain to Wright looks like the pointless addition of further epicycles to his pragmatist opponents.

Wright's suggestion—which, though I have scanted it for my purposes in this essay, is at the heart of his book—is that there are different truth predicates for different discourses. He argues that we should use a minimalist, thin truth predicate in discourse about the comic, and various thicker alternatives (such as Cognitive Command), correlated with various a priori determinable relations between other discourses and the rest of the world, for other discourses.[57] But of course for pragmatists, what Wright thinks of as permanent a priori determinable relations are just local and transitory historicosociological differences between patterns of justification and blame. These differences—subpatterns within the single overall pattern justification makes—should not, pragmatists think, be imported into the concept of truth. To do so is to do what Davidson calls "humanizing truth by making it basically epistemic."[58]

Much of what I have said can be summed up in the claim that the central issue between Wright's metaphysical activism and Davidson's quietism concerns the point of inquiry. For Wright truth, considered as a desirable noncausal relation between language and nonlanguage, is a goal of such inquiry (if only in those areas of culture, such as physical science, for which "realism" is thought appropriate). For Davidsonians, on the other hand, the most consistent position is to hold that

(a) the arguments from the indefinite plurality of ways of going on/input-output functions/conventions of representations leave no room for any such desirable non-causal relation,

(b) so there is no reason to think that even an infinite amount of justification would get us closer to such a relation,

(c) so there is nothing that can plausibly be described as a *goal* of inquiry, although the desire for further justification, of course, serves as a *motive* of inquiry.

If Dewey and Davidson were asked, "What is the goal of inquiry?" the best either could say would be that it has many different goals, none of which have any metaphysical presuppositions—for example, getting what we want, the improvement of man's estate, convincing as many audiences as possible, solving as many problems as possible. *Only* if we concede to Wright that "truth" is the name of a distinct norm will metaphysical activism seem desirable. For Dewey and Davidson, that is an excellent reason not to view it as such a norm.

Some Davidsonians might see no reason why they too should not say, ringingly, robustly, and commonsensically, that the goal of inquiry is *truth*. But they cannot say this without misleading the public. For when they go on to add that they are, of course, not saying that the goal of inquiry is correspondence to the intrinsic nature of things, the common sense of the vulgar will feel betrayed.[59] For "truth" sounds like the name of a goal only if it is thought to name a *fixed* goal—that is, if progress toward truth is explicated by reference to a metaphysical picture, that of getting closer to what Bernard Williams calls "what is there *anyway*." Without that picture, to say that truth is our goal is merely to say something like: we hope to justify our belief to as many and as large audiences as possible. But to say that is to offer only an ever-retreating goal, one that fades forever and forever when we move. It is not what common sense would call a goal. For it is neither something we might realize we had reached, nor something to which we might get closer.

We pragmatists think that philosophers who view the defense of "our realistic intuitions" as an important cultural or moral imperative are held captive by the picture of getting closer to a fixed goal. As an initial step in breaking free of this picture, we suggest following Davidson in abandoning what he calls "standard ideas of language mastery." Then one will think of such mastery as involving "no learnable common core of consistent behavior, no shared grammar or rules, no portable interpreting machine set to grind out the meaning of an arbitrary utterance."[60] Dropping these standard ideas makes it very difficult to take seriously the idea of human beings as portable representing machines that incorporate a priori knowable input-output functions.

The idea of such a machine lies behind both Wright's notion of Cognitive Command and his Kripkean suggestion that language, meaning, truth, and knowledge might all collapse together if, *horribile dictu*, it should turn out that there is no fact of the matter about what we have been meaning by "addition." But the skepticism described by Kripke's Wittgenstein holds no terrors for those who follow Davidson in abandoning the whole idea of "rules of language." Analogously, skepticism about an a priori recognizable attribute of discourses called cognitivity or representationality, and about the utility of the notions of cognitivity and representationality, holds no terrors for those who, like Bacon, Dewey, and Kuhn, see artisans and natural scientists as doing the same kind of thing: employing whatever propositional or nonpropositional tools they think may help with the problems currently before them.[61]

If, as good Darwinians, we want to introduce as few discontinuities as possible into the story of how we got from the apes to the Enlightenment, we shall reject the idea that Nature has settled on a single input-output function that, incarnated in each member of our species, enables us to represent our environment accurately. For that idea requires that Nature herself has divided up the causal swirl surrounding these organisms into discrete inputs and has adopted a particular input-output function as distinctively hers—a function whose detection enables us to offer justification according to Nature's own criteria (or, as Wright would say, Commands) rather than to those of transitory and local audiences. So, for Darwinians, there is an obvious advantage in *not* dividing the activities of these organisms into the cognitive, representational ones and the others. This means that there is an obvious advantage in dropping the idea of a distinct goal or norm called "truth"—the goal of scientific inquiry, but not, for example, of carpentry. On a Deweyan view, the difference between the carpenter and the scientist is simply the difference between a workman who justifies his actions mainly by reference to the movements of matter and one who justifies his mainly by reference to the behavior of his colleagues.

In previous essays—in particular one called "Science as Solidarity"[62]—I have urged that the romance and the idealistic hopes that have traditionally been elaborated in a rhetoric of "the pursuit of objective truth" can be equally well elaborated in a rhetoric of social solidarity—a rhetoric that romanticizes the pursuit of intersubjective, unforced agreement among larger and larger groups of interlocutors. But I agree with those who insist that the former rhetoric is that of contemporary common sense. So I think that pragmatism should not claim to be a commonsensical philosophy. Nor should it appeal, as David Lewis suggests metaphysics must appeal, to intuition as final arbiter.

If contemporary intuitions are to decide the matter, "realism" and representationalism will always win, and the pragmatists' quietism will seem intellectually irresponsible. So pragmatists should not submit to their judgment. Instead, they should see themselves as working at the interface between the common sense of their community, a common sense much influenced by Greek metaphysics and by monotheism, and the startlingly counterintuitive self-image sketched by Darwin, and partially filled in by Dewey. They should see themselves as involved in a long-term attempt to change the rhetoric, the common sense, and the self-image of their community.

The pragmatist who says, "The difference between justification and truth makes no difference, except for the reminder that justification to one audience is not justification to another"—the claim I put in her mouth at the beginning of this essay—has not yet said enough. For there is another difference: justification does not call for metaphysical activism but truth, as understood by contemporary, representationalist common sense, does. The pragmatist regrets the prevalence of this representationalist picture and of the "realist" intuitions that go with it, but she cannot get rid of these unfortunate cultural facts by more refined analyses of contemporary common sense. She cannot appeal to neutral premises or to widely shared beliefs.

She is in the same situation as are atheists in overwhelmingly religious cultures. Such people can only hope to trace the outlines of what Shelley calls "the gigantic shadows which futurity casts upon the present." They foresee a time when the notions of Divine Will and of Cognitive Command will, for similar reasons, have been replaced by that of a Free Consensus of Inquirers. But, in the meantime, the pragmatist who urges our culture to abandon metaphysical activism cannot argue that such activism is inconsistent with a mass of our other beliefs, any more than ancient Greek atheists could say that sacrificing to the Olympians was inconsistent with a mass of other Greek beliefs. All the pragmatist can do is the sort of thing they did: she can point to the seeming futility of metaphysical activity, as they pointed to the seeming futility of religious activity.

In the end, we pragmatists have no real arguments against the intuitions to which books like Wright's *Truth and Objectivity* appeal. All we have are rhetorical questions like: Are all those epicycles really worth the trouble? What good do the intuitions you painstakingly salvage do us? What practical difference do they make?[63] But such rhetorical questions have been instruments of sociocultural change in the past, and may be again.

Notes

1. Of course, when the question is not about deciding what to believe now, but about explaining what has happened, the distinction between justification and truth is useful: we often explain our failures by saying, "I was quite justified in believing that, but unfortunately it was not true." But though useful, it is not essential. We can explain our failure equally well by saying "What I thought would happen did not," and in many other ways.

2. However, what there is to be said about justification is local rather than global: quite different, unconnected things have to be said about justification in, for example, mathematics, jurisprudence, and astrology. So philosophers are hardly the people to say it. This point chimes with Michael Williams's argument (in his *Unnatural Doubts: Epistemological Realism and the Basis of Scepticism* [Oxford: Blackwell, 1991]) that "knowledge" is neither the name of a natural kind nor the topic of useful global theorizing. I am indebted to Williams for the realization that the Cartesian notion of a natural, ahistorical, and transcultural "order of reasons" is essential to Descartes's

"dreaming" argument, and more generally to both epistemological skepticism and the feasibility of epistemology as a discipline.

3. Not all. Some idealists argued that all truths are true by virtue of their correspondence to a single object (the Absolute), thereby eviscerating the idea of correspondence.

4. Of course, a host of contemporary philosophers (notably Ruth Millikan, David Papineau, and Fred Dretske) have retained the notion of "inner representation" and interpreted it biologistically, as a matter of the evolutionarily designed ability of an organism to respond differentially to different stimuli. In contrast, followers of Wilfred Sellars (such as George Pitcher, David Armstrong, Daniel Dennett, and myself) lump the neurological arrangements that make possible such differential responses to differential stimuli together with the internal states of (for example) thermostats. We treat perceptions as dispositions to acquire beliefs and desires rather than as "experiences" or "raw feels," and hence we disagree with Thomas Nagel that there is "something it is like" to have a perception. I see the Sellarsian strategy we employ as an example of the pragmatist habit of refusing to recognize the existence of troublemaking entities. This habit strikes nonpragmatists like Nagel as a refusal to face up to the facts.

As I suggest at the end of this essay, we pragmatists too want to be faithful to Darwin. But we think that the Millikan-Papineau-Dretske revivification of the notion of "representation" is an insufficiently radical way of appropriating Darwin's insight. These philosophers want to reconcile Darwin with Descartes's and Locke's "way of ideas." In contrast, we want to follow up on Dewey's suggestion that Darwin has made Descartes and Locke obsolete.

5. *Pragmatism and the Meaning of Truth* (Cambridge, MA: Harvard University Press, 1975), 106.

6. Ibid., 42. James also, unfortunately, said a lot of other, conflicting things about truth—such as that it consists in some kind of agreement between ideas and reality. In "Dewey between Hegel and Darwin" (reprinted in *Truth and Progress: Philosophical Papers*, vol. 3 [Cambridge: Cambridge University Press, 1998]), I argue that Dewey was wise to avoid saying the latter sort of thing and to eschew analyses or definitions of "truth" or of "true."

7. Two recent books show how this suggestion can be worked out in detail: Barry Allen's *Truth in Philosophy* (Cambridge, MA: Harvard University Press, 1993) and Robert Brandom's *Making It Explicit* (Cambridge, MA: Harvard University Press, 1994).

8. For an account of this strategy, see Hilary Putnam's "Does the Disquotational Theory Solve All Problems?" in his *Words and Life* (Cambridge, MA: Harvard University Press, 1994), 264–278. Putnam there criticizes two philosophers whom he construes as disquotationalists—Paul Horwich and Michael Williams—for remaining in the grip of a "positivistic picture" and for being closet reductionists. This is a criticism he has often made of me (see, e.g., "The Question of Realism," 295–312, in the same volume). On Putnam's view, all three of us ignore the need to admit the existence of genuine "directedness" and "intentionality." I am not sure whether Putnam would make the same criticism of Davidson.

9. R. Rorty, "Pragmatism, Davidson and Truth," in E. LePore, ed., *Truth and Interpretation: Perspectives on the Philosophy of Donald Davidson* (Oxford: Blackwell, 1986), 333–368. This article is reprinted in my *Objectivity, Relativism, and Truth* (Cambridge: Cambridge University Press, 1991).

10. D. Davidson, "The Structure and Content of Truth," *Journal of Philosophy* 87, no. 6 (1990): 279–328. This article comprises Davidson's Dewey Lectures.

11. Ibid., 287.

12. Ibid.

13. Ibid., 295.

14. Ibid.

15. Ibid., 322.

16. Ibid., 323.

17. Ibid., 320.

18. A good statement of the view that you *can* separate these is Wright's description of metaphysical realism, as asserting the possibility that "despite the apparent cognitive richness of our lives, we are somehow so situated as not to be enabled to arrive at the concepts which fundamentally depict the character of the real world and the nature of our interaction with it" ("On Putnam's Proof That We Are Not Brains in a Vat," in P. Clark and B. Hale, eds., *Reading Putnam* [Oxford: Blackwell, 1994], 238). Assuming that "fundamentally depict the character of ..." means "are required to tell the truth about," then Davidson is committed to saying that this situation cannot arise: there can never be what Wright calls "a thought whose truth would make a mockery of humankind and its place in nature" (ibid., 240). The worst that can happen is that people whose language we are quite capable of learning (the Galactics, say) might offer us some astonishingly impressive substitutes for our present beliefs about selected special topics (e.g., the microstructure of matter or how to achieve world peace).

19. Davidson, "Structure," 309. Some commentators on Davidson have taken a truth condition to be a nonlinguistic state of affairs, a fact rather than a sentence in the truth theorist's language—despite Davidson's polemic against the notion of "fact" in "True to the Facts," in *Inquiries into Truth and Interpretation* (Oxford: Clarendon Press, 1984), 36–54.

20. Davidson, "Structure," 309.

21. Michael Williams in *Unnatural Doubts* suggests that an inability to "account for the truth-conduciveness of justification" will lead to skepticism (231). My view, and the one I am attributing to Davidson, is that what leads to skepticism is the initial assumption of truth-conduciveness rather than the failure of attempts to back up this assumption. So I deny Williams's claim that "it is surely an essential feature of epistemic justification that justifying a belief makes it more likely to be true" (229). I enlarge on this denial in "Sind Aussagen universelle Geltungsansprüche?," *Deutsche Zeitschrift für Philosophie* 42, no. 6 (1994): 975–988, a criticism of Habermas's and Apel's views on truth.

22. For his repudiation of the notion of "representation," see Davidson's "The Myth of the Subjective," in M. Krausz, ed., *Relativism: Interpretation and Confrontation* (Notre Dame, IN: University of Notre Dame Press, 1989), 165–166.

23. But I may be missing something here, and my blind spot may conceal a real and important disagreement between Davidson's views and my version of pragmatism. For in "Structure," Davidson says that "since the concept of truth is central to the theory [i.e., to an empirical theory that entails T-sentences], we are justified in saying that truth is a crucially important explanatory concept" (313). It does not look particularly central to me. As I see it, what Davidson calls a "theory of truth" could equally well be called "a theory of complex behavior" or "a theory of justificatory behavior." Granted that the production of the sort of biconditionals Tarski called "T-sentences" is the whole point of the theory, I am not sure why the production of these sentences illustrates the centrality, or the crucial importance, of the concept of truth.

I am quite willing to withdraw my 1986 claim that "true" has no explanatory use, which was a misleading way of putting the point that "It's true!" is not a helpful explanation of why science works or of why you should share one of my beliefs. But although the sort of theory to which Davidson thinks "the concept of truth" central is indeed explanatory, it seems to me somewhat awkward and unnecessary to pick out a given concept that is explicated by reference to such theories and say that *it* has a crucial explanatory role. Avoiding such favoritism would be more congruent with Davidson's fundamental point that a theory of truth is automatically a theory of meaning and of rationality—as well as with his doctrine that every intensional concept is intertwined with every other such concept.

Another way of locating the point at which Davidson and I may differ is that he thinks it significant that we use the same word to designate what is preserved by valid inference as we use to caution people that beliefs justified to us may not be justified to other, better audiences. As far as I can see, there is no deep reason why "true" is used to do both of these jobs, why one of the words that we use to describe the pattern of behavior necessarily exhibited by language users (logical inference) should also be one of the words we use to caution people that they may be believing something that better-advised people would not believe. So I see no reason to look behind both uses for some feature of the *meaning* of "true" which makes that word suitable for both assignments. If I could see such a reason, I might be in a better position to appreciate what Davidson means by the "centrality" of the concept and to see why he speaks of himself as "filling in the content" of this concept.

24. Davidson, "Structure," 319.

25. Ibid., 325.

26. C. Wright, *Truth and Objectivity* (Cambridge, MA: Harvard University Press, 1992), 202.

27. Ibid., 19.

28. Ibid., 21.

29. Ibid., 23.

30. Ibid., 34.

31. Ibid., 17.

32. Ibid., 16.

33. Ibid., 17.

34. Wright identifies the claim that to possess truth is "to meet a normative constraint distinct from assertoric warrant" with the claim that "truth is a genuine property" (ibid., 35). I avoid the issue of whether truth is a property—an issue that seems to me to boil down eventually, just as Wright says, to the question "one norm or two?" I agree with what Davidson says about this issue ("Structure," 285).

35. This line of argument is often employed against, for example, a Hobbesian reductionist who says that the actions I think are motivated by my desire to be a good citizen are really motivated by my fear of sanctions. Hobbes's and Thrasymachus's strong point is that a causal explanation of my action that does not refer to good citizenship may be as useful as one that does. Their opponent's strong point is that the need for causal explanation is not our only motive for attributing motives.

36. These last six paragraphs are heavily indebted to Bjorn Ramberg and Barry Smith. They replace a section of an earlier version of this essay, a version read and discussed by Smith and Ramberg. Ramberg kindly conveyed Smith's (well-taken) criticisms of that version to me and suggested ways to avoid these criticisms—suggestions I have gratefully adopted.

37. Wright, *Truth and Objectivity*, 72.

38. Ibid., 75.

39. Ibid., 86.

40. Ibid., 83.

41. Ibid., 91.

42. Ibid., 93.

43. I cannot figure out how somebody who invokes a priori knowledge as blithely as Wright does can say, equally blithely, that "apriority generally is an artifact of description" (ibid., 129).

44. Wright has read Kuhn too, of course, and discusses "theory-ladenness" in some detail. But the upshot of his discussion is rather disappointing: "The hope must be either that we can yet win through to some purified notion of an observation statement, one that does not involve 'theory-ladenness' of the sort which is giving the trouble, or—more likely—that the Cognitive Command constraint can and must be refined in some way while remaining faithful to its motivation in the idea of representational function. I have no easy solution to suggest" (167–168).

This passage is typical of Wright's hope to smooth over the anomalies that arise from attempts to make explicit the presuppositions of traditional, intuitive distinctions. Pragmatists rejoice in no longer needing to invoke those distinctions or to have those intuitions. So what looks like undesirable quietism to Wright looks like vigorous philosophical progress to them. This is the same sort of dialectical standoff that obtained between Leibniz and Newton. Newton shrugged off, quietistically, many traditional Aristotelian problems. Leibniz insisted that such shrugs were symptoms of intellectual irresponsibility and that metaphysical, as well as physical, explanations were required.

45. "If our interest is in the question whether comic discourse, *by virtue of its very content*, is fitted to express the products of a seriously representational mode of function, then any constraint designed to capture that idea must, it seems, be so formulated that satisfying it requires the possibility of a priori knowledge that the relevant conditions are met" (ibid., 94). In Wright's usage, it seems to me, the "concepts content of a discourse" and "a priori knowledge about that discourse" are mutually definable. For the only way one would know whether one had zeroed in on the content of a discourse, as opposed to the mechanisms of its production, would be to figure out what could be known about that discourse a priori. For Quinean holists like Davidson, of course, these mutually definable concepts are equally dubious.

46. "Quietism makes at least one important contribution, viz., the insight that it is a metaphysical hypostasis of notions like truth and assertion to write their applicability within a discourse into the substance of a realist view about its subject matter" (ibid., 204).

47. Ibid., 207.

48. Ibid., 208.

49. Ibid., 208.

50. Ibid., 77. Elsewhere Wright speaks of "the kind of state of affairs conferring truth on *P*" (117). The homiletic tone of "between the statement and its truth-maker" recurs when Wright says that "where we deal in a purely cognitive way with objective matters, the opinions which we form are in no sense optional or variable as a function of permissible idiosyncrasy, but are *commanded* of us" (146). Contrast the *libertinisme erudit* implicit in the concluding words of Davidson's "Structure": "Truth thus rests in the end on belief and, even more ultimately, on the affective attitudes" (326).

51. See Davidson, *Inquiries into Truth*, 194, for his rejection of the idea of "truth makers." See also, in the same volume, his 1969 essay "True to the Facts," which contrasts the Tarskian notion of a sentence being satisfied by objects that can be individuated without the use of the sentence with that of "a sentence being made true by a fact." Since writing that essay, however, Davidson has dropped the claim that the former notion gives us any sort of correspondence account of truth.

52. Wright seems to be speaking to this issue when, in a pregnant, compressed, and baffling footnote, he says that "it seems just plain obvious that the reaction-dependence of rules, the ceaseless involvement of our sub-cognitive natures in our step-by-step appreciation of the requirements of rules which Wittgenstein emphasizes, cannot be at ease with the mythology of the epistemically transparent yet fully substantial propositional object" (226). He suggests that the moral to be drawn from Wittgenstein may be that "something irreducibly *human and sub-cognitive* actively contributes to our engagement with any issue at all—a contribution ... presumed shared among thinkers who engage the issue in question" (227). If that is what Wittgenstein told us, he chose a remarkably roundabout way of saying that we can presume that our interlocutors' bodies respond to the environment pretty much as ours do. One difference between Wright and Davidson is that Davidson would, I think, see no point in distinguishing between a cognitive nature or level and a noncognitive nature or level, for the same reasons he sees none in distinguishing between scheme and content, or between subject and object, or between "knowing a language and knowing our

way around the world generally" ("A Nice Derangement of Epitaphs," in Lepore, *Truth and Interpretation*, 445–446). From his point of view, such distinctions hypostatize two descriptions, one in propositional and one in nonpropositional terms, of the same events.

I confess, however, that Davidson's attachment to the doctrine of the indeterminacy of translation, and his related insistence that there is a philosophically interesting difference between the intentional and the nonintentional, suggest that he qualifies the thoroughgoing antidualism I am attributing to him here. I discuss this attachment in "Davidson's Mental-Physical Distinction," forthcoming in L. Hahn, ed., *The Philosophy of Donald Davidson*, The Library of Living Philosophers (La Salle, IL: Open Court).

53. Wright, *Truth and Objectivity*, 211.

54. See ibid., 227.

55. Ibid., 229–230.

56. Ibid., 230.

57. "There are a *variety* of features that may be possessed by minimally truth-apt discourses, any of which may contribute in some measure towards clarifying and substantiating realist preconceptions about it ... A basic realism about a discourse (of course, the epithets 'realism' and 'anti-realism' come to seem less and less happy from a pluralistic perspective) would be the view that it is qualified by *no* interesting feature serving to give point to an intuitive realism about it—that it deploys minimally truth-apt contents, and that's the whole of the matter" (ibid., 141–142).

58. Davidson, "Structure," 298.

59. For a good example of the outrage that results from such betrayal, see J. Searle, "Rationality and Realism: What Is at Stake?," *Daedalus* 122, no. 4 (1993): 55–83. Searle believes that there are ways of getting around the traditional problems with the notion that truth is accuracy of representation (65–66) and that those of us (he mentions Kuhn and Derrida, as well as myself) who think these problems insoluble are, by departing from what he calls the "Western Rationalistic Tradition," endangering the universities. I reply to Searle's article in "John Searle on Realism and Relativism" (*Truth and Progress*, chap. 3).

60. Davidson, "A Nice Derangement," 445. Dropping these ideas also makes it very difficult to get excited about Wittgenstein's rule-following argument. For freedom from these ideas permits one to see it as simply a version (adapted to the needs of those who still take the notion of "rules of language" seriously) of a generic argument against the existence of any relation that is both natural (i.e., not simply a product of contingent human practices) and noncausal. That is the sort of relation which representationalists are constantly invoking: For the Sellarsian version of this argument, see Brandom, *Making It Explicit*, and my "Robert Brandom on Social Practices and Representations," in *Truth and Progress*, chap. 6.

61. Kuhn summed up his claim that science should be thought of as problem solving by saying, "Whether or not individual practitioners are aware of it, they are trained to and rewarded for solving intricate puzzles—be they instrumental, theoretical, logical or mathematical—at the interface between their phenomenal world and their community's beliefs about it" ("Afterwords," in P.

Horwich, ed., *World Changes: Thomas Kuhn and the Nature of Science* [Cambridge, MA: MIT Press, 1993], 338). Like Dewey, Kuhn thought that a historicosociological account of the origin of these interfaces and these puzzles can replace a metaphysical account of the nature of representation. "I aim," he says, "to deny all meaning to claims that successive scientific beliefs become more and more probable or better and better approximations to the truth and simultaneously to suggest that the subject of truth claims cannot be a relation between beliefs and a putatively mind-independent or 'external' world" (ibid., 330).

62. Included in my *Objectivity, Relativism, and Truth*.

63. Putnam thinks we have more, namely demonstrations of the incoherence of nonpragmatic positions. In *Words and Life* (Cambridge, MA: Harvard University Press, 1994) he explains "incoherence" as the fact that "attempts at a clear formulation of the [metaphysical realist] position never succeed—because there is no real content there to be captured" (303). I think that clarity is a matter of familiarity rather than a property whose presence or absence can be demonstrated, and that Wright, Bernard Williams, and others find clear as the noonday sun what Putnam finds irremediably unclear. So I prefer to talk of lack of convenience rather than lack of clarity. James Conant discusses the metaphilosophical issue between Putnam and myself in his introduction to *Words and Life* (xxx–xxxi).

IV   Tarski's Theory and Its Importance

Introduction

Michael P. Lynch, Nathan Kellen, and Jeremy Wyatt

Most philosophers would agree that Alfred Tarski's work on truth has been immensely influential. But that is where agreement generally ends, for the point of Tarski's theory, its applicability to philosophical concerns, and its very nature are all deeply disputed.

When discussing Tarski's importance, it is crucial to distinguish two influential elements of his work that are often conflated. The first is what Tarski (chapter 14) called his *material adequacy condition* for a theory of truth. This is Tarski's famous *Convention T*, which involves the schema (T). Tarski proposed that it was a minimal condition of any theory of truth that it entail all sentences of the following form:

(T) X is true if and only if p.

Here p is a variable for a sentence, X is a name of that sentence, and the "if and only if" denotes an extensional equivalence. Instances of (T) therefore include the following:

"Roses are red" is true if and only if roses are red.

"Violets are blue" is true if and only if violets are blue.

Tarski was not the first to note that biconditionals of this form capture something very basic about our concept of truth (see, e.g., Frank Plumpton Ramsey in chapter 16). But he was the first to employ schema (T) as a test for truth theories. Since schema (T) articulates something very basic about our concept of truth, Tarski reasoned, any adequate theory of truth must logically entail every instance of this schema in the language in which the truth predicate is being defined.

It is important to realize, however, that (T) is not Tarski's *definition* of truth.[1] His definition is the second and more important element of Tarski's work on truth. While (T) does not comprise Tarski's definition of truth, he did believe that each instance of (T) is "a partial definition of truth." Each instance defines truth for the sentence in question—for example, "Roses are red." Thus, if the language contained only the sentences used in the examples above, we could give a complete definition of truth by simply conjoining the above instances of (T). However, Tarski was interested in languages in which it is possible to have an infinite number of sentences. For this reason, he aimed to supply one general definition of truth that would be extensionally equivalent to the logical conjunction of an infinite number of instances of (T).

Tarski had three goals in presenting a theory of truth. First, he obviously wanted a theory that would meet the material adequacy condition. Second, he wanted to make the concept of truth physically respectable. In the 1930s, when Tarski first developed his theory, verificationist philosophers were openly suspicious of semantic notions like truth. Like the verificationists, Tarski subscribed to the physicalist view that any concept worth having can be completely defined in terms that refer only to physical and mathematical entities. As a result, Tarski set himself the task of defining truth in this way for certain formal languages, which he took to be adequate for the physical sciences and mathematics.

Finally, Tarski wanted a theory that was immune to the destructive impact of the Liar Paradox. We can formulate this paradox informally by drawing on sentence (1):

(1) This sentence is false.

From this seemingly innocuous sentence, a contradiction follows. It seems that (1) must be either true or false; but if it is either, then it is both true and false. After all, if (1) is true, then it is false, because it says that it is false. But if it is false, then it must be true, since once again it says that it is false. So (1) is both true and false, which is a contradiction.[2]

Tarski argues that natural languages, like English, are subject to the Liar Paradox because they are "semantically closed." That is, they contain semantic predicates like "true" and "false" that can apply to the language's own sentences. Tarski therefore restricts his definition of truth to *semantically open* languages, whose semantic predicates apply only to sentences of languages other than themselves. Liar sentences like (1) can't be expressed in such a language.

If we adopt this strategy, then when we define truth for a semantically open language L_1, we must use another semantically open language L_2. That is, we must distinguish between the language for which we want to define truth (the *object language*) and the language in which we express that definition (the *metalanguage*). When we state our definition in the metalanguage, we must use words like "true" to mean true in L_1 (that is, true in the object language). In short, to avoid the Liar Paradox, Tarski believed that a definition of "true" must not be expressed in the language for which the concept is being defined. We must always climb up to a metalanguage to define truth for the language below.

With this qualification in place, Tarski defines truth as a relation, which he calls "satisfaction," that links expressions and objects: "A sentence is true if it is satisfied by all objects and false otherwise."[3] His definition relies on the idea that while a language has a potentially infinite number of sentences, those sentences are constructed from a finite vocabulary. The rough idea is first to define the basic elements of the language and then to build up the definition from there by means of a procedure known as recursion. A recursive definition consists of one or more clauses that specify the most basic members of a particular set, followed by further clauses that show how other members of the set are built out of the more basic members. As long as there is a finite number of types of basic members of the set and a finite number of ways that these can be combined to form new (nonbasic) members, an infinite number of nonbasic members of the set can be defined by this procedure.

In his definition, Tarski took the basic expressions of the languages he was interested in to be *sentential functions*, or *open sentences* such as "*x* loves *y*" or "*y* is a philosopher." We can then say that satisfaction relates sentential functions to objects, roughly as follows. If "*x* is red" is the sentential function and a particular rose is the object, then the rose *satisfies* "*x* is red" just when the rose is red. Simplifying greatly, what Tarski showed is that once we define satisfaction for the simplest types of sentential functions in this way, we can use the truth-functional operators ("and," "or," "not," etc.) and quantifiers ("all" and "some") to define "satisfies," and hence "true," for any complete sentence (e.g., "Elizabeth planted red roses and yellow sunflowers" or "All roses are red") in the object language.

We should highlight two features of Tarski's definition in particular. First, it must be stressed that the languages that concerned Tarski, such as the languages of deductive logic, are entirely formal. Not only are such languages semantically open in the sense explained above, they contain none of the ambiguity and vagueness that riddle ordinary languages such as English or Polish. Second, it is crucial to Tarski's definition that it is not a *general* definition of "true" as it applies to any language L but rather a definition of "true in L_1," "true in L_2," and so on. This is a consequence not only of Tarski's meta/object language distinction but also of the fact that his truth definitions rely on extensional definitions of the basic expressions (for instance, the predicates) of the object language. Object languages with extensionally different basic expressions will therefore require distinct definitions of "true."

These two features of Tarski's theory have caused many philosophers to wonder whether it is at all relevant to the philosophical problem of defining the ordinary concept of truth. After all, the ordinary languages that we speak are messy, rife with ambiguity and vagueness, and subject to paradox. Furthermore, a definition of "true in L_1," "true in L_2," and so on may seem to miss the point of defining "true," in the same way that definitions of "the proper legal ruling on Wednesday" and "the proper legal ruling on Thursday" don't give us a definition of "proper legal ruling" (see Blackburn 1984, 266–267). We want to know what all the relativized definitions have in common; that is, we want a general definition of "true."

In his seminal essay on Tarski, Hartry Field (chapter 15) argues that we should think of Tarski's truth definition as having two parts. The first part involves definitions of what it is for a name to *denote* an object, for a predicate to *apply to* some class of objects, and for a function symbol to be *fulfilled by* a pair of objects. Field refers collectively to these relations as relations of *primitive denotation*. The second part then consists of a recursive definition of "true" in terms of primitive denotation.

According to Field, Tarski's truth definition, when thought of in this way, can be applied to natural languages so long as we take the truth-bearers to be sentence tokens, or individual utterances. However, Field also argues that if we think of Tarski's truth definition in this way, then we must admit that Tarski did not actually succeed in incorporating truth into a physicalist picture of the world. Instead, Tarski reduced truth to other *semantic* notions which aren't themselves adequately reduced. In particular, Field's point is that Tarski merely offers "list-like" definitions of denotation, applica-tion, and fulfillment that don't reduce or explain these crucial notions. He argues that to reduce truth to purely physical terms, we must go beyond these list-like definitions. A promising route, Field suggests, is to employ causal theories of reference to this end.

If we follow Field, then we might think that Tarski's theory amounts to (or should amount to) a correspondence theory in which "correspondence" is cashed out in terms of causal relations between our uses of words and the world (see the introduction to part I). Whether Tarski's theory does in fact amount to a correspondence theory of truth is a difficult question. Tarski himself argues that his theory, insofar as it meets the mate-rial adequacy condition, does accord with the fundamental intuitions behind the cor-respondence theory. But it is unclear whether this entails that the theory itself can be called a correspondence account of truth. For alternative interpretations on which Tar-ski's theory fits more with deflationary theories of truth, see, for example, Quine (1986) and Soames (1999), and for further discussion, see Schantz (1998) and Horwich (2010).

Notes

1. Indeed, he wouldn't have regarded a schema like (T) as being capable of serving as a definition.

2. The Liar Paradox is frustrating because while (1) is odd sounding, it is more difficult than it looks to say what, if anything, is wrong with it. It seems like a perfectly meaningful sentence, even though it is self-referential. After all, the sentence "This sentence is in English" is self-referential, and it looks to be meaningful. For a discussion of the "meaningless strategy" and its connections to theories of truth, see Beall (2001) and Armour-Garb (2001).

Further, the premises that we used to derive a contradiction from (1) seem eminently respect-able: a sentence is true when and only when things are as it says they are, and every sentence is either true or false. Indeed, Kripke (1975) has shown that the Liar Paradox can arise in the context of rather normal-sounding conversation. Given these facts, it is not surprising that the paradox remains a formidable problem for any theory of truth.

Moreover, it seems that we don't even need self-reference to generate Liar-like paradoxes, as Stephen Yablo (1985, 1993) has argued.

3. As Tarski points out in note 15 of his essay in this volume, various technical details require that the definition actually be put in terms of sequences of objects—for example, truth is satisfaction

by all sequences of objects (see also Tarski [1933a] 1983). For a user-friendly explanation of the point of this provision, and of Tarski's theory in general, see Kirkham (1992, chap. 5).

Further Reading

Achourioti, T., Galinon, H., Martínez-Fernández, J., and Fujimoto, K., eds. 2015. *Unifying the Philosophy of Truth*. Dordrecht: Springer.

Armour-Garb, B. 2001. "Deflationism and the Meaningless Strategy." *Analysis* 61(4): 280–289.

Asay, J. 2013. *The Primitivist Theory of Truth*, chap. 7. Cambridge: Cambridge University Press.

Barnard, R., and Ulatowski, J. 2016. "Tarski's 1944 Polemical Remarks and Naess' 'Experimental Philosophy.'" *Erkenntnis* 81(3): 457–477.

Beall, Jc. 2001. "A Neglected Deflationist Approach to the Liar." *Analysis* 61(2): 126–129.

Black, M. 1948. "The Semantic Conception of Truth." *Analysis* 8: 49–63.

Blackburn, S. 1984. *Spreading the Word*. Oxford: Oxford University Press.

Burgess, A., and J. Burgess. 2011. *Truth*, chap. 2. Princeton, NJ: Princeton University Press.

Davidson, D. 2001. *Inquiries into Truth and Interpretation*. New York: Oxford University Press.

Davidson, D. 2005a. *Truth and Predication*. Cambridge, MA: Harvard University Press.

Davidson, D. 2005b. *Truth, Language, and History*. Oxford: Oxford University Press.

Etchemendy, J. 1988. "Tarski on Truth and Logical Consequence." *Journal of Symbolic Logic* 53: 51–79.

Etchemendy, J. 1990. *The Concept of Logical Consequence*. Cambridge, MA: Harvard University Press.

Fox, J. 1989. "What Were Tarski's Truth Definitions For?" *History and Philosophy of Logic* 10: 165–179.

García-Carpintero, M. 1996. "What Is a Tarskian Definition of Truth?" *Philosophical Studies* 82(2): 113–144.

Glanzberg, M. 2015. "Representation and the Modern Correspondence Theory of Truth." In S. Gross, N. Tebben, and M. Williams, eds., *Meaning without Representation: Essays on Truth, Expression, Normativity, and Naturalism*, 81–102. New York: Oxford University Press.

Gómez-Torrente, M. 2019. "Alfred Tarski." *Stanford Encyclopedia of Philosophy*. https://plato.stanford.edu/entries/tarski/.

Gupta, A., and J. Martínez-Fernández. 2005. "Field on the Concept of Truth: Comment." *Philosophical Studies* 124(1): 45–58.

Haack, S. 1978. *Philosophy of Logics*, chap. 7. Cambridge: Cambridge University Press.

Halbach, V. 2011. *Axiomatic Theories of Truth*, chap. 3. Cambridge: Cambridge University Press.

Heck, R. 1997. "Tarski, Truth, and Semantics." *Philosophical Review* 106(4): 533–554.

Hintikka, J. 1975. "A Counterexample to Tarski-Type Truth-Definitions as Applied to Natural Languages." *Philosophia* 5: 207–212.

Hodges, W. 2018. "Tarski's Truth Definitions." *Stanford Encyclopedia of Philosophy*. https://plato .stanford.edu/entries/tarski-truth/.

Horsten, L. 2011. *The Tarskian Turn*. Oxford: Oxford University Press.

Horwich, P. 2010. "A Minimalist Critique of Tarski." In *Truth-Meaning-Reality*, 79–97. Oxford: Clarendon Press.

Keuth, H. 1978. "Tarski's Definition of Truth and the Correspondence Theory." *Philosophy of Science* 45: 420–430.

Kirkham, R. 1992. *Theories of Truth*, chaps. 5, 6, 9. Cambridge, MA: MIT Press.

Kripke, S. 1975. "Outline of a Theory of Truth." *Journal of Philosophy* 72: 690–716. Reprinted as chap. 4 of *Philosophical Troubles: Collected Papers*, vol. 1. Oxford: Oxford University Press, 2011.

McDowell, J. 1978. "Physicalism and Primitive Denotation: Field on Tarski." *Erkenntnis* 13: 137–152.

Mou, B. 2001. "The Enumerative Character of Tarski's Definition of Truth and Its General Character in a Tarskian System." *Synthese* 126(1–2): 91–121.

Patterson, D. 2002. "Theories of Truth and Convention T." *Philosophers' Imprint* 2: 1–16.

Patterson, D., ed. 2008. *New Essays on Tarski and Philosophy*. Oxford: Oxford University Press.

Peregrin, J., ed. 1999. *Truth and Its Nature (If Any)*. Dordrecht: Springer.

Popper, K. 1979. "Philosophical Comments on Tarski's Theory of Truth." In *Objective Knowledge: An Evolutionary Approach*, rev. ed., 319–340. Oxford: Clarendon Press.

Putnam, H. 2015. "Naturalism, Realism, and Normativity." *Journal of the American Philosophical Association* 1(2): 312–328.

Quine, W. V. O. 1986. *Philosophy of Logic*. 2nd ed. Cambridge, MA: Harvard University Press.

Ray, G. 2018. "Tarski on the Concept of Truth." In M. Glanzberg, ed., *The Oxford Handbook of Truth*, 695–717. Oxford: Oxford University Press.

Schantz, R. 1998. "Was Tarski a Deflationist?" *Logic and Logical Philosophy* 6: 157–172.

Sher, G. 1999. "What Is Tarski's Theory of Truth?" *Topoi* 18(2): 149–166.

Soames, S. 1999. *Understanding Truth*. New York: Oxford University Press.

Tarski, A. (1933a) 1983. "The Concept of Truth in Formalized Languages." In J. Corcoran, ed., and J. H. Woodger, trans., *Logic, Semantics, Metamathematics: Papers from 1923–1938*, 152–278. 2nd ed. Indianapolis: Hackett.

Tarski, A. (1933b) 1983. "The Establishment of Scientific Semantics." In J. Corcoran, ed., and J. H. Woodger, trans., *Logic, Semantics, Metamathematics: Papers from 1923–1938*, 401–408. 2nd ed. Indianapolis: Hackett.

Tarski, A. 1969. "Truth and Proof." *Scientific American* 220: 63–67.

Ulatowski, J. 2016. "Ordinary Truth in Tarski and Naess." In A. Kuzniar and J. Odrowąż-Sypniewska, eds., *Uncovering Facts and Values*, 67–90. Leiden: Brill.

Ulatowski, J. 2017. *Commonsense Pluralism about Truth: An Empirical Defence.* Cham, Switzerland: Palgrave Macmillan.

Woleński, J. "The Semantic Theory of Truth." *Internet Encyclopedia of Philosophy.* https://www.iep.utm.edu/s-truth/.

Yablo, S. 1985. "Truth and Reflection." *Journal of Philosophical Logic* 14(3): 297–349.

Yablo, S. 1993. "Paradox without Self-Reference." *Analysis* 53: 251–252.

14   The Semantic Conception of Truth and the Foundations of Semantics

Alfred Tarski

This paper consists of two parts; the first has an expository character, and the second is rather polemical.

In the first part I want to summarize in an informal way the main results of my investigations concerning the definition of truth and the more general problem of the foundations of semantics. These results have been embodied in a work which appeared in print several years ago.[1] Although my investigations concern concepts dealt with in classical philosophy, they happen to be comparatively little known in philosophical circles, perhaps because of their strictly technical character. For this reason I hope I shall be excused for taking up the matter once again.[2]

Since my work was published, various objections, of unequal value, have been raised to my investigations; some of these appeared in print, and others were made in public and private discussions in which I took part.[3] In the second part of the paper I should like to express my views regarding these objections. I hope that the remarks which will be made in this context will not be considered as purely polemical in character, but will be found to contain some constructive contributions to the subject.

In the second part of the paper I have made extensive use of material graciously put at my disposal by Dr. Marja Kokoszyńska (University of Lwów). I am especially indebted and grateful to Professors Ernest Nagel (Columbia University) and David Rynin (University of California, Berkeley) for their help in preparing the final text and for various critical remarks.

I   Exposition

1   The Main Problem—A Satisfactory Definition of Truth

Our discussion will be centered around the notion[4] of *truth*. The main problem is that of giving a *satisfactory definition* of this notion, i.e., a definition which is *materially adequate* and *formally correct*. But such a formulation of the problem, because of its generality, cannot be considered unequivocal, and requires some further comments.

In order to avoid any ambiguity, we must first specify the conditions under which the definition of truth will be considered adequate from the material point of view. The desired definition does not aim to specify the meaning of a familiar word used to denote a novel notion; on the contrary, it aims to catch hold of the actual meaning of an old notion. We must then characterize this notion precisely enough to enable anyone to determine whether the definition actually fulfills its task.

Secondly, we must determine on what the formal correctness of the definition depends. Thus, we must specify the words or concepts which we wish to use in defining the notion of truth; and we must also give the formal rules to which the definition should conform. Speaking more generally, we must describe the formal structure of the language in which the definition will be given.

The discussion of these points will occupy a considerable portion of the first part of the paper.

2   The Extension of the Term "True"

We begin with some remarks regarding the extension of the concept of truth which we have in mind here.

The predicate *"true"* is sometimes used to refer to psychological phenomena such as judgments or beliefs, sometimes to certain physical objects, namely, linguistic expressions and specifically sentences, and sometimes to certain ideal entities called "propositions." By "sentence" we understand here what is usually meant in grammar by "declarative sentence"; as regards the term "proposition," its meaning is notoriously a subject of lengthy disputations by various philosophers and logicians, and it seems never to have been made quite clear and unambiguous. For several reasons it appears most convenient to *apply the term "true" to sentences*, and we shall follow this course.[5]

Consequently, we must always relate the notion of truth, like that of a sentence, to a specific language; for it is obvious that the same expression which is a true sentence in one language can be false or meaningless in another.

Of course, the fact that we are interested here primarily in the notion of truth for sentences does not exclude the possibility of a subsequent extension of this notion to other kinds of objects.

3   The Meaning of the Term "True"

Much more serious difficulties are connected with the problem of the meaning (or the intension) of the concept of truth.

The word *"true,"* like other words from our everyday language, is certainly not unambiguous. And it does not seem to me that the philosophers who have discussed this concept have helped to diminish its ambiguity. In works and discussions of philosophers we meet many different conceptions of truth and falsity, and we must indicate which conception will be the basis of our discussion.

We should like our definition to do justice to the intuitions which adhere to the *classical Aristotelian conception of truth*—intuitions which find their expression in the well-known words of Aristotle's *Metaphysics*:

> To say of what is that it is not, or of what is not that it is, is false, while to say of what is that it is, or of what is not that it is not, is true.

If we wished to adapt ourselves to modern philosophical terminology, we could perhaps express this conception by means of the familiar formula:

> The truth of a sentence consists in its agreement with (or correspondence to) reality.

(For a theory of truth which is to be based upon the latter formulation the term "correspondence theory" has been suggested.)

If, on the other hand, we should decide to extend the popular usage of the term "*designate*" by applying it not only to names, but also to sentences, and if we agreed to speak of the designata of sentences as "states of affairs," we could possibly use for the same purpose the following phrase:

> A sentence is true if it designates an existing state of affairs.[6]

However, all these formulations can lead to various misunderstandings, for none of them is sufficiently precise and clear (though this applies much less to the original Aristotelian formulation than to either of the others); at any rate, none of them can be considered a satisfactory definition of truth. It is up to us to look for a more precise expression of our intuitions.

4   A Criterion for the Material Adequacy of the Definition[7]

Let us start with a concrete example. Consider the sentence "*snow is white*." We ask the question under what conditions this sentence is true or false. It seems clear that if we base ourselves on the classical conception of truth, we shall say that the sentence is true if snow is white, and that it is false if snow is not white. Thus, if the definition of truth is to conform to our conception, it must imply the following equivalence:

> The sentence "snow is white" is true if, and only if, snow is white.

Let me point out that the phrase "*snow is white*" occurs on the left side of this equivalence in quotation marks, and on the right without quotation marks. On the right side we have the sentence itself, and on the left the name of the sentence. Employing the medieval logical terminology we could also say that on the right side the words "*snow is white*" occur in *suppositio formalis*, and on the left in *suppositio materialis*. It is hardly necessary to explain why we must have the name of the sentence, and not the sentence itself, on the left side of the equivalence. For, in the first place, from the point of view of the grammar of our language, an expression of the form "*X is true*" will not become a meaningful sentence if we replace in it "*X*" by a sentence or by anything other than a name—since the subject of a sentence may be only a noun or an expression functioning like a noun. And, in the second place, the fundamental conventions regarding the use of any language require that in any utterance we make about an object it is the name of the object which must be employed, and not the object itself. In consequence, if we wish to say something about a sentence, for example, that it is true, we must use the name of this sentence, and not the sentence itself.[8]

It may be added that enclosing a sentence in quotation marks is by no means the only way of forming its name. For instance, by assuming the usual order of letters in our alphabet, we can use the following expression as the name (the description) of the sentence "*snow is white*":

> the sentence constituted by three words, the first of which consists of the 19th, 14th, 15th, and 23rd letters, the second of the 9th and 19th letters, and the third of the 23rd, 8th, 9th, 20th, and 5th letters of the English alphabet.

We shall now generalize the procedure which we have applied above. Let us consider an arbitrary sentence; we shall replace it by the letter "*p.*" We form the name of this sentence and we replace it by another letter, say "*X.*" We ask now what is the logical relation between the two sentences "*X is true*" and "*p.*" It is clear that from the point of view of our basic conception of truth these sentences are equivalent. In other words, the following equivalence holds:

> (T) *X* is true if, and only if, *p*.

We shall call any such equivalence (with "*p*" replaced by any sentence of the language to which the word "*true*" refers, and "*X*" replaced by a name of this sentence) an "*equivalence of the form* (T)."

Now at last we are able to put into a precise form the conditions under which we will consider the usage and the definition of the term "*true*" as adequate from the material point of view: we wish to use the term "*true*" in such a way that all equivalences of the form (T) can be asserted, and *we shall call a definition of truth "adequate" if all these equivalences follow from it.*

It should be emphasized that neither the expression (T) itself (which is not a sentence, but only a schema of a sentence) nor any particular instance of the form (T) can be regarded as a definition of truth. We can only say that every equivalence of the form (T) obtained by replacing "*p*" by a particular sentence, and "*X*" by a name of this sentence, may be considered a partial definition of truth, which explains wherein the truth of this one individual sentence consists. The general definition has to be, in a certain sense, a logical conjunction of all these partial definitions.

(The last remark calls for some comments. A language may admit the construction of infinitely many sentences; and thus the number of partial definitions of truth referring to sentences of such a language will also be infinite. Hence to give our remark a precise sense we should have to explain what is meant by a "logical conjunction of infinitely many sentences"; but this would lead us too far into technical problems of modern logic.)

5   Truth as a Semantic Concept

I should like to propose the name *"the semantic conception of truth"* for the conception of truth which has just been discussed.

Semantics is a discipline which, speaking loosely, *deals with certain relations between expressions of a language and the objects* (or "states of affairs") *"referred to" by those expressions*. As typical examples of semantic concepts we may mention the concepts of *designation, satisfaction*, and *definition* as these occur in the following examples:

> the expression "the father of his country" designates (denotes) George Washington
>
> snow satisfies the sentential function (the condition) "x is white"
>
> the equation "$2 \cdot x = 1$" defines (uniquely determines) the number 1/2

While the words *"designates," "satisfies,"* and *"defines"* express relations (between certain expressions and the objects "referred to" by these expressions), the word *"true"* is of a different logical nature: it expresses a property (or denotes a class) of certain expressions, viz., of sentences. However, it is easily seen that all the formulations which were given earlier and which aimed to explain the meaning of this word (cf. sections 3 and 4) referred not only to sentences themselves, but also to objects "talked about" by these sentences, or possibly to "states of affairs" described by them. And, moreover, it turns out that the simplest and the most natural way of obtaining an exact definition of truth is one which involves the use of other semantic notions, e.g., the notion of satisfaction. It is for these reasons that we count the concept of truth which is discussed here among the concepts of semantics, and the problem of defining truth proves to be closely related to the more general problem of setting up the foundations of theoretical semantics.

It is perhaps worth while saying that semantics as it is conceived in this paper (and in former papers of the author) is a sober and modest discipline which has no pretensions of being a universal patent-medicine for all the ills and diseases of mankind, whether imaginary or real. You will not find in semantics any remedy for decayed teeth or illusions of grandeur or class conflicts. Nor is semantics a device for establishing that everyone except the speaker and his friends is speaking nonsense.

From antiquity to the present day the concepts of semantics have played an important role in the discussions of philosophers, logicians, and philologists. Nevertheless, these concepts have been treated for a long time with a certain amount of suspicion. From a historical stand-point, this suspicion is to be regarded as completely justified. For although the meaning of semantic concepts as they are used in everyday language seems to be rather clear and understandable, still all attempts to characterize this meaning in a general and exact way miscarried. And what is worse, various arguments in which these concepts were involved, and which seemed otherwise quite correct and based upon apparently obvious premises, led frequently to paradoxes and antinomies. It is sufficient to mention here the *antinomy of the liar*, Richard's *antinomy of definability* (by means of a finite number of words), and Grelling-Nelson's *antinomy of heterological terms*.[9]

I believe that the method which is outlined in this paper helps to overcome these difficulties and assures the possibility of a consistent use of semantic concepts.

6   Languages with a Specified Structure

Because of the possible occurrence of antinomies, the problem of specifying the formal structure and the vocabulary of a language in which definitions of semantic concepts are to be given becomes especially acute; and we turn now to this problem.

There are certain general conditions under which the structure of a language is regarded as *exactly specified*. Thus, to specify the structure of a language, we must characterize unambiguously the class of those words and expressions which are to be considered *meaningful*. In particular, we must indicate all words which we decide to use without defining them, and which are called "*undefined* (or *primitive*) *terms*"; and we must give the so-called *rules of definition* for introducing new or *defined terms*. Furthermore, we must set up criteria for distinguishing within the class of expressions those which we call "*sentences*." Finally, we must formulate the conditions under which a sentence of the language can be *asserted*. In particular, we must indicate all *axioms* (or *primitive sentences*), i.e., those sentences which we decide to assert without proof; and we must give the so-called *rules of inference* (or *rules of proof*) by means of which we can deduce new asserted sentences from other sentences which have been previously asserted. Axioms, as well as sentences deduced from them by means of rules of inference, are referred to as "*theorems*" or "*provable sentences*."

If in specifying the structure of a language we refer exclusively to the form of the expressions involved, the language is said to the *formalized*. In such a language theorems are the only sentences which can be asserted. At the present time the only languages with a specified structure are the formalized languages of various systems of deductive logic, possibly enriched by the introduction of certain nonlogical terms. However, the field of application of these languages is rather comprehensive; we are able, theoretically, to develop in them various branches of science, for instance, mathematics and theoretical physics.

(On the other hand, we can imagine the construction of languages which have an exactly specified structure without being formalized. In such a language the assertability of sentences, for instance, may depend not always on their form, but sometimes on other, non-linguistic factors. It would be interesting and important actually to construct a language of this type, and specifically one which would prove to be sufficient for the development of a comprehensive branch of empirical science; for this would justify the hope that languages with specified structure could finally replace everyday language in scientific discourse.)

The problem of the definition of truth obtains a precise meaning and can be solved in a rigorous way only for those languages whose structure has been exactly specified. For other languages—thus, for all natural, "spoken" languages—the meaning of the problem is more or less vague, and its solution can have only an approximate character. Roughly speaking, the approximation consists in replacing a natural language (or a portion of it in which we are interested) by one whose structure is exactly specified, and which diverges from the given language "as little as possible."

7 The Antinomy of the Liar

In order to discover some of the more specific conditions which must be satisfied by languages in which (or for which) the definition of truth is to be given, it will be advisable to begin with a discussion of that antinomy which directly involves the notion of truth, namely, the antinomy of the liar.

To obtain this antinomy in a perspicuous form,[10] consider the following sentence:

The sentence printed in this paper on p. 271, l. 16, is not true.

For brevity we shall replace the sentence just stated by the letter "*s.*"

According to our convention concerning the adequate usage of the term "*true,*" we assert the following equivalence of the form (T):

(1) "*s*" is true if, and only if, the sentence printed in this paper on p. 271, l. 16, is not true.

On the other hand, keeping in mind the meaning of the symbol "*s,*" we establish empirically the following fact:

(2) "*s*" is identical with the sentence printed in this paper on p. 271, l. 16.

Now, by a familiar law from the theory of identity (Leibniz's law), it follows from (2) that we may replace in (1) the expression "*the sentence printed in this paper on p. 271, l. 16*" by the symbol "*s.*" We thus obtain what follows:

(3) "*s*" is true if, and only if, "*s*" is not true.

In this way we have arrived at an obvious contradiction.

In my judgment, it would be quite wrong and dangerous from the standpoint of scientific progress to depreciate the importance of this and other antinomies, and to treat them as jokes or sophistries. It is a fact that we are here in the presence of an absurdity, that we have been compelled to assert a false sentence (since (3), as an equivalence between two contradictory sentences, is necessarily false). If we take our work seriously, we cannot be reconciled with this fact. We must discover its cause, that is to say, we must analyze premises upon which the antinomy is based; we must then reject at least one of these premises, and we must investigate the consequences which this has for the whole domain of our research.

It should be emphasized that antinomies have played a preeminent role in establishing the foundations of modern deductive sciences. And just as class-theoretical antinomies, and in particular Russell's antinomy (of the class of all classes that are not members of themselves), were the starting point for the successful attempts at a consistent formalization of logic and mathematics, so the antinomy of the liar and other semantic antinomies give rise to the construction of theoretical semantics.

8   The Inconsistency of Semantically Closed Languages[7]

If we now analyze the assumptions which lead to the antinomy of the liar, we notice the following:

I.   We have implicitly assumed that the language in which the antinomy is constructed contains, in addition to its expressions, also the names of these expressions, as well as semantic terms such as the term "*true*" referring to sentences of this language; we have also assumed that all sentences which determine the adequate usage of this term can be asserted in the language. A language with these properties will be called "*semantically closed*."

II. We have assumed that in this language the ordinary laws of logic hold.

III. We have assumed that we can formulate and assert in our language an empirical premise such as the statement (2) which has occurred in our argument.

It turns out that the assumption (III) is not essential, for it is possible to reconstruct the antinomy of the liar without its help.[11] But the assumptions (I) and (II) prove essential. Since every language which satisfies both of these assumptions is inconsistent, we must reject at least one of them.

It would be superfluous to stress here the consequences of rejecting the assumption (II), that is, of changing our logic (supposing this were possible) even in its more elementary and fundamental parts. We thus consider only the possibility of rejecting the assumption (I). Accordingly, we decide *not to use any language which is semantically closed* in the sense given.

This restriction would of course be unacceptable for those who, for reasons which are not clear to me, believe that there is only one "genuine" language (or, at least, that all "genuine" languages are mutually translatable). However, this restriction does not affect the needs or interests of science in any essential way. The languages (either the formalized languages or—what is more frequently the case—the portions of everyday language) which are used in scientific discourse do not have to be semantically closed. This is obvious in case linguistic phenomena and, in particular, semantic notions do not enter in any way into the subject matter of a science; for in such a case the language of this science does not have to be provided with any semantic terms at all. However, we shall see in the next section how semantically closed languages can be dispensed with even in those scientific discussions in which semantic notions are essentially involved.

The problem arises as to the position of everyday language with regard to this point. At first blush it would seem that this language satisfies both assumptions (I) and (II), and that therefore it must be inconsistent. But actually the case is not so simple. Our everyday language is certainly not one with an exactly specified structure. We do not know precisely which expressions are sentences, and we know even to a smaller degree which sentences are to be taken as assertible. Thus the problem of consistency has no exact meaning with respect to this language. We may at best only risk the guess that a language whose structure has been exactly specified and which resembles our everyday language as closely as possible would be inconsistent.

9 Object-Language and Meta-Language

Since we have agreed not to employ semantically closed languages, we have to use two different languages in discussing the problem of the definition of truth and, more generally, any problems in the field of semantics. The first of these languages is the language which is "talked about" and which is the subject matter of the whole discussion; the definition of truth which we are seeking applies to the sentences of this language. The second is the language in which we "talk about" the first language, and in terms of which we wish, in particular, to construct the definition of truth for the first language. We shall refer to the first language as *"the object-language,"* and to the second as *"the meta-language."*

It should be noticed that these terms "object-language" and "meta-language" have only a relative sense. If, for instance, we become interested in the notion of truth applying to sentences, not of our original object-language, but of its meta-language, the latter becomes automatically the object-language of our discussion; and in order to define truth for this language, we have to go to a new meta-language—so to speak, to a meta-language of a higher level. In this way we arrive at a whole hierarchy of languages.

The vocabulary of the meta-language is to a large extent determined by previously stated conditions under which a definition of truth will be considered materially adequate. This definition, as we recall, has to imply all equivalences of the form (T):

(T) X is true if, and only if, p.

The definition itself and all the equivalences implied by it are to be formulated in the meta-language. On the other hand, the symbol "p" in (T) stands for an arbitrary sentence of our object-language. Hence it follows that every sentence which occurs in the object-language must also occur in the meta-language; in other words, the meta-language must contain the object-language as a part. This is at any rate necessary for the proof of the adequacy of the definition—even though the definition itself can sometimes be formulated in a less comprehensive meta-language which does not satisfy this requirement.

(The requirement in question can be somewhat modified, for it suffices to assume that the object-language can be translated into the meta-language; this necessitates a certain change in the interpretation of the symbol "p" in (T). In all that follows we shall ignore the possibility of this modification.)

Furthermore, the symbol "X" in (T) represents the name of the sentence which "p" stands for. We see therefore that the meta-language must be rich enough to provide possibilities of constructing a name for every sentence of the object-language.

In addition, the meta-language must obviously contain terms of a general logical character, such as the expression "if, and only if."[12]

It is desirable for the meta-language not to contain any undefined terms except such as are involved explicitly or implicitly in the remarks above, i.e.: terms of the object-language; terms referring to the form of the expressions of the object-language, and used in building names for these expressions; and terms of logic. In particular, we desire *semantic terms* (referring to the object-language) *to be introduced into the meta-language only by definition*. For, if this postulate is satisfied, the definition of truth, or of any other semantic concept, will fulfill what we intuitively expect from every definition; that is, it will explain the meaning of the term being defined in terms whose meaning appears to be completely clear and unequivocal. And, moreover, we have then a kind of guarantee that the use of semantic concepts will not involve us in any contradictions.

We have no further requirements as to the formal structure of the object-language and the meta-language; we assume that it is similar to that of other formalized languages known at the present time. In particular, we assume that the usual formal rules of definition are observed in the meta-language.

10 Conditions for a Positive Solution of the Main Problem

Now, we have already a clear idea both of the conditions of material adequacy to which the definition of truth is subjected, and of the formal structure of the language in which this definition is to be constructed. Under these circumstances the problem of the definition of truth acquires the character of a definite problem of a purely deductive nature.

The solution of the problem, however, is by no means obvious, and I would not attempt to give it in detail without using the whole machinery of contemporary logic. Here I shall confine myself to a rough outline of the solution and to the discussion of certain points of a more general interest which are involved in it.

The solution turns out to be sometimes positive, sometimes negative. This depends upon some formal relations between the object-language and its meta-language; or, more specifically, upon the fact whether the meta-language in its logical part is "*essentially richer*" than the object-language or not. It is not easy to give a general and precise definition of this notion of "essential richness." If we restrict ourselves to languages based on the logical theory of types, the condition for the meta-language to be "essentially richer" than the object-language is that it contain variables of a higher logical type than those of the object-language.

If the condition of "essential richness" is not satisfied, it can usually be shown that an interpretation of the meta-language in the object-language is possible; that is to say, with any given term of the meta-language a well-determined term of the object-language can be correlated in such a way that the assertible sentences of the one language turn out to be correlated with assertible sentences of the other. As a result of this interpretation, the hypothesis that a satisfactory definition of truth has been formulated in the meta-language turns out to imply the possibility of reconstructing in that language the antinomy of the liar; and this in turn forces us to reject the hypothesis in question.

(The fact that the meta-language, in its non-logical part, is ordinarily more comprehensive than the object-language does not affect the possibility of interpreting the former in the latter. For example, the names of expressions of the object-language occur in the meta-language, though for the most part they do not occur in the object-language itself; but, nevertheless, it may be possible to interpret these names in terms of the object-language.)

Thus we see that the condition of "essential richness" is necessary for the possibility of a satisfactory definition of truth in the meta-language. If we want to develop the theory of truth in a meta-language which does not satisfy this condition, we must give up the idea of defining truth with the exclusive help of those terms which were indicated above (in section 8). We have then to include the term *"true,"* or some other semantic term, in the list of undefined terms of the meta-language, and to express fundamental properties of the notion of truth in a series of axioms. There is nothing essentially wrong in such an axiomatic procedure, and it may prove useful for various purposes.[13]

It turns out, however, that this procedure can be avoided. For *the condition of the "essential richness" of the meta-language proves to be, not only necessary, but also sufficient for the construction of a satisfactory definition of truth*; i.e., if the meta-language satisfies this condition, the notion of truth can be defined in it. We shall now indicate in general terms how this construction can be carried through.

11 The Construction (in Outline) of the Definition[14]

A definition of truth can be obtained in a very simple way from that of another semantic notion, namely, of the notion of *satisfaction*.

Satisfaction is a relation between arbitrary objects and certain expressions called *"sentential functions."* These are expressions like *"x is white," "x is greater than y,"* etc. Their formal structure is analogous to that of sentences; however, they may contain the so-called free variables (like *"x"* and *"y"* in *"x is greater than y"*), which cannot occur in sentences.

In defining the notion of a sentential function in formalized languages, we usually apply what is called a "recursive procedure"; i.e., we first describe sentential functions of the simplest structure (which ordinarily presents no difficulty), and then we indicate the operations by means of which compound functions can be constructed from simpler ones. Such an operation may consist, for instance, in forming the logical disjunction or conjunction of two given functions, i.e., by combining them by the word "*or*" or "*and*." A sentence can now be defined simply as a sentential function which contains no free variables.

As regards the notion of satisfaction, we might try to define it by saying that given objects satisfy a given function if the latter becomes a true sentence when we replace in it free variables by names of given objects. In this sense, for example, snow satisfies the sentential function "*x is white*" since the sentence "*snow is white*" is true. However, apart from other difficulties, this method is not available to us, for we want to use the notion of satisfaction in defining truth.

To obtain a definition of satisfaction we have rather to apply again a recursive procedure. We indicate which objects satisfy the simplest sentential functions; and then we state the conditions under which given objects satisfy a compound function—assuming that we know which objects satisfy the simpler functions from which the compound one has been constructed. Thus, for instance, we say that given numbers satisfy the logical disjunction "*x is greater than y or x is equal to y*" if they satisfy at least one of the functions "*x is greater than y*" or "*x is equal to y.*"

Once the general definition of satisfaction is obtained, we notice that it applies automatically also to those special sentential functions which contain no free variables, i.e., to sentences. It turns out that for a sentence only two cases are possible: a sentence is either satisfied by all objects, or by no objects. Hence we arrive at a definition of truth and falsehood simply by saying that *a sentence is true if it is satisfied by all objects, and false otherwise.*[15]

(It may seem strange that we have chosen a roundabout way of defining the truth of a sentence, instead of trying to apply, for instance, a direct recursive procedure. The reason is that compound sentences are constructed from simpler sentential functions, but not always from simpler sentences; hence no general recursive method is known which applies specifically to sentences.)

From this rough outline it is not clear where and how the assumption of the "essential richness" of the meta-language is involved in the discussion; this becomes clear only when the construction is carried through in a detailed and formal way.[16]

12 Consequences of the Definition

The definition of truth which was outlined above has many interesting consequences.

In the first place, the definition proves to be not only formally correct, but also materially adequate (in the sense established in section 4); in other words, it implies all equivalences of the form (T). In this connection it is important to notice that the conditions for the material adequacy of the definition determine uniquely the extension of the term "*true.*" Therefore, every definition of truth which is materially adequate would necessarily be equivalent to that actually constructed. The semantic conception of truth gives us, so to speak, no possibility of choice between various non-equivalent definitions of this notion.

Moreover, we can deduce from our definition various laws of a general nature. In particular, we can prove with its help the *laws of contradiction and of excluded middle,* which are so characteristic of the Aristotelian conception of truth; i.e., we can show that one and only one of any two contradictory sentences is true. These semantic laws should not be identified with the related logical laws of contradiction and excluded middle; the latter belong to the sentential calculus, i.e., to the most elementary part of logic, and do not involve the term "*true*" at all.

Further important results can be obtained by applying the theory of truth to formalized languages of a certain very comprehensive class of mathematical disciplines; only disciplines of an elementary character and a very elementary logical structure are excluded from this class. It turns out that for a discipline of this class *the notion of truth never coincides with that of provability*; for all provable sentences are true, but there are true sentences which are not provable.[17] Hence it follows further that every such discipline is consistent, but incomplete; that is to say, of any two contradictory sentences at most one is provable, and—what is more—there exists a pair of contradictory sentences neither of which is provable.[18]

13 Extension of the Results to Other Semantic Notions

Most of the results at which we arrived in the preceding sections in discussing the notion of truth can be extended with appropriate changes to other semantic notions, for instance, to the notion of satisfaction (involved in our previous discussion), and to those of *designation* and *definition.*

Each of these notions can be analyzed along the lines followed in the analysis of truth. Thus, criteria for an adequate usage of these notions can be established; it can be shown that each of these notions, when used in a semantically closed language according to those criteria, leads necessarily to a contradiction;[19] a distinction between the object-language and the meta-language becomes again indispensable; and the "essential richness" of the meta-language proves in each case to be a necessary and sufficient condition for a satisfactory definition of the notion involved. Hence the results obtained in discussing one particular semantic notion apply to the general problem of the foundations of theoretical semantics. Within theoretical semantics we can define and study some further notions, whose intuitive content is more involved and whose semantic origin is less obvious; we have in mind, for instance, the important notions of *consequence, synonymity,* and *meaning.*[20]

We have concerned ourselves here with the theory of semantic notions related to an individual object-language (although no specific properties of this language have been involved in our arguments). However, we could also consider the problem of developing *general semantics* which applies to a comprehensive class of object-languages. A considerable part of our previous remarks can be extended to this general problem; however, certain previous remarks can be extended to this general problem; however, certain new difficulties arise in this connection, which will not be discussed here. I shall merely observe that the axiomatic method (mentioned in section 10) may prove the most appropriate for the treatment of the problem.[21]

II Polemical Remarks

14 Is the Semantic Conception of Truth the "Right" One?

I should like to begin the polemical part of the paper with some general remarks.

I hope nothing which is said here will be interpreted as a claim that the semantic conception of truth is the "right" or indeed the "only possible" one. I do not have the slightest intention to contribute in any way to those endless, often violent discussions on the subject: "What is the right conception of truth?"[22] I must confess I do not understand what is at stake in such disputes; for the problem itself is so vague that no definite solution is possible. In fact, it seems to me that the sense in which the phrase "the right conception" is used has never been made clear. In most cases one gets the impression that the phrase is used in an almost mystical sense based upon the belief that every word has only one "real" meaning (a kind of Platonic or Aristotelian idea), and that all the competing conceptions really attempt to catch hold of this one meaning; since, however, they contradict each other, only one attempt can be successful, and hence only one conception is the "right" one.

Disputes of this type are by no means restricted to the notion of truth. They occur in all domains where—instead of an exact, scientific terminology—common language with its vagueness and ambiguity is used; and they are always meaningless, and therefore in vain.

It seems to me obvious that the only rational approach to such problems would be the following: We should reconcile ourselves with the fact that we are confronted, not with one concept, but with several different concepts which are denoted by one word; we should try to make these concepts as clear as possible (by means of definition, or of an axiomatic procedure, or in some other way); to avoid further confusions, we should agree to use different terms for different concepts; and then we may proceed to a quiet and systematic study of all concepts involved, which will exhibit their main properties and mutual relations.

Referring specifically to the notion of truth, it is undoubtedly the case that in philosophical discussions—and perhaps also in everyday usage—some incipient conceptions of this notion can be found that differ essentially from the classical one (of which the semantic conception is but a modernized form). In fact, various conceptions of this sort have been discussed in the literature, for instance, the pragmatic conception, the coherence theory, etc.[6]

It seems to me that none of these conceptions have been put so far in an intelligible and unequivocal form. This may change, however; a time may come when we find ourselves confronted with several incompatible, but equally clear and precise, conceptions of truth. It will then become necessary to abandon the ambiguous usage of the word "*true*," and to introduce several terms instead, each to denote a different notion. Personally, I should not feel hurt if a future world congress of the "theoreticians of truth" should decide—by a majority of votes—to reserve the word "*true*" for one of the non-classical conceptions, and should suggest another word, say, "*frue*," for the conception considered here. But I cannot imagine that anybody could present cogent arguments to the effect that the semantic conception is wrong and should be entirely abandoned.

15 Formal Correctness of the Suggested Definition of Truth

The specific objections which have been raised to my investigations can be divided into several groups; each of these will be discussed separately.

I think that practically all these objections apply, not to the special definition I have given, but to the semantic conception of truth in general. Even those which were leveled against the definition actually constructed could be related to any other definition which conforms to this conception.

This holds, in particular, for those objections which concern the formal correctness of the definition. I have heard a few objections of this kind; however, I doubt very much whether anyone of them can be treated seriously.

As a typical example let me quote in substance such an objection.[23] In formulating the definition we use necessarily sentential connectives, i.e., expressions like "*if* ... , *then*," "*or*," etc. They occur in the definiens; and one of them, namely, the phrase "*if, and only if*" is usually employed to combine the definiendum with the definiens. However, it is well known that the meaning of sentential connectives is explained in logic with the help of the words "*true*" and "*false*"; for instance, we say that an equivalence, i.e., a sentence of the form "*p if, and only if, q*," is true if either both of its members, i.e., the sentences represented by "*p*" and "*q*," are true or both are false. Hence the definition of truth involves a vicious circle.

If this objection were valid, no formally correct definition of truth would be possible; for we are unable to formulate any compound sentence without using sentential connectives, or other logical terms defined with their help. Fortunately, the situation is not so bad.

It is undoubtedly the case that a strictly deductive development of logic is often preceded by certain statements explaining the conditions under which sentences of the form "*if p, then q*," etc., are considered true or false. (Such explanations are often given schematically, by means of the so-called truth-tables.) However, these statements are outside of the system of logic, and should not be regarded as definitions of the terms involved. They are not formulated in the language of the system, but constitute rather special consequences of the definition of truth given in the meta-language. Moreover, these statements do not influence the deductive development of logic in any way. For in such a development we do not discuss the question whether a given sentence is true, we are only interested in the problem whether it is provable.[24]

On the other hand, the moment we find ourselves within the deductive system of logic—or of any discipline based upon logic, e.g., of semantics—we either treat sentential connectives as undefined terms, or else we define them by means of other sentential connectives, but never by means of semantic terms like "*true*" or "*false.*" For instance, if we agree to regard the expressions "*not*" and "*if ..., then*" (and possibly also "*if, and only if*") as undefined terms, we can define the term "*or*" by stating that a sentence of the form "*p or q*" is equivalent to the corresponding sentence of the form "*if not p, then q.*" The definition can be formulated, e.g., in the following way:

(*p* or *q*) if, and only if, (if not *p*, then *q*).

This definition obviously contains no semantic terms.

However, a vicious circle in definition arises only when the definiens contains either the term to be defined itself, or other terms defined with its help. Thus we clearly see that the use of sentential connectives in defining the semantic term "*true*" does not involve any circle.

I should like to mention a further objection which I have found in the literature and which seems also to concern the formal correctness, if not of the definition of truth itself, then at least of the arguments which lead to this definition.[25]

The author of this objection mistakenly regards scheme (T) (from section 4) as a definition of truth. He charges this alleged definition with "inadmissible brevity, i.e., incompleteness," which "does not give us the means of deciding whether by 'equivalence' is meant a logical-formal, or a non-logical and also structurally non-describable relation." To remove this "defect" he suggests supplementing (T) in one of the two following ways:

(T') *X* is true if, and only if, *p* is true,

or

(T") *X* is true if, and only if, *p* is the case (i.e., if what *p* states is the case).

Then he discusses these two new "definitions," which are supposedly free from the old, formal "defect," but which turn out to be unsatisfactory for other, non-formal reasons.

This new objection seems to arise from a misunderstanding concerning the nature of sentential connectives (and thus to be somehow related to that previously discussed).

The author of the objection does not seem to realize that the phrase *"if, and only if"* (in opposition to such phrases as *"are equivalent"* or *"is equivalent to"*) expresses no relation between sentences at all since it does not combine names of sentences.

In general, the whole argument is based upon an obvious confusion between sentences and their names. It suffices to point out that—in contradistinction to (T)—schemata (T') and (T") do not give any meaningful expressions if we replace in them *"p"* by a sentence; for the phrases *"p is true"* and *"p is the case"* (i.e., *"what p states is the case"*) become meaningless if *"p"* is replaced by a sentence, and not by the name of a sentence (cf. section 4).[26]

While the author of the objection considers schema (T) "inadmissibly brief," I am inclined, on my part, to regard schemata (T') and (T") as "inadmissibly long." And I think even that I can rigorously prove this statement on the basis of the following definition: An expression is said to be "inadmissibly long" if (i) it is meaningless, and (ii) it has been obtained from a meaningful expression by inserting superfluous words.

16   Redundancy of Semantic Terms—Their Possible Elimination

The objection I am going to discuss now no longer concerns the formal correctness of the definition, but is still concerned with certain formal features of the semantic conception of truth.

We have seen that this conception essentially consists in regarding the sentence *"X is true"* as equivalent to the sentence denoted by *"X"* (where *"X"* stands for a name of a sentence of the object-language). Consequently, the term *"true"* when occurring in a simple sentence of the form *"X is true"* can easily be eliminated, and the sentence itself, which belongs to the meta-language, can be replaced by an equivalent sentence of the object-language; and the same applies to compound sentences provided the term *"true"* occurs in them exclusively as a part of the expressions of the form *"X is true."*

Some people have therefore urged that the term *"true"* in the semantic sense can always be eliminated, and that for this reason the semantic conception of truth is altogether sterile and useless. And since the same considerations apply to other semantic notions, the conclusion has been drawn that semantics as a whole is a purely verbal game and at best only a harmless hobby.

But the matter is not quite so simple.[27] The sort of elimination here discussed cannot always be made. It cannot be done in the case of universal statements which express the fact that all sentences of a certain type are true, or that all true sentences have a certain property. For instance, we can prove in the theory of truth the following statement:

All consequences of true sentences are true.

However, we cannot get rid here of the word *"true"* in the simple manner contemplated.

Again, even in the case of particular sentences having the form *"X is true"* such a simple elimination cannot always be made. In fact, the elimination is possible only in those cases in which the name of the sentence which is said to be true occurs in a form that enables us to reconstruct the sentence itself. For example, our present historical knowledge does not give us any possibility of eliminating the word "*true*" from the following sentence:

The first sentence written by Plato is true.

Of course, since we have a definition for truth and since every definition enables us to replace the definiendum by its definiens, an elimination of the term "*true*" in its semantic sense is always theoretically possible. But this would not be the kind of simple elimination discussed above, and it would not result in the replacement of a sentence in the meta-language by a sentence in the object-language.

If, however, anyone continues to urge that—because of the theoretical possibility of eliminating the word "*true*" on the basis of its definition—the concept of truth is sterile, he must accept the further conclusion that all defined notions are sterile. But this outcome is so absurd and so unsound historically that any comment on it is unnecessary. In fact, I am rather inclined to agree with those who maintain that the moments of greatest creative advancement in science frequently coincide with the introduction of new notions by means of definition.

17 Conformity of the Semantic Conception of Truth with Philosophical and Common-Sense Usage

The question has been raised whether the semantic conception of truth can indeed be regarded as a precise form of the old, classical conception of this notion.

Various formulations of the classical conception were quoted in the early part of this paper (section 3). I must repeat that in my judgment none of them is quite precise and clear. Accordingly, the only sure way of settling the question would be to confront the authors of those statements with our new formulation, and to ask them whether it agrees with their intentions. Unfortunately, this method is impractical since they died quite some time ago.

As far as my own opinion is concerned, I do not have any doubts that our formulation does conform to the intuitive content of that of Aristotle. I am less certain regarding the later formulations of the classical conception, for they are very vague indeed.[28]

Furthermore, some doubts have been expressed whether the semantic conception does reflect the notion of truth in its common-sense and everyday usage. I clearly realize (as I already indicated) that the common meaning of the word "*true*"—as that of any other word of everyday language—is to some extent vague, and that its usage more or less fluctuates. Hence the problem of assigning to this word a fixed and exact meaning is relatively unspecified, and every solution of this problem implies necessarily a certain deviation from the practice of everyday language.

In spite of all this, I happen to believe that the semantic conception does conform to a very considerable extent with the common-sense usage—although I readily admit

I may be mistaken. What is more to the point, however, I believe that the issue raised can be settled scientifically, though of course not by a deductive procedure, but with the help of the statistical questionnaire method. As a matter of fact, such research has been carried on, and some of the results have been reported at congresses and in part published.[29]

I should like to emphasize that in my opinion such investigations must be conducted with the utmost care. Thus, if we ask a high-school boy, or even an adult intelligent man having no special philosophical training, whether he regards a sentence to be true if it agrees with reality, or if it designates an existing state of affairs, it may simply turn out that he does not understand the question; in consequence his response, whatever it may be, will be of no value for us. But his answer to the question whether he would admit that the sentence *"it is snowing"* could be true although it is not snowing, or could be false although it is snowing, would naturally be very significant for our problem.

Therefore, I was by no means surprised to learn (in a discussion devoted to these problems) that in a group of people who were questioned only 15% agreed that *"true"* means for them *"agreeing with reality,"* while 90% agreed that a sentence such as *"it is snowing"* is true if, and only if, it is snowing. Thus, a great majority of these people seemed to reject the classical conception of truth in its "philosophical" formulation, while accepting the same conception when formulated in plain words (waiving the question whether the use of the phrase the same conception is here justified).

18 The Definition in Its Relation to "The Philosophical Problem of Truth" and to Various Epistemological Trends

I have heard it remarked that the formal definition of truth has nothing to do with "the philosophical problem of truth."[30] However, nobody has ever pointed out to me in an intelligible way just what this problem is. I have been informed in this connection that my definition, though it states necessary and sufficient conditions for a sentence to be true, does not really grasp the "essence" of this concept. Since I have never been able to understand what the "essence" of a concept is, I must be excused from discussing this point any longer.

In general, I do not believe that there is such a thing as "the philosophical problem of truth." I do believe that there are various intelligible and interesting (but not necessarily philosophical) problems concerning the notion of truth, but I also believe that they can be exactly formulated and possibly solved only on the basis of a precise conception of this notion.

While on the one hand the definition of truth has been blamed for not being philosophical enough, on the other a series of objections have been raised charging this definition with serious philosophical implications, always of a very undesirable nature. I shall discuss now one special objection of this type; another group of such objections will be dealt with in the next section.[31]

It has been claimed that—due to the fact that a sentence like "snow is white" is taken to be semantically true if snow is *in fact* white (italics by the critic)—logic finds itself involved in a most uncritical realism.[32]

If there were an opportunity to discuss the objection with its author, I should raise two points. First, I should ask him to drop the words "*in fact,*" which do not occur in the original formulation and which are misleading, even if they do not affect the content. For these words convey the impression that the semantic conception of truth is intended to establish the conditions under which we are warranted in asserting any given sentence, and in particular any empirical sentence. However, a moment's reflection shows that this impression is merely an illusion; and I think that the author of the objection falls victim to the illusion which he himself created.

In fact, the semantic definition of truth implies nothing regarding the conditions under which a sentence like (1):

(1) Snow is white

can be asserted. It implies only that, whenever we assert or reject this sentence, we must be ready to assert or reject the correlated sentence (2):

(2) The sentence "snow is white" is true.

Thus, we may accept the semantic conception of truth without giving up any epistemological attitude we may have had; we may remain naive realists, critical realists or idealists, empiricists or metaphysicians—whatever we were before. The semantic conception is completely neutral toward all these issues.

In the second place, I should try to get some information regarding the conception of truth which (in the opinion of the author of the objection) does not involve logic in a most naive realism. I would gather that this conception must be incompatible with the semantic one. Thus, there must be sentences which are true in one of these conceptions without being true in the other. Assume, e.g., the sentence (1) to be of this kind. The truth of this sentence in the semantic conception is determined by an equivalence of the form (T):

The sentence "snow is white" is true if, and only if, snow is white.

Hence in the new conception we must reject this equivalence, and consequently we must assume its denial:

The sentence "snow is white" is true if, and only if, snow is not white (or perhaps: snow, in fact, is not white).

This sounds somewhat paradoxical. I do not regard such a consequence of the new conception as absurd; but I am a little fearful that someone in the future may charge this conception with involving logic in a "most sophisticated kind of irrealism." At any rate, it seems to me important to realize that every conception of truth which is incompatible with the semantic one carries with it consequences of this type.

I have dwelt a little on this whole question, not because the objection discussed seems to me very significant, but because certain points which have arisen in the discussion should be taken into account by all those who for various epistemological reasons are inclined to reject the semantic conception of truth.

Notes

1. Compare Tarski [2] (see bibliography at the end of the paper). This work may be consulted for a more detailed and formal presentation of the subject of the paper, especially of the material included in sections 6 and 9–13. It contains also references to my earlier publications on the problems of semantics (a communication in Polish, 1930; the article Tarski [1] in French, 1931; a communication in German, 1932; and a book in Polish, 1933). The expository part of the present paper is related in its character to Tarski [3]. My investigations on the notion of truth and on theoretical semantics have been reviewed or discussed in Hofstadter [1], Juhos [1], Kokoszyńska [1] and [2], Kotarbiński [2], Scholz [1], Weinberg [1], et al.

2. It may be hoped that the interest in theoretical semantics will now increase, as a result of the recent publication of the important work Carnap [2].

3. This applies, in particular, to public discussions during the I. International Congress for the Unity of Science (Paris, 1935) and the Conference of International Congresses for the Unity of Science (Paris, 1937); cf., e.g., Neurath [1] and Gonseth [1].

4. The words "notion" and "concept" are used in this paper with all of the vagueness and ambiguity with which they occur in philosophical literature. Thus, sometimes they refer simply to a term, sometimes to what is meant by a term, and in other cases to what is denoted by a term. Sometimes it is irrelevant which of these interpretations is meant; and in certain cases perhaps none of them applies adequately. While on principle I share the tendency to avoid these words in any exact discussion, I did not consider it necessary to do so in this informal presentation.

5. For our present purposes it is somewhat more convenient to understand by "expressions," "sentences," etc., not individual inscriptions, but classes of inscriptions of similar form (thus, not individual physical things, but classes of such things).

6. For the Aristotelian formulation see Aristotle [1], Γ, 7, 27. The other two formulations are very common in the literature, but I do not know with whom they originate. A critical discussion of various conceptions of truth can be found, e.g., in Kokoszyński [1] (so far available only in Polish), 123ff., and Russell [1], 362ff.

7. For most of the remarks contained in sections 4 and 8, I am indebted to the late S. Leśniewski who developed them in his unpublished lectures in the University of Warsaw (in 1919 and later). However, Leśniewski did not anticipate the possibility of a rigorous development of the theory of truth, and still less of a definition of this notion; hence, while indicating equivalences of the form (T) as premises in the antinomy of the liar, he did not conceive them as any sufficient conditions for an adequate usage (or definition) of the notion of truth. Also the remarks in section 8

regarding the occurrence of an empirical premiss in the antinomy of the liar, and the possibility of eliminating this premiss, do not originate with him.

8. In connection with various logical and methodological problems involved in this paper the reader may consult Tarski [6].

9. The antinomy of the liar (ascribed to Eubulides or Epimenides) is discussed here in sections 7 and 8. For the antinomy of definability (due to J. Richard) see, e.g., Hilbert and Bernays [1], vol. 2, 263ff.; for the antinomy of heterological terms see Grelling and Nelson [1], 307.

10. Due to Professor J. Łukasiewicz (University of Warsaw).

11. This can roughly be done in the following way. Let S be any sentence beginning with the words *"Every sentence."* We correlate with S a new sentence S^* by subjecting S to the following two modifications: we replace in S the first word, *"Every,"* by *"The"*; and we insert after the second word, *"sentence,"* the whole sentence S enclosed in quotation marks. Let us agree to call the sentence S "(self-)applicable" or "non-(self-)applicable" dependent on whether the correlated sentence S^* is true or false. Now consider the following sentence:

> Every sentence is non-applicable.

It can easily be shown that the sentence just stated must be both applicable and non-applicable; hence a contradiction. It may not be quite clear in what sense this formulation of the antinomy does not involve an empirical premiss; however, I shall not elaborate on this point.

12. The terms "logic" and "logical" are used in this paper in a broad sense, which has become almost traditional in the last decades; logic is assumed here to comprehend the whole theory of classes and relations (i.e., the mathematical theory of sets). For many different reasons I am personally inclined to use the term "logic" in a much narrower sense, so as to apply it only to what is sometimes called elementary logic, i.e., to the sentential calculus and the (restricted) predicate calculus.

13. Cf. here, however, Tarski [3], 5f.

14. The method of construction we are going to outline can be applied—with appropriate changes—to all formalized languages that are known at the present time; although it does not follow that a language could not be constructed to which this method would not apply.

15. In carrying through this idea a certain technical difficulty arises. A sentential function may contain an arbitrary number of free variables; and the logical nature of the notion of satisfaction varies with this number. Thus, the notion in question when applied to functions with one variable is a binary relation between these functions and single objects; when applied to functions with two variables it becomes a ternary relation between functions and couples of objects; and so on. Hence, strictly speaking, we are confronted, not with one notion of satisfaction, but with infinitely many notions; and it turns out that these notions cannot be defined independently of each other, but must all be introduced simultaneously.

To overcome this difficulty, we employ the mathematical notion of an infinite sequence (or, possibly, of a finite sequence with an arbitrary number of terms). We agree to regard satisfaction, not as a many-termed relation between sentential functions and an indefinite number of objects, but as a binary relation between functions and sequences of objects. Under this assumption the formulation of a general and precise definition of satisfaction no longer presents any difficulty; and a true sentence can now be defined as one which is satisfied by every sequence.

16. To define recursively the notion of satisfaction, we have to apply a certain form of recursive definition which is not admitted in the object-language. Hence the essential richness of the meta-language may simply consist in admitting this type of definition. On the other hand, a general method is known which makes it possible to eliminate all recursive definitions and to replace them by normal, explicit ones. If we try to apply this method to the definition of satisfaction, we see that we have either to introduce into the meta-language variables of a higher logical type than those which occur in the object-language; or else to assume axiomatically in the meta-language the existence of classes that are more comprehensive than all those whose existence can be established in the object-language. See here Tarski [2], 393ff., and Tarski [5], 110.

17. Due to the development of modern logic, the notion of mathematical proof has undergone a far-reaching simplification. A sentence of a given formalized discipline is provable if it can be obtained from the axioms of this discipline by applying certain simple and purely formal rules of inference, such as those of detachment and substitution. Hence to show that all provable sentences are true, it suffices to prove that all the sentences accepted as axioms are true, and that the rules of inference when applied to true sentences yield new true sentences; and this usually presents no difficulty.

On the other hand, in view of the elementary nature of the notion of provability, a precise definition of this notion requires only rather simple logical devices. In most cases, those logical devices which are available in the formalized discipline itself (to which the notion of provability is related) are more than sufficient for this purpose. We know, however, that as regards the definition of truth just the opposite holds. Hence, as a rule, the notions of truth and provability cannot coincide; and since every provable sentence is true, there must be true sentences which are not provable.

18. Thus the theory of truth provides us with a general method for consistency proofs for formalized mathematical disciplines. It can be easily realized, however, that a consistency proof obtained by this method may possess some intuitive value—i.e., may convince us, or strengthen our belief, that the discipline under consideration is actually consistent—only in case we succeed in defining truth in terms of a meta-language which does not contain the object-language as a part (cf. here a remark in section 9). For only in this case the deductive assumptions of the meta-language may be intuitively simpler and more obvious than those of the object-language—even though the condition of essential richness will be formally satisfied. Cf. here also Tarski [3], 7.

The incompleteness of a comprehensive class of formalized disciplines constitutes the essential content of a fundamental theorem of K. Gödel; cf. Gödel [1], 187ff. The explanation of the fact that the theory of truth leads so directly to Gödel's theorem is rather simple. In deriving Gödel's result from the theory of truth we make an essential use of the fact that the definition of truth cannot be given in a meta-language which is only as rich as the object-language (cf. note 17); however, in establishing this fact, a method of reasoning has been applied which is very closely related to that used (for the first time) by Gödel. It may be added that Gödel was clearly guided in his proof by certain intuitive considerations regarding the notion of truth, although this notion does not occur in the proof explicitly; cf. Gödel [1], 174f.

19. The notions of designation and definition lead respectively to the antinomies of Grelling-Nelson and Richard (cf. note 9). To obtain an antinomy for the notion of satisfaction, we construct the following expression:

> The sentential function X does not satisfy X.

A contradiction arises when we consider the question whether this expression, which is clearly a sentential function, satisfies itself or not.

20. All notions mentioned in this section can be defined in terms of satisfaction. We can say, e.g., that a given term designates a given object if this object satisfies the sentential function "x *is identical with T*" where "*T*" stands for the given term. Similarly, a sentential function is said to define a given object if the latter is the only object which satisfies this function. For a definition of consequence see Tarski [4], and for that of synonymity—Carnap [2].

21. General semantics is the subject of Carnap [2]. Cf. here also remarks in Tarski [2], 388f.

22. Cf. various quotations in Ness [1], 13f.

23. The names of persons who have raised objections will not be quoted here, unless their objections have appeared in print.

24. It should be emphasized, however, that as regards the question of an alleged vicious circle the situation would not change even if we took a different point of view, represented, e.g., in Carnap [2]; i.e., if we regarded the specification of conditions under which sentences of a language are true as an essential part of the description of this language. On the other hand, it may be noticed that the point of view represented in the text does not exclude the possibility of using truth tables in a deductive development of logic. However, these tables are to be regarded then merely as a formal instrument for checking the provability of certain sentences; and the symbols "*T*" and "*F*" which occur in them and which are usually considered abbreviations of "*true*" and "*false*" should not be interpreted in any intuitive way.

25. Cf. Juhos [1]. I must admit that I do not clearly understand von Juhos' objections and do not know how to classify them; therefore, I confine myself here to certain points of a formal character. Von Juhos does not seem to know my definition of truth; he refers only to an informal presentation in Tarski [3] where the definition has not been given at all. If he knew the actual definition, he would have to change his argument. However, I have no doubt that he would discover in this definition some "defects" as well. For he believes he has proved that "on ground of principle it is impossible to give such a definition at all."

26. The phrases "*p is true*" and "*p is the case*" (or better "*it is true that p*" and "*it is the case that p*") are sometimes used in informal discussions, mainly for stylistic reasons; but they are considered then as synonymous with the sentence represented by "*p.*" On the other hand, as far as I understand the situation, the phrases in question cannot be used by von Juhos synonymously with "*p*"; for otherwise the replacement of (T) by (T') or (T'') would not constitute any "improvement."

27. Cf. the discussion of this problem in Kokoszyńska [1], 161ff.

28. Most authors who have discussed my work on the notion of truth are of the opinion that my definition does conform with the classical conception of this notion; see, e.g., Kotarbiński [2] and Scholz [1].

29. Cf. Ness [1]. Unfortunately, the results of that part of Ness' research which is especially relevant for our problem are not discussed in his book; compare p. 148, footnote 1.

30. Though I have heard this opinion several times, I have seen it in print only once and, curiously enough, in a work which does not have a philosophical character—in fact, in Hilbert and Bernays [1], vol. 2, 269 (where, by the way, it is not expressed as any kind of objection). On the other hand, I have not found any remark to this effect in discussions of my work by professional philosophers (cf. note 1).

31. The remaining sections of Tarski's original article have been omitted in this reprinting.—Eds.

32. Cf. Gonseth [1], 187f.

References

Aristotle. [1]. *Metaphysics* (*Works*, vol. 5). English translation by W. D. Ross. Oxford, 1908.

Carnap, R. [1]. *Logical Syntax of Language*. London, 1937.

Carnap, R. [2]. *Introduction to Semantics*. Cambridge, 1942.

Gödel, K. [1]. "Über formal unentscheidbare Sätze der *Principia Mathematica* und verwandter Systeme, I." *Monatshefte für Mathematik und Physik* 38 (1931): 173–198.

Gödel, K. [2]. "Über die Länge von Beweisen." *Ergebnisse eines mathematischen Kolloquiums* 7 (1936): 23–24.

Gonseth, F. [1]. "Le Congrès Descartes. Questions de Philosophie scientifique." *Revue thomiste* 44 (1938): 183–193.

Grelling, K., and Nelson, L. [1]. "Bemerkungen zu den Paradoxien von Russell und Burali-Forti." *Abhandlungen der Frie'schen Schule*, n.s., 2 (1908): 301–334.

Hilbert, D., and Bernays, P. [1]. *Grundlagen der Mathematik*. 2 vols. Berlin, 1934–1939.

Hofstadter, A. [1]. "On Semantic Problems." *Journal of Philosophy* 35 (1938): 225–232.

Juhos, B. von. [1]. "The Truth of Empirical Statements." *Analysis* 4 (1937): 65–70.

Kokoszyńska, M. [1]. "Über den absoluten Wahrheitsbegriff und einige andere semantische Begriffe." *Erkenntnis* 6 (1936): 143–165.

Kokoszyńska, M. [2]. "Syntax, Semantik und Wissenschaftslogik." *Actes du Congrès International de Philosophie Scientifique* 3 (1936): 9–14.

Kotarbiński, T. [1]. *Elementy teorji poznania, logiki formalnej i metodologji nauk* [*Elements of Epistemology, Formal Logic, and the Methodology of Sciences*, in Polish]. Lwów, 1929.

Kotarbiński, T. [2]. "W sprawie pojęcia prawdy" [Concerning the Concept of Truth, in Polish]. *Przeglgd filozoficzny* 37 [n.d.]: 85–91.

Lindenbaum, A., and Tarski, A. [1]. "Über die Beschranktheit der Ausdrucksmittel deduktiver Theorien." *Ergebnisse eines mathematischen Kolloquiums* 7 (1936): 15–23.

Nagel, E. [1]. Review of Hofstadter [1]. *Journal of Symbolic Logic* 3 (1938): 90.

Nagel, E. [2]. Review of Carnap [2]. *Journal of Philosophy* 39 (1942): 468–473.

Ness, A. [1]. "'Truth' as Conceived by Those Who Are Not Professional Philosophers." *Skrifter utgitt av Det Norske Videnskaps—Akademi i Oslo, II. Hist.—Filos. Klasse* 4 (1938).

Neurath, O. [1]. "Erster Internationaler Kongress für Einheit der Wissenschaft in Paris 1935." *Erkenntnis* 5 (1935): 377–406.

Russell, B. [1]. *An Inquiry into Meaning and Truth*. New York, 1940.

Scholz, H. [1]. Review of *Studia philosophica*, Vol. I. *Deutsche Literaturzeitung* 58 (1937): 1914–1917.

Tarski, A. [1]. "Sur les ensembles définissables de nombres réels, 1." *Fundamenta mathematicae* 17 (1931): 210–239.

Tarski, A. [2]. "Der Wahrheitsbegriff in den formalisierten Sprachen." [German translation of a book in Polish, 1933.] *Studia philosophica* 1 (1935): 261–405.

Tarski, A. [3]. "Grundlegung der wissenschaftlichen Semantik." *Actes du Congrès International de Philosophie Scientifique* 3 (1936): 1–8.

Tarski, A. [4]. "Über den Begriff der logischen Folgerung." *Actes du Congrès International de Philosophie Scientifique* 7 (1937): 1–11.

Tarski, A. [5]. "On Undecidable Statements in Enlarged Systems of Logic and the Concept of Truth." *Journal of Symbolic Logic* 4 (1939): 105–112.

Tarski, A. [6]. *Introduction to Logic*. New York, 1941.

Weinberg, J. [1]. Review of *Studia philosophica*, Vol. I. *Philosophical Review* 47 (1937): 70–77.

15 Tarski's Theory of Truth

Hartry Field

In the early 1930s there was prevalent, among scientifically minded philosophers, the view that semantic notions such as the notions of truth and denotation were illegitimate: that they could not or should not be incorporated into a scientific conception of the world. But when Tarski's work on truth became known, all this changed. Popper wrote, "As a result of Tarski's teaching, I no longer hesitate to speak of 'truth' and 'falsity'";[1] and Popper's reaction was widely shared.[2]

A philosopher who shared Popper's reaction to Tarski's discoveries would presumably argue as follows. "What Tarski did was to define the term 'true,' using in his definitions only terms that are clearly acceptable. In particular, he did not employ any undefined semantic terms in his definitions. So Tarski's work should make the term 'true' acceptable even to someone who is initially suspicious of semantic terms."

This contention has an initial plausibility, but I will argue that it is radically wrong. My contrary claim will be that Tarski succeeded in reducing the notion of truth *to certain other semantic notions*; but that he did not in any way explicate these other notions, so that his results ought to make the word "true" acceptable only to someone who already regarded these other semantic notions as acceptable.

By claiming that Tarski merely reduced truth to other semantic notions, I don't mean to suggest that his results on truth are trivial. On the contrary, I think that they are extremely important, and have applications not only to mathematics but also to linguistics and to more directly philosophical problems about realism and objectivity. I think, however, that the real value of Tarski's discoveries for linguistics and philosophy is widely misunderstood, and I hope to eradicate the most central misunderstandings by clarifying and defending the claim that Tarski merely reduced truth to other semantic notions.

I

I believe that Tarski presented his semantic theory in a very misleading way, one which has encouraged the misinterpretations just alluded to. In this section I will present Tarski's theory as I think he should have presented it. However, I do not expect instant agreement that this new way is better than the old, and so I will use the name "Tarski*" for a logician who gave the sort of semantic theory I will now sketch. Later in the paper I will compare Tarski*'s semantics to the semantics that the real Tarski actually gave; by doing this I will cast light on the issues raised in my introductory paragraphs.

In sketching Tarski*'s theory, I will focus my attention on a particular object language L. The language L that I choose will be a quantificational language with names ('c_1,' 'c_2,' ...), one-place function symbols ('f_1,' 'f_2,' ...), and one-place predicates ('p_1,' 'p_2,' ...). The language of course cannot be viewed as an "uninterpreted" language, i.e., as just a bunch of strings of meaningless marks, for then there would be no truth to worry about. Instead, the language should be regarded as something that people actually speak or write; and it is because the speakers speak or write the way they do that the words of the language have the meaning they have.[3]

Initially I will follow Tarski in supposing that in L "the sense of every expression is unambiguously determined by its form,"[4] i.e., that whenever two speakers use the same name (or one speaker uses it on two occasions) they are referring to the same thing, that whenever two speakers use the same sentence either both are saying something true or neither is, etc. In these circumstances it makes sense to speak of the names of the language denoting things (a name denotes whatever the users of the name refer to) and the sentences being true or false (true when speakers who use it say something true by so doing.) The more general situation, in which there are expressions whose "sense" is not determined wholly by their form, will be dealt with later. (We'll see that it is one of the advantages of Tarski*'s semantics that it can easily handle this more general situation).

The syntax of L can be given by two recursive definitions: first we define the *singular terms* by saying that all names and variables are singular terms, and a function symbol followed by a singular term is a singular term; then we define the *formulas* by saying that a predicate followed by a singular term is a formula, as is the negation of a formula, the conjunction of two formulas, and the universal quantification of a formula with any variable. The *sentences*, or *closed formulas*, are then singled out in the usual way.

Now we can proceed to Tarski*'s semantics. Rather than characterize truth directly, we characterize it relative to some assignment of objects to the variables, say s_k to 'x_k.' The idea is going to be to treat the variables, or at least the free variables, as sort of "temporary names" for the objects assigned to them. So we proceed by fixing a sequence $s = <s_1, s_2, ...>$ of objects, to be assigned to 'x_1,' 'x_2,' ..., respectively; and we want to say what it is for a formula to be true$_s$, i.e., true relative to the assignment s. As a preliminary we say what it is for a term to denote$_s$ an object, i.e., to denote it relative to the assignment s. The denotation of 'x_k' relative to s is evidently s_k, for this is the object assigned to 'x_k.' But what is the denotation relative to s of 'c_k'? Evidently what objects are assigned to the variables here is irrelevant, and the denotation$_s$ of 'c_k' is some fixed object that users of the language refer to when they use the name 'c_k.' Just what this object is depends on facts we have not yet been given about the use of 'c_k.' Similarly there are facts we have not yet been given about the use of 'p_k' and 'f_k' which we need in order to fix the truth value of sentences containing them. For 'p_k' the relevant facts concern the extension of the predicate—what objects the predicate *applies to*—for it is this which affects the truth value of all utterances containing 'p_k.' For 'f_k,' the relevant facts concern what pairs of objects *fulfill* that function symbol—in the sense that the pair (John Adams, John Quincy Adams) and every other father-son pair fulfill the function symbol 'father of.'

With these points in mind it is now easy to give an inductive characterization of denotations:

T1 (A)   1. 'x_k' denotes$_s$ s_k.

2. 'c_k' denotes$_s$ what it denotes.

3. $\ulcorner f_k(e) \urcorner$ denotes$_s$ an object a if and only if

(i)   there is an object b that e denotes$_s$ and

(ii) 'f_k' is fulfilled by $<a, b>$.

(Here 'e' is a variable ranging over expressions of L.) Similarly we define 'true$_s$' for formulas—what Tarski calls satisfaction of a formula by s:

(B)   1. $\ulcorner p_k (e) \urcorner$ is true$_s$ if and only if

(i)   there is an object a that e denotes$_s$ and

(ii) 'p_k' applies to a.

2. $\ulcorner \sim e \urcorner$ is true$_s$ if and only if e is not true$_s$.

3. $\ulcorner e_1 \wedge e_2 \urcorner$ is true$_s$ if and only if e_1 is true$_s$ and so is e_2.

4. $\ulcorner \forall x_k (e) \urcorner$ is true$_s$ if and only if for each sequence s^* that differs from s at the kth place at most, e is true$_{s^*}$.

This completes the characterization of truth relative to an assignment of objects to the variables. In the case of sentences it is easily seen that we get the same results whatever such assignment we pick; we can say

(C) A sentence is true if and only if it is true$_s$ for some (or all) s.

This completes my elaboration of Tarski*'s "truth definition" T1 for L—or his *truth characterization* (TC), as I prefer to call it. What is its philosophical significance? The obvious answer, and the correct one, I think, is that the TC reduces one semantic notion to three others. It explains what it is for a sentence to be true in terms of certain semantic features of the primitive components of the sentence: in terms of what it is for a name to denote something, what it is for a predicate to apply to something, and what it is for a function symbol to be fulfilled by some pair of things. It is convenient to introduce the expression "primitively denotes" as follows: every name *primitively denotes* what it denotes; every predicate and every function symbol *primitively denotes* what it applies to or is fulfilled by; and no complex expression primitively denotes anything. In this terminology, what T1 does is to explain truth in terms of primitive denotation. Similarly we can explain denotation for arbitrary closed singular terms [such as '$f_1(c_1)$'] in terms of primitive denotation, i.e., in terms of the semantic features of the names and function symbols from which the complex singular term is composed—we merely say that a closed singular term denotes an object a if it denotes$_s$ a for some (or all) s, where denotation$s$ is defined as before. We see then that *Tarski*'s semantics explains the semantic properties of complex expressions* (e.g., truth value for sentences, denotation for complex singular terms) *in terms of semantic properties of their primitive components.*

To explain truth in terms of primitive denotation is, I think, an important task. It certainly doesn't answer *every* question that anyone would ever want answered about truth, but for many purposes it is precisely what we need. For instance, in model theory we are interested in such questions as: given a set Γ of sentences, is there any way to choose the denotations of the primitives of the language so that every sentence of Γ will come out true given the usual semantics for the logical connectives?[5] For questions such as this, what we need to know is how the truth value of a whole sentence depends on the denotations of its primitive nonlogical parts, and that is precisely what T1 tells us. So *at least for model-theoretic purposes*, Tarski*'s TC is precisely the kind of explication of truth we need.

I want now to return to a point I mentioned earlier, about Tarski's restriction to languages in which "the sense of every expression is unambiguously determined by its form." Natural languages are full of expressions that do not meet this requirement. For instance, different tokens of "John takes grass" can differ in "sense"—e.g., one token may be uttered in saying that John Smith smokes marijuana, and another may be uttered in saying that John Jones steals lawn material, and these differences may give rise to differences of truth value in the tokens. (I say that a complete[6] token of a sentence is true if the person who spoke or wrote that token said something true by so doing; I also say that a name token denotes an object if the person who spoke or wrote the token referred to the object by so doing.) The prevalence of such examples in natural languages raises the question of whether Tarski's type of semantic theory is applicable to languages in which the sense is *not* determined by the form; for if the answer is no, then Davidson's very worth-while project[7] of giving truth characterizations for natural languages seems doomed from the start.

It seems clear that if we stick to the kind of TC that Tarski actually gave (see next section), there is no remotely palatable way of extending TC's to sentences like "John takes grass." But if we use TC's like T1 there is no difficulty at all. The only point about languages containing "John" or "grass" or "I" or "you" is that for such languages "true," "denotes," and other semantic terms make no clear sense as applied to expression types; they make sense only as applied to tokens. For this reason we have to interpret clause (B)2 of T1 as meaning

A token of $\ulcorner \sim e \urcorner$ is true$_s$ if and only if the token of e that it contains is not true$_s$,

and similarly for the other clauses. Once we interpret our TC in this way in terms of tokens, i.e., individual occasions of utterance, that TC works perfectly: someone who utters "John is sick" (or "I am sick") says something true if and only if his token of "sick" applies to the person he refers to by "John" (or by "I"); and the fact that other speakers (or this speaker on other occasions) sometimes refer to different things when they use "John" (or "I") is beside the point.

This analysis leaves entirely out of account the ways in which "I" and "John" differ: it leaves out of account, for instance, the fact that a token of "I" always denotes the speaker who produced it. But that is no objection to the analysis, for the analysis purports merely to explain truth in terms of primitive denotation; it does not purport to say anything about primitive denotation, and the differences between "I" and "John" (or their analogues in a language like L) are purely differences of how they denote. (The word "I" denotes according to the simple rule mentioned two sentences back; "John" denotes according to much more complex rules that I have no idea how to formulate.)

Of course, the fact that a theory of denotation for a word like "I" is so simple and obvious, makes it possible to alter the TC so that the theory of denotation for such a word is built into the TC itself—such a course is adopted, for instance, by Davidson at the end of "Truth and Meaning." I myself prefer to preserve the analogies of the word "I" to words that function less systematically, e.g., "we," "she," and "John." How one treats "I" is more or less a matter of taste; but the less systematic words I've just mentioned cannot be handled in the way that Davidson handles "I," and the only reasonable way I can see to handle them is the way I have suggested: use a truth characterization like T1 (except stated in terms of tokens rather than types), and leave it to a separate theory of primitive denotation to explain the relevant differences between tokens of "John" that denote John Adams and tokens of "John" that denote John Lennon, and between tokens of "bank" that apply to things along rivers and tokens of "bank" that apply to the Chase Manhattan.[8]

There are other advantages to T1 besides its ability to handle ambiguous sentences, i.e., sentences for which the sense is not determined by the form. For instance, Tarski required that the vocabulary of the language be fixed once and for all; but if we decide to give truth characterizations of type T1, this is unnecessary: all that is required is that the general structure of the language be fixed, e.g., that the semantic categories[9] (name, one-place predicate, etc.) be held constant. In other words, if a language already contained proper names, the invention of a new name to baptize an object will not invalidate the old TC; though introduction of a name into a hitherto nameless language will.

To show this, we have merely to reformulate the given TC so that it does not rely on the actual vocabulary that the language contains at a given time, but works also for sentences containing new names, one-place predicates, etc., that speakers of the language might later introduce. To do this is trivial: we define denotation$_s$ by

1. The kth variable denotes$_s$ s_k.
2. If e_1 is a name, it denotes$_s$ what it denotes.
3. If e_1 is a singular term and e_2 is a function symbol, then $\ulcorner e_2(e_1) \urcorner$ denotes$_s$ a if and only if

   (i) as before, and

   (ii) e_2 is fulfilled by $<a, b>$.

And we can generalize the definition of truth$_s$ in a similar manner.[10] This shows that, in giving a TC, there is no need to utilize the particular vocabulary used at one temporal stage of a language, for we can instead give a more general TC which can be incorporated into a diachronic theory of the language (and can also be applied directly to other languages of a similar structure). *If*, that is, we accept the modification of Tarski proposed in this section.

II

The kind of truth characterization advocated in the previous section differs from the kind of TC Tarski offered in one important respect. Tarski stated the policy "I shall not make use of any semantical concept if I am not able previously to reduce it to other concepts" (CTFL 152–153), and this policy is flagrantly violated by T1: T1 utilizes unreduced notions of proper names denoting things, predicates applying to things, and function symbols being fulfilled by things.

Tarski's truth characterizations, unlike T1, accorded with his stated policy: they did not contain any semantic terms like "applies to" or "denotes." How did Tarski achieve this result? Very simply: first, he translated every name, predicate, and function symbol of L into English; then he utilized these translations in order to reformulate clauses 2 and 3(ii) of part (A) of the definition and clause 1(ii) of part (B). For simplicity, let's use '$\overline{c}_1$,' '$\overline{c}_2$,' etc. as abbreviations for the English expressions that are the translations of the words 'c_1,' 'c_2,' ... of L: e.g.: if L is simplified German and 'c_1' is "Deutschland," then 'c_1' is an abbreviation for "Germany." Similarly, let '$\overline{f}_1$' abbreviate the translation into English of the word 'f_1' of L, and let '$\overline{p}_1$' abbreviate the translation of 'p_1' into English. Then Tarski's reformulated truth definition will read as follows:

T2 (A) 1. as before

2. 'c_k' denotes$_s$ $\bar{c}_k$

3. $\ulcorner f_k(e) \urcorner$ denotes$_s$ a if and only if

(i) as before

(ii) a is $\bar{f}_k(b)$

(B) 1. $\ulcorner p_k(e) \urcorner$ is true$_s$ if and only if

(i) as before

(ii) $\bar{p}_k(a)$

2–4. as before

(C) as before

What T2 is like depends of course on the precise character of the translations of the primitives that are utilized. For instance, if we translate 'c_1' as "the denotation of 'c_1,'" translate 'p_1' as "is something that 'p_1' applies to," etc., then T2 becomes identical with T1. This of course is *not* what Tarski intended. What Tarski intended is that T2 not contain unexplicated semantic terms, and if we are to get this result we must not employ any semantic terms in our translations.[11]

But other restrictions on translations are also necessary: if we were to translate "Deutschland" as "Bertrand Russell," a truth characterization T2 that was based on this translation would grossly misrepresent L. In order to state the matter more generally, I introduce the term "coreferential": two singular terms are coreferential if they denote the same thing; two predicative expressions are coreferential if they have the same extension, i.e., if they apply to the same things; and two functional expressions are coreferential if they are fulfilled by the same pairs. It is then easily seen that any departure from coreferentiality in translation will bring errors into T2. For instance, suppose we translate the foreign predicate "glub" as "yellow," and suppose "glub" and "yellow" are not *precisely* coreferential; then clause (B)$_1$ will say falsely that "glub(x)" is true of just those objects which are yellow.

Let us say, then, that

(1) An adequate translation of a primitive e_1 of L into English is an expression e_2 of English such that

(i) e_1 and e_2 are coreferential, and

(ii) e_2 contains no semantic terms.

This notion of an adequate translation is of course a semantic notion that Tarski did not reduce to nonsemantic terms. But that is no objection to his characterization T2 (at least, it isn't obviously an objection), for the notion of an adequate translation is never built into the truth characterization and is not, properly speaking, part of a theory of truth. On Tarski's view we need to adequately translate the object language into the meta-language in order to give an adequate theory of truth for the object language; this means that the notion of an adequate translation is employed in the methodology of giving truth theories, but it is not employed in the truth theories themselves.

In what follows I shall assume that the language L with which we are dealing is so related to English that all its primitives *can* be adequately translated into English, according to the standards of adequacy set forth in (1). (This is another restriction that we avoid if we give TC's of the type T1; quite a significant restriction, I think.) If we then suppose that the translation given ('$\bar{c}_1$' for 'c_1,' etc.) is one of the adequate translations, then T2, like T1, is a correct recursive characterization of truth for the language L. There is, of course, a simple procedure for transforming recursive characterizations such as these into explicit characterizations. To carry the procedure through in these cases would be pretty complicated, but it could be done; so we could regard T1 (or T2) as implicitly specifying a metalinguistic formula '$A_1(e)$' (or '$A_2(e)$'), and saying that an utterance e of L is true if and only if $A_1(e)$ (or $A_2(e)$). If we regard T1 and T2 as written in this form, then the key difference between them is that '$A_1(e)$' contains *semantic terms and* '$A_2(e)$' *does not*. The question then arises: is the fact that '$A_2(e)$' does not contain semantic terms an advantage of T2 over T1? If so, then *why* is it an advantage?

In order to discuss the possible advantages of T2 over T1, I think we have to go beyond mathematical considerations and focus instead on linguistic and other "philosophical" matters. It is not enough to say that T2 *defines* truth without utilizing semantic terms, whereas T1 defines it only in other semantic terms: this is not enough until we say something more about the purpose of definition. If the purpose of giving a "definition" of truth is to enable you to do model theory, then the elimination of semantic terms from T1 gives no advantage. For what purpose do we want definitions for which the elimination of semantic terms is useful?

One purpose to which definitions are sometimes put is in explaining the meaning of a word. This of course is very vague, but I think it is clear enough to enable use to recognize that neither T1 nor T2 has very much to do with explaining the meaning of the word "true." This is especially obvious for T2: a T2-type truth definition works for a single language only, and so if it "explains the meaning of" the word "true" as applied to that language, then for *any* two languages L_1 and L_2, the word "true" means something different when applied to utterances of L_1 than it means when applied to utterances of L_2! I make this point not in criticism of T2, but in criticism of the idea that the significance of T2 can be explained by saying that it "gives the meaning of" the word "true."

We still need to know what purpose a truth characterization like T1 or T2 could serve that would give someone reason to think that a TC without unexplicated semantic terms would be better than a TC with unexplicated semantic terms. Tarski hints at such a purpose in one place in his writings, where he is discussing the importance of being able to define the word "true," as opposed to merely introducing axioms to establish the basic properties of truth. If a definition of semantic notions such as truth could not be given, Tarski writes,

> ... it would then be difficult to bring [semantics] into harmony with the postulates of the unity of science and of physicalism (since the concepts of semantics would be neither logical nor physical concepts).[12]

This remark seems to me to be of utmost importance in evaluating the philosophical significance of Tarski's work, and so I will now say something about the general philosophical issues it raises. When this is done we will be in a better position to understand Tarski's choice of T2 over T1.

III

In the early 1930s many philosophers believed that the notion of truth could not be incorporated into a scientific conception of the world. I think that the main rationale for this view is hinted at in the remark of Tarski's that I quoted at the end of the last section, and what I want to do now is to elaborate a bit on Tarski's hint.

In the remark I have quoted, Tarski put a heavy stress on the doctrine of physicalism: the doctrine that chemical facts, biological facts, psychological facts, and semantical facts, are all explicable (in principle) in terms of physical facts. The doctrine of physicalism functions as a high-level empirical hypothesis, a hypothesis that no small number of experiments can force us to give up. It functions, in other words, in much the same way as the doctrine of mechanism (that all facts are explicable in terms of *mechanical* facts) once functioned: this latter doctrine has now been universally rejected, but it was given up only by the development of a well-accepted theory (Maxwell's) which described phenomena (electromagnetic radiation and the electromagnetic field) that were very difficult to account for mechanically, and by amassing a great deal of experiment and theory that together made it quite conclusive that mechanical explanations of these phenomena (e.g., by positing "the ether") would never get off the ground. Mechanism has been empirically refuted; its heir is physicalism, which allows as "basic" not only facts about mechanics, but facts about other branches of physics as well.[13] I believe that physicists a hundred years ago were justified in accepting mechanism, and that, similarly, physicalism should be accepted until we have convincing evidence that there is a realm of phenomena it leaves out of account. Even if there *does* turn out to be such a realm of phenomena, the only way we'll ever come to know that there is, is by repeated efforts and repeated failures to explain these phenomena in physical terms.

That's my view, anyway, but there are philosophers who think that it is in order to reject physicalism now. One way of rejecting physicalism is called "vitalism": it is the view that there are irreducibly biological facts, i.e., biological facts that aren't explicable in nonbiological terms (and hence, not in physical terms). Physicalism and vitalism are incompatible, and it is because of this incompatibility that the doctrine of physicalism has the methodological importance it has for biology. Suppose, for instance, that a certain woman has two sons, one hemophilic and one not. Then, according to standard genetic accounts of hemophilia, the ovum from which one of these sons was produced must have contained a gene for hemophilia, and the ovum from which the other son was produced must not have contained such a gene. But now the doctrine of physicalism tells us that there must have been a *physical* difference between the two ova that explains why the first son had hemophilia and the second one didn't, if the standard genetic account is to be accepted. We should not rest content with a special biological predicate "has-a-hemophilic-gene"—rather, we should look for nonbiological facts (chemical facts; and ultimately, physical facts) that underlie the correct application of this predicate. That at least is what the principle of physicalism tells us, and it can hardly be doubted that this principle has motivated a great deal of very profitable research into the chemical foundations of genetics.

So much for vitalism; now let us turn to other irreducibility doctrines that are opposed to physicalism. One such irreducibility doctrine is Cartesianism: it is the doctrine that there are irreducibly mental facts. Another irreducibility doctrine has received much less attention than either vitalism or Cartesianism, but it is central to our present concerns: this doctrine, which might be called "semanticalism," is the doctrine that there are irreducibly semantic facts. The semanticalist claims, in other words, that semantic phenomena (such as the fact that "Schnee" refers to snow) must be accepted as primitive, in precisely the way that electromagnetic phenomena are accepted as primitive (by those who accept Maxwell's equations and reject the ether); and in precisely the way that biological phenomena and mental phenomena are accepted as primitive by vitalists and Cartesians. Semanticalism, like Cartesianism and vitalism, posits nonphysical primitives, and as a physicalist I believe that all three doctrines must be rejected.

There are two general sorts of strategy that can be taken in rejecting semanticalism, or Cartesianism, or vitalism. One strategy, illustrated two paragraphs back in discussing vitalism, is to try to explicate the terms of a biological theory in nonbiological terms. But there is another possible strategy, which is to argue that the biological terms are illegitimate. The second strategy seems reasonable to adopt in dealing with the following predicate of (reincarnationist) biology: "*x* has the same soul as *y*." A physicalist would never try to find physical or chemical facts that underlie reincarnation; rather, he would reject reincarnation as a myth.

Since biological theory is as well developed as it is, we usually have a pretty good idea which biological terms require explication and which require elimination. When we turn to psychology and semantics, however, it is often not so obvious which strategy is the more promising. Thus in semantics, physicalists agree that all *legitimate* semantic terms must be explicable nonsemantically—they think in other words that there are no irreducibly semantic facts—but they disagree as to which semantic terms are legitimate. That disagreement has become fairly clear in recent years in the theory of meaning, with the work of Quine: the disagreement is between those physicalists who would look for a nonsemantic basis for terms in the theory of meaning, and those who would follow Quine in simply throwing out those terms. Our concern, however, is not with the theory of meaning, but with the theory of reference, and here the disagreement has been less clear, since there haven't been many physicalists who openly advocate getting rid of terms like "true" and "denotes." There were such physicalists in the early 1930s; part of the importance of Tarski's work was to persuade them that they were on the wrong track, to persuade them that we should explicate notions in the theory of reference nonsemantically rather than simply get rid of them.

The view that we should just stop using semantic terms (here and in the rest of this paper, I mean terms in the theory of reference, such as "true" and "denotes" and "applies to") draws its plausibility from the apparent difficulty of explicating these terms nonsemantically. People utter the sounds "Electrons have rest mass but photons don't," or "Schnee ist weiss und Gras ist grün," and we apply the word "true" to their utterances. We don't want to say that it is a primitive and inexplicable fact about these utterances that they are true, a fact that cannot be explicated in nonsemantic terms; this is as unattractive to a physicalist as supposing that it is a primitive and inexplicable fact about an organism at a certain time that it is in pain. But how could we ever explicate in nonsemantic terms the alleged fact that these utterances are true? *Part* of the explication of the truth of "Schnee ist weiss und Gras ist grün," presumably, would be that snow is white and grass is green. But this would only be part of the explanation, for still missing is the connection between snow being white and grass being green on the one hand, and the German utterance being true on the other hand. It is this connection that seems so difficult to explicate in a way that would satisfy a physicalist, i.e., in a way that does not involve the use of semantic terms.

If, in face of these difficulties, we were ever to conclude that it was *impossible* to explicate the notions of truth and denotation in nonsemantic terms, we would have either to give up these semantic terms or else to reject physicalism. It seems to me that that is essentially what Tarski is saying in the quotation at the end of the last section, and I have tried to make it plausible by sketching analogies to areas other than semantics. Tarski's view, however, was that, for certain languages at least, semantic terms *are* explicable nonsemantically, and that truth definitions like T2 provide the required explication. It is understandable that as far as *philosophical* purposes go Tarski should think that T1 leaves something to be desired: after all, it merely explicates truth in terms of other semantic concepts; but what good does that do if those other concepts can't be explicated nonsemantically? T2, then, has a strong prima facie advantage over T1. In the next section I will show that it is not a genuine advantage.

IV

The apparent advantage of T2 over T1, I have stressed, is that it appears to reduce truth to nonsemantic terms; and I *think* this is why Tarski wanted to give a truth definition like T2 rather than like T1. This interpretation makes sense of Tarski's remark about physicalism, and it also explains why someone who was certainly not interested in "meaning analysis" as that is usually conceived would have wanted to give "definitions" of truth and would emphasize that, in these "definitions," "I will not make use of any semantical concept if I am not able previously to reduce it to other concepts." In any case, the problem of reducing truth is a very important problem, one which T1 and T2 provide a partial solution to, and one which T2 *might* be thought to provide a full solution to; and it is not at all clear what *other* interesting problems T2 could be though to solve better than T1.

In Tarski's own exposition of his theory of truth, Tarski put very little stress on the problem of reduction or on any other problem with a clear philosophical or mathematical motivation; instead, he set up a formal criterion of adequacy for theories of truth without any serious discussion of whether or why this formal criterion is reasonable. Roughly, the criterion was this:[14]

(M) Any condition of the form

(2) $(\forall e)[e \text{ is true} \equiv B(e)]$

should be accepted as an adequate definition of truth if and only if it is correct and '$B(e)$' is a well-formed formula containing no semantic terms. (The quantifiers are to be taken as ranging over expressions of one particular language only.)

The "only if" part of condition M is not something I will contest. It rules out the possibility of T1 *by itself* being an adequate truth definition; and it is right to do so, if the task of a truth definition is to reduce truth to nonsemantic terms, for T1 provides only a *partial* reduction. (To complete the reduction we need to reduce primitive denotation to nonsemantic terms.) T2, on the other hand, meets condition M; so either T2 is superior to T1 as a reduction, or else condition M is too weak and the "if" part of it must be rejected. My own diagnosis is the latter, but the other possibility seems initially reasonable. After all, how could condition M be strengthened? We might try requiring that '$B(e)$' be not only *extensionally* equivalent to 'e is true,' but *intensionally* equivalent to it; but this clearly won't do, for even if we grant that there is an intelligible notion of intensional equivalence, our concern is not with analyzing the meaning of the word "true" but with performing a reduction. A clear and useful standard of equivalence that is stronger than extensional equivalence but not so strong as to rule out acceptable reductions is unknown at the present time, so I know no way to improve on condition M. My view is that we have a rough but useful concept of reduction which we are unable to formulate precisely; but I must admit that the alternative view, that extensional equivalence is adequate, has an initial appeal.

A closer look, however, will reveal quite conclusively that extensional equivalence is not a sufficient standard of reduction. This can be seen by looking at the concept of valence. The valence of a chemical element is an integer that is associated with that element, which represents the sort of chemical combinations that the element will enter into. What I mean by the last phrase is that it is possible—roughly, at least—to characterize which elements will combine with which others, and in what proportions they will combine, merely in terms of their valences. Because of this fact, the concept of valence is a physically important concept, and so if physicalism is correct it ought to be possible to explicate this concept in physical terms—e.g., it ought to be possible to find structural properties of the atoms of each element that determine what the valence of that element will be. Early in the twentieth century (long after the notion of valence had proved its value in enabling chemists to predict what chemical combinations there would be) this reduction of the concept of valence to the physical properties of atoms was established; the notion of valence was thus shown to be a physicalistically acceptable notion.

Now, it would have been easy for a chemist, late in the last century, to have given a "valence definition" of the following form:

(3) $(\forall E)(\forall n)(E$ has valence $n \equiv E$ is potassium and n is +1, or ... , or E is sulphur and n is $-2)$

where in the blanks go a list of similar clauses, one for each element. But, though this is an extensionally correct definition of valence, it would not have been an acceptable reduction; and had it turned out that nothing else was possible—had all efforts to explain valence in terms of the structural properties of atoms proved futile—scientists would have eventually had to decide either (a) to give up valence theory, or else (b) to replace the hypothesis of physicalism by another hypothesis (chemicalism?). It is part of scientific methodology to resist doing (b); and I also think it is part of scientific methodology to resist doing (a) as long as the notion of valence is serving the purposes for which it was designed (i.e., as long as it is proving useful in helping us characterize chemical compounds in terms of their valences). But the methodology is not to resist (a) and (b) by giving lists like (3); the methodology is to look for a real reduction. This is a methodology that has proved extremely fruitful in science, and I think we'd be crazy to give it up in linguistics. *And I think we are giving up this fruitful methodology, unless we realize that we need to add theories of primitive reference to T1 or T2 if we are to establish the notion of truth as a physicalistically acceptable notion.*

I certainly haven't yet given much argument for this last claim. I *have* argued that the standard of extensional equivalence doesn't guarantee an acceptable reduction; but T2 is obviously not trivial to the extent that (3) is. What *is* true, however, is roughly that T2 minus T1 is as trivial as (3) is. One way in which this last claim can be made more precise is by remembering that really we often apply the term "valence" not only to elements, but also to configurations of elements (at least to stable configurations that are not compounds, i.e., to radicals). Thus, if we abstract from certain physical limitations on the size of possible configurations of elements (as, in linguistics, we usually abstract from the limitations that memory, etc., impose on the lengths of possible utterances), there is an infinite number of entities to which the term "valence" is applied. But it is an important fact about valence that the valence of a configuration of elements is determined from the valences of the elements that make it up, and from the way they're put together. Because of this, we might try to give a recursive characterization of valence. First of all, we would try to characterize all the different *structures* that configurations of elements can have (much as we try to characterize all the different grammatical structures before we give a truth definition like T1 or T2). We would then try to find rules that would enable us to determine what the valence of a complicated configuration would be, given the valences of certain less complicated configurations that make it up and the way they're put together. If we had enough such rules, we could determine the valence of a given configuration given only its structure and the valences of the elements that make it up. And if we like, we can transform our recursive characterization of valence into an explicit characterization, getting

(V1) $(\forall c)(\forall n)(c$ has valence $n \equiv B(c, n))$.

The formula '$B(c, n)$' here employed will still contain the term "valence," but it will contain that term only as applied to elements, not as applied to configurations. Thus our "valence definition" V1 would characterize the valence of the complex *in terms of the valences of the simple.*

It would now be possible to eliminate the term "valence" from '$B(c, n)$,' in either of two ways. One way would be to employ a genuine reduction of the notion of valence for elements to the structural properties of atoms. The other way would be to employ the pseudo-reduction (3). It is clear that we could use (3) to give a trivial reformulation V2 of V1, which would have precisely the "advantages" as a reduction that T2 has over T1. (V2, incidentally, would also have one of the disadvantages over V1 that T2 has over T1: V1 does not need to be overhauled when you discover or synthesize new elements, whereas V2 does.)

That is a sketch of one way that the remark I made two paragraphs back about "T2 minus T1" could be made more precise. But it is somewhat more fruitful to develop the point slightly differently: doing this will enable me to make clearer that there is unlikely to be *any* purpose that T2 serves better than T1 (not merely that T2 is no better at reduction).

To get this result I'll go back to my original use of the term "valence," where it applies to elements only and not to configurations. And what I will do is compare (3) not to Tarski's theory of *truth*, but to Tarski's theory of *denotation* for names; the effect of this on his theory of truth will then be considered. Tarski states his theory of denotation for names in a footnote, as follows:

> To say that the name x denotes a given object a is the same as to stipulate that the object a ...
> satisfies a sentential function of a particular type. In colloquial language it would be a function
> which consists of three parts in the following order: a variable, the word "is" and the given
> name x. (CTFL 194)

This is actually only part of the theory, the part that defines denotation in terms of satisfaction; to see what the theory looks like when all semantic terms are eliminated, we
must see how satisfaction is defined. The definition is given by the (A) and (B) clauses
of T2, for, as I've remarked, "satisfaction" is Tarski's name for what I've called "truth$_s$."
What Tarski's definition of satisfaction tells us is this: for any name N, an object a satisfies the sentential function $\ulcorner x_1$ is $N\urcorner$ if and only if a is France and N is "France" or ...
or a is Germany and N is "Germany." Combining this definition of satisfaction (for
sentential functions of form $\ulcorner x_1$ is $N\urcorner$) with the earlier account of denotation in terms
of satisfaction, we get:

(DE) To say that the name N denotes a given object a is the same as to stipulate that
either a is France and N is "France," or ... , or a is Germany and N is "Germany."

This is Tarski's account of denotation for English proper names. For foreign proper
names, the definition of denotation in terms of satisfaction needs no modification
(except that the "is" must be replaced by a name of a foreign word, say "ist" for German). Combining this with the definition (again given by T2) of satisfaction for foreign
sentential functions like $\ulcorner x_1$ ist $N\urcorner$, we get:

(DG) To say that the name N denotes a given object a is the same as to stipulate
that either a is France and N is "Frankreich," or ... , or a is Germany and N is
"Deutschland."

DE and DG have not received much attention in commentaries on Tarski, but in fact
they play a key role in his semantic theory; and it was no aberration on Tarski's part
that he offered them as theories of denotation for English and German names, for *they
satisfy criteria of adequacy exactly analogous to the criteria of adequacy that Tarski accepted for
theories of truth*.[15] Nevertheless, it seems clear that DE and DG do not really reduce denotation to nonsemantic terms, any more than (3) reduces valence to nonchemical terms.

What would a real explication of denotation in nonsemantic terms be like? The
"classical" answer to this question (Russell's) is that a name like "Cicero" is "analytically linked" to a certain description (such as "the denouncer of Catiline"); so to explain
how the name "Cicero" denotes what it does you merely have to explain

i. the process by which it is linked to the description (presumably you bring in facts
about how it was learned by its user, or facts about what is going on in the user's
brain at the time of the using) and

ii. how the description refers to what it does

Because of (ii), of course, the project threatens circularity: the project is to explain how names refer in terms of how descriptions refer; but the natural way to explain how descriptions refer is in terms of how they're built up from their significant parts,[16] and how those significant parts refer (or apply, or are fulfilled), and those significant parts will usually include names. But Russell recognized this threat of circularity, and carefully avoided it: he assumed that the primitives of the language were to be partially ordered by a relation of "basicness," and that each name except a most basic ("logically proper") name was to be analytically linked to a formula containing only primitives more basic than it. The most basic primitives were to be linked to the world without the intervention of other words, by the relation of acquaintance.

This classical view of how names (and other primitives) latch onto their denotations is extremely implausible in many ways (e.g., it says you can refer only to things that are definable from "logically proper" primitives; it requires that there be certain statements, such as "If Cicero existed then Cicero denounced Catiline," which are analytic in the sense that they are guaranteed by linguistic rules and are immune to revision by future discoveries). I conjecture that it is because of the difficulties with this classical theory, which was the only theory available at the time that Tarski wrote, that Tarski's pseudo-theories DE and DG seemed reasonable—they weren't exciting, but if you wanted something exciting you got logically proper names. The diagnosis that any attempt to explain the relation between words and the things they are about must inevitably lead to either a wildly implausible theory (like Russell's) or a trivial theory (like Tarski's) seems to be widely accepted still; but I think that the diagnosis has become less plausible in recent years through the development of *causal* theories of denotation by Saul Kripke[17] and others. According to such theories, the facts that "Cicero" denotes Cicero and that "muon" applies to muons are to be explained in terms of certain kinds of causal networks between Cicero (muons) and our uses of "Cicero" ("muon"): causal connections both of a social sort (the passing of the word "Cicero" down to us from the original users of the name, or the passing of the word "muon" to laymen from physicists) and of other sorts (the evidential causal connections that gave the original users of the name "access" to Cicero and give physicists "access" to muons). I don't think that Kripke or anyone else thinks that *purely* causal theories of primitive denotation can be developed (even for proper names of past physical objects and for natural-kind predicates); this however should not blind us to the fact that he has suggested a kind of factor involved in denotation that gives new hope to the idea of explaining the connection between language and the things it is about. It seems to me that the possibility of *some such* theory of denotation (to be deliberately very vague) is essential to the joint acceptability of physicalism and the semantic term "denotes," and that denotation definitions like DE and DG merely obscure the need for this.

It might be objected that the purpose of DE and DG was not reduction; but what was their purpose? One answer might be that (DE) and (DG) enable us to eliminate the word "denote" whenever it occurs. ("To explain is to show how to eliminate.") For instance,

(4) No German name now in use denotes something that does not yet exist

would become

(4′) For any name N now in use, if N is "Frankreich" then France already exists, and ... , and if N is "Deutschland" then Germany already exists

provided that (DG) is a correct and complete list of the denotations of all those German proper names that have denotations. It seems reasonably clear that we could specify a detailed procedure for transforming sentences like (4) into materially equivalent sentences like (4′). A similar claim could be made for the "valence definition" (3). Such a valence definition makes it possible to eliminate the word "valence" from a large class of sentences containing it, and in a uniform way. For instance,

(5) For any elements A and B, if one atom of A combines with two of B, then the valence of A is -2 times that of B.

is materially equivalent to

(5′) For any elements A and B, if one atom of A combines with two of B, then either A is sodium and B is sodium and $+1 = -2 \, (+1)$, or ... , or A is sulphur and B is sodium and $-2 = -2 \, (+1)$, or ...

provided that (3) is a correct and complete list of valences. So if anyone ever wants to eliminate the word "denote" or the word "valence" from a large class of English sentences by a uniform procedure, denotation definitions and valence definitions are just the thing he needs. There are, however, sentences from which these words are not eliminable by the sketched procedure. For instance, in semantics and possibly in chemistry there are problems with counterfactuals, e.g., "If 'Germany' had been used to denote France, then ..." Moreover, there are special problems affecting the case of semantics, arising from the facts

i.   that the elimination procedure works only for languages in which nothing is denoted that cannot be denoted (without using semantic terms) in one's own language,

ii. that it works only for languages that contain no ambiguous names, and

iii. that the denotation definitions provide no procedure for eliminating "denote" from sentences where it is applied to more than one language; e.g., it gives no way of handling sentences like "'Glub' denotes different things in different languages."

But, subject to these three qualifications (plus perhaps that involving counterfactuals), the elimination procedure for "denote" is every bit as good as that for "valence."

What value did Tarski attach to such transformations? Unfortunately he did not discuss the one about valences, but he did discuss the one that transforms "Smith used a proper name to denote Germany" into something logically equivalent to "Smith uttered 'Deutschland.'" And it is clear that to this definition he attached great philosophical importance. After defining semantics as "the totality of considerations concerning those concepts which, roughly speaking, express certain connexions between the expressions of a language and the objects and states of affairs referred to by those expressions" (ESS 401), he says that with his definitions, "the problem of establishing semantics on a scientific basis is completely solved" (ESS 407). In other places his claims are almost as extravagant. For instance, the remark about physicalism that I quoted at the end of section II is intended to apply to denotation as well as to truth: if definitions of denotation like DE and DG could not be given, "it would ... be impossible to bring [semantics] into harmony with ... physicalism" (ESS 406); but because of these definitions, the compatibility of the semantic concept of denotation with physicalism is established. By similar standards of reduction, one might prove that witchcraft is compatible with physicalism, as long as witches cast only a finite number of spells: for then "cast a spell" can be defined without use of any of the terms of witchcraft theory, merely by listing all the witch-and-victim pairs.

In other places Tarski makes quite different claims for the value of his denotation definitions. For example:

> We desire semantic terms (referring to the object language) to be introduced into the metalanguage only by definition. For, if this postulate is satisfied, the definition of truth, or of any other semantic concept [including denotation, which Tarski had already specifically mentioned to be definable], will fulfill what we intuitively expect from every definition; that is, it will explain the meaning of the term being defined in terms whose meaning appears to be completely clear and unequivocal.[18]

But it is no more plausible that DE "explains the meaning of" "denote" as applied to English, or that DG "explains the meaning of" "denote" as applied to German, than that (3) "explains the meaning of" "valence"—considerably *less* so in fact, since for "valence" there is no analogue to the conclusions that "denote" means something different when applied to English than it means when applied to German. In fact, it seems pretty clear that denotation definitions like DE and DG have no philosophical interest whatever. But what conclusions can we draw from this about Tarski's *truth* definitions like T2? I think the conclusion to draw is that T2 *has no philosophical interest whatever that is not shared by* T1. How this follows I will now explain.

We have seen that Tarski advocated theories of denotation for names that had the form of mere lists: examples of his denotation definitions were DE and DG, and for language L his denotation definition would take the following form:

(D2) $(\forall e)(\forall a)[e$ is a name that denotes $a \equiv (e$ is 'c_1' and a is $\bar{c}_1)$ or $(e$ is 'c_2' and a is $\bar{c}_2)$ or ...]

where into the dots go analogous clauses for every name of L. Similarly, we can come up with definitions of application and fulfillment which are acceptable according to Tarski's standards, and which also have the form of mere lists. The definition of application runs:

(A2) $(\forall e)(\forall a)[e$ is a predicate that applies to $a \equiv (e$ is 'p_1' and $\bar{p}_1(a))$ or $(e$ is 'p_2' and $\bar{p}_2(a))$ or ...].

Similarly, we can formulate a list-like characterization F2 of fulfillment for the function symbols. Clearly neither A2 nor F2 is of any more theoretical interest than D2.

Tarski, I have stressed, accepted D2 as part of his semantic theory, and would also have accepted A2 and F2; and this fact is quite important, since D2, A2, and F2 together with T2 imply T1. In other words, T1 is simply a weaker version of Tarski's semantic theory; it is a logical consequence of Tarski's theory. Now, an interesting question is what you have to add to T1 to get the rest of Tarski's semantic theory. Suppose we can find a formula R that we can argue to be of no interest whatever, such that Tarski's semantic theory $(T2 \wedge D2 \wedge A2 \wedge F2)$ is logically equivalent to $T1 \wedge R$. It will then follow that the whole interest of Tarski's semantic theory lies in T1—the rest of his semantic theory results simply by adding to it the formula R, which (I have assumed) has no interest whatever. And if there is nothing of interest in the conjunction $T2 \wedge D2 \wedge A2 \wedge F2$ beyond T1, certainly there can be nothing of interest in T2 alone beyond T1.

An example of such a formula R is $D2 \wedge A2 \wedge F2$: it is obvious that Tarski's semantic theory is logically equivalent to $T1 \wedge D2 \wedge A2 \wedge F2$. Because of this, *any interest in Tarski's semantic theory over T1 must be due to an interest in D2 or A2 or F2 (or to confusion): in this sense* $D2 \wedge A2 \wedge F2$ *is "T2 minus T1."* But I've already argued that D2, A2, and F2 have no theoretical interest whatever, and so that establishes that T2 has no theoretical interest whatever that is not shared by T1.

V

Much of what I've said in this paper gains plausibility by being put in a wider persepctive, and so I now want to say a little bit about why we want a notion of truth. The notion of truth serves a great many purposes, but I suspect that its original purpose—the purpose for which it was first developed—was to aid us in utilizing the utterances of others in drawing conclusions about the world. To take an extremely simple example, suppose that a friend reports that he's just come back from Alabama and that there was a foot of snow on the ground there. Were it not for his report we would have considered it extremely unlikely that there was a foot of snow on the ground in Alabama—but the friend knows snow when he sees it and is not prone to telling us lies for no apparent reason, and so after brief deliberation we conclude that probably there *was* a foot of snow in Alabama. What we did here was first to use our evidence about the person and his situation to decide that he probably said something true when he made a certain utterance, and then to draw a conclusion from the truth of his utterance to the existence of snow in Alabama. In order to make such inferences, we have to have a pretty good grasp of (i) the circumstances under which what another says is likely to be true, and (ii) how to get from a belief in the truth of what he says to a belief about the extralinguistic world.

If this idea is right, then two features of truth that are intimately bound up with the purposes to which the notion of truth are put are (I) the role that the attempt to tell the truth and the success in doing so play in social institutions, and (II) the fact that normally one is in a position to assert of a sentence that it is true in just those cases where one is in a position to assert the sentence or a paraphrase of it. It would then be natural to expect that what is involved in communicating the meaning of the word "true" to a child or to a philosopher is getting across to him the sorts of facts listed under (I) and (II); for those are the facts that it is essential for him to have an awareness of if he is to put the notion of truth to its primary use (child) or if he is to get a clear grasp of what its primary use is (philosopher).

I think that this natural expectation is correct, and that it gives more insight than was given in sections II and IV into why it is that neither T1 nor T2 can reasonably be said to explain the meaning of the term "true"—even when a theory of primitive reference is added to them. First consider (I). The need of understanding the sort of thing alluded to in (I), if we are to grasp the notion of truth, has been presented quite forcefully in Michael Dummett's article "Truth,"[19] in his analogy between speaking the truth and winning at a game. It is obvious that T1 and T2 don't explain anything like this (and in fact Dummett's fourth paragraph, on Frege-style truth definitions, can be carried over directly to T1 and T2).

The matter might perhaps be expressed in terms of assertibility conditions that one learns in learning to use the word "true": part of what we learn, in learning to use this word, is that in cases like that involving the friend from Alabama there is some prima facie weight to be attached to the claim that the other person is saying something true. But there are also *other* assertibility conditions that one learns in learning the word "true," assertibility conditions which have received considerable attention in the philosophical literature on truth. To begin with, let's note one obvious fact about how the word "true" is standardly learned: we learn how to apply it to utterances of our own language first, and when we later learn to apply it to other languages it is by conceiving the utterances of another language more or less on the model of utterances of our own language. The obvious model of the first stage of this process is that we learn to accept all instances of the schema

(T) X is true if and only if p

where 'X' is replaced by a quotation-mark name of an English sentence S and 'p' is replaced by S. This must be complicated to deal with ambiguous and truth-value-less sentences, but let's ignore them. Also let's ignore the fact that certain pathological instances of (T)—the Epimenides-type paradoxical sentences—are logically refutable. Then there is a sense in which the instances of (T) that we've learned to assert determine a unique extension for the predicate "true" as applied to sentences of our own language.[20] Our views about what English sentences belong to this unique extension may be altered, but as long as we stick to the instances of (T) they cannot consistently be altered without also altering our beliefs in what those sentences express. This fact is extremly important to the functions that the word "true" serves (as the Alabama example illustrates).

In stressing the assertibility conditions for simple sentences containing the word "true," I have followed Quine (ibid., 138); for, like him, I believe that such assertibility conditions are enough to make the term "true" reasonably clear. But now it might be asked, "Then why do we need causal (etc.) theories of reference? The words 'true' and 'denotes' are made perfectly clear by schemas like (T). To ask for more than these schemas—to ask for causal theories of reference to nail language to reality—is to fail to recognize that we are at sea on Neurath's boat: we have to work *within* our conceptual scheme, we can't glue it to reality from the outside."

I suspect that this would be Quine's diagnosis—it is strongly suggested by §6 of *Word and Object*, especially when that is taken in conjunction with some of Quine's remarks about the inscrutibility of reference and truth value, the underdetermination of theories, and the relativity of ontology. It seems to me, however, that the diagnosis is quite wrong. In looking for a theory of truth and a theory of primitive reference we *are* trying to explain the connection between language and (extralinguistic) reality, but we are *not* trying to step outside of our theories of the world in order to do so. Our accounts of primitive reference and of truth are not to be thought of as something that could be given by philosophical reflection prior to scientific information—on the contrary, it seems likely that such things as psychological models of human beings and investigations of neurophysiology will be very relevant to discovering the mechanisms involved in reference. *The reason why accounts of truth and primitive reference are needed is not to tack our conceptual scheme onto reality from the outside; the reason, rather, is that without such accounts our conceptual scheme breaks down from the inside.* On our theory of the world it would be extremely surprising if there were some nonphysical connection between words and things. Thus if we could argue from our theory of the world that the notion of an utterer's saying something true, or referring to a particular thing, cannot be made sense of in physicalist terms (say, by arguing that any semantic notion that makes physicalistic sense *can* be explicated in Skinnerian terms, and that the notions of truth and reference *can't* be explicated in Skinnerian terms), then to the extent that such an argument is convincing we ought to be led to conclude that, if we are to remain physicalists, the notions of truth and reference must be abandoned. No amount of pointing out the clarity of these terms helps enable us to escape this conclusion: "valence" and "gene" were perfectly clear long before anyone succeeded in reducing them, but it was their reducibility and not their clarity before reduction that showed them to be compatible with physicalism.

The clarity of "valence" and "gene" before reduction—and even more, their *utility* before reduction—did provide physicalists with substantial reason to think that a reduction of these terms was possible, and, as I remarked earlier, a great deal of fruitful work in physical chemistry and chemical genetics was motivated by the fact. Similarly, insofar as semantic notions like "true" are useful, we have every reason to suspect that they will be reducible to nonsemantic terms, and it is likely that progress in linguistic theory will come by looking for such reductions. (In fact, the fruitfulness of Tarski's work in aiding us to understand language is already some sign of this, even though it represents only a partial reduction.) Of course, this sort of argument for the prospects of reducing semantic notions is only as powerful as our arguments for the utility of semantic terms; and it is clear that the question of the utility of the term "true"—the purposes it serves, and the extent to which those purposes could be served by less pretentious notions such as warranted assertibility—needs much closer investigation.

All these remarks require one important qualification. The notion of valence, it must be admitted, is *not* reducible to nonchemical terms on the *strictest* standards of reduction, but is only *approximately* reducible; yet, in spite of this, we don't want to get rid of the notion, since it is still extremely useful in those contexts where its approximate character isn't too likely to get in the way and where if we did not approximate we'd get into quantum-mechanical problems far too complex for anyone to solve. (Moreover, considerations about the purposes of the notion of valence were sufficient to show that the notion of valence would only be approximately reducible: for the utility of the notion of valence is that it aids us in approximately characterizing which elements will combine with which and in what proportions; yet it is obvious that no *precise* such characterization is possible.)

Similarly, it may well be that a detailed investigation into the purposes of the notion of truth might show that these purposes require only an approximate reduction of the notion of truth. Still, to require an approximate reduction is to require quite a bit; after all, "is a reincarnation of" isn't even approximately reducible to respectable biology, and "electromagnetic field" is not approximately reducible to mechanics. Obviously the notion of approximate reduction needs to be made more precise (as in fact does the notion of strict, or nonapproximate, reduction); but even without making it so, I think we can see that T2 is no more of an approximate reduction than is V2, since D2 ∧ A2 ∧ F2 is no more of an approximate reduction than is (3). In other words, the main point of the paper survives when we replace the ideal of strict reduction by the ideal of approximate reduction.

It should be kept carefully in mind that the Quinean view that all we need do is clarify the term "true," in the sense that this term is clarified by schema T (or by schema T plus a theory of translation to handle foreign languages; or by schema T plus the sort of thing alluded to in connection with Dummett), is *not* Tarski's view. Tarski's view is that we have to provide a truth characterization like T2 (which, when we choose as our object language L a "nice" fragment of our own language, can be shown correct merely by assuming that all instances of schema T are valid—cf. note 14); and such a truth characterization does much more than schema T does. It does not do everything that Tarski ever claimed for it, for Tarski attached much too much importance to the pseudo-theories D2, A2, and F2; but even when we "subtract" such trivialities from his truth characterization T2, we still get the very interesting and important truth characterization T1. T1, I believe, adequately represents Tarski's real contribution to the theory of truth, and in doing this it has a number of positive advantages over T2 (in addition to the important negative advantage I've been stressing, of preventing extravagant claims based on the fact that T2 contains no semantic terms). First of all, T1, unlike T2, is applicable to languages that contain ambiguities and languages that contain terms not adequately translatable into English. Second, T1, unlike T2, can be used in diachronic linguistics: it doesn't need overhauling as you add new words to the language, provided those new words belong to the same semantic category as words already in the language. Third, I think that the reason why Tarski's theory of truth T2 has seemed so uninteresting to so many people is that it contains the vacuous semantic theories D2, A2, and F2 for the primitives of the language. By expressing the really important features of Tarski's results on truth, and leaving out the inessential and uninteresting "theories" of the semantics of the primitives, T1 should make the philosophical importance of Tarski's work more universally recognized.

Notes

This paper grew out of a talk I gave at Princeton in the fall of 1970, where I defended T1 over T2. Donald Davidson and Gilbert Harman—and later, in private conversation, John Wallace—all came to the defense of T2, and their remarks have all been of help to me in writing the paper. I have also benefited from advice given by Michael Devitt, Paul Benacerraf, and especially David Hills.

1. *Logic of Scientific Discovery* (New York: Basic Books, 1968), 274.

2. Cf. Carnap's "Autobiography," in P. A. Schilpp, ed., *The Philosophy of Rudolf Carnap* (La Salle, IL: Open Court, 1963), 61.

3. It is sometimes claimed that Tarski was interested in languages considered in abstraction from all speakers and writers of the language; that the languages he was dealing with are abstract entities to be specified by giving their rules. This seems incorrect: Tarski was interested in giving the semantics of languages that mathematicians had been writing for years; and only as a result of Tarski's work was it then possible for philosophers like Carnap to propose that the clauses of a Tarski-type truth definition for such languages be called rules of the languages and be used in defining the languages as abstract entities.

4. "The Concept of Truth in Formalized Languages" (CTFL), in *Logic, Semantics, and Metamathematics* (*LSM*) (New York: Oxford University Press, 1956), 166.

5. Actually in model theory we are interested in allowing a slightly unusual semantics for the quantifiers: we are willing to allow that the quantifier not range over everything. We could build this generalization into our truth definition, by stipulating that in addition to the denotations of the nonlogical symbols we specify a universe U, and then reformulating clause (B)4 by requiring that the *k*th member of *s** belong to U. If we did this, then it would be the range of the quantifiers as well as the denotations of the nonlogical primitives that we would have explained truth in terms of.

6. An *incomplete* sentence token is a sentence token which [like the occurrence of "$2+2=4$" inside "$\sim (2+2=4)$"] is part of a larger sentence token.

7. "Truth and Meaning," *Synthese* 17, no. 3 (September 1967): 304–323, 314–315.

8. Note that the claims I've been making are intended to apply only to cases where different tokens have different semantic features; they are not intended to apply to cases of indeterminacy, i.e., to cases where a particular name token or predicate token has no determinate denotation or extension. To deal with indeterminacy requires more complex devices than I employ in this paper.

9. The notion of a semantic category is Tarski's: cf. CTFL, 215.

10. To do so in the obvious way requires that we introduce semantic categories of negation symbol, conjunction symbol, and universal-quantification symbol; though by utilizing some ideas of Frege it could be shown that there is really no need of a separate semantic category for each logical operator. The use of semantic categories in the generalized truth characterization raises important problems which I have had to suppress for lack of space in this paper.

11. For simplicity, I have assumed that L itself contains no semantic terms.

12. "The Establishment of Scientific Semantics" (ESS), in *LSM*, 406.

13. This, of course, is very vague, but most attempts to explicate the doctrine of physicalism more precisely result in doctrines that are very hard to take seriously [e.g., the doctrine that for every acceptable predicate '$P(x)$' there is a formula '$B(x)$' containing only terminology from physics, such that '$\forall x(P(x) \equiv B(x))$' is true]. Physicalism should be understood as the doctrine (however precisely it is to be characterized) that guides science in the way I describe.

14. Tarski actually gives a different formulation, the famous Convention T, evidently because he does not think that the word "correct" ought to be employed in stating a criterion of adequacy. First of all Tarski writes

> … we shall accept as valid every sentence of the form
> [T] The sentence *x* is true if and only *p*

> where '*p*' is to be replaced by any sentence of the language under investigation and '*x*' by any individual name of that sentence provided this name occurs in the metalanguage (ESS, 404).

Is Tarski's policy of accepting these sentences as "valid" (i.e., true) legitimate? It seems to me that it is, in a certain special case. The special case is where

I. The object language is a proper part of the metalanguage (here, English).

II. The object language contains no paradoxical or ambiguous or truth-value-less sentences.

In this special case—and it was the case that Tarski was primarily concerned with—I think it will be generally agreed that all instances of Schema T hold. From this, together with the fact that only grammatical sentences are true, we can argue that, if a necessary and sufficient condition of form (2) has the following consequences:

(a) Every instance of Schema T

(b) The sentence "$(\forall x)$ (x is true $\supset S(x)$)," where '$S(x)$' formulates (correct) conditions for an utterance of L to be a sentence

then that necessary and sufficient condition is correct. Let's say that a "truth definition" for L (a necessary and sufficient condition of truth in L) *satisfies Convention T* if it has all the consequences listed under (a) and (b). Then, restating: when L is a language for which I and II hold, then any truth definition satisfying Convention T is correct; and since only quite uncontroversial assumptions about truth are used in getting this result, anyone will admit to the correctness of a truth characterization satisfying Convention T. If we use the term "formally correct definition" for a sentence of form (2) in which '$B(e)$' contains no semantic terms, this means that a formally correct definition that satisfies Convention T is bound to satisfy Condition M (when the language L satisfies I and II). As far as I can see, this is the only motivation for Convention T; if so, we can discredit Convention T by discrediting Convention M.

Tarski sometimes states a more general form of Convention T, which applies to languages that do not meet restriction I: it is what results when one allows as instances of Schema T the results of replacing 'p' by a *correct translation* of the sentence that the name substituted for 'x' denotes (in some sense of "correct translation" in which correctness requires preservation of truth value). But then the advantage of the ungeneralized form of Convention T (viz., that anything satisfying it wears its correctness on its face, or more accurately, on the faces of its logical consequences) is lost.

15. A sentence of the form '$(\forall N)(\forall x)[N$ denotes $x \equiv B(N,x)]$' *satisfies convention D* if it has as consequences every instance of the schema 'y denotes z' in which 'y' is to be replaced by a quotation-mark name for a name N, and 'z' is to be replaced by (an adequate translation of N into English, i.e.) a singular term of English that contains no semantic terms and that denotes the same thing that N denotes. Clearly DE and DG are not only extensionally correct, they also satisfy Convention D. Presumably philosophers who are especially impressed with Convention T will be equally impressed with this fact, but they owe us a reason why satisfying Convention D is of any interest.

16. For example, by extending our definition of denotation$_s$ to descriptions by:

$\ulcorner \imath x_k\, e \urcorner$ denotes$_s$ a if and only if [for each sequence s^* which differs from s at the kth place at most, e is true$_{s^*}$ if and only if the kth member of s^* is a].

and then defining denotation in terms of denotation$_s$ by stipulating that a closed term denotes an object if and only if it denotes$_s$ that object for some (or all) s.

17. Some of Kripke's work on names will be published shortly in D. Davidson and G. Harman, eds., *Semantics of Natural Language* (Dordrecht: Reidel, 1971). What I've said about Russell's view is influenced by some of Kripke's lectures on which his paper there is based.

18. "The Semantic Conception of Truth and the Foundations of Semantics," *Philosophy and Phenomenological Research* 4, no. 3 (March 1944): 341–375, 351.

19. *Proceedings of the Aristotelian Society* 59 (1958/1959): 141–162 (reprinted as chapter 11 in this volume—Eds.).

20. Cf. W. V. Quine, *From a Logical Point of View* (New York: Harper & Row, 1961), 136.

V Deflationary Theories

Introduction

Jeremy Wyatt

Truth theorists have tended to puzzle a great deal over the metaphysical question of truth's nature. In doing so, they have approached the study of truth much as a chemist might approach the study of a newly discovered compound, asking, "What is the underlying essence of truth, and how should we uncover it?" Frank Ramsey (1927, 157) summed up the contrasting, deflationary outlook on truth by suggesting that "there really is no separate problem of truth but merely a linguistic muddle." Ramsey's contention is that we can easily dispel the metaphysical puzzles related to truth by attending more carefully to the *language* that we use to talk about truth. In doing so, we adopt the mindset of a linguist, asking, "How do we speak (and think) about truth, and why, exactly, do we speak (and think) in this way?" This pronounced focus on language is in line with the spirit of much early analytic philosophy, and it has informed the work of every deflationist who has endeavored to build upon Ramsey's ideas.

Deflationists contend that when we systematically analyze our talk about truth (henceforth, *truth-talk*), we will discover that the nature of truth is much simpler than truth theorists have traditionally assumed. Moreover, we will discover that, contrary to many traditional truth theorists, we can't appeal to truth in order to explain philosophically interesting phenomena. These two theses—that truth is *metaphysically simple* and *explanatorily inert*—are at the heart of the deflationary programme.

In pursuing this programme, deflationists have put forward a number of importantly different theories of truth-talk. Despite their differences, these theories all spring from a basic contention about how truth-talk behaves.

Let a *direct truth ascription* be an ascription of truth to a sentence, proposition, or utterance to which the ascription directly refers (or at least seems to directly refer). Direct truth ascriptions will then include assertive utterances of the following "true"-containing sentences:[1]

(1) It is true that France is in Europe.

(2) The sentence "France is in Europe" is true.

(3) James's assertion that France is in Europe is true.

(4) That France is in Europe is true.

(5) James: France is in Europe.

    Susan: That is true.

We can call the core thesis about truth-talk that has inspired the development of deflationism the *Equivalence Principle*:[2]

> (EQ) A direct truth ascription is equivalent to the sentence, proposition, or utterance that figures therein.

As we'll see, it is illuminating to interpret deflationists as setting out to *sharpen* (EQ) by pinpointing a specific equivalence relation and then incorporating that relation into (EQ).

We'll begin with an overview of the deflationary theories that will be defended in part V, focusing on the sharpenings of (EQ) that they deliver. We'll also trace their implications regarding the nature of truth and the nature of the bearers of truth. We'll then have a look at some of the major objections that deflationists must confront.[3]

The Redundancy Theory

Ramsey is often credited with developing, in 1927, the first deflationary account of truth-talk. This account is standardly called the *redundancy theory*, and it sharpens (EQ) in terms of the following schema (see also chapter 16):[4]

> (EQ$_{RED}$) "It is true that p" is synonymous with "p."

According to the redundancy theorist, a sentence of the form "It is true that p" is synonymous with a sentence of the form "p." That is, sentences of these respective forms have exactly the same meaning—or in terms more congenial to Ramsey, they express exactly the same judgment. Consider, for instance:

(6) It is true that France is in Europe.

The redundancy theorist holds that "It is true that France is in Europe" has precisely the same meaning as "France is in Europe." Specifically, both sentences mean that France is in Europe.

If this is right, then it would seem that to properly understand truth-talk, we need not take truth to be a *property* that we ascribe to sentences (or to anything else). In this way, the redundancy theorist aims to deflate the metaphysical ambitions of traditional theories of truth. Similarly, if we refrain from taking truth to be a property, we can likewise refrain from taking entities of *any* sort (sentences, propositions, utterances, etc.) to serve as truth-bearers.[5]

The Performative Theory

A standard complaint about the redundancy theory is that it makes the fact that English contains the word "true" rather mysterious. If, for example, "It is true that France is in Europe" just means that France is in Europe, then why would we bother using this sentence, rather than the shorter "France is in Europe?" In chapter 17, P. F. Strawson develops an answer to this query. In doing so, he offers the following sharpening of (EQ):

(EQ$_{PER}$) To say that an assertion is true is not to make a further assertion but to make the same assertion.

Strawson aims to establish two main points in connection with (EQ$_{PER}$). The first is in the spirit of the redundancy theory. It is that as (EQ$_{PER}$) indicates, if one makes a direct truth ascription, then one is not (contrary to appearances, and to Tarski) speaking about any sort of truth-bearer. Consider, for instance:

(7) James: Latisha is a trustworthy person.

Susan: What you say is true.

It initially seems that Susan is speaking about what James said. However, Strawson would point out that if Susan makes precisely the same assertion as James, then this can't be right. After all, James clearly doesn't speak about anything that he said, but rather speaks about Latisha. Thus, Strawson would argue, we should take Susan to have asserted, like James, simply that Latisha is a trustworthy person.

At this stage, the standard complaint crops up—if (EQ$_{PER}$) is true, then what is the point of using truth-talk? Strawson suggests that we standardly use truth-talk to perform speech acts *other than assertion* which do relate to what other speakers have said. These include affirming, granting, agreeing, confirming, and admitting. In connection with (7), for instance, we might say that Susan not only asserted that Latisha is a trustworthy person, but also confirmed what James said—namely, that Latisha is a trustworthy person. Since Strawson highlights the pragmatic or performative effects of truth-talk, his account is often called the *performative theory* of truth.

Admittedly, the performative theory is not widely endorsed by contemporary philosophers. In fact, Strawson himself eventually rejected the theory. It may be that a more promising successor can be crafted, but this remains to be seen.[6]

Disquotationalism

A third deflationary analysis of truth-talk, pioneered by Willard Van Orman Quine in 1970, is *disquotationalism*.[7] Quine takes the truth-bearers to be *eternal sentences*—that is, sentences that receive a determinate, unchanging truth-value. Provided that there are such sentences, it is clear that we sometimes *use* them and that by contrast, we sometimes *mention* them. Suppose, for instance, that I assertively utter:

(8) Mount Etna is in Italy.

In doing so, I use the sentence (8) and I speak about Mount Etna. By contrast, I might also assertively utter:

(9) "Mount Etna is in Italy" is an English sentence.

In this case, I mention the sentence that I previously used and I say that it is an English sentence.

Quotation marks thus serve as a device for mentioning sentences and other linguistic expressions. To use Quine's metaphor, quotation marks allow us to *ascend* from speaking about the nonlinguistic world to speaking about our language. Quine's contention is that when one predicates truth of a quoted sentence, one thereby cancels the effect of quoting the sentence—that is, one *disquotes* the sentence. In doing so, one *descends* back to talk about the nonlinguistic world.

To illustrate, consider:

(10) "Mount Etna is in Italy" is true.

If I assertively utter (10), Quine would admit, then I appear to be ascribing a property *truth* to the sentence "Mount Etna is in Italy."[8] However, Quine would argue that I'm actually speaking not about a sentence but simply about Mount Etna—in particular, I'm saying that Mount Etna is in Italy. This means that in cases like (10), the truth predicate is dispensable, an insight that traces back to the redundancy theory. This disquotational conception of truth can be captured using what is standardly called the *Disquotation Schema*:[9]

(EQ_{DIS}) "S" is true iff S.

Despite cases like (10), however, Quine doesn't take the truth predicate to *always* be dispensable. "The truth predicate," he says in chapter 18, "proves invaluable when we want to generalize along a dimension that cannot be swept out by a general term."

Suppose, for instance, that I want to expand upon the idea that "Hitoshi is sitting or it is not the case that Hitoshi is sitting" is a *tautology*. I can't do this, Quine suggests, by replacing "Hitoshi is sitting" with a variable and then binding that variable with a universal quantifier. The reason is that, according to Quine, such a variable must range over *objects*, yet sentences such as "Hitoshi is sitting" don't refer to objects. What I can do, however, is bring in the truth predicate and make the generalization "Every sentence of the form 'S or it is not the case that S' is true." In this way, for Quine, the truth predicate earns its keep by serving (together with quantifiers like "every") as a *device of generalization*.

In chapter 19, Jc Beall puts forward his own brand of disquotationalism, according to which the truth predicate is *transparent*. Beall's transparency conception generates the following sharpening of (EQ):

(EQ$_{\text{DISB}}$) A direct truth ascription to sentence "*S*" is intersubstitutable with "*S*" in all non-intensional contexts.

Regarding the metaphysics of truth, Beall is a good deal more informative than disquotationalists have tended to be. He grants that a disquotationalist of his sort can happily take truth to be a property. However, he argues that if they do, then they should hold that truth is merely an "emergent logical property."[10]

Prosententialism

The deflationary theory known as *prosententialism* rests on the notion of a *prosentence*, which is due to Franz Brentano.[11] One often uses a pronoun such as "he," "she," or "it" to refer to an entity to which one or one's interlocutor has previously referred using a noun. This is what happens in the following exchange:

(11) James: Latisha went to the market.

    Susan: Did she buy some bread?

In (11), James uses the noun "Latisha" to refer to Latisha. Susan's use of "she" then *inherits* the referent of "Latisha"—namely, Latisha herself. "Latisha" is for this reason called the *anaphoric antecedent* of this occurrence of "she." Just as pronouns take nouns as their antecedents, prosentences take sentences as their antecedents. This means that a prosentence, like a pronoun, can inherit the content of a sentence that was used at an earlier point in a given conversation.

Dorothy Grover, together with Joseph Camp and Nuel Belnap, was the first to defend prosententialism. Consider:

(12) James: Jupiter is a planet.

    Susan: That is true.

Grover proposes that we take Susan's direct truth ascription in (12) to be a prosentence and as such, to inherit the content of "Jupiter is a planet." The result is that both sentences have the same content—namely, that Jupiter is a planet. More generally, the basic idea behind Grover's prosententialism is:[12]

(EQ$_{\text{PRO}}$) Direct truth ascriptions inherit the contents of their sentential antecedents.

Grover takes prosentences containing "true" to be unanalyzable wholes that in particular do not have a subject-predicate-style logical form. Accordingly, Grover's prosententialism, like the redundancy and performative theories, provides us with a reason to dispense with both the property *truth* and the notion of a truth-bearer.

In chapter 20, Grover adumbrates her prosentential approach. She also endeavors to explain how a prosententialist should analyze occurrences of truth-talk in explanations while retaining the view that we don't use such talk to speak about a property *truth*.

Minimalism

Since 1990, Paul Horwich has arguably served as the most prominent representative of the deflationary programme. In an expansive body of work, Horwich defends what he calls the *minimalist conception* of truth. The centerpiece of the minimalist conception is what Horwich dubs the *Equivalence Schema*:

(EQ$_{MIN}$) The proposition that p is true iff p.

Regarding the role of (EQ$_{MIN}$) in the minimalist conception, it's helpful to focus on two details. The first is that Horwich employs (EQ$_{MIN}$) in offering an account of the possession conditions of the *concept* of truth. Horwich's contention is that to possess this concept, one must, in essence, be disposed to accept every instance of (EQ$_{MIN}$) in the absence of supporting argumentation. In this sense, (EQ$_{MIN}$)'s instances are meant to be *conceptually basic*. This delivers the result that to think about truth, one needn't be disposed to accept any propositions about correspondence, facts, coherence, practical success, and so on. What's required is merely a disposition to accept a host of comparatively banal propositions—for example, that the proposition that tables are solid is true iff tables are solid.

Horwich also takes the class of (nonpathological) instances of (EQ$_{MIN}$) to constitute the axioms of his theory of truth, which he calls the *minimal theory of truth*. This means that if Horwich is asked to explain what truth is, his basic reply will be, "The proposition that tables are solid is true iff tables are solid, and the proposition that chocolate is salty is true iff chocolate is salty, and so forth." This reply is compatible, Horwich argues, with taking truth to be a property. However, he contends that *truth* is merely an "insubstantial" property whose its nature isn't especially interesting . In chapter 21, Horwich defends the minimalist conception against a wide range of influential objections. In chapter 24, I offer an extended discussion of what deflationists such as Horwich mean, or ought to mean, in claiming that truth is an "insubstantial" property.[13]

Substitutionalism

It is useful to see Christopher Hill's *substitutionalism* as being, in part, a reaction to perceived inadequacies in the minimalist conception. Horwich's minimal theory of truth is meant to serve as a definition of truth. In particular, Horwich takes the class of (EQ$_{MIN}$)'s (nonpathological) instances to *implicitly* define truth. Since there are infinitely many such instances—one for each of the infinitely many propositions—the minimalist conception provides an implicit, infinitary definition of truth.

Hill expresses sympathy with a well-known criticism of the minimalist conception which relates to this feature of the view. Anil Gupta (1993) famously argued that the minimalist's implicit, infinitary definition of truth won't suffice to explain our acceptance of certain *general* claims involving truth—for example, that a conjunction is true iff both of its conjuncts are true.[14] To remedy this defect, Hill proposes that those who favor minimalism should instead endorse an *explicit, finite* definition of truth.

The central feature of Hill's definition is that it contains an existential, *substitutional quantifier* Σ which binds the propositional variable p:[15]

(EQ$_{SUB}$) For any thought x, x is true iff $(\Sigma p)(x = $ the thought that p and p).

In chapter 22, Hill explains in detail how he thinks about substitutional quantification and, in particular, why we don't have to analyze substitutional quantifiers in terms of truth. This, of course, is necessary for (EQ$_{SUB}$) to get off of the ground, as this definition would otherwise be viciously circular. He also details his more general substitutional approach to semantic relations, including reference and semantic correspondence. This approach, he argues, serves to curb the reasonable temptation to reduce semantic relations to empirical relations.[16]

Fictionalism

Over approximately the past 15 years, Bradley Armour-Garb and James Woodbridge have defended a *fictionalist* account of truth-talk, which they describe (chapter 23) as a *semantic pretense-involving fictionalist* (or SPIF) account. While Armour-Garb and Woodbridge acknowledge the novelty of their SPIF account, they also maintain that it neatly systematizes signature deflationary ideas about truth.

Deflationists urge us to recognize that when we engage in truth-talk, we don't speak about a significant property *truth*. However, as we've seen, deflationists must grapple with the fact that truth-talk does seem to enable us to speak about such a property. Consider:

(13) That Venus is a star is true.

If I assertively utter (13), then it seems as though I'm ascribing the property *truth* to the proposition that Venus is a star, and most ordinary speakers would presumably take *truth* to be a rather important and complex property.

The deflationist, say Armour-Garb and Woodbridge, should reply that when we assertively utter sentences like (13), it is merely *as if* we are speaking about *truth*. This appearance is generated by the principles of a game of make-believe that governs our use of truth-talk. Similarly, they hold that it is merely as if we are speaking about propositions when we use expressions like "That Venus is a star."

According to Armour-Garb and Woodbridge, someone who assertively utters a sentence like (13) actually speaks about matters that have nothing to do with *truth* or propositions. They (indirectly) assert not that the proposition that Venus is a star has the property *truth*, but simply that Venus is a star. That Venus is a star thus constitutes what Armour-Garb and Woodbridge call the *serious content* of their assertion. More generally, Armour-Garb and Woodbridge's SPIF account generates the following sharpening of (EQ):

(EQ$_{FIC}$) The serious content of a direct truth ascription of the form "That *p* is true" is equivalent to that of the sentence "*P*."

Regarding the purpose of truth-talk, Armour-Garb and Woodbridge take a recognizably deflationary line. They argue that truth-talk enables us to say things that we couldn't say without adding complicated logical tools (e.g., substitutional quantification and infinite conjunctions and disjunctions) to our language.[17]

Let's now take stock of the deflationary theories that we've surveyed by laying out the sharpenings of (EQ) that they deliver.

Overview of deflationary theories.

Theory	Sharpening of (EQ)
Redundancy theory	"It is true that *p*" is synonymous with "*p*"
Performative theory	To say that an assertion is true is not to make a further assertion but to make the same assertion
Disquotationalism (Quine)	"*S*" is true iff *S*
Disquotationalism (Beall)	A direct truth ascription to sentence "*S*" is intersubstitutable with "*S*" in all non-intensional contexts
Prosententialism (Grover)	Direct truth ascriptions inherit the contents of their sentential antecedents
Minimalism	The proposition that *p* is true iff *p*
Substitutionalism	For any thought *x*, *x* is true iff (Σp)(*x* = the thought that *p* and *p*)
Fictionalism	The serious content of a direct truth ascription of the form "That *p* is true" is equivalent to that of the sentence "*P*"

Major Objections to Deflationary Theories

It should be apparent that the landscape of deflationary theories of truth is remarkably rich and diverse. Just as diverse are the challenges that have been raised against such theories, a number of which are discussed in part V. Here is a summary that will provide a taste of this range of challenges:[18]

- *Truth-conditional semantics:* Deflationists face a variety of challenges related to their contention that truth is explanatorily inert. One of these involves truth-conditional semantics. It is common practice for linguists to take the meaning of a sentence to involve its truth conditions and to likewise take the meaning of a subsentential expression to involve the contribution that it makes to the truth conditions of sentences in which it appears. If we conceive of linguistic meaning along these lines, then it seems that we explain the nature of meaning by appealing to truth. This, however, runs contrary to the ambitions of deflationists. In this way, deflationary truth theories look to run against the grain of mainstream programmes in linguistics.[19]

- *The success argument:* Hilary Putnam first advanced the *success argument* against deflationism.[20] This argument centers on the plausible thought that having true beliefs can make it more probable that one will get what one desires. Suppose, for instance, that we are dealing with an everyday case in which Bill desires to get a bottle of beer. If Bill has true beliefs about the locations of bottles of beer in his vicinity, then it is more probable that Bill will in fact get a bottle of beer than if he had false beliefs about this issue. In so describing this case, however, it seems that we have cast truth in an explanatory role. As a result, deflationists are again under pressure to uphold their contention that truth is explanatorily inert.[21]

- *Nonconservativeness:* Stewart Shapiro (1998) has suggested that we should regiment the thought that truth is explanatorily inert using the notion of *conservativeness*. Put simply, a theory T_1 is conservative over a theory T_2 iff there are no T_2 statements that are provable using T_1 but aren't provable using T_2 alone. If T_1 is nonconservative over some theory T_2, it thus seems that the notions in T_1 enjoy an important sort of explanatory power. Shapiro argues that (given a first-order relation of logical consequence), an adequate disquotational theory of truth will be nonconservative over Peano Arithmetic, which suggests that the notion of truth does actually enjoy explanatory power.[22]

- *Assertion:* In chapter 25, Dorit Bar-On and Keith Simmons discuss the influential Fregean idea that "to assert is to present as true." They argue that deflationists about the concept of truth can't accommodate this idea, insofar as it entails that we must invoke truth to explain the nature of assertion. As a result, it seems that such deflationists are unable to account for the relationship between truth and assertion.

- *Truth-value gaps:* It's plausible that some sentences are neither true nor false; these are often called *truth-value gaps*. One potential example is sentences that contain a nonreferring name, such as "Atlantis had many inhabitants." The instance of the Disquotation Schema (EQ_{DIS}) which involves this sentence is:

(14) "Atlantis had many inhabitants" is true iff Atlantis had many inhabitants.

Now if "Atlantis had many inhabitants" is a truth-value gap, then it would seem that an ascription of truth to this sentence is *false* since the sentence isn't true (or false). But then (14) isn't true, since its left-hand side is false, whereas its right-hand side is neither true nor false. In this way, the existence of truth-value gaps looks to jeopardize disquotationalism and, in similar fashion, other deflationary approaches to truth.[23]

- *Semantic paradox:* Lastly, deflationists face a host of problems related to the *semantic paradoxes*, the most infamous of which is the *Liar paradox*. To see how this paradox affects disquotationalists in particular, consider the sentence:[24]

(L) *"L"* is false.

   Sentence *"L"* says of itself that it is false, so the instance of (EQ_{DIS}) that involves *"L"* will read:

(15) *"L"* is true iff *"L"* is false.

Using classical logical rules and the assumption that if a sentence is false then its negation is true, we can easily prove a contradiction from (15)—namely, that *"L"* and its negation *"not-L"* are both true. This, of course, is an unhappy result for the disquotationalist, and other deflationary theories look to face similar problems.[25]

Notes

1. Künne (2003, sec. 2.1.5) draws a related distinction between "propositionally revealing" and "propositionally unrevealing truth declarations."

2. See Burgess and Burgess (2011, 33–34) for a kindred account of deflationism.

3. In addition to the theories covered here, we should note the distinctive deflationary approaches defended by Künne (2003, sec. 6.2) and Horsten (2011).

4. Similar ideas about truth were put forward by earlier thinkers, including Aristotle and Frege. However, it is controversial whether these thinkers are committed to deflationary accounts of truth. In this connection, see the deflationary, Madhyamaka Buddhist account of truth that is sketched by Priest, Siderits, and Tillemans (2011).

   A number of authors have contested the attribution of the redundancy theory to Ramsey. See Le Morvan (2004); Frápolli (2013, chap. 6); the references therein; and Sullivan and Johnston (2018).

   The letter p functions in (EQ_{RED}) as a *schematic letter*—i.e., as a placeholder for English sentences. "It is true that" is usually called either the *truth connective* or the *truth operator*.

5. For additional discussion of the redundancy theory, see Ayer (1946, chap. 5); Odegard (1977); Baldwin (1991); Hugly and Sayward (1992, 1993); Künne (2003, chap. 2) and the references therein; and Horwich (2010, chap. 2, secs. 5–6).

6. On the evolution of Strawson's views, see Künne (2003, sec. 2.2.1). On potential successors to the performative theory, see Kraut (1993) and Schroeder (2010).

7. In addition to chapter 18, see Quine (1986, chap. 1; 1987, 212–216).

8. Following standard practice, we'll use italics to denote properties.

9. Here, "iff" stands for the relation of material equivalence.

10. For additional defenses of disquotationalism, see Leeds (1978); Field (1986, 1994); and Horsten and Leigh (2017). For critiques of disquotationalism, see, e.g., David (1994); Heck (2005); and Horwich (2010, chap. 2, sec. 11).

11. Brentano (1966, 45).

12. Grover's story regarding quantified truth ascriptions is a bit more complex; see Grover (1992, chap. 3) for details. For an importantly different variety of prosententialism, see Brandom (1994, chap. 5). For additional discussions of prosententialism, see Künne (2003, chap. 2) and the references therein; Båve (2009); Horwich (2010, chap. 2, secs. 9–10); and Frápolli (2013).

13. For a critical overview of minimalism, see Hoffmann (2010).

14. Horwich replies to this criticism in chapter 21 of this volume.

15. As Hill indicates, he prefers to follow Frege in using "thought," rather than "proposition."

16. For further discussion of substitutionalism, see the symposium in *Philosophy and Phenomenological Research* 72(1) (2006), as well as the exchange between Hill (2016) and McGee (2016).

17. For discussion of Armour-Garb and Woodbridge's fictionalist program, see the symposium in *Analysis* 78(4) (2018).

18. For additional challenges, see Boghossian (1990); Wright (1992, chap. 1); Misak (2007); Lynch (2009, chap. 6); Mou (2009, chap. 5); Edwards (2018); Jago (2018, chap. 1); Moltmann (2018); and Barnard and Ulatowski (2019). For additional overviews of challenges for deflationism, see Kirkham (1992, chap. 10); Künne (2003, chaps. 2, 4, 6); Armour-Garb and Beall (2005); Bar-On and Simmons (2006); Raatikainen (2006); Stoljar and Damnjanovic (2010); Armour-Garb (2012a); Wrenn (2015, chap. 6); and Azzouni (2018).

19. For further discussion, see Dummett (chapter 11 in this volume); Burgess (2011); Löwenstein (2012); Dodd (2013, 317–318); and Gross (2015) and the references therein.

20. Putnam (1978, 4, lecture II, and part III).

21. For an overview of reactions to the success argument, see Armour-Garb (2012a, secs. 2.2, 2.3). See also Kapus (2007) and Gamester (2018) and the references therein. Putnam (1978, lecture II) also develops a variant of this argument that turns on the success of scientific theories.

22. For further discussion of this challenge, see Cieśliński (2017); Murzi and Rossi (2018); and the references therein.

23. See chapter 11 in this volume; Hugly and Sayward (1992, 1993); and Greenough (2010) and the references therein.

24. Recall that Tarski sets out a version of this paradox in section 7 of chapter 14 in this volume.

25. For further discussion, see chapters 18, 19, 21, 22, and 23 in this volume, as well as Beall and Armour-Garb (2005); Beall and Glanzberg (2008); Field (2008); and Cieśliński (2017) and the references therein. For an excellent resource on the semantic paradoxes and formal theories of truth, see Beall, Glanzberg, and Ripley (2018).

Further Reading

Armour-Garb, B. 2012a. "Challenges to Deflationary Theories of Truth." *Philosophy Compass* 7(4): 256–266.

Armour-Garb, B. 2012b. "Deflationism (about Theories of Truth)." *Philosophy Compass* 7(4): 267–277.

Armour-Garb, B., and Beall, Jc. 2005. "Deflationism: The Basics." In B. Armour-Garb and Jc Beall, eds., *Deflationary Truth*, 1–29. Chicago: Open Court.

Ayer, A. J. 1946. *Language, Truth, and Logic*. London: Gollancz.

Azzouni, J. 2018. "Deflationist Truth." In M. Glanzberg, ed., *The Oxford Handbook of Truth*, 477–502. Oxford: Oxford University Press.

Baldwin, T. 1991. "Can There Be a Substantive Account of Truth?" In N. Cooper and P. Engel, eds., *New Inquiries into Meaning and Truth*, 21–39. New York: St. Martin's Press.

Barnard, R., and Ulatowski, J. 2019. "Does Anyone Really Think That ⌜φ⌝ Is True if and Only if φ?" In A. Aberdein and M. Inglis, eds., *Advances in Experimental Philosophy of Logic and Mathematics*, 145–171. London: Bloomsbury.

Bar-On, D., and Simmons, K. 2006. "Deflationism." In E. Lepore and B. C. Smith, eds., *The Oxford Handbook of Philosophy of Language*, 607–630. Oxford: Oxford University Press.

Båve, A. 2009. "Why Is a Truth-Predicate Like a Pronoun?" *Philosophical Studies* 145(2): 297–310.

Beall, Jc, and Armour-Garb, B. 2005. *Deflationism and Paradox*. Oxford: Oxford University Press.

Beall, Jc, and Glanzberg, M. 2008. "Where the Paths Meet: Remarks on Truth and Paradox." *Midwest Studies in Philosophy* 32(1): 169–198.

Beall, Jc, Glanzberg, M., and Ripley, D. 2018. *Formal Theories of Truth*. Oxford: Oxford University Press.

Boghossian, P. 1990. "The Status of Content." *Philosophical Review* 99(2): 157–184.

Brandom, R. 1994. *Making It Explicit: Reasoning, Representing, and Discursive Commitment*. Cambridge, MA: Harvard University Press.

Brentano, F. 1966. *The True and the Evident*. Edited by R. M. Chisholm and translated by R. M. Chisholm, I. Politzer, and K. R. Fischer. London: Routledge and Kegan Paul.

Burgess, A. 2011. "Mainstream Semantics + Deflationary Truth." *Linguistics and Philosophy* 34(5): 397–410.

Burgess, A., and Burgess, J. 2011. *Truth*. Princeton, NJ: Princeton University Press.

Cieśliński, C. 2017. *The Epistemic Lightness of Truth: Deflationism and Its Logic*. Cambridge: Cambridge University Press.

David, M. 1994. *Correspondence and Disquotation*. Oxford: Oxford University Press.

Dodd, J. 2013. "Deflationism Trumps Pluralism!" In N. Pedersen and C. Wright, eds., *Truth and Pluralism: Current Debates*, 298–322. Oxford: Oxford University Press.

Edwards, D. 2018. *The Metaphysics of Truth*. New York: Oxford University Press.

Field, H. 1986. "The Deflationary Conception of Truth." In G. MacDonald and C. Wright, eds., *Fact, Science, and Morality*, 55–117. Malden, MA: Blackwell.

Field, H. 1994. "Deflationist Views of Meaning and Content." *Mind* 103(411): 249–285.

Field, H. 2008. *Saving Truth from Paradox*. Oxford: Oxford University Press.

Frápolli, M. J. 2013. *The Nature of Truth: An Updated Approach to the Meaning of Truth Ascriptions*. Dordrecht: Springer.

Gamester, W. 2018. "Truth: Explanation, Success, and Coincidence." *Philosophical Studies* 175(5): 1243–1265.

Greenough, P. 2010. "Deflationism and Truth-Value Gaps." In Wright and Pedersen, eds., *New Waves in Truth*, 115–125.

Gross, S. 2015. "Does the Expressive Role of 'True' Preclude Deflationary Davidsonian Semantics?" In S. Gross, N. Tebben, and M. Williams, eds., *Meaning without Representation: Essays on Truth, Expression, Normativity, and Naturalism*, 47–63. Oxford: Oxford University Press.

Grover, D. 1992. *A Prosentential Theory of Truth*. Princeton, NJ: Princeton University Press.

Gupta, A. 1993. "Minimalism." *Philosophical Perspectives* 7: 359–369.

Heck, R. 2005. "Truth and Disquotation." *Synthese* 142(3): 317–352.

Hill, C. 2016. "Deflationism: The Best Thing since Pizza and Quite Possibly Better." *Philosophical Studies* 173(12): 3169–3180.

Hoffmann, G. 2010. "The Minimalist Theory of Truth: Challenges and Concerns." *Philosophy Compass* 5(10): 938–949.

Horsten, L. 2011. *The Tarskian Turn*. Oxford: Oxford University Press.

Horsten, L., and Leigh, G. 2017. "Truth is Simple." *Mind* 126(501): 195–232.

Horwich, P. 1998. *Truth*. 2nd ed. Oxford: Oxford University Press.

Horwich, P. 2010. *Truth-Meaning-Reality*. Oxford: Oxford University Press.

Hugly, P., and Sayward, C. 1992. "Redundant Truth." *Ratio* 5(1): 24–37.

Hugly, P., and Sayward, C. 1993. "Two Concepts of Truth." *Philosophical Studies* 70(1): 35–58.

Jago, M. 2018. *What Truth Is*. Oxford: Oxford University Press.

Kapus, J. 2007. "Truth, Deflationism, and Success." In S. Voss and D. Moran, eds., *Proceedings of the Twenty-First World Congress of Philosophy*, vol. 6, 85–91. Ankara: Philosophical Society of Turkey.

Kirkham, R. 1992. *Theories of Truth: A Critical Introduction*. Cambridge, MA: MIT Press.

Kraut, R. 1993. "Robust Deflationism." *Philosophical Review* 102(2): 247–263.

Künne, W. 2003. *Conceptions of Truth*. Oxford: Oxford University Press.

Leeds, S. 1978. "Theories of Reference and Truth." *Erkenntnis* 13(1): 111–129.

Le Morvan, P. 2004. "Ramsey on Truth and Truth on Ramsey." *British Journal for the History of Philosophy* 12(4): 705–718.

Löwenstein, D. 2012. "Davidsonian Semantics and Anaphoric Deflationism." *Dialectica* 66(1): 23–44.

Lynch, M. 2009. *Truth as One and Many*. New York: Oxford University Press.

McGee, V. 2016. "Thought, Thoughts, and Deflationism." *Philosophical Studies* 173(12): 3153–3168.

Misak, C. 2007. "Pragmatism and Deflationism." In C. Misak, ed., *New Pragmatists*, 68–90. Oxford: Oxford University Press.

Moltmann, F. 2018. "Truth Predicates, Truth Bearers, and Their Variants." *Synthese*. https://doi.org/10.1007/s11229-018-1814-8.

Mou, B. 2009. *Substantive Perspectivism: An Essay on Philosophical Concern with Truth*. Dordrecht: Springer.

Murzi, J., and Rossi, L. 2018. "Conservative Deflationism?" *Philosophical Studies* 177(2): 535–549.

Odegard, D. 1977. "Truth and Redundancy." *Mind* 86(343): 333–344.

Priest, G., Siderits, M., and Tillemans, T. 2011. "The (Two) Truths about Truth." In *The Cowherds, Moonshadows: Conventional Truth in Buddhist Philosophy*, 131–150. New York: Oxford University Press.

Putnam, H. 1978. *Meaning and the Moral Sciences*. New York: Routledge and Kegan Paul.

Quine, W. V. O. 1986. *Philosophy of Logic*. 2nd ed. Cambridge, MA; Harvard University Press.

Quine, W. V. O. 1987. *Quiddities: An Intermittently Philosophical Dictionary*. Cambridge, MA: Belknap Press of Harvard University Press.

Raatikainen, P. 2006. "Problems of Deflationism." In T. Aho and A.-V. Pietarinen, eds., *Truth and Games in Logic and Language (Acta Philosophica Fennica)*, vol. 78, 175–185. Helsinki: Societas Philosophica Fennica.

Ramsey, F. 1927. "Facts and Propositions." *Proceedings of the Aristotelian Society Supplementary* 7(1): 153–170.

Schroeder, M. 2010. "How to Be an Expressivist about Truth." In Wright and Pedersen, eds., *New Waves in Truth*, 282–298.

Shapiro, S. 1998. "Proof and Truth: Through Thick and Thin." *Journal of Philosophy* 95(10): 493–521.

Stoljar, D., and Damnjanovic, N. 2010. "The Deflationary Theory of Truth." *Stanford Encyclopedia of Philosophy*. https://plato.stanford.edu/entries/truth-deflationary/.

Sullivan, P., and Johnston, C. 2018. "Judgments, Facts, and Propositions: Theories of Truth in Russell, Wittgenstein, and Ramsey." In M. Glanzberg, ed., *The Oxford Handbook of Truth*, 150–192. Oxford: Oxford University Press.

Wrenn, C. 2015. *Truth*. Cambridge: Polity Press.

Wright, C. 1992. *Truth and Objectivity*. Cambridge, MA: Harvard University Press.

Wright, C. D., and Pedersen, N. J. L. L., eds. 2010. *New Waves in Truth*. New York: Palgrave Macmillan.

16 The Nature of Truth

Frank Plumpton Ramsey

1 What Is Truth?

What is truth? What character is it that we ascribe to an opinion or a statement when we call it "true"? This is our first question, but before trying to answer it let us reflect for a moment on what it means. For we must distinguish one question, "what is *truth*?," from the quite different question "what is *true*?" If a man asked what was true, the sort of answer he might hope for would either be as complete an enumeration as possible of all truths, i.e., an encyclopaedia, or else a test or criterion of truth, a method by which he could know a truth from a falsehood. But what we are asking for is neither of these things, but something much more modest; we do not hope to learn an infallible means of distinguishing truth from falsehood but simply to know what it is that this word "true" means. It is a word which we all understand, but if we try to explain it, we can easily get involved, as the history of philosophy shows, in a maze of confusion.[1]

One source of such confusion must be eliminated straight away; besides the primary meaning in which we apply it to statements or opinions, the word "true" can also be used in a number of derived and metaphorical senses which it is no part of our problem to discuss. Obscure utterances such as "Beauty is truth, truth beauty" we shall make no attempts to elucidate, and confine ourselves to the plain work-a-day sense in which it is true that Charles I was beheaded and that the earth is round.

First we have to consider to what class of things the epithets "true" and "false" are primarily applied, since there are three classes which might be suggested. For we use "true" and "false" both of mental states,[2] such as beliefs, judgments, opinions or conjectures; and also of statements or indicative sentences; and thirdly according to some philosophers we apply these terms to "propositions," which are the objects of judgments and the meaning of sentences, but themselves neither judgments nor sentences.

According to the philosophers who believe in them, it is these propositions which are true or false in the most fundamental sense, a belief being called true or false by an extension of meaning according as what is believed is a true or a false proposition. But in as much as the existence of such things as these propositions is generally (and to my mind rightly) doubted, it seems best to begin not with them but with the mental states of which they are the supposed objects, and to discuss the terms true and false in their application to these mental states, without committing ourselves before we need to any doubtful hypothesis about the nature of their objects.

The third class consisting of statements or indicative sentences is not a serious rival, for it is evident that the truth and falsity of statements depends on their meaning, that is on what people mean by them, the thoughts and opinions which they are intended to convey. And even if, as some say, judgments are no more than sentences uttered to oneself, the truth of such sentences will still not be more primitive than but simply identical with that of judgments.

Our task, then, is, to elucidate the terms true and false as applied to mental states, and as typical of the states with which we are concerned we may take for the moment beliefs. Now whether or not it is philosophically correct to say that they have propositions as objects, beliefs undoubtedly have a characteristic which I make bold to call *propositional reference*. A belief is necessarily a belief that something or other is so-and-so,[3] for instance that the earth is flat; and it is this aspect of it, its being "that the earth is flat" that I propose to call its propositional reference. So important is this character of propositional reference that we are apt to forget that a belief has any other aspects of characters at all, and when two men both believe that the earth is flat we say they have the same belief, though they may believe it at different times for different reasons and with different degrees of conviction and use different languages or systems of imagery; if the propositional references are the same, if they are both "beliefs that" the same thing, we commonly ignore all other differences between them and call them the same belief.

It is usual in logic to express this resemblance between the two men's beliefs not by saying as I do that they have the same propositional reference, but by calling them beliefs in the same proposition; to say this is not however to deny the existence of such a character as propositional reference, but merely to put forward a certain view as to how this character should be analysed. For no one can deny that in speaking of a belief as a belief that the earth is flat we are ascribing to it some character; and though it is natural to think that this character consists in a relation to a proposition; yet, since this view has been disputed, we shall start our inquiry from what is undoubtedly real, which is not the proposition but the character of propositional reference. We shall have to discuss its analysis later, but for our immediate purposes we can take it without analysis as something with which we are all familiar.

Propositional reference is not, of course, confined to beliefs; my knowledge that the earth is round, my opinion that free trade is superior to protection, any form of thinking, knowing, or being under the impression that—has a propositional reference, and it is only such states of mind that can be either true or false. Merely thinking of Napoleon cannot be true or false, unless it is thinking *that* he was or did so and so; for if the reference is not propositional, if it is not the sort of reference which it takes a sentence to express, there can be neither truth nor falsity. On the other hand not all states which have propositional reference are either true or false; I can hope it will be fine to-morrow, wonder whether it will be fine to-morrow, and finally believe it will be fine to-morrow. These three states all have the same propositional reference but only the belief can be called true or false. We do not call wishes, desires or wonderings true, not because they have no propositional reference, but because they lack what may be called an affirmative or assertive character, the element that is present in thinking that, but absent in wondering whether. In the absence of some degree of this character we never use the words "true" or "false," though the degree need be only of the slightest and we can speak of an assumption as true, even when it is only made in order to discover its consequences. For states with the opposite character of denial we do not naturally use the words "true" or "false," though we can call them correct or incorrect according as beliefs with the same propositional reference would be false or true.

The mental states, [then,] with which we are concerned, those, namely, with propositional reference and some degree of the affirmative character, have unfortunately no common name in ordinary language. There is no term applicable to the whole range from mere conjecture to certain knowledge, and I propose to meet this deficiency[4] by using the terms *belief* and *judgment* as synonyms to cover the whole range of [mental] states in question [although this involves a great widening of their ordinary meanings] and not in their ordinary narrower meanings.

It is, then, in regard to beliefs or judgments that we ask for the meaning of truth and falsity, and it seems advisable to begin by explaining that these are not just vague terms indicating praise or blame of any kind, but have a quite definite meaning. There are various respects in which a belief can be regarded as good or bad; it can be true or false, it can be held with a higher or a low degree of confidence, for good or for bad reasons, in isolation or as part of a coherent system of thought, and for any clear discussion to be possible it is essential to keep those forms of merit distinct from one another, and not to confuse them by using the word "true" in a vague way first for one and then for another. This is a point on which ordinary speech is sounder than the philosophers; to take an example of Mr. Russell's, someone who thought that the present Prime Minister's name began with B would think so truly, even if he had derived his opinion from the mistaken idea that the Prime Minister was Lord Birkenhead; and it is clear that by calling a belief true, we neither mean nor imply that it is either well-grounded or comprehensive and that if these qualities are confused with truth as they are, for instance, by Bosanquet,[5] any profitable discussion of the subject becomes impossible. The kind of merit in a belief to which we refer in calling it true can be easily seen to be something which depends only on its propositional reference;[6] if one man's belief that the earth is round is true so is anyone else's belief that the earth is round, however little reason he may have for thinking so.

After these preliminaries we must come to the point: what *is* the meaning of "true"? It seems to me that the answer is really perfectly obvious, that anyone can *see* what it is and that difficulty only arises when we try to *say* what it is, because it is something which ordinary language is rather ill-adapted to express.

Suppose a man believes that the earth is round; then his belief is true because the earth *is* round; or generalising this, if he believes that *A* is *B* his belief will be true if *A* is *B* and false otherwise.

It is, I think, clear that in this last sentence we have the meaning of truth explained, and that the only difficulty is to formulate this explanation strictly as a definition. If we try to do this, the obstacle we encounter is that we cannot describe all beliefs as beliefs that *A* is *B* since the propositional reference of a belief may have any number of different more complicated forms. A man may be believing that all *A* are not *B*, or that if all *A* are *B*, either all *C* are *D* or some *E* are *F*, or something still more complicated. We cannot, in fact, assign any limit to the number of forms which may occur, and must therefore be comprehended in a definition of truth; so that if we try to make a definition to cover them all it will have to go on forever, since we must say that a belief is true, if supposing it to be a belief that *A* is *B*, *A* is *B*, or if supposing it to be a belief that *A* is not *B*, *A* is not *B*, or if supposing it to be a belief that either *A* is *B* or *C* is *D*, either *A* is *B* or *C* is *D*, and so on ad infinitum.

In order to avoid this infinity we must consider the general form of a propositional reference of which all these forms are species; any belief whatever we may symbolise as a belief that *p*, where "*p*" is a variable sentence just as "A" and "B" are variable words or phrases (or terms as they are called in logic). We can then say that a belief is true if it is a belief that *p*, and *p*.[7] This definition sounds odd because we do not at first real- ize that "*p*" is a variable *sentence* and so should be regarded as containing a verb; "and *p*" sounds nonsense because it seems to have no verb and we are apt to supply a verb such as "is true" which would of course make nonsense of our definition by apparently reintroducing what was to be defined. But "*p*" really contains a verb; for instance, it might be "*A* is *B*" and in this case we should end up "and *A* is *B*" which can as a matter of ordinary grammar stand perfectly well by itself.

The same point exactly arises if we take, not the symbol "*p*," but the relative pro- noun which replaces it in ordinary language. Take for example "what he believed was true." Here what he believed was, of course, something expressed by a sentence con- taining a verb. But when we represent it by the pronoun "what" the verb which is really contained in the "what" has, as a matter of language, to be supplied again by "was true." If however we particularize the form of belief in question all need for the words "was true" disappears as before and we can say "the things he believed to be connected by a certain relation were, in fact,[8] connected by that relation." As we claim to have defined truth we ought to be able to substitute our definition for the word "true" wherever it occurs. But the difficulty we have mentioned renders this impos- sible in ordinary language which treats what should really be called *pro-sentences* as if they were *pronouns*. The only pro-sentences admitted by ordinary language are "yes" and "no," which are regarded as by themselves expressing a complete sense, whereas "that" and "what," even when functioning as short for sentences, always require to be supplied with a verb: this verb is often "is true" and this peculiarity of language gives rise to artificial problems as to the nature of truth, which disappear at once when they are expressed in logical symbolism, in which we can render "what he believed is true" by "if p was what he believed, p."

So far we have dealt only with truth; what about falsity? The answer is again simply expressible in logical symbolism, but difficult to explain in ordinary language. There is not only the same difficulty that there is with truth but an additional difficulty due to the absence in ordinary language of any simple uniform expression for negation. In logical symbolism, for any proposition symbol p (corresponding to a sentence), we form the contradictory $\neg p$ (or $\sim p$ in *Principia Mathematica*); but in English we often have no similar way of reversing the sense of a sentence without considerable circumlocution. We cannot do it merely by putting in a "not" except in the simplest cases; thus "The King of France is not clever" is ambiguous, but on its most natural interpretation means "There is a King of France but he is not clever" and so is not what we get by simply denying "The King of France is clever"; and in more complicated sentences such as "if he comes, she will come with him" we can only deny either by a method special to the particular form of proposition, like "if he comes, she will not *necessarily* come with him" or by the general method of prefixing "It is not true that," "it is false that" or "It is not the case that," where [again] it looks as if two new ideas, "truth" and "falsity," were involved, but in reality we are simply adopting a round-about way of applying *not* to the sentence as a whole.

Consequently our definition of falsity (to believe falsely is to believe p, when $\neg p$) is doubly difficult to put into words; but to argue that it is circular, because it defines falsity in terms of the operation of negation which cannot always be rendered in language without using the word "false," would simply be a confusion. "False" is used in ordinary language in two ways: first as part of a way of expressing negation, correlative to the use of "true" as a purely stylistic addition (as when "it is true that the earth is round" means no more than that the earth is round); and secondly as equivalent to not true, applied to beliefs or other states of mind having propositional references or derivatively to sentences or other symbols expressing those states of mind. The use we are trying to define is the second, not the first, which in the guise of the symbol $\neg p$ we are taking for granted and propose to discuss later under the head of negation.[9]

Our definition that a belief is true if it is a "belief that p" and p, but false if it is a "belief that p" and $\neg p$ is, it may be remarked, substantially that of Aristotle, who considering only the two forms "A is" and "A is not" declared that "To say of what is, that it is not, or of what is not, that it is, is false, while to say of what is that it is, and of what is not that it is not, is true."[10]

Although we have not yet used the word "correspondence" ours will probably be called a Correspondence Theory of Truth. For if A is B we can speak according to common usage of the fact that A is B and say that it corresponds to the belief that A is B in a way in which if A is not B there is no such fact corresponding to it. But we cannot describe the nature of this correspondence until we know the analysis of propositional reference, of "believing that A is B." Only when we know the structure of belief can we say what type of correspondence it is that unites true beliefs and facts. And we may well be sceptical as to there being any simple relation of correspondence applicable to all cases or even if it is always right to describe the relation as holding between the "belief that p" and the "fact that p"; for instance if the belief is disjunctive as it is when Jones thinks that Smith is either a liar or a fool, are we to say that it is made true by a "disjunctive fact," "the fact," namely, "that Smith is either a liar or a fool"? [If we believe that reality contains no such mere "either-or" we shall have to modify our account.] Or if we hold it absurd to believe that reality contains such a mere either-or, what does the belief correspond to?

But the prospect of these difficulties need not distress us or lead us to suppose that we are on a wrong track in adopting what is, in a vague sense, a correspondence theory of truth. For we have given a clear definition of truth which escapes all these difficulties by not appealing to a notion of correspondence at all. A belief that p, we say, is true if and only if p; for instance a belief that Smith is either a liar or a fool is true if Smith is either a liar or a fool and not otherwise. It seems, indeed, possible to replace this definition by a periphrasis about the correspondence of two facts; but if such a periphrasis is not ultimately legitimate that does not prove that our definition is wrong, but merely that it should not strictly be called a correspondence theory and that a statement of it in terms of correspondence should be regarded as merely an inaccurate popular explanation. Truth, we say, is when a man believes that A is B and A is B, whether or not such an occurrence can be accurately described as a correspondence between two facts; failure to describe it in terms of correspondence cannot show that it never occurs and is not what we mean by truth.

This account of truth is merely a truism, but there is no platitude so obvious that eminent philosophers have not denied it, and at the risk of wearying the reader we shall insist on our truism once more.

Let us take three statements like this:

The earth is round.

It is true that the earth is round.

Anyone who believes that the earth is round believes truly.

It is really obvious that these statements are all equivalent, in the sense that it is not possible to affirm one of them and deny another without patent contradiction; to say, for instance, that it is true that the earth is round but that the earth is not round is plainly absurd.

Now the first statement of the three does not involve the idea of truth in any way, it says simply that the earth is round. [In the second we have to prefix "It is true that," which is generally added not to alter the meaning but for what in a wide sense are reasons of style and does not affect the meaning of the statements.] Thus we can use it rather like "although" in conceding a point but denying a supposed consequence, "It is true that the earth is round, but still ... ," or again we often use it when what we say has been questioned: "Is that true?" "Yes, it is perfectly true." [But in the last case the phrase "it is true that the earth is round" is changing from simply meaning that the earth is round ...]

The meaning of the second, on the other hand, is less clear: it may be a mere synonym for the first, but more often contains some reference to the possibility of someone believing or saying that the earth is round. We are thinking not merely that the earth is round, but that because it is round anyone[11] who believes or says that it is round believes or says truly. We have passed from the first of our statements to the third. But the third amounts in a sense to no more than the first, and it is merely the first thought of in connection with the possibility of someone saying or believing it. To take a parallel case, we can say simply "The weather in Scotland was bad in July," or we can think of that fact in reference to its possible effect on one of our friends and say instead "If you were in Scotland in July, you had bad weather." So too we can think of the earth being round as a possible subject of belief and say "If you think the earth is round, you think truly" and this amounts to no more than that the earth has the quality you think it has when you think it is round, i.e. that the earth is round.

All this is really so obvious that one is ashamed to insist on it, but our insistence is rendered necessary by the extraordinary way in which philosophers produce definitions of truth in no way compatible with our platitudes, definitions according to which the earth can be round without its being true that it is round.[12] The reason for this lies in a number of confusions of which it must be extremely hard to keep clear if we are to judge by their extraordinary prevalence. In the rest of this chapter we shall be occupied solely with the defence of our platitude that a belief that p is true if and only if p, and in an attempt to unravel the confusions that surround it.

The first type of confusion arises from the ambiguity of the question which we are trying to answer, the question "what is truth?" which can be interpreted in at least three different ways. For in the first place there are some philosophers who do not see any problem in what is *meant* by "truth," but take our interpretation of the term as being obviously right, and proceed under the title of "what is truth?" to discuss the different problem of giving a general criterion for distinguishing truth and falsehood. This was for instance Kant's interpretation[13] and he goes on quite rightly to say that the idea of such a general criterion of truth is absurd, and that for men to discuss such a question is as foolish as for one to milk a he-goat while another holds a sieve to catch the milk.

And secondly even when we agree that the problem is to define truth in the sense of explaining its meaning, this problem can wear two quite different complexions according to the kind of definition with which we are prepared to be content. Our definition is one in terms of propositional reference, which we take as a term already understood. But it may be held that this notion of propositional reference is itself in need of analysis and definition, and that a definition of truth in terms of so obscure a notion represents very little if any progress. If a belief is identified as what Mr. Jones was thinking at 10 o'clock in the morning, and we ask what is meant by calling the belief so identified a true belief, to apply the only answer we have so far obtained we need to know what Mr. Jones' belief was a "belief that"; for instance, we say that if it was a belief that the earth is flat, then it was true if the earth is flat. But to many this may seem merely to shirk the hardest and most interesting part of the problem, which is to find out how and in what sense those images or ideas in Mr. Jones' mind at 10 o'clock constitute or express a "belief that the earth is flat." Truth, it will be said, consists in a relation between ideas and reality, and the use without analysis of the term "propositional reference" simply conceals and shirks all the real problems that this relation involves.

This charge must be admitted to be just, and an account of truth which accepts the notion of propositional reference without analysis cannot possibly be regarded as complete. For all the many difficulties connected with that notion are really involved in truth which depends on it: if, for instance, "propositional reference" has quite different meanings in relation to different kinds of belief (as many people think) then a similar ambiguity is latent in "truth" also, and it is obvious that we shall not have got our idea of truth really clear until this and all similar problems are settled.

But though the reduction of truth to propositional reference is a very small part and much the easiest part of its analysis, it is not therefore one which we can afford to neglect. [Not only is it essential to realize that truth and propositional reference are not independent notions requiring separate analysis, and that it is truth that depends on and must be defined *via* reference not reference *via* truth.[14]] For not only is it in any event essential to realise that the problem falls in this way into two parts,[15] the reduction of truth to reference and the analysis of reference itself, and to be clear which part of the problem is at any time being tackled, but for many purposes it is only the first and easiest part of the solution that we required; we are often concerned not with beliefs or judgments as occurences at particular times in particular men's minds, but with, for instance, *the* belief or judgment "all men are mortal"; in such case the only definition of truth we can possibly need is one in terms of propositional reference, which is presupposed in the very notion of *the* judgment "all men are mortal"; for when we speak of *the* judgment "all men are mortal" what we are really dealing with is any particular judgment on any particular occasion which has that propositional reference, which is a judgment "that all men are mortal." Thus, though the psychological difficulties involved in this notion of reference must be faced in any complete treatment of truth, it is well to begin with a definition which is sufficient for a great many purposes and depends only on the simplest considerations.

And whatever the complete definition may be, it must preserve the evident connection between truth and reference, that a belief "that p" is true if and only if p. We may deride this as trivial formalism, but since we cannot contradict it without absurdity, it provides a slight check on any deeper investigations that they must square with this obvious truism.

Notes

1. How difficult the problem is may be judged from the fact that in the years 1904–1925 Mr. Bertrand Russell has adopted in succession five different solutions of it.

2. I use "state" as the widest possible term, not wishing to express any opinion as to the nature of beliefs etc.

3. Or, of course, that something is not so and so, or that if something is so and so, something is not such and such, and so on through all the possible forms.

4. [It should perhaps be remarked that the late Professor Cook Wilson held that these mental states do not in fact belong. (Square brackets indicate remarks F. P. Ramsey made on the manuscript—Eds.)] It should, however, be remarked that according to one theory this is not really a deficiency at all, since the states in question have nothing important in common. Knowledge and opinion have propositional reference in quite different senses and are not species of a common genus. This view, put forward most clearly by J. Cook Wilson (but also implied by others, e.g., Edmund Husserl), is explained and considered below.

5. Bernard Bosanquet, *Logic*, 2nd ed., vol. 2 (Oxford: Oxford University Press, 1911), 282ff. Of course he sees the distinction but he deliberately blurs it, arguing that an account of truth which enables an ill-grounded statement to be true, cannot be right. His example of the man who makes a true statement believing it to be false, reveals an even grosser confusion. He asks why such a statement is a lie, and answers this by saying that "it was contrary to the system of his knowledge as determined by his whole experience at the time." Granting this, it would at most follow that coherence with the man's system of his knowledge is a mark not of *truth* (for *ex hypothesi* such a statement would have been false) but of *good faith*; and this is brought in as an argument in favour of a coherence theory of *truth*!

6. It has been suggested by Professor Moore ("Facts and Propositions," suppl., *Proceedings of the Aristotelian Society* 7 [1927]: 171–206; see p. 178) that the same entity may be both a belief that (say) the earth is round and a belief that something else; in this case it will have two propositional references and may be true in respect of one and false in respect of the other. It is not to my mind a real possibility, but everything in the present chapter could easily be altered so as to allow for it, though the complication of language which would result seems to me far to outweigh the possible gain in accuracy.

7. In Mr. Russell's symbolism

B is true :=: $(\exists p)$. B is a belief that p & p. Df

8. In a sentence like this "in fact" serves simply to show that the *oratio obliqua* introduced by "he believed" has now come to an end. It does not mean a new notion to be analyzed, but is simply a connecting particle.

9. See below. [Presumably this is a reference to the unwritten chapter on negation.—Eds.]

10. *Metaphysics*, Gamma 6: 1011b25, Mr. Ross' translation.

11. For instance the man we are talking to may have just made the point and we concede it. "Yes, it's true, as you say, that the earth is round, but____" or we may have made it and be questioned "Is that true, what you were saying, that the earth is round?" "Yes, it's perfectly true."

12. Thus according to William James a pragmatist could think both that Shakespeare's plays were written by Bacon and that someone else's opinion that Shakespeare wrote them might be perfectly true "for him" ("The Meaning of Truth," 274). On the idea that what is true for one person may not be true for another see below.

13. See *Kritik der reinen Vernunft*, "Die transzendentale Logik," Einleitung 3, A57 B82: "Die alte und berühmte Frage ... Was ist Wahrheit? Die Namenerklä rung der Wahrheit, dass sie näm-lich die Übereinstimmung der Erkenntnis mit ihrem Gegenstande sei, wird hier geschenkt und vorausgesetzt; man verlangt aber zu wissen, welches das allgemeine und sichere Kriterium der Wahrheit einer jedem Erkenntnis sei." The reason why there can be no such criterion is that every object is distinguishable and therefore has something true of it which is true of no other object. Hence there can be no guarantee of truth irrespective of the object in question.

14. [This might perhaps be denied if reference were something essentially different in the cases of true and of false beliefs; e.g., if the precise way in which a man's belief today that it will be wet to-morrow was a belief "that it will be wet to-morrow" depended on how to-morrow's weather actually turned out. But this is absurd for it would allow us to settle the weather in advance by simply considering the nature of the prophet's expectation and seeing whether it had true-reference or false-reference.]

15. It might possibly be questioned whether this division of the problem is sound, not because the truth of a belief does not obviously depend on its reference, i.e., on what is believed, but because reference might be essentially different in the two cases of truth and falsity, so that there were really two primitive ideas, true-reference and false-reference, which had to be separately analysed. In this case, however, we could tell whether a belief that A is B were true or false, without looking at A by simply seeing whether the manner in which the belief was a "belief that A is B" was that of true-reference or false-reference, and infer with certainty that to-morrow would be fine from the fact that someone believed in a particular way, the way of false-reference, that it would be wet.

17 Truth

P. F. Strawson

In the following discussion, I confine myself to the question of the truth of empirical statements. My positive thesis is an elaboration of what was said, a long time ago, by F. P. Ramsey.[1] My negative purpose is the criticism of a current misconception—the Semantic or Meta-linguistic Theory of Truth—which seems to me to repeat, in a new way, some old mistakes. In so far as this theory is simply a contribution to the construction of artificial languages, and is not intended to be regarded as relevant to the use of actual languages, I am not concerned with it. But I think the theory has been claimed by some, and it has certainly been thought by many, to throw light on the actual use of the word "true"; or (which I take to be the same claim) on the philosophical problem of truth. I think it *does* throw some light; but I think it is also seriously misleading. Nothing that follows, however, is to be taken as implying that the word "true" is *never* used in the way described by the semantic theory. It is certainly so used for some technical purposes, and may sometimes be so used for non-technical purposes as well; though I know of no such non-technical purposes.

I

In recent discussions of truth, one or both of two theses are commonly maintained. These are:

First, any sentence beginning "It is true that …" does not change its assertive meaning when the phrase "It is true that" is omitted. More generally, to say that an assertion is true is not to make any further assertion at all; it is to make the same assertion. This I shall call Thesis I.

Second, to say that a statement is true is to make a statement about a sentence of a given language, viz., the language in which the first statement was made. It is (in other and more technical terms) to make a statement in a meta-language ascribing the semantic property of truth (or the semantic predicate "true") to a sentence in an object-language. The object-sentence concerned should strictly be written in inverted commas to make it clear that we are talking *about the sentence*; and the phrase "is true" should strictly be followed by some such phrase as "in L," where "L" designates the object-language concerned. This I shall call Thesis 2.

Of these two theses, the first is true, but inadequate; the second is false, but important. The first thesis is right in what it asserts, and wrong in what it suggests. The second thesis is wrong in what it asserts, but right in what it implies. The first thesis is right in asserting that to say that a statement is true is not to make a further statement; but wrong in suggesting that to say that a statement is true is not to do something different from, or additional to, just making the statement. The second thesis is right in implying that to say that a statement is true is to do something different from just making the statement; but wrong in asserting that this "something different" consists in making a further statement, viz. a statement about a sentence.

Although both theses are sometimes maintained by the same philosopher, it is easy to see that they cannot both be correct. For if it is true that to say (1) "Moths fly by night" is to make the same assertion as to say (2) "It is true that moths fly by night," then it is false that to say (2) is to say anything about the English sentence "Moths fly by night"; i.e. false that (2) ought strictly to be written "'Moths fly by night' is true in English." If to say (2) is to make the same assertion as to say (1), then to say (2) cannot be to say anything about an English sentence; for to say (1) is not to say anything about an English sentence, but is to say something about moths.

Independently of this, one sees how misleading it is to say that the phrase "... is true" is used to talk *about sentences*, by comparing it with other phrases which certainly are used to talk about sentences (or words, or phrases). For example, someone says, in French, "Il pleut"; and someone else corrects him, saying: "'Il pleut' is *incorrect* French. 'Il pleut' is the right way of saying it." Or, criticising the style of a passage, someone says: "The sentence '....' is *badly expressed*." Similarly, one may ask what a sentence *means*, or say that a sentence is *ungrammatical, misspelt, a poor translation*. In all these cases, it is natural to say that one is talking *about a sentence*. If any statement of this kind were correctly translated into any language at all, the sentence which was being discussed would re-appear, quoted and untranslated, in the translation of the statement as a whole. Otherwise the translation would be incorrect. But it is perfectly obvious that a correct translation of any statement containing the phrase "is true" (used as it is ordinarily used) never contains a quoted and untranslated sentence to which the phrase "is true" was *applied* in the original sentence. The phrase "is true" is not *applied to* sentences; for it is not *applied to* anything.

Truth is not a property of symbols; for it is not a property.

II

The habit of calling truth a "semantic" concept ("true" a "semantical predicate") does not lessen the confusion involved in saying that "true" is a predicate of sentences; but it helps to indicate a possible source of the confusion. I shall digress briefly to explore this source. For light on the use of the word "semantic," I quote the following from Carnap's *Introduction to Semantics* (22):[2]

> By a *semantical system* we understand a system of rules, formulated in a meta-language and referring to an object-language, of such a kind that the rules determine a *truth-condition* for every sentence of the object-language. ... To formulate it in another way: the rules determine the *meaning* or *sense* of the sentences.

It will be noticed that the expressions "truth-condition" and "meaning" are used synonymously. And this suggests that even if there is no use of the phrase "is true" in which that phrase is correctly applied to (used to talk about) sentences, there is, or might be, a use of the phrase "is true if and only if," in which *this* phrase is correctly applied to (used to talk about) sentences; a use, namely, in which this phrase would be synonymous with the phrase "means that"; which certainly *is* used to talk about sentences. Suppose, for example, that we wish to give information about the meaning of the sentence "The monarch is deceased." We can do this by making the following meta-statement:

(i) "The monarch is deceased" means that the king is dead.

Here we put the sentence "The monarch is deceased" in inverted commas to indicate that we are talking about this sentence. We are making a meta-statement. And the meta-statement is contingent, for it is a contingent matter that the sentence in question has this meaning in English, or, indeed, that it has any meaning at all. To be quite strict, we perhaps ought to write it:

(ia) "The monarch is deceased" in English means that the king is dead.

If we were to translate this meta-statement into another language, none of the expressions occurring in it would remain unchanged except the quoted sentence "The monarch is deceased." That would remain unchanged; otherwise the translation would be incorrect. Now the suggestion is that we might, without unintelligibility, give the same information in exactly the same way, except that we should replace the phrase "mean that" with the phrase "is true if and only if" obtaining the contingent meta-statement:

(ii) "The monarch is deceased" is true if and only if the king is dead.

or, more strictly:

(iia) "The monarch is deceased" is true in English if and only if the king is dead.

This seems to be an intelligible procedure. All that I have said of statements (i) and (ia) will apply to statements (ii) and (iia); we shall be using the phrase "is true if and only if," in a contingent statement, to talk about a sentence. Now consider a degenerate case of such meta-statements: the case exemplified in the sentences:

(iii) "The monarch is deceased" means (in English) that the monarch is deceased.

(iv) "The monarch is deceased" is true (in English) if and only if the monarch is deceased.

It is difficult, and, perhaps, for the present purpose, not very important, to decide what status to assign to such sentences as these. Considerations which might tempt us to describe them firmly as true, contingent meta-statements are the following:

(a) Although they are of no use for telling us what the quoted sentence means, they do give us some information about it. They do at any rate indicate that the quoted sentence has some meaning in English.[3] And this is a contingent matter.

(b) These statements could be obtained from the nondegenerate cases by a quite legitimate process of translation, inference and retranslation. (Or, more simply, their correct translation into, say, French would undoubtedly yield a contingent meta-statement.)

(c) It is a contingent matter that any sentence means what it does mean, expresses the proposition it does express.[4]

Although these considerations are decisive against calling (iii) and (iv) "logically necessary,"[5] they are very inadequate grounds for calling them, without qualification, "true and contingent." For what contingent matter do they state? If we answer, taking the hint from (a), that they state merely that the quoted sentence has some meaning in English, then their form (the use of the expression "means that") is utterly mislead-ing. If we demand what contingent matter they state, which falls under the head of (c), no answer is possible. One cannot *state* what a sentence means without the help of another sentence.

For these reasons, I propose to continue to refer to statements (or pseudo-statements) like (iii) and (iv) not as necessary, nor as contingent, but simply as "degenerate cases" of contingent meta-statements of the type of (i) and (ii). The point is not in itself impor-tant; though it is important that no confusion should arise from it.

The next step is to notice the deceptive similarity of the use of the phrase "if and only if" in this type of contingent meta-statement to its use in expressions which are not contingent statements, but necessary or defining formulae. An example of such a formula would be: The monarch is deceased if and only if the king is dead. Here the phrase "is true" does not occur; and no part of this expression is in inverted commas. The formula itself does not give us information about the meaning of the sentence "The monarch is deceased," though the statement that it *was* a necessary formula *would* give us such information. Now the similarity of the use of the phrase "if and only if" in these necessary formulae to its use as *part* of the phrase "is true if and only if" in contingent meta-statements, may have constituted a strong temptation to split the degenerate cases of such meta-statements down the middle, and to regard what follows the phrase "if and only if" as the definiens of what precedes it; i.e. of the phrase "the sentence '... .' is true (in L)"; to regard, for example, the whole expression (iv),

"The monarch is deceased" is true if and only if the monarch is deceased,

as a specification or consequence or part[6] of a general definition of "... is true" (or of "... is true in L"). And this we in fact find; i.e. we find it said that a satisfactory general definition of truth must have as its consequences such expressions as the following:[7]

(v) "To-day is Monday" is true if and only if to-day is Monday.

(vi) "London is a City" is true if and only if London is a City.

Now we have seen that such statements as (v) and (vi) are degenerate cases of those contingent meta-statements of the type of (ii), which make use of the phrase "*is true if and only if*" as a synonym for "*means that.*" It is only *as a part of the former phrase* that the expression "*is true*" is used, in such statements, to talk about sentences. To read the degenerate cases, then, as specification, or parts, of some ideal defining formula for the phrase "is true" is to separate the phrase from the context which alone confers this meta-linguistic use upon it, and to regard the result as a model for the general use of "is true." It is to be committed to the mistake of supposing that the phrase "is true" is normally (or strictly) used as a meta-linguistic predicate. Thus misinterpreted, as defining formulae, such expressions as (v) are both fascinating and misleading. They mislead because, as we have seen, they crystallise the false Thesis 2. They fascinate because they seem to point to the true Thesis 1; for part of the expression to be defined (namely, the combination of quotation-marks and the phrase is "true") *disappears* in the definiens without being replaced by anything else. (How odd it is, incidentally, to call this definition-by-disappearance "definition"!). In this way, the view that "true" is assertively redundant is represented as somehow combined with, and dependent upon, the view that "true" is a meta-linguistic predicate of sentences. We may express, then, the main contention of the semantic theory as follows: to say that a statement is true is not to say something further *about the subject-matter* of the statement, but is to say the same thing about the subject-matter of the statement, *by means of a further statement, namely a statement about a sentence.* Now I said that Thesis 1 is true. A fortiori, a modification of Thesis 1 is true, which I shall call Thesis 1A, and which runs as follows:

> To say that a statement is true is not to say something further about the subject-matter of the statement, but, in so far as it is to say anything about that subject-matter, is to say the same thing about it.

Now Thesis 1A, but not Thesis 1, is compatible with Thesis 2. The semantic theory consists in the joint assertion of 1A and 2. I suggest that the semantic theory borrows a lot of its plausibility from the truth of 1A. We swallow 2 for the sake of 1A. I now wish to show that the unmodified thesis 1 is true, and that we therefore can and must assert 1A while rejecting 2 and, therefore, rejecting the semantic theory.

As for the muddle I have described above—the muddle of reading a degenerate case of contingent statements meta-linguistically employing the phrase *is true if and only if,* as a pseudo-defining-formula of which the definiendum consists of a quoted sentence followed by the phrase *is true*—I do not claim that this muddle represents the genesis of the semantic theory; but I do think that it, too, may have contributed to the plausibility of the theory.

III

The best way of showing that Thesis 1 is true is to correct its inadequacy. The best way of correcting its inadequacy is to discover the further reasons which have led to Thesis 2. To bring out those features of the situation which lead to the mistake of saying that the word "true" is used meta-linguistically (to talk about sentences), I want first to compare the use of "true" with that of "Yes." If you and I have been sitting together in silence for some time, and I suddenly say "Yes," you would, perhaps, look at me with surprise and answer "I didn't say anything." Of course, a man may say "Yes" to himself; and this will be a sign that he has resolved a doubt in his own mind, or come to a decision. But the normal use of "Yes" is to answer: and where no question is asked, no answer can be given. Suppose you now ask: "Was Jones there?" and I say "Yes"; there seems no temptation whatever to say that, in so answering, I am *talking about* the English sentence "Was Jones there?" So, in the case of "Yes," we have a word of which the normal use requires some linguistic occasion (a question), without there being any temptation at all to say that it is used to *talk about* the sentence of which the utterance is the occasion for its use. There is indeed a temptation to go further in the opposite direction and say that in answering "Yes" I am not talking *about* anything, not making any assertion, at all; but simply answering. In a way, this is correct; but in a way, it's wrong. For it would be perfectly correct for you, reporting our dialogue, to say of me: "He said Jones was there." So of the ordinary use of "Yes," we may say: first, that it demands a linguistic occasion, namely the asking of a question; second, that it is not used meta-linguistically, to talk about the question, but to answer it; third, that in so far as we are making an assertion at all in using it, the content of the assertion is the same as the content of the question. Now imagine a possible, and perhaps vulgarly current, use of the expression "Ditto." You make an assertion, and I say "Ditto." In so far as I assert anything, talk about anything, I talk about and assert what you talk about and assert. Of course—and this points to the inadequacy of Thesis 1 and the reason for the meta-linguistic error—to say "Ditto" is not *the same as* to make the statement in question; for, whereas I might have made the statement before anyone else had spoken, it would be meaningless for me to say "Ditto" before anyone else had spoken. "Ditto," like "Yes," requires a linguistic occasion. But again, and largely, I think, because the expression "Ditto" does not consist of a grammatical subject and a grammatical predicate, there is absolutely no temptation to say that in thus using "Ditto," I should be talking *about the sentence* you used, and the utterance of which was the linguistic occasion for my use of this expression. I am not talking about what you said (the noise you made, or the sentence you spoke, or the proposition you expressed). I am agreeing with, endorsing, underwriting what you said; and, unless you had said something, I couldn't perform *these* activities, though I could *make the assertion* you made. Now the expression "That's true" sometimes functions in just the way in which I have suggested the expression "Ditto" might function. A says "Jones was there" and B says "That's true"; and C, reporting the conversation, can correctly say: "Both A and B said that Jones was there." But the point is that B couldn't have said that Jones was there in the way he *did* say it (i.e. by the use of the expression "That's true"), unless A had previously uttered the *sentence* "Jones was there," or some equivalent sentence. It is, perhaps, *this* fact about the use (*this* use) of the word "true," together with the old prejudice that any indicative sentence must describe (be "about") something, which encourages those who have become chary of saying that truth is a property of propositions to say instead that in using the word "true," we are talking about sentences. (What I have said about the use of "That's true" applies, of course, with suitable alterations, to the use of "That's false.")

Now those who assert that "true" is a predicate of sentences have not, in general, considered these simple cases of the use of "true" (and "false"), but the more puzzling cases which lead, or seem to lead, to paradoxes: such as the case where someone utters the isolated sentence "What I am saying now is false," or writes on an otherwise clean blackboard the sentence "Every statement on this blackboard is false." The solution on meta-linguistic lines is to treat these sentences as making statements of the second order to the effect:

(1) that there is some statement of the first order written on the blackboard (or said by me now); and

(2) that any first-order statement written on the blackboard (or said by me now) is false.

By means of this distinction of orders, the distinction between meta and object-language, the puzzling sentences are said no longer *to* engender contradictions: either they are simply false, since the existential part of what they assert is false; or, alternatively, leaving out the existential part of the analysis, and treating them solely as hypotheticals, they are seen to be vacuously true, since no first-order statements occur. This solution is formally successful in avoiding the apparent contradictions. But it seems to me to achieve this success only by repeating the fundamental mistake from which the contradictions themselves arise, and also, and consequently, involving the difficulties mentioned at the beginning of this paper. That is, first, it involves the view that to say that a statement is true (or false) is to make a further, second-order, statement (thus contradicting Thesis 1); and, second, it (usually) involves the unplausibility of saying that this second-order statement is *about* a sentence or sentences. Now the point of the previous discussion of the actual use of "Yes," the possible use of "Ditto" and the actual use of "That's true" is to show that these expedients are unnecessary. When no one has spoken, and I say "Ditto," I am not making a false statement to the effect that something true has been said, nor a true statement to the effect that nothing false has been said. I am not making a statement at all; but producing a pointless utterance. When somebody has made an assertion previously, my saying "Ditto" acquires a point, has an occasion: and, if you like, you may say that I am now making a statement, repeating, in a manner, what the speaker said. But I am not making an additional statement, a meta-statement. It would perhaps be better to say that my utterance is not a statement at all, but a linguistic performance for which in the first case there was not, and in the second case there was, an occasion: so that in the first case it was a spurious, and in the second case a genuine, performance. Similarly, the words "true" and "false" normally require, as an occasion for their significant use, that somebody should have made, be making or be about to make (utter or write), some statement. (The making of the statement need not precede the use of "true": it may follow it as in the case of the expression "It is true that ..."—a form of words I shall discuss later.) But in all cases the indicative clause of which the grammatical predicate is the phrase "is true" does not in itself make any kind of statement at all (not even a meta-statement), and *a fortiori* cannot make the statement, the making of which is required as the occasion for the significant use of the words "true" or "false." This is not, as it stands, quite accurate. For an indicative sentence of which the grammatical predicate is the phrase "is true" may sometimes, as I shall shortly show, be used to make an implicit meta-statement. But when this is so, the phrase "is true" plays no part in the making of this meta-statement. The phrase "is true" *never* has a statement-making role. And when this is seen, the paradoxes vanish without the need for the meta-linguistic machinery; or at least without the need for regarding the words "true" and "false" as part of that machinery. The paradoxes arise on the assumption that the words "true" and "false" can be used to make first-order assertions. They are formally solved by the declaration that these words can be used only to make second-order assertions. Both paradoxes and solution disappear on the more radical assumption that they are not used to make assertions of any order, are not used to make assertions at all.

I said, however, that indicative sentences of which the grammatical predicate is the phrase "is true" or the phrase "is false" may be used to make an implicit meta-statement, in the making of which these phrases themselves play no part. To elucidate this, consider the following sentences:

(1) What I am saying now is false.

(2) All statements made in English are false.

(3) What the policeman said is true.

It is certainly not incorrect to regard each of these sentences as implicitly making an *existential* meta-statement, which does not involve the words "true" or "false." The implicit meta-statements in these cases might be written as follows:

(la) I have just made (am about to make) a statement.

(2a) Some statements are made in English.

(3a) The policeman made a statement.

These are all second-order assertive sentences to the effect that there are some first-order assertive sentences, uttered (a) by me, (b) in English, (c) by the policeman.

These second-order assertive sentences we can regard as part of the analysis of the sentences (1), (2) and (3). Obviously they are not the whole of their analysis. The sentence "The policeman made a statement" clearly has not the same use as the sentence "What the policeman said is true." To utter the second is to do something more than to assert the first. What is this additional performance? Consider the circumstances in which we might use the expression "What the policeman said is true." Instead of using this expression, I might have *repeated* the policeman's story. In this case, I shall be said to have *confirmed* what the policeman said. I might, however, have made exactly the same set of statements as I made in repeating his story, but have made them *before* the policeman spoke. In this case, though the assertions I have made are no different, I have not done what I did in the other case, namely "confirmed his story." So to confirm his story is not to say anything further, *about* his story, or the sentences he used in telling it, though it is to do something that cannot be done unless he has told his story. Now, unlike the confirming narrative which I might have told, the sentence "What the policeman said is true" has no use *except* to confirm the policeman's story;[8] but like the confirming narrative, the sentence does not say anything further *about* the policeman's story or the sentences he used in telling it. It is a device for confirming the story without telling it again. So, in general, in using such expressions, we are confirming, underwriting, admitting, agreeing with, what somebody has said; but (except where we are implicitly making an existential meta-statement, in making which the phrase "is true" plays no part), we are not making any assertion additional to theirs; and are *never* using "is true" to talk *about* something which is *what they said*, or the sentences they used in saying it. To complete the analysis, then, of the entire sentence (3) "What the policeman said is true," we have to add, to the existential meta-assertion, a phrase which is not assertive, but (if I may borrow Mr. Austin's word) performatory.[9] We might, e.g., offer, as a complete analysis of one case, the expression: "The policeman made a statement. I confirm it"; where, in uttering the words "I confirm it," I am not describing something I do, but *doing* something.[10] There is, then, a difference between the more complicated cases in which the phrase "is true" is preceded by a descriptive phrase, and the simpler sentences (e.g. "That's true") in which the phrase "is true" is preceded by a demonstrative. The former may be regarded as involving an implicit meta-statement, while the latter are purely confirmatory (or purely "admittive"). But in neither sort of case has the phrase "is true" any assertive (or meta-assertive) function.

There may still be some uneasiness felt at the denial that the phrase "is true" has any assertive, or descriptive, function. Partially to allay this uneasiness, I will again say something familiar, that I have said already: that is, that when I say "That's true" in response to your statement, I am in a manner making an assertion, namely the assertion you made; describing something, namely what you described. But pointing this out is quite consistent with saying that "That's true" makes no statement in its own right. It makes no meta-statement. If there is any residual uneasiness, it ought not to be allayed. For its source is the ancient prejudice that any indicative sentence is, or makes,[11] a statement. I call it a prejudice: we could, instead, make it a criterion. And there would even be no harm in adopting this criterion for "statement," if we could simultaneously divorce the word, in this strictly grammatical use, from its logic in other uses: from that logic which leads us, given a "statement," to enquire: What is it about? What does it describe? What property, or what relation, does it assert to belong to, or hold between, what entity or entities? Asking these questions when confronted with such a sentence as "What Pascal said is true," we are led to look for the entity which is *what Pascal said*; looking with cautious, contemporary eyes, we find only his words; and so are induced to say that, in using this expression, we are talking about the French sentences he wrote or spoke. It is, then, the out-of-date desire that the phrase "is true" should be some kind of a descriptive phrase, that leads to the up-to-date suggestion that the word "true" is a second-level predicate of first-level sentences. More important than simply to reject *this* view is to have the right reason for rejecting it: the reason, namely, that the phrase "is true" is not descriptive at all. If we persist that it describes (is about) something, while denying that it describes (is about) sentences, we shall be left with the old, general questions about the nature of, and tests for, truth, about the nature of the entities related by the truth-relation, and so on. Better than asking "What is the criterion of truth?" is to ask: "What are the grounds for agreement?"—for those we see to be not less various than the subjects on which an agreed opinion can be reached. And this will perhaps also discourage us from seeking to mark the difference between one kind of utterance and another by saying, for example, "Ethical utterances are not true or false." It is correct to say that utterances of any kind are true or false, if it is correct usage to signify agreement or disagreement with such utterances by means of the *expressions* "true" or "false."

Of course, the formula that I have adopted in the discussion of one use of "true" is not immune from another variant of that argument from grammar which leads to treating "true" as a descriptive word. Someone might say: in order for you to *confirm* anything, there must be some *object* of this activity; a sentence or a proposition: and to perform this activity upon this object is nothing other than to assert that the object has the property, stands in the relation, referred to by the word "true." Anyone who says this is misled partly by the fact that the verb "confirm" takes a grammatical object; and partly by the fact that the linguistic performance (of "confirming") requires, not an object, but an *occasion*—a fact which I declared to be the misunderstood element of truth in the semantic theory. Even this assertion—that there must be, or be thought to be, some kind of sign-occasion for the significant, or genuine, use of the word "true"— is not quite correct, if it means that some spoken or written utterance must occur, or be thought to occur. For it would not be incorrect, though it would be unusual, to say: "What you are thinking is true"; when nothing has been said. (But, then, a conversation *can* be carried on by glances and nods.)

IV

In philosophical discussion of this whole subject, very little attention has been paid to the actual use of "true." And I want to conclude by distinguishing some of its normal uses in a little more detail. The uses mentioned so far I was tempted to call "performatory." But this is a misnomer. A performatory word, in Austin's sense, I take to be a verb, the use of which, in the first person present indicative, seems to describe some activity of the speaker, but in fact *is* that activity. Clearly the use of "is true" does not seem to describe any activity of the speaker; it *has seemed* to describe a sentence, a proposition, or statement. The point of using Austin's word at all is the fact that the phrase "is true" can sometimes be replaced,[12] without any important change in meaning, by some such phrase as "I confirm it," which is performatory in the strict sense. I shall take the substitute performatory word as a title for each of these cases; and shall speak, e.g., of the "confirmatory" or "admissive" use of "true." What commends the word as, e.g., a confirmatory device is its economy. By its means we can confirm without repeating.

The word has other, equally non-descriptive, uses. A familiar one is its use in sentences which begin with the phrase "It's true that," followed by a clause, followed by the word "but," followed by another clause. It has been pointed to me that the words "It's true that ... but ..." could, in these sentences, be replaced by the word "Although"; or, alternatively, by the words "I concede that ... but ..." This use of the phrase, then, is concessive. The inappropriateness of the meta-linguistic treatment seems peculiarly apparent here.

The purely confirmatory use is probably no more common than other uses which look much the same, but which are, I think, distinct. A man may make an assertion to you, not wanting you to confirm it, to remove the doubt of others or his own; but wanting to know that you share his belief, or his attitude. If, in this case, you say 'That's true," you are not *saying*, but *indicating*, that you do share his belief. It seems to me natural to describe this simply as "agreeing." Again, it seems to me that we very often use the phrase "That's true" to express, not only agreement with what is said, but also our sense of its novelty and force. We register the impact of what is said, much as we might register it by saying: "I never thought of that." Contrast the ironical "very true" with which we sometimes rudely greet the obvious. The use of "true" here is effectively ironical just because we normally use it to express agreement when our agreement is in doubt, or to register a sense of revelation. Sometimes, in sentences beginning "Is it true that ...?" or "So it's true that ...," we could preserve the expressive quality of the utterance by substituting the adverb "really" for the quoted phrases, at an appropriate point in the sentence; to convey, as they do, incredulity or surprise.

No doubt, the word has other functions; but those I have mentioned are probably as common as any. The important point is that the performance of these functions (and, I suspect, of all other non-technical jobs the word may do) does not involve the use of a meta-linguistic predicate; and that we *could*, with no very great violence to our language, perform them without the need for any expression which *seems* (as "is true" seems) to make a statement. For instance, the substitution of "although" for "It's true that ... but that ..." is an obvious way of dealing with the concessive use; an extension of the practice of the inarticulate election-candidate whose speech consisted of "Ditto to Mr. X" might deal with the confirmatory and, partly, with the expressive uses; and so on. The selection of the substitute-expressions would of course be governed by the propagandist consideration that they should provide the minimum encouragement to anyone anxious to mistake them for statement-making phrases, or descriptive words.

One last point: a suggestion on the reasons why the puzzle about truth has commonly got entangled with the puzzle about certainty. It is above all when a doubt has been raised, when mistakes or deceit seem possible; when the need for confirmation is felt; that we tend to make use of those certifying words of which "true" is one and of which others are "certain," "know," "prove," "establish," "validate," "confirm," "evidence" and so on. So that the question "What is the nature of truth?" leads naturally to the question "What are the tests for truth?," and this, in its turn, to the question "What are the conditions of certainty?" The historical or judicial search for truth is the search for the evidence which will set doubt at rest. The philosophical endeavour to characterise truth *in general* has tended to become the endeavour to characterise that which *in general* sets doubt at rest; really and finally at rest. Where you find the indubitable, there you find the true. And this metaphysical road branches into different paths, at the end of one of which you find the Atomic Fact, and, at the end of another, the Absolute.

Finally, I will repeat that in saying that the word "true" has not in itself any assertive function, I am not of course saying that a sentence like "His statement is true" is incorrect. Of course the word "statement" may be the grammatical subject of a sentence of which the phrase "is true" is the grammatical predicate. Nor am I recommending that we drop this usage. But for the usage, there would be no problem.

Notes

1. Ramsey, *Foundations of Mathematics* (London: Routledge and Kegan Paul, 1931), 142–143.

2. Carnap, *Introduction to Semantics* (Cambridge, MA: Harvard University Press, 1942).—Eds.

3. One can imagine another use for statements (iii) and (iv); e.g. if the object-language were written, and the meta-language spoken, English.

4. Cf. Lewy, "Truth and Significance," *Analysis* 8, no. 2 (1947): 24–27.

5. We might be tempted to call (iii) and (iv) "necessary," because it seems self-contradictory to say:

> (iiia) "The monarch is deceased" does not mean in English that the monarch is deceased.

But this would be a mistake. To say that a sentence both has some meaning or other and has no meaning at all would be to say something self-contradictory. To say that a sentence both has and has not some particular, specified meaning would be to say something self-contradictory. But (iiia) does neither of these things. The form of (iii) is appropriate to assigning, and that of (iiia) to withholding, some specific meaning. But since (iii) does not assign, (iiia) does not withhold, any specific meaning, (iiia) is not a self-contradictory, nor a false, contingent, statement; but a pseudo-statement.

6. E.g. Tarski, in "The Semantic Conception of Truth," *Philosophy and Phenomenological Research* 4 (1943–1944): 344, says:

> Every equivalence of the form (T) [(T) X is true if and only if p] obtained by replacing "p" by a particular sentence and "X" by a name of this sentence, may be considered a partial definition of truth, which explains wherein the truth of this one individual sentence consists. The general definition has to be, in a certain sense, a logical conjunction of all these partial definitions.

7. Cf. M. Black, expounding and criticising Tarski, in "The Semantic Definition of Truth,"*Analysis* 8, no. 4 (1947): 51.

8. This needs qualification. Uttered by a witness, the sentence is a *confirmation*; wrung from the culprit, it is an admission. No doubt there are other cases.

9. Cf. J. L. Austin, "Other Minds," *Proceedings of the Aristotelian Society*, suppl., 20 (1946): 169–175 for an account of some words of this class.

10. Cf. also "I admit it." To *say* this *is* to make an admission.

11. Throughout I have used such mild barbarisms as "This sentence makes a statement" as shorthand for such expressions as "Anyone who uttered this sentence would be making a statement."

12. Of course, not *simply* replaced. Other verbal changes would be necessary.

18 Truth

W. V. O. Quine

1 Vehicles of Truth

What are true or false, it will be widely agreed, are propositions. But it would not be so widely agreed were it not for the ambiguity of "proposition." Some understand the word as referring to sentences meeting certain specifications. Others understand it as referring rather to the meanings of such sentences. What looked like wide agreement thus resolves into two schools of thought: for the first school the vehicles of truth and falsity are the sentences, and for the second they are the meanings of the sentences.

A weakness of this second position is the tenuousness of the notion of sentence meanings. The tenuousness reaches the breaking point if one is persuaded of my thesis of the indeterminacy of translation (secs. 18 and 21 [in *The Pursuit of Truth*, 1990—Eds.]). Even apart from that thesis, it seems perverse to bypass the visible or audible sentences and to center upon sentence meanings as truth vehicles; for it is only by recurring to the sentence that we can say which sentence meaning we have in mind.

There was indeed a motive for pressing to the sentence meanings. Many sentences in the same or different languages are deemed to be alike in meaning, and distinctions among them are indifferent to truth; so one narrowed the field by ascribing truth rather to the meanings. This motive would be excellent if the notion of sentence meaning were not so elusive. But as matters stand we fare better by treating directly of sentences. These we can get our teeth into.

There was also a second motive, equal and opposite to the first, for pressing on to the sentence meanings; namely, that one and the same sentence can be true on some occasions and false on others. Thus "The Pope will visit Boston" was true but turned false after his last visit. "I have a headache" is true or false depending on who says it and when. Ambiguity or vagueness of terms, also, can cause the truth value of a sentence to depend in part on the speaker's intention.

Propositions, thought of as sentence meanings, were the meanings exclusively of sentences of a firmer sort, not subject to such vacillations; what we may call *eternal* sentences.[1] My obvious response, then, is that those eternal sentences themselves can serve as the truth vehicles. Just think of "I," "you," "he," "she," "here," and "there" as supplanted by names and addresses or other identifying particulars as needed. Think of tenses as dropped; we can use dates, the predicate "earlier than," and the like as needed. Think of ambiguities and vaguenesses as resolved by paraphrase—not absolutely, but enough to immobilize the truth value of the particular sentence. The truth values need not be known, but they must be stable.

The attitude is the one that is familiar in the teaching of logic. When we take illustrative sentences from everyday language and paraphrase them into the notation of truth functions and quantifiers, we think of the reference of demonstratives and personal pronouns as fixed—albeit tacitly—and we never dream of reading "$\exists x$" as "there was" or "there will be something x."

Declarative sentences thus refined—eternal sentences—are what I shall regard as truth vehicles in ensuing pages, for the most part. On the whole it is the convenient line for theoretical purposes. We must recognize, though, that it bypasses most of what counts in daily discourse as true or false, since our utterances are not for the most part thus refined. The truth vehicles directly related to behavior are not sentences as repeatable linguistic forms, but rather the individual acts of uttering them. These are for the most part univocal in truth value without benefit of paraphrase. There are just occasional failures, perhaps because some name turns out to be empty or because some vague term turns out to be indeterminate just where it matters for the utterance in question. Such utterances may be dismissed as neither true nor false.

So much by way of coming to terms with the realities of verbal behavior. Let us now return to the more conveniently manageable domain of eternal sentences, whose truth or falsity, known or unknown, is unchanging.

2   Truth as Disquotation

Such being what admit of truth, then, wherein does their truth consist? They qualify as true, one is told, by corresponding to reality. But correspondence word by word will not do; it invites the idle cluttering of reality with a bizarre host of fancied objects, just for the sake of correspondence. A neater plan is to posit *facts*, as correspondents of true sentences as wholes; but this still is a put-up job. Objects in abundance, concrete and abstract, are indeed needed for an account of the world; but facts contribute nothing beyond their specious support of a correspondence theory.

Yet there is some underlying validity to the correspondence theory of truth, as Tarski has taught us. Instead of saying that

"Snow is white" is true if and only if it is a fact that snow is white

we can simply delete "it is a fact that" as vacuous, and therewith facts themselves:

"Snow is white" is true if and only if snow is white.

To ascribe truth to the sentence is to ascribe whiteness to snow; such is the correspondence, in this example. Ascription of truth just cancels the quotation marks. Truth is disquotation.

So the truth predicate is superfluous when ascribed to a given sentence; you could just utter the sentence. But it is needed for sentences that are not given. Thus we may want to say that everything someone said on some occasion was true, or that all consequences of true theories are true. Such contexts, when analyzed logically, exhibit the truth predicate in application not to a quotation but to a pronoun, or bound variable.

The truth predicate proves invaluable when we want to generalize along a dimension that cannot be swept out by a general term. The easy sort of generalization is illustrated by generalization on the term "Socrates" in "Socrates is mortal"; the sentence generalizes to "All men are mortal." The general term "man" has served to sweep out the desired dimension of generality. The harder sort of generalization is illustrated by generalization on the clause "time flies" in "If time flies then time flies." We want to say that this compound continues true when the clause is supplanted by any other; and we can do no better than to say just that in so many words, including the word "true." We say "All sentences of the form 'If p then p' are true." We could not generalize as in "All men are mortal," because "time flies" is not, like "Socrates," a name of one of a range of objects (men) over which to generalize. We cleared this obstacle by *semantic ascent*: by ascending to a level where there were indeed objects over which to generalize, namely linguistic objects, sentences.

Semantic ascent serves also outside of logic. When Einstein propounded relativity, disrupting our basic conceptions of distance and time, it was hard to assess it without leaning on our basic conceptions and thus begging the question. But by semantic ascent one could compare the new and old theories as symbolic structures, and so appreciate that the new theory organized the pertinent data more simply than the old. Simplicity of symbolic structures can be appreciated independently of those basic conceptions.

As already hinted by the correspondence theory, the truth predicate is an intermediary between words and the world. What is true is the sentence, but its truth consists in the world's being as the sentence says. Hence the use of the truth predicate in accommodating semantic ascent.

The disquotational account of truth does not define the truth predicate—not in the strict sense of "definition"; for definition in the strict sense tells how to eliminate the defined expression from every desired context in favor of previously established notation. But in a looser sense the disquotational account does define truth. It tells us what it is for any sentence to be true, and it tells us this in terms just as clear to us as the sentence in question itself. We understand what it is for the sentence "Snow is white" to be true as clearly as we understand what it is for snow to be white. Evidently one who puzzles over the adjective "true" should puzzle rather over the sentences to which he ascribes it. "True" is transparent.

For eternal sentences the disquotational account of truth is neat, we see, and simple. It is readily extended, moreover, to the workaday world of individual utterances; thus an utterance of "I have a headache" is true if and only if the utterer has a headache while uttering it.

3   Paradox

It seems paradoxical that the truth predicate, for all its transparency, should prove useful to the point of indispensability. In the matter of paradox, moreover, this is scarcely the beginning. Truth is notoriously enmeshed in paradox, to the point of out-and-out antinomy.

An ancient form of the antinomy of truth is the Paradox of the Liar: "I am lying," or "This sentence is not true." A looser and fancier version was the paradox of Epimenides the Cretan, who said that all Cretans were liars. The underlying antinomy can be purified for logical purposes to read thus:

(1) "yields a falsehood when appended to its own quotation" yields a falsehood when appended to its own quotation.

Executing the instructions in (1), we append the nine-word expression to its quotation. The result is (1) itself. Thus (1) says that (1) itself is a falsehood. It is thus tantamount to "I am lying," but more clean-cut. It hinges only on the innocuous operations of quoting and appending and the notion of falsehood, which reduces to an innocent "not" and *true*. The truth predicate is clearly the trouble spot. The inevitable conclusion is that the truth predicate, for all its transparency and seeming triviality, is incoherent unless somehow restricted.

For further explicitness a technical turn of phrase will be convenient. The truth predicate will be said to *disquote* a sentence *S* if the form

_____ is true if and only if _____

comes out true when *S* is named in the first blank and written in the second. Thus what the disquotational account of truth says is that the truth predicate disquotes every eternal sentence. But the lesson of the antinomy is that if a language has at its disposal the innocent notations for treating of quoting and appending, and also the notations of elementary logic, then it cannot contain also a truth predicate that disquotes all its own eternal sentences—on pain of inconsistency. Its truth predicate, or its best approximation to one, must be incompletely disquotational. Specifically, it must not disquote all the sentences that contain it. That was the trouble with (1). And of course it must not disquote all the sentences containing terms by which that predicate could be paraphrased. This, apart from its special orientation to quoting and appending, is substantially what has come to be known as Tarski's Theorem. He has proved harder things.

The truth predicate loses little in general utility thereby, for it can still disquote all the eternal sentences that do not themselves contain it or other expressions to the same effect. And even these excluded applications can be accommodated by a hierarchy of truth predicates. The hierarchy begins with a predicate "$true_0$," which disquotes all sentences that contain no truth predicate or equivalent devices. A predicate "$true_1$," next, disquotes all sentences that contain no truth predicate or equivalent devices beyond "$true_0$." And so on up. It is a hierarchy of progressively more nearly perfect truth predicates. The plan dates back in a way to the early phase of Russell's theory of types (1908), by which he meant to obstruct the Paradox of the Liar among others.

4   Tarski's Construction

We saw that disquotation is loosely definitive of truth. We may now be thankful for the looseness, seeing as we do that definability of truth for a language within the language would be an embarrassment. And thus it was that Tarski undertook the perilous adventure of defining it for the language within the language, as nearly as possible, if only to see what minimum obstacle saved the situation. This was not his order of presentation, but it comes out the same.

The language chosen for the construction contains the logical notations for quantification and the truth functions and the set-theoretic notation "$x \in y$" for membership.[2] It contains also a finite lexicon, as large as you please, of predicates for natural science and daily life. Finally it contains the means, in effect, of quoting and appending, as in (1); that is, it can specify each of its single signs and it can express the concatenation of expressions.

Truth pertains to closed sentences, that is, sentences without free variables. Its analogue for open sentences is the two-place predicate of *satisfaction*. An assignment of objects to variables *satisfies* a sentence if the sentence is true for those values of its free variables.

What sort of object is an *assignment* of objects to variables? It is simply a function, or one-many *relation*, relating one and only one object to each variable—that is, to each letter, "w," "x," "y," "z," "w'," etc. A relation, in turn, is a set, or class, or *ordered pairs*. Ways are well known of defining the notation "$\langle x, y \rangle$" of ordered pairs contextually by means of epsilon and the logical particles.

Once satisfaction is defined, truth comes easily; for a closed sentence, having no free variables, is vacuously satisfied by all assignments or none according as it is true or false. We can simply define

(2) "y is true" as "$\forall x$ (x is assignment $\rightarrow x$ satisfies y)."

So Tarski's big job is to define satisfaction. First he defines it for *atomic* sentences, each of which consists of just a predicate adjoined to one or more variables. For instance an assignment satisfies the atomic sentence "$x \in y$" if and only if what is assigned to the letter "*x*" is a member of what is assigned to the letter "*y*." Correspondingly for each of the other predicates in the lexicon. An assignment satisfies an alternation of sentences, next, if and only if it satisfies one of both of them; it satisfies their conjunction if and only if it satisfies both; and it satisfies a negation if and only if it does not satisfy the sentence that is negated. Finally, an assignment satisfies an existential quantification "$\exists x(\dots x \dots)$" if and only if some assignment, matching that one except perhaps for what it assigns to "*x*," satisfies "$\dots x \dots$."

Such is Tarski's recursive or inductive definition of satisfaction. It explains satisfaction of atomic sentences outright, and it explains satisfaction of sentences of each higher grade or complexity in terms of satisfaction of their components. Universal quantification is passed over because it is expressible in terms of existential quantification and negation in familiar fashion.

5   Paradox Skirted

Clearly all the clauses of this inductive definition can be formulated within the formal language itself, except for the word "satisfies" that is being defined. Thus we have apparently defined satisfaction for the language within the language. Invoking (2), then, we have done the same for truth. This was supposed to spell contradiction.

We could even get contradiction directly from satisfaction, without the detour through (2), "truth," and (1). We have merely to ask whether assignment of the sentence "not (*x* satisfies *x*)" to the variable "*x*" satisfies the sentence "not (*x* satisfies *x*)" itself. Such is Grelling's so-called Heterological Paradox.[3]

What saves the situation is that the definition of satisfaction is inductive rather than direct. The inductive definition explains satisfaction of each specific sentence, but it does not provide a translation of "*x* satisfies *y*" with variable "*y*." Consequently it does not translate the "not (*x* satisfies *x*)" of Grelling's paradox, and does not support the truth definition (2) for variable "*y*"; it just explains truth of each specific closed sentence. It leaves the truth predicate in the same state in which the disquotational account left it; namely, fully explained in application to each specific sentence of the given language but not in application to a variable.

It was a near miss, and I turn now to a nearer one. Treating relations again as classes of ordered pairs, we can write "$\langle x, y \rangle \in z$" to mean that *x* bears the relation *z* to *y*. Now imagine the above inductive definition of satisfaction written out in our formal language, with the variable "*z*" always in place of "satisfies" and so "$\langle x, y \rangle \in z$" in place of "*x* satisfies *y*." Let the whole inductive definition, thus edited, be abbreviated as "Φz." It fixes *z* as the satisfaction relation. Evidently we arrive thus at a *direct* definition:

(3) $\exists z(\Phi z \cdot \langle x, y \rangle \in z)$

of "*x* satisfies *y*" strictly within the formal language itself. Doesn't this spell contradiction?

No. The catch this time is that there might not be any relation z such that Φz. Indeed there better not be, on pain, we see, of contradiction. The two-place predicate "satisfies" remains well defined in its inductive way, but a grasp of the predicate and how to use it carries no assurance of the existence of a corresponding abstract object, a corresponding set of ordered pairs. And, failing such a pair set, (3) fails to translate "x satisfies y." Though the satisfaction predicate is well explained even within the formal language by the recursion, it does not get reduced to the prior notation of that language. Satisfaction, and truth along with it, retain the status that truth already enjoyed under the disquotation account: clear intelligibility without full eliminability.[4]

Notes

1. In my logic books of 1940, 1941, and 1950, and revised editions down the years, my word for them was "statement"; but I became chary of it because of its customary use rather for an act. "Eternal sentence," along with "standing sentence" (sec. 4), dates from *Word and Object*. "Standing sentence" is more inclusive. "The *Times* has come" is a standing sentence, for it can command assent all day independently of interim stimulation; but it is not eternal.

2. Readers expecting a contrast between object language and metalanguage should bear in mind that I am already addressing the aforesaid perilous adventure.

3. See my *Ways of Paradox* (Cambridge, MA: Harvard University Press, 1976), 4–6.

4. The foregoing analysis is adapted from my *Philosophy of Logic* (Englewood Cliffs, NJ: Prentice-Hall, 1970), 35–46. A somewhat different analysis, in my 1952 paper "On an Application of Tarski's Theory of Truth," is called for when the set theory is of the kind that admits both sets and ultimate classes.

19 Transparent Truth as a Logical Property

Jc Beall

1 Transparent Truth

There are notoriously many so-called deflationary truth theories. I think of *transparent truth* as a sort of pure case of deflationary truth. The transparency view has it that any (declarative, etc.) sentence is intersubstitutable (in all non-intensional contexts) with the corresponding attribution of (transparent) truth to A.[1] This intersubstitutability (or, in short, 'transparency') rule is fundamental to transparent truth; it—and not some sequence of so-called T-biconditionals—is the defining rule. Whether the familiar so-called T-biconditionals are true in a language depends on the language. If a language has both a transparent truth predicate (for itself) and enjoys the truth of $A \to A$ for all sentences A in the language and some conditional $\to$ in the language, then the language also enjoys all T-biconditionals using $\to$ as their underwriting conditional;[2] but, again, there can be languages that have (their own) transparent truth predicate but lack the corresponding T-biconditionals.[3]

On the transparency account, truth is not only 'deflationary,' in the sense of not being some explanatory notion of truth, but is *see-through* in the sense above, namely, that an ascription of transparent truth to a sentence is completely intersubstitutable with the given sentence. In particular, in any theory that contains its own transparent truth predicate (i.e., has a transparent truth predicate in and for the language of the theory), ascribing (transparent) truth to a sentence does nothing more nor less than deliver an equivalent sentence—equivalent in 'semantic status' and entailments (or consequences).[4] The 'disquotationalism' of Quine [22, 23, 24], as reflected in Leeds [15], might be an early precursor (if not pioneer) of a transparency account of truth, though it is hard to tell given that a transparency view normally requires that logic be nonclassical (at least if the truth predicate is in the very language for which it is transparent in the given way). (Quine [22] notoriously suggested that nonclassical accounts of logic (-al consequence) 'changed the subject'.) For more recent defenses and discussion of transparent truth, see [3, 5, 10, 26, 28].

If, as above, a transparent truth predicate is intended to produce, for any sentence A of the language, a sentence B (say, $T\langle A\rangle$) which is equivalent in entailments to A, then the transparent truth predicate appears to express a property that does the work done by a familiar—indeed, as discussed below, *logic's*—sentential truth connective: namely, 'It is true that…'.[5] The familiar truth operator, expressed by the given connective (notation: †), takes any sentence A of the language and produces a sentence (viz., †A) which is exactly equivalent in consequences (entailments) to A itself; and the operator, understood just so, is thereby *redundant* with respect to its consequences—much as Ramsey noted [25]. A truth operator is not 'creative' or in any way 'productive' with respect to new entailments: whatever entailments the language has without the truth operator the language has with them—except for the explicit decorations involving the connective 'It is true that…'. As it turns out, the transparent truth property, unlike the truth operator, is 'creative' and 'productive' (in ways discussed below); but the similarity between the truth operator and the property of transparent truth underlies the sense in which the given property is 'logical.'

2 Deflationary Truth as a 'Logical Property'

Deflationists about truth (whether transparency theorists or otherwise) share a common negative characterization of truth: namely, that it's not itself explanatory but is often useful in expressing or voicing explanations and/or true theories generally— much in the way that logical vocabulary isn't explanatory but is useful in expressing explanations and/or true theories generally.

But then the call comes: 'But what of a *positive* characterization of truth?' And to this the idea of logical vocabulary is often invoked again.

As Jeremy Wyatt observes, "A number of deflationists have claimed that truth is a 'logical' property…. A difficulty here is that those who advance this claim rarely indicate what they take the characteristic features of logical properties to be" [29, p. 376].

And he's right. Very little is said. Wyatt proposes a natural strategy: "To rectify this, we can consider what is perhaps the most influential account of the boundary between the logical and the non-logical, that proposed by Tarski" [29, p. 376].

The Tarski-inspired approach to logical vocabulary invokes a notion of *invariance*—a notion that serves as one mathematical model of logic's 'universality' and 'topic-neutrality.' The trouble is that, as Wyatt and others note [11, 29], Tarski's proposal and the vast majority of variations on it fail to accommodate truth as being invariant (and, hence, logical). And so the challenge of specifying the sense in which deflationary truth is a *logical property* remains. There have been some efforts to meet this challenge by constructing a Tarski-inspired notion of invariance that accommodates truth;[6] however, I suggest a different course.[7]

3   Logical Vocabulary as Universal

Think of theories as so-called closed theories; they are sets of claims closed under a closure relation—a consequence or entailment relation that has standard so-called 'closure' properties. Theories can be thought of as containing two chief ingredients: a seed theory (a set of claims) and a closure relation, where the closure relation 'completes' the theory by adding all consequences of anything that's in the theory.

The task of truth-seeking theorists is accordingly twofold: put truths about the target phenomenon into one's theory, and construct the right consequence (closure) relation for the theory. If one is giving the true (and complete-as-possible) theory of what is known, one adds a bunch of claims (e.g., that $1+1=2$, that it's known that $1+1=2$, and so on). Now, if one tried to complete this theory by closing it only under logic (i.e., logical consequence), the result would be badly inadequate. To begin, claims of the form *It is known that A* would fail to entail *A*; logical consequence treats that 'form' as invalid because there is no logical vocabulary that validates it. The only vocabulary is the knowledge operator, which logic ignores (because it sees only logical vocabulary). This is why the epistemologist must construct an *extra-logical* consequence relation specific to the theory in question, a closure relation that gets the theory-specific entailments right.

What is the difference between *logical consequence* (or logical entailment) and the many, many other consequence (entailment) relations on our language? My answer to this question points to the *role* that logical consequence (i.e., logic) plays in our true theories.

Logical consequence is a closure relation like all of the other closure relations. The difference is that, to echo a long-standing tradition, logical consequence is 'universal' and 'topic-neutral.' Logic's role—unlike any other closure relation—is to be the basement-level closure relation involved in *all* of our true (and complete-as-possible) theories. Consider a picture of our many true (and complete-as-possible) theories:

$$\langle T_1, \vdash_{T1}\rangle, \langle T_2, \vdash_{T2}\rangle, \ldots, \langle T_n, \vdash_{Tn}\rangle$$

Each theory has its own consequence (closure) relation $\vdash_{T_i}$. Where is *logical* consequence in this picture? The answer: it's in each and every theory; it's at the bottom of each and every such closure relation.

On this picture, logic is 'universal' and 'topic-neutral' in straightforward ways: it doesn't matter what your true (and complete-as-possible) theory is about; logic is involved in your theory.

3.1   What Is Logical Vocabulary?

What, then, is *logical vocabulary* on this picture? The logical vocabulary is simply the vocabulary involved in all true (and complete-as-possible) theories; it's the vocabulary recognized by the basement-level closure relation.

3.2   Which Vocabulary Is Logical?

Debate is still open on this question but the answer I give points to a long-standing candidate: namely, the usual stock of first-order vocabulary (sans identity, which has always been controversial). This vocabulary contains the so-called Boolean quartet and the usual pair of (dual) first-order quantifiers:

- Boolean quartet:
  - Unary:
    - Truth operator (nullation): *it is true that...*; notation †.
    - Falsity operator (negation): *it is false that...*; notation ¬.
  - Binary:
    - Conjunction: *...and...*; notation ∧.
    - Disjunction: *...or...*; notation ∨.
- Quantifiers:
  - Universal: *Every object*; notation ∀.
  - Existential: *At least one object*; notation ∃.

And that's it. Any other vocabulary is extra-logical.

One might pause (maybe even flinch) at the listing of logic's truth (null) operator. This operator (or at least its connective, which expresses it) is almost never listed among the stock of *logical* connectives—but that's just because it's logically redundant, a point on which the so-called redundancy theory is absolutely and uncontroversially correct. Logic's truth operator takes a sentence and delivers a logically equivalent sentence. The truth operator is the dual of logic's falsity operator, where logic's falsity operator takes any sentence to its dual.[8]

While it's often omitted from the usual stock of logical vocabulary, logic's truth operator is uncontroversially among the logical vocabulary; it is uncontroversially in the vocabulary of every true and complete-as-possible theory—even if its appearance is usually implicit.

Logic's truth operator is the key to the sense in which (transparent) truth is a logical property. But what are logical properties in the current picture?

4   Two Sorts of Logical Properties

As per section 3.2, there are no predicates in the logical vocabulary (understood as universal, as above). Hence, there's no truth predicate in the logical vocabulary.

On the question of whether truth—in particular, transparent truth—is a 'logical property' a distinction is worth drawing between two sorts of logical properties.

4.1 Logical Properties (Simpliciter)

The first sort of logical property is the obvious one: *a property is logical if it's expressed by a logical predicate*. As there are no logical predicates, there are no logical properties of the first sort.

One might find it dubious that there are no predicates in logic's stock of vocabulary (e.g., it remains controversial whether there's a logical relation of identity—even if the standard presentation of mainstream first-order logic contains a binary predicate serving to express one candidate for a would-be logical identity relation). What matters for present purposes is whether there's a *truth* predicate in logic's stock of vocabulary. If there is, then the given truth predicate is in the language of every true (and complete-as-possible) theory. But there are clear-cut counterexamples against such a universal truth predicate. Witness, for (but one) example, true arithmetic—say, Peano arithmetic—which is closed under so-called classical logic. There is no truth predicate in the language of that theory, and there is certainly no transparent truth predicate— the main focus of this discussion—in that theory.[9] But this doesn't mean that there isn't a clear sense in which truth—indeed, the focus here, *transparent truth*—is a sort of logical property.

4.2 Emergent Logical Properties

For lack of a better term, *emergent logical properties* are a sort of property correlate of logical vocabulary. The term 'emergent logical properties' is not used to suggest that properties of the target sort are somehow epiphenomenal or anything of the sort; the term 'emergent' here is used only to suggest that the given properties emerge directly from some other kind of thing—in the current case, logical expressions (e.g., operators).[10]

Think of emergent logical properties in terms of a prior project:

- Project: give 'property correlates' to each of logic's Boolean operators.
- Desideratum: introduce predicates that are intersubstitutable (according to the theory of the given properties) with the logical connectives to which they correspond.

Example: take logical conjunction (viz., $\wedge$). This connective expresses an operator, not a property. The project at hand is to give a property correlate for the operator. The (binary) predicate, corresponding to the (binary) relation of logical conjunction, should be something intersubstitutable with the connective; and so we introduce (say) the binary predicate $C(x, y)$ via just such a 'transparency' rule. Where $\langle A \rangle$ and $\langle B \rangle$ are suitable names of sentences A and B,

$$C(\langle A \rangle, \langle B \rangle)$$

is intersubstitutable in all (non-intensional) contexts with

$$A \wedge B.^{11}$$

In this way, the predicate C expresses the relation extracted from the given logical operator. Which relation? An obvious answer points to the relation of *being related by logical conjunction*. This is different, of course, from *being a logical conjunction*, which is only a syntactic (unary) relation (for lack of a better term), and in any event is expressed by a unary predicate (viz., 'is a logical conjunction') rather than by the target binary predicate (viz., '...is related by logical conjunction to...'). Given the (transparency) constraint on the 'property correlate' of logical conjunction, the two claims (say)

> Grass is brown

and

> Honey bees are kind

are related by logical conjunction (expressed via C as above) just if their logical conjunction, namely,

> Grass is brown and honey bees are kind,

is true, and so just if both

> It is true that grass is brown

and

> It is true that honey bees are kind

are true, and so—via the logical redundancy of 'it is true that...'—just if both

> Grass is brown

and

> Honey bees are kind

are true, and so—via the transparency of 'is true'—just if grass is brown and honey bees are kind. So, the relation expressed by the 'new' predicate C is the relation exemplified by two claims just when their logical conjunction is true. And that's the 'emergent logical property'—in this case, 'emergent logical relation'—correlated with logic's binary conjunction operator. This is the property (relation) reflected in the transparency rule governing C.

And there is nothing peculiar about logic's conjunction operator. The same 'property correlate' project applies to each bit of logic's vocabulary; but for present purposes I focus on logic's truth operator.

5   Transparent Truth as a Logical Property

Transparent truth, defined by its transparency rule, is an emergent logical property in the sense above (section 4.2); it is motivated directly by logic's truth operator; it is the property correlate of logic's truth operator. Just as with the example of logical conjunction (which is binary), we have a unary property extracted (or abstracted) from logical nullation—that is, logic's truth operator (which is unary)—in such a way that

$T\langle A\rangle$

is intersubstitutable in all (non-intensional) contexts with

$\dagger A.$

And since $\dagger A$ is (according to logic) intersubstitutable with A, we have the usual transparency rule for every theory in which the given predicate (viz., the transparent-truth predicate) appears: $T\langle A\rangle$ and A are everywhere (non-intensional) intersubstitutable.

There is no more to say about the sense in which transparent truth is a logical property beyond its being an emergent logical property so understood. But a few features of the property, in contrast to logic's truth operator, should be highlighted.

5.1 Not Redundant

Logic's truth operator is logically redundant. The property correlate of logic's truth operator—namely, transparent truth—is not redundant in the true theories in which it appears. As deflationists have long emphasized (e.g., with respect to the generalizing role that suitable deflationary truth predicates—certainly transparent predicates—play), there are some claims in true theories that are not expressible in the theories without transparent truth.

That logic's truth operator is redundant in all true (and complete-as-possible) theories, while the corresponding truth property (viz., transparent truth) is not redundant in all such theories, is not a problem for the running account of (transparent) truth's logicality; it's a feature of the work that properties (and the predicates used to express them) can do over operators. To put the point at a linguistic level (not that it needs to be at this level): predicates (over sentences) tend to be more expressive than corresponding (e.g., sentential) operators. Witness the creative difference between the operator 'it is known that...' and the corresponding predicate '...is known'—a creative difference brought out by infamous spandrels of such predicates (see below).

5.2 Spandrels and Paradox

The operator 'It is known that...' takes *sentences* (or propositions or whatever) and makes new sentences; but it demands a sentence before you get a sentence. Predicates are very different, even if they express the property correlates of the operators in question. In particular, '...is known,' as a predicate defined over sentences,[12] takes *names* of sentences (or singular terms denoting sentences, etc.) to make a new sentence; it doesn't require a 'previously existing' sentence to make a new sentence. For example, while there's no way to get the following ticked sentence

✓ The ticked sentence is known

merely from the knowledge operator (I'm assuming that there's no available truth predicate or similar sort of predicate to do the middle work), there is a simple way to get it once the predicate '…is known' is available. (The simple way is just grammar, which counts it as grammatical.)

There is a big creative difference between operators and their property (relation) correlates; and transparent truth is no different. Such properties bring about 'spandrels'—inevitable and often unintended side effects of the given property. (In the case of truth, some spandrels are downright twisted—witness the infamous liar such as 'it is false that this sentence is true,' a construction that doesn't arise from logic's truth and falsity operators on their own. This is why logic's truth operator can be—and implicitly is—in all true theories, even classically closed ones; however, transparent truth is not similarly 'universal.')

In the end, emergent logical properties outreach their logical mate by unleashing spandrels that, in some cases (e.g., truth) put severe limits on the universality of the emergent property.

6   Some Objections and Replies

I've put forward the sense in which transparent truth is a logical property—namely, the emergent logical property understood as the property correlate of logic's truth operator.

6.1   Not General Enough

An objection to the account is that it is not general enough. The account applies only to transparent truth; it will not—at least as given (e.g., in terms of transparency constraints on emergent logical properties)—apply to deflationary truth properties generally.

The reply: true. But this is not a problem for the account; it's a problem for the other accounts of deflationary truth, which have to give their own accounts of truth's would-be logicality if they take it to be a 'logical property' at all.

6.2   Not Metaphysically Interesting

Another objection is that emergent logical properties (relations), understood per above, are not metaphysically interesting properties.

My reply: I am not sure what is involved in the notion of a metaphysically interesting property, but whatever it is, it's likely not something that should apply to a transparent-truth property—or to a suitably 'deflated' truth property generally.

Setting aside whether emergent logical properties are 'metaphysically interesting' it is worth flagging at least one interesting feature of emergent logical properties—namely, their important creative capacities that can (and, in the case of truth, do) impose wide-ranging constraints on our true theories. As per section 5.2, truth not only ushers in spandrels; it ushers in paradoxes that preclude the universality of the property—preclude the property's being expressible in all of our true theories (despite the property's being the direct property correlate of logic's universal truth operator). This constraint, brought about by the creative powers of the transparent property, has spawned a great deal of interesting work on how our true theories can navigate around the property's given constraint.[13] The property of *transparent truth* has the feature *creativity* to a degree that no other properties have, as far as I can tell. In that respect, the property 'has a feature' that may qualify it as 'metaphysically interesting' [29], but I leave that issue to future debate among those who demand 'metaphysical interest' from transparent truth.

7 Concluding Remarks

Deflationism about truth is a many-faced philosophy. A deflationary account of truth must make its face clear. In this paper I've focused on what I take to be the simplest—the purest—form of deflationary truth, namely, transparent truth. A transparency account of truth is 'deflationary' in taking the given property of truth to be non-explanatory. As for a positive account of the property of transparent truth, the usual tag 'logical property' applies, and in turn confronts the question: What's that? What's a logical property? I've aimed to answer that question in this essay. There are many other questions that confront transparent truth; but those questions are left for elsewhere.

Notes

I'm grateful to Jeremy Wyatt for very, very helpful feedback on this essay, both in written comments and via in-person discussion of relevant issues. I'm also grateful to my colleague Michael P. Lynch, who, for as long as I've known him, has pushed against my transparency conception of truth in ways that have made it clearer. Finally, my colleague Lionel Shapiro's work on truth (and logic) has influenced my own views in many ways; to him I remain grateful both for his own work in the area and especially for engagement with my work.

1. The intersubstitutability is not sameness of meaning; it's intersubstitutability with respect to truth or consequence.

2. Just use the transparency rule to substitute an ascription of transparent truth to A—say, $T\langle A\rangle$—into each direction of $A \to A$, getting $T\langle A\rangle \to A$ and its converse.

3. Some common models of transparent truth have the former (viz., a transparent truth predicate for themselves) without the latter (viz., corresponding T-biconditionals). For example, the so-called Strong Kleene model of transparent truth discussed by Saul Kripke [14] is a model of a language with its own transparent truth predicate but devoid of any derived T-biconditionals, since the Strong Kleene language itself is devoid of any conditional $\to$ for which $A \to A$ is true (for all sentences A). On the other hand, extending Kripke's Strong Kleene framework, Hartry Field's

work [10], building in some ways on work by Ross Brady [7] and Anil Gupta and Nuel Belnap [12], models a language with both its own transparent truth predicate and a conditional such that $A \rightarrow A$ is true for all A in the language. Similar (but not the same) issues arise in logically dual models of transparent truth that utilize a so-called LP [1, 2, 20] framework, including work by Jc Beall [3], Bradley Dowden [8], Robert Martin and Peter Woodruff [16], Graham Priest [20, 21], and others. In a different direction, Vann McGee's work [18] is a pioneering sort of 'truth pluralism' that combines the ideas of transparent truth together with the demands for (a separate) 'semantically useful' truth property. Timothy Maudlin's work [17] explores further implications of a transparent truth predicate, as does Leon Horsten's [13].

4. NB: That a consequence or entailment relation in a true theory might go from $P\langle A \rangle$ to a claim about the existence of sentences is not a problem for the transparency of P provided that the consequence relation also goes from any A (even ones that don't explicitly talk about sentences) to $P\langle A \rangle$. Etc.

5. Following standard usage, I use 'connective' and 'predicate' throughout this essay for the expressions in the language's syntax that express operators and relations (or properties), respectively. (This isn't to say that all connectives express operators—that is, functions of a certain sort—but they're the only sort of connectives under discussion.)

6. The recent approach by Bonnay and Galinon [6], which takes up Wyatt's challenge, may work as a way of accommodating the idea that truth is logical (qua a sort of invariance). I think that this approach is the best candidate for those who want to tie the would-be logicality of truth to a Tarski-inspired invariance notion; but I shall suggest a different path.

7. I should emphasize that I think that one clear sense of 'logical property' is given by saying that truth is fully 'characterized by consequence behavior'—that is, that it's a property fully characterized by the entailments in which it figures in true theories. I do not clearly see the need to say more than just that; but philosophers such as Edwards [9], Wyatt [29], and others have argued that more needs to be said if the truth property is to be a 'metaphysically interesting property'—a desideratum not to be readily expected in the work of truth deflationists generally or especially in the work of disquotationalists or transparent-truth theorists. (See section 6 for more on the 'metaphysically interesting' demand.) Even so, this essay aims to say at least a little bit more on how to think of the (transparent) truth property's being 'logical'—at least from a transparent-truth perspective.

8. E.g., $\neg \dagger A$ to $\neg A$, $\neg\neg A$ to $\dagger A$, and similarly $\neg(A \vee B)$ to $\neg A \wedge \neg B$, etc. [4, 19].

9. If Peano arithmetic had a transparent truth predicate in (and for) the language of the theory then the theory couldn't be coherently closed under classical logic (it would 'explode' into the trivial theory, which contains every sentence of the given language of the theory); but true Peano arithmetic is classically (and non-trivially!) closed. If one rejects that true Peano arithmetic is (non-trivially) classically closed, just change the example to some true, classically closed (non-trivial!) theory. (That such true and complete-as-possible theories are closed under classical logic is not to suggest that logical consequence itself—the universal, basement-level consequence relation involved in all of our true theories—is per the classical-logic account. Transparent truth theorists reject as much due to familiar paradox—more on which below.)

10. Stephen Schiffer has written about what he calls 'pleonastic properties' [27]. I think that Schiffer's notion is subsumed by the more general idea of (what I'm calling) 'emergent properties,' but Schiffer's full theoretical framework around 'pleonastic entities' should not be read into the following discussion. (Thanks to Jeremy Wyatt for prompting this note.)

11. Of course, given that logic's truth operator is logically redundant, the transparency rule for C (above) is equivalent to the '†'-adorned rule in which $C(\langle A \rangle, \langle B \rangle)$ is intersubstitutable with $\dagger A \wedge \dagger B$. But what might be useful to recall is that transparent truth (say, T) is itself supposed to be intersubstitutable, and so the rule for C (above) is also equivalent to the 'T'-adorned rule in which $C(\langle A \rangle, \langle B \rangle)$ is intersubstitutable with $T \langle A \wedge B \rangle$.

12. One can put all of this in terms of propositions if one wishes, but the 'creative' difference between operators and predicates remains the same.

13. Beall, Glanzberg, and Ripley [5] give a short introductory survey of some of the interesting work prompted by the emergent logical property of (transparent) truth.

References

[1] Asenjo, F. G. 1966. "A Calculus of Antinomies." *Notre Dame Journal of Formal Logic* 7(1): 103–105.

[2] Asenjo, F. G., and Tamburino, J. 1975. "Logic of Antinomies." *Notre Dame Journal of Formal Logic* 16(1): 17–44.

[3] Beall, Jc. 2009. *Spandrels of Truth*. Oxford: Oxford University Press.

[4] Beall, Jc. 2017. "There Is No Logical Negation: True, False, Both, and Neither." *Australasian Journal of Logic* 14(1). https://ojs.victoria.ac.nz/ajl/article/view/4025.

[5] Beall, Jc, Glanzberg, M., and Ripley, D. 2018. *Formal Theories of Truth*. Oxford: Oxford University Press.

[6] Bonnay, D., and Galinon, H. 2018. "Deflationary Truth Is a Logical Notion." In M. Piazza and G. Pulcini, eds., *Truth, Existence, and Explanation: FilMat 2016 Studies in the Philosophy of Mathematics*, 71–88. Cham, Switzerland: Springer.

[7] Brady, R. 2006. *Universal Logic*. Vol. 109. CSLI Lecture Notes, Stanford, CA.

[8] Dowden, B. H. 1984. "Accepting Inconsistencies from the Paradoxes." *Journal of Philosophical Logic* 13(2): 125–130.

[9] Edwards, D. 2013. "Truth as a Substantive Property." *Australasian Journal of Philosophy* 91(2): 279–294.

[10] Field, H. 2008. *Saving Truth from Paradox*. Oxford: Oxford University Press.

[11] Galinon, H. 2015. "Deflationary Truth: Conservativity or Logicality?" *Philosophical Quarterly* 65(259): 268–274.

[12] Gupta, A., and Belnap, N. 1993. *The Revision Theory of Truth*. Cambridge, MA: MIT Press.

[13] Horsten, L. 2011. *The Tarskian Turn: Deflationism and Axiomatic Truth*. Cambridge, MA: MIT Press.

[14] Kripke, S. 1975. "Outline of a Theory of Truth." *Journal of Philosophy* 72: 690–716.

[15] Leeds, S. 1978. "Theories of Reference and Truth." *Erkenntnis* 13(1): 111–129.

[16] Martin, R. L., and Woodruff, P. W. 1975. "On Representing 'True-in-L' in L." *Philosophia* 5: 217–221.

[17] Maudlin, T. 2004. *Truth and Paradox: Solving the Riddles*. New York: Oxford University Press.

[18] McGee, V. 1991. *Truth, Vagueness, and Paradox*. Indianapolis, IN: Hackett Publishing.

[19] Paoli, F. 2015. "Bilateralism Meets Minimalism." Lecture presented at the CLMPS, Helsinki, August 2015.

[20] Priest, G. 1979. "The Logic of Paradox." *Journal of Philosophical Logic* 8: 219–241.

[21] Priest, G. 2006. *In Contradiction*. 2nd ed. Oxford: Oxford University Press.

[22] Quine, W. V. O. 1970. *Philosophy of Logic*. Upper Saddle River, NJ: Prentice-Hall.

[23] Quine, W. V. O. 1987. *Quiddities*. Cambridge, MA: Harvard University Press.

[24] Quine, W. V. O. 1992. *Pursuit of Truth*. Rev. ed. Cambridge, MA: Harvard University Press.

[25] Ramsey, F. P. 1927. "Facts and Propositions." *Proceedings of the Aristotelian Society* 7(1): 153–170.

[26] Ripley, D. 2012. "Conservatively Extending Classical Logic with Transparent Truth." *Review of Symbolic Logic* 5(2): 354–378.

[27] Schiffer, S. 2003. *The Things We Mean*. Oxford: Oxford University Press.

[28] Shapiro, L. 2011. "Deflating Logical Consequence." *Philosophical Quarterly* 61(243): 320–342.

[29] Wyatt, J. 2016. "The Many (Yet Few) Faces of Deflationism." *Philosophical Quarterly* 66(263): 362–382.

The Prosentential Theory: Further Reflections on Locating Our Interest in Truth

Dorothy Grover

There are charges that deflationists have separated truth from the important issues.[1] It has also been charged that deflationary theories of truth are "philosophically more boring" than might be expected.[2] Such complaints will seem unequivocal to those who locate all that's interesting about truth in a truth property. But arguing from the perspective of a deflationist, I will show why both charges are misconceived. In addressing the first charge, I will demonstrate, for a variety of contexts, the expressibility that a deflationary truth predicate provides. My goal will be to explain *how a* prosentential theorist has the option of subscribing to theses that place importance on truth, should he or she want to do that. This exploration will also serve to show that the *neutrality* of the prosentential theory with respect to the importance of truth is not a *denial* that truth is important. In addressing the second charge, I will remind readers of the challenge that deflationary theories pose for truth-property theories and of the advantage of not encumbering inquiry with the task of identifying a truth property.

1 The Prosentential Theory

I begin with a brief review of the prosentential account of the role of the truth predicate.[3]

I initially employed the concept of a prosentence (introduced by analogy with pronouns) to provide a reading of the anaphoric occurrences of bound propositional variables. Consider, for example, the following formula:

$\neg \exists p$ (Albert believes that p and p).

A reading in English will look like the following:

There is nothing such that Albert believes it is true, and it is true.

More colloquially, we might say this:

Nothing Albert believes is true.

"It is true" is used in providing a reading in English because it can accomplish the same kinds of logical connections that bound propositional variables accomplish, for each provides ways of making the logical connections we need for expressing generalizations. The basic claim of the prosentential theory is that "it is true" and "that is true" function as prosentences in English. Much as pronouns are used for generalizing with respect to nominal positions, so "it is true" tends to be used for generalization with respect to sentence positions. "That is true," on the other hand, tends to be used much as "pronouns of laziness" are used, but whereas a pronoun occupies a position that a noun occupies, "that is true" occupies a sentential position. This means that in simple cases, "that is true" stands in for, and anaphorically connects with, something else that has been said in the context. For example, "that is true" has "December 20 is the longest day" as its antecedent in the following dialogue:

Mary: December 20 is the longest day.

Tom: That is true, but only in the Southern Hemisphere.

Similarly, "she" has the name "Janet" as its antecedent in this context:

   Because Janet likes to ski, she will not want to go hiking with us.

Just as "she" picks up its referent from the name "Janet," so "that is true" will acquire its content from Mary's statement. Tom in effect is saying, but with anaphoric overtones, "December 20 is the longest day, but only in the Southern Hemisphere." This is partially what it is for "that is true" to function as a prosentence. In the above dialogue, "that is true" is used to say (with anaphoric overtones) something about December 20 and not something about a property of a sentence. In this lies an important difference between the prosentential account and those deflationary theories that represent "true" as a metalinguistic predicate. The prosentential truth predicate typically keeps discourse at the level of the "object language,"[4] which means that if extralinguistic matters are being discussed, they remain the topic of discussion when "true" is used. By contrast, other deflationary theories (e.g., Horwich 1990) represent "true" as functioning at the level of the metalanguage.

   Prosentences can be modified, as in, "that was true," "that might be true," and "what is true?" For example:

Tom: That was true last year, but this year the longest day is December 21.

In such simple cases, the modified prosentence can be said to stand in for a modified form of the antecedent, which in this case would be "December 20 is the longest day," while the modified form would be "December 20 was the longest day last year." This prosentential picture serves to explain many pragmatic features of our truth talk, features highlighted in Strawson (1950). For example, in this context, use of "that is true" allows Tom to implicitly acknowledge that it has already been mentioned that December 20 is the longest day. Anaphoric devices seem essential if we are to establish the connections needed for communication, for they facilitate the process whereby different speakers are able to talk about, and know they are talking about, the same things; they also provide logical connections needed for generalization.[5]

I will often appeal to the fact that generalizations have instances. Remember that "it is true" tends to be used for generalization, as in the following:

> I believe all that he said, but if you have reason to think some of it-is-not-true, let us know immediately.[6]

I have found that in those cases where "true" is used to express a generalization, the form of the prosentential reading is often more effectively conveyed (to those with a background of logic) through a paraphrase that uses bound propositional variables. In this case the propositional variable paraphrase could take the following form:

> $\forall p$ (if he said that p, then I believe that p, but if you have reason to think that not p, then tell us immediately)

Its instances will include this:

> Because he said that the nuclear reactor would be safe at the turn of the millennium, I believe it will be safe, but if you have reason to think the nuclear reactor will not be safe at the turn of the millennium, let us know immediately.

I will continue to offer paraphrases using propositional quantifiers and variables.

Just as an account of the functioning of pronouns will be neutral with respect to many philosophical questions, so also the prosentential theory will be *neutral*. That is, the prosentential theory does not itself yield answers to general philosophical questions about meaning and communication, the status of science, realism, and so on.

The prosentential theory has been classified as a deflationary theory, a theory that denies there is (a need for) a truth property. This seems to follow from the fact that deflationary theories claim that the truth predicate has primarily a logical role. For if our use of the truth predicate is explained in some way in terms of anaphora, that is, in terms of "true" as a prosentence-forming predicate, it can no longer be assumed *without argument* that "true" must have a property-ascribing role. The prosentential theory, together with other deflationary proposals, poses a significant challenge for truth-property theorists, for it puts the onus on property theorists to show that the truth predicate ascribes a property.[7] The challenge has been taken seriously. Devitt (1984) and Field (1986), for example, have responded with the suggestion that if truth can be shown to have an explanatory role, then we need a truth property. Accordingly, they have offered suggestions for the explanatory role.

Another wrinkle also needs to be considered. I considered the possibility in Grover (1977) that a property-ascribing role might be "superimposed" on the anaphoric role. There are several reasons why I reject this possibility. First, I have not found an account of a truth property that is plausible, nor do I see a need for a property.[8] This is one reason why I have advanced, and continue to advance, the prosentential alternative. And except in the context of formal languages, I do not see an appropriate identification of the property's bearers. I have now also given reasons for thinking that the problem of inconsistency that seems to arise with Liar sentences is only introduced if a property-ascribing role is everywhere superimposed on the prosentential role (Grover 1977).[9] Since I see no reason to superimpose a property-ascribing role, and good reasons not to, I will continue to classify the prosentential theory as a deflationary theory. The assumption that the truth predicate has only a logical role leaves the relative neutrality of the theory intact. The only exception to the neutrality thesis is that the prosentential theory denies that there is a substantive truth property.

2 Separation

Before beginning my defense that the prosentential theory does not separate truth from interesting and important philosophical issues, I must acknowledge that some aspects of the prosentential theory encourage philosophers to think that truth has been separated from all that is interesting and important. There is the fact that the prosentential theory, along with other deflationary theories, has been referred to as a theory of *truth*.[10] Described as a theory of *truth*, philosophers might reasonably expect the prosentential theory to provide answers to those questions that have been associated with other theories of truth: philosophical questions about meaning, belief, assertion, and the success of science, perhaps. However, as I have explained above, the prosentential theory provides only a theory of the truth predicate and is neutral on theories of meaning, belief, and so on. Denying the need for a substantive truth property also encourages the view that truth has been separated from the important issues, especially among those property theorists who think that no truth property means no truth.

    These features (its classification as a theory of *truth*, its neutrality, and the denial of a substantive truth property) certainly seem to suggest that the prosentential theory must separate truth from the important issues. How, then, can I claim that a prosentential theorist has the option of affirming the importance of truth in the event that he or she might want to?

    My answer appeals to the fact that a prosententialist can accept that we have cognitive attitudes toward what-is-true and toward what-might-be-true, where "true" is read as a prosentence-forming predicate. Indeed, my point will be that those concerned with the importance of truth would do well to use a prosentential predicate in formulating general questions and stating general theses in their approach to the "big" philosophical issues.

    In my first paper on locating our interest in truth (Grover 2001), I respond to Misak's (1998) charges of separation by showing that a prosentential theorist can accept claims like "Our survival depends on having knowledge of what-is-true" and "The goal of inquiry is to determine what-is-true." Note that on a prosentential reading, "what-is-true," just like "Snow is white" and "Electrons carry a negative charge," is ordinarily used to talk about extralinguistic things. The only difference is that "what-is-true" involves a generalization—a generalization like that in "Our survival depends on having knowledge whether *p*, for many *p*." The latter says that our survival depends on having knowledge: perhaps knowledge of the date of the longest day, the charge on electrons, the state of the ozone layer, and so on. Note that the instances of "The goal of inquiry is to determine what-is-true" include "The goal of inquiry is to determine whether December 20 is the longest day." A prosentential theorist can also convey an interest in what-is-true (the truth) by asking questions: Could all human life be destroyed by a nuclear accident? Is the effect of pollution on the ozone layer irreversible? Does music increase intellectual performance? These are questions concerning how the world is, questions that are instances of the question "What-is-true?"

3   What Is a Theory of Truth?

In this section I will show why I think a deflationary theorist can (consistently) explore the "big" issues, even to the extent of endorsing a theory of *truth*. But, first, if the prosentential theory is not a theory of *truth* and the correspondence theory is presumably not either (there being no truth property), where will we find a theory of truth?

In addressing Misak's concerns, I distinguished among *theories of the truth predicate*, *theories of what-is-true*, and *theories of theories of what-is-true*. The prosentential theory, together with theories that advance views concerning the logic of the truth predicate, are theories of the truth predicate. To the extent that science, creative endeavors, and value statements purport to tell us what-is-true—that is, tell us the way the world is—they are each theories of what-is-true. It would go too much against tradition to call theories of what-is-true (for example, scientific theories) theories of truth, but it would not be a mistake to do so.

Theories of theories of what-is-true are better candidates for being called theories of truth. Included are theories that tell us about the status of theories purporting to be theories of what-is-true. For example, they tell us whether theorists who claim to tell us about how the world is do indeed tell us how the world is. Does science tell us what-is-true? Should we follow Strawson (1985) in according legitimacy to the humanistic standpoint that we, as persons, occupy? Philosophy of science is one area of philosophy that yields theories of theories of what-is-true. Theories that address questions as to whether moral statements and literary statements tell us about the world also fall under this heading. So while theories of what-is-true and theories of theories of what-is-true address issues of truth, they do so in different ways. Theories of what-is-true are typically (though not always) concerned with determining how the extralinguistic world is, while theories of theories of what-is-true are concerned with identifying the assumptions of inquiry itself as well as with assessing the methods used to determine what-is-true. The prosentential theory, in its attempt to describe the role of "true," qualifies not only as a theory of the truth predicate but also as a theory of what-is-true; it is not, however, a theory of theories of what-is-true. Theories of assertion and belief, which may make significant appeals to truth, will usually qualify as theories of what-is-true but not as theories of theories of what-is-true, except insofar as they are incorporated in theories of theories of what-is-true.

Note that the debates that arise among theorists of what-is-true and among theorists who assess the status of theories of what-is-true are much more complex than those arising among competing correspondence theorists. The latter focus on language-world connections or meaning, without concern for determining how the world is—that is, without trying to determine, for example, whether electrons have a charge, whether pollution affects the ozone layer, or whether any objects are basic in the physical universe. Of course, issues of language arise in debates among theorists of theories of what-is-true. But this is because issues of language and meaning are intertwined with issues in ontology and epistemology. I borrow a couple of questions from Kuhn (1970, 184) to illustrate the subtleties involved: "Did Einstein show that simultaneity was relative, or did he alter the notion of simultaneity itself? Were those who heard paradox in the phrase 'relativity of simultaneity' simply wrong?" While some of the hardest language questions may arise in our consideration of what-is-true, questions in the philosophy of language are not usually the primary focus of either theories of what-is-true or theories of theories of what-is-true. I assume that the primary focus is to determine whether p (for many p); it is primarily our interest in extralinguistic matters that motivates the task of assessing the subtleties of communication and our assumptions and methodology when determining whether p.

Truth-property theorists may be tempted to jump in and claim that theorists of theories of what-is-true are *really* identifying a truth property of sentences. But this is to miss the prosentential point that our interest in truth amounts to no more or less than our interest in knowing the way the world is. Any focus on sentences, or even utterances, is only a means to this end. Furthermore, I follow Tarski (1936) in thinking that it is only in the context of formal languages that extensions for "true" and "false" can be defined. While formal languages have many important uses and formal language analyses provide invaluable insight into the subtleties and logical structure of natural languages, I believe that they are not stand-alone languages of communication. This is because formal languages have been trimmed of essential features needed for communication.[11] So an extension for "true" in a formal language has limited, though very important, interest.

Some deflationists—for example, Horwich (1990) and Quine (1970, 10–13)—assume that "true" *is* a metalinguistic predicate and that "true" has an extension. I accept this possibility for formal languages. For Quine, at least, it is the canonical language that matters, anyway. As I have argued elsewhere (Grover 1975, 1990a), use of a metalinguistic predicate can be incorporated in the prosentential account. But note, in formal languages, instances of the T-schema, "'p' is true iff p," will be relied on to bring talk of sentences back to talk about the way the world is. We need this connection, facilitated by a deflationary "true," if formal languages are to be useful for more than just symbol-pushing maneuvers.

But let's return to the present focus of our interest in truth. Can deflationists (those who deny there is a truth property) endorse a theory of truth? That is, can deflationists endorse a theory of theories of what-is-true? Certainly they can. Quine's realist view of science (which is quite independent of his deflationary view of the truth predicate) qualifies as a theory of a theory of what-is-true. Consider, for example, the realist view expressed here:

> But I also expressed, at the beginning, my unswerving belief in external things—people, nerve endings, sticks, stones. This I reaffirm. I believe also, if less firmly, in atoms and electrons and in classes. Now how is all this robust realism to be reconciled with the barren scene that I have just been depicting? The answer is naturalism: the recognition that it is within science itself, and not in some prior philosophy, that reality is to be identified and described. (Quine 1981, 21)

Whereas I see Quine as able to defend both a deflationary view of the truth predicate and a view of science according to which it describes the world, O'Leary-Hawthorne and Oppy (1997) think there is an inherent problem. They argue that Quine needs a supersense of truth. (They introduce the supersense of truth as follows: "The 'no super sense' theory claims that, if one has entertained the question whether P and come to a decision, there is no interesting further sorting procedure to be undertaken whether 'P' is true, 'P' correspondences to reality and so on" [O'Leary-Hawthorne and Oppy 1997, 180].[12]) The addition of a supersense of truth contradicts the spirit of Quine's deflationism. O'Leary-Hawthorne and Oppy (1997) make their criticism this way:

> Quine assigns a thin role to the ordinary truth predicate, according to which it is merely a device for generalizing "along a dimension that cannot be swept out by a general term." He also holds there are discourses which do not "limn the truth." Given that we have the same need for generality in those other discourses too, there is considerable pressure here to introduce a supersense of "truth." (181)

I do not know why O'Leary-Hawthorne and Oppy think limning the truth calls for a supersense of truth. I can only think they do not recognize a deflationary "true" in the phrase "limn the truth." Since no bibliographic reference is provided, I asked Peter Hylton for a suggestion. He directed me to a passage in *Word and Object* that probably provides the basis of Hawthorne and Oppy's remark: "If we are limning the true and ultimate structure of reality, the canonical scheme for us is the austere scheme that knows no quotation but direct quotation and no propositional attitudes but only the physical constitution and behavior of organisms" (Quine 1960, 221).

On a deflationary reading, "truth" (in "limn the truth") and "true" (in "limning the true") would be used to express a generalization. If we are "limning the true and ultimate structure of reality," we are providing illumination on the way the world is. For Quine, this is the task of science, for it is science that enlightens us as to whether p: science has the task of telling us whether electrons exist and if they do, whether they have mass, and so on. And so I interpret Quine as recommending that his austere canonical language be the language of inquiry into what-is-true, the language of science.

The fact that Quine's remarks can be interpreted as employing a deflationary truth predicate shows that he can consistently be a deflationist while at the same time endorsing a view according to which we should look to science to determine what-is-true. Because Quine can use a deflationary predicate to state his position that science determines whether a proposition is true, he remains consistent with the no-supersense position. So, though Quine has significant views about truth (he has a theory of theories of what-is-true), this is consistent with his deflationary view. Having said this, I am fully aware, as I mentioned earlier, that the task of determining whether p (for any p) is very complex, raising in the long run, as it does, the deepest of issues in metaphysics, epistemology, and language.

4   Linguistic Competence and the Concept of Truth

How might a prosententialist respond to criticism that claims that "the concept of truth" is important? This question arises because O'Leary-Hawthorne and Oppy use the phrase "the concept of truth" throughout their commendable critique of deflationary theories. Consider how they identify a version of a minimalist view of truth:

> One such candidate is that "is true" has a thin conceptual role: *mere possession of the concept of truth* contributes little or nothing to our understanding of the structure of reality and our relationship to it. The most radical version of this thesis will maintain that our grasp of other central cognitive concepts—belief, assertion, meaning, proposition, statement, translation, synonymy, fact, declarative sentence, negation, propositional connective, deep structure, logical form, semantics, etc.—is never explained in terms of the concept of truth; it will maintain further that deployment of the concept of truth does not, in and of itself, immediately commit us *a priori* to any interesting metaphysical theses. (1997, 174)

And then for the purpose of distinguishing further versions of minimalism, O'Leary-Hawthorne and Oppy raise the following questions.

> How much does our understanding of various aspects of our conceptual scheme depend on our grasping the concept of truth? Does the making of judgments at all require possession of the concept of truth, as the Fregean idea of judgment—as advancement from thought to truth value—might suggest? Does a grasp of logical laws depend upon possession of the concept of truth? (1997, 178)

Philosophers who talk of a concept of truth assume concepts must be grasped if a property-ascribing predicate is to be properly applied. As deflationists deny that there is a truth property, they will also deny there is such a concept of truth. Because the property theorist's concept-of-truth talk is not easily adapted to the deflationist context, I need to find some other avenue of common ground if I am to provide a constructive response to O'Leary-Hawthorne and Oppy's remarks. They think that aspects of linguistic competence (a grasp of cognitive concepts, making judgments, a grasp of logical laws) require a grasp of the concept of truth.[13] For comparison, I will delineate two ways in which a prosententialist might appeal to an understanding of true and "what-is-true" in assessing linguistic competence.

We can certainly understand or fail to understand use of the truth predicate. For while most of us use the predicate appropriately, there could be people who do not have "true" in their vocabulary. Young children come to mind, since just as there will be a stage at which a child cannot use pronouns satisfactorily, so she may not be able to use "true" correctly. So my first suggestion for drawing a comparison will be that a speaker can be judged to have a certain level of linguistic competence when she has mastered our use of the word "true," as well as use of its derivatives.

Connecting back to the specific remarks of Hawthorne and Oppy, we can note that such an understanding "contributes little or nothing to our understanding of the structure of reality." For just as our understanding of pronouns does not give us insight into the structure of reality, so also our understanding of how to use the word "true," in itself, does not give us insight into the structure of reality. Nor will this feature (lack of insight) suffice for separating off a version of minimalism, because all deflationists will agree that an understanding of the use of "true" does not lead to special insights. But deflationists will claim that the theoretical understanding that we offer of "true" as having a logical role will help us sort through philosophical issues that have previously been encumbered by truth-property talk.

I remarked earlier that a prosententialist can use the truth predicate to talk about cognitive attitudes toward what-is-true and what-might-be-true. We can know what-is-true, wonder if we believe what-is-true, try to assert only what-is-true, be confused as to what-is-true, question whether p, for some p, and so on. We can also question whether a speaker can determine what is true on any occasion; that is, we can question whether a given speaker is able to determine whether p, for some p.

On occasion, some of us have trouble determining the difference between fantasy and reality, but there can be more serious failures. I have in mind cases where there is a complete failure to distinguish between what-is-true and what-is-false. This would mean that the speaker cannot tell whether snow is white, whether grass is green, whether she has a bank account, and so on. This seems to be the situation with people who have been referred to as *chatterboxes* or *blatherers* (Pinker 1994, 50–54).[14]

Chatterboxes have been described as "linguistic idiot savants—people with good language and bad cognition" (Pinker 1994). They can speak in syntactically well-formed sentences, string sentences together to make a story, and have impressive vocabularies, but they have limited cognitive contact with reality. There are reports of a 14-year-old who "chats on" about the trouble she has been having with the bank, the bank statements she has received, a joint account she has with her boyfriend, plans to go and talk with the bank, and so on. But she doesn't have a bank account or a boyfriend. Indeed, chatterboxes are described as being "incompetent at ordinary tasks like tying shoes, telling left from right, adding two numbers, drawing a bicycle, suppressing their natural tendency to hug strangers" (Pinker 1994, 52). So though chatterboxes string sentences together in a relatively coherent way, their interactions with the world are seriously undeveloped. These cognitive shortcomings seem to show that chatterboxes have little or no *propositional knowledge*.

With respect to the issues to hand, it would seem possible that a chatterbox might correctly follow the syntax of "true" and "false" to the extent that she can create well-formed sentences containing these words, perhaps as a parrot or robot might. But there is an important sense in which she hasn't really latched onto language. For if a chatterbox could not tell whether p, for any p, it would seem she could not have a goal of speaking the truth. This in turn would suggest that she could neither be described as making assertions, nor as knowing what counts as an answer to a question. Being able to determine, for at least some instances, whether snow is white, grass is green, and so on is clearly an essential ingredient of acquiring cognitive attitudes. (I assume that linguistic competence at the level of making assertions and asking questions involves the acquisition of other cognitive abilities.)

There is now a better match with the concerns of O'Leary-Hawthorne and Oppy. They think our grasp of cognitive concepts is to be explained in terms of the possession of the concept of truth—an ability to apply the truth predicate. Analogously, a prosententialist has the option of endorsing the thesis that a competent speaker must be able to tell whether p, for some p. That is, linguistic competence requires propositional knowledge, knowledge of some truths. O'Leary-Hawthorne and Oppy's implied claim that possession of the concept of truth contributes to our understanding of reality also has an analogue. A prosententialist has the option of endorsing the trivially true thesis that a speaker must be able to tell what-is-true in at least some instances if she is to "understand the structure of reality and our relationship to it."

It is interesting to note a contrast at this stage. In my first example I hypothesized that at a certain stage a child might have some communication abilities but not have either "true" or "false" in her vocabulary. If the child's communication skills are otherwise reasonably developed, it would be sensible to say that she knows whether p for at least some p. In the case of chatterboxes, the reverse happens. A chatterbox may (in some limited sense) have "true" and "false" in her vocabulary but not be able to tell whether p, for any p. The former may be linguistically competent, while the latter is not.

Note a difference between O'Leary-Hawthorne and Oppy's property-ascribing account of linguistic competence and the one I am proposing. O'Leary-Hawthorne and Oppy seem to think that linguistic competence depends on our having grasped the concept of truth, which means (I am supposing) that we should know when sentences or statements have the property of being true. But the example of the child who is acquiring language shows that a speaker might be reasonably linguistically competent yet not have "true" in her vocabulary. The prosentential account opens up the alternative that linguistic competence requires that a speaker be able to determine whether p, for some p. That is, a linguistically competent speaker should be able to determine, in a "sufficient number" of cases, whether snow is white, whether grass is green, whether she has a bank account, and so on. There is no requirement that "true" be included in the speaker's vocabulary or, in O'Leary-Hawthorne and Oppy's sense, that there be a grasp of the concept of truth.[15]

Once again, we have seen that a prosentential theorist can employ the truth predicate in talking about interesting and important issues. Not only can we can describe cognitive attitudes in terms of attitudes toward what-is-true, what-might-be-true, and so on. We can adopt, for example, the view that we are linguistically competent only if we have an ability to question and/or assert what-is-true.

5 Explanatory Role

Another charge that has often been made (in the context of the charge that deflationists separate truth from interesting issues) is to the effect that can make no appeal to truth in an explanation of the success of science.

O'Leary-Hawthorne and Oppy (1997) present this particular concern as a hypothetical scenario, as follows:

> Suppose, for example, that science is converging on truth. Must it be simply illegitimate to explain the success of science in terms of this convergence, no matter what the context? ... Bald claims about the non-explanatory value of truth are normally accompanied by little more than a few examples. What we need is a theory of explanation which sets clear standards of explanatoriness and which provides some general account of why it is that truth cannot meet those standards. (182)

O'Leary-Hawthorne and Oppy assume that deflationists deny that truth has an explanatory role in the hypothesized situation in which science converges. Certainly, deflationists have denied that convergence in science would show an explanatory role for a truth property. I, for one, have criticized Putnam's argument (1978, lectures II and III) that convergence in scientific theories is best explained by a correspondence account of truth and Field's (1986) attempts to discover an explanatory need for a correspondence truth property.

Initially, those who subscribed to the thesis that "true" ascribed a property tended to make the following inference:

The word "true" is used in (scientific) explanation.

So truth is a property with an explanatory role.

But such an appeal ignores the alternative of a deflationary reading of the word "true."[16] And so, initially, I responded by pointing out the possibility of a prosentential reading. Prompted by O'Leary-Hawthorne and Oppy's remarks, I now elaborate on the prosententialist position by showing that deflationists can certainly hold that truth can be important in explanations. Rather than construing explanations as appealing to a truth property, deflationists can construe explanations as appealing to what-is-true (the way the world is) and/or cognitive attitudes we have toward what-is-true, what-might-be-true, and so on.

Recall that prosentences function a bit like pronouns (when used anaphorically) and bound variables. One thing this means is that truth talk ordinarily proceeds at the level of the object language, rather than at the level of a metalanguage: truth talk is ordinarily (but not always) used to talk about how the extralinguistic world is. This feature of a prosentential account of "true" will be most pertinent in my account of truth in explanations, just as it has been in the other cases considered.

Let us consider an example. Suppose, with respect to a certain subject matter (like cooking), that Sally's predictions are true, while Blake's are sometimes false. And suppose that the explanation of this difference is that Sally's relevant assumptions are true, while some of Blake's relevant assumptions are false. (It might be that Sally has more cooking experience and so she is able to predict on the basis of knowledge, while Blake has little experience and must make wild guesses.[17]) To make the prosentential structure explicit, I rephrase so that the word true is used in the prosentence "it-is-true."

1. Each relevant assumption Sally makes, when predicting what will enhance the flavor of a dish, is such that it-is-true. (Using propositional variables and omitting a few details, we can write this as follows: for any p, Sally assumes that p only if p.)

2. At least one relevant assumption Blake makes, when predicting what will enhance the flavor of a dish, is such that it-is-false. (There is a p, Blake assumes that p, and not p.)

3. Each prediction Sally makes with respect to flavor is such that it-is-true, while at least one of Blake's predictions is such that it-is-false. ((For any p, Sally predicts that p only if p) and (there is a q, Blake predicts that q, and not q).[18])

Because quantifiers bind the prosentences, we need to examine an instance of this explanation to see what is going on. Suppose that Sally and Blake have been asked to predict whether it makes a difference to the flavor of a dish if the garlic is sliced or minced. Then we have the following argument:

a. Based on experience, Sally knows that sliced garlic enhances the flavor of soup, pasta, and fish dishes better than minced garlic does, and these are her assumptions.

b. Making a wild guess, Blake assumes that it makes no difference to the flavor of dishes whether garlic is sliced or minced. (Blake wonders if minced garlic might have the edge since recipes usually suggest using minced garlic, but then he also wonders if this suggestion is made in the interest of providing an easy recipe.)

c. Sliced garlic enhances the flavor of soup, pasta, and fish dishes better than minced garlic.

d. Sally's prediction is that sliced garlic enhances the flavor of a bean casserole better than minced garlic. Blake predicts that sliced garlic is no better than minced garlic.

e. Sliced garlic enhances the flavor of a bean casserole better than minced garlic.

The task was to explain why Sally's predictions are true and Blake's are false. The explanation is that Sally's assumptions are based on relevant experience and are true, while Blake's are not so based and some of his assumptions are false. But note that in (a) through (c) of the explanation "true" is not used. Rather, we learn something about each of the following:

- The assumptions that Sally and Blake make
- The extralinguistic context in which Sally and Blake made their predictions: the enhanced flavor that results from using sliced garlic, rather than minced garlic, in soup, pasta, and fish dishes
- The cognitive basis on which Sally made her assumptions: her knowledge of the effects that sliced and minced cloves of garlic have on flavor[19]
- The cognitive basis on which Blake made his assumptions: his limited knowledge of cooking with garlic

I believe that causal, statistical, or (just) plausible connections are implicitly appealed to also. These might concern constancy in the effects of sliced and minced garlic on the flavor of a range of dishes.

The list contains no use of a truth predicate because I replaced the bound occurrences of the prosentence "it-is-true" in (1) through (3) with sentences not containing prosentences (for example, with "sliced garlic enhances the flavor of soup better than minced garlic"). So the prosentential reading has explanations like the above, appealing to worldly details and cognitive attitudes toward the way the world is or might be. In contrast to property theorists' accounts, the prosentential account keeps the explanation in the object language, so to speak.[20]

Does absence of the use of the word "true" mean that truth does not have a role in the explanation? Not quite, because we require that an explanation only appeal to what-is-true. In my example, (1), (2), (a), (b), and (c) should tell us what-is-true. So when we evaluate an explanation, we *do* pay attention to *truth*: we want to know what-is-true; we want to know what features of the world serve to explain the explanandum. It is in at least this sense that truth is important in explanations.

I doubt that these grounds suffice for saying truth has an *explanatory role*.[21] But even if we were to say that truth has an explanatory role in the sense just delineated, I would not yet have addressed the challenge that O'Leary-Hawthorne and Oppy posed. For the above would assign truth an explanatory role in *every* satisfactory explanation. O'Leary-Hawthorne and Oppy focused on a role that the truth property is said to have in only a select group of explanations.

The challenge was to explain why Sally's predictions were true and Blake's false. This is where a property theorist jumps in with the claim that the truth property explains why it is that Sally comes up with a true prediction and Blake does not. It is not just a question of it being true that Sally made certain assumptions; the assumptions themselves are true. But, of course, for a prosentential theorist, saying that Sally's assumptions are true is not to characterize her assumptions as having the property truth. In my example we have premises like this:

Sally assumed that sliced garlic enhances the flavor of soup better than minced garlic does, and it-is-true.

This says, but without the anaphoric overtones, something like the following:

Sally assumed that sliced garlic enhances the flavor of soup better than minced garlic does, and sliced garlic enhances the flavor of soup better than minced garlic does.

The prosentential reading presents the explanation as appealing not only to the fact that Sally made a certain assumption but also to features of the world (what-is-true). There is also an appeal to the circumstances under which Sally adopted the assumptions she makes.[22] Truth has a role in explanations not because we appeal to an explanatory truth property but because we appeal (among other things) to features of the world we consider relevant to the world's being as predicted. An appeal to a truth property would provide an irrelevant detour.

Some opponents to this prosentential account may wish to focus on the fact that Sally's assumptions did not come out of the blue but were arrived at through experience. It was not just by chance that she had the assumptions she had and that her assumptions were true. Sally had relevant knowledge. This suggests that there is an appeal in the explanation to connections between her cognitive attitudes and how things are in the world.[23] Perhaps there are, somewhere here, the language-world connections that correspondence theorists have tried to characterize. But the issues seem far from those of the correspondence theorist: the question as to whether Sally's assumptions are wild guesses, or evidentially based, is surely an issue for epistemologists; correspondence theorists have characteristically addressed issues of meaning.

I suggest that the proposed explanation of the success of science would come out similarly. (I will not address the issue of convergence, because I do not know what philosophers are trying to capture with this concept.) Let us suppose a simple case in which the laws of the science and the observations of the scientists are all true. The explanation of the fact (if it is a fact) that the science yields true predictions will thus appeal to the fact that science has laws that tell us what-is-true and also to the fact that the reported observations of scientists tell us what-is-true. As far as I can see, nothing would be gained by introducing an appeal to correspondence properties of the sentences that state the laws or describe the observations.

While I have not addressed many other questions and doubts that critics have expressed of deflationary theories, I hope that the above succeeds in presenting a slightly less sketchy account of how it is that a prosentential theorist has the wherewithal to take a position on the importance of truth. This in turn should also show that the approach of deflationists would help philosophers think more clearly about issues that most of us regard as central in philosophy.

Notes

I thank Jerry Kapus for his insightful criticisms and suggestions on an earlier draft of this paper.

1. In a very interesting paper on deflationism and pragmatist truth, Misak (1998) has charged deflationists with separating truth from the interesting and important issues.

2. O'Leary-Hawthorne and Oppy (1997, 170).

3. Readers who are unfamiliar with the prosentential theory are referred to Grover (1992) for a better introduction. I also recommend Robert Brandom's account of the theory, together with his elaborations (1994, 301–333).

4. I put "object language" in shudder quotes because, unless we are employing a formal language, the phrase is used metaphorically. I use "metalinguistic language" similarly.

5. While several of my early papers (reprinted in Grover 1992) cover details of the prosentential thesis, there remains much work to be done in working out the syntactical details, as Wilson (1990) has ably shown. It is a little reassuring to know that the syntax of pronouns has not yet been adequately explained either.

6. I use the hyphens to emphasize a prosentential reading of the truth predicate.

7. I do not mean to suggest that only property theorists must argue for their assumptions.

8. I must admit that a problem I have in responding to correspondence theorists in general is that I do not really know what would qualify as a correspondence theory. I think (as undoubtedly everyone does) that sequences of marks on paper and sequences of sounds do acquire properties as they come to be used for communication. It would be helpful to have more information about which among these provide the kind of property that correspondence theorists seek.

There have been suggestions for a correspondence property, but I have not found them satisfactory. In Grover (1990), I presented a critique of Field's suggestion. Field's theory has the same language-world connections for true and false sentences. I have always assumed that a correspondence theory would have different language-world connections for true and false sentences. Kirkham (1992) and David (1994) define correspondence truth in terms of "obtains," but neither of them explains "obtains." This is a serious omission because "obtains" serves as a replacement for "true." (My reviews of their books, in Grover [1995] and Grover [1997], raise this difficulty.) The shortcomings of Russell's proposals are well known.

Deflationists are left with only the constructive approach: that of showing how well philosophers are served by a deflationary truth predicate.

9. But see Kapus (1991) for a critique of my claims. I am not persuaded by his argument that inconsistency threatens the prosentential theory because I reject his assumptions with respect to content. I leave my defense until such time as I have developed my ideas on language.

10. Though I myself have referred to the prosentential theory as a theory of truth, I now think that doing so was misleading. I return to this issue in the next section.

11. I am presently working on a project that addresses some of the differences between formal and natural languages.

12. Note that O'Leary-Hawthorne and Oppy's "*P*" is used differently from my lower-case "*p*." Their "*P*" is (almost always) a placeholder in schemas. Instances of the schema are generated through substitution of sentences for "*P*."

13. I am assuming that O'Leary-Hawthorne and Oppy think the answer is "Yes" to the questions "Does making judgments at all require the possession of the concept of truth ...?" and "Does a grasp of logical laws depend on possession of the concept of truth?"

14. I thank my colleague Charles Chastain for having drawn my attention to this literature several years ago.

15. A dogged property theorist may respond with the charge that a speaker cannot know that snow is white, for example, unless she knows that white *applies* to snow. What's the role of "applies"? This question reintroduces the debate between deflationists and property theorists, but this time the focus will be on "applies."

16. Not everyone is guilty; see, for example, Devitt (1984). O'Leary-Hawthorne and Oppy also appreciate that something more is needed since they attempt to establish a truth property.

17. I have space to consider just the one scenario, but there are variations on this example that could be entertained. For example, we might suppose that Sally and Blake have the same background of experience and yet Sally's predictions are true and Blake's false. It might then be explained that Sally comes up with better hypotheses and why. Or it could be that Blake has a poor memory or that he pays little attention to the flavor of food.

18. Not having expertise in the subject of explanation, I can only surmise that there must be a significant connection between events appealed to in the explanation and the event being

explained. In the present case, Sally's prediction of enhanced flavor cannot be explained in terms of Sally's (true) beliefs that $2+2=4$, and $3+7=10$. An explanation must presumably be based on assumptions that make it reasonable that she arrived at the predictions she does. I have used "relevant" to cover whatever features must be included.

19. I assume that Sally has relevant knowledge. If she had only been able to make wild guesses, then we might say that there is no explanation for her success beyond being lucky. I also assume that the effect of garlic on bean dishes is somewhat similar to its effect on other dishes.

20. This is how I construe this kind of explanation. Of course, there are explanations of linguistic matters in which one will want to appeal to "metalinguistic" properties.

21. Again, not having expertise in the area of explanation, I am inclined to accept the suggestion that properties are the only candidates for an explanatory role.

22. By contrast, for the property theorist, there is an appeal in the explanation of the fact that Sally's assumption is characterized as being true; truth, as a property, performs some explanatory work.

23. It is difficult for me to develop a stronger case for the opposition because, as I have mentioned in an earlier note, I am not quite sure how the correspondence theory is supposed to go. Because I do, of course, think that there are connections between the extralinguistic world and our acquiring language and cognitive attitudes, I cannot try to forestall correspondence theorists by claiming that language-world connections have *no* place in explanations. For example, perhaps a version of the causal theory of perception will feature in some explanations of the predictions of Sally and Blake. Whichever way this might come out, my guess is that the situation is much more complex than any correspondence theorist has so far represented it. As Jerry Kapus has said in a comment (personal communication) in this section of the paper, there are matters here that all of us have to address.

References

Brandom, R. B. 1994. *Making It Explicit: Reasoning, Representing, and Discursive Commitment.* Cambridge, MA: Harvard University Press.

David, M. 1994. *Correspondence and Disquotation: An Essay on the Nature of Truth.* Oxford: Oxford University Press.

Devitt, M. 1984. *Realism and Truth.* Princeton, NJ: Princeton University Press.

Field, H. 1986. "The Deflationary Conception of Truth." In G. Macdonald and C. W. Wright, eds., *Fact, Science, and Morality: Essays on A. J. Ayer's Language, Truth, and Logic*, 83–107. Oxford: Blackwell.

Grover, D. 1977. "Inheritors and Paradox." *Journal of Philosophy* 74: 590–604. Reprinted in Grover (1992).

Grover, D. 1990a. "On Two Deflationary Truth Theories." In M. Dunn and A. Gupta, eds., *Truth or Consequences: Essays in Honor of Nuel Belnap*, 1–17. Dordrecht: Kluwer Academic Publishers. Reprinted in Grover (1992).

Grover, D. 1990b. "Truth and Language-World Connections." *Journal of Philosophy* 87: 671–687. Reprinted in Grover (1992).

Grover, D. 1992. *A Prosentential Theory of Truth*. Princeton, NJ: Princeton University Press.

Grover, D. 1995. Review of *Theories of Truth: A Critical Introduction*, by Richard Kirkham. *Philosophy and Phenomenological Research* 55: 3.

Grover, D. 1997. Review of *Correspondence and Disquotation*, by Marian David. *Journal of Symbolic Logic* 62: 326–328.

Grover, D. 2001. "On Locating Our Interest in Truth." In R. Schantz, ed., *What Is Truth?*, 120–132. Berlin: de Gruyter.

Grover, D, Camp, J. L., and Belnap, N. D. 1975. "A Prosentential Theory of Truth." *Philosophical Studies* 27: 73–124. Reprinted in Grover (1992).

Horwich, P. 1990. *Truth*. Oxford: Blackwell.

Kapus, J. 1991. "The Liar and the Prosentential Theory of Truth." *Logique et Analyse* 34: 283–291.

Kikham, R. L. 1992. *Theories of Truth: A Critical Introduction*. Cambridge, MA: MIT Press.

Kuhn, T. S. 1970. *The Structure of Scientific Revolutions*. Chicago: University of Chicago Press.

Misak, C. 1998. "Deflating Truth: Pragmatism vs. Minimalism." *Monist* 81(3): 407–425.

O'Leary-Hawthorne, J., and Oppy, G. 1997. "Minimalism and Truth." *Noûs* 31(2): 170–196.

Pinker, S. 1994. *The Language Instinct*. New York: William Morrow.

Putnam, H. 1978. *Meaning and the Moral Sciences*. London: Routledge and Kegan Paul.

Quine, W. V. 1960. *Word and Object*. Cambridge, MA: MIT Press.

Quine, W. V. 1970. *The Philosophy of Logic*. New York: Harper and Row.

Quine, W. V. 1981. *Theories and Things*. Cambridge, MA: Harvard University Press.

Strawson, P. F. 1950. "Truth." *Proceedings of the Artistotelian Society*, suppl., 24: 129–156.

Strawson, P. F. 1985. *Skepticism and Naturalism: Some Varieties*. New York: Columbia University Press.

Tarski, A. 1936. "The Concept of Truth in Formalized Languages." In A. Tarski, ed., and J. H. Woodger, trans., *Logic, Semantics, Metamathematics: Papers from 1923–1938*, 152–278. Oxford: Clarendon Press, 1956.

Wilson, K. 1990. "Some Reflections on the Prosentential Theory of Truth." In J. M. Dunn and A. Gupta, eds., *Truth or Consequences: Essays in Honor of Nuel Belnap*, 19–32. Dordrecht: Kluwer Academic Publishers.

21 A Defense of Minimalism

Paul Horwich

My objective in this chapter is to clarify and defend a certain "minimalist" thesis about truth: roughly, that the meaning of the truth predicate is fixed by the schema, "The proposition *that p* is true if and only if p."[1] The several criticisms of this idea to which I wish to respond are to be found in the work of Davidson, Field, Gupta, Richard, and Soames, and in a classic paper of Dummett's. But before addressing these criticisms let me begin by saying something more about the thesis itself.

Consider biconditionals like

<snow is white> is true ↔ snow is white

and

<lying is wrong> is true ↔ lying is wrong[2]

—that is, instances of the *equivalence schema*

<p> is true ↔ p

It can be argued that such biconditionals are *epistemologically fundamental*—we do not arrive at them, or seek to justify our acceptance of them, on the basis of anything more obvious or more immediately known. It can be argued, in addition, that our underived inclination to accept these biconditionals is the source of *everything else* we do with the truth predicate. For example, from the premises

What he said is that he was abducted

and

What he said is true

we are prepared to infer

He was abducted

This particular use of the word "true" is explained by supposing that we first employ Leibniz's Law to get from our pair of premises to

<He was abducted> is true

and then invoke the relevant instance of the equivalence schema. And, more generally, it can be made plausible that no further fact about the truth predicate—nothing beyond our allegiance to the equivalence schema—is needed to explain *any* of our ways of using it. It is for this reason that we are entitled to conclude that the meaning of "true" is determined by that schema. For, plausibly, the property of a word that constitutes its having the particular meaning that it has should be identified with the property that explains the *symptoms* of its possessing that meaning—and these symptoms are the various characteristic ways in which the word is used.[3] Thus my minimalist thesis is the product of two prior claims: first, that our underived endorsement of the equivalence schema is explanatorily fundamental with respect to the overall use of the truth predicate; and second, that the meaning of any word is engendered by the fact about it that explains its overall use.

This line of thought can be challenged at various points and no doubt stands in need of considerable further support.[4] But my main aim here is not to defend my *route* to the minimalist conclusion, but rather to defend that conclusion itself: namely, that the meaning of "true" stems from the equivalence schema. For most of the recent objections to this thesis do not target any particular rationale for it, but purport to demonstrate that the thesis itself cannot be correct. However, before addressing these objections, let me help to prepare the ground for my replies to them by saying a little more to clarify just what the proposal is, and is not, intended to encompass.

Several different kinds of theory, with very different explanatory objectives, might appropriately be labeled "theories of truth." So it is important to be clear about what sort of theoretical work the minimalist proposal is not meant to do and should not be blamed for failing to do. In the first place, it is not intended to provide an *explicit definition* of the word "true," neither descriptive nor stipulative; it does not offer a way of re-articulating the contents of sentences containing the word; indeed, it implies that no such reformulations are possible.[5] In the second place, the proposal does not amount to a substantive *reductive theory* of the property of being true—something in the style of "water is H_2O"—which would tell us how truth is constituted at some underlying level. Again, it suggests that the search for such a theory would be misguided. And in the third place, it is not a "theory of truth" in the sense of a set of fundamental theoretical postulates on the basis of which all other facts about truth can be explained.[6] Its immediate concern is with the *word* "true" rather than with truth itself. It purports to specify which particular non-semantic fact about that word is responsible for its meaning what it does; and the fact it so identifies is, roughly speaking, the role of that word in the equivalence schema.

Now let me turn to an array of objections. I will look at one difficulty raised by Hartry Field, three devised by Anil Gupta, one due to Mark Richard, a couple that I put to myself, an old but still influential objection of Michael Dummett's, and two posed by Donald Davidson. My discussion of each of these problems will be brief—merely indicating the lines along which I think the response should be given, rather than giving it in full. In some cases these responses will be somewhat concessive—involving certain significant adjustments of the minimalist thesis.

Objection 1: The minimalist proposal would leave it mysterious how we are able to attribute meanings to sentences that predicate truth of *untranslatable* foreign statements. If an utterance V is known to mean (say) *that dogs bark*, then (according to the proposal) the sentence "V is true" (or "V expresses a truth") might be interpreted as saying roughly *that dogs bark*. However, given an utterance, U, that cannot be translated into our language, the proposal enables us to attach no meaning at all to "U is true"—even though it surely *would* be meaningful. So the minimalist proposal is defective. (Field[7])

But, as I stressed from the outset, the minimalist form of deflationism does not offer an explicit or contextual definition of "true": it does not purport to provide a way of reformulating or re-articulating the content of each sentence containing the word "true." On the contrary, it insists that no such a thing is possible. So one cannot reasonably complain that the minimalist proposal fails to yield a conceptual analysis of the sentence "U is true."

One certainly *could* complain if the proposal implied that this sentence lacked meaning—but it has no such implication. It aims to specify the underlying use-property in virtue of which the truth predicate means what it does. To that end, it identifies certain deployments of that predicate as explanatorily fundamental and hence meaning-constituting—namely, those that appear in instances of the equivalence schema. But other tokens of the word may perfectly well have the very same meaning, as long as their deployment is partially explained by the fundamental ones. Thus if a person reasons inductively to "U expresses something true" on the basis of the fact that the other assertions of the speaker—those that *can* be translated—have turned out to be true (where that depends on the equivalence schema), then that person uses the truth predicate with a constant meaning, one that is engendered by the schema.

Objection 2: The equivalence schema is not strong enough to identify the meaning of the truth predicate, because exactly parallel schemata are satisfied by predicates that do not mean the same as "true." For example, instances of the schema, "<p> is true-and-not-red ↔ p," are just as obviously correct as instances of the equivalence schema (since, obviously, no proposition is red). But "is true and not red" is not a strict *synonym* of the truth predicate. More generally, the schema, "<p> is f ↔ p," will be endorsed relative to a variety of predicates, "f," that possess somewhat different meanings from one another; therefore, for no given "f," can it be that our acceptance of instances of "<p> is f ↔ p" is what fixes the meaning of "f." (Gupta[8])

Indeed. However, according to minimalism, what fixes the meaning of the truth predicate is *not* merely our *allegiance* to the equivalence schema but, in addition, the fact that this allegiance is the use that is explanatorily fundamental—i.e. the fact that our endorsement of the equivalence schema is the *basic law of use* for "true", accounting for its overall deployment. Certainly there are parallel schemata, constructed with other predicates in place of "true", that are no less acceptable. However, in every such case our commitment to the schema is not what explains the predicate's overall deployment; rather, that commitment is itself explained by the predicate's meaning-constituting use.

For example, our acceptance of instances of "<p> is glub ↔ p"—where "glub" abbreviates "true and not red"—is a consequence of three more basic commitments: (i) our endorsing the equivalence schema for "true", (ii) our accepting "No proposition is red", and (iii) our accepting "x is glub ↔ x is true and not red". The meaning of "glub" is given by (iii), rather than by the "glub"-schema. Only in the case of the *truth* predicate does the schema capture what is explanatorily basic in our usage of the predicate. So only in *that* case is the schema meaning-constituting.

Objection 3: The minimalist proposal implies *either* that the word "true" will never be fully understood *or* that the meaning of each person's truth predicate depends on, and varies with, whatever else is in his vocabulary. For the proposal is tantamount to the definition:

x is true ≡ [x = <dogs bark> & dogs bark; or
                  x = <pigs fly> & pigs fly; or
                  … and so on]

Therefore, if the "and so on" is intended to cover *all* propositions, then—since some of them must involve concepts that no one possesses—the meaning of "true" will not be fully known to anyone. And if, alternatively, the definition of each person's truth predicate is supposed to cover only those propositions he himself can currently grasp, then, as new concepts are deployed and new terms coined, his definition of "true" will change. But neither of these alternative implications of minimalism is acceptable. Surely our understanding of the truth predicate is both complete and constant. (Gupta[9])

Agreed. But my proposal is perfectly consonant with such intuitions, because it is not at all equivalent to the above alleged definition. As already emphasized, the minimalist thesis does not offer anything like an explicit definition. Rather it purports to specify the fact of usage that provides the truth predicate with its meaning. That fact of usage, it claims, is the explanatory role of our inclination to accept instances of the equivalence schema—a fact that remains fixed as the rest of our language evolves. So, for example, at the moment that the term, "tachyon," enters our language, we become inclined to accept

<tachyons go backwards in time> is true ↔ tachyons go backwards in time.

But this is merely one more application of a single and invariable regularity—our inclination to accept any instance of the schema that we understand. That inclination preceded the introduction of the term "tachyon" and was in no way altered by it. Thus the minimalist thesis implies neither that the meaning of the word "true" can't be fully grasped, nor that it changes with expansions of our vocabulary.[10]

Objection 4: Our reliance on the equivalence schema will not suffice to explain our commitment to *general* facts about truth. Consider, for example, "All propositions of the form, <p→p>, are true." No doubt our *particular* logical convictions of that form, together with our acceptance of the equivalence schema, can explain, *for any single proposition*, why we take it to be true that this proposition implies itself. Thus we can explain, given our logical commitment to "dogs bark→dogs bark," why we also accept "The proposition *that dogs bark→dogs bark* is true." But we have not thereby explained how the above *generalization* is reached. Therefore our allegiance to the equivalence schema does not really suffice to account for *all* uses of the truth predicate. So that practice does not fix the meaning of "true," contrary to what the minimalist maintains. (Gupta, Soames[11])

Granted, if all uses of "true" are to be accounted for, it will not be enough *merely* to cite our allegiance to the equivalence schema. Further explanatory premises will be needed. But this is an obvious and familiar point. Note, for example, the reference above to our acceptance of "dogs bark→dogs bark" in explaining why we accept "The proposition *that dogs bark→dogs bark* is true." That is perfectly consistent with minimalism because the further explanatory factor makes no mention of the word "true." So perhaps the present objection can be defused in the same way?

In other words, it remains to be seen whether or not the extra factors needed to account for our acceptance of *generalizations* explicitly concern the word "true." Only if they do can one conclude that the explanatorily adequate regularities of use governing "true" must go beyond our underived acceptance of "<p> is true ↔ p"—so that minimalism is defective. But we have been given no reason to think that this is so. On the contrary, there is good reason to suspect that it isn't so.

Suppose it were the case that whenever anyone is disposed to hold, concerning each F, that it is G, then he comes, on that basis, to believe that every F is G. Our disposition to accept, for each proposition of a certain form, that it is true would then suffice to explain our acceptance of the generalization, "Every proposition of that form is true."

Now this particular response to the objection can't be right as it stands, because the proposed extra explanatory premise is glaringly incorrect. It is *not* always the case that having shown, for each F, that it is G, one will inevitably come to the belief that all Fs are G. After all, such demonstrations may well coincide with the mistaken conviction that not all the Fs have been considered. Imagine, for example, that someone mistakenly suspects that there are mountains higher than Everest. He might nevertheless be able to show, of every actual mountain, that it is no higher than Everest; but he does not believe the generalization that all mountains have that property.

However, a modified version of this strategy is much more promising. Let us restrict the proposed extra premise to kinds of entity, F, and properties, G, that satisfy the following condition:

> We cannot conceive of there being additional Fs—beyond those Fs we are disposed to believe are G—which we would not have the same sort of reason to believe are Gs.

This restriction is satisfied when (a) it is essential to our conception of the Fs to maintain that all Fs result from the application of certain operations to certain basic Fs (thus Fs might be propositions, numbers, or sets); and (b) given any such F, there is a uniform way of proving it to be G.

Thus a more plausible version of our extra premise would run along the following lines:

> Whenever someone is disposed to accept, for any proposition of structural type F, that it is G (and to do so for uniform reasons) then he will be disposed to accept that every F-proposition is G.

And this will do the trick. We are indeed disposed to accept, for any proposition of the form, $<p \rightarrow p>$, that it is true. Moreover, the rules that account for these acceptances are the same, no matter which proposition of that form is under consideration. So it is now possible to infer that we accept that all such propositions are true, and hence to explain why we do so.

Thus we have a sound explanatory premise which, in conjunction with our commitment to "$<p>$ is true $\leftrightarrow$ p," will enable us to explain our acceptance of generalizations about truth. And since that premise does not mention the word, "true," the need for it does nothing to suggest that the basic (hence, meaning-constituting) use of it must exceed the bounds set by minimalism.[12]

Objection 5: Certain people (mostly philosophers) do *not* in fact have a completely general inclination to endorse the equivalence schema. Some hold that ethical pronouncements fail to yield acceptable instances. Others take that view of contingent statements about the future, or of applications of vague predicates to borderline cases, or of sentences containing empty names. But all these people nevertheless mean the same thing as we do by the word "true." After all, we might argue with them about "Whether ethical pronouncements can be true?"—yet each of us expresses the issue in just that way. Consequently, it cannot be that to understand the English truth predicate one must have an inclination to accept *every* instance of the schema. (Richard[13])

Notice that the present objection is not that certain instances of the equivalence schema actually *are* incorrect, or that some of them are unhesitatingly rejected by everyone. The point rather is that even if someone—perhaps, mistakenly—has no inclination to *accept* a certain class of instances he might nonetheless *understand* them exactly as we do. And so we have to conclude, it would seem, that an endorsement of the *general* schema is *not* what provides the word "true" with its meaning.

But this conclusion is unwarranted. For we can invoke *social externalism* in order to reconcile our minimalist thesis with the facts under consideration. The rough idea is that a word is a social entity with a certain public meaning, and each member of the linguistic community can (if he wants) deploy the word with that meaning—even if his own usage of it diverges radically from everyone else's. What fixes that shared meaning is the basic use that *predominates* within the community (or, in the case of a technical term, within the sub-community in which it is deployed). After all, it is such "predominant basic use" that translation mappings are attempting to preserve.

Now, our word "true" is not a merely technical term. And most people's use of it is unaffected by philosophical fretting, so tends to be governed by the *full* equivalence schema. Therefore, its shared meaning derives from that characteristic. And even those few who are inclined to reject certain instances of it are nonetheless using the truth predicate with that shared meaning.

Objection 6: But what about the notorious *paradox*-inducing instances of the schema— e.g. the one that results from applying it to the statement *that this very statement is not true?* It is easy to prove that such instances lead to contradiction. As a consequence, many of us have learned not to accept them. Indeed, most people, *were* they to grasp the relevant proofs, *would* agree that those instances are unacceptable. Thus our meaning what we do by "true" does not require us (or most of us, or the "experts" among us) to have a disposition to accept *every* instance of the equivalence schema.

It seems to me that this point is correct, but not devastating. One way of accommodating it is to concede that the meaning of "true" does not derive from an *entirely* unrestricted equivalence schema. Rather, it might be said, the basic meaning-constituting practice is merely to accept patently nonparadoxical instances—instances concerning propositions, like <snow is white> and <lying is wrong>, that make no mention of truth. Given these, we are then tempted to generalize and to accept *all* instances of the schema. But when this conclusion is found to lead into contradiction, the retreat back to a more constrained schema need involve no revision of the meaning-constituting use of "true."

However, there's an alternative strategy—one that strikes me as preferable. Instead of linking the meaning of "true" with the disposition to wholeheartedly accept a certain restricted class of instances, we might link it with the *defeasible inclination* to accept *any* instance. We might suppose that, in paradoxical cases, this inclination is over-ridden; but that it nonetheless continues to exist—sustaining the sense of paradox.

Objection 7: Mightn't there be a linguistic community in which the very existence of truth is widely debated—in which some people are disposed to accept some (or all) instance of their equivalence schema—"<p> is schmoo ↔ p"—but some reject it altogether, and most are simply not sure? And isn't it natural to report them (as I just did) as questioning the reality of *truth*? Wouldn't their word "schmoo" mean exactly the same as our "true"?

If so, then the social externalism of meaning will not suffice to rescue minimalism. The moral will be, rather, that there must be some way of using "true" that (a) is implicit in, but *weaker* than, an endorsement of the equivalence schema, (b) is displayed by the community of truth-debaters and by ourselves, and (c) constitutes what we communitites mean by that word. And this conclusion would seem to be at odds with minimalism.

However, there is a natural minimalist way to implement it. We must appreciate that even the truth-sceptics are prepared sometimes to *suppose for the sake of argument* (what they do not actually believe) that certain things are "schmoo." And when they do this, they will proceed—within the context of this supposition—to "accept" their equivalence schema. In addition, when they suppose, again merely for the sake of argument, that *some* schema of the form, "<p> is Φ ↔ p", holds, they will be prepared to infer (relative to that supposition) instances of "<p> is schmoo ↔ p." Moreover, we non-skeptics also follow these rules—but using "true" instead of "schmoo."[14] Thus we have here a way of deploying the equivalence schema that is shared by skeptics and non-skeptics alike, and this is what we can take to provide the truth predicate with its meaning.

Objection 8: Truth is valuable: we ought to pursue it and we ought to avoid false belief. But these normative sentiments are not contained in (nor can they be extracted from) instances of "<p> is true ↔ p," which merely tell us *when* beliefs possess the property of being true, and are completely silent on the question of whether its possession is desirable. Consequently, our concept of truth is not fully captured by the equivalence schema; so the minimalist proposal is false. (Dummett[15])

On the contrary, the equivalence schema *is* able to account for the value of truth. To see this, consider specific norms of belief such as

It is desirable that (one believe *that wombats fly* ↔ wombats fly)

Clearly our commitments to norms like this one have nothing to do with the concept of truth; for that concept is completely absent from their articulation. Nor is there any reason to suppose that the concept of truth will need to be deployed in explaining *why* we accept them.

Let us then imagine that all such specific normative commitments are somehow explained.[16] Suppose, that is, we can account for our attachment to all norms of the form

It is desirable that (one believe *that p* ↔ p)

Given our a priori knowledge of the equivalence schema, we will then be able to explain our attachment to every norm of the form

It is desirable that (one believe <p> ↔ <p> is true)

that is, to every norm of the form

It is desirable that (one believe x ↔ x is true)

But this engenders (via the mechanism discussed in the response to Objection 4) a commitment to the generalization

(x) (It is desirable that (one believe x ↔ x is true)

—or, in English, to the principle

It is desirable to believe what is true and only what is true

Thus the value we attach to true belief is explained by the role of truth as a device of generalization—which is itself explained perfectly by the equivalence schema.

Objection 9: The minimalist proposal implies that the meaning of the word, "true", depends on the meaning of the expressions, "the proposition that ..." For someone's acceptance of, for example, "The proposition *that Hesperus rotates* is true if and only if Hesperus rotates" manifests a standard understanding of the truth predicate only to the extent that its component, "The proposition that ...", is being understood in the standard way. Thus minimalism implies that one must *already* understand "that"-clauses—i.e. one must understand sentences of the form "u expresses the proposition *that p*"—in order to be in a position to acquire the concept of truth. But this surely gets things the wrong way round! Surely the intimately related notions of meaning and proposition must be analysed in terms of truth (or better, perhaps, must be *replaced* by truth-conditional notions). More specifically, we must suppose that, insofar as there are any facts of the form

u means (says, expresses the proposition) *that p*

they consist in facts of the form

u is true (i.e. expresses a truth) if and only if p

Thus truth is conceptually prior to meaning, contrary to what is required by the minimalist proposal. (Davidson[17])

Davidson gives three reasons for thinking that TRUTH is a more basic concept than MEANING.

First, he infers it from the idea that there are sentences (such as "That is red") whose meaning-constituting assertibility conditions are to accept those sentences only when they are *true*.

But this inference involves several mistakes:

(1) It neglects the fact that, for each specific sentence, "p", of that special sort, the assertibility condition is, "One should accept 'p' only if p"—in which *the concept of truth is not deployed*. This concept is needed only by the theoretician who wishes to

make the *general* point that there are sentences of that kind (i.e. to be accepted only when true). It isn't needed to formulate any particular assertibility condition.

(2) His rationale wrongly presupposes that meaning-constituting regularities of use are *explicitly* known by the speakers of a language. Even if the truth predicate *were* to be needed in order to articulate the fact about a person that underlies her understanding of some word, we could not conclude that she herself would have to possess the concept of truth.

(3) Davidson confuses the conditions for understanding particular non-semantic sentences, like "That is red," with the real issue here—namely, the conditions for understanding "that"-clauses, for grasping the concept of "proposition". Remember that his thesis was that one cannot have the concept of meaning without possessing the concept of truth. Thus the issue is *not* whether one can have various non-semantic concepts—such as "red"—without the concept of truth.

Davidson's second stated reason for thinking that TRUTH is conceptually prior to MEANING is that *someone's affirmation of a sentence can be justified only if he believes that the sentence is true.* Thus it would seem that the concept of ASSERTIBILITY CONDITION—i.e. of when one is justified in assenting to a sentence—presupposes the concept of truth. And, in that case, one cannot go along with a deflationary order of explanation: which would go from assertibility conditions, to meanings, to truth.

But, in fact, this sequence of conceptual dependencies coheres perfectly well with the normative constraint on public affirmation, to which Davidson calls attention. For note first that S's believing *that "p" is true* is equivalent to S's accepting the sentence, "'p' is true," which, given deflationism, correlates with S's accepting "p". In addition— and this is the basic norm here—S *should* assent publicly to "p" only if he privately accepts it. It then follows, as Davidson says, that S should assent to "p" if and only if he believes it to be true. However, the just-given account of why this norm holds does not preclude that the meanings of terms be constituted by the conditions in which sentences containing them are (or should be) accepted.

It might be protested that what we call "accepting" a sentence is simply a matter, as Davidson would say, of "holding it true." So, relative to the deflationist's "acceptance-conditions" account of meaning, it may appear that the notion of truth is, after all, prior to the notion of proposition. But this use of the term, "holding true," is a somewhat misleading one, given that the intended commitment—"holding"—is to a sentence that does not contain the truth predicate. The notion needed here is simply that of *relying on* a sentence as a premise in inference (both theoretical and practical), and that psychological role may be explicated without bringing in the notion of truth.[18]

Davidson's third motivation is his attachment to a direction of explanation which goes from (i) facts about the circumstances that cause the acceptance (= "holding true") of sentences, to (ii) facts about their truth conditions, to (iii) facts about their meanings.

But among the many obstacles to working out such an idea there is one that has proven notoriously difficult to navigate around. The problem is to articulate a conception of "truth condition" that is strong enough. For, given a *material* construal of "if", "p" may very well be true *if and only if* q, without *meaning* that q. And stronger construals of "if and only if" merely make the counterexamples slightly harder to construct.[19]

Objection 10: "That"-clauses cannot be regarded as referring expressions, because there is no way of seeing how their referents would be determined by the referents of their component words. Therefore, sentences like "The proposition *that Hesperus rotates* is true", insofar as they are construed as predicating truth of the propositions to which "that"-clauses refer, are in fact unintelligible. But if such truth ascriptions (so construed) are unintelligible, then the minimalist proposal cannot be correct. (Davidson[20])

Davidson's basis for maintaining that alleged referents of "that"-clauses would not be determinable by the referents of the parts of these clauses is that—as Frege observed—substitution of co-referential terms (e.g. putting "Phosphorus" in place of "Hesperus") within a "that"-clause occurring in some sentence (e.g. "Mary believes that Hesperus rotates") will not always preserve the sentence's truth value. But why does he not continue to follow Frege's line of reasoning, and conclude that an expression within a "that"-clause does not have its *standard* referent, but instead refers to the *meaning* (i.e. "sense") of that expression? Why not identify the referent of "that Hesperus rotates" with the meaning of "Hesperus rotates" and identify the referents (in that context) of the contained words "Hesperus" and "rotates" with *their* meanings?

The reason given is that the meanings of words in "that"-clauses are just their normal meanings. After all, we understand "The proposition that Hesperus rotates" only if we understand the isolated sentence "Hesperus rotates." And in the biconditional, "The proposition *that Hesperus rotates* is true ↔ Hesperus rotates," the two occurrences of "Hesperus rotates" are clearly supposed to be understood in the same way. But in that case—since meaning determines reference—how could words in "that"-clauses fail to have their standard referents? And if they do have their standard referents then "that"-clauses cannot refer, since what would be determined by those standard referents would be the *wrong* thing (e.g. "that Hesperus rotates" would acquire the same referent as "that Phosphorus rotates").

However, there's a pretty obvious response to this anti-Fregean story. We can simply deny that meaning *all by itself* determines reference. We can allow—and this, of course, is completely uncontroversial—that the referent of a term is fixed in part by the *context* in which it occurs. More specifically, we might say that the admittedly uniform meaning of "Hesperus" yields one referent (the planet) for standard (non-opaque) occurrences of the word, and that it yields a different referent (the meaning, or sense, of "Hesperus") for occurrences of the word within the context of a "that"-clause.

It's worth emphasizing that although our Fregean response is far from problem-free, it is not being introduced ad hoc, merely for the sake of a certain theory of truth. After all, ordinary language is full of "that"-clauses (e.g. in attributions of belief). And there is no available strategy for dealing with them that is evidently less problematic than Frege's—namely, to suppose that they designate entities (nowadays called "propositions"), and that each of our "attitude" attributions asserts that a certain psychological relation (of believing, or conjecturing, or stating, etc.) holds between a person and one of these entities (so designated).

Finally, the question arises, if one *were* to prefer a non-Fregean semantics for "that"-clauses, why it could not be deployed by minimalists? Consider, for example, an approach suggested by Davidson's "paratactic" analysis of "S says that p."[21] We might interpret

The proposition *that Hesperus rotates* is true

as

The proposition expressed by *this*—Hesperus rotates—is true

—where "Hesperus rotates" is uttered as an aside. Thus the equivalence schema would become:

The proposition expressed by *this* (- p -) is true $\leftrightarrow$ p.

Or, along similar lines, we might reformulate it as:

The proposition expressed by the *immediately following* sentence-token is true $\leftrightarrow$ p[22]

Therefore, even if Davidson's squeamishness about Fregean "that"-clauses were correct—and my first response argued that it is not—the minimalist proposal can be salvaged. For its truth schema may be articulated in one of the two ways just mentioned.

The *full* minimalist picture of truth includes considerably more than the thesis I have been defending in this chapter. It involves, besides the present claim about how the meaning of "true" is constituted, an affiliated view about the *function* of the truth predicate (namely—as illustrated in response to Objection 8—that it is merely a device of generalization), an affiliated view about the *underlying nature* of truth (namely, that there is no such thing), and an affiliated view about the general shape of the basic theory that will best explain all the facts about truth (namely, that its postulates are instances of the equivalence schema). I have not attempted to elaborate or establish these further minimalist doctrines. However, since what I have been concerned with here is the central component of minimalism, my defense of that thesis, if successful, provides important support for the view as a whole.[23]

Notes

This chapter is a considerably revised version of a paper published, under the same title, in M. Lynch, ed., *The Nature of Truth* (Cambridge, MA: MIT Press, 2001), which was itself a revision of an earlier paper, written for the conference on Truth that took place in Leuwen in 2000, and published with the other conference papers in V. Halbach and L. Horsten, eds., "Truth," special issue, *Synthese* 126 (2001): 149–165.

1. For a thorough discussion of the relationship between *deflationism* and *minimalism* about truth, see "Varieties of Deflationism," in Horwich, *Truth-Meaning-Reality* (Oxford: Oxford University Press, 2010), 13–34. But here, for convenience, is a summary. Deflationism is the somewhat vague idea that truth is not a "substantive" property, that no reductive theory of it should be anticipated, and that our grasp of the truth predicate comes from our appreciation of the trivial way that each statement specifies its own condition for being true. But philosophers who sympathize with this general point of view disagree amongst themselves about how best to elaborate it. Minimalism is one such strategy—the one defended here and previously articulated in my *Truth*, 2nd ed. (Oxford: Oxford University Press, 1998). Besides minimalism, the main alternative forms of deflationism about truth are: (1) *disquotationalism*, according to which sentences (rather than propositions) should be regarded as the bearers of truth, and the schema, "p" is true ↔ p, will be the core of what defines the truth predicate; (2) *prosententialism*, which denies that "true" is a genuine (logical) predicate, and which stresses instead the analogy between a pronoun and "That is true" (insofar as both inherit their content from some other contextually salient expression); (3) *the redundancy theory*, whereby "The proposition *that p* is true" means exactly the same as "p"; (4) *the sentence-variable analysis*, which analyses truth-talk in terms of quantification into sentence positions—"x is true" means "(∃p)(x = <p> & p)"; and (5) *Tarski's theory*, which explains the truth of each sentence of a language in terms of the referential properties of its components (characterized disquotationally) and the logical structure in which they are embedded. The relative advantages of the minimalist version of deflationism are elaborated in "Varieties of Deflationism." In a nutshell, its merits are that (a) it deals with our *actual* concept of truth, rather than some allegedly superior one; (b) it does not attempt to explain truth in terms of notions that should themselves be explained in terms of truth (e.g. substitutional quantification); (c) it recognizes that there is no call for an *explicit* definition of truth; (d) it can countenance the attribution of truth to propositions whose logical forms we do not know; and (e) it does justice to the role of truth as a device of generalization.

2. "<p>" abbreviates "the proposition that p"; and "↔" is the *material* biconditional.

3. This view of how meaning-constituting properties are to be identified is an instance of the general idea that an underlying property U constitutes a relatively superficial property S when U's being co-extensive with S explains why possession of S has the symptoms that it does. My speaking of S as being *constituted* by U in those circumstances, rather than as being *identical* to U, requires a fine-grained conception of "property" whereby two predicates stand for the same property only when they have the same meaning. This way of speaking does not preclude also deploying a more coarse-grained conception whereby, if fine-grained property U constitutes fine-grained property S, then each of them is associated with a single coarse-grained property.

4. For justification of the claim that the equivalence schema is explanatorily fundamental, see *Truth*, 50–51. For justification of the use theory of meaning, see my *Meaning* (Oxford: Clarendon Press, 1998), chap. 3; *Reflections on Meaning* (Oxford: Oxford University Press, 2004), chap. 2;

and "Regularities, Rules, Meanings, Truth Conditions, and Epistemic Norms," in *Truth-Meaning-Reality*, 113–142.

5. To claim that "x is true ↔ x is F" is the explicit definition of the truth predicate (where "F" might be replaced with "in correspondence with reality," "verifiable," "useful," etc.) is to claim that our acceptance of such a principle is explanatorily fundamental with respect to our overall use of that predicate. But such a claim is incompatible with the minimalist thesis according to which it is rather our endorsement of the equivalence schema that is explanatorily basic.

6. There is, however, a plausible theory of truth itself that is closely affiliated with the minimalist account of the meaning-constitution of the word, "true." Arguably, the axioms of the fundamental theory of truth itself—those that will provide the best explanation (i.e. simplest derivation) of all facts about truth—are instances of "<p> is true ↔ p." For (a) such axioms would appear to suffice (in conjunction with theories of other matters) to explain every other fact about truth; and (b) it is hard to imagine a simpler body of principles on the basis of which those instances could themselves be explained. For further discussion see *Truth*, 25–31, 50–51.

7. H. Field, "Critical Notice: Paul Horwich's *Truth*," *Philosophy of Science* 59 (1992): 321–330. The importance of being able to attribute truth to untranslatable statements has been emphasized by Stewart Shapiro. See his "The Guru, the Logician, and the Deflationist," *Noûs* 37 (2003): 113–132.

8. This objection was put to me by Gupta in October 1992, and appears in note 17 of his "Deflationism, the Problem of Representation, and Horwich's Use Theory of Meaning," *Philosophy and Phenomenological Research* 67 (November 2003): 654–666.

9. A. Gupta, "A Critique of Deflationism," *Philosophical Topics* 21 (1993): 57–81; and his "Minimalism," *Philosophical Perspectives* 7 (1993): 359–369.

10. A further objection of Anil Gupta's—one that I *do* think is correct—is that our underived endorsement of the equivalence schema will not explain our refusal to apply truth to things such as Julius Caesar (i.e. it won't explain our confident acceptance of sentences like "Julius Caesar was not true"). To accommodate this point we can suppose that the explanatorily-basic, meaning-constituting facts about "true" include, not merely our underived allegiance to the equivalence schema, but also our underived acceptance of the principle, "Only propositions are true".

11. Gupta, "Minimalism." This objection has also been forcefully articulated by Scott Soames in his "The Truth about Deflationism," in E. Villanueva, ed., *Philosophical Issues*, vol. 8 (Atascadero, CA: Ridgeview, 1997), 1–44. See also P. Casalegno, "Some Remarks on Deflationism" (unpublished paper, University of Milan). A version of the problem was raised by Tarski in section 5 of "The Concept of Truth in Formalized Languages," in *Logic, Semantics, Metamathematics: Papers from 1923 to 1938* (Oxford: Oxford University Press, 1958), 152–278.

12. For an extended response to the above "generalization" problem, see "A Minimalist Critique of Tarski," in *Truth-Meaning-Reality*, 79–98.

13. M. Richard, "Deflating Truth," in Villanueva, *Philosophical Issues*, 8:57–78. See also M. Richard, *When Truth Gives Out* (Oxford: Oxford University Press, 2008), for further elaboration of his anti-minimalistic perspective.

14. This idea (generalized from TRUTH to other meanings) is elaborated in section 5 of "Ungrounded Reason," in *Truth-Meaning-Reality*, 197–224.

15. M. Dummett, "Truth," *Proceedings of the Aristotelian Society* 59(1) (1958–1959): 141–162.

16. I would argue that the basis for our commitment to these specific norms is both *pragmatic*—insofar as we are more likely to get what we want if we abide by them—and *moral*—the value of truth for its own sake. For more, see my "The Value of Truth," in *Truth-Meaning-Reality*, 57–78.

17. D. Davidson, "The Folly of Trying to Define Truth," *Journal of Philosophy* 87 (1996): 267–278.

18. See my *Meaning*, 84–86, for a sketch of how this can be done.

19. For further discussion of this final point see "Deflating Compositionality," in *Reflections on Meaning* (Oxford: Oxford University Press, 2005), 201, and "Semantics: What's Truth Got to Do with It?," in *Truth-Meaning-Reality*, 143–166.

20. D. Davidson, "The Folly of Trying to Define Truth," *Journal of Philosophy* 93 (1996): 263–278.

21. He proposes that "S says that dogs bark" be construed as "S's utterance same-says *that*. Dogs bark."—where the demonstrative in the speaker's supposed first sentence refers to the subsequent utterance of "Dogs bark." See Davidson's "On Saying That," collected in his *Inquiries into Truth and Interpretation* (Oxford: Oxford University Press, 1984), 93–108.

22. Clearly these formulations still trade in *propositions*! However, Davidson is careful to emphasize that his complaint about minimalism is *not* its commitment to such things. His point, rather, is that *if* they exist, then the logical form of what designates them must be "The proposition expressed by u" (instead of "The proposition that p"). Perhaps he would be prepared to analyze this along the lines of "The class of utterances that *same-say* u".

In addition to Davidson's critique of minimalism, which focuses on the way that propositions are *designated*, there are several objections to the very *existence* of propositions—objections that a minimalist must be able to rebut. The main ones are (1) that propositions lack satisfactory identity conditions; (2) that *false* propositions do not exist (because any actual combination of objects and properties would amount to a *fact*); (3) that propositions are ontologically weird and explanatorily unnecessary. For discussion of some of these issues, see the end of "Varieties of Deflationism." For a more complete discussion see *Truth*, 86–97, 106.

23. I am most grateful to Harry Field and Michael Lynch for their feedback on the material here.

22 A Substitutional Theory of Truth, Reference, and Semantic Correspondence

Christopher Hill

I will begin by sketching a deflationary theory of truth that I present in greater detail in an earlier work, *Thought and World* (Hill 2002). The principal target of the theory is the concept of propositional truth—that is, the concept that figures in claims like *the proposition that snow is white is true*. The theory that I will sketch is deflationary in that its centerpiece is a logical concept, the notion of substitutional quantification. I hope the present sketch will make the theory more accessible.

After presenting this substitutional account of truth, I will show how to extend it so as to encompass semantic relations. My main targets will be reference and semantic correspondence, construed as a relation between propositions and facts or states of affairs; but as I will show, it is possible to generalize the account I will give of these two relations to include others, such as the relation that a general concept bears to the property it expresses. Since my analysis of semantic relations is based largely on substitutional quantification, it can be combined easily with the earlier account of truth to provide a fully general theory of truth conditional semantic properties. I call the resulting theory *semantic substitutionalism*, or *substutionalism* for short.

Now if substitutionalism is sound, our truth conditional semantic concepts are *thin* concepts. Most of their content derives from substitutional quantification, which (as I will argue) is closely related to ordinary objectual quantification, and therefore counts as a logical device. Many people, however, have thought that concepts like truth, reference, and semantic correspondence are *thick* concepts, possessed of a robust share of empirical meaning, and this has led them to reject deflationary theories like substitutionalism. After presenting substitutionalism, I will consider this opposing view at some length. In some cases, it derives from a desire to "naturalize" concepts and propositions by reducing them to more basic phenomena, such as words and sentences in a language of thought, and/or a desire to naturalize semantic properties and relations by reducing them to properties and relations that are manifestly empirical. In other cases, the objection derives from the perception that semantic concepts play essential and substantial roles in laws of nature, and therefore in the explanations of empirical phenomena that the laws support, together with the companion view that this would be impossible unless semantic concepts were substantive concepts with a full share of empirical meaning. I will argue that these sources of the opposing view fail to provide it with an adequate rationale. To be sure, substitutionalism makes no effort to "naturalize" semantic relations: it makes no attempt to reduce them to empirical relations like causation and information. As we will see, however, it undercuts the perception that there is a *need* for reduction of semantic relations by showing that they can be fully explained in terms of notions that are transparently legitimate. It removes the main grounds for metaphysical or epistemological concern about the relations. Moreover, substitutionalism is fully capable of accounting for the role that semantic concepts play in laws of nature, and therefore in the explanations that invoke those laws.

There are other sources of the idea that semantic concepts are empirically robust that I will not be able to discuss in the present essay. One of these additional sources is the perception that we can best explain the intuitions that motivate semantic externalism, such as the intuition that the ability to refer to water presupposes that an agent stands in a causal or informational relation to actual samples of water, by supposing that reference is reducible to an empirical relation like causation or information. I criticize this perception in *Thought and World*. Another important source is the view that it is reference and other relations that provide us with our cognitive purchase on specific portions of extramental reality, together with the view that this would be impossible unless semantic relations were empirically robust. I discuss this view in "How Concepts Hook onto the World."

Although I will be much concerned with propositions, I will generally use the term "thought" in place of the term "proposition," hoping thereby to avoid some ambiguities. In my view, thoughts are the things that serve as the objects of propositional attitudes, and that are expressed by sentences when we use them to make assertions. Further, following Frege, I take thoughts to have a mereological structure—for example, I take the thought that snow is white to consist of the concept *snow*, the concept *white*, and a predicate-forming device corresponding to the word "is." A thought is individuated in part by its logical organization and in part by the concepts that serve as its constituents. I will not offer a detailed theory of concepts, but will presuppose that it is somehow possible to explain how concepts are individuated in terms of long-armed conceptual roles. More specifically, I will presuppose that concepts are individuated in part by core aspects of their internal cognitive roles and in part by the roles they play in encoding information about the external world.

I A Substitutional Theory of Truth

Paul Horwich explains truth in terms of thoughts that have the following form:

(T) The thought that p is true just in case p.

To be more precise, he offers an implicit definition of truth that has infinitely many clauses, one for each of the thoughts of form (T) (Horwich 1998). This theory can account for many fundamental facts about the concept of truth. Consider, for example, the fact that we have a priori knowledge of (1):

(1) The thought that love is blind is true just in case love is blind.

Horwich's theory can easily explain this fact: (1) is a component of a definition, so *of course* it can be known a priori. But more: unlike Tarski's theory, Horwich's account can explain why (1) is a triviality—that is, why we can come to know it without drawing on a complex theory of syntax, and without engaging in laborious argumentation.

Unfortunately, despite having these virtues, Horwich's theory is inadequate. As is inevitable, given that it offers only an implicit definition, it fails to fix the extension of the concept of truth. What is much worse, it is incapable of explaining our a priori appreciation of certain generalizations about truth—for example, the generalization that a disjunction is true just in case at least one of its disjuncts is true. If one is to explain our knowledge of this generalization, one must show that it can be derived from other generalizations that we know. It follows that if a definition of truth is to play a role in explaining our knowledge of the generalization, the definition must itself be general in form. But Horwich does not use a generalization to define truth. Instead he uses a host of particular propositions, each of which explains what it is for a specific thought to be true. (This problem was first pointed out by Anil Gupta in a searching examination of Horwich's theory (Gupta 1993). For further discussion of Horwich's theory, see Hill 2011.)

Seeking to avoid these difficulties, substitutionalism uses substitutional quantification to enfold all of the clauses of Horwich's implicit definition into a single explicit definition. To be specific, it defines propositional truth as follows:

(S) For any thought x, x is true just in case $(\Sigma p)(x = $ the thought that p and $p)$.

Like Horwich's theory, (S) can easily explain the a priori character of (1), and also its triviality, for it is an easy matter to derive (P) from (S), and (1) follows immediately from (P) by universal instantiation:

(P) (Πp)(the thought that p is true just in case p).

(S) also has other advantages. It completely fixes the extension of the concept of truth; and since it is a generalization, it provides a basis for explaining our knowledge of other general propositions in which the concept of truth plays a role. Also, it dovetails beautifully with a very plausible account of the cognitive function of the concept of truth. Quine and other writers have argued convincingly that we need the concept of truth because it provides us with the ability to endorse a large set of thoughts without having to endorse each member of the set individually, and with the ability to endorse single thoughts without having to formulate the thoughts explicitly (Quine 1970). (For additional discussion of the motivation for the concept of truth, see the introduction to my *Meaning, Mind, and Knowledge*, 2014.) In short, according to Quine, the concept of truth is a device that enables general and indefinite endorsements. Assuming that this view is correct, the concept of truth is fundamentally akin to the substitutional quantifiers, for it is clear that the universal substitutional quantifier is a device that enables general endorsements (consider *(Πp)(if Joe asserts that p, then p)*), and that the existential substitutional quantifier is a device that enables indefinite endorsements (consider *(Σp) (Fermat's Last Theorem = the thought that p and p)*). In effect, then, since (S) implies that there is a deep relationship between truth and substitutional quantification, (S) ratifies Quine's view and provides additional support for it.

The idea that truth can be analyzed in terms of substitutional quantification is far from novel; but the idea has never been received with much enthusiasm, because it has seemed that definitions like (S) are implicitly circular. The reason for this perception is the belief that it is necessary to explain substitutional quantifiers by describing the truth conditions of thoughts that contain them. Thus, for example, it has been held that it is necessary to explain the existential substitutional quantifier by a proposition like (2):

(2) A thought of the form *(Σp)(... p ...)* is true just in case at least one substitution instance of the matrix *(... p ...)* is true.

(2) makes essential use of the concept of propositional truth. Accordingly, if (2) was the basis of our grasp of the existential substitutional quantifier, it would be entirely inappropriate to view (S) as a definition of truth.

Substitutionalism responds to this concern in two more or less independent ways. First, it calls attention to the fact that substitutional quantification appears to be present in our commonsense conceptual scheme. Consider the following propositions:

(3) It holds without exception that if Kurt believes that things stand thus and so, then things do stand thus and so.

(4) Generally speaking, when Kurt maintains that matters are arranged in such-and-such a way, matters really are arranged in such-and-such a way.

(5) If Kurt predicts that so-and-so, then, whatever so-and-so may be, it turns out that so-and-so.

(6) It never fails: if Kurt maintains that things stand thus and so, and Peter contradicts him, maintaining instead that matters are arranged in such-and-such a way, then whatever the particular nature of their respective contentions, it turns out to be the case that things stand thus and so, and that matters are *not* arranged in such-and-such a way.

Grover, Camp, and Belnap speak of *prosentences*, meaning thereby to indicate components of sentences that are counterparts of pronouns (Grover, Camp, and Belnap 1975). Equally one might say that certain components of thoughts are *prothoughts*. A prothought stands in a position that could be occupied by a whole thought. Examples are *things stand thus and so, matters are arranged in such and such a way,* and *so-and-so.*

Now it is extremely plausible that these prothoughts have the role of substitutional variables in (3)–(6), and extremely plausible also that the quantifiers that bind them are substitutional quantifiers. Thus, it is clear, for example, that (3) summarizes an infinite sheaf of thoughts that have the same form as (7):

(7) If Kurt believes that the universe is expanding, then the universe is expanding.

To see this, observe that it is clearly appropriate to infer (7) and all other thoughts of the same form from (3). Observe also that the quantifier *it holds without exception that* provides no ground for inferring thoughts from (3) that do not have the same form as (7). One may of course infer other thoughts from (3), such as the disjunction of (3) and the thought that snow is white, but one cannot justify those additional inferences by appealing to the logical powers of the quantifier.

One might reply that these facts do not establish conclusively that *it holds without exception that* is a substitutional quantifier. They can all be explained, it might be said, by supposing that it is an objectual quantifier that ranges over a domain consisting of propositions. This reply is initially plausible, but reflection shows that it will not work. The hypothesis that *it holds without exception that* is an objectual quantifier is ruled out by the fact that, as (3) shows, it can bind variables that occur in hyperintensional contexts. This is a distinctive mark of substitutional quantifiers. Unlike their objectual brethren, substitutional quantifiers can reach inside ascriptions of propositional attitudes, operators like *it has been proved that*, and even quotation marks. Since *it holds without exception that* binds a variable that is governed by *believes that* in (3), it must be a substitutional quantifier.

It appears, then, that substitutional quantification plays a role in commonsense logic. But this means that it is possible to explain the formal substitutional quantifiers Σ and Π without resorting to (2). One can explain them by simply equating them with commonsense counterparts.

In addition to this first truth-independent way of assigning meaning to the formal substitutional quantifiers, there is also a second such way. Since the substitutional quantifiers are logical concepts, it is possible to confer meaning on them by formulating rules that are to govern their use in inference. More specifically, it is possible to confer meaning on each formal quantifier by stating two rules of inference for it—a rule that specifies the conditions under which it is permissible to *introduce* the quantifier (that is, the conditions under which it is permissible to infer a thought containing the quantifier from another thought), and the conditions under which it is appropriate to *eliminate* the quantifier (that is, the conditions under which it is appropriate to infer another thought from a thought containing the quantifier). Substitutionalism provides introduction and elimination rules for both the existential substitutional quantifier and the universal substitutional quantifier. Here, for example, are its introduction and elimination rules for the propositional existential quantifier:

Existential Introduction

(... *T* ...)   (... **q** ...)
———————   ———————
(Σ**p**)(... **p** ...)   (Σ**p**)(... **p** ...)

Here *T* is a particular, determinate thought, and (... *T* ...) is the thought that comes from replacing all free occurrences of the propositional variable **p** in the open thought (... **p** ...) with *T*. Further, **q** is a propositional variable, and (... **q** ...) is the open thought that comes from replacing all free occurrences of the propositional variable p in the open thought (... **p** ...) with free occurrences of **q**.

Existential Elimination

(Σ**p**)(... **p** ...)
If (... **q** ...), then *T*

———————

T

Here *T* is a thought, **q** is a propositional variable, and (... **q** ...) is the open thought that comes from replacing all free occurrences of the propositional variable **p** in the open thought (... **p** ...) with free occurrences of **q**. Further, for Existential Elimination to be properly performed, **q** must satisfy three additional conditions: (i) it cannot have a free occurrence in *T*; (ii) it cannot have a free occurrence in (Σ**p**)(... **p** ...); and (iii) it cannot have a free occurrence in any premise on which the thought *T* depends.

In proposing an explanation in terms of introduction and elimination rules, I am simply following a long tradition, which stems from Gerhard Gentzen, in the philosophy of logic. Moreover, it can reasonably be claimed that the rules I am proposing are entirely appropriate, given that the quantifiers are to be counterparts of the common-sense concepts *some* and *all*. Rules like the present ones are structurally akin to rules that can be seen on reflection to govern *some* and *all*. There are only two differences. One is that the rules proposed by substitutionalism are intended to bind variables that stand in positions that can be occupied by thoughts. In their most usual deployments, *some* and *all* bind variables in positions that can be occupied by singular terms. The other difference has to do with the fact that the substitutional rules are meant to govern substitutional quantifiers. As noted a bit earlier, substitutional quantifiers differ from their objectual colleagues in that they can bind variables that stand in hyperintensional contexts. It is of course necessary to allow for this difference in formulating rules of inference. One can do so by formulating the rules for substitutional quantifiers in such a way that they apply to *all* contexts—to florid hyperintensional contexts as well as to prosaic extensional contexts. The substitutional rules have precisely this character. Thus, for example, the rule of Existential Introduction permits passage from the hyperintensional thought *Kate believes that Jon is talking* to the thought *(Σp)(Kate believes that p)*. On the other hand, in formulating rules for objectual quantifiers it is necessary to restrict their deployment to extensional contexts.

To summarize: Substitutionalism characterizes the formal substitutional quantifiers Σ and Π by formulating rules that are to govern their use in inference. The rules in question are structurally akin to the rules that govern the commonsense objectual quantifiers *some* and *all*. These rules can be seen on reflection to be constitutive of the concepts of existential and universal quantification. That is why they have received the approval of generations of logicians. To be sure, the substitutional rules have some features that are not present in normal codifications of the logic of *some* and *all*, but these differences were to be expected, given that substitutional quantifiers are meant to bind propositional variables, and given also that they are meant to be substitutional quantifiers.

II   A Substitutional Theory of Semantic Relations

I will now offer substitutional accounts of our relational semantic concepts, starting with the following analyses of reference, denotation, and expression:

(R) For every object x and every object y, x refers to y if and only if (Σa)(the concept of a is a singular concept and $x=$ the concept of a and $y=a$).

(D) For every object x and every object y, x denotes y if and only if (ΣF)(the concept of a thing that is F is a monadic general concept and $x=$ the concept of a thing that is F and y is an F).

(E) For every object x and every object y, x expresses y if and only if (ΣF)(the concept of a thing that is F is a monadic general concept and $x=$ the concept of a thing that is F and $y=$ the property F-ness).

In addition to these analyses of relational concepts that apply to concepts, substitutionalism also offers an analysis of semantic correspondence, a relational concept that applies to whole thoughts. It runs as follows:

(SC) For any thought x and any state of affairs y, x semantically corresponds to y if and only if $(\Sigma p)(x=$ the thought that p and $y=$ the state of affairs that p).

Arguably (SC) delivers all of the truths about semantic correspondence that guide and motivate our use of the concept. Thus, it can be used to derive every proposition of the form *The thought that p semantically corresponds to the state of affairs that p.*

Once (SC) is in hand, it is possible to introduce a correspondence-based concept of truth via the following definition:

(CT) For any thought x, x is true if and only if there is a state of affairs y such that (a) x semantically corresponds to y, and (b) y actually obtains.

I leave it to the reader to decide whether (CT) is a better account of our ordinary concept of truth than the account provided by (S). I myself favor (S) on grounds of simplicity, but there are many philosophers who prefer an account like (CT). My present point is that substitutionalism can do full justice to correspondence intuitions. (CT) is virtually identical to standard versions of the correspondence theory.

III Substitutionalism and Reduction

Turning now to the explanation and defense of this theory of semantic relations, I begin by emphasizing that theory is *not* intended to fulfill the reductionist dreams of naturalistically-minded philosophers. Beginning with Bertrand Russell, twentieth-century philosophers sought accounts of the aboutness of mental states and the reference of words that would naturalize them. Some hoped to reduce the relations to dispositions to apply concepts and words to objects; others to reduce them to relations definable in terms of the concept of information; and still others to reduce them to teleosemantic relations. The motivation for these reductionist programs was complex, but generally speaking, it included a desire to lay to rest worries originating with Brentano as to whether reference and other semantic relations might pose a threat to physicalism and the unity of science. It is after all quite impressive, and also quite puzzling, that reference can connect the mind to such disparate phenomena as wars fought in the distant past, bridges that will be built next year, particles that are imperceptible, and abstract entities like colors and shapes. How can a single relation be so marvelously promiscuous? It is also puzzling that while reference generally links concepts to single items, or to single sets of items, empirical relations tend to link concepts to multiple entities. We observe this difference, for example, when we compare reference to the empirical relation *encodes information about*: while the concept of Barack Obama refers to Obama and nothing else, the concept encodes information about a number of things, including Obama, retinal images of Obama, and thalamic projections of such images. It is not surprising that philosophers have been concerned that reference might somehow transcend the natural world, thereby posing substantial epistemological and metaphysical challenges. There were many eloquent expressions of this concern in the twentieth century. Here is Fodor's formulation: "It's hard to see … how one can be a Realist about intentionality without also being, to some extent or other, a Reductionist. If the semantic and the intentional are real properties of things, it must be in virtue of their identity (or maybe their supervenience on?) properties that are themselves *neither* intentional *nor* semantic. If aboutness is real, it must really be something else" (Fodor 1987, 97).

My treatment of semantic relations has a completely different motivation, and a completely different content, than the aforementioned reductionist proposals. Instead of explaining reference and semantic correspondence in terms of empirical relations that are of interest to science, the theory maintains that they are induced by certain formal, mereological relations among concepts. Consider the theory's definition of reference:

(R) For every object x and every object y, x refers to y if and only if (Σa)(the concept of a is a singular concept and $x=$ the concept of a and $y=a$).

(R) defines a relation between concepts and objects, but it does so by exploiting a fact about our practice of forming canonical names for concepts. The concept that serves as a name for the concept C is formed by attaching the concept-forming operator *the concept of* to C. Thus, for example, the concept that serves as the canonical name for the concept *Abraham Lincoln* is formed by prefixing the operator *the concept of* to *Abraham Lincoln*. Because of this fact about our practice, the canonical name for the concept C can be said to contain C as a constituent. (R) exploits this formal relationship between the canonical name of C and C itself. The same is true, mutatis mutandis, of the definition that substitutionalism provides for the concept of semantic correspondence:

(SC) For any thought x and any state of affairs y, x semantically corresponds to y if and only if $(\Sigma p)(x=$ the thought that p and $y=$ the state of affairs that p).

(SC) defines a relation between thoughts and states of affairs, but it does so by exploiting the fact that the concepts that serve as our canonical names for thoughts share constituents with the concepts that serve as our canonical names for states of affairs. The canonical name *the proposition that p* shares the thought p with the canonical name *the state of affairs that p*.[1]

It is of course perfectly appropriate to invoke formal relations between names in specifying a relation between objects. If someone writes the names of certain people on index cards, he can then specify a relation between the people by pairing the cards. To be sure, not every pairing of names can be counted on correspond to a pairing of objects: the procedure can be trusted to work only when one has grounds for thinking that the named objects actually exist. But we have the appropriate existential assurances in the case of (R) and (SC). We know both that the concept of Abraham Lincoln exists and that Abraham Lincoln exists, and we have similar knowledge about every pair that we regard as standing in the relation of reference. Equally, we know both that the thought that Abraham Lincoln was wise exists and that the state of affairs that Abraham Lincoln was wise exists, and we have similar knowledge about every pair that we regard as standing in the correspondence relation.[2]

It is clear that neither (R) nor (SC) counts as a naturalization. A naturalization of a semantic relation would explain the relation in terms of other relations that are empirically or mathematically robust. It is clear that neither (R) nor (SC) attempts to do this. Fortunately, it is equally clear that there is nothing metaphysically questionable about the relations defined by (R) and (SC), and that there are no challenges associated with grasping them epistemically. Like any other relations, the relations defined by (R) and

(SC) can be seen as collections of ordered pairs—or, to be precise, as functions that map possible worlds onto collections of ordered pairs. The only thing that is unusual about them is that they are made salient by, and specified by appeal to, formal relations between names of the objects that figure in the pairs. The relations themselves are no more mysterious, and no more in need of a legitimizing naturalization, than the function that maps each possible world onto the set consisting of the pairs <1, 2>, <2, 3>, and <3, 1>. Moreover, to gain epistemic access to them, one simply has to take note of the formal relations between names that are invoked in (R) and (SC).

It appears, then, that there is no problem with using formal properties of representations to define relations. Still, it might be objected that there is a problem with supposing that concepts and thoughts have formal properties. I have presupposed that the concept a is a constituent of the concept *the concept of a*, and that the thought p is a constituent of both the concept *the thought that p* and the concept *the state of affairs that p*. More generally, I have presupposed that concepts and thoughts have roughly the same combinatorial capacities as words and sentences in a spoken language. It might be doubted that these presuppositions are appropriate. After all, there are prominent theories of concepts that make no mention of combinatorial powers. This is true, for example, of the theories that seek to explain the role of concepts in categorization by representing them as prototypes or sets of exemplars. Moreover, psychologists who favor connectionist architectures have often maintained that we can live without the assumption that the mind uses representations with syntactic structures. Is it risky to view concepts as having word-like syntactic properties in trying to explain their semantic properties?

It would be difficult to work out a theory of concepts that reconciles their combinatorial capacities with their other powers, such as their role in categorization; but challenging though it may be to devise such a theory, I think we have no choice but to seek one. For it is essential to assume that concepts have word-like syntactic properties if we are to account for the roles that thoughts play in inference. The thought that $2+2=\sqrt{16}$ has different inferential properties than the thought that $2+2=4$, even though the two thoughts are a priori equivalent, and the same is true of the thought that Bill and Edith live here and the thought that it's not the case that either Bill doesn't live here or Edith doesn't live here. It is easy to establish experimentally that this is so—for example, by showing that it takes longer to process inferences involving the thought that $2+2=\sqrt{16}$ than to process inferences involving the thought that $2+2=4$. Now differences of these sorts can be explained by supposing, first, that the thoughts I have cited are composed of different concepts, and second, that their constituent concepts have different inferential roles. Thus, we can explain why inferences involving the thought that $2+2=\sqrt{16}$ take longer to process than inferences involving the thought that $2+2=4$ by supposing that the first thought contains the concept of $\sqrt{16}$, and that this concept has different inferential powers than the concept of 4. Further, we can explain this difference between the two concepts by supposing that the concept of

√16 has a different constituent structure than the concept of 4, and by pointing to the inferential powers of its constituents. These explanations are satisfactory—so much so that it is hard to imagine a future science of mind that would not avail itself of them. Hence, as Frege appreciated, whatever difficulties may attend the doctrine, it appears that we are compelled to acknowledge that concepts and thoughts resemble linguistic expressions in having a syntactic organization.

To summarize: A number of philosophers have believed it necessary to "legitimize" semantic relations by reducing them to empirically robust relations that are better understood. They have hoped to reduce the number of problems confronting philosophy by showing that semantic relations do not give rise to any *new* or *proprietary* epistemological or metaphysical concerns. I have tried to offer an alternative perspective, according to which semantic relations are epistemologically and metaphysically legitimate because it is possible to define them explicitly using only logical devices that are reasonably well understood. These definitions exploit formal properties of our canonical names of concepts, thoughts, and states of affairs, but this is perfectly acceptable. The practice of exploiting formal properties of representations in specifying relations is familiar and straightforward.

This is perhaps the place to acknowledge that substitutionalism does not protect the concept of truth and other semantic concepts from paradoxes. On the contrary, all of the familiar semantic paradoxes can be derived easily from the definitions of semantic concepts that substitutionalism provides. Moreover, it is possible to derive paradoxes directly from the rules of inference that govern the substitutional quantifiers (Hill 2002, 121–126). Substitutionalism has a paradoxical core.

Now in view of these difficulties, it cannot be claimed that substitutionalism disposes of *all* of the problems associated with truth and the semantic relations. It protects them from most of the worries that motivated semantic reductionism, but it doesn't show that they are altogether innocuous.

In considering this fact, it is useful to distinguish between the enterprise of analyzing our commonsense semantic concepts, and the enterprise of revising our commonsense concepts in ways that prevent the derivation of paradoxes. One reason for seeing the two enterprises as distinct is the intuitive appeal of the principles that lead to the paradoxes. Until we appreciate that they have unacceptable consequences, these principles seem obviously correct. Indeed, they seem to be forced upon us. This strongly suggests that they are constitutive of our everyday semantic concepts, which of course means that the paradoxes are constitutive of those concepts as well.

Another reason for seeing the enterprises as distinct is that theories of truth that succeed in blocking the paradoxes, such as Kripke's theory of grounding and Gupta and Belnap's revision theory, are extremely complex, presupposing considerable amounts of logic and mathematics. (See Kripke 1975 and Gupta and Belnap 1993.) It simply isn't believable that commonsense concepts could harbor such complexity. Now in the version I am proposing here, substitutionalism is concerned exclusively with analyzing our commonsense semantic concepts. Accordingly, it is a virtue rather than a fault that it provides a basis for deriving the standard semantic paradoxes. Indeed, since our commonsense concepts seem to be inherently paradoxical, substitutionalism would fail to reach its objective if its definitions did not lead to contradictions.

To emphasize the main point, I mean to be proposing substitutional analyses, not rational reconstructions. But it should be mentioned that it is also possible to use substitutional quantifiers in reconstructive efforts. To do so, it would be necessary to revise the rules of inference for the quantifiers in such a way as to block the derivation of contradictions. Fortunately, there are ways of doing this. To be more specific, the standard solutions to the semantic paradoxes can be adapted so as to block the derivation of paradoxes involving the substitutional quantifiers (McGee 2000). To be sure, it is not yet clear *which* ideas about the semantic paradoxes are best, and it is therefore not yet clear how best to revise substitutional quantification. Those questions are still under active investigation. But it is reasonable to suppose that they have answers, and that current research is gradually leading us to them. If this is so, then it will someday be possible to use substitutional quantification to construct counter-parts of our current concepts that are *altogether* free from difficulties.

IV Substitutionalism and the Laws of Folk Psychology

Reflection shows that the laws of folk psychology include many principles like the following:

Law of informational uptake: If C is a concept that refers to a perceptually accessible object, o, and x is an agent who possesses C, then x is disposed to form beliefs involving C as a result of acquiring perceptual information about o.

First law of reliable indication: If an agent x comes to believe that p as a result of immediate inference from a perceptual experience, then, where z is the state of affairs that corresponds semantically to the thought that p, it is quite likely that z is actual, and quite likely also that z is a distal cause of the fact that x comes to believe that p.

Second law of reliable indication: If an agent x comes to believe that p as a result of immediate inference from an episodic memory, then, where z is the state of affairs that corresponds semantically to the thought that p, it is quite likely that z is actual, and quite likely also that z is a distal cause of the fact that x comes to believe that p.

First law of reliable inference: If it is the case (a) that x arrives at the thought w from the thoughts $y_1, \ldots, y_n$ by deductive inference, and (b) that w and $y_1, \ldots, y_n$ correspond semantically to the states of affairs u and $z_1, \ldots, z_n$, respectively, then it is quite likely that u is logically implied by $z_1, \ldots, z_n$.

Second law of reliable inference: If it is the case (a) that x arrives at time T at the thought w by inductive inference from the thoughts $y_1, \ldots, y_n$, (b) that w corresponds semantically to the state of affairs u, where u involves a future time T', and (c) that $y_1, \ldots, y_n$ correspond semantically to $z_1, \ldots, z_n$, then the conditional probability $P(u/z_1, \ldots, z_n)$ is quite likely to be high.

First law of desire: If N is a need such that in x's experience instances of the property P have consistently fulfilled N, then, generally speaking, on those occasions when N is particularly pressing and x's perceptual state carries information to the effect that there is an instance of P in the current environment, x forms a desire that semantically corresponds to a state of affairs involving x's obtaining that instance of P.

Second law of desire: If x desires that p, and does so because the prospect of its being the case that p has an intrinsic appeal, then, where z is the state of affairs that corresponds semantically to the thought that p, it is quite likely that z is similar to states of affairs that have fulfilled one of x's needs in the past or to states of affairs that have caused x to experience some form of pleasure in the past.

Law of action: If x desires that p, then, where u is the state of affairs that corresponds semantically to the thought that p, and $z_1, \ldots, z_n$ are the states of affairs that correspond semantically to x's beliefs, x is disposed to act in ways that would tend to bring about u in possible worlds in which $z_1, \ldots, z_n$ were actual.

Now I wish to claim that these laws, together with similar laws involving our other semantic concepts, are partly responsible for the perception that semantic relations are robustly empirical. Inspection shows that two semantic relations, reference and semantic correspondence, figure prominently in the laws, and reflection shows that the contributions they make to the laws are essential. Moreover, the laws imply that there are stable and systematic links between these semantic relations and thick empirical relations like indication and information. To be more specific, they imply that the former relations enjoy nomological tracking relationships to the latter. But if this is so, then the former relations must themselves be empirical. How could it be otherwise?

I will respond to this line of thought by arguing that it misconstrues the role that semantic concepts play in the foregoing generalizations. They don't add to the empirical content of the generalizations by bringing additional empirical relations to the fore, but rather enable a level of generality that could otherwise be achieved only by using substitutional quantification. In arguing for this interpretation of the laws, I will focus on the following simplified version of the Law of Informational Uptake:

($) If C is a nominal concept that refers to a perceptually accessible object o, then C is used to encode perceptually acquired information about o.

I will maintain that it is actually quite reasonable to suppose that ($) depends obliquely on a mereological relationship between names of concepts and names of perceptually accessible objects. As the reader will appreciate, it is possible to adapt everything I will say about ($) to other laws containing semantic concepts, and in particular, to all of the laws that are considered earlier.

($) is concerned with a semantic relation, but it is also concerned with a range of facts involving an empirical relation—the relation that a nominal concept bears to an object when the former is used to encode perceptually acquired information about the latter. Suppose that we wish to consider a particular fact in which this empirical relation plays a role. Suppose, for example, that we wish to consider the fact that the nominal concept that refers to my brother in law, Mike, bears the relation to Mike. To do this we must entertain the following thought:

> (#) The concept of Mike is used to encode perceptually acquired information about Mike.

(#) involves two singular concepts—*the concept of Mike* and *Mike*. It is clear that these singular concepts are linked by a formal, mereological relationship: the former concept is obtained from the latter by combining it with the concept-forming operator *the concept of*. Thus, we have used a pair of concepts that stand in a formal, mereological relationship to describe a fact involving a thick empirical relation. Moreover, it is not an accident that we have done this. We were concerned to describe a relationship between an object and a concept of that object. Clearly, if we are to reach a goal of this sort, we must make use of a concept that refers to the object and a concept that refers to the concept. But where *C* is any concept, if we are to form a concept that refers to *C*, the simplest and most straightforward way to proceed is to combine *C* with the operator *the concept of*. Thus, given that we were concerned to describe a relationship between Mike and a concept that refers to Mike, it was natural to make use of two concepts that were linked by a formal, mereological relation.

Now when we reflect on (#), we see that it illustrates a general pattern. There are countless informational relationships between concepts and objects like the one that is described by (#), and our canonical descriptions of these facts will all have the same form as (#). In short, there are countless true propositions like (#). Clearly, it is desirable to have some way of summarizing these propositions. Substitutional quantification provides us with a way of doing this:

> (%) (Π*a*) (if the concept of *a* is a nominal concept and *a* is a perceptually accessible object, the concept of *a* is used to encode perceptually acquired information about *a*).

We can use substitutional quantification to summarize the class of true propositions like (#) because all such propositions involve names of objects and names of concepts, and the former names are constituents of the latter.

Now it can be shown that if reference is defined substitutionally, in the way indicated in section II by (R), then the substitutional generalization (%) is equivalent to the objectual generalization ($). In effect, (%) uses substitutional quantification to accomplish what ($) accomplishes by deploying the concept of reference and objectual quantification. In view of this fact, we can claim to have an explanation of why reference enjoys the stable and systematic relationship to perceptually acquired information that is captured by ($). As we have seen, it is a consequence of our convention for forming canonical names for concepts that we are able to use substitutional quantification to describe the general pattern that is illustrated by (#). Given that the concept of reference simply provides us with an alternative means of describing this same pattern, it is inevitable that there be a stable and systematic relationship between reference and information.

This completes the argument. The key idea is that ($) does not use the concept of reference to bring a new empirical relation into the picture, but rather to achieve a desired level of generality in representing a set of facts about the use of concepts to encode information—a level of generality that could otherwise be achieved only by using substitutional quantification.

As noted earlier, this argument can be generalized so as to apply to all of the laws that are cited earlier. In its most general form, it fully and decisively undercuts the impression that the laws provide the foundation of a case for viewing semantic relations as contingent and empirical, and by the same token, it shows that it is impossible to argue from the representational powers of the mind to a conclusion that is at odds with substitutionalism.

Notes

This chapter is largely a composite of the two contributions I made to a symposium on my book *Thought and World* (Hill 2006a, 2006b). The first two sections of the present chapter correspond to a précis of *Thought and World* that opened the symposium, and the remaining sections correspond to parts of my replies to my fellow symposiasts, Marian David, Anil Gupta, and Keith Simmons. I am grateful to these philosophers for their illuminating comments, and also to Gupta for reviewing drafts of the précis and my replies.

1. In *Thought and World* (Hill 2002) this proposal concerning semantic correspondence is accompanied by explanations of the logical properties of the concepts *the thought that* and *the state of affairs that*. One might expect that my explanation of the latter concept would treat it as expressing the function that maps the thought that p onto the state of affairs that p, for every *p*. But this is not the case, for a very good reason: if I had taken that line, my account of semantic correspondence would have been circular. The function in question is tantamount to the relation of semantic correspondence, so it would be circular to invoke it in a definition of the relation. Instead, I take concepts of the form *the state of affairs that p* as abbreviations for descriptions of the form *the state of affairs x such that, necessarily, x is actual just in case p*. See *Thought and World*, 46–48.

2. There is an argument in *Thought and World* (Hill 2002, 41–46) which is designed to show that we do in fact know that states of affairs exist.

References

Fodor, J. A. 1987. *Psychosemantics*. Cambridge, MA: MIT Press.

Grover, D., Camp, J. L., Jr., and Belnap, N. 1975. "A Prosentential Theory of Truth." *Philosophical Studies* 27: 73–125.

Gupta, A. 1993. "Minimalism." *Philosophical Perspectives* 7: 359–369.

Gupta, A., and Belnap, N. 1993. *The Revision Theory of Truth*. Cambridge, MA: MIT Press.

Hill, C. S. 2002. *Thought and World: An Austere Portrayal of Truth, Reference, and Semantic Correspondence*. Cambridge: Cambridge University Press.

Hill, C. S. 2006a. "Precis of *Thought and World*." *Philosophy and Phenomenological Research* 72: 174–181.

Hill, C. S. 2006b. "Replies to Marian David, Anil Gupta, and Keith Simmons." *Philosophy and Phenomenological Research* 72: 205–222.

Hill, C. S. 2011. Review of Paul Horwich, *Truth-Meaning-Reality*. *Mind* 120: 1262–1270.

Hill, C. S. 2014. "How Concepts Hook onto the World." In *Meaning, Mind, and Knowledge*, 66–96. Oxford: Oxford University Press.

Horwich, P. 1998. *Truth*. 2nd ed. Oxford: Oxford University Press.

Kripke, S. A. 1975. "Outline of a Theory of Truth." *Journal of Philosophy* 72: 690–716.

McGee, V. 2000. "The Analysis of 'x Is True' as 'For Every p, if x = "p," Then p.'" In A. Chapuis and A. Gupta, eds., *Circularity, Definition, and Truth*, 255–272. New Delhi: Indian Council for Philosophical Research.

Quine, W. V. 1970. *Philosophy of Logic*. Englewood Cliffs, NJ: Prentice-Hall.

23 Deflationism as Alethic Fictionalism via a SPIF Account of Truth-Talk

Bradley Armour-Garb and James A. Woodbridge

The aim of this chapter is to explain, motivate, and provide the central details of a specific version of what has come to be called *alethic fictionalism*—namely, a fictionalist account of truth (or, more accurately, of truth-*talk*, that fragment of discourse that involves the truth-predicate and other alethic-locutions[1]). Our particular brand of alethic fictionalism is sometimes described as a "pretense theory of truth," and a catchphrase for our view is "truth is a pretense."[2] But a more precise label for the view that we will present is "semantic pretense-involving fictionalism about truth-talk."[3] Our endorsement of this view (for short, our *SPIF* account) stems from our belief that deflationism is the right approach to take on the topic of truth. This already shifts the focus away from any property of truth, since deflationism "about truth" (or, as we will call this view, *T-deflationism*) is best understood as an approach to analyzing truth-talk. We arrive specifically at our SPIF account of truth-talk because we also think that versions of T-deflationism should be understood as a kind of fictionalism (which, again, puts the focus on discourse, rather than metaphysics) and because we maintain that a SPIF account is the best variety of fictionalism to apply specifically to truth-talk. We will explain some of our reasons for holding these beliefs below, laying out the basics of our SPIF account of truth-talk and highlighting the merits of endorsing our particular account of that talk.

1 T-Deflationism and Representational Aides

To motivate understanding T-deflationism as a kind of fictionalism about truth-talk, we begin with a general thesis that has been employed to motivate fictionalism about certain other fragments of discourse, that of *expressive indispensability*, namely:

> (EI) We need to enlist certain aspects of X-talk, as a means for expressing certain claims that we could not otherwise express.[4]

In the case specifically of truth-talk, we can see (EI) in effect in our widely acknowledged need to enlist the truth-predicate, which *appears* to commit us to a property of truth, as a means for expressing certain claims (to be discussed below) that we otherwise could not—or, at least, could not so easily—express.

The impetus for moving to a fictionalist account of truth-talk begins with the T-deflationist's thought that what we are trying to say through our use of truth-talk has nothing to do with any property of truth per se and, in fact, but for certain *expressive limitations*, could be expressed without an appeal to any such property. Moreover, such expressive needs have nothing to say about truth—its nature or even its existence—or about whether there need be any such property in order to express what we aim to convey. So, while truth-*talk* does appear to be *expressively* indispensable, truth, qua property, may well be *theoretically* dispensable.[5]

The connection between understanding the notion of truth in this way (as theoretically dispensable but expressively indispensable) and alethic fictionalism is as follows. Suppose that we can explain the expressive advantages of employing truth-talk, and suppose, with T-deflationists, that these expressive purposes exhaust our use of that talk. Suppose, finally, that what we are trying to get across through our use of truth-talk is not *about* any property of truth, in the sense that what we aim to convey itself has nothing to do with any such property. In that case, because 'true'—the notion of truth, as it occurs in truth-talk—serves essentially in the indirect expression of facts that are not about any property of truth, it simply functions as what Stephen Yablo (2005) calls a "representational aid[e]." As we understand things, when the central locutions of some fragment of discourse function as representational aides in this way—to allow speakers to make *as if* they are talking about one thing for the purposes of talking about something else indirectly, via implementing what we call *semantic redirection*—that just *is* for that fragment of discourse to operate via some element of fiction.

According to the line of reasoning just sketched, T-deflationists should see truth-talk as operating through some element of fiction, effecting some sort of semantic redirection away from a face-value reading of its instances. After all, T-deflationists acknowledge the *expressive* indispensability of truth-talk, but they do not then go on to conclude that the truth-predicate is "ontologically serious." Rather, they hold that the truth-predicate functions as a device that allows speakers to talk indirectly about other matters, facilitating the expression of facts that are not about truth.

2 Semantic Pretense-Involving Fictionalism

We take the above to provide some reason for concluding that T-deflationism should be understood as a type of fictionalism.[6] But there are several species and varieties of fictionalism, and it is important to recognize that not all fictionalist accounts are the same. For present purposes, the most relevant distinction within fictionalism is that between the perhaps more familiar prefix-fictionalism and the newer pretense-involving variety.[7] With respect to most fragments of discourse, there are general reasons for worrying about prefix-fictionalist accounts.[8] Accounts of this sort are highly restricted in the semantic redirection they can implement, being able only to indicate how things are according to or within the fiction cited in the story-prefix. They also typically turn out to be cases of what we call *error-theoretic fictionalism* (ETF), which involves attributing error theories of the discourse being analyzed.[9] We contrast the class of ETF accounts with *pretense-involving fictionalism* (PIF), a kind of fictionalism on which it is possible for utterances from a fragment of discourse so analyzed to make serious claims about the world indirectly. Within the latter approach, we favor *semantic* pretense-involving fictionalism—SPIF—over an alternative *pragmatic* version.[10]

Our SPIF approach involves postulating a semantic mechanism at work in the linguistic functioning of the relevant fragment of discourse, involving a special but familiar kind of pretense: *make-believe*. Make-believe games (e.g., the classic children's games of "mudpies," cowboys and Indians, cops and robbers, etc.) involve pretenses of two types. In the first type, certain pretenses are stipulated, or *expressly pretended*—typically about the props that are employed in the game of make-believe (e.g., globs of mud counting as pies, sticks counting as horses, fingers counting as pistols, etc.). The second type involves pretenses that are "generated from reality" via the game of make-believe's *principles of generation* (e.g., it is to be pretended that someone has put a pie in the oven whenever she has put a glob of mud into the hollow stump). These principles are rules for the make-believe that establish a systematic dependency between some of what is to be pretended—that is, which pretenses are *prescribed*—and real-world conditions that are, as it were, outside of the game.[11] Postulating such dependencies as holding for the claims from some discourse can explain how speakers can use utterances from the discourse to say indirectly things that the utterances appear unsuited to say. This is done by making utterances that, in a sense, *belong* to a game of make-believe involving the characteristic locutions of the discourse. A typical merit of the approach is that it allows speakers to use readily available, familiar linguistic resources—ordinary object-talk, predication, and objectual quantification—in order to make much more complicated and technical claims indirectly.[12]

In general, a SPIF account of some apparently problematic discourse appeals to make-believe to implement semantic redirection away from a face-value reading of the sentences of the discourse. On our view, sentences from a target discourse that merit a SPIF account are "semantically infelicitous" on a face-value reading. The fact that the sentences still function linguistically is then explained in terms of semantic redirection away from this face-value reading, with the notion of fiction we appeal to—make-believe—playing a pivotal role in the redirection. As we see it, this generates what we call the "serious content" of that utterance—namely, what it can be used to say about the real world outside of the make-believe.[13]

In the "games" that our SPIF accounts posit, we take the props to be certain linguistic items, and the principles of generation that we lay out specify the real-world conditions that prescribe the pretenses displayed in the uses of those props (i.e., the relevant locutions). The systematic dependency established between the appropriateness of the pretense-involving utterances in question and the obtaining of certain real-world conditions outside of the make-believe is what allows SPIF accounts to avoid being error-theoretic and, unlike with prefix-fictionalism, allows utterances from discourses so analyzed to be about the real world instead of just being about how things are "according to the fiction."

3 Our SPIF Account of Truth-Talk

According to our SPIF account of truth-talk, we talk *as if* there were a property of truth though this fragment of discourse operates with complete indifference as to whether there really is any such property.[14] More specifically, we speak as if we are describing things as having or lacking properties, named "truth" and "falsity," in order to express other (more complicated) content (or M-conditions—see note 13) indirectly. On our view, truth-talk is underwritten by a game of make-believe, one that allows us to use familiar linguistic resources in order to specify, indirectly, certain complex M-conditions, the direct specification of which would involve technical and unfamiliar linguistic and logical devices that ordinary language does not explicitly contain. The kinds of devices that we have in mind include schematic sentence variables and substitutional quantifiers ('Π' and 'Σ', understood as means for encoding potentially infinite conjunctions and potentially infinite disjunctions, respectively).

As we noted above, make-believe, including that described in our SPIF account of truth-talk, involves two kinds of *prescribed* pretenses—namely, stipulated background pretenses that are expressly pretended and additional pretenses that are systematically *generated from reality* via a game's principles of generation. The make-believe that our SPIF account of truth-talk proposes as the basis of this fragment of discourse is governed, at least in part, by rules like the following.[15]

Truth-Talk Make-Believe

(T-I) The central props for the game are the linguistic expressions 'is true', 'is false', 'is not true', and their cognates (e.g., 'is correct', 'is right', 'is so', etc.), as well as the expressions 'truth' and 'falsity'. Other props include 'that'-clauses and linguistic (and cognitive-state) items that can be related to them in proposition-talk. The following pretenses are stipulated about these props:

(i) The adjectival expressions 'is true', 'is false', and so on function predicatively to describe objects as having or lacking certain properties.

(ii) The nominal expression 'truth' picks out the property attributed with the expression 'is true' (and 'falsity' picks out the property attributed with the expression 'is false').

(iii)   The most basic objects that directly have or lack the properties that 'is true', etc. attribute are abstract, mind- and language-independent entities called *propositions*. Other kinds of objects (e.g., linguistic items) can have the properties that 'is true', and so on attribute only derivatively, in virtue of expressing a proposition that has the relevant property.

(T-II) Πp(The pretenses displayed in an utterance of ⌜(The proposition) that p is true⌝ are prescribed iff p).

(T-III) Πp(The pretenses displayed in an utterance of ⌜(The proposition) that p is false⌝ are prescribed iff ¬ p).

(T-IV) Πp(If S_1 and S_2 are sentences that are alike except (in some transparent context) one has a subsentence ⌜p⌝ where the other has ⌜⟨p⟩ is true⌝ then one can directly infer S_1 from S_2 and S_2 from S_1).

(T-V) Πp(If S_1 and S_2 are sentences that are alike except (in some transparent context) one has a subsentence ⌜¬ p⌝ where the other has ⌜⟨p⟩ is false⌝ then one can directly infer S_1 from S_2 and S_2 from S_1).

In our SPIF account of truth-talk, the first rule, (T-I), states the stipulated, *expressly made-believe*, background pretenses for the make-believe,[16] while rules (T-II) and (T-III) are the central principles of generation for the game. Rules (T-IV) and (T-V) are further principles that explicitly codify certain consequences of rules (T-II) and (T-III) that are crucially important for the truth- and falsity-predicates playing their more important expressive roles. To show how a game of make-believe based on these rules can account for all of the expressive roles that the truth-predicate plays in various forms of truth-talk while adhering to T-deflationist commitments, we will briefly explain the operation of these rules and their implications.

3.1   Rule (T-I), Background Pretenses, and the Truth-Predicate

In laying out the background pretenses for the make-believe behind truth-talk, rule (T-I) identifies certain linguistic expressions as the props for the game and explains what is to be pretended *about* such props. It involves three subrules regarding these props. We will explicate these subrules in reverse order.

Rule (T-I.iii) indicates that the basic applications of 'is true' are those that combine this locution with expressions that are supposedly content-connected to propositions.[17] Thus, the pretense that underwrites truth-talk includes the *existentially creative* pretense that we claim is behind proposition-talk. Within the pretense involved in that SPIF account, 'that'-clauses emerge as the most "transparent" way (pretendedly) to name particular propositions and (pretendedly) to describe or relate things to them.[18] According to our account of truth-talk, the most basic instances will involve combining a 'that'-clause with either 'is true' or 'is false'. Call this part of discourse *transparent propositional truth-talk*. Making this part of truth-talk the discourse's core fits with standard linguistic and inferential practices with the truth-predicate.[19] Extending truth-talk beyond its basic cases, to cover applications of 'is true' to sentences, utterances, or thought-states, requires bringing in our account of the role of 'that'-clauses in meaning-attribution (or proposition-expression) claims. These extended instances of truth-talk involve taking things of these other kinds to have certain relations (e.g., the *expressing* or *meaning* relation or the *belief* relation) to propositions that are true. Explaining this sometimes requires quantifying over propositions and concatenating the truth-predicate to the bound variable; we return to this issue below, after we explain the operation of quantificational truth-talk.

Rule (T-I.ii) covers the nominal locutions peculiar to truth-talk and reveals that they, too, involve an existentially creative pretense. These expressions are stipulated to be the names for the putative properties that the predicates 'is true' and 'is false' (pretendedly) attribute to propositions. However, as we have suggested above, we maintain that, really, the operation of the discourse is indifferent as to whether there are any properties of truth and falsity—it operates *as if* there were in any case. Moreover, as we noted above (see note 18), we maintain that the putative bearers of these supposed properties, propositions, are also just an existentially creative pretense. Thus, it is only a pretense that there are such properties, as well as anything that could have them, at all. As a result, there are no uses of the expressions 'truth', 'falsity', and so on that do not involve pretense, meaning that these expressions cannot be employed in any direct specification of M-conditions.

Rule (T-I.i) involves the most fundamental background pretense of the make-believe in that it indicates that the game involves an *operational* pretense regarding the locution 'is true' (as well as 'is false', etc.). This is because it is only a pretense that 'is true' (etc.) functions as a genuinely descriptive predicate at all. We take there to be an operational pretense at work in the logico-linguistic functioning of any expression that, while serving logically or grammatically as a predicate, does not require anything of the putative objects it supposedly describes in its applications. We maintain that this pertains to 'is true' (and 'is false', etc.) because the application conditions for the truth-predicate—at least in its fundamental role in transparent propositional truth-talk—do not require anything of the putative objects supposedly described.

This is especially so in the context of T-deflationism, since T-deflationists maintain that the instances of the equivalence schema

(ES) It is true that p iff p (= That p is true iff p)

are fundamental. That is, T-deflationists claim that there is no deeper explanation, in terms of other concepts, for why these equivalences hold. But this attitude toward these equivalences also entails believing that, at least in the basic instances of truth-talk (viz., those that figure in the instances of (ES)), the applicability conditions for the expression 'is true' place no conditions on any objects putatively picked out by the (supposed) designation expressions these utterances employ, that is, by 'that'-clauses. In turn, this suggests that 'is true' also does not really function predicatively in the full, genuinely descriptive sense.

To see this, consider a basic instance of truth-talk, such as

(1) It is true that crabapples are edible.

For reasons pertaining to our inferential practices with 'that'-clauses, including 'that'-clauses in sentences of the form ⌜It is F that p⌝, we think that (1) is more perspicuously rendered as

(1′) That crabapples are edible is true.

The instance of (ES) that pertains to this sentence is

(ES₁) That crabapples are edible is true iff crabapples are edible.

If we take this biconditional to give the applicability conditions for the use of 'is true' made on the left-hand side, we can see that the conditions specified on the right-hand side place no requirements on any proposition putatively designated by the 'that'-clause employed on the left. The only things these conditions seem to require anything of are the crabapples. We conclude from this that the applicability conditions for this use of the truth-predicate—as well as for other cases of transparent propositional truth-talk—show that this locution does not actually function directly to describe anything, contrary to its surface appearances. Again, this is part of the truth-predicate's operation as a representational aide and indicates that the linguistic functioning of 'is true' involves an operational pretense. That means the pretense that implements semantic redirection in instances of truth-talk is actually about the very logico-linguistic functioning of the locution, with the result that the pretense must be taken as intrinsic to the locution's operation in any utterance.

According to the line of reasoning just given, T-deflationism involves viewing truth-talk as not genuinely predicative, not even in terms of employing a primitive predicate. Prosentential theorists, such as Robert Brandom, explicitly endorse a thesis even stronger than this, claiming that 'is true' is not even a predicate *logically* speaking.[20] But this seems too strong, since the locution functions like a predicate in inference.[21] Moreover, the instances of truth-talk look exactly like cases of genuine predication, and prosententialists offer no substantive account as to *why* they take this form. We can resolve the apparent conflict between truth-talk's surface appearances and the denial that it is genuinely predicative by recognizing the instances of truth-talk as invoking an operational pretense at the level of the logico-linguistic functioning of its central locutions. So, an account of truth-talk in terms of operational pretense fits especially well with the core commitments of T-deflationism.

As just mentioned, identifying the central pretense that the instances of truth-talk involve specifically as an operational pretense indicates that this way of talking involves pretense intrinsically. This in turn shows how our SPIF account of truth-talk avoids any version of the Problem of Error—namely, the problem of attributing massive error, both to what is said with the discourse and to speakers regarding their understanding of the status of their talk—by skirting even a modified error-theoretic interpretation. That said, there is a sense in which the instances of truth-talk are misleading on our account. Since the basic functioning of the expression 'is true' is not genuinely predicative, it is not possible to make "pretense-free" claims of the sort that (1/1') appears to make on the surface. So it is never correct to say that (1/1') is true when we take it literally (i.e., take it seriously at face value). But our account is not an error theory in any problematic sense because it is also never correct to say that (1/1') is false when we take it literally, or even that (1/1') is not true when we take it literally. The point is that we cannot take (1/1') *literally*—that is, we cannot assign it an interpretation on a face-value (which is *not* to say standard) reading. But this is because truth-talk never puts forward genuine claims about the world *directly* (i.e., without the operation of pretense). (1/1') has *no* literal (i.e., pretense-independent) content at all because the standard use of 'is true' invokes pretense intrinsically. The only content regarding the real world that we can associate with (1/1') is the serious content it puts forward indirectly, in virtue of how it is governed by a principle of generation for the make-believe. We thus turn to the operation and consequences of the game's central principles of generation, rules (T-II) and (T-III).

3.2   Rules (T-II) and (T-III) and Transparent Propositional Truth-Talk

The serious content that an instance of transparent propositional truth-talk puts forward (or specifies) comes from the operation of the make-believe's central principles of generation—specifically, rules (T-II) and (T-III). On our account, these principles of generation of the game of make-believe underlying truth-talk give the discourse a "quasi-anaphoric" functioning. This effects the sort of semantic descent that T-deflationists highlight, through a kind of collapse of the use/mention distinction, here effecting an indirect use of a sentence performed through some mention (nominalization) of it.

To illustrate how, according to the principles of generation we have offered, the most basic instances of truth-talk function in the indirect specification of M-conditions, consider again the example of truth-talk we introduced above,

(1') That crabapples are edible is true.

In (1'), 'that crabapples are edible' operates (in the context of the pretense of proposition-talk embedded in the pretense behind truth-talk) as a designation expression that (in the context of that pretense) is content-connected to the proposition that crabapples are edible. Syntactically speaking, the 'that'-clause is a nominalization of the sentence

(2) Crabapples are edible.

When assertorically uttered, a 'true'-involving sentence like (1') presents the pretenses it displays as prescribed, where pretenses being prescribed is a matter of:

(a) the particular principles of generation that govern those pretenses (here, rule (T-II)),

and

(b) whether the conditions, whose obtaining those principles make prescriptive for the pretenses, actually obtain.

Recall that rule (T-II) has it that the prescriptive conditions for the pretenses displayed in (1′) are those specified by a denominalized use of the sentence that is nominalized as the subject expression of (1′)—in this case, by a use of (2). In short, by presenting the pretenses it displays as prescribed, an assertoric utterance of (1′) specifies, indirectly, precisely the M-conditions that an assertoric utterance of (2) specifies directly.[22] Thus, the serious content put forward by an assertoric utterance of (1′) is the content put forward directly by an assertoric utterance of (2).[23]

One consequence of the principles of generation for the pretense that truth-talk invokes is that this make-believe is what we call *world-oriented*. While this type of make-believe is similar to the pretenses at work in the SPIF account of proposition-talk that we (Armour-Garb and Woodbridge 2012, 2015) have developed, in that the point of sentences that count as moves in these games has to do with how things are in the real world outside of the make-believe (as opposed to with which pretenses are part of the "world" or content of the make-believe), truth-talk is slightly different in that it is not focused on features specifically of the *props* that the game employs.[24] As we explain proposition-talk, the serious content that its instances specify has to do with certain features of the designation-expression props used in the utterances (in particular, *as* they are used in the utterances). In the case of proposition-talk, the serious content that its instances specify typically has to do with attributing certain "use" features of its definitive props ('that'-clauses) to certain other props employed in the game (utterances, cognitive states, and expressions that can be substituted for 'that'-clauses). The serious content that the instances of truth-talk specify, in contrast, does not typically have to do with features of either the definitive props of the game (the alethic-locutions) or of the other props employed ('that'-clauses). Instead, pretenses involving these props are displayed as prescribed in order to specify the (not necessarily prop-involving) M-conditions that the make-believe's principles of generation make prescriptive for those pretenses.

As should be apparent, a further consequence of our pretense account of truth-talk is that any specification of M-conditions (that obtain or fail to obtain outside of the pretense) that is accomplished by a 'true'-involving sentence will be accomplished only indirectly, via the operation of the pretenses that govern the functioning of the truth-predicate. Thus, like T-deflationism, the upshot of our SPIF account is that there are no M-conditions that involve any property of truth; the truth-predicate is a representational aide that serves in the indirect specification of M-conditions that have nothing to do with any such property. The rules for the make-believe that underwrites truth-talk make this possible by establishing an identity of serious content between an instance of transparent propositional truth-talk of the form ⌜That p is true⌝ and an assertoric utterance of a denominalized occurrence of the content-vehicle nominalized in it (viz., the sentence that goes in for 'p'). This, in turn, means that the game of make-believe behind truth-talk generates all instances of the equivalence schema

(ES) It is true that p iff p.[25]

This is an important result because, as most theorists—T-inflationists along with T-deflationists—on the topic of truth recognize, these equivalences (or variants of them) are (some of) the central principles governing truth-talk. Our pretense account has them follow directly from the functioning that truth-talk is given by the rules of the game of make-believe that underwrites it, satisfying one of the central commitments of T-deflationism.

The principles of generation for the game of make-believe that we think underwrites truth-talk make the correctness of a putative attribution of truth or falsity to some nominalized sentence a function (possibly negating) of whether the M-conditions specified by a denominalized use of that sentence obtain. Since these indirectly specified M-conditions can actually obtain, this makes it possible for instances of truth-talk to make (what we might, now *employing* the very pretense being explained, describe as) "genuinely true" claims about the world outside of the pretense. In this way, our SPIF account of truth-talk avoids any (in this context, incoherence generating) error-theoretic interpretation, along with any versions of the Problem of Error, which might plague such an interpretation.

3.3   Rules (T-IV) and (T-V) and Quantificational Truth-Talk

We now turn to the more interesting forms of truth-talk, those that manifest the important expressive role this fragment of discourse plays: the quantificational instances. We take this class to include both universal generalizations involving the truth-predicate, such as

(3) Everything Isabel says is true,

which, in the context of the pretense behind truth-talk, we understand to have the form

(4) $\forall x$(Isabel says $x \rightarrow x$ is true),

and what are sometimes called *blind truth-attributions*,[26] but which we call *opaque truth-ascriptions* (since we very well might "see" what it is that we (nontransparently) endorse (or deny) with a truth (or falsity)-ascription), such as

(5) What Corey said is true,

which, in the context of the pretense behind truth-talk, we understand as an existential quantification of the form

(6) $\exists x$(Corey said $x \wedge x$ is true).[27]

Rules (T-IV) and (T-V) make the account satisfy an important condition of adequacy for any T-deflationary theory of truth-talk, as they provide versions of rules of *intersubstitution*.[28] In the set of rules for the make-believe under consideration, rules (T-IV) and (T-V) are, in a manner of speaking, consequences of rules (T-II) and (T-III), respectively. The intersubstitution rules further capture the sense in which the serious content of a putative ascription of truth to some content-vehicle just is the serious content of the content-vehicle itself. Codifying this equivalence of serious content in rules that license general intersubstitution is important for ensuring that our pretense account yields the right serious content for the more interesting cases of truth-talk, namely, the quantificational instances. Since those instances are where expressive indispensability emerges, they are what give truth-talk its point. Accounting for them is thus a crucial condition of adequacy for any account of truth-talk.[29]

To demonstrate the importance of rules (T-IV) and (T-V) for our account, and to show how the account satisfies this condition of adequacy in virtue of them, it will help to explain further the role of intersubstitution in the truth-predicate's functioning in the expression of infinite conjunctions and infinite disjunctions. One of the central contexts in which we need 'is true' to fulfill this function is when it serves to express the kind of "extended" opaque endorsement performed in an utterance of a 'true'-involving generalization like (3), which, as we mentioned above, gets (semi-) formalized as (4). To see what serious content such a generalization puts forward, we need to unpack the quantification at work in (4), as it operates in the context of the pretense.

We explained above that, in the context of the pretense, the truth-predicate applies fundamentally to propositions. Since we maintain that, really, there are no such entities, and that propositions are just the pretense-bound "ontological shadows" of 'that'-clauses, the serious upshot of the quantification in (4) has to do with all of the 'that'-clauses that are available. Thus, we can delve more fine-grainedly into the 'x's in (4), by re-rendering them as '$\langle p \rangle$'s (where, as before, the angle brackets indicate a 'that'-clause nominalization of whatever sentence goes in for 'p') since, in the pretense, this notation still provides a variable that ranges over objects—now just restrictedly over only the "truth-bearer" objects. What the universal quantifier in (4), operating within the pretense, seriously expresses, then, is a commitment to every filling of the schema $\ulcorner$Isabel says $\langle p \rangle \rightarrow \langle p \rangle$ is true$\urcorner$. Gathering all of these together, by prefixing the schema with a universal *substitutional* quantifier governing the occurrences of 'p', we arrive at

(7) Πp(Isabel says $\langle p \rangle \rightarrow \langle p \rangle$ is true).

Since this still employs the truth-predicate, it still involves the pretense at work in truth-talk. However, it is precisely here that intersubstitution plays its role. By applying rule (T-IV) to (7), we move, from a formula that still employs the truth-predicate, to one that does not—that is,

(8) Πp(Isabel said $\langle p \rangle \rightarrow p$).

While (8) does not employ the truth-predicate, it does employ some technical devices that are not available in natural language—substitutional quantification and schematic sentence variables—in order to perform a kind of generalization on sentence-in-use positions (that of the second 'p'). This is precisely what many T-deflationists claim the truth-predicate is for—to function as a surrogate in natural language for these nonstandard logical devices, allowing speakers to express "fertile generalizations" that do not really have anything to do with truth.[30] We might offer (8) as a quasi-formal specification of the M-conditions that an utterance of (3) specifies indirectly.[31] Specifying those M-conditions in ordinary language without the truth-predicate would require uttering a gigantic conjunction of conditionals along the lines of

(9) If Isabel says that crabapples are edible, then crabapples are edible; and if Isabel says that grass is green, then grass is green; and if Isabel says that power corrupts, then power corrupts; and if Isabel says …

However, since (9) must go on to cover everything Isabel might say, and since that is an infinite number of things, it is actually impossible for us to utter (9) assertorically. But we can, and do, express a commitment to what an utterance of (9) would express by assertorically uttering (3). An utterance of (3) accomplishes this in virtue of the rules that govern truth-talk—in particular, rule (T-IV), licensing intersubstitution. Thus, on our account, in keeping with a central emphasis of T-deflationism, truth-talk provides speakers with a finite means for expressing what it would otherwise take infinite conjunctions to express, a means that still employs just the standard logical and linguistic devices of an ordinary language like English.

As we see it (and as T-deflationists would agree), allowing speakers to generalize in this new way, on sentence-in-use positions within claims, without having to incorporate new, complicated logical devices into our language, is the main, perhaps the central, purpose of truth-talk. Our appeal to pretense explains how truth-talk does this with linguistic resources that seem, on the surface, unsuited to the task (and without leaving it a brute, unexplained fact that it does this). Furthermore, our SPIF account's incorporation of intersubstitution rules (T-IV) and (T-V) within a make-believe that includes a pretense that alethic-predicates serve to attribute alethic properties provides an additional benefit for the T-deflationist. The infinite conjunction, which the rules allow a claim like (3) to express indirectly, takes on an important modal status because of the operation of the pretense. Typically, encoding an infinite conjunction with substitutional quantification ties the conjunction to a specific substitution class, so it covers only the "current" substitution instances of the schema prefixed. If new sentences are introduced into the language, with the development of new concepts and new vocabulary, they are not included in the original conjunction encoded. The pretense gives the infinite conjunction a kind of *indefinite extendability*, so that it automatically includes every new substitution instance in every possible extension of the language. It is part of the make-believe that language expansions simply "reveal" more objects (propositions) already in the domain of the objectual quantifier a claim like (3) employs. The merit of this feature is that it gives the serious content of a claim like (3) the sort of scope that the content of a universal generalization is supposed to have— one covering all instances, not just those currently expressible in our language.[32]

Much of what we have said so far regarding the role of intersubstitution in explaining the serious content put forward by an assertoric utterance of a generalization like (3) carries over to an explanation of the serious content put forward by opaque truth-ascriptions, such as

(5) What Corey said is true.

We noted above that, in the make-believe behind truth-talk, an utterance like this has the logical form of an existential claim—that is,

(6) $\exists x$(Corey said $x \wedge x$ is true).

Again, since it is part of the pretense that what is true (as well as what gets said) are propositions, and since we maintain that these putative entities are just part of the pretense, the serious point of the quantifier in (6), as it operates in the context of the pretense, has to do with what is expressed when some 'that'-clause goes in for (i.e., replaces) the 'x'. Thus, what the quantifier expresses a commitment to is some unspecified filling in of the schema $\ulcorner$ Corey said $\langle p \rangle \wedge \langle p \rangle$ is true $\urcorner$.

We can indicate such a commitment by prefixing the schema with an existential substitutional quantifier, as in

(10) Σp(Corey said $\langle p \rangle \wedge \langle p \rangle$ is true).

Here again is where intersubstitution plays its important role, as the application of rule (T-IV) takes us from this truth-involving formula to one that does not employ truth-talk, namely

(11) Σp(Corey said $\langle p \rangle \wedge p$).

We take (11) to provide a quasi-formal specification of the M-conditions that (4) specifies indirectly (albeit, again, still employing the pretense-involving discourse of proposition-talk). But, like (8), (11) employs technical devices that are not available in ordinary language. Specifying those M-conditions without recourse to those devices (or to the truth-predicate) would require the utterance of a potentially infinite disjunction of conjunctions (each specifying what Corey said and how the world is).

An opaque ascription of the truth-predicate, as in (5), thus serves as a means for endorsing what would otherwise require uttering an infinitely long sentence to endorse. When the context of an opaque truth-ascription makes it obvious which disjunct is relevant (by making it clear, e.g., what Corey said), the rest of them drop out of any processing. We might say that, technically, all of the disjuncts are included in what is expressed, but practically (or inferentially) speaking, the other disjuncts do not play any role. However, when a truth-ascription is "blind," the ability to express, in a finite manner, what it would otherwise take the entire infinite disjunction to express implements the important expressive role of opaque endorsement, a role that truth-talk incorporates into the language by including the intersubstitution license granted by rule (T-IV).

Even when the truth-predicate is not serving directly as a device for facilitating the expression of opaque endorsement, there is still a logical need for intersubstitution. Consider, for example, a sentence like

(12) If what the weatherman said is true, then you should bring your umbrella.

(employed in a conversational context where it is assumed that the weatherman said something). Here, the truth-predicate operates in the antecedent of the conditional, bracketing any expression of commitment. In the context of the pretense, (12) has the superficial form displayed in

(13) $(\exists x(\text{weatherman said } x \wedge x \text{ is true}) \rightarrow \text{you should bring your umbrella})$.

The quantification that (13) involves operates only in the antecedent, but it still applies in the context of the pretense, so we can understand its serious operation as we did above. Replacing the 'x's with '⟨p⟩'s, and indicating an unspecified filling of 'p' with the existential substitutional quantifier, we arrive at

(14) $(\Sigma p(\text{weatherman said } \langle p \rangle \wedge \langle p \rangle \text{ is true}) \rightarrow \text{you should bring your umbrella})$.

Once again, intersubstitution is crucial for getting from the truth-talk-involving (14) to something that we can consider to specify, without the pretense involved in truth-talk, the M-conditions that (12) specifies indirectly. Applying rule (T-IV) to (14) gives us the needed truth-talk-free formula,

(15) $(\Sigma p(\text{weatherman said } \langle p \rangle \wedge p) \rightarrow \text{you should bring your umbrella})$.

3.4 Non-Propositional Truth-Talk

Instances of truth-talk involving non-propositional subjects (e.g., sentences, utterances, thought-states, and so on) receive a similar analysis to that of existentially quantified instances of truth-talk. The difference is that, in the presentation of the logical form, the relevant non-propositional item will get (pretendedly) related either to a particular, specified proposition (via use of a 'that'-clause) or to what a bound variable ranges over by putative relations like *proposition-expression* or *meaning*.

In some instances of non-propositional truth-talk, the meaning or proposition-expression aspect of the truth-ascription turns out to be automatically, immediately available, in virtue of the default and immediate status of homophonic (or even extended homophonic) meaning-attribution sentences. So, in a case like

(16) 'Birds are dinosaurs' is true.

the default automatic availability of the homophonic meaning-attribution sentence

   (HMA) 'Birds are dinosaurs' means that birds are dinosaurs.

makes the first conjunct in the "official" analysis of the truth-ascription,

(17) ('Birds are dinosaurs' means that birds are dinosaurs ∧ that birds are dinosaurs is true).

trivial, in a sense. As a result, the point of the truth-ascription in (16) boils down to

(18) That birds are dinosaurs is true.

which Rule (T-II) reveals to be an indirect way of specifying the same M-conditions that are specified by

(19) Birds are dinosaurs.

Thus, in purely "home-language" cases like (16), truth-talk functions essentially in a disquotational manner.[33]

This point can be extended to other sorts of cases in which context makes it obvious what 'that'-clause would figure in the relevant meaning or proposition-expression clause (e.g., if it is obvious what meaning-attribution sentence applies regarding someone's utterance). Factoring in the relevant clause (pretendedly) relating the non-propositional item in question to a proposition, the serious content that a non-propositional instance of truth-talk puts forward indirectly is just the (serious) content that is or would be put forward by the putative content-vehicle to which the truth-predicate is being applied. This is the sense in which our account of truth-talk understands this fragment of discourse to operate quasi-anaphorically with respect to other sentences or utterances.

In other cases of non-propositional truth-ascription, where the relevant (pretended) connection to a particular proposition is not automatically apparent, truth-talk does not function in a disquotational manner (although there may be a sense in which it is still quasi-anaphoric). To see this, consider an opaque instance of truth-talk, such as

(20) 'Holzäpfel sind eßbar' is true.

Within the pretense behind truth-talk, (20) has the logical form

(21) ∃x('Holzäpfel sind eßbar' means x ∧ x is true).

We then analyze this form along the lines we applied to (6) to arrive eventually at

(22) Σp('Holzäpfel sind eßbar' means ⟨p⟩ ∧ p).

As with (8) and (11), this result of processing the truth-talk aspect of (20)/(21) would then have to be processed through our analysis of meaning-attribution sentences, to arrive at a direct specification of M-conditions along the lines of

(22*) Σp('Holzäpfel sind eßbar' has the same long-arm conceptual role as ⌜p⌝-as-the-speaker-actually-understands-it ∧ p).[34]

Direct statements of the M-conditions specified indirectly via "blind" truth-ascriptions to thought-states or utterances would be similar but would appeal to our analysis of proposition-relational/expressing talk. Once again, in these sorts of cases, truth-talk functions as a surrogate for substitutional quantification and schematic sentence variables, providing a way of incorporating the expressive power of these devices into our language without the actual technical aspects that they involve.[35]

4 Conclusions

We have claimed that T-deflationists should be alethic fictionalists about truth-talk, but given what our SPIF account says about the function and purpose of truth-talk, one might ask why we bother to offer specifically a *pretense* account of truth-talk instead of just endorsing T-deflationism.

We think that such a question, while not unexpected, belies a misunderstanding of what T-deflationism involves. On our view, the pretense approach is correlated with the *genus* of T-deflationism as a whole. The different *species* of this genus (e.g., disquotationalism, prosententialism, inference-rule deflationism, etc.) might fruitfully be viewed as attempts at cashing out principles of generation for a game of make-believe that could underwrite truth-talk. Our main reason for claiming this is the recognition that a central thesis of T-deflationism is that truth-talk serves only logical and linguistic *expressive* purposes. The alethic-locutions exist in order to provide a means for talking about other things, which are unrelated to truth. So T-deflationism *in effect* treats the alethic-locutions as representational aides, which are introduced not to express something about the world directly but rather in order to facilitate a certain kind of indirect talk about aspects of the world. For this reason we are inclined to say that understanding a way of talking in the way that T-deflationists view truth-talk just is to see it as involving a kind of fiction. We also maintain that the most fruitful way to understand a way of talking as involving an element of fiction is in terms of a SPIF account of that fragment of discourse, explaining the linguistic functioning of the talk as involving mechanisms that invoke pretense. For these reasons, we offer a SPIF account of truth-talk.

While we do not think that ordinary speakers are (or, if queried, would acknowledge) pretending anything when they employ truth-talk, an awareness of the pretense at some level could be part of our account. If it were, we would locate this awareness at the level of a *theorist*, when she aims to explain the linguistic functioning of the instances of certain fragments of discourse in expressing the serious content they put forward. We think that something like this theorist-level pretense-awareness may be present when philosophers attempt to "regiment" some fragment of discourse.[36]

Although we shall not try to establish that point here, we will provide a sense for how one might go about establishing it.

We get an initial indication of the kind of theorist-level pretense-awareness that we have postulated by considering how a truth theorist who advocates T-deflationism might deal with the issues that surround 'true'-involving generalizations. When our theorist is concerned with determining how to interpret some 'true'-involving discourse, or if she is attempting to show how one can *prove* such 'true'-involving generalizations, there is a question as to whether she is providing a *descriptive* account of our actual practices or whether she is providing a *prescriptive* account of how we should use the language. Some T-deflationists—we think, for example, of Hartry Field—relegate such a descriptive account to a branch of sociology, one they see as neither particularly interesting nor particularly relevant, given the problems they are tackling. As such, we are inclined to conclude that our regimenting theorist is offering a prescriptive, rather than a descriptive, account.

But our theorist need not go so far as to embrace some form of *revolutionary* fictionalism, claiming that, insofar as it is prescriptive, her view suggests how we might either change our language or change the practices that determine how we use truth-talk. Rather, what seems more plausible is that such a theorist is providing a *hermeneutic* fictionalist account—frequently, in the form of what might count as principles of generation for a pretense already involved in truth-talk.[37] This account makes it seem as if it is about *truth* when, in fact, it is not. On her view, there is nothing—no property (at least of the sort there would have to be)—to which the proposed principles would answer. Moreover, when such a theorist presents an account of the truth-predicate, thereby explaining the serious content of 'true'-involving sentences, we can take what she does as analogous to what we are doing in presenting our SPIF account of truth-talk.

Understanding 'principles of generation' in a suitably broad way, we might see a T-deflationist's proposal of such rules—be they instances of the T-schema, the inference rules, *'True'-In* and *'True'-Out*, or what have you—as, in effect, attempts to explain principles of generation for a pretense involved in truth-talk. So, depending on which rules or principles a T-deflationist develops for 'true', she will get various brands of T-deflationism—various species of that genus. But such a theorist need not be saying— and we do not need to construe such a theorist as saying—that these rules are what actual language users have in mind or aim to follow when they employ truth-talk. Rather, what the T-deflationist (and, by proxy, what we) should (or would) say is that what enables truth-talk to work is that it is *as if* these principles actually govern the behavior of speakers employing the locutions 'true', 'false', and so on. Insofar as the theorist is not offering principles that speakers actually, psychologically realize (any more than Alfred Tarski was, perhaps), there is a sense in which she herself is engaged in a pretense, making *as if* these principles are correct for purposes of accounting for truth-talk and for yielding the serious content of uses of 'true'-involving sentences.[38]

In this chapter we have argued that T-deflationists should be (or, perhaps, already are) pretense theorists about truth-talk, and we have provided some of the central features of our favored pretense account of that talk. But one might ask why one should be a T-deflationist at all. In order to answer this question, we must consider what the alternatives to T-deflationism might be. In order to get to the alternatives, notice that one might either accept that there is a real, robust, perhaps explanatorily important, property of truth, or one might not accept that there is any such property. One who adopts the first option would be an inflationist *about truth*.[39] One who adopts the second option would either be a deflationist or an eliminativist *about truth-talk*. As we see it, a primary reason for being a T-deflationist is because of the reasons for not adopting one of these other positions.[40]

The central issue that T-inflationists point to, as the basis for their claim that the truth-predicate expresses a substantive property, turns on the explanation of linguistic and mental content.[41] (Earlier responses to T-deflationism focused on the putative role of truth in explanations of success—either of scientific theorizing or of behavior—but we think that this earlier issue has been adequately resolved by T-deflationists.[42]) However, while truth-conditional/referential semantics is still more or less orthodoxy, it is not without gaps and problems.[43] Nor is it the only game in town (so to speak).[44] Moreover, an inflationist view about truth (and reference), according to which the truth-predicate (as well as the reference- and satisfaction-predicates) functions to attribute a substantive, explanatory property, faces the daunting task of providing a revenge-immune (and consistent) solution to the full range of *semantic pathology*. This putative phenomenon includes the familiar liar paradox—along with Curry's, Yablo's, Grelling's, and Berry's, as well as the truth-teller and a whole host of other indeterminate cases we have identified that are analogs for the rest of the putative semantic paradoxes, plus all of the dual-symptom variants of what we call the "open pair."[45]

In contrast, as part of a broadly T-deflationist package, we have provided a diagnosis and treatment of the full spectrum of (putative) semantic pathology, based on elements of the SPIF accounts we offer for talk involving each of the traditional semantic notions.[46] On our accounts, none of the sentences that appear to manifest semantic pathology has any real-world (i.e., serious) content. They therefore all turn out to be semantically defective (what we sometimes call *s-defective*), as we explain this notion.[47] These sentences have this status because of a "content-seeking" looping that arises in these cases, due to the quasi-anaphoric operation that all of the traditional semantic locutions involve,[48] one given to them by the principles of generation that govern their use, according to the games of make-believe that underlie these ways of talking. This looping keeps the "semantic reach" of these sentences entirely within the relevant make-believe, making them "purely pretend" claims that say nothing about the world outside of the game.[49] Because the problematic sentences are all thereby s-defective, they cannot serve as premises or conclusions in any arguments, nor, we argue, can they be embedded in truth-functional constructions without rendering the whole s-defective as well. This factors into the immunity that we claim our dissolution of semantic pathology has to the sorts of revenge problems that plague other responses to the liar paradox and its kin. We consider this provision of a unified, revenge-immune dissolution of the full range of semantic pathology to be one of the most important accomplishments of our project. This tidy approach to semantic pathology is unavailable to T-inflationists, who must therefore provide their own solution to the problem. We conjecture that this will be very difficult for a T-inflationist to do.[50]

Notes

1. While fictionalism is sometimes motivated by metaphysical considerations, it ought to be understood as a genus of theories in the philosophy of language, rather than in metaphysics. See Armour-Garb and Woodbridge (2015, chap. 1).

2. Woodbridge (2005) presents the original version of this sort of view.

3. See Armour-Garb and Woodbridge (2015) for the most complete presentation of our mature account of truth-talk, as well as our related accounts of talk putatively about propositions, what does and does not exist, identity and difference, reference, and predicate-satisfaction.

4. While not explicitly formulating the thesis in this way, Yablo (2005) relies on something like (EI) to argue for a particular fictionalist account of "number-talk."

5. We should note that by 'property' what we primarily have in mind here is what one intuitively might call a *robust* or *substantive* property—in David Lewis's (1983) terminology, a "sparse" property—of the sort that T-deflationists reject. As far as a Lewisian "abundant" property is concerned, we, like most theorists, accept that a "property" of that sort exists (simply as the extension of 'true'), but we think of it as a by-product of the operation of the predicate rather than anything that can do theoretical (i.e., explanatory) work. If one wants to posit "thin" properties of some other sort, as Horwich (1998) seems to do, we are agnostic about whether anything of that sort exists, although we are not inclined to endorse this type of view. We are skeptical that such a property would do any theoretical work.

6. For more on this, see Armour-Garb and Woodbridge (2014; 2015, chap. 4).

7. Prime examples of prefix-fictionalism include the accounts that Lewis (1978), Field (1989), and Rosen (1990) develop. Pretense-involving fictionalist accounts include Yablo (1996, 2005), Crimmins (1998), and Kroon (2001, 2004), all of which stem from Walton (1990). See Caddick Bourne (2013) and Armour-Garb and Woodbridge (2015, chap. 1) for more details on the distinction.

8. For some of the reasons, see Armour-Garb (2015) and Armour-Garb and Woodbridge (2015, chap. 1).

9. As seems clear, an ETF account of truth-talk would be intolerable, as it would render false all truth-ascriptions, thereby undermining the status of the T-schema, since not every instance of it would be true.

10. For pragmatic PIF accounts, see Kroon (2001, 2004). See Armour-Garb and Woodbridge (2015, chap. 2) for reasons to prefer SPIF accounts over pragmatic PIF accounts.

11. See Walton (1990) and Crimmins (1998).

12. For more on the details of make-believe and its role in semantic pretense, see Richard (2000); Woodbridge and Armour-Garb (2009).

13. In general, we call the real-world conditions specified by a sentence that sentence's *M-conditions* (*M* for "meaning"—although we could have used *W* for "worldly" instead). The serious content that a pretense-involving utterance expresses is just the M-conditions specified by the utterance. Such claims are "partially pretend" claims, since they say something about the real world; they just do so indirectly *via* semantic mechanisms that involve pretense. In contrast, pretense-free utterances specify their M-conditions directly.

14. Cf. Woodbridge (2005). In order to deflect a possible misinterpretation, we should make clear that we are not saying that being true is a matter of being pretended true. There is an important difference between claiming something is true—and the pretenses always involved in such a claim—and pretending that something is true. When we claim, or assert (e.g.) that a given sentence is true, we are not pretending that it is true.

15. There is a potential worry that is peculiar to a proposed *pretense-based* account of truth-talk, which emerges once we consider a putatively plausible reading of what pretending might involve. The worry is that we will not be able to explain truth-talk in terms of pretense because the explanations of pretense and the activity of pretending itself rely on a notion of truth. For a response to this worry, see Armour-Garb and Woodbridge (2015, chap. 7).

16. This is to say that if someone were explicitly and intentionally to engage in this game of make-believe, that person would expressly make-believe what is laid out in rule (T-I). That said, we do not think that speakers employing truth-talk do explicitly and intentionally engage in the game of make-believe we describe here, so no one is actually stipulating or expressly pretending what we specify in (T-I). As we explain in responding to what we call the *Engagement Complaint* (or, the EC), we do not offer our view as an account of speakers' attitudes or of what speakers are, or take themselves to be, doing. Rather, we claim that it is *as if* speakers employing truth-talk are actively engaged in the game of make-believe we explain here. For more on the EC and our response to it, see Armour-Garb and Woodbridge (2015, chap. 2).

17. Like most T-deflationists, we reject the standard truth-conditional/referential conception of linguistic meaning or content, in favor of a *use-theoretic* understanding. More specifically, we favor explaining meaning in terms of long-arm conceptual roles or broadly inferential roles (cf. Brandom 1994). We use the terms *content-connection* and *content-connected* to indicate whatever connection an expression has to some part of the world—the worldly entanglement aspects of the long-arm conceptual role that someone's use of the expression gives it—in virtue of which it is possible for a speaker to use the expression to talk about that part of the world. For more on *content-connectedness*, see Armour-Garb and Woodbridge (2015, chap. 2).

18. We also advocate, and have developed, a SPIF account of proposition-talk, which we cannot discuss in this chapter, but see Armour-Garb and Woodbridge (2012; 2015, chap. 3).

19. Cf. Alston (1996, 14).

20. The classic presentation of prosententialism is Grover, Camp, and Belnap (1975). Brandom's version of the approach appears in Brandom (1994, chap. 5).

21. Cf. Horwich (1998, 125).

22. This explains the sense in which the truth-conditions for a sentence are a by-product of its meaning, of which M-conditions are a significant component. As should be clear, on our view, truth-conditions have only a thin, derivative status, as conditions for the appropriate use of the truth-predicate.

23. The directness of the specification of those conditions by an assertoric utterance of (2) is an accidental feature of this case (and others like it), but it is not necessary in general. Rules (T-II) and (T-III) both allow that the sentence that goes in for the 'p' in ⌜That p is true⌝ or ⌜That p is false⌝ can itself be a pretense-involving sentence (e.g., an instance of existence-talk or of proposition-talk or even truth-talk) that specifies M-conditions only indirectly. This is the case with an utterance of "It is true that Santa Claus does not exist" or even an utterance of "It is true that it is true that crabapples are edible."

24. See Walton (1993) and Yablo (1996) on the distinction between content-oriented and prop-oriented make-believe.

25. For present purposes, this is taken to be equivalent to

(ES*) That p is true iff p.

26. Azzouni (2006).

27. Mutatis mutandis for quantificational utterances employing the falsity-predicate.

28. (T-IV) captures a form of 'True'-In and 'True'-Out, namely,

'True'-In: From $p \Rightarrow T\langle p \rangle$
'True'-Out: From $T\langle p \rangle \Rightarrow p$,

where these can be understood as representing inference rules or as capturing substitution rules, to the effect that, in all extensional (or "transparent") contexts, one can intersubstitute '$\langle p \rangle$ is true' ('p') for 'p' ('$\langle p \rangle$ is true'), where 'p' serves as a sentential variable, which can be replaced by any declarative sentence, and where the chevron brackets, '$\langle$' and '$\rangle$', serve as a device for nominalizing any sentence that goes in for 'p'. Compare Beall (2009, vii, 1, 12) on the role of intersubstitution.

29. Notice that Horwich's (1998) minimalism runs into difficulties precisely on this point, since he does not introduce an intersubstitution rule but desperately needs one, lest he lose the explanation for why, in some sense, the assertability of any utterance of the form ⌜If p, then q⌝ is conditional on one of the form ⌜If $\langle p \rangle$ is true, then $\langle q \rangle$ is true⌝ and vice versa (and ditto for their unassertability).

30. Quine (1986, 11–12); Horwich (1998, 4n1, 25–26, 32–33); Azzouni (1999, 541–544); and Field (1999, 533).

31. The specification that (8) accomplishes does, however, still involve the pretense of proposition-talk and thus is still an indirect specification, strictly speaking. Unpacking the

proposition-talk along the lines of our SPIF account of that discourse would involve moving from (8) to

(8*) Πp(Isabel assertorically uttered a sentence with the same long-arm conceptual role as ⌜p⌝-as-the-speaker-actually-understands-it → p).

For more on this, see Armour-Garb and Woodbridge (2015, chap. 3).

32. This aspect of our SPIF account of truth-talk gives T-deflationists an easier time dealing with the generalization problem (cf. Gupta 1993). An explicit appeal to pretense would allow the T-deflationist to take 'true'-involving generalizations to be actual generalizations, logically speaking, instead of just the conjunction of the instances. While the serious content of such generalizations is the totality of the instances, because this serious content also automatically incorporates any new cases that arise with the expansion of a language, it avoids taking the meaning of 'true' to change when the substitution class for the otherwise necessary substitutional quantifiers or schematic sentence variables changes. Thus, the recognition of pretense might better account for the role that 'true'-involving generalizations can play in explanations, the expression of logical laws, and so on. Cf. Woodbridge (2005, 154–161).

33. Relative to the speaker's understanding, as per Field (1994).

34. Similarly, instances of truth-talk that are propositional but *nontransparent*, such as 'Goldbach's conjecture is true', would receive an initial analysis along the lines of

Σp(Goldbach's conjecture = ⟨p⟩ ∧ p)

with the embedded sentence then getting analyzed to yield

Σp('Goldbach's conjecture' has the same singular-term long-arm conceptual role as ⌜that p⌝-as-the-speaker-actually-understands-it ∧ p).

35. Armour-Garb and Woodbridge (2015, chap. 4) also explains how our SPIF account analyzes truth-ascriptions embedded in intentional contexts.

36. For a good discussion of *regimentation*, see Azzouni (2006, 74–81).

37. On the distinction between revolutionary and hermeneutic fictionalism, see Stanley (2001) and Armour-Garb and Woodbridge (2015, chap. 1).

38. Lest a reader worry that, deep down (so to speak), we are committed to the claim that such theorists are actually engaged in (formulating or constructing) a pretense (i.e., are intentionally making as if), we note that we, as metatheorists, can describe the situation by saying it is simply *as if* they are engaged in (formulating or constructing) a pretense—that is, that they are offering rules or principles as background pretenses for a game of make-believe.

39. In general, a T-inflationist could be either a primitivist or a reductionist about truth. Since the points that we will make apply to either species of T-inflationism, we will not discuss the details behind such positions.

40. Since the expressive indispensability of truth-talk is acknowledged by all truth-theorists, we find eliminativism about such talk to be a nonstarter.

41. Cf. Davidson (1996) for an appeal to this explanatory role in an argument for primitivism about truth and Devitt (1997, 101–105) for an appeal to this explanatory role in an argument for a reductionist view of truth.

42. See Leeds (1978, 1995), Williams (1986), Field (1994), and Devitt (1997, 98–101). But see Damnjanovic (2005) and Gamster (2018) for reconsideration of this attitude.

43. Cf. Schiffer (1987) and Soames (1992).

44. See Brandom (1994).

45. See Armour-Garb and Woodbridge (2015, chaps. 5 and 6).

46. For the details, see Armour-Garb and Woodbridge (2013; 2015, chaps. 5 and 6).

47. Ibid. As we would put it, these sentences do not express any M-conditions.

48. Cf. Grover (1977)'s proposed solution to the liar paradox.

49. This is not to say that such sentences are entirely meaningless; for discussion, see Armour-Garb and Woodbridge (2015, 157–161).

50. Our thanks to Jeremy Wyatt for helpful comments and suggestions.

References

Alston, W. 1996. *A Realist Conception of Truth*. Ithaca, NY: Cornell University Press.

Armour-Garb, B. 2015. "New Problems for Modal Fictionalism." *Philosophical Studies* 172: 1201–1219.

Armour-Garb, B., and Woodbridge, J. 2012. "The Story about Propositions." *Noûs* 46: 635–674.

Armour-Garb, B., and Woodbridge, J. 2013. "Semantic Defectiveness and the Liar." *Philosophical Studies* 164: 845–863.

Armour-Garb, B., and Woodbridge, J. 2014. "From Mathematical Fictionalism to Truth-Theoretic Fictionalism." *Philosophy and Phenomenological Research* 88: 93–118.

Armour-Garb, B., and Woodbridge, J. 2015. *Pretense and Pathology: Philosophical Fictionalism and Its Applications*. Cambridge: Cambridge University Press.

Azzouni, J. 1999. "Comments on Shapiro." *Journal of Philosophy* 96: 541–544.

Azzouni, J. 2006. *Tracking Reason: Proof, Consequence and Truth*. Oxford: Oxford University Press.

Beall, Jc. 2009. *Spandrels of Truth*. Oxford: Oxford University Press.

Brandom, R. 1994. *Making It Explicit*. Cambridge, MA: Harvard University Press.

Caddick Bourne, E. 2013. "Fictionalism." *Analysis* 73: 147–162.

Crimmins, M. 1998. "Hesperus and Phosphorus: Sense, Pretense, and Reference." *Philosophical Review* 107: 1–47.

Damnjanovic, N. 2005. "Deflationism and the Success Argument." *Philosophical Quarterly* 55: 53–67.

Davidson, D. 1996. "The Folly of Trying to Define Truth." *Journal of Philosophy* 93: 263–278.

Devitt, M. 1997. *Realism and Truth*. 2nd ed. Princeton, NJ: Princeton University Press.

Field, H. 1989. *Realism, Mathematics and Modality*. Oxford: Basil Blackwell.

Field, H. 1994. "Deflationist Views of Meaning and Content." *Mind* 103: 249–285.

Field, H. 1999. "Deflating the Conservativeness Argument." *Journal of Philosophy* 96: 533–540.

Field, H. 2008. *Saving Truth from Paradox*. Oxford: Oxford University Press.

Gamster, W. 2018. "Truth: Explanation, Success, and Coincidence." *Philosophical Studies* 175: 1243–1265.

Grover, D. 1977. "Inheritors and Paradox." *Journal of Philosophy* 74: 590–604.

Grover, D., Camp, J., and Belnap, N. 1975. "A Prosentential Theory of Truth." *Philosophical Studies* 27: 73–125.

Gupta, A. 1993. "A Critique of Deflationism." *Philosophical Topics* 21: 57–81.

Horwich, P. 1998. *Truth*. 2nd ed. Oxford: Clarendon Press.

Kroon, F. 2001. "Fictionalism and the Informativeness of Identity." *Philosophical Studies* 106: 197–225.

Kroon, F. 2004. "Descriptivism, Pretense, and the Frege-Russell Problems." *Philosophical Review* 113: 1–30.

Leeds, S. 1978. "Theories of Reference and Truth." *Erkenntnis* 13: 111–129.

Leeds, S. 1995. "Truth, Correspondence, and Success." *Philosophical Studies* 79: 1–36.

Lewis, D. 1978. "Truth in Fiction." *American Philosophical Quarterly* 15: 37–46. Reprinted in *Philosophical Papers*, vol. 1, 261–280. Oxford: Oxford University Press, 1983.

Lewis, D. 1983. "New Work for a Theory of Universals." *Australasian Journal of Philosophy* 61: 343–377.

Quine, W. V. 1986. *Philosophy of Logic*. 2nd ed. Cambridge, MA: Harvard University Press.

Richard, M. 2000. "Semantic Pretense." In A. Everett and T. Hofweber, eds., *Empty Names, Fiction, and the Puzzles of Non-Existence*, 205–232. Stanford, CA: CSLI.

Rosen, G. 1990. "Modal Fictionalism." *Mind* 99: 327–354.

Schiffer, S. 1987. *Remnants of Meaning*. Cambridge, MA: MIT Press.

Soames, S. 1992. "Truth, Meaning, and Understanding." *Philosophical Studies* 65: 17–35.

Stanley, J. 2001. "Hermeneutic Fictionalism." *Figurative Language, Midwest Studies in Philosophy* 25: 36–71.

Walton, K. 1990. *Mimesis as Make-Believe*. Cambridge, MA: Harvard University Press.

Walton, K. 1993. "Metaphor and Prop-Oriented Make-Believe." *European Journal of Philosophy* 1: 39–56. Reprinted in M. Kalderon, ed., *Fictionalism in Metaphysics*, 65–87. Oxford: Oxford University Press.

Williams, M. 1986. "Do We (Epistemologists) Need a Theory of Truth?" *Philosophical Topics* 14: 223–242.

Woodbridge, J. 2005. "Truth as a Pretense." In M. Kalderon, ed., *Fictionalism in Metaphysics*, 134–177. Oxford: Oxford University Press.

Woodbridge, J., and Armour-Garb, B. 2009. "Linguistic Puzzles and Semantic Pretense." In S. Sawyer, ed., *New Waves in Philosophy of Language*, 250–284. Basingstoke: Palgrave Macmillan.

Yablo, S. 1996. "How in the World?" *Philosophical Topics* 24: 255–286.

Yablo, S. 2005. "The Myth of the Seven." In M. Kalderon, ed., *Fictionalism in Metaphysics*, 88–115. Oxford: Oxford University Press.

24   Truth and Insubstantiality: The Metaphysics of Deflationism

Jeremy Wyatt

Deflationism has left an indelible mark on the theories of truth that have emerged over the past century.[1] Deflationists, carefully observing the long-standing debates over truth's nature, enter the fray offering a metaphysically tidy path to resolution. Whereas *substantivist* theorists—including correspondence and coherence theorists, pragmatists, identity theorists, and pluralists—vigorously disagree among themselves over how to understand the essence of truth, the deflationist assures them that there is a rather simple solution to this classic problem. Deflationists differ among themselves over the precise contours of the solution, but the basic deflationary suggestion is that a truth-bearer (e.g., a proposition, sentence, or utterance) is true iff things are as it says that they are. To understand this proposal, it seems, we needn't appeal to any sort of complicated correspondence or coherence relations, we needn't talk about truth's relationship with inquiry or verification or facts, and we needn't say that truth's nature varies from domain to domain. In other words, the deflationary approach to the metaphysics of truth is meant to be illuminating in virtue of its striking metaphysical simplicity.

It is understandable, then, that deflationists have aimed primarily to develop theories of our thought and talk about truth, rather than the metaphysics of truth. However, one of the main points that I will aim to develop is that to properly understand deflationism—and in particular, the opposition between deflationism and substantivism—we need to do quite a bit of metaphysical investigation. This fact has been underappreciated by both deflationists and their critics, with the result that debates about deflationism, despite their manifest subtlety, have been somewhat impoverished. My hope, then, is that a systematic investigation of the metaphysics of deflationism will serve to productively advance these debates.

1   Moderate Deflationism versus Pure Deflationism

In investigating the metaphysics of deflationism, we need first to draw a distinction between two deflationary stances regarding the metaphysics of truth. Crispin Wright (1998, 38–39) aptly points out that deflationism, as it is typically advanced, is better described as a "tendency" than as a particular position on truth. One often hears a certain slogan associated with the deflationary tendency: that truth is not substantial/substantive/thick/weighty/chunky.[2] As with slogans generally, this claim is highly suggestive; the trouble is that it's unclear what it means. For one thing, it's at least four ways ambiguous: it might be a contention about theories of truth, the ordinary concept TRUTH, the word "true," or the property *truth*. Since our interest here is in the metaphysics of truth, we'll be concentrating on the property-level reading.[3] Of course, focusing our efforts in this way affords only a bit of clarity, as it's highly nonobvious what it would mean for *truth* to be an insubstantial property.

Certain well-known deflationists have argued, or else would hold, that there is simply no such property as *truth*.[4] This is a rather clean, eliminative position on the nature of truth, so we can call such deflationists *pure deflationists*. Pure deflationists will of course deny that *truth* is a substantial property. However, this is because for the pure deflationist, talk of truth amounts merely to *flatus vocis*—the pure deflationist denies that *truth* exists in the first place. Accordingly, if we assimilated deflationism to pure deflationism, then it would be difficult to understand why deflationists so often say that *truth* is an insubstantial property, rather than saying more straightforwardly that *truth* doesn't exist.

The interesting wrinkle here is that a number of contemporary deflationists do grant that *truth* is a real, bona fide property. Notably, Paul Horwich (1998b, 38) regards "(is) true" as a predicate and feels compelled on that account to take this expression to "stand for" *truth*, a rationale with which a number of other deflationists have expressed sympathy.[5] But, say these theorists, *truth* is no ordinary property. Unlike, for example, *being a tree* or *being made of tin*, *truth* is "insubstantial." Call someone who posits a property *truth* but holds that it is "insubstantial" a *moderate deflationist*.[6]

Moderate deflationists thus bear the burden (in contrast to pure deflationists) of explaining what it means for *truth* to be an insubstantial property. However, it turns out that moderate deflationists and their critics have been extremely equivocal on this point. There are five senses in which moderate deflationists have held, or have been taken to hold, that *truth* is insubstantial. The theses at issue here tend to be run together or erroneously assumed to logically depend upon one another. To properly evaluate the prospects of moderate deflationism, then, it's vital that we pry them apart. My contention will be that two of these theses should each be regarded as partially definitive of moderate deflationism and that neither thesis entails the other. In this sense, as we'll see, it proves to be illuminating to think of moderate deflationism as having two distinct faces.

2   Three Constraints

The theses about *truth* that have been associated with moderate deflationism are that *truth* (i) is a "metaphysically transparent" property, (ii) is a "non-explanatory" property, (iii) lacks a constitution theory, (iv) is a rather abundant property, and (v) is a "logical" property. In determining which of these theses we should actually associate with moderate deflationism, we'll need some explicit criteria. Accordingly, we'll assume in what follows that for a thesis to be characteristic of moderate deflationism, it is necessary and sufficient that it have the following three features:[7]

(a) It is a suitably deflationary claim about *truth* (the *Deflationary Constraint*);

(b) It is directly about the features of *truth*—not directly about only the features of TRUTH or "true" (the *Metaphysical Constraint*); and

(c) It is not just a special case of a thesis with features (a) and (b) (the *Special Case Constraint*).

Let me say a few words about the motivations for these constraints and the demands that they impose. I take two conditions to be individually necessary and jointly sufficient for a claim about *truth* to satisfy the Deflationary Constraint. The first is that the claim should jeopardize traditional metaphysical inquiry into *truth*'s essence to some degree. The basic thought is that deflationary claims about *truth* are meant to *deflate* something—namely, the sort of metaphysical inquiry about *truth* pursued by substantivists. We'll say more about the distinctive character of such inquiry in sections 3.2 and 3.3.

The second condition for a claim to satisfy the Deflationary Constraint is that at least one paradigmatic moderate deflationist is committed by their views on truth to endorsing it, and no paradigmatic moderate deflationist is committed by their views on truth to rejecting it. This condition ensures that the claim does indeed have a foothold in extant varieties of moderate deflationism and is available to an advocate of any such view.[8]

A pleasing consequence of this constraint is that, for instance, the claim that there are no properties isn't characteristic of moderate deflationism. While it would deflate traditional inquiry into *truth*'s nature, we rightly predict that this claim isn't *suitably* deflationary, since every moderate deflationist takes there to be at least one property—namely, *truth*.

The impetus behind the Metaphysical Constraint is that we're interested here to determine which significant features the moderate deflationist attributes to *truth*. Significant features of predicates and predicative concepts don't in general transmit to the properties that they denote. Predicative concepts—for example, SOLID—are presumably mental entities, yet some such concepts denote nonmental properties, such as *being solid*. Likewise, *being disgusting* is denoted by the French predicate "dégoûtant," though *being disgusting* is not a French (?) property. Accordingly, when seeking to determine which claims are characteristic of moderate deflationism, we'll concentrate on claims of the form "*truth* has (lacks) feature F," rather than claims of the form "*truth* is denoted by an F (non-F) predicate/concept."

Together, the Deflationary and Metaphysical Constraints ensure that the commitments we associate with moderate deflationism are both suitably deflationary and distinctively metaphysical. The Special Case Constraint enables us to center upon the *fundamental* commitments of moderate deflationism—those that constitute the core of the view—rather than upon claims that merely follow from the view's core claims. What will emerge in our discussion is that only theses (ii) and (iii) above (when suitably refined) satisfy all of these constraints. As a result, only (ii) and (iii) (once refined) are characteristic of a moderate deflationary metaphysics of *truth*. (i), (iv), and (v) are, at least in this context, red herrings. Let's now take a close look at each of the five theses.

3   Truth's Insubstantiality: Locating the Core Theses

3.1   Transparency

When developing his critique of deflationism, Michael Lynch (2009, 107) attributes to moderate deflationists the view that *truth* is a *metaphysically transparent* property in the sense that "we know all the essential facts about [*truth*] … just by grasping the concept of truth." The truth concept at issue is the actual, ordinary concept TRUTH. Accordingly, the thesis that *truth* is metaphysically transparent is meant to have a significant methodological upshot—that to gain a comprehensive picture of *truth*'s essence, we need only discern the content of our ordinary concept TRUTH. The thesis at issue here then amounts to:[9]

> (Transparent$_L$) Any actual thinker who possesses TRUTH *ipso facto* knows every essential fact about *truth*.

Nic Damnjanovic also takes moderate deflationists (he calls them "new wave deflationists") to hold that *truth* is metaphysically transparent. Yet interestingly, Damnjanovic takes the operative notion of transparency to be different from that in (Transparent$_L$). In Damnjanovic's terminology, property P is metaphysically transparent, relative to a particular concept C of P iff C is *revelatory* of P's nature. For C to be revelatory in this way is for it to be the case that "any subject *S* who grasps [C] is in a position to know the full nature of [P] without further empirical investigation or a priori argumentation."[10] Focusing on the actual, ordinary concept TRUTH, *truth*'s being metaphysically transparent in this sense would then amount to:[11]

> (Transparent$_D$) Any actual thinker who possesses TRUTH is *ipso facto* in a position to know, without further empirical inquiry or a priori argumentation, every essential fact about *truth*.

(Transparent$_L$) is stronger than (Transparent$_D$). When articulating (Transparent$_D$), Damnjanovic adopts a Williamsonian conception of being in a position to know, according to which to be in a position to know the proposition *p*, "no obstacle must block one's path to knowing *p*. If one is in a position to know *p*, and one has done what one is in a position to do to decide whether *p* is true, then one does know *p*."[12] Thus, if S knows *p*, then S is in a position to know *p* without further empirical inquiry or a priori argumentation, though not necessarily vice versa. For S might be in a position to satisfy the conditions for knowing p without relying on further empirical inquiry or a priori argumentation though S has yet to satisfy those conditions.

Lynch takes the moderate deflationist to be committed to (Transparent$_L$), while Damnjanovic takes them to be committed only to (Transparent$_D$). To which are they committed, then? In fact, to neither. Consider, for instance, what a paradigm moderate deflationist—the *minimalist*, as depicted by Horwich—will say about *truth*'s metaphysical transparency.

Let the *equivalence schema* be:

(ES) The proposition that p is true iff p.

According to the minimalist, one's possession of the actual, ordinary concept TRUTH consists, in essence, in one's disposition to accept every instance of (ES) in the absence of supporting argumentation.[13] Minimalists likewise maintain that the fundamental, essential facts about *truth* are those that are reported by the (nonparadoxical) instances of (ES).[14]

Given this, it might seem that the minimalist should hold that *truth* is metaphysically transparent, in the sense of (Transparent$_D$). They claim that if S possesses TRUTH, then S is disposed to accept every instance of (ES) in the absence of supporting argumentation. And if the essential facts about *truth* are exhausted by the (nonparadoxical) instances of (ES), then S would presumably be in a position to know every such fact without relying upon further empirical inquiry or a priori argumentation. To come to know these facts, all that S would need to do is to reflectively tease out the content of her concept of truth.

Despite its initial plausibility, however, this line of reasoning doesn't go through. An influential observation by Anil Gupta (1993, 365–366) points to the reason why. Referring to Horwich's *minimal theory of truth*, whose axioms consist of the (nonparadoxical) instances of (ES), as "MT," Gupta notices that "MT contains a biconditional for each proposition; none is excluded. The ideology of MT contains, therefore, each and every concept. It subsumes the ideology of every theory. … None of us has more than a minute fraction of the concepts employed in the biconditionals."

MT contains infinitely many axioms, one for each proposition. Many of these axioms involve concepts that are possessed by very few (if any) possessors of TRUTH. One of them, for instance, says that the proposition that the Continuum Hypothesis is independent of ZFC (Zermelo-Fraenkel set theory with the axiom of choice) is true iff the Continuum Hypothesis is independent of ZFC. Given that each such axiom reports a fundamental, essential fact about *truth*, there will then be (infinitely) many essential facts about *truth* that, according to the minimalist, few (if any) possessors of TRUTH are in a position to know without further empirical inquiry or a priori argumentation.

Hence, for the minimalist, *truth* fails to be metaphysically transparent even in the weak sense specified in (Transparent$_D$) and thus also in the stronger sense specified in (Transparent$_L$). Accordingly, both (Transparent$_D$) and (Transparent$_L$) fail to satisfy the Deflationary Constraint—at least one paradigmatic moderate deflationary view of truth entails that they are false. Lynch and Damnjanovic have misdiagnosed what moderate deflationists—specifically, minimalists—are after. Nevertheless, I think that they are onto something important. Horwich (1998b, 2, 49) famously contends that *truth* lacks a "hidden structure." I think that it's exactly right to explicate this idea by adverting to a notion of transparency. But rather than claiming that *truth* is metaphysically transparent, what the moderate deflationist should claim is that *truth* is susceptible at most to a transparent *constitution theory*.

3.2 Lack of Constitution

Whenever he explicitly specifies the sense in which he takes *truth* to be insubstantial, Horwich proposes that substantial properties are properties "for which there might well be a constitution theory."[15] Let a constitution theory for *truth* be a set of propositions of the following form (where "P" is a schematic letter):

(CT) For all *x*: *x*'s instantiating *truth* consists in *x*'s instantiating P.

Horwich, then, takes the following thesis to be central to his deflationism:[16]

(Unconstituted*) There is a property *truth*, but it is insusceptible to a constitution theory (i.e., *truth* exists, but there is no possible, true constitution theory for *truth*).

In his own treatment of deflationism, Julian Dodd (2008, 133–134) nicely explains the rationale behind (Unconstituted*):

> [According to the deflationist,] there can be no account of what truth *consists in*: there is no prospect of discovering a property *F* shared by all and only the truths, such that the truths are true because they are *F*... The deflationist's contention is stronger than a mere rejection of correspondence: it is that the *kind of project* undertaken by a correspondence theorist—the search for a property *F* explanatory of truth—is misconceived.

The deflationary intention here is to directly undermine the traditional metaphysical project in truth theory—we might call it the *essence project*—a signature aim of which is to construct an accurate constitution theory for *truth* that reveals *truth*'s complex essence. Since establishing it would deal a severe blow to that enterprise, (Unconstituted*) does satisfy one aspect of the Deflationary Constraint. The trouble, however, is that as with (Transparent$_{L/D}$), at least one paradigm moderate deflationist should actually reject (Unconstituted*). Surprisingly enough, it is again the minimalist who must do so.

Just as the axioms of the minimal theory of truth are meant to consist of the (nonparadoxical) instances of (ES), we might say that the axioms of the *minimal constitution theory of truth* (CT$_M$) consist of the (nonparadoxical) instances of:

(MCT) For all *x*: *x*'s instantiating *truth* consists in *x*'s instantiating the property that the proposition that p instantiates iff p.

The key detail here is that given their adherence to the minimal theory of truth, the minimalist should likewise maintain that all of the axioms of (CT_M) are true. For this reason, they should in fact hold that *truth* is susceptible to a kind of constitution theory.[17]

Although (Unconstituted*) fails for this reason to satisfy the Deflationary Constraint, I think that Horwich and Dodd, too, are onto something important. To see what it is, we should ask what significant differences there are between (CT_M) and, say, a familiar correspondence-theoretic constitution theory for *truth*. Let the sole axiom of this constitution theory (CT_{Corr}) be the proposition expressed by:[18]

(CCT) For all x: x's instantiating *truth* consists in x's being isomorphic to a *worldly fact*, which is composed of objects, properties and relations.

What the minimalist needs to capture, I think, is the fact that (CT_M) is rather more *obvious* than (CT_{Corr}). In doing so, they will align themselves as they intend—against the traditional project of constructing constitution theories that "reveal/uncover" *truth*'s essence. In what sense, though, is (CT_M) more obvious than (CT_{Corr})? Here's a suggestion: in judging that (CT_M) is more obvious, we rely tacitly upon a notion of transparency. In particular, we judge that anyone who possesses the concept TRUTH can, by drawing only on that concept's content, come to know that the axioms of (CT_M) are true, whereas this isn't possible with respect to (CT_{Corr}).

We're to imagine a thinker S who possesses TRUTH competently reflecting upon *truth*, wherein she asks herself, "What, precisely, is *truth*'s nature?" Given the possession-conditions that the minimalist assigns to TRUTH, their prediction is that S will adduce (perhaps *inter alia*) considerations along the lines of, "Well, the proposition that tables are solid is true iff tables are solid and the proposition that space-time is continuous is true iff spacetime is continuous and ..." for every proposition that S considers. In so reflecting, S acquires (or becomes aware of) a host of beliefs about the truth-conditions of *individual propositions*. For S to come to know that *every* axiom of (CT_M) is true on this basis, S must rely upon on an a priori, inductive inference such as:

(1) The proposition that tables are solid is true iff tables are solid and the proposition that space-time is continuous is true iff space-time is continuous and so on, for every proposition that I've considered.

(2) So every axiom of (CT_M) is true.

What's notable about this inference is that its premise is (equivalent to) a conjunction of instances of (ES). We can say, then, that an inference about *truth* is an instance of *conceptual argumentation* if its premises consist solely of propositions that one must be disposed to accept in order to possess TRUTH or conjunctions thereof. We'll say that an inference about *truth* is an instance of *nonconceptual argumentation* otherwise.[19]

We can apply the distinction between conceptual and nonconceptual argumentation in thinking about constitution theories. Say that a constitution theory for *truth* is *transparent* iff one who possesses the ordinary concept TRUTH is *ipso facto* in a position to know that its axioms are true solely on the basis of conceptual argumentation. By contrast, a constitution theory for *truth* is *opaque* iff to know that its axioms are true, one who possesses TRUTH must rely on (a priori or empirical) nonconceptual argumentation. The minimalist's position regarding the constitution of *truth*, then, should be this:

> (Unconstituted) There is a property *truth*, but it is insusceptible to an opaque constitution theory.

Note that by contrast, the correspondence theorist will likely take (CT$_{\text{Corr}}$) to be an opaque constitution theory, since one would presumably come to know that its axiom is true via nonconceptual, metaphysical argumentation about, for example, isomorphic correspondence and worldly facts. This shows that (Unconstituted) does indeed pose a serious threat to the traditional essence project. Since the minimalist is committed to this thesis and it is compatible with the other existing species of moderate deflationism, (Unconstituted) thus satisfies the Deflationary Constraint.[20] It also satisfies the Metaphysical Constraint, since it deals directly with the nature—specifically, the constitution—of *truth*. In what follows—and most significantly in section 3.3—we'll see that (Unconstituted) satisfies the Special Case Constraint as well, from which it follows that we should associate (Unconstituted) with moderate deflationism.

3.3   Lack of Explanatory Power

Turning now to the third insubstantiality thesis, it's common practice for deflationists to contend that *truth* is "non-explanatory."[21] Here, they are also driven by a desire to undercut the essence project. Traditional truth theorists sought to discover *truth*'s essence because they took *truth* to be a kind of skeleton key. They thought that uncovering *truth*'s essence would reveal significant facts about many other philosophically central topics—rationality, epistemic justification, belief, assertion, theoretical success, successful action, communication, logic, explanation, reality, and the list goes on. Such projects have encountered serious problems, to say the least, which indicates to moderate deflationists that they represent a degenerating research programme. The culprit, say moderate deflationists, is not ignorance on our part as to the essence of a property *truth* that enjoys metaphysically significant yet deeply elusive explanatory power. Rather, it is our persistent misconception that *truth* has such explanatory power at all. Put concisely, the contention here is:[22]

> (Non-Explanatory) There is a property *truth*, but *truth* lacks explanatory power in that there are no facts that are explained by facts about *truth*'s essence.

It's thus fitting that moderate deflationists have taken great pains to argue that wherever it might seem necessary to invoke *truth* to explain some important fact, we really need to do no such thing. Many of us would agree, for instance, that true beliefs (together with appropriate desires) tend to facilitate successful action. Yet a generalization such as this, argues Horwich, is "not focused on truth, not really about truth."[23]

His contention is that while we do use "true" in such explanatory contexts, we do so *only* because "true" augments the expressive power of our language, allowing us, for example, to generalize about infinite classes of propositions. Dodd concurs, holding that *truth* is "*nothing more than* that whose expression in a language gives that language a device for the formulation of indirect and generalized assertions."[24] Michael Williams pursues a similar strategy when discussing truth-conditions and Davidson's principle of charity.[25] Wolfgang Künne takes great care to offer non-truth-theoretic accounts of propositions and propositional expression.[26] And Jamin Asay appeals to considerations involving truthmaking, resemblance, and causality to argue that we can refuse to posit a sparse property *truth* "without sacrificing explanatory power."[27]

(Non-Explanatory), then, would undercut a major aim of the essence project. Since extant moderate deflationists are highly sympathetic toward this thesis, (Non-Explanatory) thus satisfies the Deflationary Constraint. It also satisfies the Metaphysical Constraint, as it's a direct (negative) claim about *truth*'s nature, rather than a claim about "true" or TRUTH. Regarding the Special Case Constraint, it's important to observe that (Non-Explanatory) and (Unconstituted) are mutually nonentailing and that for this reason, a commitment to one doesn't automatically enjoin a commitment to the other.[28]

We can illustrate this by appealing to *countermodels*. In the present sense, a "model" is just a *logically possible* state of affairs; our usage of "model," then, is much less formal than the typical usage. I take it that the states of affairs described below are consistent, since considering their details generates no impressions of inconsistency. Moreover, note that the "models" below aren't intended to be entirely deflationism-friendly— quite the contrary, since each is meant to show that one characteristically deflationary thesis is consistent with the negation of another.

First, here's a countermodel with three main features which shows that (Unconstituted) doesn't entail (Non-Explanatory):

(M_1 (i)) S possesses TRUTH iff S is disposed to accept in the absence of supporting argumentation the proposition expressed by:

(3) For all x: x's being true consists in x's representing an actual state of affairs.

(M_1 (ii)) The true constitution theory for *truth* is transparent as its sole axiom is the proposition expressed by (3).[29]

(M_1 (iii)) *Truth* enjoys explanatory power in virtue of the explanatory power enjoyed by the representation relation and states of affairs. We can, for instance, explain why it is desirable to believe the proposition that tables are solid by appealing to the desirability of believing propositions that represent (only) actual states of affairs.

The driving idea behind this model is that it is logically possible that given the details of its constitution theory, *truth* enjoys explanatory power even as that constitution theory is transparent. This would be a case in which (Unconstituted) is true yet (Non-Explanatory) is false.

Here's a second countermodel which illustrates why (Non-Explanatory) fails to entail (Unconstituted):

(M_2 (i)) *Truth* lacks explanatory power.

(M_2 (ii)) = (M_1 (i)).

(M_2 (iii)) *Truth* is susceptible to an opaque constitution theory, namely the minimal constitution theory (CT_M) (sec. 3.2).

Here, the idea is that it's logically possible that *truth*, as the minimalist claims, lacks explanatory power and that (CT_M) is the true constitution theory for *truth*, though this constitution theory is opaque. (CT_M) is an opaque constitution theory in this model because given (M_2 (ii)), S might possess TRUTH while lacking the concept PROPOSITION and thus while failing to know that propositions can bear *truth*. In order to come to know that (CT_M)'s axioms are true, S would then need to rely upon nonconceptual, a priori argumentation—namely, that which would suffice for S to know that propositions are bearers of *truth*. In this model, then, while (Non-Explanatory) is true, (Unconstituted) is false.

The overall point to appreciate here is that (Unconstituted) and (Non-Explanatory) codify two logically distinct senses in which the moderate deflationist may hold that *truth* is an insubstantial property. Given this, it follows that neither thesis is a special case of the other. Accordingly, if they alone satisfy the Deflationary and Metaphysical Constraints (as we'll maintain in section 4), then each also satisfies the Special Case Constraint.

3.4   Abundance

In recent discussions of the metaphysics of deflationism, Jamin Asay (2013, chap. 4; 2014), Douglas Edwards (2013), and Andrea Strollo (2014) have proposed that the definitive moderate deflationary thesis about *truth* is:[30]

(Abundant) *Truth* exists, but *truth* is a highly abundant/unnatural property.

This account is tempting, given that Horwich (1998b, 11, 37) explicitly contrasts *truth* with what he calls "naturalistic properties"—for example, *being a tree*. However, certain aspects of (Abundant) fail to intersect with the concerns of moderate deflationists, while the others are mere special cases of a more basic moderate deflationary commitment.

In seminal work, David Lewis (1983) took the distinction between sparse and abundant properties to be graded, with sparseness and abundance being inverses—properties are more or less sparse than other properties, and the degree to which a property is sparse is the inverse of the degree to which it is abundant. At one extreme, Lewis contended, we have properties—presumably those taken to be fundamental by our final physical theories—that are maximally sparse or, in Lewis's terminology, *perfectly natural*. At the other, we have properties—nicely exemplified by Nelson Goodman's famous property *grueness*—that are disjunctive and gerrymandered and thus maximally abundant.

To navigate this spectrum, we need diagnostics that indicate how sparse a given property is. Edwards (2013, 12) draws on three Lewisian diagnostics, taking the extent to which P is sparse to be determined by:[31]

(S1) the length of P's chain of definability from the perfectly natural properties (the length of this chain is negatively correlated with P's degree of sparseness);

(S2) whether P grounds "genuine similarities" among its bearers; and

(S3) whether P enjoys causal-explanatory power.

Part of the trouble here is that even if moderate deflationists are committed to holding that the definability chain connecting *truth* to the perfectly natural properties is rather long, certain traditional truth theorists are presumably committed to the same. If the perfectly natural properties are those that our final physical theories will take to be fundamental, it's reasonable to predict that the definability chain connecting these properties to, say, *being isomorphic to a worldly fact* would be rather long. A correspondence theorist who articulates correspondence along these lines would then agree that *truth* can't be very simply defined in terms of the perfectly natural properties. In this respect, then, (Abundant) isn't a suitably deflationary thesis about *truth* and thus fails to satisfy the Deflationary Constraint.

Admittedly, (S2) is closer to home. Moderate deflationists should deny that *truth* grounds genuine similarities among its bearers, at least if grounding is as closely tied to explanation as many have thought.[32] But what this brings to light is that if moderate deflationists are committed to (S2), this is just an upshot of their commitment to denying that *truth* enjoys explanatory power, that is, to (Non-Explanatory).

The same goes for (S3). Moderate deflationists are indeed committed to denying that *truth* enjoys causal-explanatory power.[33] But this is a consequence of their contention that *truth* lacks *any* sort of explanatory power—it's a special case of their more basic commitment to (Non-Explanatory).

What this shows is that treating (Abundant) as a core moderate deflationary commitment would create problems in connection with the Deflationary and Special Case Constraints. In one respect, (Abundant) isn't a suitably deflationary thesis, and the respects in which it is deflationary are special cases of the more fundamental (Non-Explanatory). Before drawing the conclusion that the core of moderate deflationism consists of (Unconstituted) and (Non-Explanatory), we'll consider finally a fifth claim about *truth* that has been associated with the view—that *truth* is merely "logical."

3.5 Logicality

A number of deflationists have claimed that *truth* is a "logical" property.[34] A difficulty here is that those who advance this claim rarely indicate what they take the characteristic features of logical properties to be. To rectify this, we can consider what is perhaps the most influential account of the boundary between the logical and the nonlogical, that proposed by Alfred Tarski.

Tarski's view of what he calls "logical notions" is inspired by the account of geometrical notions stemming from Felix Klein's Erlangen Program. Klein's idea is that we can classify the notions distinctive of particular branches of geometry by reference to the sorts of *transformations* under which those notions are invariant. As the term is used in this context, a transformation is a one-one function whose domain and range are each identical to the particular universe of discourse at issue.[35]

Tarski's insight is that Klein's strategy can be generalized to deliver an account of what makes a notion logical. Tarski uses "notion" rather broadly so that for him, notions approximate what we usually describe as "entities" or "things."[36] He describes his account of logical notions as follows:[37]

> Now suppose we continue [Klein's] idea, and consider still wider classes of transformations. In the extreme case, we would consider the class of all one–one transformations of the space, or universe of discourse, or "world," onto itself. What will be the science which deals with the notions invariant under this widest class of transformations? Here we will have very few notions, all of a very general character. I suggest that they are the logical notions, that we call a notion "logical" if it is invariant under all possible one–one transformations of the world onto itself.

For Tarski, then, a notion is logical just if it is invariant under all possible transformations of the world onto itself. We might call these *total transformations*, since they map the world onto the world.

A property P is logical in this sense iff where $f(x)$ is a total transformation, if $f(x)$ maps a to $f(a)$ and a instantiates P, then so does $f(a)$. A clear instance of such a property is *being self-identical*. Another plausible candidate is *being everything*. If there is an unrestricted universal quantifier $\forall$, we could take it to denote *being everything*. A total transformation $f(x)$ maps every entity a in the world onto another entity $f(a)$ in the world. Since no such entity instantiates *being everything*—every such entity is in the world, though it isn't identical to the world—for every such a, if $f(x)$ maps a to $f(a)$ and a instantiates *being everything*, then so does $f(a)$. Existence—which we could take to be denoted by the unrestricted existential quantifier $\exists$—is also a logical property in the present sense, given that the actual world contains only existent objects.

By contrast, intuitively nonlogical properties like *being a tree*, *being blue*, and *being solid* are clearly nonlogical in the present sense. There is a total transformation that maps everything in the world onto itself, except the tree in my mother's front yard and a point three miles north of the tree's base, which are mapped to one another. There is another that maps everything to itself, except the blue sweater in my closet and the green sweater in my closet, which are mapped to one another. And there is a third that maps everything to itself, except the table in my living room and the Pacific Ocean, which are mapped to one another.

So far, so good. We have in hand a conception of logical properties that classifies several intuitively logical properties as logical and several intuitively nonlogical properties as nonlogical.[38] The hypothesis to consider now is that according to the moderate deflationist, *truth* is a logical property in the Tarskian sense:

(Logical) *Truth* is invariant under all possible total transformations.

It would, in fact, be a mistake to associate (Logical) with moderate deflationism. This is because, as with (Transparent$_{L/D}$) and (Unconstituted*), the minimalist is committed to denying (Logical). Supposing with the minimalist that propositions exist, there is a total transformation that maps the proposition that tables are solid to the proposition that $7 + 5 = 13$. Since tables are, in fact, solid, the former instantiates *truth*, according to the minimalist, in contrast to the latter. This shows that for the minimalist, *truth* isn't invariant under all possible total transformations.[39] For this reason, (Logical) fails to satisfy the Deflationary Constraint.

It may be that when they talk about the logicality of *truth*, moderate deflationists have some non-Tarskian conception of logicality in mind that would satisfy the Deflationary, Metaphysical, and Special Case Constraints. If so, then their burden is to indicate what precisely this conception amounts to. Since at present no such conception has been forthcoming, I propose (defeasibly) that we refrain from associating the claim that *truth* is logical with moderate deflationism.[40]

4   Understanding Moderate Deflationism

I hope in this discussion to have shed some light on what is at stake in contemporary debates about deflationary theories of truth.[41] We've distinguished two fundamental senses in which the moderate deflationist might take *truth* to be an insubstantial property. They might regard *truth* as being insusceptible to an opaque constitution theory or as being devoid of explanatory power. A consequence of this analysis is that there are two theses about *truth* that are each partially definitive of the view. We can say approximately that being a moderate deflationist amounts to endorsement of the following conjunction:

(MD) There is a property *truth*, but it is insusceptible to an opaque constitution theory and lacks explanatory power.

A more perspicuous way to think about moderate deflationism, however, is to treat it as consisting of two separable faces. One is a moderate deflationist to the fullest degree, we can say, if one endorses both (Unconstituted) and (Non-Explanatory). Yet as we noted in section 3.3, one might reasonably endorse one of these theses while rejecting the other. Both theses satisfy the Deflationary and Metaphysical Constraints, meaning that an advocate of either aims to jeopardize the essence project by advancing a distinctively metaphysical claim about *truth*. We should thus think of someone who endorses one but not the other as being a moderate deflationist—though not to the fullest degree. Accordingly, I suggest that there are three basic ways to be a moderate deflationist:

(i)   Endorse both (Unconstituted) and (Non-Explanatory);

(ii) Endorse (Unconstituted) and reject (Non-Explanatory); or

(iii) Endorse (Non-Explanatory) and reject (Unconstituted).

If this is correct, then when we reflect on debates about deflationary accounts of *truth*'s nature, we don't simply face the question "Should we be moderate deflationists?" Rather, the particularly fascinating question that confronts us is: "To what degree and in which senses (if any) should we be moderate deflationists?"

Notes

1. The material in this chapter is adapted from that in Wyatt (2016).

2. See, for instance, Grover (1992, 23); Price (1998, 241); Wright (1998, 34); Williams (2002, sec. 4); Horwich (2005, 70; 2010, 14; 2013, 57); Edwards (2013); and Jago (2018, chap. 1).

3. I'll use small caps to refer to concepts, quotation marks to refer to linguistic expressions, and italics to refer to properties. For an interesting treatment of substantivism and deflationism as methodologies for inquiry, see Sher (2016a, chap. 7; 2016b).

4. These include Ramsey (1927); Ayer (1946); Quine (1948, 1970, 1987); Strawson (1950 and chap. 17 in this volume); Grover (1992); and Brandom (2005). Cf. Armour-Garb and Woodbridge (chapter 23 in this volume) and Scharp (2020).

5. See Williams (2002, sec. 4); Künne (2003, 90); Dodd (2008, sec. 3.1, 136–137); and Price (2011, 256–257). Horsten (2011, 2) and Asay (2013, 104, 106) offer similar rationales. McGinn (2000, chap. 5) takes truth to be a property, though he denies (contentiously) that he is a deflationist. Likewise, I suspect that Hill is willing to posit *truth*, given that he takes TRUTH to be a "monadic predicative concept" (Hill 2002, 23), though the evidence is too thin to be certain. Since among these theorists Horwich's views are the most thoroughly developed, we'll often use those views as a test case.

6. Other theorists who have expressed sympathy for moderate deflationism include Ramsey (1991); McGrath (1997); Soames (1999); and Beall (2015 and chapter 19 in this volume).

7. Cp. the methodology that Horwich (2010, chap. 2, note 3) proposes for characterizing deflationism.

8. Note, then, that we allow for the possibility that a certain claim is characteristic of moderate deflationism as such, though only some moderate deflationists explicitly endorse it; we'll address this matter in section 4.

9. (Transparent$_L$) (and (Transparent$_D$)) could be strengthened to mention all *possible* thinkers, but this wouldn't substantially affect our discussion.

10. Damnjanovic (2010, 48).

11. Wright (chap. 29 in this volume, sec. 1) advances a similar conception of what *truth*'s metaphysical transparency would involve. Alston (2002), I take it, would deny that *truth* is metaphysically transparent in either sense.

12. Williamson (2000, 95).

13. Horwich (1998a, 103–104; 1998b, 121, 126, 128–129). For Hotwich's later refinement of this account, see Horwich (2010, 42, 47–48, chap. 3, note 10).

14. Horwich (1998b, 136; 2010, 80). Horwich eventually (1998b, 43) adds a further axiom, that propositions are the sole bearers of *truth*. We can safely set this aside here.

15. Horwich (1998b, 143).

16. For discussion of this thesis, see David (1994, 65–66); Dodd (2008, 133–134); and Horwich (2010, chap. 1, 13, 15–16, 38; 2013, 57, 59). For related discussion, see Devitt (1991, 31–32); Horwich (1998a, 10, 29, 42, 104, 107, 113, 123; 2005, 75); Wright (1998, 34–39, note 9); Rasmussen (2014, sec. 1.4.2); and Thomasson (2014, 208).

17. Strictly, Horwich (1998a, 10, 29; 1998b, 121, 143; 2010, chap. 1, sec. 2, 38; 2013, 59) takes a constitution theory for *truth* to be a single proposition of the form (CT). Given this conception of constitution theories for *truth*, the important result here is that the minimalist should take *truth* to be susceptible to *infinitely many* constitution theories of the form (MCT). It's easy to verify that the set of these propositions is transparent, according to the minimalist, in a sense analogous to that sketched below—one who possesses TRUTH is *ipso facto* in a position to know solely on the basis of conceptual argumentation that its members are true. For our purposes, then, we also could have adopted this characterization of constitution theories.

18. For the notion of a worldly fact, see Dodd (2008). Cp. the correspondence theory in Wittgenstein (1961).

19. Note, then, that the notion of conceptual argumentation should also interest deflationists who rely on schemas other than (ES)—for example, "Sentence 'S' (of language L) is true iff S."

20. Indeed, I take Williams (2002, 151), Künne (2003, 92), Dodd (2008), and Asay (2013, 117–118, 126–127, 131) to have sympathies toward (Unconstituted).

21. For discussion of this and the analogous claim about TRUTH, see, for example, Bar-On and Simmons (chapter 25 in this volume); Leeds (1978, esp. secs. 3 and 4); Field (1986, 67, 76, secs. 4.2–5.4; 1994, postscript, sec. 7); Devitt (1991); Grover (1992, sec. 3.1); Horwich (1998b, chap. 3; 2010, 6–7, 13–16); Shapiro (1998); Mou (2000); Brandom (2005); Künne (2008, sec. 13); Lynch (2009, 107, 111); and Horsten (2011, sec. 7.4).

22. Cp. Williams (2002, 158) and Lynch (2009, 108).

23. Horwich (1998b, 141).

24. Dodd (2008, 133, and chap. 6, sec. 8).

25. Williams (2002, sec. 5).

26. Künne (2003, sec. 5.1.1, 373; 2008, sec. 13).

27. Asay (2013, sec. 4.2, 108).

28. This isn't to contend that there are no interesting inductive or abductive relations between them—perhaps there are. The point remains, though, that they are mutually nonentailing.

29. Note that (3)'s form deviates harmlessly from that of (CT).

30. For the sake of continuity, I'll mostly follow Edwards, Asay, and Strollo in speaking about truth being highly abundant, rather than "highly unnatural," though the latter terminology may be preferable in this context. See Edwards (2018, chaps. 2 and 3, sec. 7.5) for a revision of his earlier account.

31. Admittedly, there are other conceptions of natural/sparse properties that might be considered here; see, for example, Schaffer (2004) and Dorr and Hawthorne (2013). These deserve further scrutiny, but because it has been specifically developed in connection with truth, I'll concentrate on the proposal in Edwards (2013) here.

32. See, for example, Fine (2012).

33. See Damnjanovic (2005; 2010, esp. sec. 3.1) for discussion of some related complications that are compatible with this suggestion.

34. See Beall (chapter 19 in this volume); McGinn (2000, chap. 5); Künne (2003, 91, 338; 2008, 130; though he calls truth a "quasi-logical" or "broadly logical" property); and Damnjanovic (2005, 2010). For related discussion, see Field (1986, 76; 1992, 322; 1994, sec. 5); Horwich (1998b, 2–5, 142; 2010, chap. 5, note 5); Hill (2002, 22); Horsten (2011, secs. 5.2.3, 10.2.1); Beall (2013); Strollo (2014, 62); Galinon (2015); Eklund (2017); Bonnay and Galinon (2018); and Scharp (2020).

35. Tarski (1986, 146).

36. Tarski (1986, 147). Tarski intends, though, to exclude linguistic and conceptual entities from the class of notions.

37. Tarski (1986, 149).

38. This conception may not simply mirror common philosophical opinion as to which properties—for example, *being a unicorn* or *being a conjunctive proposition*—are (non-)logical. This can be reasonably regarded as a cost, yet as Sher (2008, esp. 308–324) points out, the Tarskian conception of logicality fares rather well in connection with other important desiderata such as systematicity and linguistic and mathematical fruitfulness.

39. This result clearly generalizes to any theory of truth that entails the (nonparadoxical) instances of (ES).

40. Note in this connection that the claim that *truth* is denoted by a "formal" truth predicate whose meaning is defined inferentially à la Beall (2009, 5; 2013) would fail to satisfy the Metaphysical Constraint. The same goes for the claim that *truth* is logical in virtue of being denoted by a logical truth predicate, in the sense of Bonnay and Galinon (2018).

By contrast, it seems to me that Beall's proposal in chapter 19 does satisfy the Metaphysical Constraint (even as it would be good to know more about the nature of "emergent logical properties"). However, I would point out, echoing an observation that Beall makes in section 6.1 of the chapter, that his proposal seems not to satisfy the Deflationary Constraint. This is because moderate deflationists who deny that "is true" is transparent—for example, Horwich (1998b; 2010, chap. 5), given his response to the Liar paradox—will accordingly deny that *truth* is an emergent logical property in Beall's sense. Perhaps there is a variant of Beall's proposal that would be appealing to all moderate deflationists, but this would need to be spelled out. This result doesn't, of course, detract from the interest of Beall's proposal. It just shows that we shouldn't take moderate deflationists *as such* to be committed to regarding *truth* as an emergent logical property.

41. For discussion of some concerns that I can't address here, see Wyatt (2016, sec. 5); Eklund (2017); and Edwards (2018, sec. 3.5).

References

Alston, W. 2002. "Truth: Concept and Property." In R. Schantz, ed., *What Is Truth?*, 11–26. New York: de Gruyter.

Armour-Garb, B., and Beall, Jc, eds. 2005. *Deflationary Truth*. Chicago: Open Court.

Asay, J. 2013. *The Primitivist Theory of Truth*. Cambridge: Cambridge University Press.

Asay, J. 2014. "Against *Truth*." *Erkenntnis* 79(1): 147–164.

Ayer, A. J. 1946. *Language, Truth, and Logic*. London: Gollancz.

Beall, Jc. 2009. *Spandrels of Truth*. Oxford: Oxford University Press.

Beall, Jc. 2013. "Deflated Truth Pluralism." In N. Pedersen and C. D. Wright, eds., *Truth and Pluralism: Current Debates*, 323–338. Oxford: Oxford University Press.

Beall, Jc. 2015. "Non-detachable Validity and Deflationism." In C. Caret and O. Hjortland, eds., *Foundations of Logical Consequence*, 276–285. Oxford: Oxford University Press.

Bonnay, D., and Galinon, H. 2018. "Deflationary Truth Is a Logical Notion." In M. Piazza and G. Pulcini, eds., *Truth, Existence, and Explanation: FilMat 2016 Studies in the Philosophy of Mathematics*, 71–88. Cham, Switzerland: Springer.

Brandom, R. 2005. "Expressive versus Explanatory Deflationism about Truth." In Armour-Garb and Beall (2005), 237–257.

Damnjanovic, N. 2005. "Deflationism and the Success Argument." *Philosophical Quarterly* 55(218): 53–67.

Damnjanovic, N. 2010. "New Wave Deflationism." In C. D. Wright and N. J. L. L. Pedersen, eds., *New Waves in Truth*, 45–58. New York: Palgrave Macmillan.

David, M. 1994. *Correspondence and Disquotation*. Oxford: Oxford University Press.

Devitt, M. 1991. *Realism and Truth*. 2nd ed. Princeton, NJ: Princeton University Press.

Dodd, J. 2008. *An Identity Theory of Truth*. New York: Palgrave Macmillan.

Dorr, C., and Hawthorne, J. 2013. "Naturalness." In K. Bennett and D. Zimmerman, eds., *Oxford Studies in Metaphysics*, vol. 8, 3–77. New York: Oxford University Press.

Edwards, D. 2013. "Truth as a Substantive Property." *Australasian Journal of Philosophy* 91(2): 279–294.

Edwards, D. 2018. *The Metaphysics of Truth*. New York: Oxford University Press.

Eklund, M. 2017. "What Is Deflationism about Truth?" *Synthese*. https://doi.org/10.1007/s11229 -017-1557-y.

Field, H. 1986. "The Deflationary Conception of Truth." In G. MacDonald and C. Wright, eds., *Fact, Science, and Morality*, 55–117. Malden, MA: Blackwell.

Field, H. 1992. "Critical Notice: Paul Horwich's *Truth*." *Philosophy of Science* 59: 321–330.

Field, H. 1994. "Deflationist Views of Meaning and Content." *Mind* 103(411): 249–285. Reprinted, with postscript, in Armour-Garb and Beall (2005), 50–110.

Fine, K. 2012. "Guide to Ground." In F. Correia and B. Schneider, eds., *Metaphysical Grounding: Understanding the Structure of Reality*, 37–80. Cambridge: Cambridge University Press.

Galinon, H. 2015. "Deflationary Truth: Conservativity or Logicality?" *Philosophical Quarterly* 65(259): 268–274.

Grover, D. 1992. *A Prosentential Theory of Truth*. Princeton, NJ: Princeton University Press.

Gupta, A. 1993. "Minimalism." *Philosophical Perspectives* 7: 359–369.

Hill, C. 2002. *Thought and World: An Austere Portrayal of Truth, Reference, and Semantic Correspondence*. Cambridge: Cambridge University Press.

Horsten, L. 2011. *The Tarskian Turn: Deflationism and Axiomatic Truth*. Cambridge, MA: MIT Press.

Horwich, P. 1998a. *Meaning*. Oxford: Blackwell.

Horwich, P. 1998b. *Truth*. 2nd ed. Oxford: Oxford University Press.

Horwich, P. 2005. *Reflections on Meaning*. Oxford: Oxford University Press.

Horwich, P. 2010. *Truth-Meaning-Reality*. Oxford: Oxford University Press.

Horwich, P. 2013. *Wittgenstein's Metaphilosophy*. Oxford: Oxford University Press.

Jago, M. 2018. *What Truth Is*. Oxford: Oxford University Press.

Künne, W. 2003. *Conceptions of Truth*. Oxford: Oxford University Press.

Künne, W. 2008. "The Modest, or Quantificational, Account of Truth." *Studia Philosophica Estonica* 1(2): 122–168.

Leeds, S. 1978. "Theories of Truth and Reference." *Erkenntnis* 13(1): 111–129.

Lewis, D. 1983. "New Work for a Theory of Universals." *Australasian Journal of Philosophy* 61(4): 343–377.

Lynch, M. 2009. *Truth as One and Many*. Oxford: Oxford University Press.

McGinn, C. 2000. *Logical Properties: Identity, Existence, Predication, Necessity, Truth*. Oxford: Oxford University Press.

McGrath, M. 1997. "Weak Deflationism." *Mind* 106(421): 69–98.

Mou, B. 2000. "A Metaphilosophical Analysis of the Core Idea of Deflationism." *Metaphilosophy* 31(3): 262–286.

Price, H. 1998. "Three Norms of Assertibility, or How the MOA Became Extinct." *Philosophical Perspectives* 12: 41–54.

Price, H. 2011. *Naturalism without Mirrors*. Oxford: Oxford University Press.

Quine, W. V. O. 1948. "On What There Is." *Review of Metaphysics* 2(1): 21–38.

Quine, W. V. O. 1970. *Philosophy of Logic*. 2nd ed. Englewood Cliffs, NJ: Prentice-Hall.

Quine, W. V. O. 1987. *Quiddities: An Intermittently Philosophical Dictionary*. Cambridge, MA: Belknap Press of Harvard University Press.

Ramsey, F. 1927. "Facts and Propositions." *Proceedings of the Aristotelian Society*, suppl., 7(1): 153–170.

Ramsey, F. 1991. *On Truth: Original Manuscript Materials (1927–1929) from the Ramsey Collection at the University of Pittsburgh*. Edited by N. Rescher and U. Majer. Dordrecht: Kluwer Academic Publishers.

Rasmussen, J. 2014. *Defending the Correspondence Theory of Truth*. Cambridge: Cambridge University Press.

Schaffer, J. 2004. "Two Conceptions of Sparse Properties." *Pacific Philosophical Quarterly* 85(1): 92–102.

Shapiro, S. 1998. "Proof and Truth: Through Thick and Thin." *Journal of Philosophy* 95(10): 493–521.

Scharp, K. 2020. "Conceptual Engineering for Truth: Aletheic Properties and New Aletheic Concepts." *Synthese*. https://doi.org/10.1007/s11229-019-02491-4.

Sher, G. 2008. "Tarski's Thesis." In D. Patterson, ed., *New Essays on Tarski and Philosophy*, 300–339. Oxford: Oxford University Press.

Sher, G. 2016a. *Epistemic Friction: An Essay on Knowledge, Truth, and Logic*. Oxford: Oxford University Press.

Sher, G. 2016b. "Substantivism about Truth." *Philosophy Compass* 11(12): 818–828.

Soames, S. 1999. *Understanding Truth*. Oxford: Oxford University Press.

Strawson, P. F. 1950. "Truth." *Proceedings of the Artistotelian Society*, suppl., 24: 129–156.

Strollo, A. 2014. "How Simple Is the Simplicity of Truth? Reconciling the Mathematics and the Metaphysics of Truth." In F. Bacchini, S. Caputo, and M. Dell'Utri, eds., *New Frontiers in Truth*, 161–175. Newcastle upon Tyne: Cambridge Scholars.

Tarski, A. 1986. "What Are Logical Notions?" *History and Philosophy of Logic* 7(2): 143–154.

Thomasson, A. 2014. "Deflationism in Semantics and Metaphysics." In A. Burgess and B. Sherman, eds., *Metasemantics: New Essays on the Foundations of Meaning*, 185–213. Oxford: Oxford University Press.

Williams, M. 2002. "On Some Critics of Deflationism." In R. Schantz, ed., *What Is Truth?*, 146–158. New York: de Gruyter.

Williamson, T. 2000. *Knowledge and Its Limits*. Oxford: Oxford University Press.

Wittgenstein, L. 1961. *Tractatus Logico-Philosophicus*. Translated by D. F. Pears and B. F. McGuinness. New York: Routledge and Kegan Paul.

Wright, C. 1998. "Truth: A Traditional Debate Reviewed." In C. Misak, ed., "Pragmatism," special issue, *Canadian Journal of Philosophy* 28, suppl. 1: 31–74.

Wyatt, J. 2016. "The Many (Yet Few) Faces of Deflationism." *Philosophical Quarterly* 66(263): 362–382.

25 The Use of Force against Deflationism: Assertion and Truth

Dorit Bar-On and Keith Simmons

Deflationists share a core negative claim that truth is not a genuine, substantive property. Deflationism can be seen in part as a form of eliminativism: we can eliminate the property of truth from our ontological inventory. This is the distinctive claim of what we will call *metaphysical deflationism*. But anyone who accepts metaphysical deflationism must still make sense of our pervasive truth-*talk*. What is it we are doing when we call something true, if we are not ascribing a genuine property? What is the meaning of the word "true"? What are its main uses or functions? And how should we understand the *concept* of truth and the role it plays in both ordinary and philosophical discourse? An acceptable deflationism must supplement the negative metaphysical claim with an account of the word "true" as well as an account of our concept of truth.

In what follows, we wish to keep separate three deflationary claims that, it seems to us, have been run together in the literature. There is first the metaphysical claim common to all deflationists that truth is not a genuine property. Second, there is the particular account of various everyday uses of the word "true" (or the phrase "is true"). Deflationary accounts of "true" vary widely: the common metaphysical core fans out into disquotationalism, minimalism, the redundancy theory, the prosentential theory, and more. Call this *linguistic deflationism*. Third, there is what we will call *conceptual deflationism*: the claim that an acceptable deflationary account of "true" will give us *all* there is to know or understand about the concept of truth and its potential explanatory role. A thoroughgoing deflationary account of truth will go beyond the negative metaphysical claim and the positive linguistic account of "true": it will also maintain that the concept of truth is a "thin" concept that can play no substantive explanatory role in our conceptual scheme. As recently presented by Williams (1999), deflationists share the idea that the function of truth-talk is "*wholly* expressive, never *explanatory*": truth-talk *only* serves to allow us "to endorse or reject sentences (or propositions) that we cannot simply assert." "What makes deflationary views deflationary," Williams claims, "is their insistence that the importance of truth-talk is *exhausted* by its expressive function."[1]

Deflationists and their opponents often seem to take it that conceptual deflationism falls out of metaphysical and linguistic deflationism. If metaphysical deflationism is right, then we cannot assign the property of being true as the meaning of "true," and we cannot explain our understanding of "true" as consisting in the apprehension of this property. Now suppose we accept this or that deflationary account of "true." Shouldn't we further accept that the account exhausts our understanding of the concept of truth? But if so, then in explicating any seemingly truth-related concept, we can appeal to nothing more than the preferred deflationary account of "true." The concept of truth can thus bear no substantive conceptual connections to other concepts of interest to us, such as meaning, validity, belief, assertion, verification, explanation, practical success, and so on. We will thus be left with a deflated concept of truth—a "thin" concept whose understanding is exhausted by the deflationary account of "true," a concept that is isolated from all other concepts of interest to us and can play no substantive explanatory role with respect to them.

In this paper, we do not plan to take metaphysical deflationism to task. We put to one side the deflationist claim that we stand to gain nothing from appealing to a substantive property of truth. We also do not plan to challenge linguistic deflationism by criticizing the success of particular deflationist treatments of "true." Our main concern is with conceptual deflationism: the claim that our understanding of truth is fully exhausted by this or that particular deflationary account of "true," so that a deflated, "thin" concept of truth is all that we need in our conceptual scheme. In our view, even if it is granted that paradigmatic uses of "is true" can be treated in a deflationary way, this does not show that we have no need for a richer concept of truth than is allowed by deflationary accounts. As against the conceptual deflationist, it can be argued that there are ineliminable connections between truth and other concepts. For example, it might be argued that an account of *linguistic meaning* cannot be provided without invoking the notion of truth.[2] Our main interest in this paper is in the illocutionary notion of *assertion*. We will argue that there is a conceptual link between truth and assertion that cannot be broken, and that our understanding of the concept of assertion requires more than a deflated concept of truth. So much the worse, then, for conceptual deflationism.

I   Deflating Truth

As we have presented conceptual deflationism, it is committed to the claim that truth cannot play any substantive explanatory role. If this is so, the deflationist ought to tell us what to make of various apparent connections between truth and other concepts of interest to us. It has been claimed that the deflationist can readily endorse such connections.[3] To set the scene, let us consider two apparent platitudes that tie together the notions of truth, truth-aptness, assertion and belief. First, if a sentence is truth-apt—that is, either true or false—and I utter it sincerely, then I have made an assertion. Second, "assertion has the following analytical tie to belief: if someone makes an assertion, and is supposed sincere, it follows that she has a belief whose content can be captured by means of the sentence used" (Wright 1992, 14). Consequently, there is an apparently platitudinous tie (perhaps an analytic one) between truth-aptness and belief: a sentence is truth-apt only if it can be used to give the content of a belief. From a commonsensical point of view, this is just what we would expect. If I sincerely utter the truth-apt sentence "Aardvarks amble," it seems that I have asserted it; and it further seems that I have said what I believe about the world, where the content of my belief is given by the sentence "Aardvarks amble."

According to Jackson et al. (1994, 294), platitudinous conceptual connections must be preserved by any good analysis:

> When we do conceptual analysis we have to respect platitudinous connections. They are the very stuff that conceptual analyses are made from. In analyzing a concept our aim is to capture the network of platitudes that surround that concept, and so capture its meaning.

Jackson et al. (1994, 296–297) think we can adopt a certain view of conceptual analysis that they regard as "minimal." The view is this: when we analyze a concept, the analysis should comprise all the platitudes about the concept and nothing more. Call this view *platitude-respecting minimalism*. The view is minimal in the sense that it supposedly requires us to make no controversial assumptions.

In particular, a platitude-respecting minimalist *about truth* will embrace platitudinous conceptual ties between truth, truth-aptness, assertion and belief. These ties, though platitudinous, may be quite substantial, according to Jackson et al. (1994). For example, to show that a sentence is truth-apt, it needs to be shown "that the state an agent is in when she is disposed to utter a sentence … bears the relations to information, action and rationality required for the state to count as a belief. This is a substantial matter" (Jackson et al. 1994, 296). So the platitude-respecting minimalist will endorse substantive connections between truth and other concepts.

If, as Jackson et al. (1994) assume, platitude-respecting minimalism is a version of deflationism, then we cannot maintain the general claim that deflationists isolate truth from other concepts. But platitude-respecting minimalism should *not* count as a genuine form of deflationism. Deflationists do not take platitudes about truth as their starting point. Rather, deflationists are motivated by the thought that much of what is said about truth, about its nature and role and connections to other concepts, is radically misguided. Apparent platitudes about truth cannot be taken at face value. Instead, they are to be regarded with some suspicion—it may be these very platitudes that encourage the thought that truth is a substantive notion. Indeed, it seems that the deflationist would reject the basic methodology of platitude-respecting minimalism, given its commitment to incorporating everyday platitudes into the theoretical analysis of truth. The commonsense platitudes can mislead us into thinking that truth is a substantive, explanatory notion. Yet, if conceptual deflationism is right, there is nothing more to our understanding of truth than what is captured by a preferred deflationist account of "true."

For a test case, consider the following apparent platitude: *true beliefs engender successful action*.[4] On its face, this "fact about truth"[5] seems to forge substantial links between truth, belief, and action. But according to the deflationist, this appearance is misleading: we need only a deflationary account of truth to explain the role of truth in this thesis. Consider Horwich's (1990) account of such "facts about truth." The axioms of Horwich's minimal theory of truth are all and only the instances of the sentence schema:

The proposition that *p* is true if and only if *p*,

instances like "The proposition that penguins waddle is true if and only if penguins waddle." The denominalizing function of "true" embodied in these axioms exhausts what there is to be said by way of explaining truth—no other notions enter into the theory. The minimal theory of truth is *"a theory of truth that is a theory of nothing else."*[6] Moreover, it is a *complete* theory of truth—we are not to gain *further* understanding of truth by appeal to anything other than the equivalences. In particular, alleged platitudes that make use of truth locutions cannot be regarded as in any way *enhancing* our understanding of truth. By the same token, if we resort to truth-talk in our explication of other concepts, we cannot expect the notion of truth to contribute to our understanding of those concepts beyond what is afforded by the minimal theory, since "all of the facts whose expression involves the truth predicate may be explained ... by assuming no more about truth than instances of the equivalence schema" (Horwich 1990, 24). In particular, Horwich argues that this is so far the thesis that true beliefs engender successful action. Horwich considers the following instance:

> If all Bill wants is to have a beer, and he thinks that merely by nodding he will get one, then, if his belief is true, he will get what he wants.

At one point in his explanation, Horwich makes "the familiar psychological assumption" that if one has a desire, and believes that a certain action will satisfy that desire, one will perform the action.[7] That is, conceptual connections are assumed between belief, desire, and action. But *all* that is assumed about truth in Horwich's explanation is its denominalizing role. In the course of the explanation, we move from "The proposition that if Bill nods then Bill has a beer is true" to "If Bill nods then Bill has a beer"; and a little later we move from "Bill has a beer" to "The proposition that Bill has a beer is true." These are the only steps where truth has a role to play, and it is the role given to it by the equivalence schema.

This style of explanation, says Horwich, may be universalized to show how in general true beliefs lead to successful action. And beyond that, it extends to all other facts involving "true." The explanation of all these facts will, according to Horwich's minimalism, appeal to no more about truth than is given by the instances of the T-schema.

In explaining these facts, we will not improve our grasp of truth, or deepen our understanding of it. Nor does the explanation of other concepts invoke anything more than what we've described as a "thin" concept of truth—what is captured by the minimalist definition. We presumably learn more about, for example, the concepts of belief, desire and action by an improved understanding of their interrelations. But there will be no such improvement in the case of truth: the equivalence schema tells us all there is to know about truth, and it exhausts all that the notion of truth can contribute to our understanding of any other concept. In this sense, truth is isolated from other concepts.

This isolationism is not peculiar to Horwich's minimalism. Consider disquotationalism. According to the disquotationalist, there is no more to the truth of, say, the sentence "Aardvarks amble" than is given by the disquotation of its quote-name. One can think of the so-called T-sentence

"Aardvarks amble" is true if and only if aardvarks amble

as a partial definition of "true": the biconditional defines "true" with respect to the sentence "Aardvarks amble." And all such T-sentences together constitute an exhaustive and complete definition of "true."

The idea behind the disquotational view is sometimes put this way: to say that a sentence is true is really just an indirect way of saying the sentence itself. To say that the sentence "Penguins waddle" is true is just an indirect way of saying that penguins waddle. This prompts the question: Why not dispense with the truth-predicate in favor of direct talk about the world? The disquotationalist will respond by pointing to generalizations such as "Every sentence of the form 'p or not p' is true" and to truth-ascriptions such as "What Joe said is true." In the case of the generalization, we could dispense with the truth-predicate here if we could produce an infinite conjunction of sentences of the form "p or not p": aardvarks amble or aardvarks do not amble, and bison bathe or bison don't bathe, or … But we cannot produce such an infinite conjunction, and instead we achieve the desired effect by generalizing over sentences, and then bringing those sentences back down to earth by means of the truth-predicate.[8] In cases like "What Joe said is true," where the target utterance is picked out by means other than a quote-name, "true" serves to express an infinite disjunction:

What Joe said = "s_1" and s_1, or

What Joe said = "s_2" and s_2, or …

where "s_1," "s_2," … are quote-names of the sentences of Joe's language. The truth-predicate, says the disquotationalist, is a logical device: a device for disquotation, and for expressing infinite conjunctions and disjunctions.[9] There is no more to the meaning of "true" than its disquotational role. And moreover there is no more to our understanding of the concept of truth than an understanding of the disquotational role of the truth-predicate. If the concept of truth is a "thin" concept in this sense, then it can make no substantive contribution to our understanding of assertion, meaning, belief, or any other concept in this cluster. Explanations of these notions that make use of the truth-predicate can avail themselves only of its role as a logical device of disquotation.

In this vein, Field, a leading disquotationalist, observes that it may *seem* as though we need to appeal to truth to characterize the realist doctrine that "there might be ... sentences of our languages that are true that we will never have reason to believe" (Field 1999, 369) (where the realist is contrasted with the anti-realist, who identifies truth with some notion of justifiability). However, Field claims that the role of truth in such a characterization is "purely logical" (1999: 369). But for our finite limitations, the realist doctrine *could* be expressed without use of a truth-predicate via an infinite disjunction (where each disjunct is of the form "*p* and we will never have reason to believe *p*"). And Field thinks that appeal to truth in general claims such as that there is "a 'norm' of asserting and believing the truth" is merely disquotational.[10] The idea is that such general claims are in effect abbreviations for infinite conjunctions. The disquotationalist denies the concept of truth any substantive explanatory role.

Or consider Ramsey's redundancy theory. According to Ramsey, truth and falsity are ascribed to propositions, where the propositions may be given explicitly (as in "It is true that Caesar was murdered") or indirectly (as in "He is always right"). In the first case, the word "true" is readily eliminated: "It is evident that 'It is true that Caesar was murdered' means no more than that Caesar was murdered" (Ramsey 1927, 106). "True" and "false" are merely terms "which we sometimes use for emphasis or for stylistic reasons, or to indicate the position occupied by the statement in our argument" (Ramsey 1927, 106). Beyond this, "true" is redundant, and clearly has no substantive connections to other concepts. In the second case, it is not so obvious that "true" is eliminable:

> Thus if I say "He is always right," I mean that the propositions he asserts are always true, and there does not seem to be any way of expressing this without using the word "true." But suppose we put it thus "For all p, if he asserts p, p is true," then we see that the propositional function p is true is simply the same as p, as e.g. its value "Caesar was murdered is true" is the same as "Caesar was murdered." (Ramsey 1927, 106)

So in the second case too, Ramsey says, "true" is eliminable. Ramsey dismisses any problem about what it is for a proposition or judgment to be true—just make the judgment. For Ramsey, the real question is what is involved in making a judgment in the first place. Ramsey's essentially behavioristic approach to belief and judgment makes connections to various concepts, including *use* and *commitment*; but as far as truth is concerned, there is no place in this account for anything but a "thin" concept of truth.

For Ramsey, "true" is an eliminable predicate. For the prosententialist, it is not even a predicate at all,[11] but rather a component of *prosentences*. In the discourse:

Mary: Chicago is large.

John: If that is true, it probably has a large airport.

the expression "that is true" is a prosentence, which shares its content with its antecedent, namely "Chicago is large." On the prosentential view, "true" serves as a purely grammatical prosentence-forming operator. Under the prosententialist analysis, it does not survive as a discrete term expressing a separable concept that could stand in relations to other concepts.

These various deflationary accounts—minimalism, disquotationalism, the redundancy theory, and prosententialism—differ in various ways. They differ, for example, over the utility of the truth-predicate, the bearers of truth, and the grammar of "true." But their proponents share an *isolationist* view of truth: the claim that a complete account of truth will proceed independently of the concepts to which truth is traditionally tied—meaning, belief, assertion, and the rest. As Hill (2002, 4) puts it, an acceptable form of deflationism will maintain that "there is no particular set of concepts that one must acquire prior to acquiring the concept of truth"; it will present "truth as autonomous and presuppositionless."[12] Moreover, to explain facts whose statements involve truth-locutions all we need to assume about truth, according to the deflationist, is what falls out of the preferred deflationist account of "true." Isolationism cuts both ways: our understanding of truth is exhausted by the deflationary account, and truth in turn has no role in explaining other concepts, beyond the purely logical or grammatical role assigned to it by the deflationary account. Any appeal to substantive connections between truth and other concepts is based on a mistaken, inflated idea of truth.

We take isolationism to be a component of any genuine form of deflationism. It is telling that leading deflationists such as Horwich and Field explicitly spell out the isolationist consequences of their deflationary theories. But "deflationism" is a slippery term, with no agreed fixed extension—perhaps there are those who would still want to count platitude-respecting minimalism as a kind of deflationism. To avoid terminological distractions, we describe our target as *conceptual deflationism*: the view that a deflationary account of "is true" (be it minimalist, disquotationalist, prosententialist, or some other) will give us *all* there is to know or understand about the concept of truth and its explanatory role. As explained at the outset, we think that conceptual deflationism should be kept distinct from both *metaphysical deflationism* (which eliminates the property of truth from our ontological inventory) and *linguistic deflationism* (which offers this or that deflationary account of various everyday uses of the word "true"). To defend conceptual deflationism it is not enough to give arguments for the futility of appealing to a metaphysically robust relation obtaining between items we call "true" and something else (reality, facts, the way things are). Nor is it enough to provide a recipe for eliminating "is true" from our everyday discourse in which we apply it to sentences or other items. We need to see how to deflate the explanatory role apparently played by truth in elucidations of various concepts of interest to us. In what follows, our principal focus will be *assertion*. We will be arguing that understanding assertion requires more than the "thin" concept of truth afforded by deflationary accounts.

Before turning to assertion, however, it may be useful to clarify further what we take to be at stake regarding conceptual deflationism. An analogy might help. Consider for example the predicate "is good." Many philosophers would deny that there is a *sui generis* non-natural property denoted by this predicate. Some of them—call them "ethical reductionists"—propose to identify the property of being good with some natural property (though they disagree amongst themselves on *which* natural property it is). Other philosophers, however, might deny that "is good" denotes *any* property, natural or not. These philosophers—call them "ethical eliminativists"—might suggest that we can eliminate the property of being good from our ontological inventory altogether; for there is no single feature that is shared by all and only things we call good. The eliminativist owes us a story about ethical discourse. What is it that we're doing when we call something "good"? What is the meaning of "is good" as it is used in everyday discourse? And so on. An *ethical expressivist*, for example, might suggest that "is good" serves an expressive function—perhaps it is used to express approval, or some other pro-attitude. Crude as this map may be, we hope it can serve to recall familiar debates in metaethics. What is relevant about the ethical case for our purposes is the fact that it would seem implausible to claim that goodness is a "thin" concept—that it serves no explanatory role save what can be captured by some purely formal specification of the things that "is good" applies to, and that it bears no rich connections to other concepts. Contemporary ethical noncognitivists, it seems, want to preserve the explanatory role of ethical concepts and to exhibit the place each of them occupies in a complex and rich network of concepts that hold interest for us.[13]

As we see it, deflationists tend to overlook the possibility of an analogous position regarding truth. Eager to eliminate truth from our ontology and impressed by this or that deflationary treatment of "is true," they have lost sight of the place the concept of truth occupies in our conceptual scheme. Yet it seems to us that metaphysical deflationism and linguistic deflationism, taken either separately or together, do *not* entail conceptual deflationism. This is what we hope to show below.

II Truth and the Force of Assertion

Frege writes: "When we inwardly recognize that a thought is true, we are making a judgement: when we communicate this recognition, we are making an assertion" (Frege 1979, 139).[14] Making a judgment, Frege emphasized, must be sharply distinguished from the entertaining of a thought—we must not confuse merely predicating with judging. And, in parallel, assertion must be sharply distinguished from the mere expression or articulation of a thought. This is reflected in Frege's judgment sign—from the *Begriffsschrift*. The horizontal stroke—the so-called "content-stroke"—combines the symbols following it into a whole thought; the vertical stroke—the "judgment-stroke"—expresses the recognition or affirmation that this thought is *true*.

> If we *omit* the little vertical stroke at the left end of the horizontal stroke, then the judgement is to be transformed into *a mere complex of ideas;* the author is not expressing his recognition or non-recognition of the truth of this. (Frege 1879, 1–2)

Sometimes the mere expression of a thought is all that matters. In section 2 of the *Begriffsschrift*, Frege points out that one might present the thought that unlike magnetic poles attract one another merely for hypothetical consideration—one's intention is "just to produce in the reader the idea of the mutual attraction of unlike magnetic poles—so that, e.g., he may make inferences from this thought and test its correctness on the basis of these" (Frege 1879, 2). Or the thought might be the antecedent of a conditional; as Frege (1979, 185–186) puts it, "Even if the whole compound sentence is uttered with assertoric force, one is still asserting neither the truth of the thought in the antecedent nor that of the thought in the consequent." Or again, it might be what Frege (1979, 130) calls a "mock thought" of fiction.

But, says Frege, the logician has no interest in mock thoughts[15] or, more generally, in the mere presentations of thoughts: "The thing that indicates most clearly the essence of logic is the assertoric force with which a sentence is uttered" (Frege 1979, 252). And, according to Frege, assertoric force is to be understood in terms of truth: to assert that *p* is to present *p* as true (or, as Frege sometimes puts it, *to express one's acknowledgement of* p *as true*, or *to express one's affirmation of* p *as true*).

Frege's view of assertion is a natural one. When I assert that penguins waddle, I am not merely predicating waddling of penguins (where, for Frege, "merely predicating waddling of penguins" is that component common to *stating* that penguins waddle, *asking* or *wondering* whether penguins waddle, *promising* to make it so that penguins waddle, and so on). Nor am I merely presenting the thought that penguins waddle for consideration. There are many speech-acts I can perform that involve a given thought: I can suppose it, propose it, float it, question it. I can also express a thought in the course of asserting (or questioning, or supposing, etc.) a compound proposition, such as a conditional or disjunction. Frege plausibly claims that the distinguishing mark of assertion—what sets it apart from other speech-acts—is the fact that when I assert something, I present a certain thought *as true*.

Commenting on this aspect of Frege's view, Dummett says:

> When we make an assertion we are not merely uttering a sentence with determinate truth-conditions understood by the hearer, and hence with a particular truth-value; that, after all, we should do if the sentence expressed only part of what we were asserting—for instance, if it were the antecedent of a conditional. We are also, rightly or wrongly, saying that the sentence is true. This activity of asserting that the thought we are expressing is true is *sui generis:* it is not a further determination of the truth-conditions of the sentence, which remain unchanged whether we are asserting it to be true or not, but rather something which we *do* with a sentence whose truth-conditions have already been fixed. This is not the only thing we can do with a sentence: we can use it in giving a definition, in asking a question (of

the kind requiring the answer "Yes" or "No"), or in the course of telling a story. (Dummett 1978, 106)

The kind of "doing" Dummett is speaking of here—which he associates with Frege's notion of the force of an utterance, as opposed to its sense—is not restricted to speech-acts. It has its analogue in thought. Frege also wanted to distinguish the mere entertaining of a thought from the making of a *judgment*. And here again, the difference is to be captured in terms of *truth*. To judge that *p*, as opposed to merely entertaining the thought that *p*, or considering whether *p*, is to take *p* to be *true*. Moreover, judging, entertaining, considering, and so on, are attitudes or mental acts involving a single kind of entity—a *thought*. And, as Dummett points out, Frege's characterization of thoughts itself also appeals to the notion of truth:

> What, then, distinguishes thoughts from other constituents of our mental life, from mental images, ideas, feelings, desires, impulses, and the rest? That was the question Frege asked, and was the first to strive to answer: and his first step toward an answer was to say that thoughts, and only they, are apt to being characterized as being true or as being false. (Dummett 1993, 154)

The notion of truth, then, has a central role to play in Frege's account of assertion, judgment, and thought.[16]

The foregoing serves to usher in the following challenge for the conceptual deflationist: to explain how to achieve a proper theoretical understanding of what it is to assert or judge that *p* without help from the concept of truth. What is it, for the deflationist, to put forward a thought with the force of an assertion or judgment? What is it that one is *doing* when one judges or asserts *p*, as opposed to merely supposing it, or considering it, and so on? And, in the mental realm specifically, what is it that distinguishes having a *thought* from other kinds of mental episode? Frege suggests that in answering these questions we ourselves, as theorists, must appeal to a notion of truth.

How might the deflationist respond? Consider disquotationalism or Horwich's minimalism. According to this kind of deflationary view, the function of "true" is exhausted by its disquotational or denominalizing role. For example, "true" contributes no more than its denominalizing role to an explanation of why true beliefs engender successful action. Now consider the thesis that to assert is to present as true. The thesis invokes a certain concept—that of *presenting as true*—in a natural explanation of assertion. It also involves the use of the truth-predicate; in Horwich's terms, it is a fact about "true" that needs to be explained. With the denominalizing role of "true" in mind, a deflationist might claim that the thesis that *to assert that* p *is to present* p *as true* is equivalent to the thesis that *to assert that* p *is to present* p. This commits us to the claim that to present *p* as true is just to present *p*; for example, to present as true the thought that aardvarks amble is just to present the thought that aardvarks amble.[17] But this claim is false, for there are many ways to present a thought. I can present a thought as worthy of your consideration, or as a conjecture, or as a remote possibility, or as outrageous—and I can also present it as true. Presenting as true is just one way of presenting. So this cannot be the right way to denominalize away "true" in the locution "present as true."

It might be suggested that the correct denominalizing move is a wholesale "semantic descent": to present the proposition that aardvarks amble as true is just to present aardvarks as ambling. Here not only truth drops out, but so does the proposition (or thought, or sentence) that is said to be presented as true.[18] The claim "to assert that aardvarks amble is to present the proposition that aardvarks amble as true" is just a roundabout way of saying "to assert that aardvarks amble is to present aardvarks as ambling." But what is it to present aardvarks as ambling? One way of understanding this claim is as saying that we present the worldly mammals, aardvarks, as engaging in a certain kind of activity, as when a zoo-keeper gestures toward ambling aardvarks. But this clearly will not do as an explanation of assertion. (Asserting that aardvarks amble does not require the presence of ambling aardvarks; that is part of the point of assertion.)[19] A more plausible way of understanding the present suggestion is as saying that presenting aardvarks as ambling is a matter of *re*presenting aardvarks a certain way—as, well, ambling. But not any old form of representing would do the trick of capturing what is distinctive about asserting (or judging) that aardvarks amble, as opposed to, say, merely pointing to or drawing a picture of (or forming a mental image of) ambling aardvarks. The kind of representing that is relevant to assertion is surely "factual" representation: representing things *as being so*, or describing things *as they are*. But it seems that the very same task will face the deflationist, this time with respect to representation: how to understand what it is *to represent as being so*, which is a special kind of representing, just as presenting as true is a special kind of presenting. It does not seem that a deflationist would want to trade truth-talk in favor of unreconstructed talk of "the way things are" or "its being thus and so," etc. So the detour via representation will be of no help to the deflationist.

We cannot, then, denominalize away "true" as it appears in "present as true." The point applies equally well to the other locutions that Frege employs. It is implausible to claim that Frege's uses of "true" in "express one's recognition that *p* is true" or "express one's acknowledgement of *p* as true," or "express one's affirmation of *p* as true" are redundant; one can recognize or acknowledge or affirm a thought in various ways. And if it is insisted that to recognize (acknowledge, affirm) is just the same as to recognize as true (acknowledge as true, affirm as true), then the involvement of truth should instead be regarded as implicit. For now the notions *recognize, acknowledge,* and *affirm* must be understood respectively along the lines of *apprehend as true, register as true,* and *put forward as true.* "True" in the theorist's mouth still cannot be disquoted or denominalized away, and the deflationist must find another tack.

According to the present objection, we are to explain what it is to assert in terms of presenting as true, and the deflationist does not have the resources to accommodate this explanation. But a deflationist might respond as follows:

I accept that there is an undeniable connection between assertion and truth. But it is mis-leading to present the connection in terms of the slogan *to assert is to present as true*. Better to reverse the order: *to present as true is to assert*. Assertion is not to be characterized in terms of truth; rather, our use of the predicate "true" is to be characterized in terms of assertion. The objection gets the direction of explanation the wrong way around.

The idea is this: to predicate "true" of a sentence (or a thought, or a proposition) *is just to assert the sentence* (*thought, proposition*). To say:

"Penguins waddle" is true

is just to assert the sentence "Penguins waddle." We assert the sentence, we present it as true, by predicating "true" of it. Ayer puts it this way:

> To say that a proposition is true is just to assert it, and to say that it is false is just to assert its contradictory. And this indicates that the terms "true" and "false" connote nothing, but func-tion in the sentence simply as marks of assertion and denial. And in that case there can be no sense in asking us to analyze the concept of "truth." (Ayer 1936, 88–89)[20]

This is what we may call an *illocutionary* form of deflationism. We use "true" not to describe sentences or propositions, but rather to perform the speech-act of asser-tion. The term "true" is not really a property-denoting predicate; nor does it express a concept that stands in need of analysis, or can play an explanatory role in the expla-nation of assertion. The illocutionary deflationist will take on board the equivalence thesis, and agree that the content of '"Aardvarks amble" is true" is no different from that of "Aardvarks amble." But though "true" does not add content, it does introduce assertoric force: to say "'Aardvarks amble' is true" is to produce an assertion with the content that aardvarks amble.

We can understand Ayer as suggesting that "true" and "false" play a role very similar to that played by *explicit performatives*. Saying "*p* is true" is equivalent to saying "I *assert p.*" But on this reading of Ayer's proposal, his remark that "there can be no sense in asking us to analyze the concept of 'truth'" seems wrong. For we (theorists of language) do seek analyses of explicit performatives such as "assert." Perhaps Ayer would say that what makes no sense is to seek a *particular* kind of analysis: one which pairs up with "is true" a special worldly property—the property of being true. It is a mistake—a kind of category mistake—to engage in that kind of search, since calling something "true" is not predicating a property of it; rather it is articulating a kind of act one is performing in putting *p* forward. If so, Ayer is also advocating what we earlier called metaphysical deflationism: the denial that there is any need to populate our ontology with a substan-tive property of truth to serve as the extension of our truth-predicate.

Like Ayer, Frege emphasizes the illocutionary aspect or role of truth. Frege regards truth as belonging to the same family of concepts as assertion and judgment. Truth is associated with what we *do* when we use language and when we think, rather than with the content of what we say or think. Moreover, Frege famously endorses the equivalence thesis, that "p" and "'p' is true" are equivalent in content.[21] So is Frege a deflationist (as is often supposed), perhaps an illocutionary deflationist? No: it is striking that Frege is fundamentally opposed to illocutionary deflationism, and deflationism more generally.

At the core of disquotationalism, minimalism and the redundancy theory is the familiar equivalence thesis—for instance, "Sea-water is salt" is equivalent to "'Sea-water is salt' is true" (or "The proposition that sea-water is salt is true"). And Frege certainly endorses this equivalence. In his terms, both sentences express the same thought, and "the word 'true' is not an adjective in the ordinary sense" (Frege 1979, 251). Frege writes:

> If I attach the word "salt" to the word "sea-water" as a predicate, I form a sentence that expresses a thought. To make it clearer that we have only the expression of a thought, but that nothing is meant to be asserted, I put the sentence in the dependent form "that sea-water is salt."... With the word "true" the matter is quite different. If I attach this to the words "that sea-water is salt" as a predicate, I likewise form a sentence that expresses a thought. For the same reason as before I put this also in the dependent form "that it is true that sea-water is salt." The thought expressed in these words coincides with the sense of the sentence "that sea-water is salt." So the sense of the word "true" is such that it does not make any essential contribution to the thought. (Frege 1979, 251)

Predicating "true" of a sentence makes no difference to the thought expressed: it is the same thought. But according to Frege, "true" also makes no difference to the *force* with which the thought is expressed. Frege immediately goes on to say: "If I assert 'it is true that sea-water is salt,' I assert the same thing as if I assert 'sea-water is salt.' This enables us to recognize that the assertion is not to be found in the word 'true'" (Frege 1979, 251). If one's deflationary view of "true" is based on the equivalence thesis, then according to Frege "true" cannot be the mark of assertion. Indeed, Frege says that "there is no word or sign in language whose function is simply to assert something" (Frege 1979, 185).

Frege is explicitly opposed to illocutionary deflationism, and for good reason. If one accepts the equivalence thesis, there is no difference between asserting that *p* and asserting that *p* is true. Further, the locution "*p* is true" can occur as the antecedent of a conditional, where it cannot be produced with assertoric force—as in "If it is true that aardvarks amble, then ..." Further still, I can say "It is true that aardvarks amble" with a variety of different illocutionary forces—I can be supposing, conjecturing, pretending, or acting. Frege writes:

> One can, indeed, say: "The thought, that 5 is a prime number, is true." But closer examination shows that nothing more has been said than in the simple sentence "5 is a prime number." The truth claim arises in each case from the form of the declarative sentence, and when the latter lacks its usual force, e.g. in the mouth of an actor upon the stage, even the sentence "The thought that 5 is a prime number is true" contains only a thought, and indeed the same thought as the simple "5 is a prime number." (Frege 1892, 64)

The use of "true" doesn't produce assertoric force; rather, "even where we use the form of expression 'it is true that ...' the essential thing is really the assertoric form of the sentence" (Frege 1979, 129). So although Frege appears to give a deflationary account of the word "true," he explicitly rejects illocutionary deflationism.

Moreover, Frege's remarks about *truth* seem inhospitable to conceptual deflationism. For example:

> Truth is obviously something so primitive and simple that it is not possible to reduce it to anything still simpler. (Frege 1979, 129)

> The goal of scientific endeavour is *truth*. (Frege 1979, 2; emphasis in the original)

> Logic is the science of the most general laws of truth. (Frege 1979, 128)

> It is the striving for truth that drives us always to advance from the sense to the reference. (Frege 1892, 63)

Clearly we must distinguish what Frege says about the word "true," and what he says about truth. Frege writes:

> If I assert that the sum of 2 and 3 is 5, then I thereby assert that it is true that 2 and 3 make 5. So I assert that it is true that my idea of Cologne Cathedral agrees with reality, if I assert that it agrees with reality. Therefore it is really by using the form of an assertoric sentence that we assert truth, and to do this we do not need the word "true." (Frege 1979, 129)

We do *not* "assert truth" (as Frege puts it) by predicating "true" or by prefixing the operator "It is true that." Rather, we assert truth by *using a sentence with assertoric force*: "In order to put something forward as true, we do not need a special predicate: we need only the assertoric force with which the sentence is uttered" (Frege 1979, 233). Science aims at the truth, and "logic is the science of the most general laws of truth"—but it does not follow that science or logic is concerned with the word "true": "what logic is really concerned with is not contained in the word 'true' at all but in the assertoric force with which a sentence is uttered" (Frege 1979, 252).

How should we understand Frege on truth? One way is that truth is a simple, unanalyzable yet substantive primitive that is implicated ("asserted") not by the use of any special word or phrase that *denotes* it, but only by utterances made with the appropriate kind of illocutionary force—assertoric force. A second way is suggested by Greimann (2004, 431): "truth is a constituent of the assertoric force with which assertoric sentences are normally uttered."[22] In either case, truth is bound up with assertion in a way that vitiates conceptual deflationism. For, on either way of reading Frege, grasp of the concept of truth cannot be exhausted by any deflationary account of "true"; it requires understanding the fundamental connection between truth and assertion. So, while Frege explicitly embraces the equivalence thesis, which is common to all *linguistic* deflationists, he should be seen as denying *conceptual* deflationism, along with its isolationist commitments. Far from assigning no explanatory role to the concept of truth, or isolating it from other theoretical concepts of interest, he takes it to be a central notion in his philosophy of language and thought, intimately interwoven with other central notions.

We think that Frege teaches us a very important lesson. Deflationism about the word "true" is one thing, deflationism about the concept of truth quite another. Frege endorses the equivalence thesis about "true." He denies that "true" introduces descriptive content when appended to sentences or thoughts. He also denies that the use of "true" introduces any illocutionary force, or plays the role of an explicit performative. But for all that Frege is not a conceptual deflationist.

To fully appreciate Frege's lesson, it is helpful to distinguish uses of "true" in a language we theorize about from uses of "true" in the language in which we do our theorizing. Deflationists typically focus on uses of "true" in locutions such as '"Aardvarks amble' is true" (where "true" applies to the quote-name of sentences), "Socrates' last utterance was true" (where "true" is applied to a sentence picked out by means other than its quote-name), and "Everything Plato said was true" (where "true" is applied to a domain of sentences). Call these *first-order* uses of "true." In these uses, "true" is applied to sentences (or utterances, or propositions). Disquotationalists, minimalists and redundancy theorists aim to provide accounts of all first-order uses of "true," accounts which attribute to "true" a disquotational or denominalizing or prosentence-forming role. It may even be claimed that "true" can in principle be extruded altogether from the language; for example, as we saw in connection with disquotationalism, it might be claimed that if only we could handle infinite lists, "true" could be replaced by infinite disjunctions and conjunctions.

Given a language from which "true" is in this way eliminable, it is tempting to conclude that there is no substantive role for the concept of truth to play regarding this language. After all, with the word "true" eliminated, we do not even have a term to express the concept of truth. If "true" is to be regarded merely as a device for forming infinite disjunctions and conjunctions, then it can easily seem that a deflated, "thin" concept of truth is all we need. It might seem that linguistic deflationism brings conceptual deflationism in its train.

Accept for the moment that first-order uses of "true" can be handled in a deflationary way. From this it does not follow that we have done away with the concept of truth. As we continue to reflect on or theorize about a language and its practitioners, we may turn to the speech-act of assertion. We may say, following Frege, that to assert is to put forward as true. Here is the word "true" again, appearing in the language in which we theorize.[23] In our mouth, the word "true" is not used as a disquotational or denominalizing or prosentential device. We are not even purporting to describe some sentence or thought. This is not a first-order use, and it cannot be disquoted away. Our use of the word is what we may call a *reflective* or *explanatory use*; it is made in the course of offering a general explanation of what speakers are *doing* when they use language in certain ways. We are not *calling* any specific sentence true, nor are we making oblique reference to some set of sentences and saying of its members that they are true. Rather, we are trying to identify a distinguishing feature of a class of *acts*—assertions (or in the mental case, judgments).

We should emphasize that the role we are assigning to the concept of truth is reserved for reflective, explanatory uses of "true." We do not take a stand on first-order uses of "true"; for the sake of argument, we are willing to accept a deflationary account of first-order uses. At the same time, we are not claiming that explanatory uses of "true" are the sole province of high-level theorizing about language. Reflective or explanatory uses of "true" need not be technical or recherché. For example, the claim that to assert is to present as true seems intuitive and natural enough.[24]

Our present focus is on uses of the concept of truth in contexts which do not involve *calling* something true. If Frege is right, truth is implicated in the assertoric force with which a sentence is uttered. For what is distinctly characteristic of acts of assertion is that they present a thought as true. So when we explain assertion, we ourselves use a truth-locution and employ the concept of truth. Thus, even if we grant, as does Frege, that first-order uses of "true" submit to the equivalence thesis, we may need to employ the concept of truth for explanatory purposes. As we have seen, Frege is not at all shy about using truth-locutions in an explanatory way in connection with assertion, logic and science. He does *not* accept a deflationary view of the *concept* of truth.

We can get at the same point by imagining a language which has no semantic vocabulary at all. A Fregean explanation of key phenomena of this language in terms of truth may still be in order. Speakers of the language, we may suppose, will make assertions, and we will want to explain what distinguishes a speaker's assertion that *p* from other speech-acts—wondering whether *p*, joking that *p*, and the rest. For Frege, as long as we have assertoric force, we have truth. An act of assertion puts forward a thought as true; assertions advance us from sense to reference, from the thought to the True. There is no understanding of what it is to assert without the notion of truth.[25]

It is worth emphasizing that the involvement of truth with assertion, on the Fregean story, does not emerge through the use of "true" to ascribe a property to a sentence, or a thought. If Frege is right, when we say that assertion is presenting as true, we are not ourselves describing a sentence or a thought a certain way—*by ascribing truth to it*. The Fregean point is precisely that presenting as true (that is, asserting) is *not* a matter of ascribing a property to a sentence or thought, but rather is a special kind of *doing* or *act*, different from conjecturing, or surmising, or wondering, etc. Thus contrast:

(i)   presenting the thought that *p as* true

with

(ii) presenting the thought that *p is* true.

The deflationist can claim that (ii) is equivalent to:

(ii′) presenting the thought that *p*

since in (ii) "true" is applied to a particular thought. But it is not plausible to equate (i) with (ii′), for the familiar reason that presenting as true is just one way of presenting. In (i), "true" qualifies the kind of presenting at issue, not the thought presented. Frege's "presenting as true" is intended to characterize a class of acts that more often than not do not themselves involve calling something true; that is, Frege's explanandum is not primarily acts that involve first-order uses of "true." And explanatory uses of truth-locutions themselves do not involve appending "true" to a citation (direct or indirect) of a sentence or a thought. What implicates the concept of truth is our use of "presenting as true," which does not involve calling anything true, either.[26]

To sum up: even if "true" in its first-order uses is correctly treated by the linguistic deflationist, truth may nevertheless be a substantive concept, one that we invoke as we reflect on the nature of language use. If, like Frege, you are deflationist about first-order uses of "true" but you think asserting is presenting as true, you have not yet combined a truth-based account of assertion with a genuine form of conceptual deflationism.

III Assertion as Taking-True

Frege's lesson is this: you can be a deflationist about "true" (in its first-order uses) but not a deflationist about the concept of truth. But it is not clear where Frege stands on the metaphysical issue regarding truth. On the one hand, many of his remarks suggest that he thinks we get nowhere in our understanding of truth by pairing with the predicate "is true" some property that all and only true items share. On the other hand, Frege's talk of truth as "something primitive and simple" may suggest that he is reifying truth as a special, irreducible property. So some may argue that Frege's rejection of conceptual deflationism goes hand in hand with his attraction to metaphysical inflationism. However, next we will consider the view of a self-proclaimed deflationist, Robert Brandom, who is in our sense both a linguistic *and* a metaphysical deflationist,[27] but who is *not*—we will argue—a conceptual deflationist. Brandom's case will show us that Frege's lesson can be strengthened: you can be a deflationist about "true" *and* deny the existence of a property of truth, and still fail to be a deflationist about the concept of truth.

Throughout *Making It Explicit*, Brandom equates asserting with *taking-true* or *putting forward as true*. For example:

> Everyone ought to agree that asserting is putting forward a sentence as true. (Brandom 1994, 231)

> The attitude of taking-true is just that of acknowledging an assertional commitment. … A theory of asserting and assertional commitment is a theory of taking-true. (Brandom 1994, 202)

Of the claim or principle that a theory of asserting is a theory of taking-true, Brandom writes:

> This principle can be exploited according to two different orders of explanation: moving from a prior notion of truth to an understanding of asserting (or judging) as taking, treating, or putting forward *as* true, or moving from a notion of asserting to a notion of truth as what one is taking, treating, or putting forward a claim *as*. (Brandom 1994, 202)

Brandom rejects the former order of explanation, since he thinks it accords truth a more basic explanatory role than it deserves. Instead, Brandom endorses the latter way of exploiting the principle, that of "starting with an antecedent notion of assertional significance and then moving via that principle to an understanding of what is involved in talk of truth" (Brandom 1994, 232). Notice the shift here to "talk of truth." Frege has prepared us to be wary of this move to truth-talk—an account of "true," if it is confined to what we've called *first-order* uses, may tell us nothing about truth's involvement with assertion. So in what follows we will be interested not only in the adequacy of Brandom's treatment of the word "true"; we will also be interested in the relevance of that treatment to assertion.

We turn first to Brandom on "is true" and truth-talk. Brandom takes to heart the pragmatists' idea "that in calling something true, one is *doing* something, rather than, or in addition to, *saying* something" (Brandom 1994, 287). According to Brandom, the pragmatists are motivated by the special relation that exists between the force of an act of *taking as true* and the force of a straightforward assertion (see Brandom 1994, 288). Brandom makes the same observation as Frege: "In asserting 'It is true that *p*,' one asserts that *p*, and vice versa. The force or significance of the two claims is the same" (Brandom 1994, 288). Frege drew the conclusion that "true" cannot be the mark of assertion. Brandom draws a different conclusion: "true" *makes explicit* what is implicit in the act of assertion. When we assert "Aardvarks amble," we take it as true that aardvarks amble. When we assert '"Aardvarks amble' is true," we are asserting the same thing as before—but we are now making explicit our formerly implicit attitude of taking-true. Brandom writes: "Semantic vocabulary is used merely as a convenient way of making explicit what is already implicit in the force or significance that attaches to the content of a speech act or attitude" (Brandom 1994, 82). This is *not* to endorse illocutionary deflationism: Brandom is not claiming that predicating "true" of a proposition *introduces* or *produces* an assertion. It is just that what was already implicit is now made explicit; nothing new is added.

Now, according to Brandom, "true" is *force-redundant.* The assertion that *p* is true merely preserves the force of the assertion that *p*. As long as the truth locution is freestanding, and not, say, the antecedent of a conditional, force-redundancy is a central phenomenon of truth-talk (see Brandom 1994, 299). But this, Brandom says, cannot be the whole story about "true." Recall Frege's observation: there are uses of truth locutions that are not assertoric—consider, for example, the locution '"Penguins waddle' is true" in the conditional "If 'Penguins waddle' is true, then penguins waddle." Brandom offers "a more general redundancy view that has the force redundancy of freestanding truth-takings as a consequence" (Brandom 1994, 299). This is the prosentential theory of truth, according to which "... is true" is a prosentence-forming operator.[28] Prosentenccs are analogous to pronouns: just as "She stopped" differs from "Mary stopped" in its explicit dependence on a token of "Mary" as its anaphoric antecedent, so the prosentence "'Penguins waddle' is true" differs from "Penguins waddle" in its dependence upon an antecedent (perhaps the token of "Penguins waddle" that it contains)—but there is no difference of semantic content between the prosentence and its anaphoric antecedent. According to the prosentential theory, truth locutions have the same semantic content as their antecedents whatever the context—whether, for example, they are freestanding or antecedents of conditionals. Moreover, according to Brandom, content-redundancy entails force-redundancy:

> Intersubstitutability of "it is true that p" and "p" in *all* occurrences, embedded or not, is sufficient to yield force redundancy in freestanding uses as a consequence. If two asserted contents are the same, then the significance of asserting them in the same pragmatic context should be the same. (Brandom 1994, 300)

This last claim of Brandom's seems correct: given content redundancy, force-redundancy seems to follow. If "Aardvarks amble" and "'Aardvarks amble' is true" share the same content, then the force of uttering one in a given context will be the same as uttering the other in that same context. But then how can content-redundancy yield the kind of connection between "true" and assertoric force that Brandom is claiming? That is, how can it be maintained that "true" makes explicit what is already implicit in the force that attaches, specifically, to assertion? Suppose I *conjecture* that aardvarks amble. Given the content-redundancy of truth, and holding the context fixed, if we substitute "that 'aardvarks amble' is true" for "that aardvarks amble," there will be no difference of force. The force will still be that associated with an act of conjecturing. But surely we should *not* now conclude that the addition of "is true" makes explicit what we are *doing* when we conjecture. That is, the use of "is true" here cannot be taken as signaling that we're putting p forward *with the force of a conjecture*. Given the prosentential account, "true" is content-redundant and force-redundant. But if that is so, then there can be no privileged connection between truth and assertion, as Frege thought. We can no more say that "true" makes it explicit what we are doing when we are asserting than we can say that "true" makes it explicit what we are doing when we are conjecturing or supposing or entertaining a thought. On a content-redundancy view such as prosententialism, there can be no general link between truth and force, and in particular no link between truth and assertoric force. The point generalizes to other deflationary accounts—for example, disquotationalism and minimalism. Given the claimed equivalence of "Aardvarks amble" and "'Aardvarks amble' is true" (or "Aard-varks amble" and "The proposition that aardvarks amble is true"), their intersubstitut-ability in a given pragmatic context will not affect the force in any way, whatever that force may be. Treated along these deflationary lines, the truth-predicate is quite inert with respect to force, and it cannot function to make explicit what we are doing when we engage in this or that speech-act.

But this breaks the link that Brandom claims to exist between my assertional act of *taking-true* and the word "true." In endorsing the pragmatic force-based approach to truth for freestanding uses (as opposed, for example, to embedded uses in the antecedent of a conditional), Brandom writes: "On the pragmatic line being considered, it is the practical significance or force of asserting that defines taking-true, and this sense of taking-true accounts for our use of 'true'" (Brandom 1994, 297–298). But if uses of "true" are accounted for along prosentential lines, then those uses cannot be explained in terms of *taking-true*. For the prosententialist, "true" is content-redundant, and thereby force-redundant. So the word "true" has no link to assertoric force, or any other kind of force. And in the other direction, a prosentential account of "true" has no tendency to provide a deflationary understanding of *truth-taking*. (Indeed, as we shall see below, Brandom's own account of truth-taking is far from deflationary.) Again, we should heed Frege's warning not to assume too quickly that a deflationary account of "true" will bear on truth's involvement with assertion. Deflationary accounts of first-order uses of "true" will have the result that to conjecture that p is true is to do no more than to conjecture that p, to wonder whether p is true is to do nothing other than to wonder whether p, and so on for the various available illocutionary forces. Content redundancy brings force-redundancy in its train. But this does nothing to address the explanatory claim that links assertoric force, specifically, to presenting as true (or to Brandom's own taking-true). To deflate *that* claim it is not enough to be able to substitute "p" for "p is true." We need to be able to substitute "presenting" for "presenting as true" in our explanation, and we need to be able to substitute "taking" for "taking true." And we have argued that deflationary treatments of "is true" have not shown us how to do that. Thus, we may accept that the verbal separation of sentences or thoughts into the "true" ones and the rest is not a substantial separation that aims to identify some common feature shared by all and only items falling under "true." For all that, it may still be the case—and indeed we've argued that it is the case—that the separation of acts into truth presentings and the rest, or the separation of attitudes into truth-takings and the rest, *is* a substantial one.[29]

So let us now turn to the attitude of *truth-taking* or *taking as true*. Even if the prosen-tential theory of the word "true" is correct—indeed, even if we can eliminate altogether all first-order uses of the word "true" from the language—still the notion of *taking as true* remains, and with it the concept of truth. In Brandom's phrase, truth here is "what one is taking, treating, or putting forward a claim *as*" (Brandom 1994, 202) when one asserts. At this point, then, the deflationist needs a suitably deflationary account of *taking as true* and the associated concept of truth.

But this is not something that Brandom provides. Brandom is dismissive of an inflated respect for truth—but truth-taking is an altogether different matter: "Talk about the cardinal importance of concern with truth is a dispensable façon de parler. What actually matters is the pragmatic attitude of *taking-true* or putting forward as true, that is, judging or asserting" (Brandom 1994, 82). Here, as in many other places, Brandom identifies taking-true with asserting—and so Brandom's account of asserting is at the same time an account of taking-true or putting forward as true (recall Brandom's remark that a theory of asserting is a theory of taking-true). And this theory of asserting or taking-true is *not* a deflationary one. What are we doing when we assert or put forward a sentence as true? Brandom's general answer is that we are undertaking a certain kind of commitment. The commitment may be expressed in terms of the Sellarsian notion of the practice of giving and asking for reasons:

> The kind of commitment that a claim of the assertional sort is an expression of is something that can stand in need of (and so be liable to the demand for) a reason; and it is something that can be offered as a reason. (Brandom 1994, 167)

It is a necessary condition of assertional commitments that they play the dual role of justifier and subject of demand for justification; assertions "are fundamentally fodder for *inferences*" (Brandom 1994, 168). Brandom's account of asserting or taking as true goes forward in terms of commitments, inferences, entitlements, justificatory responsibilities—clearly this is not a deflationary account of *taking-true*.

There is a *phenomenalist* aspect to Brandom's account (see Brandom 1994, 291ff.). Brandom explicitly rejects a metaphysical account of truth, and instead aims for a phenomenalistic understanding of truth. We are to start not with truth, but with *takings*-true (just as a phenomenalist might start not with what is represented but with representings of it). This strategy may lead to the rejection of any metaphysically robust *property* of truth serving as the extension of "true" in its ordinary first-order uses. But it does not permit us to dispense with the *concept* of truth altogether. That concept still figures in. Taking-true is a distinctive attitude, a special kind of taking; presenting as true is a special kind of presenting. And our use of "true" in these locutions indicates what it is that is distinctive about this kind of presenting. Truth is what we take or present a claim *as* when we assert, whether or not we think that truth is a special feature shared by all true claims. Truth is thus bound up with the attitude of taking as true—and we have seen that Brandom's treatment of that attitude is far from deflationary.

Brandom may lay claim to metaphysical deflationism, and to a prosententialist deflationism about "true," but for all that he is *not* a conceptual deflationist.[30] As a theorist of language, he still needs to invoke the concept of truth to explain certain of our linguistic doings, even if there is no substantive property of truth shared by all and only things we (properly) call true, and even if the word "true" in its first-order uses is redundant. Put together Brandom's metaphysical deflationism and his redundancy account of "true," and you still won't have enough to break the conceptual connections between assertion and truth, or to deflate the concept of truth.

In treating truth phenomenalistically, Brandom does not free himself of the concept of truth—indeed, neither does he free himself of the word "true." For what are we to make of the occurrences of "true" in such locutions as "to assert is to take as true or to put forward as true"? As we suggested earlier, in locutions like these we are making *explanatory* uses of "true," as opposed to *first-order* uses. These explanatory uses cannot be treated along prosentential lines. Here "true" is not a prosentence-forming operator, and there is no anaphoric antecedent. In claiming that to assert *p* is to put forward *p* as true, we say something about the *act of asserting* a sentence; we do not explicitly or obliquely call some antecedent sentence true. Brandom does acknowledge that there are uses of the truth-predicate that his theory cannot handle. As examples, he cites uses of the substantive "truth," as in "Truth is one, but beliefs are many" and "Truth is a property definable in the language of some eventual physics" (Brandom 1994, 323). But these uses of "true," Brandom argues, are the result of a mistake: a false analogy is drawn between "true" and ordinary predicates, with the result that a property of truth is hypostatized. Brandom writes: "It is no defect in the anaphoric account not to generate readings of the fundamentally confused remarks that result" (Brandom 1994, 324). But the anaphoric account does not generate a reading of "When we assert *p* we put forward *p* as true," and Brandom surely will not regard *this* claim as confused.

Is there a way of maintaining both Brandom's account of assertion and conceptual deflationism? One option would be to deny that *taking-true* or *putting forward as true* have any connection to truth. But this seems at best implausible and at worst contradictory. It is clear that Brandom himself does not endorse this option. He shares the pragmatist's commitment to phenomenalism about truth, that "once one understands what it is to take or treat something as true, one will have understood as well the concept of truth" (Brandom 1994, 291); being true "is to be understood as being *properly* taken-true" (Brandom 1994, 291).[31] It is clear that Brandom seeks an account of truth—a pragmatic account that proceeds from the attitude of taking-true. There is no getting rid of the concept of truth: it is one of Brandom's explananda. This point is reinforced by Brandom's treatment of assertion and knowledge. According to Brandom, "assertions have the default status and significance of implicit knowledge claims" (Brandom 1994, 201). Consequently, says Brandom, some account must be given of the truth condition on knowledge. The question then is: "What is the social-deontic attitude corresponding to the truth condition on attributions of knowledge?" (Brandom 1994, 202). The aim is not to deflate truth, but to explain truth's connection to knowledge within the pragmatic framework of commitments and entitlements.[32] This project, we have argued, is quite distinct from that of providing a deflationary account of "true."

Brandom's pragmatic project could be seen as similar in some ways to that of the ethical noncognitivist who tries to explain our use of an ethical term such as "good." The noncognitivist wants to explain ethical discourse without invoking a substantive property of goodness—a worldly feature (whether irreducibly moral or reducible to some natural feature or features). Toward that end the noncognitivist might invoke a human attitude of "taking-to-be-good" as the more basic explanatory notion, in terms of which our moral attitudes and behavior, as well as aspects of our moral discourse (such as our calling things good) may be explained. The noncognitivist may further try to *reduce* the attitude of taking-to-be-good to some other psychological attitudes or propensities. But if she were to do so, it doesn't seem to us that this would amount to a "conceptual deflation" of the notion of goodness, or of taking-to-be-good. For the noncognitivist's reductive success might itself serve to reveal the richness of the relevant notions, and their connections to other ones in our conceptual scheme. (If the concept of goodness were merely a "thin" concept, whose understanding is exhausted by its mastery as a purely formal or grammatical device, the noncognitivist reductive or reconstructive task would be a very easy one indeed![33])

Another option open to the conceptual deflationist is to embrace Brandom's account of assertion—the pragmatic account of assertion that proceeds in terms of commitments, entitlements, inferences, and social-deontic attitudes—and bypass any identification of assertion with taking-true. The idea is that if we take the account this way, we have an account of assertion that is entirely independent of truth. Since truth makes no appearance, the account may seem to be compatible with conceptual deflationism. However, there are at least three problems with this option. First, it may be objected that this is a purely verbal maneuver. We can withhold the claim that to assert is to take as true. But withholding the claim does not make it false. Perhaps all we have really done is to reconstruct in pragmatic terms the notion of taking-true under a different name, under the name of assertion. At issue isn't the word "true," but an allegedly explanatory notion that we invoke using that word in certain claims about the use of language. Second, even if assertion is pulled apart from notions like *taking-true, putting forward as true, presenting as true*, those notions still stand in need of explanation. What is it to put forward a proposition as true? It seems for all the world that this is the speech-act of assertion. But suppose it isn't. Then it is a distinct speech-act that is characterized in terms of truth. And, as we have seen, truth's involvement in *taking-true* or *putting forward as true* is not explained by a deflationary account of the (first-order uses) of the word "true." As long as we need the concept of truth to explain certain speech-acts, we must reject conceptual deflationism.

Third, consider Brandom's account of assertion taken in a way that bypasses truth altogether. According to this pragmatic account, when I assert that aardvarks amble I take on certain commitments and responsibilities. But what is it about the act of asserting that generates these inferential commitments and justificatory responsibilities?

Why are they not generated when I suppose, conjecture, or ask a question? The answer seems obvious: it's because when I assert that aardvarks amble, I'm putting forward that proposition *as true,* as the way things are. I'm not putting it forward as something to be assumed for the sake of argument, or as something to be questioned, or as something that is possible—I'm putting it forward as true. This is what distinguishes assertion from other speech-acts, and this is what generates the commitments and responsibilities identified by the pragmatic account. It is no accident that taking-true and its cognates figure so centrally in Brandom's account. We cannot make proper sense of the pragmatic account of assertion without appreciating the role that the concept of truth plays in our understanding of assertoric force.

In our introduction we cited Williams's claim that, according to deflationary views, the function of truth-talk is "*wholly* expressive, never *explanatory*" (Williams 1999, 547). If our argument against conceptual deflationism is right, then truth-talk *does* have an explanatory function, *contra* the deflationist. It is not the case that the distinctive function of "true" is only to allow us "to endorse or reject sentences (or propositions) that we cannot simply assert" (Williams 1999, 547).

We conclude that a thorough-going deflationism is incompatible with an adequate account of assertion. This is not to say that we must abandon a deflationary account of the word "true"—Frege holds out the possibility that we can explain assertion while endorsing linguistic deflationism (for first-order uses of "true"). And it is not to say that we must abandon metaphysical deflationism—Brandom provides a rich account of assertion in terms of truth-taking while maintaining both metaphysical and linguistic deflationism. But it is to say that we must abandon conceptual deflationism. Perhaps there is no robust property of truth, and perhaps first-order uses of "true" are redundant, but if we are to understand what we do when we assert, we cannot dispense with the concept of truth.[34]

Notes

1. Williams (1999, 547); emphasis in the original.

2. See Bar-On, Horisk, and Lycan (2000).

3. See Jackson, Oppy, and Smith (1994).

4. This "fact about truth" is considered by Horwich (1990, 23–24).

5. The phrase is Horwich's; see Horwich (1990, 221ff.).

6. Horwich (1990, 26); emphasis in the original.

7. See Horwich (1990, 24).

8. See Quine (1970, 12).

9. For example, see Leeds (1978, 120–121n10); Field (1986, 58); Resnik (1990, 412); and David (1994, 107, chap. 4).

10. See Field (1999, 369).

11. "Truth, to coin a phrase, isn't a real predicate" (Grover, Camp, and Belnap 1975, 97).

12. Hill (2002, 3–4) recommends a version of minimalism, and regards deflationism in general as a view that "truth is philosophically and empirically neutral, in the sense that its use carries no substantive philosophical or empirical commitments."

13. For influential contemporary versions of ethical noncognitivism, see, for example, Gibbard (1990) and Blackburn (1993). It could be argued that Ayer, an early and well-known proponent of emotivism, did have hopes of "deflating" the concept of goodness (and other ethical concepts). But Ayer's version of ethical noncognitivism is notoriously riddled with difficulties, in good part because of its failure to do justice to the role played by ethical concepts in our conceptual scheme. (Ram Neta has drawn our attention to a view of Geach [1956] according to which "good" is merely a grammatical device—a predicate modifier—which does not represent a substantive concept.)

14. The emphasis is Frege's. Frege says the same thing at a number of places. For example: "Once we have grasped a thought, we can recognize it as true (*make a judgement*) and give expression to our recognition of its truth (*make an assertion*)" (Frege 1979, 185).

15. "The logician does not have to bother with mock thoughts, just as a physicist, who sets out to investigate thunder, will not pay any attention to stage-thunder" (Frege 1979, 130).

16. Dummett also urges a conceptual connection between assertion and truth, but stresses the reverse direction: "Without doubt, the source of the concept [of truth] lies in our general conception of the linguistic practice of assertion" (Dummett 1991, 165).

17. We have expressed the claim here in terms of presenting a thought as true—but one could equally well put the claim in terms of presenting a sentence as true, or a proposition as true.

18. We owe this suggestion to Dean Pettit.

19. Even if one *can* present ambling aardvarks in the absence of ambling aardvarks (perhaps via some form of "deferred ostension"), there is still the problem of identifying what has been conveyed in this way: is it the *general* claim that aardvarks amble or the *particular* claim that there are some ambling aardvarks about? There is also a question how to regard particular claims such as "Asserting that aardvarks amble is presenting aardvarks as ambling" and "Asserting that penguins waddle is presenting penguins as waddling," and so on, as instances of the general claim "To assert that *p* is to present *p* as true," since the particular claims are not the result of any suitable substitution for *p*.

20. Strawson's variant of the redundancy theory identifies a performative role for "true": we use "true" to perform speech-acts such as endorsing, agreeing, and conceding, as well as asserting. See Strawson (1950).

21. See for example Frege (1956) in Blackburn and Simmons (1999, 88): "The sentence 'I smell the scent of violets' has just the same content as the sentence 'It is true that I smell the scent of violets.'"

22. Greimann's article provides an excellent discussion of Frege on the expressive, illocutionary, cognitive and explanatory functions of truth.

23. In a similar vein, Dummett (1991, 167), remarking on the explanatory role of the concept of truth, has suggested that truth belongs with "second-level concepts, used to comment on our employment of our language."

24. Ted Parent has pointed out to us that, if one endorses a deflationary account of first-order uses of "true" and accepts our claim that reflective or theoretical uses cannot be deflated, one may have to opt for a non-uniform account of the truth-locutions for any language that permits both types of uses. This raises issues that go beyond the scope of this paper. We are here only concerned to argue that *even if we* were to accept a deflationary treatment of first-order uses of "true," we would still have reason to reject conceptual deflationism.

25. A similar point can be made about the link between truth and meaning via the notion of truth-conditions. For an argument that any explanation of meaning requires appeal to truth-conditions, and a discussion of the issues this raises for a deflationist, see Bar-On et al. (2000). Dummett has famously argued that a deflationist about truth *cannot* appeal to the notion of truth-conditions in explaining meaning. For an early statement, see Dummett's "Truth" in Dummett (1978, 7). Patterson (2003) argues that deflationism can be sanguine about the explanatory role of truth-conditions, as long as the deflationist account is confined to the role of "true" in the *object language*. He argues, however, that Dummett is right about the incompatibility of a truth-conditional account with what he calls "metalanguage deflationism." While we find Patterson's overall line congenial, we think his main point is better understood in terms of our distinction between first-order uses and explanatory uses of truth-locutions.

26. We thank Matthew Chrisman and Thomas Hofweber for remarks that have prompted this clarification. We should distinguish the schematic form φ-*ing the thought that* p *is true* and φ-*ing the thought that* p *as true*, where φ stands for a speech-act. The former is arguably equivalent to φ-*ing the thought that* p. But, in sharp contrast, the status of the latter seems to shift according to the value of φ. Although we won't pursue it here, for some values the result is nonsensical (consider *questioning whether the thought that p as true*). For other values, the result is the speciation of a genus—in particular, this is so for the case of interest to us, *presenting as true* or *taking as true*. It is less clear to us whether there are well-formed values that are equivalent to φ-*ing the thought that p*.

27. See e.g. Brandom (1994, chap. 5, sec. 2, entitled "Semantic Deflationism"). Brandom's linguistic deflationism takes the form of prosententialism, and he explicitly denies that there is a property of truth; see, for example, Brandom (1994, 325).

28. Brandom departs from the original prosentential theory, according to which "… is true" is a syncategorematic fragment of a semantically atomic generic prosentence "that is true" (see Brandom 1994, 305).

29. This goes back to the point of clarification offered toward the end of section II.

30. Brandom does not claim to be a conceptual deflationist—but then he does not separate it off from other forms of deflationism in the way that we have. His willingness to place the notion of

taking as true and its cognates in so central a position might suggest that he would reject conceptual deflationism; on the other hand he embraces deflationism without any apparent reservation. Brandom interpretation aside, we are urging that Brandom's account of assertion is incompatible with conceptual deflationism.

31. Brandom writes: "Being true is then to be understood as being properly taken-true (believed). It is this idea that is built on here, jettisoning the details of the classical pragmatist account of belief or taking-true, and substituting for it the account of assertion and doxastic discursive commitment introduced in Chapter 3" (Brandom 1994, 291).

32. Brandom also ties truth to other notions, for example *successful action*. See Brandom (1994, 527–529).

33. But see note 13.

34. We wish to thank Matthew Chrisman, Thomas Hofweber, Ted Parent, and Dean Pettit for reading a draft of the paper and providing very helpful comments.

References

Ayer, A. J. 1936. *Language, Truth, and Logic*. London: Victor Golancz.

Bar-On, D., Horisk, C., and Lycan, W. 2000. "Deflationism, Meaning, and Truth-Conditions." *Philosophical Studies* 101: 128.

Blackburn, S. 1993. *Essays on Quasi-realism*. New York: Oxford University Press.

Blackburn, S., and Simmons, K., eds. 1999. *Truth*. Oxford: Oxford University Press.

Brandom, R. 1994. *Making It Explicit*. Cambridge, MA: Harvard University Press.

David, M. 1994. *Correspondence and Disquotation*. New York: Oxford University Press.

Dummett, M. 1978. *Truth and Other Enigmas*. Cambridge, MA: Harvard University Press.

Dummett, M. 1991. *The Logical Basis of Metaphysics*. Cambridge, MA: Harvard University Press.

Dummett, M. 1993. *The Seas of Language*. Oxford: Clarendon Press.

Field, H. 1986. "The Deflationary Conception of Truth." In G. MacDonald and C. Wright, eds., *Fact, Science, and Morality: Essays on A. J. Ayer's* Language, Truth and Logic, 55–117. Oxford: Basil Blackwell.

Field, H. 1999. "Deflationist Views of Meaning and Content." In S. Blackburn and K. Simmons, eds., *Truth*, 351–391. Oxford: Oxford University Press.

Frege, G. 1879. "Begriffsschrift (Chapter I)." Reprinted in P. Geach and M. Black, eds., *Translations from the Philosophical Writings of Gottlob Frege*, 1–20. Oxford: Basil Blackwell, 1960.

Frege, G. 1892. "On Sense and Reference." Reprinted in P. Geach and M. Black, eds., *Translations from the Philosophical Writings of Gottlob Frege*, 56–78. Oxford: Basil Blackwell, 1960.

Frege, G. 1956. "The Thought: A Logical Inquiry." Reprinted in S. Blackburn and K. Simmons, eds., *Truth*. Oxford: Oxford University Press, 1999.

Frege, G. 1979. *Posthumous Writings*. Oxford: Basil Blackwell.

Geach, P. 1956. "Good and Evil." *Analysis* 17: 33–42.

Gibbard, A. 1990. *Wise Choice, Apt Feelings*. Cambridge, MA: Harvard University Press.

Greimann, D. 2004. "Frege's Puzzle about the Cognitive Function of the Concept of Truth." *Inquiry* 47: 425–442.

Grover, D., Camp, J., and Belnap, N. 1975. "A Prosentential Theory of Truth." *Philosophical Studies* 27: 73–125.

Hill, C. 2002. *Thought and World*. Cambridge: Cambridge University Press.

Horwich, P. 1990. *Truth*. Oxford: Basil Blackwell.

Jackson, F., Oppy, G., and Smith, M. 1994. "Minimalism and Truth Aptness." *Mind* 103: 287–302.

Leeds, S. 1978. "Theories of Reference and Truth." *Erkenntnis* 13: 111–129.

Patterson, D. 2003. "Deflationism and the Truth Conditional Theory of Meaning." *Philosophical Studies* 124(3): 271–294.

Quine, W. V. 1970. *Philosophy of Logic*. Englewood Cliffs, NJ: Prentice-Hall.

Ramsey, F. P. 1927. "Facts and Propositions." *Proceedings of the Aristotelian Society*, suppl., 7(1): 153–170.

Resnik, M. 1990. "Immanent Truth." *Mind* 99: 405–424.

Strawson, P. 1950. "Truth." Reprinted in S. Blackburn and K. Simmons, eds., *Truth*, 162–182. Oxford: Oxford University Press, 1999.

Williams, M. 1999. "Meaning and Deflationary Truth." *Journal of Philosophy* 96: 545–564.

Wright, C. 1992. *Truth and Objectivity*. Cambridge, MA: Harvard University Press.

VI Primitivist and Identity Theories

Introduction

Michael P. Lynch, Jeremy Wyatt, and Junyeol Kim

The essays in part VI address *primitivist* and *identity theories* of truth. The basic contention advanced by primitivists is that in developing theories that involve the notion of truth—for instance, theories of the nature of truth or theories of linguistic meaning or mental representation—we should take truth to be an unanalyzed, primitive notion. This approach to truth is of course a stark departure from many of the approaches that we've encountered thus far, according to which truth is a complex notion, an understanding of which requires detailed philosophical analysis.

In coming to grips with identity theories of truth, it is particularly helpful to contrast them with correspondence theories. Correspondence theorists often distinguish between truth-bearers (e.g., propositions, sentences, or beliefs) and the facts in the world with which they may correspond, or fail to correspond. For such correspondence theorists, truth-bearers and facts are meant not only to be numerically distinct, but distinct in *kind*.

A contrasting picture is memorably put forward by John McDowell (1994, 27):

> There is no ontological gap between the sort of thing one can mean, or generally the sort of thing one can think, and the sort of thing that can be the case. When one thinks truly, what one thinks *is* what is the case. So since the world is everything that is the case (as [Wittgenstein] once wrote), there is no gap between thought, as such, and the world.

This is the picture that is definitive of identity theories of truth. According to the identity theorist, if a proposition is true, then the reason it is true is that it is numerically *identical* (and thus also identical in kind) with a fact. The result of this way of thinking about truth is a closing of the "ontological gap," as McDowell describes it, between truth-bearers and reality that we find in correspondence theories.

Primitivist Theories

G. E. Moore famously held that the concept GOOD was a simple, unanalyzable concept. Like the concept YELLOW, Moore argued that GOOD could not be defined using any more fundamental concepts. In this sense, Moore took GOOD to be basic. It is less well known that Moore (and Russell) briefly flirted with a similar view about truth—namely, that truth is a "simple unanalysable property which is possessed by some propositions and not by others" (Moore 1953, 261).

Although Moore later abandoned this primitivist view of truth, the view that truth is a primitive concept has recently seen something of a comeback. Its classic advocate is Donald Davidson (chapter 26). According to Davidson, previous attempts to supply substantive content to the concept of truth—attempts like those of correspondence and coherence theorists, for example—are either subject to counterexample or devoid of content themselves. This is exactly what primitivism tells us to expect: these theories have failed to define truth because it can't be defined. Davidson adds two other points. First, he notes that our inability to reduce truth to a more basic set of concepts is hardly surprising. The concept of truth is already so basic to our thought that without it we might not have any concepts at all. Second, Davidson takes Tarski's work (chapter 14) to prove that the truth predicate is indefinable. Tarski contends that we can apply the truth predicate to the sentences of a language only if we relativize its application to that language. Thus, Tarski defines not "true" but "true-in-L_1," "true-in-L_2," and so on. About truth itself, Davidson argues, Tarski can say nothing.

Jamin Asay (chapter 27) is the most recent defender of primitivism. Sharply distinguishing between the concept TRUTH and the property *truth* (compare Alston's discussion in chapter 3), Asay defends a primitivist account of the former. Specifically, Asay characterizes primitivism as the thesis that "the concept of truth cannot be defined, reduced, or analyzed into concepts that are themselves more basic or fundamental than truth." He offers an overview of several arguments for primitivism as well as a number of objections to the view.

The argument for primitivism that Asay finds most compelling turns on an apparent insight due to Gottlob Frege. This is the idea that the concept TRUTH is omnipresent, insofar as it is a structural component of every propositional thought whatsoever. If TRUTH is omnipresent in this sense, Asay argues, then it follows that any attempted definition of TRUTH will contain TRUTH in its definiens, which means that any such definition will be circular. In this way, whenever we attempt to define TRUTH in terms of more basic concepts, we find that our definitional spade is turned.

Both Davidson and Asay are concerned to distinguish primitivism from deflationism. This project is important, since deflationists also take traditional theories of truth to come up short. A key idea here is that primitivists can take the concept TRUTH to enjoy explanatory power, while deflationists (or least deflationists about the concept TRUTH) cannot. Davidson, for instance, takes truth to be crucial to meaning; unless we appeal to truth, we cannot explain meaning in terms of truth-conditions, as Davidson maintains that we should. Asay takes the concept TRUTH to be explanatorily indispensable for explaining a number of phenomena (e.g., knowledge, belief, assertion, conjecture, meaning, pretense, and sincerity).

While they take the concept TRUTH to enjoy explanatory power, both Davidson and Asay refuse to give any sort of robust metaphysical explanation of the property *truth*. Instead of offering a metaphysics of *truth*, Davidson suggests that we should investigate the relations in which TRUTH stands to other important concepts. Similarly, Asay claims that primitivism as a theory about the concept TRUTH does not carry a commitment to taking *truth* to be a substantial property.

Identity Theories

In chapter 28, Jennifer Hornsby offers an influential defense of an identity theory of truth. With primitivists like Davidson and Asay, Hornsby holds that truth cannot be analyzed in accordance with any of the traditional theories. Nevertheless, she does think that it is possible to offer an illuminating account of the metaphysics of truth. Drawing on some suggestions from John McDowell, she argues that true "thinkables" are identical to facts.

By "thinkables," Hornsby means the contents of our thoughts, as opposed to the thinking of those thoughts. If one takes the contents of our thoughts to be propositions, then Hornsby's identity theory amounts to the view that true propositions are identical with facts. This means that her theory is not an epistemic theory; it is not required, for instance, that true propositions be justifiable or knowable. Moreover, her theory entails that truth does not—as it does according to correspondence theories—involve a relation between a proposition and a truthmaker of some sort. There is no gap between true thinkables and the way the world is; indeed, the mind and the world seem to envelop each other. Even so, Hornsby's identity theory looks to be committed to a metaphysically robust property of truth. To this extent, the theory serves as an additional alternative to deflationism.

Further Reading

Primitivist Theories

Asay, J. 2013. *The Primitivist Theory of Truth*. Cambridge: Cambridge University Press.

Asay, J. 2018. "TRUTH: A Concept Unlike Any Other." *Synthese*. https://doi.org/10.1007/s11229 -017-1661-z.

Baldwin, T. 1997. "Frege, Moore, Davidson: The Indefinability of Truth." *Philosophical Topics* 25: 1–18.

Brons, L. 2015. "Wang Chong, Truth, and Quasi-pluralism." *Comparative Philosophy* 6: 129–148.

Cartwright, R. 1987. "A Neglected Theory of Truth." In *Philosophical Essays*, 71–95. Cambridge, MA: MIT Press.

Davidson, D. 1990. "The Structure and Content of Truth." *Journal of Philosophy* 87: 279–328.

Fisher, A. R. J. 2014. "Examination of Merricks' Primitivism about Truth." *Metaphysica* 15: 281–298.

Frege, G. 1918. "Der Gedanke. Eine Logische Untersuchung." In *Beiträge zur Philosophie des deutschen Idealismus* 1 (1918–1919), 58–77. Translated by P. Geach and R. Stoothoff as "Thoughts: A Logical Enquiry," and reprinted in M. Beaney, ed., *The Frege Reader*, 325–445. Malden, MA: Blackwell, 1997.

Frege, G. 1979. "Logik." Originally unpublished. In H. Hermes, F. Kambartel, and F. Kaulbach, eds., with the assistance of G. Gabriel and W. Rödding, *Posthumous Writings*, trans. P. Long and R. White, with the assistance of R. Hargreaves, 137–163. Chicago: University of Chicago Press.

Greimann, D. 2000. "Explicating Truth: Minimalism and Primitivism." *Journal for General Philosophy of Science* 31: 133–155.

McGinn, C. 2000. *Logical Properties: Identity, Existence, Predication, Necessity, Truth*, chap. 5. Oxford: Oxford University Press.

McLeod, A. 2018. "Appendix: Replies to Brons and Mou on Wang Chong and Pluralism." In Bo Mou, ed., *Philosophy of Language, Chinese Language, Chinese Philosophy: Constructive Engagement*, 322–340. Leiden: Brill.

Merricks, T. 2007. *Truth and Ontology*. Oxford: Oxford University Press.

Moore, G. E. 1953. *Some Main Problems in Philosophy*. London: Allen and Unwin.

Patterson, D. 2010. "Truth as Conceptually Primitive." In C. D. Wright and N. J. L. L. Pedersen, eds., *New Waves in Truth*, 13–29. New York: Palgrave Macmillan.

Russell, B. 1904. "Meinong's Theory of Complexes and Assumptions (III)." *Mind* 13: 509–524.

Salis, P. 2019. "Anaphoric Deflationism, Primitivism, and the Truth Property." *Acta Analytic* 34: 117–134.

Sosa, E. 1993. "Epistemology, Realism, and Truth: The First Philosophical Perspectives Lecture." *Philosophical Perspectives* 7: 1–16.

Wrenn, C. 2004. "Truth and Other Self-Effacing Properties." *Philosophical Quarterly* 54: 577–586.

Identity Theories

Baldwin, T. 1991. "The Identity Theory of Truth." *Mind* 100: 35–52.

Candlish, S. 1995. "Resurrecting the Identity Theory of Truth." *Bradley Studies* 1: 116–124.

Candlish, S. 1999a. "Identifying the Identity Theory of Truth." *Proceedings of the Aristotelian Society* 99: 233–240.

Candlish, S. 1999b. "A Prolegomenon to an Identity Theory of Truth." *Philosophy* 74: 199–220.

Candlish, S., and Damnjanovic, N. 2018. "The Identity Theory of Truth." In M. Glanzberg, ed., *The Oxford Handbook of Truth*, 259–282. Oxford: Oxford University Press.

David, M. 2002. "Truth and Identity." In J. K. Campbell, M. O'Rourke, and D. Shier, eds., *Meaning and Truth: Investigations in Philosophical Semantics*, 124–141. New York: Seven Bridges Press.

Dodd, J. 1995. "McDowell and Identity Theories of Truth." *Analysis* 55: 160–165.

Dodd, J. 1999. "Hornsby on the Identity Theory of Truth." *Proceedings of the Aristotelian Society* 99(2): 225–232.

Dodd, J. 2008. *An Identity Theory of Truth*. New York: Palgrave Macmillan.

Engel, P. 2001. "The False Modesty of the Identity Theory of Truth." *International Journal of Philosophical Studies* 9(4): 441–458.

Gaskin, R. 2015. "The Identity Theory of Truth." *Stanford Encyclopedia of Philosophy*. https://plato .stanford.edu/entries/truth-identity/.

Hornsby, J. 1999. "The Facts in Question: A Response to Dodd and Candlish." *Proceedings of the Aristotelian Society* 99: 241–245.

Johnston, C. 2013. "Judgment and the Identity Theory of Truth." *Philosophical Studies* 166: 381–397.

McDowell, J. 1994. *Mind and World*. Cambridge, MA: Harvard University Press.

Moore, G. E. 1899. "The Nature of Judgement." *Mind* 8: 176–193.

Sher, G. 2013. "Introduction to and Commentary on Jennifer Hornsby's 'Truth: the Identity Theory.'" Virtual issue, *Proceedings of the Aristotelian Society* 1: 204–213.

Sullivan, P. 2005. "Identity Theories of Truth and the *Tractatus*." *Philosophical Investigations* 28: 43–62.

26   The Folly of Trying to Define Truth

Donald Davidson

In the *Euthyphro*, Socrates asks what holiness is, what "makes" holy things holy. It is clear that he seeks a definition, a definition with special properties. He spurns the mere provision of examples or lists, asking in each case what makes the examples examples, or puts an item on the list. He rejects merely coextensive concepts ("something is holy if and only if it is dear to the gods"): what makes something dear to the gods is that it is holy, but not vice versa. The dialogue ends when Socrates begs Euthyphro to enlighten him by coming up with a satisfactory answer; Euthyphro decides he has another appointment.

The pattern of attempted definition, counterexample, amended definition, further counterexample, ending with a whimper of failure, is repeated with variations throughout the Socratic and middle Platonic dialogues. Beauty, courage, virtue, friendship, love, temperance are put under the microscope, but no convincing definitions emerge. The only definitions Plato seems happy with are tendentious characterizations of what it is to be a sophist. He also gives a few trivial samples of correct definitions: of a triangle; of mud (earth and water).

In the *Theaetetus*, Plato attempts to define empirical knowledge. Like many philosophers since, he takes knowledge to be true belief plus something more—an account that justifies or warrants the belief. It is the last feature which stumps him (again foreshadowing the subsequent history of the subject). It seems no more to occur to Plato than it has to most others that the combination of causal and rational elements that must enter into an analysis of justified belief (as it must into accounts of memory, perception, and intentional action) may in the nature of the case not be amenable to sharp formulation in a clearer, more basic, vocabulary.

What is important in the present context, however, is the fact that in attempting to define knowledge, it is only with the concept of warrant that Plato concedes defeat. He does not worry much about the equal involvement of knowledge with truth and belief.

Again, though, Plato was simply blazing a trail that other philosophers over the ages have followed: you follow his lead if you worry about the concept of truth when it is the focus of your attention, but you pretend you understand it when trying to cope with knowledge (or belief, memory, perception, and the like). We come across the same puzzling strategy in David Hume and others, who forget their skepticism about the external world when they formulate their doubts concerning knowledge of other minds. When a philosopher is troubled by the idea of an intentional action, he would be happy if he could analyze it correctly in terms of the concepts of belief, desire, and causality, and he does not for the moment worry too much about those (at least equally difficult) concepts. If memory is up for analysis, the connections with belief, truth, causality, and perhaps perception, constitute the problem, but these further concepts are pro tem taken to be clear enough to be used to clarify memory, if only the connections could be got right. It is all right to assume you have an adequate handle on intention and convention if your target is meaning. I could easily go on.

There is a lesson to be learned from these familiar, though odd, shifts in the focus of philosophical puzzlement. The lesson I take to heart is this: however feeble or faulty our attempts to relate these various basic concepts to each other, these attempts fare better, and teach us more, than our efforts to produce correct and revealing definitions of basic concepts in terms of clearer or even more fundamental concepts.

This is, after all, what we should expect. For the most part, the concepts philosophers single out for attention, like truth, knowledge, belief, action, cause, the good and the right, are the most elementary concepts we have, concepts without which (I am inclined to say) we would have no concepts at all. Why then should we expect to be able to reduce these concepts definitionally to other concepts that are simpler, clearer, and more basic? We should accept the fact that what makes these concepts so important must also foreclose on the possibility of finding a foundation for them which reaches deeper into bedrock.

We should apply this obvious observation to the concept of truth: we cannot hope to underpin it with something more transparent or easier to grasp. Truth is, as G. E. Moore, Bertrand Russell, and Gottlob Frege maintained, and Alfred Tarski proved, an indefinable concept. This does not mean we can say nothing revealing about it: we can, by relating it to other concepts like belief, desire, cause, and action. Nor does the indefinability of truth imply that the concept is mysterious, ambiguous, or untrustworthy.

Even if we are persuaded that the concept of truth cannot be defined, the intuition or hope remains that we can characterize truth using some fairly simple formula. What distinguishes much of the contemporary philosophical discussion of truth is that though there are many such formulas on the market, none of them seems to keep clear of fairly obvious counterexamples. One result has been the increasing popularity of minimalist or deflationary theories of truth—theories that hold that truth is a relatively trivial concept with no "important connections with other concepts such as meaning and reality."[1]

I sympathize with the deflationists; the attempts to pump more content into the concept of truth are not, for the most part, appealing. But I think the deflationists are wrong in their conclusion, even if mostly right in what they reject. I shall not pause here to give my reasons for refusing to accept correspondence theories, coherence theories, pragmatic theories, theories that limit truth to what could be ascertained under ideal conditions or justifiably asserted, and so on.[2] But since I am with the deflationists in being dissatisfied with all such characterizations of truth, I shall say why deflationism seems to me equally unacceptable.

Aristotle, as we all know, contended that

(1) To say of what is that it is not, or of what is not that it is, is false, while to say of what is that it is, or of what is not that it is not, is true.

When Tarski[3] mentions this formulation in 1944, he complains that it is "not sufficiently precise and clear," though he prefers it to two others:

(2) The truth of a sentence consists in its agreement with (or correspondence to) reality.

(3) A sentence is true if it designates an existing state of affairs (ibid., p. 343).

In 1969, Tarski[4] again quotes (1), and adds,

> The formulation leaves much to be desired from the point of view of precision and formal correctness. For one thing, it is not general enough; it refers only to sentences that "say" about something "that it is" or "that it is not"; in most cases it would hardly be possible to cast a sentence in this mold without slanting the sense of the sentence and forcing the spirit of the language. (ibid., p. 63)

He adds that this may be the reason for such "modern substitutes" for Aristotle's formulations as (2) and (3).

In the *Wahrheitsbegriff*, however, Tarski[5] prefers the following informal statement:

(4) A true sentence is one which says that the state of affairs is so and so, and the state of affairs indeed is so and so (ibid., p. 155).

It seems to me that Aristotle's formulation is clearly superior to (2), (3), and (4); it is more in accord with Tarski's own work on truth; and Tarski's comment that (1) is "not general enough" is strangely out of keeping with the spirit of his own truth definitions.

(1) is superior to (2)–(4) for three reasons. First, (3) and (4) mention states of affairs, thus suggesting that postulating entities to correspond to sentences might be a useful way of characterizing truth. ("A true sentence is one that corresponds to the facts," or "If a sentence is true, there is a state of affairs to which it corresponds.") But facts or states of affairs have never been shown to play a useful role in semantics, and one of the strongest arguments for Tarski's definitions is that in them nothing plays the role of facts or states of affairs. This is not surprising, since there is a persuasive argument, usually traced to Frege (in one form) or Kurt Gödel (in another), to the effect that there can be at most one fact or state of affairs. (This is why Frege said all true sentences name the True.) Tarski's truth definitions make no use of the idea that a sentence "corresponds" to anything at

all. We should not take seriously the mention of "states of affairs" in such remarks of Tarski's[6] as this: "[S]emantical concepts express certain relations between objects (and states of affairs) referred to in the language discussed and expressions of the language referring to those objects" (ibid., p. 403).

A second reason for preferring Aristotle's characterization of truth is that it avoids the awkward blanks marked by the words "so and so" in Tarski's version (4); one is hard pressed to see how the blanks are to be filled in. Aristotle's formula, on the other hand, sounds much like a generalization of Tarski's convention-T.

The third reason for preferring Aristotle's characterization is that it makes clear what the other formulations do not, that the truth of a sentence depends on the inner structure of the sentence, that is, on the semantic features of the parts. In this it is once again closer to Tarski's approach to the concept of truth.

Tarski's convention-T, which he understandably substitutes for the rough formulas I have been discussing, stipulates that a satisfactory definition of a truth predicate "is true" for a language L must be such as to entail as theorems all sentences of the form

s is true-in-L if and only if p

where "s" is replaced by the description of a sentence, and "p" is replaced by that sentence, or a translation of the sentence into the metalanguage. Since it is assumed that there is an infinity of sentences in L, it is obvious that, if the definition of the truth predicate is to be finite (Tarski insisted on this), the definition must take advantage of the fact that sentences, though potentially infinite in number, are constructed from a finite vocabulary. For the languages Tarski considered, and for which he showed how to define truth, all sentences can be put into the form of an existential quantification, or the negation of an existential quantification, or a truth-functional compound of such sentences. So how "incomplete," from Tarski's point of view, is Aristotle's formulation (1)? It deals with four cases. There are the sentences that "say of what is that it is not": in modern terms it is a false sentence that begins, "It is not the case that there exists an x such that … ." An example might be: "There does not exist an x such that $x=4$." Then there are sentences that "say of what is not that it is"; for example, "There exists an x such that $x=4$ & $x=5$." There are sentences that "say of what is that it is"; for example "There exists an x such that $x=4$." And, finally, there are sentences that "say of what is not that it is not"; for example, "It is not the case that there exists an x such that $x \neq x$." According to the classical formulation, sentences of the first two kinds are false and of the second two kinds are true. Tarski is so far in agreement. What would Tarski add? Just the truth-functional compounds (beyond those involving negation) of the types of sentences already mentioned; these are true or false on the basis of the truth or falsity of the kinds of sentences already provided for. Of course, Tarski also showed in detail how the truth or falsity of the first four types of sentences depended in turn on their structure.

Thus, the classical formulation regarded as an informal characterization is "incomplete" in only a minimal way compared to Tarski's own work, and is better than Tarski's informal attempts to state the intuitive idea. Needless to say, someone might question the extent to which natural languages can be adequately characterized using such limited resources; but this is a comment equally applicable to Tarski.

Despite his nod in the direction of a correspondence theory, in which sentences are said to correspond to facts, Tarski ought not to be considered as giving comfort to serious partisans of correspondence theories, nor should Aristotle. For neither Aristotle's formula nor Tarski's truth definitions introduce entities like facts or states of affairs for sentences to correspond to. Tarski does define truth on the basis of the concept of satisfaction, which relates expressions to objects, but the sequences that satisfy sentences are nothing like the "facts" or "states of affairs" of correspondence theorists, since if one of Tarski's sequences satisfies a closed sentence, thus making it true, then that same sequence also satisfies every other true sentence, and thus also makes it true, and if any sequence satisfies a closed sentence, every sequence does.[7]

If Tarski is not a correspondence theorist (and he certainly does not hold a coherence theory or a pragmatic theory or a theory that bases truth on warranted assertability), is he a deflationist? Here opinions differ widely: W. V. Quine thinks he is, and so does Scott Soames. John Etchemendy thinks Tarski simply says nothing about truth as a semantic concept, and Hilary Putnam, though for somewhat different reasons, agrees.[8]

If Tarski has said "all there is to say" about truth, as Stephen Leeds, Paul Horwich, and Soames all contend, and Quine has strongly hinted, then a sort of deflationary attitude is justified; this is not quite the same as the "redundancy" view, but close to it. The redundancy view, taken literally, is the same as the disquotational view taken literally: we can always substitute without loss a sentence for that same sentence quoted, and followed by the words "is true." What Tarski added, as Michael Williams and others have pointed out, is a way of predicating truth of whole classes of sentences, or of sentences to which we do not know how to refer; you may think of this as an elaboration of the redundancy theory in that it allows the elimination of the truth predicate when applied to sentences of a language for which that predicate has been defined.

At the same time that we credit Tarski with having shown how to make sense of remarks like "The English sentence Joan uttered about Abbot was true" or "Everything Aristotle said (in Greek) was false" or "The usual truth table for the conditional makes any conditional true that has a false antecedent," we have to recognize that this accomplishment was accompanied by a proof that truth cannot (given various plausible assumptions) be defined in general; there can be no definition of "For all languages L, and all sentences s in L, s is true in L if and only if … s … L … ." In other words, Tarski justified the application of a truth predicate to the sentences of a particular language only by restricting its application to the sentences of that language. (It is ironic that in much recent writing on deflationary theories, Tarski has been taken to have lent support to the idea that there is a single, simple, even trivial, concept of truth.)

A deflationary attitude to the concept of truth is not, then, encouraged by reflection on Tarski's work. One can adopt the line advanced by Putnam and Etchemendy that Tarski was not even doing semantics, despite his insistence that he was; but this construal of Tarski does not support a deflationary theory: it simply denies the relevance of Tarski's results to the ordinary concept of truth. If, on the other hand, one takes Tarski's truth definitions to say something about the relations of specific languages to the world, one cannot at the same time claim that he has told us all there is to know about the concept of truth, since he has not told us what the concept is that his truth definitions for particular languages have in common.

I think that Tarski was not trying to define *the* concept of truth—so much is obvious—but that he was *employing* that concept to characterize the semantic structures of specific languages. But Tarski did not indicate how we can in general reduce the concept of truth to other more basic concepts, nor how to eliminate the English predicate "is true" from all contexts in which it is intelligibly applied to sentences. Convention-T is not a rough substitute for a general definition: it is part of a successful attempt to persuade us that his formal definitions apply our single pretheoretical concept of truth to certain languages. Deflationists cannot, then, appeal to Tarski simply because he demonstrated how to handle the semantics of quantification for individual languages. Leeds, Horwich, Williams, and others who have contended that all Tarski did was reveal the usefulness of an otherwise dispensable concept are wrong. They are right that we need a truth predicate for the purposes they, along with Tarski, mention; but they fail to note the obvious fact that at the same time Tarski solved one problem he emphasized another: that he had not, and could not, given the constraints he accepted, define or fully characterize truth.

Over the years, Quine has said a number of things about truth, but there has been, from early days until the most recent, what seems a consistent embrace of a deflationary attitude. Thus, Quine has made much of the "disquotational" aspect of the truth predicate, the fact that we can get rid of the predicate "is true" after the quotation of an English sentence simply by removing the quotation marks as we erase the truth predicate. As Quine put it in *From a Logical Point of View*,[9] we have a general paradigm, namely,

(T) "___" is true-in-*L* if and only if ___

which, though not a definition of truth, serves to endow "true-in-*L*" with "every bit as much clarity, in any particular application, as is enjoyed by the particular expressions of *L* to which we apply [it]. Attribution of truth in particular to 'Snow is white' ... is every bit as clear to us as attribution of whiteness to snow" (ibid., p. 138). In *Word and Object*, Quine[10] remarks that "To say that the statement 'Brutus killed Caesar' is true, or that 'The atomic weight of sodium is 23' is true, is in effect simply to say that Brutus killed Caesar, or that the atomic weight of sodium is 23" (ibid., p. 24). The theme is repeated thirty years later in *Pursuit of Truth*:[11] "there is surely no impugning the disquotation account; no disputing that "Snow is white" is true if and only if snow is white. Moreover, it is a full account; it explicates clearly the truth or falsity of every clear sentence" (ibid., p. 93). "Truth," he summarizes, "is disquotation" (ibid., p. 80). On this matter, Quine has not changed his mind.

It is the disquotational feature of truth, in Quine's opinion, which makes truth so much clearer a concept than meaning. Comparing theory of meaning and theory of reference, Quine says that they constitute "two provinces so fundamentally distinct as not to deserve a joint appellation at all."[12] The former deals with such tainted topics as synonymy, meaning, and analyticity. The concepts treated by the latter, which include truth, are by contrast "very much less foggy and mysterious." For although "true-in-*L*" for variable "*L*" is not definable, "what we do have suffices to endow 'true-in-*L*,' even for variable '*L*,' with a high enough degree of intelligibility so that we are not likely to be averse to using the idiom" (ibid., pp. 137–138). "What we do have is, of course, the paradigm (T) and the expedient general routine" due to Tarski for defining "true-in-*L*" for particular languages.

The disquotational feature of truth, wedded to the thought that this may exhaust the content of the concept of truth, encourages the idea that truth and meaning can be kept quite separate. But can they in general? Scattered remarks in Quine's work suggest otherwise. In 1936, Quine published the brilliant and prescient "Truth by Convention."[13] In it he remarks that "in point of meaning … a word may be said to be determined to whatever extent the truth or falsehood of its contexts is determined" (ibid., p. 89). It is hard to see how truth could have this power of determining meaning if the disquotational account were all there were to say about truth. Other passages in Quine suggest the same idea: "First and last, in learning language, we are learning how to distribute truth values. I am with Davidson here; we are learning truth conditions."[14] Or again, "Tarski's theory of truth [is] the very structure of a theory of meaning."[15]

Up to a point it may seem easy to keep questions of truth and questions of meaning segregated. Truth we may think of as disquotational (in the extended Tarski sense) and therefore trivial; meaning is then another matter, to be taken care of in terms of warranted assertability, function, or the criteria for translation. This is the line followed, for example, by Horwich in his recent book *Truth* (op. cit.), by Soames,[16] and by Lewis.[17] It may, at least at one time, have been Quine's view. In *Word and Object*, in a passage that immediately precedes the remark that to say that the sentence "Brutus killed Caesar" is true is in effect simply to say that Brutus killed Caesar, Quine despairs of a substantive concept of truth, and concludes that we make sense of a truth predicate only when we apply it to a sentence "in the terms of a given theory, and seen from within the theory" (op. cit., p. 24). This is, I think, what Quine means when he says that truth is "immanent." The point is not merely that the truth of a sentence is relative to a language; it is that there is no transcendent, single concept to be relativized.[18]

Most recently, however, Quine muses that truth "is felt to harbor something of the sublime. Its pursuit is a noble pursuit, and unending"; he seems to agree: "Science is seen as pursuing and discovering truth rather than as decreeing it. Such is the idiom of realism, and it is integral to the semantics of the predicate 'true.'"[19]

I turn now to Horwich's version of deflationism, for he seems to me to have accepted the challenge other deflationists have evaded, that of saying something more about an unrelativized concept of truth than we can learn from Tarski's definitions. Horwich's brave and striking move is to make the primary bearers of truth propositions—not exactly a new idea in itself, but new in the context of a serious attempt to defend deflationism. He is clear that he cannot provide an explicit definition of a truth predicate applying to propositions, but he urges that we really have said all there is to know about such a predicate (and hence the predicate it expresses) when we grasp the fact that the "uncontroversial instances" of the schema:

The proposition that p is true if and only if p

exhaust its content. (The limitation to "uncontroversial instances" is to exclude whatever leads to paradox.) The schema is taken as an axiom schema: the totality of its instances constitute the axioms of his theory.

This theory is, of course, incomplete until the controversial instances are specified in a non-question-begging way; and since the set of axioms is infinite, it does not meet one of Tarski's requirements for a satisfactory theory of truth. But perhaps the first difficulty can be overcome, and the second may be viewed as the price of having an unrelativized concept of truth. There are, further, the doubts many of us have about the existence of propositions, or at least of the principles for individuating them.

All these considerations give me pause, but I plan to ignore them here. I want to give deflationism its best chance, since it seems to me to be the only alternative to a more substantive view of truth, and most substantive views are in my opinion, as in Horwich's, clear failures. But although I enthusiastically endorse his arguments against correspondence, coherence, pragmatic, and epistemic theories, I cannot bring myself to accept Horwich's "minimal" theory.

I have two fundamental problems with Horwich's theory, either of which alone is reason to reject it if it cannot be resolved; and I do not myself see how to resolve them.

The first problem is easy to state: I do not understand the basic axiom schema or its instances. It will help me formulate my difficulty to compare Horwich's axiom schema with Tarski's informal (and ultimately supplanted) schema:

"___" is true if and only if ___

Tarski's objection (among others) is that you cannot turn this into a definition except by quantifying into a position inside quotation marks. The complaint ends up with a question about the clarity of quotations: How does what they refer to depend on the semantic properties of their constituents? It has sometimes been proposed to appeal to substitutional quantification, and one may wonder why Horwich cannot generalize his schema:

(*p*) (the proposition that *p* is true if and only if *p*)

by employing substitutional quantification. But here Horwich quite rightly explains that he cannot appeal to substitutional quantification to explain truth, since substitutional quantification must be explained by appeal to truth.

Why, though, does Horwich not try generalizing his schema by quantifying over propositions? The answer should be: because then we would have to view ordinary sentences as singular terms *referring* to propositions, not as *expressing* propositions. This brings me to the crux: How are we to understand phrases like "the proposition that Socrates is wise"? In giving a standard account of the semantics of the sentence "Socrates is wise," we make use of what the name "Socrates" names, and of the entities of which the predicate "is wise" is true. But how can we use these semantic features of the sentence "Socrates is wise" to yield the reference of "the proposition that Socrates is wise"? Horwich does not give us any guidance here. Could we say that expressions like "the proposition that Socrates is wise" are semantically unstructured, or at least that after the words "the proposition that" (taken as a functional expression) a sentence becomes a semantically unstructured name of the proposition it expresses? Taking this course would leave us with an infinite primitive vocabulary, and the appearance of the words "Socrates is wise" in two places in the schema would be of no help in understanding the schema or its instances. A further proposal might be to modify our instance of the schema to read:

The proposition expressed by the sentence "Socrates is wise" is true if and only if Socrates is wise.

But following this idea would require relativizing the quoted sentence to a language, a need that Horwich must circumvent.

So let me put my objection briefly as follows: the same sentence appears twice in instances of Horwich's schema, once after the words "the proposition that," in a context that requires the result to be a singular term, the subject of a predicate, and once as an ordinary sentence. We cannot eliminate this iteration of the same sentence without destroying all appearance of a theory. But we cannot *understand* the result of the iteration unless we can see how to make use of the same semantic features of the repeated sentence in both of its appearances–make use of them in giving the semantics of the schema instances. I do not see how this can be done.

My second difficulty with Horwich's theory is more dependent on my own further convictions and commitments. Horwich recognizes that to maintain that truth has, as he says, "a certain purity," he must show that we can understand it fully in isolation from other ideas, and we can understand other ideas in isolation from it. He does not say there are no relations between the concept of truth and other concepts; only that we can understand these concepts independently. There are several crucial cases so far as I am concerned, since I do not think we can understand meaning or any of the propositional attitudes without the concept of truth. Let me pick one of these: meaning.

Since Horwich thinks of truth as primarily attributable to propositions, he must explain how we can also predicate it of sentences and utterances, and he sees that to explain this without compromising the independence of truth, we must understand meaning without direct appeal to the concept of truth. On this critical matter, Horwich is brief, even laconic. Understanding a sentence, he says, does not *consist* in knowing its truth conditions, though if we understand a sentence we usually *know* its truth conditions. Understanding a sentence, he maintains, consists in knowing its "assertability conditions" (or "proper use"). He grants that these conditions may include that the sentence (or utterance) be true. I confess I do not see how, if truth is an assertability condition, and knowing the assertability conditions *is* understanding, we can understand a sentence without having the concept of truth.

I realize, however, that this is disputed territory, and that heavy thinkers like Michael Dummett, Putnam, and Soames, following various leads suggested by Ludwig Wittgenstein and H. P. Grice, believe that an account of meaning can be made to depend on a notion of assertability or use which does not in turn appeal to the concept of truth.

My hopes lie in the opposite direction: I think the sort of assertion that is linked to understanding already incorporates the concept of truth: we are *justifed* in asserting a sentence in the required sense only if we believe the sentence we use to make the assertion is true; and what ultimately ties language to the world is that the conditions that typically cause us to hold sentences true *constitute* the truth conditions, and hence the meanings, of our sentences. This is not the place to argue this. For now I must simply remark that it would be a shame if we had to develop a theory of meaning for a speaker or a language independently of a theory of truth for that speaker or language, since we have at least *some* idea how to formulate a theory of truth, but no serious idea how to formulate a theory of meaning based on a concept of assertability or use.

I conclude that the prospects for a deflationary theory of truth are dim. Its attractions seem to me entirely negative: it avoids, or at least tries to avoid, well-marked dead ends and recognizable pitfalls.

Let me suggest a diagnosis of our aporia about truth. We are still under the spell of the Socratic idea that we must keep asking for the *essence* of an idea, a significant *analysis* in other terms, an answer to the question what *makes* this an act of piety, what *makes* this, or any, utterance, sentence, belief, or proposition true. We still fall for the freshman fallacy that demands that we *define* our terms as a prelude to saying anything further with or about them.

It may seem pointless to make so much of the drive to define truth when it is unclear who is trying to do it: not Tarski, who proves it cannot be done; not Horwich, who disclaims the attempt. Who, then, *admits* to wanting to define the concept of truth? Well, that is right. But. But the same ugly urge to define shows up in the guise of trying to provide a brief criterion, schema, partial but leading hint, in place of a strict definition. Since Tarski, we are leery of the word "definition" when we are thinking of a concept of truth not relativized to a language, but we have not given up the definitional urge. Thus, I see Horwich's schema on a par *in this regard* with Dummett's notion of justified assertability, Putnam's ideally justified assertability, and the various formulations of correspondence and coherence theories. I see all of them as, if not attempts at definitions in the strict sense, attempts at *substitutes* for definitions. In the case of truth, there is no short substitute.

Now I want to describe what I take to be a fairly radical alternative to the theories I have been discussing and (with unseemly haste) dismissing. What I stress here is the *methodology* I think is required rather than the more detailed account I have given elsewhere. The methodology can be characterized on the negative side by saying it offers no definition of the concept of truth, nor any quasi-definitional clause, axiom schema, or other brief substitute for a definition. The positive proposal is to attempt to trace the connections between the concept of truth and the human attitudes and acts that give it body.

My methodological inspiration comes from finitely axiomatized theories of measurement, or of various sciences, theories that put clear constraints on one or more undefined concepts, and then prove that any model of such a theory has intuitively desired properties—that it is adequate to its designed purpose. Since among the models will be all sorts of configurations of abstract entities, and endless unwanted patterns of empirical events and objects, the theory can be applied to, or tested against, such specific phenomena as mass or temperature only by indicating how the theory is to be applied to the appropriate objects or events. We cannot demand a precise indication of how to do this; finding a useful method for applying the theory is an enterprise that goes along with tampering with the formal theory, and testing its correctness as interpreted.

We are interested in the concept of truth only because there are actual objects and states of the world to which to apply it: utterances, states of belief, inscriptions. If we did not understand what it was for such entities to be true, we would not be able to characterize the contents of these states, objects, and events. So in addition to the formal theory of truth, we must indicate how truth is to be predicated of these empirical phenomena.

Tarski's definitions make no mention of empirical matters, but we are free to ask of such a definition whether it fits the actual practice of some speaker or group of speakers–we may ask whether they speak the language for which truth has been defined. There is nothing about Tarski's definitions that prevents us from treating them in this way except the prejudice that, if something is called a definition, the question of its "correctness" is moot. To put this prejudice to rest, I suggest that we omit the final step in Tarski's definitions, the step that turns his axiomatizations into explicit definitions. We can then in good conscience call the emasculated definition a theory, and accept the truth predicate as undefined. This undefined predicate expresses the *general*, intuitive, concept, applicable to any language, the concept against which we have always surreptitiously tested Tarski's definitions (as he invited us to do, of course).

We know a great deal about how this concept applies to the speech and beliefs and actions of human agents. We use it to interpret their utterances and beliefs by assigning truth conditions to them, and we judge those actions and attitudes by evaluating the likelihood of their truth. The empirical question is how to determine, by observation and induction, what the truth conditions of empirical truth vehicles are. It bears emphasizing: absent this empirical connection, the concept of truth has no application to, or interest for, our mundane concerns, nor, so far as I can see, does it have any content at all.

Consider this analogy: I think of truth as Frank Ramsey thought of probability. He convinced himself, not irrationally, that the concept of probability applies in the first instance to propositional attitudes; it is a measure of degree of belief. He went on to ask himself: How can we make sense of the concept of degree of belief (subjective probability)? Subjective probability is not observable, either by the agent who entertains some proposition with less than total conviction and more than total disbelief, or by others who see and question him. So Ramsey axiomatized the pattern of preferences of an idealized agent who, more or less like the rest of us, adjusts his preferences for the truth of propositions (or states of affairs or events) to accord with his values and beliefs. He stated the conditions on which a pattern of such preferences would be "rational," and in effect proved that, if these conditions were satisfied, one could reconstruct from the agent's preferences the relative strengths of that agent's desires and subjective probabilities. Ramsey did not suppose everyone is perfectly rational in the postulated sense, but he did assume that people are nearly enough so, in the long run, for his theory to give a content to the concept of subjective probability—or probability, as he thought of it.

A brilliant *strategy*! (Whether or not it gives a correct analysis of probability.) The concept of probability—or at least degree of belief—unobservable by the agent who has it and by his watchers, linked to an equally theoretical concept of cardinal utility, or subjective evaluation, and both tied to simple preference by the axiomatic structure. Simple preference in turn provides the crucial empirical basis through its manifestations in actual choice behavior.

We should think of a theory of truth for a speaker in the same way we think of a theory of rational decision: both describe structures we can find, with an allowable degree of fitting and fudging, in the behavior of more or less rational creatures gifted with speech. It is in the fitting and fudging that we give content to the undefined concepts of subjective probability and subjective values—belief and desire, as we briefly call them; and, by way of theories like Tarski's, to the undefined concept of truth.

A final remark. I have deliberately made the problem of giving empirical content to the concept of truth seem simpler than it is. It would be *relatively* simple if we could directly observe—take as basic evidence—what people *mean* by what they say. But meaning not only is a more obscure concept than that of truth; it clearly involves it: if you know what an utterance means, you know its truth conditions. The problem is to give *any* propositional attitude a propositional content: belief, desire, intention, meaning.

I therefore see the problem of connecting truth with observable human behavior as inseparable from the problem of assigning contents to all the attitudes, and this seems to me to require a theory that embeds a theory of truth in a larger theory that includes decision theory itself. The result will incorporate the major norms of rationality whose partial realization in the thought and behavior of agents makes those agents intelligible, more or less, to others. If this normative structure is formidably complex, we should take comfort in the fact that the more complex it is, the better our chance of interpreting its manifestations as thought and meaningful speech and intentional action, given only scattered bits of weakly interpreted evidence.

Notes

1. These words are quoted from Michael Dummett's jacket blurb for Paul Horwich's *Truth* (Cambridge, MA: MIT Press, 1991). This is not, of course, Dummett's view.

2. I spell out my reasons for rejecting such views in "The Structure and Content of Truth," *Journal of Philosophy* 87, no. 6 (June 1990): 279–328.

3. A. Tarski, "The Semantic Conception of Truth," *Philosophy and Phenomenological Research* 4 (1944): 342–360. [Reprinted as chapter 14 in this volume.—Eds.]

4. A. Tarski, "Truth and Proof," *Scientific American* 220 (1969): 63–77.

5. A. Tarski, "The Concept of Truth in Formalized Languages," in *Logic, Semantics, Metamathematics: Papers from 1923 to 1938*, trans. J. H. Woodger (Oxford: Clarendon Press, 1956), 152–278 (originally published in German in 1936).

6. Tarski, "The Establishment of Scientific Semantics," in *Logic, Semantics, Metamathematics*, 401–408.

7. At one time I suggested calling Tarski's concept of truth a correspondence theory on the strength of the role of sequences in satisfying closed sentences, but I subsequently withdrew the suggestion as misleading. For the suggestion, see my "True to the Facts," in *Inquiries into Truth and Interpretation* (New York: Oxford University Press, 1984). For the retraction, see "Afterthoughts, 1987," in A. Malichowski, ed., *Reading Rorty* (Cambridge: Blackwell, 1990), 120–138.

8. For references, and further discussion, see my "The Structure and Content of Truth."

9. W. V. Quine, *From a Logical Point of View* (Cambridge, MA: Harvard University Press, 1961).

10. W. V. Quine, *Word and Object* (Cambridge, MA: MIT Press, 1960).

11. W. V. Quine, *Pursuit of Truth* (Cambridge, MA: Harvard University Press, 1990).

12. Quine, *From a Logical Point of View*, 130.

13. Reprinted in W. V. Quine, *The Ways of Paradox, and Other Essays* (Cambridge, MA: Harvard University Press, 1976).

14. W. V. Quine, *The Roots of Reference* (La Salle, IL: Open Court, 1974), 65.

15. W. V. Quine, "On the Very Idea of a Third Dogma," in *Theories and Things* (Cambridge, MA: Harvard University Press, 1981), 38.

16. S. Soames, "What Is a Theory of Truth?," *Journal of Philosophy* 81, no. 8 (August 1984): 411–429.

17. D. Lewis, "Languages and Language," in K. Gunderson, ed., *Minnesota Studies in the Philosophy of Science*, vol. 7 (Minneapolis: University of Minnesota Press, 1975), 3–35.

18. The preceding paragraphs on Quine are partly quoted and partly adapted from a longer and more detailed study of Quine on truth: "Pursuit of the Concept of Truth," in P. Leondardi and M. Santambrogio, eds., *On Quine: New Essays* (New York: Cambridge University Press, 1995). The relevant pages are 7–10.

19. W. V. Quine, *From Stimulus to Science* (Cambridge, MA: Harvard University Press, 1995), 67.

27 Primitivism about Truth

Jamin Asay

1 Introduction

Some theories of truth aim to analyze it in terms of further notions such as correspondence, coherence, or warrant. Some theories of truth aim to deflate its philosophical significance. The form of primitivism that I defend rejects both approaches. It takes truth to be a primitive, fundamental concept. In other words, the concept of truth cannot be defined, reduced, or analyzed into concepts that are themselves more basic or fundamental than truth. But that is not to say that truth is philosophically insignificant. Primitivism takes truth to be of paramount philosophical and explanatory significance precisely because it is unanalyzable.

Primitivism, in some form or other, is analytic philosophy's first theory of truth. "What true is," writes Frege, "I hold to be indefinable" (1979, 174). G. E. Moore said the same thing about truth that he more famously said about the good: "Truth is itself a simple concept" (1899, 182). For a time, Bertrand Russell embraced a primitivist perspective, which he understood as the belief that "truth and falsehood … are ultimate, and no account can be given of what makes a proposition true or false" (1906–1907, 49). Given the century's worth of debate, insight, and argument about the nature of truth that followed these early statements of primitivism, we are now in a position to give a more precise characterization and defense of the primitivist theory of truth. My goal in this chapter is to offer what I take to be the most perspicuous statement and defense of primitivism.[1]

I begin by identifying the form of primitivism that I find the most defensible, which I accomplish by way of continual reference to the distinctions between concepts and properties, and between substantive and deflationary views about truth. Then I present some of the arguments that favor primitivism. I conclude by answering some familiar objections that have been lodged against the view.

2 What Is Primitivism?

The primitivism I defend is that the concept of truth is fundamental: it is an explanatorily indispensable concept that cannot be defined, analyzed, or otherwise explicated in terms of concepts that are still more fundamental. This analysis relies on three notions or distinctions: (1) concepts (as opposed to properties), (2) fundamentality relations between concepts, and (3) a distinction between explanatorily indispensable and dispensable concepts. I examine these three in turn.

The first key to understanding primitivism is the distinction between the *concept* and *property* of truth (hereafter, respectively, TRUTH and *truth*). Whatever else they are, concepts are the tools our minds use to think and communicate. The range of thoughts we can think and express is a function of the concepts we possess. Understanding the nature of these concepts and how they relate to one another is one traditional project of philosophy. One way of better understanding one's mind is by better understanding the concepts under its employ. Properties, whatever else they are, are the (typically shared) features that belong to objects. Properties are the ways that objects are. My belief that puffins possess colorful beaks has the property of being true; the sentence "Pangolins founded the Smithsonian" does not.

When I say that truth is primitive, I am referring to TRUTH, not *truth*. On my view, to say that the property *truth* is primitive is to say that it is a metaphysically basic property, something akin to how we might think about *electric charge* in physics. If truth-bearers (whether they be sentences, beliefs, propositions, or all of the above) are true in virtue of possessing a fundamental property *truth*, then there is no further question as to why a truth-bearer is true or what makes it true. "Some penguins live in Australia," on this view, is true because it possesses a particular fundamental property, not because of the existence of the flightless birds that live on Kangaroo Island or because the sentence expresses a proposition that corresponds to some fact or obtaining state of affairs. One way to think about this view is that it makes the matter of which truth-bearers are true brute: there is no explanation to be given of why some sentences are true and others false, save for their possession of these two fundamental properties of the universe, *truth* and *falsity*. I know of no philosopher who both carefully distinguishes between concepts and properties and endorses the primitiveness of *truth*.[2] Doing so renders the matter of which truth-bearers are true a massive metaphysical mystery.

The issue of whether *truth* is a fundamental property is a separate matter from the issue of whether TRUTH is a fundamental concept. To say that TRUTH is fundamental is to say that it cannot be defined, analyzed, or reduced in terms of further concepts that are still more fundamental. My characterization of primitivism is therefore committed to some notion of fundamentality that obtains between concepts. The basic idea I have in mind here is that concepts stand in a hierarchical structure, with some concepts—the primitive ones—located at the ground level. To possess concepts at the higher, more derivative, levels, one must already possess the concepts connected to them at the lower levels of the structure. Concepts are more fundamental the lower on the hierarchy they stand. For example, the concept BACHELOR is derivative, as it's defined in terms of the further concepts MALE and UNMARRIED (which are themselves, presumably, dependent on still more fundamental concepts). One can possess the latter two concepts without possessing the first, but not vice versa. To say that TRUTH is primitive, then, is to say that there is no concept that is more fundamental than it. Possession of TRUTH does not require possession of any other concept (such as CORRESPONDENCE or COHERENCE, say), though possessing TRUTH may well be necessary for possessing all sorts of other concepts (such as BELIEF, KNOWLEDGE, MEANING, etc.) if those concepts are defined in terms of TRUTH. There may be other concepts that are maximally fundamental, alongside TRUTH. Whether these concepts are themselves interconnected (as in Strawson 1992) or better thought of as independent conceptual "atoms" is a further question; the primitivist claim is simply that TRUTH is a member of the most fundamental set of concepts.

My characterization of primitivism is not just that TRUTH is fundamental, but that it is explanatorily indispensable. In saying so, I emphasize that primitivism is a substantive, nondeflationary theory of truth. Deflationists with respect to the concept TRUTH hold that the concept fundamentally has an expressive purpose rather than an explanatory one (Horwich 1990; Williams 1999).[3] We can elucidate this idea in a variety of ways. A common theme in deflationist thinking is that we have words like "true" in our language not to enable us to express a special class of ideas involving truth, but to facilitate the expression of thoughts that have nothing to do with truth. To say that it's true that dodos have gone extinct is just another way of expressing the idea that dodos have gone extinct. To say that not everything Freddo says is true is just a more convenient way of saying that Freddo said that frogs are mammals (though frogs aren't mammals), or Freddo said that aquariums are tools of oppression (though aquariums aren't tools of oppression), and so on. "True," in other words, adds *convenience* rather than *content* to our language.

Another aspect of the conceptually deflationary view is that TRUTH doesn't stand in any explanatorily significant relationships to other concepts. Consider the connection between KNOWLEDGE and TRUTH: S knows that p only if "p" is true. Truth is a necessary ingredient of knowledge. But this doesn't show that the relationship between the two concepts is explanatorily significant. The reason is that the connection between knowledge and truth merely illustrates the expressive utility of truth, and nothing more. What it is to say that knowledge requires truth is that someone knows that snow is white only if snow is white, and someone knows that snow is soft only if snow is soft, and someone knows that snow is solid only if snow is solid, and so forth. It's *true* to say that knowledge and truth are connected, but saying so is no concession to substantivism about TRUTH.

Contrast the epistemological case with how Davidson, another advocate of primitivism, approaches the concept of meaning. He writes: "While Tarski intended to analyse the concept of truth by appealing (in Convention T) to the concept of meaning (in the guise of sameness of meaning, or translation), I have the reverse in mind. I considered truth to be the central primitive concept, and hoped, by detailing truth's structure, to get at meaning" (1984, xiv). Davidson is here committing to the view that the concepts TRUTH and MEANING are explanatorily connected, with the latter being dependent upon the former. A Davidsonian theory of meaning does not appeal to truth simply as a device that enables more convenient expression. Rather, it takes it as a theoretical primitive that we must presuppose if we are to understand the nature of linguistic meaning. Deflationists deny that TRUTH is related to other concepts in this way.

The theoretical purpose of allowing something into one's stock of primitives is to put it to work in one's theorizing. So it would be odd to believe that truth is conceptually primitive but explanatorily bankrupt. The primitivism that I endorse accepts, alongside Davidson, that TRUTH does enjoy rich conceptual connections to other significant notions. Start analyzing notions like knowledge, belief, assertion, conjecture, meaning, pretense, and sincerity, and it won't be long until one starts appealing to truth in order to explicate these other concepts. Now, that such connections exist does not automatically reveal that the links are explanatorily significant (as with the case of knowledge above). But it's important to note that when the connections do appear to be significant, primitivists, unlike deflationists, can accept the appearances at face value. Deflationists labor under the burden of revealing how all connections between truth and other notions are simply due to truth's expressive conveniences. (This is one major goal of Horwich [1990].) By contrast, primitivists welcome the discovery of substantive connections between TRUTH and other concepts, as this is exactly what we should expect from one of our bedrock, most fundamental concepts.

3   Arguments for Primitivism

There are a variety of ways that one might go about defending the claim that TRUTH is primitive. In this section I survey a number of such arguments, in ascending order of what I take to be their philosophical significance.

3.1   Elimination

One straightforward way of defending primitivism is by way of elimination. If one can show that all the other theories of truth are defective, then perhaps we can settle for primitivism. This might be the route of choice for those who, like Horwich (1990), believe primitivism to be "perhaps the least attractive conclusion" in the theory of truth, a view that "can be the resort only of those who feel that the decent alternatives have been exhausted" (10). I do not share this pessimistic view, and thus prefer arguments that speak to the independent plausibility of primitivism. Still, there is no shortage of dissatisfaction with the more familiar theories of truth. Many purported definitions of truth are thought to be subject to counterexample. Some belief could be a part of a maximally coherent worldview and yet be false; some belief could be incredibly useful, or find a home within some finalized scientific theory, and yet be false. If such things are possible, then truth cannot be analyzed in these sorts of coherentist or pragmatist ways. A familiar charge from alethic pluralists is that even the correspondence theory is subject to counterexample: there are no facts, for example, to which mathematical and moral truths correspond (Lynch 2009). Furthermore, if notions such as coherence, correspondence, utility, or finalized science are articulated in a way that avoids the counterexamples, there lingers a suspicion that these refined notions avoid the counterexamples only by covertly smuggling in the concept of truth. Such is Russell's critique of coherentism: it can't render "true" and "coherent" necessarily coextensive without presupposing "a more usual meaning of truth and falsehood in constructing its coherent whole, and that this more usual meaning, though indispensable to the theory, cannot be explained by means of the theory" (1906–1907, 33). Douglas Patterson (2010) also adopts this line of critique, arguing that the familiar theories of truth attain extensional adequacy only at the expense of circularity.

The elimination strategy also needs to take account of pluralist and deflationary theories, offering compelling objections against them that do not in turn apply to primitivists. I believe there are such objections (I offer them against deflationists and pluralists in, respectively, Asay [2013, 2018a]), but I will not address them here, since I think the elimination strategy is of limited dialectical value. It's better to focus on arguments that don't treat primitivism as a view of last resort.

3.2   Foundationalism

One direct argument for primitivism begins with the fact that some concepts need to be primitive and suggests that TRUTH may be such a concept. Davidson (1990) succinctly captures the sentiment of this argument, claiming that TRUTH is "as clear and basic a concept as we have. ... Why on earth should we expect to be able to reduce truth to something clearer or more fundamental?" (135–136). This closely mirrors foundationalist arguments in epistemology, which aim to establish that there must be basic beliefs providing the source of all further justification.

Primitivism presupposes that concepts stand in dependency relationships with one another. The concept BACHELOR depends on the concepts MALE and UNMARRIED, and so is not itself primitive. What of the concepts on which it depends? The concept UNMARRIED seems to depend on the concept MARRIAGE. So what about MARRIAGE? It seems that there are three possibilities: (1) it doesn't depend on any further concept and so is primitive; (2) it depends on further concepts yet to be mentioned; (3) it depends on concepts already mentioned, such as BACHELOR.

Option (3) is traditionally taken to be problematic, as it proves these conceptual dependencies run in a circle. If the dependency at issue is transitive (such that if A depends upon B, and B depends upon C, then A depends upon C) and irreflexive (such that if A depends upon B, then B doesn't depend upon A), then we can't have conceptual circles like this. If BACHELOR depends on UNMARRIED, and UNMARRIED depends on MARRIAGE, then BACHELOR depends on MARRIAGE. But if BACHELOR depends on MARRIAGE, then MARRIAGE doesn't depend on BACHELOR. So option (3) is ruled out. Option (1) seems implausible, since we can account for MARRIAGE in terms of the politically recognized unions that constitute it; MARRIAGE is hardly a contender for conceptual bedrock. So that leaves option (2), and the question of fundamentality arises for those further concepts, whatever they turn out to be: Are they fundamental, or still further analyzable? Presumably, we cannot take option (2) forever—that would be to instigate an infinite regress of concepts, each one more fundamental than the next. Eventually, then, we must take option (1) for some concepts. If there are to be no infinite regresses or conceptual circles, we must eventually land on some conceptual primitives.

Having established that there are conceptual primitives, we now need to consider what we should expect them to be like. Here are a few suggestions. The primitive concepts are the ones we need in order to have other concepts. So we should expect the primitive concepts to be highly general and of wide application.[4] In logic, the idea of topic neutrality is often invoked to capture what is distinctive about logical concepts: notions like conjunction, disjunction, and the like aren't *about* any specific domain of thought. They apply, in virtue of their generality, across all domains of thought. The same is true of truth. Any domain of thought, where thought is taken to involve the contemplation and expression of truth-evaluable contents, is a domain where truth is relevant. In fact, the idea that truth is a logical property, rather than a naturalistic or metaphysical property, is a familiar one (e.g., Horwich 1990, 38). Concepts that are limited to only certain domains of thought are less likely to be paradigm cases of primitive concepts. Truth, by way of its generality, is a strong contender for such status.

Given their foundational nature, we should also expect primitive concepts to be connected to a large number of derivative concepts. After all, the function of the foundational concepts, taken together, is to provide a basis for understanding the nature of all concepts whatsoever. The fact that TRUTH shares conceptual connections with so many other concepts is yet another indicator that it deserves a spot among the most fundamental concepts. As already noted, truth is not far from our explorations of many other topics. What is knowledge? The right kind of possession of the truth. What is assertion? Putting forward one's thoughts as being true. What is the meaning of a sentence? The conditions under which it is true. What is a belief? A representational mental state whose aim is the truth. What is the aim of science? Achieving the truth. Again, primitivism may not be necessary in order to explain all these various conceptual connections; some of them (but not all) are open to straightforward deflationary analysis.[5] The present point is that we should expect our conceptual foundations to reveal themselves all over our conceptual scheme, and that is precisely what we find with TRUTH.

3.3   Omnipresence

I now turn to one final argument for primitivism. I call it the *omnipresence* argument, and I take my inspiration for it from Frege. The basic idea is that TRUTH forms part of the structure of every thought that carries propositional content—it is thus omnipresent in all our truth-evaluable thoughts. But if so, then any attempt to define truth must make use of judgments that already employ truth. So any purported definition of truth is circular. Hence, truth cannot be analyzed in terms of more basic concepts.

As I shall explain, I take the omnipresence argument to be a metaphysical counterpart to an epistemologically focused argument that Frege offers. In his essay "The Thought," Frege (1956) presents an argument for the conclusion that truth cannot be defined. It begins as a refutation of the correspondence theory, then generalizes:

> Can it not be laid down that truth exists when there is correspondence in a certain respect? But in which? For what would we then have to do to decide whether something were true? We should have to inquire whether it were true that an idea and a reality, perhaps, corresponded in the laid-down respect. And then we should be confronted by a question of the same kind and the game could begin again. So the attempt to explain truth as correspondence collapses. And every other attempt to define truth collapses too. For in a definition certain characteristics would have to be stated. And in application to any particular case the question would always arise whether it were true that the characteristics were present. So one goes round in a circle. Consequently, it is probable that the content of the word "true" is unique and indefinable. (291)

The argument can be viewed as uncovering either a vicious circularity or a vicious regress. If truth consists in some further characteristics, then to determine whether or not something is true, we have to determine whether or not it has those further characteristics. But the new investigation is just an investigation into whether it's true that the candidate truth possesses those further characteristics. So our investigation into truth by means of the further characteristics leads us to another investigation into truth. We can continue that investigation in terms of the same further characteristics, but the question will keep coming back to truth. Of course, we know plenty about the world, and which truth-bearers are true. This knowledge would seem to be impossible, however, if truth were definable.

For Frege (1979), "Predicating [truth] is always included in predicating anything whatever" (236). So "is true" can't be analyzed in terms of other predicates since those predicates are already intertwined with truth. Predicating "is a mammal" of Elijah the echidna is just to predicate "is true" of "Elijah the echidna is a mammal." This insight is key to appreciating primitivism, but I think Frege unhelpfully casts the idea in epistemic terms in his argument. There are two epistemic assumptions underlying the argument, and I suspect that both are false.[6]

Frege's first assumption in the argument is that epistemic priority follows conceptual priority. That is to say, if some concept C is analyzed in terms of concept A, then to determine whether C applies to something one must first determine whether A applies to it. So if truth is analyzed in terms of correspondence with fact, then to determine whether something is true one must first determine whether it corresponds with fact. As a general epistemic principle, this sort of priority cannot be correct. Suppose I want to know if Ms. Marzipan is married. I'm not sure exactly how to analyze the concept MARRIAGE, but I know one way of completing the epistemic chore at hand: ask Marzipan. I can learn from testimony whether or not "is married" applies to Marzipan; the question of which concepts constitute MARRIAGE is beside the point, epistemically speaking. There are plenty of weaker claims we can make. If truth really is defined by correspondence to fact, then in learning that something is true, one can thereby come to know that something corresponds to the facts. And vice versa. In fact, this epistemic symmetry is what gives the lie to the stronger priority claim that we must learn which concepts apply to something by means of those concepts' analyses. But the stronger claim is needed to generate the vicious regress that Frege intends: to learn that p is true, we have to learn that p is A, and that means learning that it's true that p is A, and to learn that we have to learn that it's A that p is A, which just is to learn that it's true that it's A that p is A, and so on. My present point is that whatever the means are by which we learn any of these claims in the regress, we thereby enable ourselves to learn all of them. And the way we learn that p is true need not have anything to do with A at all. (We can just ask a reliable source about p.)

The second false assumption involves an even less plausible form of epistemic priority. So even if we granted Frege's first assumption—that we come to know whether a concept applies by coming to know whether the concept's constituents apply—it would not help him complete the argument. The following is an example of the kind of regress that Frege deploys:

(1) "Elijah is an echidna" is true.

(2) "Elijah is an echidna" corresponds with the facts.

(3) "'Elijah is an echidna' corresponds with the facts" is true.

(4) "'Elijah is an echidna' corresponds with the facts" corresponds with the facts.

(5) "'"Elijah is an echidna" corresponds with the facts' corresponds with the facts" is true.

...

Frege's first assumption about epistemic priority is that (2) is prior to (1). (2) provides an analysis of (1) and so takes epistemic precedent. So to come to know (1), one must first come to know (2). But, the regress must keep going for the argument to be successful. To come to know (2), one must first come to know (3), and so on. The question facing Frege is why (3) ought to come before (2), just as (2) comes before (1). It's true that (2) is true if and only if (3) is true. But what Frege needs to establish is that (3) is epistemically prior to (2). But that is independently implausible, *even if* Frege is right that (2) comes before (1). Put another way: the epistemic priority that would allow (2) to come before (1) is not the kind of priority that would allow him to infer that (3) comes before (2). Neither purported priority is particularly plausible.

Here's another way of appreciating the point. (1) and (2) can be thought of as being "joined together" by means of the biconditional schema:

"p" is true if and only if "p" corresponds with the facts.

Of course, the connection between truth and correspondence (according to correspondence theorists) is not merely material equivalence. Correspondence reveals the nature of truth, and thus Frege takes the right-hand side to be epistemically prior. I have questioned the legitimacy of that inference, but it's easy to appreciate why one might appeal to it. But now consider how (2) and (3) are connected. What joins them together is different; it's the familiar truth schema:

"p" is true if and only if p.

To launch the epistemic regress, Frege now needs the left-hand side (e.g., (3)) to be epistemically prior to the right-hand side (e.g., (2)). Even if it exists (which I have already doubted), the epistemic priority of CORRESPONDENCE WITH FACT over TRUTH does nothing to justify the epistemic priority of "'p' is true" over "p." If anything, claims that p would seem to be more conceptually basic than claims that "p" is true. The latter carries the same conceptual content of "p," plus seemingly more. Hence, even if (2) must come before (1), and (4) must come before (3), it doesn't follow that (3) must come before (2), and (5) must come before (4).

Despite these objections, which I take to be conclusive against Frege's argument, I believe that there is a nearby argument that does establish primitivism. Suppose that Frege is right in the general idea that predications of truth are always, in some sense, present whenever predications take place. One explanation of that fact is that truth is already a part of every act of predication and so is omnipresent.

Here, then, is my understanding of omnipresence.[7] I first suppose that our propositional thoughts (i.e., our thoughts whose contents are given by propositions) are constituted by their component concepts. For me to think the thought that echidnas are mammals, I must have the concepts ECHIDNA and MAMMAL. Sometimes these concepts speak to the *content* of the thought in question: the thought that echidnas are mammals is about echidnas and mammals. But concepts can also contribute to the *structure* of a thought. To think the thought that echidnas are mammals and penguins are birds, one needs the concept CONJUNCTION, although the thought in question is not about conjunction. Omnipresence is the thesis that TRUTH is a structural component of every propositional thought.

Another way of spinning the omnipresence idea is that the concept of truth is what enables us to engage in propositional thought. Without a concept of truth, we can't think in terms of propositions. Concepts are the tools that our minds use to think thoughts, so a concept that is a part of each and every thought is a concept that we must have in order to engage in any particular thought at all. So to advocate omnipresence is to advocate the claim that we must have a concept of truth if we are to engage in propositional thought. That is to say, anyone who asserts, believes, denies, hypothesizes, lies, or pretends must possess TRUTH.[8]

The best evidence for omnipresence comes from Frege's (1956) observation that "nothing is added to the thought by my ascribing to it the property of truth" (293). Contemplate whether or not the United States and Canada will merge in 2076. Now contemplate whether or not it's true that the United States and Canada will merge in 2076. There is no difference between these imaginings. Suppose a mathematician commits to the claim that there is no set whose cardinality is strictly between that of the integers and the real numbers; this mathematician is also committed to the claim that it's true that there is no set whose cardinality is strictly between that of the integers and the real numbers. If I believe that pigeons outnumber puffins in Paraguay, then it's true to say of me that I believe that it's true that pigeons outnumber puffins in Paraguay. One way to capture all these observations is to claim that the sentence forms "p" and "It is true that p" express the same thing. The reason that "adding" truth to our thoughts adds nothing is that truth is *already there*.

According to this perspective, TRUTH is at the forefront of our propositional thought. This should not be all that surprising. What are we *doing* when we engage in propositional thought? We're engaging the truth. Propositions are the truth-apt contents of our thought. When we believe or assert a proposition, we're taking a stand on what we take to be true. The difference between an imagistic thought of green grass and a propositional thought that grass is green is that the latter is related to truth. Omnipresence offers an understanding of what it is for a thought to be a *propositional, truth-apt* thought: it involves TRUTH in its structure.

If omnipresence is true, then every propositional thought presupposes TRUTH. Just as all our thoughts about dogs token DOG, all our thoughts about anything whatsoever token TRUTH. So any thought that might purport to define TRUTH already presupposes TRUTH. Thus, any attempt at defining TRUTH is circular. But a circular definition is not a definition in terms of concepts that are more fundamental. So TRUTH is primitive.

4 Objections to Primitivism

The most common objections against primitivism about truth fault it for being a form of primitivism. Earlier I cited Horwich's attitude that primitivism is a theory of last resort (1990, 10), a sentiment shared by Künne (2003, 18). The idea behind such a response is that offering an analysis—any analysis—is always better than accepting that no analysis can be offered. This response misses the point I made earlier in connection with the foundationalist argument—namely, that some concepts need to be primitive, lest all conceptual analyses run in circles or launch regresses. So a methodology that always favors analyses is flawed. Furthermore, those offering this sort of objection need an argument as to why TRUTH is a particularly bad candidate for fundamentality. I've argued that it's a particularly good candidate, given its centrality, generality, and topic-neutrality.

Similar objections suggest that accepting that truth is primitive is tantamount to believing that "there is nothing significant to say about truth" (Vision 2004, 45). This claim is a non sequitur. It assumes that the only significant things to say about a concept involve its conceptual analysis. But consider the theoretical role that primitive concepts play: together, they provide the foundations for understanding every other concept we have. In so doing, they provide us an abundance of noteworthy claims. Davidson stresses this fact in his defense of primitivism, showcasing how taking truth to be primitive enables one to take substantive stands on belief, desire, causality, action, and other significant topics (see chapter 26 in this volume).

Finally, there is the idea that taking truth to be primitive is to shroud it with "impenetrable mysteriousness" (Horwich 1998, 10). The thought seems to be that we only understand concepts by way of their decomposition, so to fail to analyze is to fail to understand. But this attitude gets the notion of a primitive concept exactly backward. The primitive concepts are likely to be those most familiar to us, since they are the ones that enable us to have all our other concepts. Merricks successfully refutes this objection, noting that if primitiveness renders a concept mysterious, then it should render all concepts built out of primitives mysterious, thus resulting in *all* concepts being mysterious. Since all concepts aren't mysterious, primitive concepts qua primitive concepts aren't mysterious (2007, 185).

This family of objections to TRUTH being primitive relies on false understandings of the nature of primitive concepts in general and their theoretical role. However, it's worth noting that parallel objections against a primitive *property* of truth may be defensible—I issued such an objection above. Taking the property *truth* to be primitive makes it out to be a fundamental property of a truth-bearer. Its role is to explain why certain objects in the world share a certain property; the primitivist about *truth* says that all truths share this fundamental property, and that's why they're true. One might think that the truth of "Lemons are sour" and "Spinach is bitter" has to do with the chemical properties of the foods in question, but this turns out to be incorrect according to the *metaphysical* primitivist about truth. This primitivist view maintains that the truth-values of truth-bearers are brute and inexplicable. In other words, it makes the matter of what's true and what's false metaphysically mysterious.

The better way to object to *conceptual* primitivism about truth is to show how it doesn't pay. Theories justify their sets of fundamentals by showing off what dividends they pay. My view is that primitivism brings with it a treasure trove of theoretical advantages. It avoids the complicated metaphysical commitments that accompany other traditional theories of truth and is not constantly on the defensive, as deflationists are, trying to show how various alethic phenomena can be accounted for in innocu-ous, deflationism-friendly ways. The right way to object to primitivism is to admit that we need conceptual primitives but then show that it's not theoretically lucrative to include TRUTH among them. Sets of fundamental concepts that eschew TRUTH need to be shown to offer significant theoretical advantages. Objections of this form are not easily substantiated, for they involve careful accounting of how competing sets of primitives stack up against each other. They certainly require more sophistication than the casual, brusque dismissals that primitivism more commonly attracts.

5   Connections to Metaphysics

I have said very little about metaphysics in this essay, and that is for good reason. The primitivism I defend is limited to the concept of truth. Taking there to be a substantial, fundamental metaphysical property of truth is disastrous, as it amounts to saying that there are no informative explanations available as to why truths are true. But what does the conceptual primitivist have to say about the metaphysical implications of truth? Correspondence theories are often thought to be in service of metaphysical realism, and coherence theories are considered a natural ally to idealism. Pluralist theories take as their raison d'être the hope of demonstrating the different ontological bases for dif-ferent domains. My conceptual primitivist seems to take on no commitments regarding the metaphysics of truth.

In this respect, conceptual primitivism resembles deflationism. Primitivists, like deflationists, accept that one's theory of truth does not settle the metaphysical ques-tion of what provides the grounds for something's being true. Primitivism about TRUTH, after all, is a thesis concerning the cognitive abilities of mental agents and the relations that must obtain between their various cognitive tools. So primitivists can accept the metaphysically deflationary idea that there is no common, unified explanation to be found as to why true truth-bearers are true. Roughly put, "p" is true because p, and "q" is true because q. What p and q come to, metaphysically speaking, is a question for metaphysics and depends upon what "p" and "q" are about and what ontological com-mitments they introduce. What primitivists should reject is that their truth comes to the same thing, like "correspondence with the facts," or what have you.

Primitivism about TRUTH, then, is a fundamentally metaphysically neutral view. It doesn't side with realism or anti-realism; it doesn't reject metaphysics altogether or embrace it. It does, I believe, rightly hold that metaphysical questions are best sepa-rated from the issues that surround the concept of truth. Metaphysical investigation into the grounds of truths is yet another form of inquiry that presupposes TRUTH. Other theories of truth are forced into metaphysically treacherous territory by spreading their ontological commitments across all domains of thought. For example, while corre-spondence theorists may easily motivate the existence of their corresponding objects (be they facts or something else), for some domains they are hard-pressed to find available objects in, say, mathematics. This is the "scope problem" familiar from discussions about pluralism (e.g., Lynch 2009). Pluralists respond to the problem by assigning different truth properties to different domains; I respond by rejecting the idea that we need properties of truth at all to account for why truth-bearers are true. Taking TRUTH to be primitive doesn't force one to take this deflationary stance regarding alleged substantive properties of truth, but it does free one up to do so. The right response for those of us who find truth to be of the highest philosophical significance is to identify that idea with the centrality that truth plays in our conceptual scheme.

Notes

1. I offer a more thorough history and defense of primitivism in Asay (2013).

2. Several do the latter without doing the former. Among them are Moore and Russell, as well as contemporary writers such as McGinn (2000) and Merricks (2007).

3. Given the distinction between concepts and properties, deflationism about the property *truth* is a separate matter. I defend metaphysical deflationism, understood as the view that *truth* is a merely abundant property (Asay 2014). That is, *truth* is not a metaphysically significant property that accounts for the genuine resemblances between objects, the causal goings-on in the world, and what makes truth-bearers true. One can take TRUTH to be an indispensable component of our conceptual repertoire without also supposing it to correspond to some metaphysically significant property. Indeed, one purpose of drawing the distinction between concepts and properties is to enable a subtler appreciation of the various ways in which truth is or isn't deflated.

4. Other examples might include identity, existence, and necessity.

5. See Bar-On and Simmons (2007; see also chapter 25 in this volume) for an argument that deflationists cannot account for the relationship between truth and assertion.

6. For a somewhat different interpretation, see Kremer (2000).

7. See Asay (2018b) for a more complete defense of this perspective.

8. As a result, my view has empirical implications, in that it's an empirical matter as to which creatures possess which concepts. It's not straightforward, however, that omnipresence can be directly tested by empirical methods. The falsifier would be someone who could assert, believe, and contemplate but didn't possess TRUTH. But there is no independent means of identifying who possesses a certain concept in the absence of (philosophical) views as to what it is to possess that concept.

References

Asay, J. 2013. *The Primitivist Theory of Truth*. Cambridge: Cambridge University Press.

Asay, J. 2014. "Against *Truth*." *Erkenntnis* 79: 147–164.

Asay, J. 2018a. "Putting Pluralism in Its Place." *Philosophy and Phenomenological Research* 96: 175–191.

Asay, J. 2018b. "TRUTH: A Concept Unlike Any Other." *Synthese*. https://doi.org/10.1007/s11229 -017-1661-z.

Bar-On, D., and K. Simmons. 2007. "The Use of Force against Deflationism: Assertion and Truth." In D. Greimann and G. Siegwart, eds., *Truth and Speech Acts: Studies in the Philosophy of Language*, 61–89. New York: Routledge.

Davidson, D. 1984. "Introduction." In *Inquiries into Truth and Interpretation*, xii–xx. Oxford: Clarendon Press.

Davidson, D. 1990. "Afterthoughts, 1987." In A. R. Malachowski, ed., *Reading Rorty: Critical Responses to* Philosophy and the Mirror of Nature *(and Beyond)*, 134–138. Oxford: Basil Blackwell.

Frege, G. 1956. "The Thought: A Logical Inquiry." Translated by A. M. Quinton and M. Quinton. *Mind*, n.s., 65: 289–311.

Frege, G. 1979. *Posthumous Writings*. Edited by H. Hermes, F. Kambartel, and F. Kaulbach, with the assistance of G. Gabriel and W. Rödding. Translated by P. Long and R. White, with the assistance of R. Hargreaves. Oxford: Basil Blackwell.

Horwich, P. 1990. *Truth*. Oxford: Basil Blackwell.

Horwich, P. 1998. *Truth*. 2nd ed. Oxford: Clarendon Press.

Kremer, M. 2000. "Judgment and Truth in Frege." *Journal of the History of Philosophy* 38: 549–581.

Künne, W. 2003. *Conceptions of Truth*. Oxford: Clarendon Press.

Lynch, M. P. 2009. *Truth as One and Many*. Oxford: Clarendon Press.

McGinn, C. 2000. *Logical Properties: Identity, Existence, Predication, Necessity, Truth*. Oxford: Clarendon Press.

Merricks, T. 2007. *Truth and Ontology*. Oxford: Clarendon Press.

Moore, G. E. 1899. "The Nature of Judgment." *Mind*, n.s., 8: 176–193.

Patterson, D. 2010. "Truth as Conceptually Primitive." In C. D. Wright and N. J. L. L. Pedersen, eds., *New Waves in Truth*, 13–29. New York: Palgrave Macmillan.

Russell, B. 1906–1907. "On the Nature of Truth." *Proceedings of the Aristotelian Society*, n.s., 7: 28–49.

Strawson, P. F. 1992. *Analysis and Metaphysics: An Introduction to Philosophy*. Oxford: Oxford University Press.

Vision, G. 2004. *Veritas: The Correspondence Theory and Its Critics*. Cambridge, MA: MIT Press.

Williams, M. 1999. "Meaning and Deflationary Truth." *Journal of Philosophy* 96: 545–564.

28 Truth: The Identity Theory

Jennifer Hornsby

I want to promote what I shall call (unoriginally, and for the sake of its having a name) "the identity theory of truth."[1] I suggest that other accounts put forward as theories of truth are genuine rivals to it, but are unacceptable.

A certain conception of *thinkables* belongs with the identity theory's conception of *truth*. I introduce these conceptions in section I by reference to John McDowell's *Mind and World*, and I show why they have a place in an identity theory, which I introduce by reference to Frege. In section II I elaborate on the conception of thinkables; and by adverting to interpretive accounts of speakers, I introduce a perspective from which the identity theory's merits can be revealed.

I

I.1

McDowell introduced the notion of a think*able* in order to fend off a particular objection to the following claim (1994, 27):

> There is no ontological gap between the sort of thing one can ... think, and the sort of thing that can be the case. When one thinks truly, what one thinks *is* what is the case. ... [T]here is no gap between thought, as such, and the world.

Someone who objects to this supposes that, by denying any gap between thought and the world, one commits oneself to a sort of idealism. But such an objector confuses people's thinkings of things with the contents of their thoughts. If one says that there is no ontological gap between thoughts and what is the case, meaning by "thoughts" cognitive activity on the part of beings such as ourselves, then one is indeed committed to a sort of idealism: one has to allow that nothing would be the case unless there were cognitive activity—that there could not be a mindless world. But someone who means by "thoughts" the contents of such activity, and who denies a gap between thoughts and what is the case, suggests only that what someone thinks can be the case.

> To say that there is no gap between thought, as such, and the world, is just to dress up a truism in high-flown language. All the point comes to is that one can think, for instance, *that spring*

has begun, and that the very same thing, that spring has begun, can be the case. That is truistic, and it cannot embody something metaphysically contentious. ... (Ibid.)

In order to avoid the ambiguity in "thought" which would be exploited if a meta-physically contentious idealism were reached, McDowell suggests using the word "thinkables" for what may be thought. My policy here will be to use the word "think-able" generally, in place of any of the more familiar "content," "proposition" or "Thought." Further reasons for this choice of word will show up in due course.

McDowell's demonstration that his position avoids a simple idealism may strike some people as an inadequate defence. I think that it can help to defend it to locate it by reference to debates about truth. One may view the quotations from McDowell as encouraging an identity theory of truth.[2] This says that true thinkables are the same as facts. True thinkables then make up the world of which McDowell speaks when he dresses up a truism. The world is "everything that is the case," or "a constellation of facts," as McDowell puts it, following Wittgenstein.

I.2

The identity theory is encapsulated in the simple statement that true thinkables are the same as facts. But it may be wondered how that statement could amount to a *theory* of truth: "If someone asks what truth is, and receives an answer which helps itself to the idea of a fact, then hasn't she been taken round a very small circle?" Yes. But the simple statement on its own is not supposed to tell us anything illuminating. A conception of truth can be drawn out from an elaboration of what the simple statement can remind us of. And, as we shall see, the conception can be set apart from the conceptions of other accounts that go by the name of theories of truth.

The identity theory is not vacuous. It cannot be vacuous because it takes a stand on what the bearers of truth are, calling them thinkables. This is not an uncontentious stand. For there are philosophers who have told us that the notion of proposition (and thus of thinkable) is so dubious that we should take the truth-bearers to be sentences.[3] The identity theory proceeds without such doubts, taking it for granted that we can make adequate sense of what is meant when someone says, for instance, "She told me something that isn't true."[4] And the identity theory not only asks us to under-stand such "something"s in appreciating where truth is applicable, but it also asks us to understand such "something"s in saying what truth's applicability consists in. Cer-tainly there is no illumination at the point at which the word "fact" is resorted to in order to say what this applicability consists in. But the identity theory makes definite commitments nonetheless.[5]

I.3

Whether or not its title to be a theory can be made out, it may be unclear why the word "identity" belongs in it. What could be the point in saying that true thinkables *are the same as* facts, rather than—more simply and apparently to the same effect—that true thinkables *are* facts?[6]

A familiar argument in Frege (1918) may help to show the point. It is an argument against the correspondence theory of truth. Frege introduces it with the words "It might be supposed ... that truth consists in the correspondence of a picture with what it depicts." "This is contradicted, however," he says, and then argues by *reductio* (18–19):

> A correspondence ... can only be perfect if the corresponding things coincide and so just are not different things at all. ... [I]f the first did correspond perfectly with the second, they would coincide. But this is not at all what people intend when they define truth as the correspondence of an idea with something real. For in this case it is essential precisely that the reality shall be distinct from the idea. But then there can be no complete correspondence, no complete truth. So nothing at all would be true; for what is only half true is untrue.

Putting this only slightly differently, we hear Frege saying: if truth were explicated in terms of any relation, it would have to be identity, since anything less than a candidate for truth's coincidence with a putatively corresponding thing would lead to the intolerable conclusion that there is no truth. Someone who takes herself to think that true thinkables correspond to the facts has it right, then, only if she actually means that any true thinkable is the same as some fact—which is what the identity theorist says.

Frege's argument has a sequel. This starts by showing how Frege thinks his opponent will respond. The opponent asks (p. 19):

> But can't it be laid down that truth exists where there is correspondence in a certain respect?

Here it is conceded that truth cannot be unspecified correspondence, so to speak. The problem with taking truth to be unspecified correspondence is that there can be correspondence in this respect, or that respect, or that other respect, so that there can be less or more correspondence according as there is correspondence in fewer or more respects; but there can't *in any analogous way* be more or less truth.[7] The opponent supposes that he can get out of this difficulty by picking on one respect of correspondence. To this Frege has a response.

> But in which [respect]? What would we then have to do to decide whether something were true? We should have to inquire whether an idea and a reality, perhaps, corresponded in a laid-down respect. And then we should have to confront a question of the same kind, and the game would begin again. So the attempt to explain truth as correspondence collapses. (19)

If there was something distinct from a thinkable (a reality, say) such that establishing that some relation obtained between it and the thinkable was a way of getting to know whether the thinkable was true, then someone could be in the position of knowing what is known when the thinkable is known, yet of still not knowing whether it was true. But of course one could never be in that position: to discover whether *p* is already to discover whether it is true that *p*.

This reveals a general difficulty about defining truth—the difficulty which shows up "when we confront the same question again."

> In a definition certain characteristics would have to be stated. And in application to any particular case the question would always arise whether it were true that the characteristics were present.

"Consequently," Frege concludes, "it is probable that the word 'true' is unique and indefinable" (19).

When one follows Frege's argument through to this general conclusion, about the definability of truth, explicit opposition to the correspondence theory is lost: the correspondence theorist's definition fails to meet a constraint on any adequate definition; but it turns out not to be alone in that failure. Frege accordingly might be thought to have argued against an especially naive correspondence theory in the first instance, and then turned to opposing the whole idea of truth's definability. But there can be a point in thinking of Frege's initial argument as meant to show that a correspondence theory in particular—and *any* correspondence theory—is untenable. This is an argument which is sound only if the identity theory escapes its *reductio*. It is the initial argument whose conclusion can be dressed up in high-flown language: there cannot be an ontological gap between thought ("an idea") and the world ("something real"). Given the sequel to the initial argument, the high-flown language can hardly point us toward any substantial theory of truth: truth's indefinability prevents us from thinking that truth has a nature that a theory could spell out. The high-flown language, then, serves only to remind us that a metaphysical stand is taken when an identity theory is endorsed.

I.4

The identity theory, at any rate, is distinguishable from any correspondence theory. And the identity theory is worth considering to the extent to which correspondence theories are worth avoiding. I think that correspondence theories *need* to be avoided. I mean by this not merely that they are incorrect, but that people are apt to believe them.

It is common for philosophers to speak as if a correspondence theory of truth had no metaphysical import whatever. We are sometimes told that the idea of correspondence is recorded in a series of platitudes that any theorist of truth has to respect. Simon Blackburn has spoken of the phrase "corresponds to the facts" as sometimes a piece of Pentagonese—a paraphrase of "is true" deployed with the purpose of saying something important sounding (1984, 255). But of course this is not all that has ever been read into the phrase. Someone who says "re-rendered it operational" for "got it going again," may be criticized for needless portentousness, but not on other grounds; but when "corresponds to the facts" gets in, the phrase's wordiness should not be the only source of doubt.

Certainly there are glosses on "is true" that are platitudinous: "is a fact" is one such—the one that the identity theory singles out for attention. Perhaps it is also a platitude that true sentences say how things are. And this again is unobjectionable, so long as the "things" in question are ordinary objects of reference: the true sentence "that book is red," for example, says something about how things are by saying how one of the things (sc. that book) is (sc. red). This platitude then points up the independence of thinking from what there is. Whether you want to know the book's colour, or to know something of what I think about the book, you have to think of something that is not sustained in existence by your thinking. Still, the thing to which you are then related (that book) is obviously not a correspondence theorist's candidate for the correspondent of a truth-bearer.[8] The platitudes about truth do not record the correspondence theorist's claims about it.

From the point of view introduced by the identity theory, it will be distinctive of correspondence theorists to seek items located outside the realm of thinkables, and outside the realm of ordinary objects of reference, but related, some of them, to whole thinkables. The idea is widespread, and it takes various guises. In the Russell of *An Inquiry into Meaning and Truth* (1940), the basic correspondents are percepts. Percepts can be "surveyed but not defined"; utterances appropriately associated with them get their particular meanings from them; and propositions, the truth-bearers, can be constructed out of percepts. In the Quine of *Philosophy of Logic* (1970), the correspondents are cosmic distributions of particles. "Two sentences agree in objective information, and so express the same proposition, when every cosmic distribution of particles over space-time that would make either sentence true would make the other true as well" (4). These very different candidates for things that make sentences true—percepts and particle distributions—reflect the very different obsessions of Russell and Quine, epistemological and cosmic. But what is common to their accounts, despite this vast difference, is a willingness to reconstruct thinkables from posited entities of a different sort, entities which make things true. Percepts and particle distributions, then, are supposed to be items which we can specify independently of an account of thinkables, items which may confer truth upon a thinkable. When they are introduced, however, we cannot hold onto the truism that inspires the identity theory. The fact (as it is) that autumn has begun, if it were to be a cosmic distribution of particles, would not be the same as what I think when I think (truly) that autumn has begun.

It is evident now that the words "corresponds with" do not have to be in play for an ontological gap between thought and the world to open up. This is something that we see in formulations used over the years by Michael Dummett and Crispin Wright in stating the semantic anti-realist's case. Their formulations often appear to invoke a conception of a truthmaker which will suit a correspondence theorist but which an identity theorist cannot allow.[9] Dummett asked "If it were impossible to know the truth of some true statement, how could there be anything which *made* that statement true?" Wright spoke of "a truth-conferrer for a sentence": in the case where the truth of the sentence cannot be known, he said that this is something that "the world fails to deliver up." And he spoke of "the states of affairs" that are in question when a sentence is undecidable as things that "could not be encountered." These ways of speaking give rise to an image of something with which a thinkable might have connected up, but a something which we are expected to think of the world as taking sole responsibility for. This is the image that an identity theory may help to rid us of. For when the conditions for the truth of a sentence are supplied by an identity theorist, nothing is brought in besides the thinkable that is expressed by the sentence itself. By introducing "sources of truth," "truth conferrers" and "states of affairs," Dummett and Wright drive a wedge between what is demanded by a thinkable and what is demanded by a thinkable that is true. The identity theorist leaves no room for any wedge at this point.

Of course these remarks about Dummett and Wright do not get to grips with the position which was their concern. But they can illustrate a point—that philosophers' formulations are apt to create an outlook which is forsworn when an identity theory displaces a correspondence theory. I hope that they also suggest how the identity theory may displace forms of anti-realism more subtle than the crass idealism which results from equating thinkables with thinkings of them.

II

II.1

It would be laborious to attempt to show that the identity theory is incompatible with all things irrealist. In order to show that it embodies nothing metaphysically contentious, I shall attempt only to reveal its actual compatibility with a perfectly common-sense realism.

McDowell's rebuttal of any simple idealism emphasizes the independence of thinkables from thinkings. One way to grasp this independence is to see that there are (so to speak) more thinkables than there are thinkings. I suspect that those who find the theory problematic are apt to suppose that it could be part of common sense that there are (so to speak) more facts than there are true thinkables. If this is right about where the opposition lies, then further reflections on the identity theory, if they are to serve as a defence, must expand on the notion of a thinkable. By the identity theorist's lights, our grasp of the notion of a fact cannot exceed our grasp of the notion of a true thinkable. But someone who wishes to express doubts on that score might be helped by having it made apparent how generous the notion of a thinkable nonetheless is.

II.2

There can seem to be an immediate obstacle, however, to *any* account of thinkables—of the contents, the meaningful things that bear truth. Quine's attack on the Myth of the

Museum (1960) is directed against the assumption that there could be things external to thought and meaning, lodged like exhibits in the mind, whose relations to other things could constitute the foundations of meaning. The identity theorist agrees with Quine about the incoherence of the hope that intersubjective sameness of meaning might be explained in terms of relations with things external to thought and meaning.

From the identity theorist's point of view the correspondents of correspondence theories of truth play the same role as the exhibits in the museum of the mind: they are items located beyond the bounds of human play with concepts, in terms of which one is supposed to explain meaning. Quine, speaking of cosmic distributions of particles over space-time, said that the item assigned to one sentence as a condition of its truth is the same as the item assigned to another sentence as a condition of *its* truth if and only if the two sentences have the same meaning. But such items as cosmic distributions of particles are in the same boat as items in the mind's museum according to the identity theory: neither can be used in the reconstruction of thinkables from something else.

If one countenances the cosmic items, but is led by the problems of the items in the mind's museum to think that ordinary talk of meaning is unsupported, then one may invoke a double standard. Quine tells us that a second class standard is appropriate so long as we are tolerant of such everyday psychological talk as involves any notion of a thinkable (1960, sec. 45). But he said that we can, and in science we must, employ a first class standard; it is then that objective information, corresponding to (say) cosmic distributions of particles, can do duty for thinkables, Quine thinks. The upshot of this is hard to make coherent. For the view of everyday reports of people's psychological states which is required by Quine's lower standard for them is not a view that can be sustained by someone who takes herself (for instance) to seek the truth in some area. A person's being an enquirer of any sort requires that she be interpretable as aiming at gleaning the facts, and we have no conception of what that is excepting as we can think of her as more generally intelligible—as apt to perceive things, and to think them, and to draw conclusions. We cannot then be in a position to make statements about Quine's first-class reality but of refusing (according to the same standard) to make any statements which say, for instance, what people are doing when they are investigating that reality. The identity theory helps to make this difficulty with the Quinean picture vivid. The first-class standard was meant to be the standard of genuine facts; the second-class standard was to be invoked when the language of thinkables was used. But if any fact is the same as some true thinkable, then we cannot endorse facts and despise thinkables.

II.3

It can seem as though the identity theorist had nowhere to turn for an account of thinkables. At least there is nowhere to turn for an account besides an investigation of other predications to them—predications other than "is true." This brings me to further reasons (which I said I would come to) for using the term "thinkable."

"Thinkable" is a word for a sort of things to which a person can be related in various modes. I say that the Labour Party will win the next election. I have just said something (that Labour will win) which many now believe, which a good few hope, which John Major fears. The example then shows that thinkables can be beliefs, hopes and fears. They are called beliefs when thought of in connection with one psychological attitude towards them; they are called hopes or fears when thought of in connection with other attitudes. They are thought of as propositions when thought of as propounded.[10] A modal term, like "thinkable," may serve to remind one of the variety of relations here: it is not only thought which relates to think*ables*, because a thinkable can be believed and hoped, for instance. (And just as we must not confuse a thinkable with a thinking, so we must not confuse a thinkable with someone's believing one, or with someone's hoping one.)

Besides "___ is true," then, there are predicates of thinkables, such as "___ is believed by Tony," "___ is hoped by members of the crowd." Yet other predicates of thinkables show people as related to them by their speech acts: a statement, for instance, is what we call a thinkable when we think of it in connection with someone's making a statement. "Thinkable" gives a word for what is truth-evaluable which is indifferent between the case where the evaluable thing is presented as the object of a state of a thinker's mind and the case where it is presented as having been put into words. But it is the linguistic expression of thinkables which we are bound to focus on, if we are to find anything of a systematic sort to say about them. One aim of theories of meaning is to show the significance of sentences as systematically dependent on properties of the words that make them up: theories of meaning, one might say, treat of thinkables' composition. The productivity of language, which can be revealed in its theory of meaning, then points towards another reason for using a modal notion, and speaking of think*ables*. Someone in possession of a theory of meaning for some language can say what was expressed in the use of any of the sentences on some list, composed from some stock of words; and is in a position to see that there are other things that would be expressed in the use of other sentences, not on the list, but composed only from words in the same stock. A theory of meaning, though its data are uses of actual sentences, is a theory which speaks to potential uses—to what would be said if some hitherto unused sentence of the language were used. There are actually unused sentences, which, just like the sentences we have given voice to or heard or read, express thinkables.

This suggests the place to look if we want to expand on the notion of a thinkable. We cannot postulate meanings in the mind or correspondents in the world. But we can look to the actual practices of language users. And we shall be reminded here of an idea first recommended by Donald Davidson—that we might put to work, as a theory of meaning of the language of some speakers, a definition of truth for the language which enables the interpretation of those speakers. Davidson's claim that a definition of truth for a language can serve as its theory of meaning depended in part on his thinking that

Tarski had shown a way of displaying the recurrent significance of words—by treating words as having characteristics which affect the truth of sentences they come into.[11] In the present context, much of the importance of the idea of deploying such a definition of truth for a language is the view of predications of thinkables it affords. Where an account of a language's workings is interpretive of its speakers, it enables the theorist to give expression, in the case of any sentence in the language and any speaker of it, to the thinkable expressed by the speaker using that sentence. It thus gives the theorist the resources to say what speakers are doing when they use their language.[12]

An interpretive account of speakers is not narrowly linguistic. For speakers' productions of sentences cannot be seen as intelligible expressions of thinkables except as speakers are seen to have some purpose in producing the sentences. And any hypothesis about the purpose of a person who uses words on some occasion goes hand in hand not only with a hypothesis about the thinkable then expressed but also with hypotheses about her mental states—about how *belief* and *desire* and the other attitudes relate her to thinkables—and with hypotheses also about the states of mind of audiences to her speech, and of all the others who use the language on other occasions.

The imaginary theorist, who compiles the facts about words that could put one in a position to understand foreign speakers, would be involved not only in making attributions to speakers of psychological attitudes and speech acts towards thinkables, but also, and inevitably, in taking a view of the truth of the thinkables to which speakers are then taken to be related. One cannot generally take a view about what someone's purposes are without having some view of which of those purposes are achieved; people intentionally do what they try to do to the extent that the beliefs which explain their doing what they do are true (are believings of true thinkables, that is). Of course the word "true" does not have to be dragged in in order to see someone's taking an attitude towards a thinkable as working as it does. One can just as well say "She believed that the plane took off at 9, and the plane took off at 9" as one can say "She believes that the plane took off at 9 and that is true." But insofar as an interpretive account requires more than the idea of people's relations to thinkables, and more than the idea of interconnections between those relations, it requires grasp of the distinction involved in assessments of thinkables as true or false. The view of thinkables that emerges, then, in trying to expand on the notion, is one in which some thinkables are taken to be (the same as) facts.

The study of interpretive accounts affords a distinctive perspective on the application of "is true" to thinkables. "True" can be treated as having a role alongside a variety of psychological predicates; but it is not itself treated as a psychological predicate, of course.[13]

II.4

Discussions of coming to understand a foreign language sometimes assume its speakers to be more ignorant than the theorist: the facts at the theorist's disposal go beyond any of which the interpreted people are apprised. But this assumption is not essential to the idea of an interpretive account. Contemplating interpretive accounts shows the accept-ability of a conception of potential uses of language expressive of thinkables outside one's ken, and some of which are facts.

One might think inductively here. Over the centuries, human knowledge, at least in some spheres, has expanded, and its expansion has been assisted by the introduction of new concepts, for instance in the formulation of scientific theories. If one believes that human knowledge will continue to expand, one is entitled to predict that thinkables which none of us here and now is capable of thinking will come to be known. One may envisage a theorist interpreting a language of the future: its speakers would think things, and the theorist, in coming to understand them, would learn from them. She could come to have access to facts, which in her present situation she is not even equipped to express.

Here one thinks of thinkables in connection with expanding knowledge. And it might then be supposed that the facts are to be circumscribed by reference to what is known by an ideal knower, at the limit, as it were, of an inductive series of more and more knowledgeable beings. But acceptance of unthought thinkables, some of which are facts, requires no such supposition. The supposition requires an understanding of the ideal situation for arriving at knowledge. And this can only be a situation in which all sources of error are eliminated or taken account of—a situation, that is to say, in which one is sure to believe what is *true*. Perhaps we can gesture towards such an ideal. But since we can explain it at best in terms of an antecedent notion of truth, the style of thinking used here to uncover a conception of facts can lend no support to an epis-temic theory of truth.[14]

The conception of unthought thinkables elicited here does not depend upon any settled opinion about human ambitions or limitations, but only upon an idea of intel-ligible others from whom one could learn. It evidently yields a generous conception of facts, to which an identity theorist is entitled. I hope, then, that the identity theory emerges as a defensible theory of truth, in keeping with our commonsensically realist view about the extent of facts independent of us.[15]

Answers to philosophers' questions about the relation between language and the world have traditionally taken a form that we now call theories of truth. I have not meant to develop any new theory here. Indeed, I do not think that we need a theory of truth, save insofar as we may go astray without one. I have promoted the identity theory because I think that we have to find a position from which to avoid the false dilemmas that theories currently on offer present us with. Nowadays many suppose that philosophers *either* endorse some version of a correspondence theory *or* have to say distinctively deflationary things about truth.[16] I hope that reflection on the iden-tity theory shows that dissension from correspondence theories, and indeed from all theories that purport to analyze truth, is independent of a deflationary attitude toward truth. The identity theory, by prompting questions about the nature of thinkables, provides us with a perspective from which many other theories appear indefensible.[17]

Notes

1. For "the identity theory" in recent and contemporary philosophy, see Candlish (1995).

2. I do not say that McDowell himself would see a point in viewing them thus.

3. The doubts are induced by Quine's attack on propositions, which I touch on in section II.2; see also notes 6 and 10. I think that someone who had never encountered logic or semantics might have encountered predications of truth to thinkables without encountering predications of truth to sentences; and the question *what truth is* surely concerns a concept which might feature in a language about which logicians and semanticists had never had anything to say. At a minimum, then, a philosopher who takes *truth* primarily as a property of sentences must say something about what appear to be its predication to thinkables. Although I accord priority to thinkables' truth here, I acknowledge that, when returning answers to particular philosophical questions, the application of "true" to sentences is indispensable: see section II. I acknowledge also that what appear to be predications of truth to thinkables may be treated as no such thing, as in the prosentential theory (see note 6). *Pro hac vice* I talk as if the surface appearances were sustainable.

4. In saying that the identity theorist proceeds without doubts, I do not deny that hard work has to be done to give accounts of what appears to be talk about propositions/thinkables. An identity theory of truth evidently places constraints on such accounts. See e.g. Rumfitt's (1993) account of the construction of propositions: Rumfitt's constructionalism goes hand in hand with a paratactic treatment of the logical form of sentences containing "that"-clauses; but his kind of constructionalism might be entertained outside the context of such treatment.

5. Candlish says, of what he calls a "modest" identity theory, that it is "completely uninteresting— trivial ... precisely because it has no independent conception of a fact to give content to the identity claim" (1995, 107). Candlish assesses the theory as if it had the ambitions of a definition. But what I call "the identity theory" has no such ambitions; its interest derives from what it can be seen, from what it says, to be opposed to philosophically. Candlish allows that an *im*modest ("robust") identity theory might be interesting: its interest could derive from its "independent conception of facts," independent, that is, of the conception of thinkables, or truth-bearers. For my own part, I cannot see a point in thinking that such a theory deserves the name of *identity* theory. (Here I disagree with Dodd [1995], from whom Candlish takes the robust/modest distinction. There is much about which Dodd and I agree, however: see Dodd and Hornsby [1992].) Addition to note, 1999: In the three discussion papers in *Proceedings of the Aristotelian Society* 2 (1999): 225–245, Dodd (among other things) says why he considers my position to be that of a robust theorist, Candlish (among other things) contrasts my position with Dodd's, and I respond to Dodd and Candlish. See also Dodd (2000).

6. The introduction of "identity" might seem to have the consequence of upping the ontological stakes (so that thinkables are to be treated as OBJECTS). That is not so. When we have understood, for example, "She does it in one way, and he does it in another way," we have also made sense of "They don't do it the *same* way"—but not at the expense of treating either things that are done or ways of doing them as OBJECTS. I think that hostility to propositions derives partly from Quine's assumption that all quantification is objectual or (in Quine's own sense) substitutional. This

assumption has seemed to have the consequence that unless we give a Quinean substitutional account of these "something"s, we shall be forced to treat propositions as OBJECTS, in a sense of the term caught up with a particular understanding of singular reference. But Quine's assumption is not compulsory: see e.g. Davies (1981, chap. 6, sec. 3). Some of the interest of the prosentential theory of truth, defended in Grover (1992) and Brandom (1994), derives from the directness of its challenge to Quine's assumption.

The identity theory is not formulated in order to take a stand on the logical form of predications of truth. If taken to reveal logical form, it would take an erroneous stand—the one which is contradicted by Frege's remark that "'true' is not a relative term." Comparison with Russell's Theory of Descriptions may be helpful here. In the analysis of "the" provided by Russell, the word "the" is not treated as the simple quantifier which, presumably, so far as logical form is concerned, it is. One point of giving the analysis which Russell's theory states is to show what is involved in seeing "the" as a quantifier, and to show which quantifier it is. Something analogous goes on when "identity" is introduced into an account of truth. Just as Russell's theory can present the negative semantical claim that "the" does not combine with predicates to form names, so the identity theory of truth can present its own negative metaphysical claims—claims such as emerge from seeing how the identity theory arises out of rejection of a correspondence theory.

One point of a formulation including "same" might be to draw attention to the principles of distinctness of facts presupposed to the theory: those principles cannot allow a coarser grain to facts than to thinkables. (This means that it is not a target of the so-called slingshot argument; see Neale [1995].) A naive account of facts, attractive to those who seek facts in line with a correspondence conception, might incorporate the principle: Where $a=b$, "Fb" does not express a different fact from "Fa." Such a principle, obviously, is at odds with the identity theorist's conception of facts. (In Neale's terms: "the fact that ( )=the fact that ( )" is –PSST.)

7. Frege pointed out that "with every property of a thing is joined a property of a [thinkable], namely that of truth" (1918, 20). For illustration, suppose that Fred is tall. Putting it in Frege's way, a property of Fred (being tall) is joined to a property of a thinkable: if Fred is indeed tall, then a true thinkable is put forward when Fred is said to be tall. But if this is correct, then it can seem that we should allow that *truth* can have any of the features which the property of *being tall* can have, so that if *being tall* admits of degrees (if x can be to some extent tall), then *truth* admits of degrees (it can be to some extent true that x is tall). But now it seems that Frege appreciates a characteristic of "true" which ensures that, when treated as a predicate, it will seem to admit of degrees, if any does. This makes me think that when Frege invokes the claim that what is half-true is untrue, he is relying on the thought that any *relation* introduced to account for truth cannot be a relation which admits of degrees. And that is why I say that there cannot *in any analogous way* be more or less truth.

8. Davidson used to say that a relation like Tarskian *satisfaction* could provide the language-world links sought by a correspondence theorist of truth. But Davidson now regards this as a mistake (1990, 302). It must indeed be a mistake if opposition to correspondence theories can be combined with thought about mind-independent objects.

9. See Dummett (1976, 61), in the version reprinted in Dummett (1993). A different sort of illustration may be got from Jackson, Oppy, and Smith (1994). They argue for the compatibility of

versions of non-cognitivism (in ethics, say) with minimalism about truth. They follow Michael Devitt in characterizing minimalism as holding that "terms for truth and falsity are linguistic devices for talking about reality by appending the truth predicate." Their claim then is that it might not be that any old sentence is such as to talk about reality: non-cognitivists, they say, "precisely deny that (e.g.) ethical sentences talk about reality." But someone who is opposed to correspondence theories in all their versions will not allow this "talking about reality." Suppose that Devitt had characterized minimalism by saying that truth and falsity are terms for going on talking while adding a word or two. Would Jackson et al. (1994) then have said "Non-cognitivists precisely deny that (e.g.) ethical sentences are used in talking"?

This example may serve to show how easily ideas of correspondence get in through the back door.

10. It seems worth remembering that propounding is a propositional attitude, and that Quinean hostility to propositions is hostility equally to beliefs (say). Because the opposition to certain abstract conceptions of thinkables has typically been directed against things called propositions, we find philosophers whose attitude towards beliefs and statements is one of acceptance, but towards propositions is one of rejection. (See e.g. David [1994], 12.) Of course it might be stipulated that the term "proposition" is to mean what is meant by those who use the term illicitly. But short of making such a stipulation, it will be hard to justify an attitude of hostility peculiarly to propositions.

11. Davidson 1967. I use "*definition* of truth" here as Davidson did there; and this allows me to avoid using "theory of truth" ambiguously. (It seems impossible to avoid all possible ambiguity, however. Where a theory of truth [in the only sense of that phrase I use here] purports to give a definition [as the identity theory I defend does not], it purports to give a definition of *truth*; but of course what it purports to give is not a definition of the sort Tarski showed one how to construct, which was a definition of *truth-in-L* for a particular language L.)

One makes no assumptions about Tarski's own intentions in saying that Tarski in fact showed us a way to construct a definition of truth for L that can be used to do something that a theory of meaning for L has to do. (Etchemendy [1988] has an understanding of Tarski's purpose which leads to a view of a definition of truth for a language which encourages a deflationary attitude to truth.)

12. I cannot here do more than take for granted a vast body of literature which shows the workability of definitions of truth for languages having natural languages' features. See, e.g. further papers in Davidson (1984). Davidson's idea has been endorsed by many others, of whom, in the present connection, McDowell should be mentioned; see, for example, McDowell (1976).

13. Cp. Davidson (1990, 287): "the concept of truth has essential connections with the concepts of belief and meaning"; and "what Tarski has done for us is to show in detail how to describe the kind of pattern truth must make." Davidson himself thinks that the empirical evidence we need in order to identify the pattern must avoid, in the first instance "states with (as one says) a propositional object." Davidson, then, would not be happy with the introduction of, "as one says," propositional objects (i.e. thinkables) at the outset. This explains why his objections to Paul Horwich begin at an earlier point than my own do. For his part, Davidson has a theory of verbal interpretation to elaborate: see Davidson (1990). To question the need for this would take

me too far afield. But I can try to state Davidson's view in my own terms: such a theory of verbal interpretation has to be understood from the standpoint of someone contemplating an interpretive account in order that such contemplation should ensure that a philosophically adequate conception of truth is elicited.

14. Here I am thinking of, for example, the theory which seems to be endorsed in Putnam (1981), which says that truth is an idealization of rational acceptability (see chapter 12 in this volume). In later writings (e.g. Putnam 1990), Putnam asks us to read the remarks he makes in supporting his Internal Realism as meant only to convey a picture, rather than as a theory of truth.

15. The remarks of this section are intended to go further than those of McDowell (reported in sec. I.1)—further towards showing that it is not a difficulty for the identity theory that it circumscribes the world using the notion of a thinkable. Although offered in defence of the claim that an identity theorist has a commonsensically realist conception of facts, they are not offered as a defence of any "Realism" meriting a capital "R." In defending his "Internal Realism" (see note 14), Putnam's target was "Metaphysical Realism," a doctrine which the identity theory is evidently also opposed to.

Of course it is possible to think that a defence even of commonsense realism is required: Michael Dummett has long urged this. Dummett (1990) thinks of the "tacit acquisition of the concept [of truth]" as involving "a conceptual leap … just because this is so, it is open to challenge" (200, in 1993 reprint). The leap, Dummett says, is one "we all [made] at an early stage in our acquisition of our mother tongues": it involves a transition from the "justifiability condition of an assertion to the truth-condition of the statement asserted" (198). Now Dummett's own understanding of the conceptual leap is shown in his speaking of the notion of justification as "cruder" and of truth as "more refined." But Dummett's opponent may resist any picture of the concept of truth as got from something cruder—as if there were something which might be added to justifiability to get truth, so that the child at some stage had to acquire the added extra. (The identity theorist seems bound to resist this, since she cannot allow *truth*'s applicability to be separated from *thinkability*.) Against Dummett, it may be said that the child who comes to belong to a community of speakers (a systematic account of whose uses of sentences deploy the concept of truth) is drawn into practices in which the concept already has a place. Evidently in saying this, one still does not supply the defence which Dummett seeks. But perhaps it helps to make it clear that one can reject Dummett's story about the acquisition of the concept of truth while acknowledging that truth is indeed in an obvious sense more demanding than justifiability.

16. The reader of David (1994), for example, is invited to accept a correspondence theory of truth on the basis of a demonstration of the untenability of disquotationalism. The dilemmas are sometimes well concealed. For instance, "robustness" may be taken to accrue to truth, or "factualism" to a discourse that is "truth-apt" as soon as some assumed tenet of "minimalism" is denied, and then correspondence conceptions are introduced along with talk of robustness or factualism.

17. Note, 1999: For further discussion of why the identity theory should be incompatible with a deflationary attitude toward truth, see part III (16–22) of Hornsby (1997), from which the present was got by editing and extraction: *Proceedings of the Aristotelian Society* 97 (1997): 1–24. A

"deflationary attitude" is held both by minimalists about truth like Horwich ([1990], and his paper in this volume) and by pragmatists of Rorty's sort (1995, reprinted in this volume).

References

Blackburn, S. 1984. *Spreading the Word*. Oxford: Clarendon Press.

Brandom, R. 1994. *Making It Explicit*. Cambridge, MA: Harvard University Press.

Candlish, S. 1995. "Resurrecting the Identity Theory of Truth." *Bradley Studies* 1: 116–124.

David, M. 1994. *Correspondence and Disquotation*. Oxford: Oxford University Press.

Davidson, D. 1967. "Truth and Meaning." Reprinted in Davidson 1984.

Davidson, D. 1969. "True to the Facts." Reprinted in Davidson 1984.

Davidson, D. 1984. *Inquiries into Truth and Interpretation*. Oxford: Clarendon Press.

Davidson, D. 1990. "The Structure and Content of Truth." *Journal of Philosophy* 87: 279–329.

Davies, M. 1981. *Meaning, Quantification, Necessity*. London: Routledge and Kegan Paul.

Dodd, J. 1995. "McDowell and Identity Theories of Truth." *Analysis* 55: 160–165.

Dodd, J. 2000. *An Identity Theory of Truth*. New York: St. Martin's Press.

Dodd, J., and Hornsby, J. 1992. "The Identity Theory of Truth: Reply to Baldwin." *Mind* 101: 319–322.

Dummett, M. 1976. "What Is a Theory of Meaning? II." In G. Evans and J. McDowell, eds., *Truth and Meaning: Essays in Semantics*, 67–137. Oxford: Clarendon Press.

Dummett, M. 1990. "The Source of the Concept of Truth." In G. Boolos, ed., *Meaning and Method: Essays in Honour of Hilary Putnam*, 1–16. Cambridge: Cambridge University Press. Page references are to the version reprinted in M. Dummett, *The Seas of Language*, 188–201. Oxford: Oxford University Press, 1993.

Etchemendy, J. 1988. "Tarski on Truth and Logical Consequence." *Journal of Symbolic Logic* 53: 51–79.

Frege, G. 1918. "The Thought." Quotations are taken from the translation by A. M. and M. Quinton, as reprinted in P. F. Strawson, ed., *Philosophical Logic*. Oxford: Oxford University Press, 1967.

Grover, D. 1992. *A Prosentential Theory of Truth*. Princeton, NJ: Princeton University Press.

Hornsby, J. 1997. "Truth: The Identity Theory." *Proceedings of the Aristotelian Society* 97: 1–24.

Horwich, P. 1990. *Truth*. Oxford: Blackwell.

Jackson, F., Oppy, G., and Smith, M. 1994. "Minimalism and Truth Aptness." *Mind* 103: 287–302.

McDowell, J. 1976. "Truth Conditions, Bivalence and Verificationism." In G. Evans and J. McDowell, eds., *Truth and Meaning: Essays in Semantics*, 42–66. Oxford: Clarendon Press.

McDowell, J. 1994. *Mind and World*. Cambridge, MA: Harvard University Press.

Neale, S. 1995. "The Philosophical Significance of Gödel's Slingshot." *Mind* 104: 761–825.

Putnam, H. 1981. *Reason, Truth, and History*. Cambridge: Cambridge University Press.

Putnam, H. 1990. "A Defense of Internal Realism." In *Realism with a Human Face*, 30–42. Cambridge, MA: Harvard University Press.

Quine, W. V. 1960. *Word and Object*. Cambridge, MA: MIT Press.

Quine, W. V. 1970. *Philosophy of Logic*. Englewood Cliffs, NJ: Prentice-Hall.

Rorty, R. 1995. "Is Truth a Goal of Enquiry? Davidson vs. Wright." *Philosophical Quarterly* 45: 281–300.

Rumfitt, I. 1993. "Content and Context: The Paratactic Theory Revisited and Revised." *Mind* 102: 429–454.

Russell, B. 1940. *An Inquiry into Meaning and Truth*. London: Allen and Unwin.

VII Pluralist and Replacement Theories

Introduction

Michael P. Lynch, Jeremy Wyatt, and Nathan Kellen

Even a fairly quick perusal of most of the essays in this volume can leave one with the impression that the debate over truth has reached an impasse. On one side are the substantive accounts of truth, such as correspondence, coherence, pragmatist, verificationist, primitivist, and identity theories. On the other are the many varieties of deflationism. Since both approaches are riddled with problems, one senses a stalemate.

In one way or another, all of the essays in this section discuss ways to think about truth that look beyond the traditional theories. A common thread is that the failure of familiar substantive theories of truth needn't lead to a thoroughgoing deflationism. Broadly speaking, these authors discuss two alternatives: pluralism—according to which truth has different natures in different domains—and replacement theories—according to which the concept of truth is defective and must thus be replaced with a concept, or team of concepts, that are free from its defects.

Pluralist Theories

Alethic pluralism can be briefly described as the view that there is more than one way of being true. A central motivation for this view is that it allows us to capture insights from both *realist* (e.g., correspondence) and *anti-realist* (e.g., coherence and pragmatist) theories of truth.

Pluralists typically stress that the contents of our beliefs are very diverse. We can believe all sorts of things: that two plus two equals four, that murder is wrong, that grass is green, that *Guernica* is haunting, or that it is logically impossible for God to be omnipotent. Very plausibly, our beliefs about physical objects are responsive to mind-independent, physical reality. This is the central insight of correspondence theories of truth. By contrast, it is notoriously problematic to think of, for example, arithmetic, moral, aesthetic, or modal beliefs in a similar fashion.[1]

Nevertheless, as Crispin Wright influentially argues in chapter 29, truth seems like a standard of correctness for all of our beliefs. This entails that all of our beliefs are subject to a uniform standard of normative assessment. As Michael Lynch points out, this fact looks to present us with an important task: to develop a theory of truth that acknowledges our beliefs' *semantic diversity* as well as their *cognitive unity*.

The basic pluralist suggestion at this stage is straightforward: rather than taking correspondence to be the nature of truth in all domains, we should allow that truth in some domains—for example, the mathematical or moral domains—has a nature closer to what the pragmatists and the coherence theorists have traditionally taken it to be. In short, the nature of truth is correspondence in some domains but not in all.

In their respective contributions, the leading pluralists Crispin Wright and Michael P. Lynch (chapter 30) frame their theories by drawing a firm distinction between the *concept* of truth and the *property*, or properties, that are picked out by this concept. Wright and Lynch characterize the concept of truth using a body of *platitudes*, or *truisms* about truth—for example, "To assert is to present as true" (Wright) and "True propositions are those that are correct to believe" (Lynch).

As Wright puts the idea, the pluralist, like the deflationist, adopts a *minimalist* view of the concept of truth according to which this concept can be fully characterized by way of platitudes about truth. When comparing his view to Wright's, Lynch suggests that both he and Wright take the concept of truth to be a *functional* concept. In doing so, they hold that the basic platitudes about truth specify a particular functional role—the *truth-role*.

By contrast, both Wright and Lynch take the properties that are picked out by the concept of truth—that is, the properties that play the truth-role—to be quite substantial. Wright devotes much of his rich discussion to the question of how best to capture the spirit of the pragmatist conception of truth. After discussing and ultimately rejecting Putnam's version of that view, Wright suggests that the basic insight behind pragmatism can be captured by the idea of *superassertibility*. In essence, a proposition is superassertible just when it is enduringly justified. That is, a superassertible proposition is one whose justification is never defeated or overridden by future evidence.

Wright argues that with respect to certain domains of discourse, superassertibility satisfies the various platitudes that constitute our analytical theory of truth. In particular, he proposes that superassertibility may constitute truth in any discourse where it is a priori that all the truths of that discourse are knowable. Moral and comic discourse, according to Wright, are possible examples of discourses of this kind. It then follows that in some discourses truth needn't be understood in terms of a relation between statements and objects. Moral truth, for example, can be understood as an epistemic property of moral statements.

Lynch and Douglas Edwards (chapter 31) present two different ways of sharpening the basic pluralist picture. In his contribution, Lynch raises three distinct questions, which he claims that any pluralist theory must answer:

(1) How do we identify the properties by virtue of which propositions are true?

(2) How are these properties related to the property of truth itself?

(3) What determines which of these properties a proposition must have in order to be true?

The view that emerges from Lynch's answers to these questions is often called *manifestation functionalism*. This view has it that the properties by virtue of which propositions are true are the properties that play the truth-role. These properties have the features that are mentioned in the platitudes about truth, which Lynch calls the *truish features*. The property of truth itself is distinguished by the fact that it is the only such property that has the truish features *essentially*, rather than accidentally. Moreover, two features of a given proposition determine which of these properties it must have in order to be true—its logical structure and its subject matter.

Edwards's guiding insight is an analogy between truth and winning that first emerges in the work of Michael Dummett (chapter 11 in this volume). Following Dummett, Edwards suggests that truth is analogous to winning: just as the aim of believing is to believe what's true, the aim of a game is to win. However, he points out that what it is to win looks to differ from game to game (e.g., chess and baseball). Similarly, he contends, what it is to be true differs from domain to domain. Using this comparison between truth and winning, Edwards articulates what he takes to be an attractively simplified variety of alethic pluralism. A central component of this view is the relation that Edwards calls *determination*. This relation is meant to link the property of truth itself to what Edwards calls the *truth-determining properties*.

Lynch and Edwards (as well as Wright, on one interpretation; though cf. the proposal in Wright [2013]) represent what is often called *moderate alethic pluralism*. Moderate pluralists, like traditional theorists of truth, hold that there is a single, generic property of truth that is exemplified by all true propositions, regardless of their domain. Lynch, for instance, holds that this single, generic property is the property that has the truish features essentially.

Filippo Ferrari, Sebastiano Moruzzi, and Nikolaj Jang Lee Linding Pedersen (chapter 32) reject moderate pluralism in favor of an alternative approach that is standardly called *strong alethic pluralism*. The strong pluralist parts company with the moderate pluralist in holding that as a matter of fact, there is no generic truth property. Instead, strong pluralists maintain that there is a plurality of properties that reduce or constitute truth only within particular domains.

It's often thought that strong pluralism founders on problems related to *mixed discourse*, including the problems of *mixed compounds* and *mixed inferences*.[2] Regarding the former, the basic worry is that if there is no generic truth property that is exemplified by all true propositions, then it's not clear how we could legitimately say, for example, that a mixed conjunction like "Two plus two equals four and murder is wrong" is true. Regarding the latter, the worry is that unless we can appeal to such a generic truth property, we'll be unable to explain why a mixed inference such as the following is valid:[3]

(1) Wet cats are funny.

(2) This cat is wet.

(3) Therefore, this cat is funny.

In defense of strong pluralism, Ferrari, Moruzzi, and Pedersen offer new responses to these challenges that are embedded within a version of strong pluralism that they call *austere pluralism*.

The eminent philosopher Simon Blackburn (chapter 33) investigates alethic pluralism by situating the view within the history of philosophy and raising an important objection against it.[4] Like the pluralist, Blackburn sees the need to account for the semantic diversity and cognitive unity of our beliefs and other cognitive states. However, he maintains that we don't need to endorse alethic pluralism to do so. According to Blackburn, the pluralist is guilty of *double-counting* insofar as they take both content and truth to come in a variety of forms. Instead, Blackburn argues, we can capture the diversity of our thought in terms of differences in content and attitude alone. When accounting for the cognitive unity of our thought, Blackburn maintains that we needn't go beyond the sort of deflationism that is championed by Paul Horwich.

Replacement Theories

Pluralism represents one way to move beyond traditional debates about truth. Kevin Scharp (chapter 34) defends a rather different alternative, which is often called a *replacement theory* of truth. Scharp's views on truth are motivated primarily by the semantic paradoxes, including Yablo's paradox, Curry's paradox, and the Liar paradox. The Liar paradox, for example, arises because of sentences like:

(L) This sentence is false.

Assuming classical logic and the validity of the following two principles, it is straightforward to derive a contradiction from (L):[5]

(T-In) If ϕ, then "ϕ" is true.

(T-Out) If "ϕ" is true, then ϕ.

To address the Liar, one might argue that English (or the relevant fragment thereof) is governed by a subclassical logic in which the Liar reasoning is invalid.[6] Or one might argue that (L) is somehow defective and hence unsuitable for use in reasoning, or even that (L) is context-sensitive in a way that blocks the Liar reasoning.[7]

Scharp rejects all of these familiar strategies and a number of others besides. Rather, he retains classical logic and maintains that (T-In) and (T-Out) are constitutive principles of the concept TRUTH. He accordingly contends that TRUTH is an inconsistent concept in that some of its constitutive principles—namely, (T-In) and (T-Out)—have untrue instances.[8] Because TRUTH is an inconsistent concept, says Scharp, we shouldn't rely on TRUTH in theoretical contexts—for example, when offering theories of meaning for natural languages. Rather, we should rely on a pair of successor concepts ASCENDING TRUTH and DESCENDING TRUTH that are governed, respectively, by analogues of (T-In) and (T-Out):

(AT) If ϕ, then "ϕ" is ascending true.

(DT) If "ϕ" is descending true, then ϕ.

To use a familiar metaphor, the problem with TRUTH, for Scharp, is that it allows us to climb both up and down Ramsey's ladder—to infer "ϕ" from "'ϕ' is true," and vice versa. To avoid paradox-generated contradiction, we must discard Ramsey's ladder and rest content with an ascending escalator and a descending escalator. The former allows us only to semantically ascend from "ϕ" to "'ϕ' is true," while the latter allows us only to semantically descend from "'ϕ' is true" to "ϕ."

Scharp's replacement theory, as developed in chapter 34, is similar, in interesting ways, to both pluralist and deflationary theories of truth. One of Scharp's ambitions in his essay is to investigate whether there is any property *truth*. In doing so, he draws on what he describes as 12 "logical platitudes" about truth, which include (T-In) and (T-Out). Insofar as he relies on platitudes about truth, Scharp's methodology is notably similar to that of pluralists such as Wright, Lynch, Edwards, and Ferrari, Moruzzi, and Pedersen.

Scharp goes on to observe that no property satisfies all of these logical platitudes. He also argues that while there are properties that satisfy some of them, none is very similar to what we would ordinarily regard as the property *truth*. In light of these considerations, Scharp concludes that there simply is no property *truth*. This result is good news for strong pluralists since they deny that there is a generic truth property. Unlike strong pluralists, however, Scharp doesn't commit to domain-specific truth properties. This result should also be welcomed by deflationists such as Ayer, Brandom, Grover, Quine, and certain time slices of Ramsey and Strawson, as they also maintain that there is no such property as *truth*.

Finally, in his critique of replacement theories, Alexis Burgess (chapter 35) argues against the idea that we need to give up on the concept of truth. Burgess is willing to grant, for the sake of argument, that our concept of truth (as well as related concepts like the concept of reference) is inconsistent. However, he resists Scharp's conclusion that we must therefore replace this concept. Instead, Burgess uses a metasemantic principle that he finds in the work of Matti Eklund to argue that our ordinary concept of truth is suitable to use in both theoretical and ordinary contexts. In defending this argument, Burgess draws inventively on David Lewis's response to Putnam's model-theoretic argument as well as mathematical work on the semantic paradoxes.

Notes

1. This gives rise to what Lynch (2009, chap. 2) calls the *scope problem* for correspondence theories of truth.

2. The literature on alethic pluralism and mixed discourse is rather extensive. Touchstones include Tappolet (1997, 2000); Beall (2000); Sher (2005); Pedersen (2006); Edwards (2008, 2009); Cotnoir (2009); Lynch (2009); Cotnoir (2013); Wyatt (2013); Yu (2017); Kim and Pedersen (2018); and Gamester (2019).

3. This example is due to Tappolet (1997, 209).

4. This objection is importantly similar to what is often called the *Quine-Sainsbury objection*: see Pedersen and Wright (2018, sec. 4.2). See also Williamson (1994, sec. 5); Sainsbury (1996); Haack (2005, 2008, 2014); Azzouni (2010, chap. 4); Smith (2010); Dodd (2013); Asay (2018); and Blackburn (chapter 33 in this volume). For a response to Blackburn's objection, see Lynch (2018).

5. For additional discussion of the Liar paradox, see the introductions to Parts IV and V and the references therein.

6. See Priest (2006a, 2006b); Field (2008); Beall (2009).

7. See Glanzberg (2001, 2004); Berk (2004); Shapiro (2006); and Simmons (2007).

8. Cf. the inconsistency theories defended by Badici and Ludwig (2007); Eklund (2007); Patterson (2009); and Burgess (2018).

Further Reading

Pluralist Theories

Asay, J. 2018. "Putting Pluralism in Its Place." *Philosophy and Phenomenological Research* 96: 175–191.

Azzouni, J. 2010. *Talking about Nothing: Numbers, Hallucinations, and Fictions*. Oxford: Oxford University Press.

Barnard, R., and Horgan, T. 2013. "The Synthetic Unity of Truth." In Pedersen and Wright 2013, 180–196.

Beall, Jc. 2000. "On Mixed Inferences and Pluralism about Truth Predicates." *Philosophical Quarterly* 50: 380–382.

Beall, Jc. 2009. *Spandrels of Truth*. Oxford: Oxford University Press.

Brons, L. 2018. "Wang Chong, Truth, and Quasi-pluralism and Postscript: Reply to McLeod." In Mou 2018a, 341–370.

Cotnoir, A. 2009. "Generic Truth and Mixed Conjunctions: Some Alternatives." *Analysis* 63: 473–479.

Cotnoir, A. 2013. "Validity for Strong Pluralists." *Philosophy and Phenomenological Research* 83: 563–579.

Cotnoir, A., and Edwards, D. 2015. "From Truth Pluralism to Ontological Pluralism and Back." *Journal of Philosophy* 112: 113–140.

Dodd, J. 2013. "Deflationism Trumps Pluralism!" In Pedersen and Wright 2013, 298–322.

Edwards, D. 2008. "How to Solve the Problem of Mixed Conjunctions." *Analysis* 68: 143–149.

Edwards, D. 2009. "Truth-Conditions and the Nature of Truth: Re-solving Mixed Conjunctions." *Analysis* 69(4): 684–688.

Edwards, D. 2018. *The Metaphysics of Truth*. Oxford, Oxford University Press.

Edwards, D. n.d. "Pluralist Theories of Truth." *Internet Encyclopedia of Philosophy*. https://www.iep .utm.edu/plur-tru/.

Engel, P. 2013. "Alethic Functionalism and the Norm of Belief." In Pedersen and Wright 2013, 69–86.

Ferrari, F. 2018. "Normative Alethic Pluralism." In Wyatt, Pedersen, and Kellen 2018, 145–168.

Ferrari, F., and Moruzzi, S. 2018. "Ecumenical Alethic Pluralism." *Canadian Journal of Philosophy* 49(3): 368–393.

Gamester, W. 2019. "Logic, Logical Form, and the Disunity of Truth." *Analysis* 79(1): 34–43.

Haack, S. 2005. "The Unity of Truth and the Plurality of Truths." *Principia* 9: 87–110. Reprinted as chap. 3 of S. Haack, *Putting Philosophy to Work*. Amherst, NY: Prometheus Books, 2013.

Haack, S. 2008. "The Whole Truth and Nothing but the Truth." *Midwest Studies in Philosophy* 32(1): 20–35.

Haack, S. 2014. "Nothing Fancy: Some Simple Truths about Truth in the Law." In *Evidence Matters*, chap. 12. Cambridge: Cambridge University Press.

Horgan, T., and Barnard, R. 2006. "Truth as Mediated Correspondence." *The Monist* 89: 31–50.

Kim, S., and Pedersen, N. 2018. "Strong Truth Pluralism." In Wyatt, Pedersen, and Kellen 2018, 107–130.

Lynch, M. 2009. *Truth as One and Many*. Oxford: Oxford University Press.

Lynch, M. 2018. "Truth Pluralism, Quasi-realism and the Problem of Double-Counting." In Wyatt, Pedersen, and Kellen 2018, 63–84.

McLeod, A. 2018. "Pluralism about Truth in Early Chinese Philosophy: A Reflection on Wang Chong's Approach and Appendix: Replies to Brons and Mou on Wang Chong and Pluralism." In Mou 2018a, 295–340.

Mou, B. 2018a. *Philosophy of Language, Chinese Language, Chinese Philosophy: Constructive Engagement*. Leiden: Brill.

Mou, B. 2018b. "Rooted and Rootless Pluralist Approaches to Truth: Two Distinct Interpretations of Wang Chong's Account and Postscript: Normative Character of Semantic Truth." In Mou 2018a, 371–399.

Mou, B. 2019. *Semantic-Truth Approaches in Chinese Philosophy: A Unifying Pluralist Account.* Lanham, MD: Lexington Books.

Pedersen, N. 2006. "What Can the Problem of Mixed Inferences Teach Us about Alethic Pluralism?" *The Monist* 89: 103–117.

Pedersen, N. 2010. "Stabilizing Alethic Pluralism." *Philosophical Quarterly* 60: 92–108.

Pedersen, N. 2012. "Recent Work on Alethic Pluralism." *Analysis* 72: 588–607.

Pedersen, N. 2014. "Pluralism×3: Truth, Logic, Metaphysics." *Erkenntnis* 79: 259–277.

Pedersen, N., and Lynch, M. P. 2018. "Truth Pluralism." In M. Glanzberg, ed., *The Oxford Handbook of Truth*, 543–575. Oxford: Oxford University Press.

Pedersen, N., and Wright, C. D., eds. 2013. *Truth and Pluralism: Current Debates.* New York: Oxford University Press.

Pedersen, N., and Wright, C. D. 2018. "Pluralist Theories of Truth." *Stanford Encyclopedia of Philosophy.* https://plato.stanford.edu/entries/truth-pluralist/.

Sainsbury, M. 1996. "Crispin Wright: Truth and Objectivity." *Philosophy and Phenomenological Research* 56(4): 899–904.

Sher, G. 2005. "Functional Pluralism." *Philosophical Books* 46: 311–330.

Sher, G. 2016. *Epistemic Friction: An Essay on Knowledge, Truth, and Logic.* Oxford: Oxford University Press.

Smith, N. J. J. 2010. "Review of *Truth as One and Many*." *Analysis* 70(1): 191–193.

Tappolet, C. 1997. "Mixed Inferences: A Problem for Pluralism about Truth Predicates." *Analysis* 57: 209–210.

Tappolet, C. 2000. "Truth Pluralism and Many-Valued Logics: A Reply to Beall." *Philosophical Quarterly* 50: 382–385.

Ulatowski, J. 2017. *Commonsense Pluralism about Truth: An Empirical Defence.* London: Palgrave Macmillan.

Williamson, T. 1994. "A Critical Study of *Truth and Objectivity*." *International Journal of Philosophical Studies* 30: 130–144.

Wright, C. 1992. *Truth and Objectivity.* Cambridge, MA: Harvard University Press.

Wright, C. 2013. "A Plurality of Pluralisms." In Pedersen and Wright 2013, 123–153.

Wright, C. D. 2005. "On the Functionalization of Pluralist Approaches to Truth." *Synthese* 145: 1–28.

Wright, C. D. 2010. "Truth, Ramsification, and the Pluralist's Revenge." *Australasian Journal of Philosophy* 88: 265–283.

Wright, C. D. 2012. "Is Pluralism about Truth Inherently Unstable?" *Philosophical Studies* 159: 89–105.

Wright, C. D., and Pedersen, N. J. L. L., eds. 2010. *New Waves in Truth*. New York: Palgrave Macmillan.

Wyatt, J. 2013. "Domains, Plural Truth, and Mixed Atomic Propositions." *Philosophical Studies* 166: 255–236.

Wyatt, J. 2018. "Truth in English and Elsewhere: An Empirically-Informed Functionalism." In Wyatt, Pedersen, and Kellen 2018, 169–196.

Wyatt, J., Pedersen, N. J. L. L., and Kellen, N., eds. 2018. *Pluralisms in Truth and Logic*. London: Palgrave Macmillan.

Yu, A. 2017. "Logic for Alethic Pluralists." *Journal of Philosophy* 114: 277–302.

Replacement Theories

Bacon, A. 2019. "Scharp on Replacing Truth." *Inquiry* 62(4): 370–386.

Badici, E., and Ludwig, K. 2007. "The Concept of Truth and the Semantics of the Truth Predicate." *Inquiry* 50: 622–638.

Beall, Jc, Glanzberg, M., and Ripley, D. 2018. *Formal Theories of Truth*, chap. 8. Oxford: Oxford University Press.

Berk, L. 2004. "The Liar, Context, and Logical Form." *Journal of Logic, Language, and Information* 13(3): 267–286.

Burgess, A. 2018. "Truth in Fictionalism." In M. Glanzberg, ed., *The Oxford Handbook of Truth*, 503–516. Oxford: Oxford University Press.

Eklund, M. 2007. "Meaning-Constitutivity." *Inquiry* 50(6): 559–574.

Eklund, M. 2019. "Inconsistency and Replacement." *Inquiry* 62(4): 387–402.

Field, H. 2008. *Saving Truth from Paradox*. Oxford: Oxford University Press.

Glanzberg, M. 2001. "The Liar in Context." *Philosophical Studies* 103: 217–251.

Glanzberg, M. 2004. "A Contextual-Hierarchical Approach to Truth and the Liar Paradox." *Journal of Philosophical Logic* 33(1): 27–88.

Greenough, P. 2019. "Conceptual Marxism and Truth." *Inquiry* 62(4): 403–421.

Patterson, D. 2009. "Inconsistency Theories of Semantic Paradox." *Philosophy and Phenomenological Research* 79: 387–422.

Pinder, M. 2019. "Scharp on Inconsistent Concepts and Their Engineered Replacements, or: Can We Mend These Broken Things?" *Inquiry*. https://doi.org/10.1080/0020174X.2019.1688181.

Priest, G. 2006a. *Doubt Truth to Be a Liar.* Oxford: Oxford University Press.

Priest, G. 2006b. *In Contradiction: A Study of the Transconsistent.* 2nd ed. Oxford: Oxford University Press.

Ripley, D. 2014. "Replacing Truth." *Notre Dame Philosophical Reviews.* http://ndpr.nd.edu/news /48851-replacing-truth/.

Scharp, K. 2013. *Replacing Truth.* Oxford: Oxford University Press.

Scharp, K. 2019. "Replies to Bacon, Eklund, and Greenough on *Replacing Truth.*" *Inquiry* 62(4): 422–475.

Shapiro, L. 2006. "The Rationale behind Revision-Rule Semantics." *Philosophical Studies* 129(3): 477–515.

Simmons, K. 2007. "Revenge and Context." In Jc Beall, ed., *Revenge of the Liar,* 345–367. Oxford: Oxford University Press.

29 Minimalism, Deflationism, Pragmatism, Pluralism

Crispin Wright

1 Minimalism and Deflationism: An Overview

Deflationists have offered views about truth differing significantly in detail. But they characteristically maintain that as far as philosophy is concerned, there is nothing to say about truth that is not captured by a suitably generalized form of one (or both) of the following two schemata:

(ES) It is true that P iff P.

(DS) "P" is true iff P.

And they maintain that this point in turn entails deflation—that the traditional metaphysical debates about truth, as well as more recent ones, are about nothing substantial.

It is worth noting that these are separable claims. Someone could allow that the two schemata—the Equivalence Schema (ES), for propositions, and the Disquotational Schema (DS), for sentences—are each a priori correct[1] and (together) somehow fully encapsulate all proper uses of the truth predicate without conceding that (it follows therefrom that) truth is somehow not a proper object of further philosophical enquiry, that no further metaphysical or semantic issues arise. Conversely, someone broadly in agreement with the antimetaphysical spirit of deflationism might hold that a correct characterization of the use of the truth predicate demands something more complicated than the two schemata.

The minimalist view about truth that I here defend rejects each of these deflationist claims, contending both that the two schemata are insufficient to capture all that should properly be reckoned as belonging to the concept of truth and that the antimetaphysical message of deflationism, globally applied, represents a philosophical mistake.[2] Still, there are points of affinity between minimalism and deflationism. Minimalism agrees that, as far as the *conceptual* analysis of truth is concerned, matters should proceed by reference to a set of basic a priori principles in which (ES) and (DS) are preeminent candidates for inclusion and agrees, too, that aptitude for truth and falsity goes with surface assertoric content and is not the kind of deep property that, for instance, expressivist views about moral judgment standardly take it to be. However, minimalism rejects the idea that the analysis of the concept of truth exhausts the philosophy of truth: rather, even if the *concept* may be fully characterized by reference to certain basic a priori principles concerning it, the question of which *property* or *properties* of propositions, or sentences, realize the concept can still sensibly be raised for every discourse in which truth has application. Not that an answer to this question has necessarily to provide an identification of truth in the form "*x* is true iff *x* is *F*." Minimalism only requires that each discourse that deals in truth-apt claims is associated with such a property whose character need not be fully determinable just from the list of basic principles serving to characterize the concept but which, relative to the discourse in question, serves as truth by dint of satisfying those principles. The fuller characterization of this property will depend on specific features of the particular discourse, and it will ultimately depend on these features whether or not the relevant truth property can be explicitly identified by, for instance, a biconditional of the type above.[3]

Minimalism thus incorporates a potential *pluralism* about truth, in the specific sense that what property serves as truth may vary from discourse to discourse. And it is this point which allows it to provide hospitality for the discussion of metaphysical—realist or antirealist—ideas that have fuelled those other traditional conceptions of truth that deflationists sought to undermine from the start. This potential pluralism is itself in opposition to the more traditional positions, insofar as they claim to uncover *the* universal nature of truth, something common to all truth-apt discourse. But it can still allow that some regions of discourse may be subject to a truth property congenial to broadly realist thinking about them, while in other regions the character of the truth property may be more congenial to antirealism.

All this may seem to suggest that the key difference between minimalism and deflationism resides in the fact that while the latter concedes the significance of the predicate "true" and hence grants that there is a discussible *concept* of truth, it holds—in contrast to minimalism—that there is no *property* of truth: no property that all truths in a given area have in common.[4] This view of the matter would be encouraged by some of the literature in the field, but it is not the happiest way of putting the differences. For once the currency of a concept of truth is granted, it ought to be allowed that all truths have at least the following property in common: the property of falling under this concept.[5] No doubt this move may not illustrate the most natural or fruitful way of conceiving the relationship between concepts and their associated properties in general. But, for all that, it would be misleading to suggest that (most) deflationists would embrace the view that "Coal is black" and "Snow is white" have no more in common than do coal and snow.

The real distinction, then, between minimalism and deflationism in respect of the issue whether truth is a property is not that deflationism cannot consistently allow that it is, but rather that minimalism allows more: precisely, that the character of the property may not be transparent from the analysis of the concept. So in this respect there is a rough analogy with the relationship—to have recourse to a tired but useful example—between the concept of water and the property (that of being composed of H_2O molecules, I suppose) that it denotes. Not that minimalism suggests that it should comparably be an a posteriori matter what property truth (locally) is. It will be a matter for further *conceptual* reflection—of a sort I will try to illustrate in the sequel—what (kind of) property best fulfills (locally) the role circumscribed by the concept. (That is why the water analogy is imperfect.)

This kind of substantial distinction between a concept, *F*, and the property it denotes, being *F*, is called for whenever we stand in need of some sort of general explanation of a characteristic of items that are F that cannot be elicited solely from materials directly implicated in those items falling under the concept in question.[6] To take a simple instance, suppose, to pursue the tired example, that the concept of water is a natural-kind concept after the fashion of Putnam's well-known paradigm: that it is, for example, given as the concept of that colorless, odorless, tasteless liquid that is typically found in lakes and rivers, assuages thirst, and so on. If we allow that it makes good sense to ask *why* water typically presents with the surface features mentioned in its concept, we accept that there is a good explanatory question that cannot, obviously, be answered by appeal to water's falling under its concept, since we are asking for an explanation of the very features involved in its so doing. To allow the legitimacy of the question thus involves conceiving of whatever makes water what it is as distanced from the characteristics presented in its concept—as something that can potentially be invoked in explaining their habit of co-occurrence. But what makes water what it is is just its having the property of being water.

Now, it is plausible enough that there are no such explanations that might be given by appeal to the "thin" truth property that we envisaged the deflationist as admitting—the property of *falling under the concept of truth*—that we could not equally well give by appeal to the concept of truth itself. What the minimalist should claim, accordingly, in contradistinction to the deflationist, is that there *are* certain legitimate explanatory burdens that can be discharged only if we appeal to a property (or properties) of truth conceived in a more substantial sense of "property."[7] And note that this claim can be true—in contrast with the situation of the kinds of explanation that might be given by appeal to the property of being water—even if truth, locally or globally, admits of no naturalistic (physicalistic) reduction. (It all depends on whether the things that need explaining are themselves so reducible.) As we shall see in due course, however, the minimalist's argument has no connection with the question of the feasibility of any such reduction.[8]

2   The Inflationary Argument

The inflationary argument is to the effect that the legitimacy of thinking of truth, in any particular discourse, as substantial in a fashion deflationism cannot accept, is already guaranteed by the very principles characterizing the concept of truth to which deflationism gives centre stage—at least when they are taken in conjunction with certain further uncontroversial principles. Thus minimalism does not just go beyond what deflationism allows but contends in addition that deflationism is incoherent: that, in coupling the thesis that (ES) and/or (DS) yield(s) a complete account of truth with the contention that truth is a property only in the etiolated sense we have just reviewed, its proponents withdraw with one hand what they just tabled with the other.

   We begin with the observation that truth-apt contents, or sentences expressing such contents, demand a distinction between circumstances under which asserting them is warranted and those under which it is not. And competent thought and talk requires an ability to tell the difference: I need to be able to tell which assertions I am warranted in making in a given state of information and which I am not. So if I am warranted in asserting P, that fact will be recognizable to me, and I will thereby be warranted in claiming that I am so warranted. Conversely, if I am warranted in thinking that the assertion of P is warranted, I will be beyond relevant—that is, epistemic—reproach if I go on to assert it. But that is to say that I will be warranted in doing so. We accordingly obtain:

> There is warrant for thinking that [it is warrantedly assertible that P] iff there is warrant for thinking that [P].

Given the Equivalence Schema, this will in turn yield:

> There is warrant for thinking that [it is warrantedly assertible that P] iff there is warrant for thinking that [it is true that P].

And now, since warranted assertibility is, in a perfectly trivial sense, a normative property—a property possession or lack of which determines which assertions are acceptable and which are not—it follows that truth is too. For by the above equivalence, to be warranted in thinking that P is true has exactly the same normative payload as being warranted in thinking that it is warrantedly assertible. Moreover, our finding is that truth, as characterized by the schemata, and warranted assertibility *coincide in positive normative force*.

   That is hardly a startling finding. But the relevant point is not the result itself but its provenance: that truth's being normative in the fashion noted is not merely plausible anyway but is a consequence of what ought to be uncontroversial considerations about the concept of assertibility and a central tenet of deflationism: the conceptual necessity of the Equivalence Schema. However, given only the further assumption that any

P apt for truth has a significant negation that is likewise apt for truth, the Equivalence Schema will also entail any instance of the following *Negation Equivalence*:[9]

(NE) It is true that [not-*P*] iff it is not true that [*P*].

And this shows that, coincident in positive normative force though they may be, we cannot in general *identify* truth and warrant. For most propositions about most subject matters allow of neutral states of information: states of information in which there are neither warrants for asserting *P* nor for asserting its negation. In any such case, an invalid schema results if we substitute "is warrantedly assertible" for "is true" in (NE). More specifically, if the propositions that make up the substitution class for *P* allow in principle of neutral states of information, the following conditional is *not* valid:

It is warrantedly assertible that [not-*P*] if it is not warrantedly assertible that [*P*].

Thus, we can already conclude from (NE), and hence from (ES), that truth and warranted assertibility, even if coinciding in positive normative force, are *potentially divergent in extension*.[10]

It is an immediate consequence of this observation that for any assertoric practice that allows the definition, on the contents of the moves it permits, of a truth property satisfying (ES)—that is, for any assertoric practice whatever—there must be a further kind of distinction between circumstances in which making these moves is in good standing and circumstances in which it is not—a distinction that need not coincide with the distinction between circumstances in which such a move can warrantedly be made and those in which it cannot. The concept of truth as characterized by (ES) precisely calls for a norm—a way an assertion may be in good standing—which warrant is essentially warrant to suppose satisfied but which, because of the point about potential extensional divergence, may nevertheless not be satisfied when an assertion is warranted (or may be satisfied when it is not). And a fully intelligent participation in such practices will involve grasping that they essentially involve submission to a standard the meeting of which need not just be a matter of possessing warrants for the claim that it is met.

Minimalism now claims that these facts about assertoric practices stand in need of explanation. In particular, it maintains that it needs to be explained what this further norm of correctness amounts to in such a way that it becomes clear how it and warranted assertibility, although potentially divergent in extension, coincide in normative force: how it can be that warrant is essentially warrant to think that this other norm is satisfied when there is no guarantee that they are always *co*-satisfied. And such an explanation, it is contended, while it will have to do much more than this, must at least begin by finding something for the truth of a proposition to consist in, a property that it can intelligibly have although there may currently be no reason to suppose that it has it, or may intelligibly lack even though there is reason to think that it has it.

Warrant can then be required to be whatever gives a (defeasible) reason to think that a proposition has that property.

The deflationist account of truth would appear, however, to have no resources to give such an explanation. For all we can elicit from the Equivalence Schema is the *problem*. The point of the inflationary argument is precisely that the basic principles on which deflationism builds its account spawn the concept of a norm—a way a proposition can be in good or bad standing, as I put it a moment ago—that contrasts with its current evidential status. But these principles keep silence when the question is raised, What does the satisfaction or nonsatisfaction of this new norm consist in, and how can it fail to be a substantial property?

So at any rate the inflationary argument contends. But the deflationist is likely to believe that she has a good response. "There is no silence on the point," she will reply. "On the contrary, my theory is very explicit about what the satisfaction of your 'norm' consists in. The proposition that snow is white satisfies it just if snow is white; the proposition that grass is green satisfies it just if grass is green, the proposition that there is no life on Mars satisfies it just if there is no life on Mars ..." However, this response is, of course, to no avail unless we *already* understand the difference between the proposition, for example, that there is no life on Mars and the proposition that that proposition is warranted. And clearly this distinction cannot be recovered from any contrast between the circumstances under which the two propositions are *respectively* warranted, since—as in effect noted right at the start of the argument—there is none.

The difference between them resides, rather, precisely in a difference in correctness conditions of another sort (whisper: *truth* conditions): in order to understand the contrast between the two propositions, I precisely have to understand that the former is in principle hostage to a kind of failure that can occur even when it is warranted, and that will not then affect the latter. So the debate is rapidly brought back to the point before the deflationist made her putative "good response," with the minimalist charging her to explain (i) how the relevant contrast can so much as exist unless there is something substantial in which such failure—or more happily, success—consists, and (ii) how a *grasp* of the contrast can anywhere be possible unless we are familiar with a (perhaps local) property that behaves as the concept characterized by the basic principles demands.

The kind of move we just envisaged a deflationist making is, of course, pure deflationist stock-in-trade. Supporters of deflationism characteristically view the whole debate as turning on whether it can be shown that all legitimate uses of the word "true" can somehow be explained on the basis of the Equivalence Schema (and/or the Disquotational Schema) together with a repertoire of contexts free of "true" and its cognates, and they put all their effort and (often considerable) ingenuity into the attempt to show that these uses can be so explained.[11] But success in this project is entirely beside the point if the contents of the relevant "true"-free contexts, to which deflationists simply help themselves, cannot be explicated by construing them merely as subject to norms of assertibility but demand an additional truthlike constraint. Deducing some aspect of our use of the predicate "true" by appeal just to the Equivalence Schema and certain "true"-free contexts cannot just be assumed to have reductive significance without further ado. The initial position in the debate is one in which nothing yet stands against the opposed thought that, instead of reading the Equivalence Schema from left to right, as if to eliminate the truth property, we should read it from right to left, as highlighting the fact that, implicit in any content in the range of "P," there is already a tacit invocation of the norm of truth. Deflationism needs to get to grips with this reading: to make a case that no implicit prior grasp of the concept of truth, nor implicit reference to a property that the concept denotes, lurks buried in the materials to which its "explanations" appeal. The thrust of the inflationary argument is that no such convincing case can be made—that whether or not we can somehow eliminate or otherwise "deflate" the *word*, a corresponding property, and its contrast with assertibility, is part and parcel of assertoric content itself.[12]

3   Pragmatism and Pluralism (I): Peirce and Putnam

Let me now be a little more explicit about how minimalism opens up prospects for a pluralistic conception of truth. Above, I spoke approvingly of the idea, of which the deflationist proposals can be seen as one example, that as far as the conceptual analysis of truth is concerned, matters should proceed by reference to a set of basic a priori principles variously configuring or bearing on the concept. Many philosophers, from Frege to Davidson, have, of course, doubted whether truth allows of any illuminating philosophical analysis. But their skepticism has been driven largely by the traditional notion that success in this project would have to consist in the provision of a satisfactory necessary-and-sufficient-conditions analysis of the concept, and there is clearly some scope for relaxation of that model. After all, such a necessary-and-sufficient-conditions analysis, even if it could be provided, would only culminate in one particular a priori—presumably, conceptually necessary—claim. Why should not other such claims—even if not biconditional or identity claims—provide illumination of essentially the same kind? To be sure, if one wants a priori conceptual clarity about what truth—or beauty, or goodness, etc.—is, then the natural target is an identity (or a biconditional). But perhaps the sought-for reflective illumination can be equally well— if less directly—provided by the assembly of a body of conceptual truths that, without providing any reductive account, nevertheless collectively constrain and locate the target concept and sufficiently characterize some of its relations with other concepts and its role and purposes.

What should such principles be for the case of truth? The method here should be initially to compile a list, including anything that chimes with ordinary a priori thinking about truth—what I shall call a *platitude*—and later to scrutinize more rigorously for deductive articulation and for whether candidates do indeed have the right kind of conceptual plausibility. So we might begin by including, for instance,

- the transparency of truth—that to assert is to present as true and, more generally, that any attitude to a proposition is an attitude to its truth—that to believe, doubt, or fear, for example, that *P* is to believe, doubt, or fear that *P* is true. (*Transparency*)

- the epistemic opacity of truth—incorporating a variety of weaker and stronger principles: that a thinker may be so situated that a particular truth is beyond her ken, that some truths may never be known, that some truths may be unknowable in principle, etc.[13] (*Opacity*)

- the conservation of truth-aptitude under embedding: aptitude for truth is preserved under a variety of operations—in particular, truth-apt propositions have negations, conjunctions, disjunctions, etc., which are likewise truth-apt. (*Embedding*)

- the Correspondence Platitude—for a proposition to be true is for it to correspond to reality, accurately reflect how matters stand, "tell it like it is," etc. (*Correspondence*)

- the contrast of truth with justification—a proposition may be true without being justified, and vice versa. (*Contrast*)

- the timelessness of truth—if a proposition is ever true, then it always is, so that whatever may, at any particular time, be truly asserted may—perhaps by appropriate transformations of mood or tense—be truly asserted at any time. (*Stability*)

- that truth is absolute—there is, strictly, no such thing as a proposition's being more or less true; propositions are completely true if true at all. (*Absoluteness*)

The list might be enlarged, and some of these principles may anyway seem controversial. Moreover, it can be argued that the Equivalence Schema underlies not merely the first of the platitudes listed—Transparency—but the Correspondence Platitude[14] and, as we have seen in discussion of deflationism, the Contrast Platitude as well.

There's much to be said about this general approach to conceptual analysis, and many hard and interesting questions arise, not least, of course, about the epistemological provenance of the requisite basic platitudes. But such questions arise on *any* conception of philosophical analysis, which must always take for granted our ability to recognize basic truths holding a priori of concepts in which we are interested.

Let us call an account based on the accumulation and theoretical organization of a set of such platitudes concerning a particular concept an *analytical theory* of the concept in question.[15] Then the provision of an analytical theory of truth in particular opens up possibilities for a principled pluralism in the following specific way: in different regions of thought and discourse, the theory may hold good a priori of—may be satisfied by—different properties. If this is so, then always provided the network of platitudes integrated into the theory is sufficiently comprehensive, we should not scruple to say that truth may consist in different things in different such areas: in the possession of one property in one area, and in that of a different property in another. For there will be nothing in the idea of truth that is not accommodated by the analytical theory, and thus no more to a concept's presenting a truth property than its validating the ingredient platitudes. In brief, the *unity* in the concept of truth will be supplied by the analytical theory, and the *pluralism* will be underwritten by the fact that the principles composing that theory admit of *variable collective realization*.

An illuminating case study for these ideas is provided by pragmatist conceptions of truth. In a very famous passage, C. S. Peirce writes,

> Different minds may set out with the most antagonistic views, but the progress of investigations carries them by a force outside themselves to one and the same conclusion. This activity of thought by which we are carried, not where we wish but to a fore-ordained goal, is like the operation of destiny. No modification of the point of view taken, no selection of other facts to study, no natural bent of mind even, can enable a man to escape the predestinate opinion. This great law is embodied in the conception of truth and reality. *The opinion which is fated to be ultimately agreed by all who investigate is what we mean by the truth*, and the object represented in this opinion is the real.[16]

Here Peirce seemingly believes in a predestined march toward a stable scientific consensus among "all who investigate," but the received understanding of the "Peircean" view, whether historically faithful or not, has come to be, rather, that the true propositions are those on which investigators *would* agree if—which may well not be so—it were possible to pursue enquiry to some kind of ideal limit; that

> *P* is true if and only if, were epistemically ideal conditions to obtain, *P* would be believed by anyone who investigated it.

An equally famous passage in Hilary Putnam's *Reason, Truth, and History* has regularly been interpreted as advancing the same proposal. Having rejected the identification of truth with what he calls rational acceptability, Putnam suggests that "truth is an *idealisation* of rational acceptability. We speak as if there were such things as epistemically ideal conditions, and we call a statement 'true' if it would be justified under such conditions."[17]

He explains that, as he intends the notion, "epistemically ideal conditions" are an idealization in the same way that frictionlessness is: they are conditions that we cannot actually attain, nor—he adds, interestingly—can we "even be absolutely certain that we have come sufficiently close to them." He is explicit that he is not "trying to give a formal *definition* of truth, but an informal elucidation of the notion." And he goes on to say that "the two key ideas of the idealisation theory of truth are (i) that truth is independent of justification here and now, but not independent of *all* justification. To claim a statement is true is to claim it could be justified. (ii) Truth is expected to be stable or 'convergent.'"[18]

Putnam has, of course, since officially moved a long way from these ideas.[19] But this is the nearest that he ever came to explicitly endorsing the Peircean conception, and it is clear that his words left considerable latitude for interpretation. In particular, there was no unmistakable suggestion of a key feature of the Peircean proposal: that some *single* set of "epistemically ideal conditions" would be apt for the appraisal of any statement whatever.

Putnam himself subsequently returned to emphasize that point. In the preface to *Realism with a Human Face*, he again endorsed the idea that to claim of any statement that it is true is, roughly, to claim that it could be justified were epistemic conditions good enough.[20] And he goes on to allow that "one can express this by saying that a true statement is one that could be justified were epistemic conditions ideal." But then he proceeds immediately to repudiate the idea

> that we can sensibly imagine conditions which are *simultaneously ideal* for the ascertainment of any truth whatsoever, or simultaneously ideal for answering any question whatsoever. I have never thought such a thing, and I was, indeed, so far from ever thinking such a thing that it never occurred to me even to warn against this misunderstanding. I do not by any means *ever* mean to use the notion of an "ideal epistemic situation" in this fantastic (or utopian) Peircean sense.[21]

Rather, the notion of ideal epistemic circumstances stands in need of specialization to the subject matter under consideration:

> If I say "there is a chair in my study," an ideal epistemic situation would be to be in my study, with the lights on or with daylight streaming through the window, with nothing wrong with my eyesight, with an unconfused mind, without having taken drugs or being subjected to hypnosis, and so forth, and to look and see if there is a chair there.

Indeed, we might as well drop the metaphor of idealisation altogether. Rather, "there are *better and worse* epistemic situations *with respect to particular statements*. What I just described is a very good epistemic situation with respect to the statement 'there is a chair in my study.'"[22]

These remarks might invite the following regimentation. Let us, for any proposition *P*, call the following the *Peircean biconditional* for *P*:

> *P* is true if and only if, were *P* appraised under conditions *U*, *P* would be believed,

where *U* are conditions under which thinkers have achieved some informationally comprehensive ideal limit of rational-empirical enquiry. And let us call the following the corresponding *Putnamian biconditional* for *P*:

> *P* is true if and only if, were *P* appraised under topic-specifically sufficiently good conditions, *P* would be believed.

Then we now have two contrasting pragmatist conceptions of truth to consider. And the question is, Do they—either of them—meet the standard set by our proposed minimalism: do they realize the relevant constitutive platitudes?[23]

There is an interesting difficulty about an affirmative answer. Putnam imposed what he termed a convergence requirement on his conception of truth—that there be no statement such that both it and its negation are assertible under epistemically ideal (topic-specifically sufficiently good) conditions.[24] This is to be distinguished, of course, from any requirement of *completeness*. The requirement of completeness would be that, for each statement, *either* it *or* its negation must be justified under such circumstances. There seems no good reason to impose any such completeness requirement—no particular reason why all questions that are empirical in content should become decidable under Peirce's or Putnam's respective ideal conditions. Indeed, to take seriously the indeterminacies postulated by contemporary physical theory is to consider that there is reason to the contrary. We should expect that a pragmatist would want to suspend the Principle of Bivalence for statements that would find themselves in limbo under epistemically ideal, or topic-specifically sufficiently good, conditions in this way, and ought consequently, one would imagine, to want to suspend it in any case, failing an assurance that no statements are actually in that situation.

So what is the promised difficulty? That there is, apparently, a simple inconsistency within the triad uniting either of our pragmatist biconditionals with the claim that the notion of truth it concerns complies with the minimal platitudes and the admission that certain statements may remain undecidable under epistemically ideal, or topic-specifically sufficiently good, circumstances, neither they nor their negations being justified. For, as we have seen, the minimal platitudes impose the standard Negation Equivalence:

(NE) It is true that [not-P] iff it is not true that [P].

And to allow that, even under epistemically ideal or topic-specifically sufficiently good circumstances, we might yet be in a state of information that provided warrant neither for P nor for its negation would force us to reject the right-to-left ingredient in (NE) when "true" is interpreted in accordance with either pragmatist biconditional. In other words, it seems that epistemically ideal or topic-specifically sufficiently good circumstances cannot be neutral both on a statement and its negation if the Equivalence Schema is in force over all assertoric contents, if every assertoric content has a negation that is an assertoric content, and if truth is Peircean or Putnamian.

Simple though this train of thought is, it provides, on the face of it, a devastating blow to both pragmatist proposals. Leave on one side the obvious difficulties occasioned by the undecidability of mathematical examples like, say, the generalized continuum hypothesis. Surely, it should not be true a priori even of empirical statements in general that each would be decidable—confirmable or disconfirmable—under epistemically ideal or topic-specifically sufficiently good circumstances. But the relevant minimal platitudes, for their part, presumably hold true a priori. So *if* either pragmatist proposal were a priori correct—as it has to be if it is correct at all—it would have to be a priori that if a statement failed to be justified under epistemically ideal or topic-specifically sufficiently good circumstances, its negation would be justified instead—just the thing, it seems, that cannot be a priori. Invited conclusion: such proposals incorporate mistaken a priori claims about the concept of truth, and the properties they present are hence unfitted to serve as realizers of that concept. Indeed, the point is more general: a simple extension of the argument seems to tell not just against the two tabled pragmatist proposals but against any attempt to represent truth as essentially evidentially constrained. Someone in sympathy with Dummettian antirealism, for instance, may content herself with a one-way Principle of Epistemic Constraint,

(EC) If P is true, then evidence is available that it is so,

yet still be posed an embarrassment by the argument. For if no evidence is available that P, then, contraposing on (EC), she ought to allow that it is not the case that P is true, whence, by the Negation Equivalence, its negation must count as true. So in the presence even of a one-way epistemic constraint, the unattainability of evidence for a statement is bound, it appears, to confer truth on, and hence, via (EC), to ensure the availability of evidential support for, its negation—contrary to what, someone might very well think, the antirealist could and should admit, namely, that some statements may be such that no evidence bearing upon them is available either way, even under idealized conditions of investigation. (Indeed, how do we explain the semantical antirealist's characteristic refusal to allow the unrestricted validity of the Principle of Bivalence unless it is based on precisely that admission, coupled with the insistence that truth is evidentially constrained?)

What room does such an antirealist have for maneuver here? We can take it that, unless she decides to off-load the notion of truth entirely, there is no denying the Equivalence Schema. Maybe trouble might somehow be found for the move from that to the Negation Equivalence. But the prospects do not look bright.[25] What is needed, rather, is a way to reconcile the Negation Equivalence with an insistence that truth is evidentially constrained and the admission that not every issue can be guaranteed to be decidable, even in principle. But is there any scope for such a reconciliation?

Yes, there is. There can be no denying that the Negation Equivalence commits someone who endorses (EC) to allowing (A):

(A) If no evidence is available for P, then evidence is available for its negation.

And, of course, it's extremely easy to hear this as tantamount to the admission that evidence is in principle available either for affirming P or denying it. But there is a suppressed premise in this turn of thought: the premise (B), an instance of the law of excluded middle:

(B) Either evidence is available for P or it is not.

Classically, of course, the conditional (A) is an equivalent of the disjunction (C):

(C) Either evidence is available for P, or evidence is available for its negation.

But the proof of the equivalence depends on the instance of the law of excluded middle, (B). If we may not assume that evidence either is or is not available for an arbitrary statement, then the convertibility of lack of evidence for a particular statement into evidence for its negation, demanded by the Negation Equivalence when truth is evidentially constrained, need not impose (C), and so need not be in contradiction with the a priori unwarrantability of the claim that the scales of (in principle) available evidence must tilt, sooner or later, one way or the other, between each statement and its negation.

This is a substantial result. It teaches us, in effect, that in order to sustain the claim of our two pragmatist proposals—and indeed any broadly Dummettian antirealist proposal—to offer defensible conceptions of truth, the associated package must include revisions of classical logic *of a broadly intuitionistic sort*. For otherwise there is no possibility of modeling the minimal platitudes consistently with a proper recognition that decidability is often not guaranteed even under ideal—Peircean or Putnamian—conditions.

Provided this way of surmounting the difficulty is accepted, our two pragmatist proposals remain in the field as offering two possible ways in which a property satisfying the minimal constraints on truth may be constructed out of assertibility by idealization. Of course, we have only considered just one problem, so the proposals' claim to succeed in that regard would need more detailed review. But I shelve consideration of that review to turn to another serious and independent form of difficulty confronting each of them, a difficulty that, I contend, should force a pragmatist-inclined philosopher to look for a subtly different kind of conception of truth.

Here is a generalization (and, in one respect, a simplification—see note 28) of an objection advanced by Alvin Plantinga specifically against the Peircean proposal.[26] Assume any purported account—or indeed any "informal elucidation"—of truth of the form (o):

(o) It is true that $P \leftrightarrow (Q \mathbin{\square\!\!\rightarrow} Z(P))$,

where Q expresses a general epistemic idealization, $Z(\ )$ is any condition on propositions—for instance, being judged to be true by the ideally rational and informed thinkers whose existence is hypothesized by Q, or cohering with the maximally coherent set of beliefs whose existence is hypothesized by Q, etc.—and "$\square\!\!\rightarrow$" expresses the subjunctive conditional. Since (o) is purportedly a correct elucidation of a concept, it presumably holds as a matter of conceptual necessity. Thus:

(i) Necessarily (It is true that $P \leftrightarrow (Q \mathbin{\square\!\!\rightarrow} Z(P))$).

Now suppose that (ii):

(ii) Possibly (Q & Not $Z(Q)$)

Then, by logic and the Equivalence Schema, (iii):

(iii) Possibly (It is true that Q & (Q & Not $Z(Q)$)).

But (iii) contradicts (i), with "Q" taken for P,[27] which therefore entails

(iv) Not possibly (Q & Not $Z(Q)$).

So

(v) Necessarily ($Q \rightarrow Z(Q)$).

A necessarily true conditional ought to be sufficient for the corresponding subjunctive, so:

(vi) $Q \,\square\!\!\rightarrow Z(Q)$.

So, from (i):

(vii) It is true that Q.

So by the Equivalence Schema again:

(viii) Q

The upshot is, it seems, that anyone proposing an account of truth of the shape typified by (o) must accept that the idealization Q *already obtains*. Thus, the Peircean must accept that conditions are already "epistemically ideal" (and a coherence theorist must accept that there already is a controlled, comprehensive, and coherent set of beliefs.)[28] Obviously, this is unacceptable. And it is not clear how the Peircean can respond.

However, just here is where there may seem additional point to the more modest Putnamian proposal. For the key to the proof above is the license, granted by the Peircean conception of truth in particular, to assume that the conditions that are ideal for the appraisal of the proposition U are the very conditions depicted by that proposition—it is this assumption that sanctions the substitution of "Q" for "P" in (o). Suppose instead that, with erstwhile Putnam, the pragmatist drops the idea of such a comprehensive set of epistemically ideal conditions and that (o) gives way to a range of Putnamian biconditionals:

(o') It is true that $P \leftrightarrow (Q_P \,\square\!\!\rightarrow Z(P))$.

Here Q_P is the hypothesis that conditions are sufficiently good for the appraisal specifically of P. We can advance as before to:

(iii') Possibly (It is true that Q_P & (Q_P & Not $Z(Q_P)$)).

But nothing harmful need follow unless one of our Putnamian biconditionals is:

It is true that $Q_P \leftrightarrow (Q_P \,\square\!\!\rightarrow Z(Q_P))$,

which will be available only if conditions Q_P are topic-specifically sufficiently good not merely for the appraisal of P but also for the appraisal of the proposition Q_P itself—that is, if $Q_P = Q_{QP}$. And why should that be so?

Well, but the question should be, Is it certain such an identity is *never* realized? Consider Putnam's own example: a sufficiently good epistemic situation for appraisal specifically of "There is a chair in my study." That would be, he said, to be in my study, with the lights on or with daylight streaming through the window, with nothing wrong with my eyesight, with an unconfused mind, without having taken drugs or being subjected to hypnosis, and so forth. But wouldn't these conditions likewise be sufficiently good conditions in which to appraise the claim that I was indeed in my study, with the lights on or with daylight streaming through the window, with nothing wrong with my eyesight, with an unconfused mind, without having taken drugs or being subjected to hypnosis, and so forth? Maybe not—maybe there is some condition whose addition to the list would not improve my epistemic situation with respect to "There is a chair in my study" but without which I would not be best placed to assess the complex proposition just stated. But even if so in the particular example, must that *always* be so? Unless we can see our way to justifying an affirmative answer, there can be no assurance that Plantinga's problem can be resolved by a fallback to Putnamian biconditionals.

In fact it is clear that the most basic problem with the Peircean biconditional cannot be resolved by this fallback. Plantinga made a difficulty by taking Q for P in (o). But suppose instead we take "Q will never obtain," thus obtaining:

Q will never obtain $\leftrightarrow (Q \,\square\!\!\rightarrow Z(Q$ will never obtain)).

Then if the right-hand side is interpreted as in the Peircean biconditional, we have a claim to the effect that conditions will always be less than epistemically ideal just in case thinkers who considered the matter under epistemically ideal conditions would suppose so. This is obviously unacceptable. And it is an illustration of a very general point: that no categorical claim P can be a priori (or necessarily) equivalent to a subjunctive conditional of a certain type—roughly, one whose antecedent hypothesizes conditions under which a manifestation, depicted by the consequent, of the status of P takes place—unless it is likewise a priori (or necessary) that the realization of the antecedent of the latter would not impinge on the actual truth-value of the categorical claim. More specifically, it cannot be a priori—or necessary—that

It is true that $P \leftrightarrow$ were conditions C to obtain, such and such an indicator M of P's status would also obtain

unless it is a priori (or necessary) that the obtaining of C would not bring about any change in the actual truth-value of P. For suppose that it is true that P, but that were conditions C to obtain, it would cease to be so: would M then obtain? Yes. For by hypothesis, P is actually true. So the biconditional demands that M would obtain if C did. So not-P would hold alongside conditions C and M. But in that case, M would not be an indicator of P's status in those circumstances after all. In particular, if M consists in the believing that P by suitably placed thinkers, then the effect will be that their beliefs will be *in error* under conditions *C*—exactly what the pragmatist proposal was meant to exclude.

This point—or anyway the general thought, epitomized in the phrase, "the Conditional Fallacy," that subjunctive conditional analyses are almost always unstable—is nowadays very familiar from the literature on dispositions and response-dependence.[29] What is clear for our present purpose is that it is no less a problem for Putnamian biconditionals than for Peircean ones. That is, unless it is given a priori that the implementation of conditions Q_p would not impinge on the circumstances actually conferring its truth-value on P, it cannot be supposed to hold purely in virtue of the concepts involved that

It is true that $P \leftrightarrow (Q_p \,\square\!\!\rightarrow P$ would be believed)

except at the cost of allowing that even under Q_p circumstances, P might be believed when false. And again, this is just to surrender the idea that belief under ideal circumstances is guaranteed to line up with the facts: the cardinal tenet of this kind of pragmatism.[30]

4   Pragmatism and Pluralism (II): Superassertibility

The ur-thought behind any pragmatist conception of truth is that the notion should be grounded in ordinary human practices of assessment and epistemic values. So some form of idealized assertibility is the most natural concrete interpretation of the idea. But I think that the Peircean and Putnamian conceptions idealized assertibility in the wrong direction. Warranted assertibility is assertibility relative to a state of information. So it can seem as if there is only one direction for a truth-like idealization of assertibility to assume: to wit, we have somehow to idealize the state of information involved, as both the Peircean and Putnamian proposals do in their different ways. But there is another way. Rather than ask whether a statement would be justified at the limit of ideal empirical investigation or under topic-specifically sufficiently good circumstances, whatever they are, we can ask whether an ordinary carefully controlled investigation, in advance of attaining any mythical or more practical limit, would justify the statement, and whether, once justified, that statement would continue to be so no matter how much further information were accumulated.

More carefully, another property constructible out of assertibility that is both absolute and, so it is plausible to think, may not be lost—Putnam's two desiderata—is the property of being justified by some (in principle accessible) state of information and then *remaining* justified no matter how that state of information might be enlarged upon or improved. Like Peircean truth, the characterization of this property presupposes that we understand what it is for one state of information to enlarge upon or otherwise improve another. But it does not presuppose that we grasp the idea of a limit to such improvement—a state of information that is itself beyond all improvement—or even have any general conception of what it would be for the topic-specific epistemic circumstances to be unimprovable.

So this characterization need not confront questions about the intelligibility and coherence of the idea of the Peircean limit, nor need it confront the question of how appraisal under merely topic-specifically sufficiently good conditions can guarantee the stability of a verdict, and thereby the stability of Putnamian truth.

Elsewhere I have called the property just prefigured *superassertibility*.[31] A statement is superassertible, then, if and only if it is, or can be, warranted and some warrant for it would survive arbitrarily close scrutiny of its pedigree and arbitrarily extensive increments to, or other forms of improvement of, our information.

This admittedly vague characterization makes purely formal use of the notions of "state of information," "improvement," and so on. It's natural to wonder how more concrete yet generally applicable accounts of these notions might be given. But I do not think we need to take these issues on. It is enough for our purposes if the notion of superassertibility is *relatively* clear; clear, that is, relative to whatever notion of warranted assertion is in play in the particular discourse with which we may happen to be concerned. Provided, as in all cases that interest us there will be, there are generally acknowledged standards of proper and improper assertion within the discourse, there must be sense to be attached to the idea of a statement that under certain circumstances meets the standards of proper assertion and then will or would continue to do so unless the considerations that led to its downfall were open to objection in some way. In short, wherever our discourse displays some measure of convergence about what is warrantedly assertible, a corresponding notion of *super*assertibility has to be intelligible. This notion may be unclear in various respects, but they will be respects in which the relevant notion of warranted assertibility was already unclear.

So does superassertibility qualify as a potential truth property—does it satisfy the minimal platitudes? The issues here are actually quite subtle. Let's explore some of the twists. We already noted that superassertibility is, plausibly, both absolute and stable.[32] It is uncontroversial that it is potentially divergent in extension from assertibility proper. But it merits consideration whether superassertibility and assertibility coincide in normative force. And the question, anyway, is not merely whether superassertibility has these features but whether they issue in the right kind of way from its sustaining the key platitudes.

Let's focus on the Equivalence Schema. Can a supporter of superassertibility argue compellingly for the validity of (E^s)?

(E^s) It is superassertible that P if and only if P.

If he can, then, as briefly noted above, that will arguably settle the matters of Transparency, Correspondence, and Contrast. The commutativity of superassertibility and negation—the analogue of (NE) for superassertibility—will likewise be a consequence.[33]

The matter may seem easily resolved, at least to anyone sympathetic to the idea that for a wide class of admissible substitutions for "P," it may be that P, although

no evidence is available to that effect. Such a theorist will want to object that (E^s)
cannot be valid, since it conflates right across the board the obtaining of a certain
kind of high-grade evidence for P with the obtaining of the fact. A suitably chosen
proposition—Goldbach's conjecture, say—may be undetectably true, and hence not
superassertible, and a suitably chosen superassertible proposition—perhaps that we
are not brains-in-a-vat—may be undetectably false. Since (E^s) is hostage to counterexample, so not a priori true, superassertibility has no case to be a truth property.

But the supporter of superassertibility may rejoin that, quite apart from any doubt
about the realism on which it depends, there is something unsatisfactory about the
shape of this objection. Its claim is that there is no assurance that there are no counterexamples to (E^s). But what does it take a counterexample to be? Is it a true proposition
that may not truly be claimed to be superassertible? In that case the objection asserts,
in effect, that superassertibility potentially lacks, but as a putative truth property ought
to be guaranteed to have, the property of generating a valid equivalence when substituted for "?" in the schema (F):

(F) It is true that it is ? that P iff it is true that P.

However, (F) contains two mentions of a truth property, which, if interpreted as presupposed by the objection, has to be understood as *distinct* from superassertibility. If
that doesn't seem evident, reflect that while—to one in the cast of mind that fuels the
objection—it is a possibility that Goldbach's conjecture be true without it being true
that it is superassertible (provable), it certainly isn't evident that the conjecture might
be *superassertible* without it being superassertible that it is. But if there really can be,
as minimalism suggests, a *plurality* of truth properties, qualifying as such by satisfying
certain general principles, it is only to be expected that an *illusion* of failure may be
created by selective interpretations of "true" as it occurs within those principles. It is as
if someone were to argue that physical necessity fails to qualify as a genuine notion of
necessity on the grounds that it fails to satisfy the principle

Necessarily $(A \leftrightarrow B) \vDash$ Necessarily $(A) \leftrightarrow$ Necessarily (B)

and were then to try to back up that contention by selectively interpreting the final
occurrence of "Necessarily" in terms of *logical* necessity. If we wish to determine
whether there are counterexamples to (E^s), the proper question to put, the friend of
superassertibility contends, is not whether superassertibility satisfies (F), but rather
whether it satisfies what results when the two tendentious occurrences of "true" are
replaced by ones of "?":

(G) It is ? that it is ? that P iff it is ? that P.

The question is, in effect, whether, whenever it is superassertible that P, it is superassertible that it is so, and vice versa.

Can we arbitrate this exchange? What is suspect about the shape of the original objection can be put like this. If any genuine truth property has to validate (i.e., satisfy a priori) the Equivalence Schema, then clearly, *distinct* truth properties can operate over a single discourse (or range of propositions) only if they are a priori coextensive. Plainly, then, no predicate F can express such a property in a discourse in which it is made to function alongside another predicate G that is already assumed both to validate the Equivalence Schema and to be potentially divergent in extension from F.[34] The original objection is therefore cogent only to this extent: to show that a discourse is governed by an evidentially unconstrained notion of truth is, for that reason, to show that superassertibility is not a truth property *for that discourse*.[35] But no *global* conclusion is licensed. We have to distinguish the questions (i) whether a predicate's content would enable it, under certain conditions, to function as expressing a truth property; (ii) whether, if so, the relevant conditions are met by any particular discourse; and (iii) whether they are met globally. The objection, drawing as it does on a range of examples where it is thought especially plausible that truth is evidentially unconstrained, is properly targeted against the claim of superassertibility on a positive answer to (iii). But in failing to make any distinction among the three questions, it implicitly begs the other two.

There is, however, on the other side, a similar oversimplification in the suggestion that "*the* proper question to put" is, in effect, whether

(G^s) It is superassertible that it is superassertible that P iff it is superassertible that P

holds a priori. The right perspective, rather, is this. In the presence of the Equivalence Schema, counterexamples to (E^s) are indeed all and only cases where

(F^s) It is true that it is superassertible that P iff it is true that P

also breaks down. So if (G^s) is valid, then we know that there can be no such counterexamples, and hence that (E^s) is valid, provided, but only provided *no competitor truth-property* operates alongside superassertibility—no predicate, that is, that validates the Equivalence Schema but whose coextensiveness with superassertibility is not guaranteed a priori. If there is a competitor in operation, (F^s) may fail when its occurrences of "true" are suitably interpreted, even if (G^s) is valid without restriction on "P." If there is no competitor, (G^s) and (F^s) stand or fall together. The status of (G^s) is thus highly germane to question (i). If counterexamples to it cannot be excluded a priori, then there will be no general assurance that superassertibility can function as a truth property even when we give it the fullest elbow room, as it were—even when we make no initial assumption that a competitor is operating over the discourse. On the other hand, if counterexamples to (G^s) can be excluded a priori irrespective of the range of "P," then we can return a positive answer to question (i), and the answers to questions (ii) and (iii) will then depend on whether and how widely competitor truth properties should be regarded as in operation.

So is (G^s) unrestrictedly valid? We may return a positive answer if it can be shown that to have warrant for P is to have warrant for the claim that P is superassertible, and conversely.[36] The latter direction seems unproblematic. If we have reason to regard a statement as superassertible, then we have reason to think that some (in principle accessible) state of information will stably justify the statement, no matter how added to or otherwise improved. And having reason to think that such a state of information exists is plausibly taken to have the same probative force as actually being in the state of information in question. For instance, proving that a (canonical) proof of a particular statement can be constructed is, as far as probative force is concerned, as good as constructing the proof; and there seems no reason why the point should not survive generalization to the general run of cases where we are concerned with defeasible grounds rather than conclusive ones like mathematical proof. What is less clear is that to have warrant to assert a statement must be to have warrant to regard it as superassertible. Doubtless, warrant to assert P cannot coexist with warrant to *deny* that P is superassertible, since that would be to have warrant to think that the present case for P would be defeated if we pressed matters sufficiently far, and again, that seems as much as to defeat it already. But the question to ask is, rather, whether warrant to assert P can coexist with lack of warrant to regard it as superassertible—whether one can coherently combine *agnosticism* about P's superassertibility with regarding a present case for asserting it as sufficient.

I'll outline an argument that the mooted combination of attitudes is *not* coherent, that it is precluded by certain quite basic elements in our ordinary conception of what justification for a statement or, equivalently, warrant for a belief involves. The elements involved are three. The first is that epistemic warranty does not have a sell-by date—what I am warranted in believing I remain warranted in believing *sine die* unless I acquire defeating collateral information. The second is that in warrantedly believing any statement P, a subject is thereby warranted in believing that a sound investigation, to whatever extent one is possible, would bear her out. The third I shall introduce in a moment.

Suppose I warrantedly believe that P. Now, what counts as warrant to believe a particular statement varies, of course, as a function of time, place, and background information. So what counts as corroboration of P for me if I return my attention to the matter in a year's time, say, may comprise very different considerations to those which warrant my present belief. However, by the first of the two assumptions, I will then be warranted, ceteris paribus, in believing P; and by the second, I will thereby be entitled to expect whatever sound considerations are then available to me to be corroborative just in virtue of the warrant I possessed a year before.

That establishes a conditional: if I am warranted in believing P now, then, if I acquire no other relevant information in the meantime, I will be warranted in future in expecting then available, sound considerations to bear P out. But this conditional is something that I may take myself to know now. So whenever I know its antecedent—which, as remarked earlier, I can whenever it is true, since possession of warrant should be a decidable matter—I can know that in any case where I acquire no further relevant information in the interim, certain expectations will be warranted in future. But to know that certain beliefs will be warranted in the future is, only provided one has no present reason to view them as wrong, to be warranted in holding them now. This is the third element in our ordinary conception of justification advertised above: the firm *promise* of justification for what one has no reason to doubt is already justification. So to be warranted in believing P involves having justification for believing that any subsequent, soundly conducted investigation, prior to which one has acquired no further relevant additional information, will corroborate P.

This is *close* to the desired result but doesn't quite get it. What would suffice to justify the claim that P is superassertible is warrant for the claim that *any* improvement, I^*, of my present state of information, I, will justify P. But what the foregoing establishes is only that if I am warranted in believing P, then I am warranted in claiming that any such I^* *prior to which I have acquired no further relevant additional information* will justify P. So there is a gap. But perhaps we can eliminate it, given the third assumption mooted at the end of the preceding paragraph. Say that a later state of information I^* is *first-time P-incremental* on an earlier one I for a given thinker just if prior to possessing I^*, she has no P-relevant information that she did not possess in I. So our result above was that if I am warranted in believing P in I, then I am warranted in thinking that each I^* that is first-time P-incremental on I will likewise warrant P. And now, in order to extend this result to arbitrary improvements I^* of my present state of information I, it suffices to reflect that if I^* is not first-time P-incremental on I, then it must be the terminus of a finite chain, $<I, I^2, \ldots, I^*>$, each element of which is first-time P-incremental on its immediate predecessor. (The point is simply that no matter what P-relevant information I gather between I and I^*, there has to be a first state of information in which I possess each particular item in it.) Reflect then that, by the result of the previous paragraph, in each I^k in which I am warranted in believing P, I will be warranted in believing that I will be warranted in believing P in I^{k+1}. I can know this in I and hence infer that I am warranted in believing that in I^2 I will be warranted in believing that in I^3 I will be warranted in believing ... that I will be warranted in believing P in I^*. Application of the third assumption will then let me simplify to "If I am warranted in believing P in I, then I will be warranted in believing P in any improved state of information I^*."

The contention that (G^5) holds a priori, without restriction on the range of "P," is thus very much in play, but I leave it to the reader to satisfy herself of the premises and detail of this argument, which will bear a more rigorous examination.[37] In general, though, it is hard to see how the making of warranted assertions, and the avoidance of unwarranted ones, could have any distinctive point or consequence unless warrant is taken per se to license expectations about the favourable character of subsequent states of information.[38]

5   Superassertibility as a Model of Truth

We now need to observe, finally, that it is actually not necessary, in order for superassertibility to qualify as a truth property, that it validate the platitudes unconditionally. It will be of no less significance if superassertibility turns out to validate the basic platitudes only subject to certain *additional assumptions* that, consistently with the platitudes, hold a priori for a particular discourse. Such a finding would put us in a position to say that, whether or not the platitudes are analytic of superassertibility when all occurrences of "true" are so interpreted, it is at least a possible *model* of them: it can be shown to have the features they collectively articulate when they are augmented with suppositions on whose status the platitudes themselves are silent.

How does the inquiry fare if we let it take this direction? One way of pursuing the matter begins by asking what is the relation between superassertibility and knowledge. It would be a tall order to argue unrestrictedly that whatever is superassertible can be known, not merely because one would have to vanquish the metaphysical-realist notion that even an empirically unimprovable theory might simply be mistaken, but perhaps more seriously, because the superassertibility of a statement carries no implication about the *strength* of the available evidence, which, though positive, may be enduringly weak. By contrast, it seems to me a highly intuitive claim that anything we can know is superassertible. Admittedly, this will not be so on any reliabilist conception of knowledge sufficiently extreme to abrogate all connection between knowledge and the possession of reason to believe. On such a view, one can know that P just by being a dispositionally reliable litmus of whether or not P, even if one has nothing whatever to say in support or explanation of one's believing or disbelieving P. But on any view according to which knowledge requires at least some backup with reasons, that is, with assertibility, it is surely going to require superassertibility too. I do not deny that in suitable circumstances an agent may know something on the basis of information that can in fact be defeated. But if his knowledge claim is not to be undermined by the availability of such defeating information, it is surely required that the negative effect of that information, once acquired, could itself be stably overturned.

Doubtless, the matter needs more discussion. But let me propose (K) as analytic of the concepts of knowledge and superassertibility:

(K) P is knowable $\rightarrow P$ is superassertible.

And now suppose we are dealing with a discourse in which, as we conceive, it is guaranteed a priori that each statable truth can, in favorable circumstances, be recognized as such—a discourse for which we can make nothing of the idea that truth might lie beyond all possibility of acknowledgement. Comic and, on a wide class of views about it, moral discourse are each, for instance, in this situation: there seems no sense to be attached to the idea that the comedy of a situation might elude the appreciation even of the most fortunately situated judge, or that the moral significance of an act might lie beyond human recognition, even in principle.[39] In any case, suppose that, for each assertoric content, P, in some germane class, we have it a priori that:

(L) $P \leftrightarrow P$ is knowable.

Had we the converse of (K),

P is superassertible $\rightarrow$ P is knowable,

the validity for the discourse concerned of the Equivalence Schema for superassertibility,

(E^s) It is superassertible that P if and only if P,

would, of course, be immediate. But we can skin the cat without appeal to the converse of (K) provided we are entitled to assume one half, as it were, of the commutativity of superassertibility and negation, specifically the direction from

It is superassertible that [not P]

to

Not [P is superassertible].[40]

This principle is equivalent to the inconsistency of the supposition that P and its negation might both be superassertible and is therefore uncontentious, so long as any two states of information are conceived as mutually accessible and warrant is so conceived that no state of information can warrant contradictory claims.

With this lemma in place, it is easy to see that (E^s) is good. What needs to be shown is that

P, and P is not superassertible

and

P is superassertible, and Not-P

are contradictory, just as are "P and P is not true," and "P is true and not-P." For the first, merely reflect that if P then, by (L), P is knowable; and if P is knowable, then, by (K), P is superassertible. For the second, reflect that, by the same moves, if Not-P, then Not-P is superassertible, and hence by the commutativity lemma, that it's not the case that P is superassertible, contradicting the first conjunct. Thus, granted the a priori link between knowability and superassertibility postulated by (K), it follows, for any set of contents that sustain (L) a priori, that the assertion of any of these contents is a commitment to its superassertibility and the assertion of its superassertibility is a commitment to (rejecting any denial of) the content.

Plausibly, then, for discourses all of whose contents are in that case, superassertibility satisfies the Equivalence Schema and, in the light of earlier considerations, thus plausibly presents a model of the basic platitudes.[41] And if what I said about the essential appreciability of the moral and the comic is correct, a presumption is established that moral and comic truth can be taken as species of superassertibility.[42]

One interesting effect is the perspective in which the semantical antirealism is now placed that generalizes Michael Dummett's interpretation of mathematical intuitionism. Dummett's antirealist, inspired by considerations concerning the acquisition and manifestation of understanding, contends that if the meaning of a statement is to be regarded as determined by its truth conditions, then truth cannot outrun our ability (in principle) to know. But then the thesis is that assumption (L), the equivalence of "P" and "P is knowable," holds globally for *all* intelligible assertoric contents. So, granted (K), the semantical antirealist contention becomes, in effect, that truth behaves, or ought to behave, *everywhere* in a fashion that allows it to be construed as superassertibility. And to respond to the manifestation and acquisition arguments will be to explain how the currency of a notion of truth that cannot be modeled in terms of superassertibility is distinctively displayed in certain aspects of our linguistic practice, and how such a conception of truth might be arrived at in the first place.

This seems to me a helpful perspective on the Dummettian debate. Semantical antirealism now distances itself from the almost certainly doomed project of attempting a meaning theory that proceeds in terms of an indexical notion of assertibility. Instead, it avails itself of a notion of truth, contrasting with assertibility, and an associated truth-conditional conception of meaning. But it can do this only because superassertibility is, as any antirealistically acceptable notion of truth must be, an essentially epistemically constrained notion—for if P is superassertible, it must be possible to alight on the (de facto) indefeasible state of information that makes it so and then to accumulate inductive grounds for identifying it as such.

For the purposes of pragmatism, for its part, the crucial reflection is that superassertibility is, in a clear sense, an *internal* property of the statements of a discourse—a projection, merely, of the standards, whatever they are, that actually inform belief formation and assertion within the discourse. It supplies no external norm—in a way that truth is classically supposed to do—against which our ordinary standards might themselves be measured *sub specie Dei* and might rate as adequate or inadequate. Rather, the way in which it is fashioned from our actual practices of assessment renders superassertibility as well equipped to express the aspiration for a developed pragmatist conception of truth as any other candidate known to me. If it seems to distort our thinking about truth in particular regions of discourse to conceive it in such terms, that, it seems to me, will be a measure of the local unnaturalness of pragmatism itself.

Notes

This chapter, at Michael Lynch's suggestion, revisits some of the arguments and themes of chapters 1 and 2 of my *Truth and Objectivity* (Cambridge, MA: Harvard University Press, 1993). I am grateful to Michael Lynch for giving me the opportunity to present these ideas to the readership of the present volume and for helpful suggestions about what best to include. Sven Rosenkranz also gave me extremely detailed and helpful suggestions about both contents and structure. My thanks to Harvard University Press for permission to include excerpts from *Truth and Objectivity*, and to the University of Calgary Press for permission to include passages from my paper "Truth: A Traditional Debate Reviewed," *Canadian Journal of Philosophy*, suppl., 24 (1998): 31–74, reprinted in S. Blackburn and K. Simmons, eds., *Truth* (Oxford: Oxford University Press, 1999); the official dates notwithstanding, first published in German in M. Vogel and L. Wingert, eds., *Unsere Welt gegeben oder gemacht? Menschliches Erkennen zwischen Entdeckung und Konstruktion* (Frankfurt am Main: Suhrkamp, 1999). The present chapter was completed during my tenure of a Leverhulme Personal Research Professorship. I gratefully acknowledge the support of the Leverhulme Trust.

1. That is, the Equivalence Schema and the Disquotational Schema yield instances whose truth is knowable a priori by anyone who is in a position to understand them. As is familiar, the right-to-left directions of these equivalences become contestable if truth-value gaps or many truth-values are admitted. This complication is pursued in discussion note 1 of chapter 2 of *Truth and Objectivity*. But I do not think that any deflationist should go out of her way to accommodate it, since rejection of the right-to-left direction of the Equivalence Schema flies in the face of what would seem to be an absolutely basic and constitutive characteristic of the notion of truth, that P and "It is true that P" are, as it were, attitudinally equivalent: that any attitude to the proposition that P—belief, hope, doubt, desire, fear, etc.—is tantamount to the same attitude to its truth. For if that's accepted, and if it is granted that any reservation about a conditional has to involve the taking of *differential* attitudes to its antecedent and consequent, then there simply can be no coherent reservation about $P \rightarrow$ it is true that P.

2. It's an unhappy situation that the leading contemporary theorist of deflationism, Paul Horwich, uses both "minimalism" and "deflationism" to characterize his view. However, both his use of "minimalism" and my contrasting one are now entrenched. Probably, nobody is confused.

3. This view is contrary to what is suggested by P. Horwich, *Truth*, 2nd ed. (Oxford: Clarendon Press, 1998), 143–144. Horwich there seems to conflate the substantiality of a property with the feasibility of what he calls a "theory of constitution" for this property—that is, a theory that identifies this property by means of a noncircular equation of the form "x is true iff x is F," where "F" is replaced by a predicate that does not contain any semantic terms, a fortiori no cognates of "is true." But that just seems to be a prejudice. It is evident from the example of scientific-theoretical predicates, for instance, that there can be no compelling reason to tie expression of a substantial property to explicit definability.

4. There are deflationists who go so far as to deny that "is true" is a genuine predicate at all, but most deflationists are ready to concede that there is such a thing as the concept of truth. A deflationist proposal of the first kind can be found in D. Grover, J. Camp, and N. Belnap, "A Prosentential Theory of Truth," *Philosophical Studies* 27 (1975): 73–125.

5. That is, the property of having "true" correctly predicable of them. This is presumably what Horwich has in mind when he says that truth denotes a property in the sense in which "every term that functions logically as a predicate stands for a property" (Horwich, *Truth*, 141–142).

6. See H. Putnam, "On Properties," in *Mathematics, Matter, and Method* (Cambridge: Cambridge University Press, 1975), 305–322.

7. Thus, the minimalist opposes Horwich's suggestion that truth presents a special case in that an account of the property (or properties) denoted just coincides with an account of the concept that does the denoting. See Horwich, *Truth*, 136.

8. On Horwich's interpretation of "substantive property," such reducibility is precisely a necessary condition for a property to be substantive. His suggestion that minimalism (in my sense) is based on the idea that truth is substantive on this understanding thus misconceives the position. See Horwich, *Truth*, 142–143.

9. Proof: derive the two biconditionals one gets from (ES) by respectively negating both its halves and taking "not-*P*" for "*P*." Transitivity of the biconditional then yields (NE).

10. If they were necessarily coextensive, the Negation Equivalence would have to hold for both if for either.

To offset misunderstanding, two points merit emphasis. First, warranted assertibility is here understood to be a notion that is always relativized to a particular state of information. If no such state of information is explicitly mentioned, claims involving this notion will always be understood to relate to the present state of information. Second, the modality involved in "warranted assert*ibility*" does not signify the potential possession of warrants for an assertion, but the actual possession of warrants for a potential assertion. So in particular, merely provable mathematical statements, for which we so far have no proof, do not qualify as warrantedly assertible. I believe a confusion of this distinction drives the criticisms in N. Tennant's "On Negation, Truth, and Warranted Assertibility," *Analysis* 55 (1995): 98–104.

11. Thus, for instance Horwich, *Truth*, 20–23, 139–140.

12. This is, of course, by no means the end of the dialectic. A supporter of the project of Robert Brandom's compendious *Making It Explicit* (Cambridge, MA: Harvard University Press, 1994) will believe that a suitable account of assertoric content—one sustaining the contrast between the proposition that *P* and the proposition that that proposition is assertible—can be constructed out of truth-free materials, as it were. And in his recent book *Meaning* (Oxford: Clarendon Press, 1998), Horwich himself tries—as he must—to develop a general account of meaning in which truth plays no explanatory part. I cannot pursue the problems with these approaches here. My own view is that the best deflationist response to the inflationary argument is to concede its immediate conclusion but insist that it shows no more than that the concept of truth is indeed of a dimension of (substantial) success and failure, distinct from warrant, for *each particular* proposition, but that there still need be no *single* thing in which, for any two propositions, such success or failure consists. This is indeed one way of taking the "stock-in-trade" response reviewed above. For pursuit of the issue at least some distance beyond this point, see my "Truth: A Traditional Debate Reviewed," section IV.

13. Which of these forms of opacity goes with the very concept of truth is, of course, contentious, but not that some do.

14. For elaboration of this claim, see my *Truth and Objectivity*, 24–27.

15. Readers familiar with Michael Smith's work will note a point of contact here with the conception of a *network analysis*, which he derives from Ramsey and Lewis (see, in particular, chapter 2, section 10, of Smith's *The Moral Problem* [Oxford: Basil Blackwell, 1994]). The principal contrast with the approach to truth here canvassed is that a network analysis has to be based on a comprehensive set of platitudes whose conjunction so constrains the target concept that the replacement within those platitudes of all expressions for that concept by a variable and its binding by the description operator results in a definite description that is at the service of an analytically true identity:

F-ness is the property Φ such that $\{\ldots \Phi \ldots \& \ldots \Phi \ldots \& \ldots\}$

This effectively supplies a reductive analysis of the concept *F*. An analytical theory, by contrast, need not—though it may—subserve the construction of such an analytically true identity.

16. C. S. Peirce, *Collected Papers*, vol. 8, ed. C. Hartshorne and P. Weiss (Cambridge, MA: Harvard University Press, 1935), 139; emphasis added. [See also chapter 8 in this volume—Eds.]

17. We may take it that this is the notion that is now standardly called "assertibility." Putnam's grounds for the rejection are two: first, that truth is, plausibly, timeless, whereas warranted assertibility varies as a function of the state of information ("Truth is supposed to be a property of a statement that cannot be lost, whereas justification can be lost"), and second, that assertoric warrant is, whereas truth is not, a matter of *degree*. Recall that I incorporated these points into the platitudes listed above.

18. *Reason, Truth, and History* (Cambridge: Cambridge University Press, 1981), 56. [See also chapter 12 in this volume.—Eds.]

19. For a review of the contrast between Putnam's "middle" and most recent views, see my "Truth as Sort of Epistemic: Putnam's Peregrinations," *Journal of Philosophy* 97 (2000): 335–364.

20. H. Putnam, *Realism with a Human Face*, ed. J. Conant (Cambridge, MA: Harvard University Press, 1990).

21. Putnam, *Realism with a Human Face*, viii.

22. Putnam, *Realism with a Human Face*, viii.

23. In making this distinction between the Peircean and sometime Putnamian conceptions, I intend no judgment about whether it is finally stable. As noted, Putnam's intention was that truth, as he informally elucidates it, is, in contrast to warrant, to be a stable property of propositions across time and a property that is absolute, that is not applicable in varying degree. Plainly, this intention can be fulfilled only if to have warrant for a proposition under "epistemically ideal conditions" (however that phrase be interpreted) involves having a case for it that *cannot be defeated* (else we wouldn't have stability) *or improved* (else we wouldn't have absoluteness) *by any further information*. And the only way of ensuring that both points are met would seem to be

to require that circumstances count as epistemically ideal (or topic-specifically sufficiently good) with respect to a particular statement just in case *no further information relevant to a verdict on it exists to be had.*

The force of that idea obviously depends on what "relevant" should mean in such a context. In fact, though, it is difficult to see that the term can impose any real restriction at all. For, as is very familiar, warrant is a highly systematic, holistic property of beliefs: the status of a body of information as support for a particular belief turns not simply on the character of the information and the content of the belief but on what beliefs are held as background. A flash of grey glimpsed in the woods may be evidence of the presence of a squirrel if you take yourself to be in New Jersey, say, but of a wood pigeon if you take yourself to be in Scotland. It is no exaggeration to say that any piece of information may, in the context of an appropriate epistemic background, be relevant to any particular belief. How, in consequence, are we to understand the idea of possessing *all* information relevant to a particular proposition? Doesn't it just have to mean possessing *all empirical information,* period? In this way, and notwithstanding his protestations to the contrary, Putnam's intentionally less extreme proposal may seem to slide inevitably toward the Peircean. But I make no assumption about this in what follows.

24. This requirement is superfluous, presumably, since a statement does not count as justified, in any sense that concerns us, unless the case in its favor dominates anything that counts in favor of its negation.

25. For further discussion, see my *Truth and Objectivity,* chap. 2, discussion note 1.

26. A. Plantinga, "How to Be an Anti-realist," *Proceedings and Addresses of the American Philosophical Association* 56 (1982): 47–70. Plantinga believed he had Putnam in his sights as well, but there are some issues about that, as we will see (though he would be right in any case if the suspicion expressed in note 23 is sound).

27. Assuming—surely correctly—that a subjunctive conditional, no less than an indicative, is controverted by the actual truth of its antecedent and falsity of its consequent.

28. Plantinga's version of this argument exploits the S4 principle—that what is necessary is necessarily necessary—to derive the conclusion that the idealization Q holds of necessity. But the derivability of Q, unnecessitated, is quite bad enough. A proponent of the "Peircean" conception, or a coherence account of truth, certainly would not intend that the actual obtaining of epistemically ideal conditions, or the actual existence of a maximally coherent belief set, should be consequences of the account. Indeed, these conditions are precisely thought *not* to obtain— hence the counterfactual analysis.

29. A useful explicit discussion is Robert K. Shope's "The Conditional Fallacy in Contemporary Philosophy," *Journal of Philosophy* 75 (1978): 397–413. The Conditional Fallacy is, of course, a crucial difficulty for certain classical forms of philosophical reductionism-behaviorism and phenomenalism, for instance—but like another absolutely basic structural problem for such views, the holistic interdependencies discussed in Christopher Peacocke's *Holistic Explanation* (Oxford: Clarendon Press, 1978), seems never to have been clearly appreciated during the heyday of debate about them.

30. Both pragmatist conceptions also confront a distinct worry concerning the implicit assumption that epistemically ideal or topic-specifically sufficiently good circumstances are *unique*. Only if so can the proposed conceptions of truth ensure convergence of opinion under such circumstances. But given that the relation *is evidence for* is holistically conditioned by background empirical theory, what a priori obstacle is there to the possibility that *conflicting* sets of beliefs be arrived at under epistemically ideal or topic-specifically sufficiently good conditions as a result of theorists having successfully maintained distinct theoretical backgrounds throughout the information-gathering process—so that an opinion formed about a particular statement can vary as a function of the direction in which, so to say, the idealized circumstances are approached? This thought is amplified, in rather a different context, in chapter 4 of my *Truth and Objectivity*.

31. See my *Realism, Meaning, and Truth* (Oxford: Basil Blackwell, 1987), 295–302, and *Truth and Objectivity*, passim.

32. In fact, it is stable provided the range of the "states of information" quantifier in its definition is stable. That's an assumption that would be questioned by, for instance, an antirealist about the past, or future, who contested whether we should think of the totality of states of affairs as eternal. But, of course, such an antirealist would regard the truth predicate as unstable in any case so that, in the view of such a theorist, instability stemming from that source would not disqualify superassertibility as a truth predicate. For further reflections on the matter, see *Realism, Meaning, and Truth*, 300–302.

33. Of the remaining platitudes, Embedding is presumably uncontroversial if all assertoric contents sustain it and all are apt to be superassertible. A degree of Opacity is likewise uncontroversial for superassertibility (though what degree of Opacity any truth property has to display is in any case likely to be a vexed question).

34. This is because it cannot be a priori that (P iff P is F) if it is a priori that (P iff P is G) but not a priori that (P is G iff P is F).

35. Since, trivially, if P is superassertible, there has to be evidence for P.

36. For suppose that to have warrant for A is to have warrant for B and vice versa, but for *reductio*, that A is superassertible, while B is not. Let I be a total state of information in virtue of which A is superassertible—that is, I warrants A and so does any improvement I^* of I. By hypothesis, I also warrants B. Since B is not superassertible, there must therefore be some improvement I^* of I that fails to warrant B. Since any such I^* warrants A, the supposition is contradicted. This shows that coincidence in assertibility conditions suffices for a pair of statements both being superassertible if either is. So if "P" and "'P' is superassertible" have the same assertibility conditions, (G^5) follows.

37. A beginning is made in discussion note 3 at the end of chapter 2 of *Truth and Objectivity*.

38. For further discussion of this general thought, see chapter 9, note 13, of *Realism, Meaning, and Truth*, and the other passages in that book there referred to.

39. I prescind from the complication that the bearers of comic and moral predicates may be spatially or temporally remote. Naturally, modifiers of time and place throw up the same prima

facie barriers to the acknowledgability of comic, or moral truth, broadly conceived, as they pose for discourses in general. A similar point applies, of course, to quantification.

40. The other direction may easily be established by appeal to (K) and (L) as follows:

(1) Not [P is superassertible]   hypothesis
(2) Not [P is knowable]   1 (by K)
(3) Not P 2 (by L)
(4) It is knowable that [not P]   3 (by L, not P / P)
(5) It is superassertible that [not P]   4 (by K)

A different argument for (E^s) is presented in the appendix to my "Truth: A Traditional Debate Reviewed."

41. Such a conclusion could be drawn locally, of course, even if the general validity of (K) is rejected, provided that knowledge entails superassertibility in at least some discourses of which (L) is a priori true.

42. Only a presumption, though. A discourse that meets the conditions described, and so permits superassertibility to model the platitudes characteristic of truth, may yet have other features that impose differences between the two concepts. Getting clear about what such features could be is exactly what is involved in getting clear how realist/antirealist debate is possible after minimalism about truth is accepted on both sides.

30   Three Questions for Truth Pluralism

Michael P. Lynch

1   Three Questions

Truth pluralism, as I understand it, is a *metaphysical* theory about the nature of truth. It is therefore concerned with that in virtue of which propositions are true, when they are lucky enough to be true. Monists hold that there is only one property of propositions in virtue of which they are true. Deflationists can be understood as denying that there is any such property (or any interesting property). In contrast, the pluralist seeks to widen the playing field.[1] She endorses

Pluralism: there is more than one property of propositions in virtue of which propositions (that have that property) are true.

While there are, as we'll see, a range of pluralist positions on truth, the basic idea behind most versions is that while some propositions are true in virtue of say, corresponding to reality, others may be true by virtue of possessing some epistemic property, such as:

Superwarrant: p is superwarranted just when believing p is warranted at some stage of inquiry and would remain warranted without defeat at every successive stage of inquiry.[2]

One basic motivation for pluralism—not the only motivation, but an important one—is that it has certain theoretical benefits that its rivals lack. Monist theories have always seen truth as an explanatorily rich notion: understanding the nature of truth helps us understand the nature of knowledge, content, and the norms of thought. But traditional theories face counterexamples, and counterexamples of a particular form. Such theories work well enough as accounts of how some propositions are true, but fail with regard to others. The most plausible correspondence theories, for example, are plausible when applied to propositions about the color of snow, but generate problems when applied to normative and mathematical propositions.[3] Epistemic theories—whether they are unpacked in terms of superwarrant or coherence—seem on firmer ground when applied to normative propositions, but less plausible when applied to propositions about middle-sized dry goods.

These patterns of failure have motivated many philosophers who think about truth for a living to pursue deflationism. The basic deflationary insight is that we can know all we need to know about truth by looking at its function. And that function, says the deflationist, is really very simple: our concept of truth doesn't work to pick out an interesting property of propositions, it simply serves as an expressive device: it allows us to overcome our biological limitations and generalize over infinite strings of propositions. But as most deflationists will acknowledge, they pay a price for this simple account of truth: they remove truth from our explanatory resources. We can no longer use it to help explain content, or meaning, or the norms of thought.[4]

Prima facie, the pluralist seems poised to take advantage of the other approaches' shortcomings. She claims that different propositions can be true by virtue of distinct properties. So, like the traditionalist, the pluralist can seemingly allow, if she wishes, that truth can have explanatory value. We might even be able to appeal to the different kinds of truth to explain the different kinds of content our propositional attitudes enjoy.[5] And as I will argue below, pluralism—seen in its best light—also shares a key commitment with deflationism: the idea that the key to truth's nature is through its function.

Naturally, pluralism's theoretical advantages (and its costs) are best appreciated after we get a clear sense of the view itself. Indeed, as with any new view, making sense of it is half the battle. So in this essay, I aim to clarify pluralism by concentrating on three questions any pluralist theory of truth must answer:

- How do we identify the properties in virtue of which propositions are true?
- How are those properties related to truth?
- What determines which of these properties a given proposition must have in order to be true?

Clearly, these aren't just questions for pluralists. Any substantive view of truth must face them. Nor are they the only questions facing pluralists. Yet they are certainly among the most basic. Consequently, it pays for anyone sympathetic to the view to give these questions serious attention. But my aim will not be solely clarificatory. I will make a case for a specific answer to each, building on some of the views I defend in *Truth as One and Many* (hereafter *TOM*).

2   What Makes a Theory a Theory of Truth?

Alethic pluralism is a metaphysical view of truth. Like any other metaphysics of truth, it is distinct from views about the concept of truth, or the meaning of the truth predicate, and again from an account of how we fix that predicate's reference. Nonetheless, it is clear that something needs to be said about an issue that, at the very least, is in the neighborhood of these other questions. Any non-deflationary view of truth takes it that there is some property F of true propositions in virtue of which they are true. Some of those views will take it that F *is* truth. Others may hold that truth supervenes on F. But whichever way we end up going on that question, we will need to be given some reason for thinking that F has—to put it bluntly—anything to do with truth. And that means we need some way of narrowing down the candidates for F—one that rules out obvious nonstarters.

As it turns out, this is not a question that only the pluralist must answer. Any view of truth must say something about what would qualify as a property in virtue of which propositions are true. This is because our first question is really just an instance of a more general issue. What makes a given metaphysical theory of truth a theory of *truth*, rather than a theory of some other thing?

In doing metaphysics, we are looking for real essences—we seek to understand the nature of causation, identity, mind. Yet in order to search for something, you must already know something about it—otherwise you won't know if you have found it. So in searching for the real essence of something, we must already have some beliefs about it. Call these beliefs its nominal essence. The nominal essence of something, in the sense I intend here, is the set of largely tacit beliefs we folk have about it. By appealing to those folk beliefs, or truisms, we won't learn *everything* about the object or property in which we are interested. And our later discoveries may force us to revise our preconceptions of it. But however these questions play out, keeping one eye on our folk beliefs about the thing about which we are curious will hopefully tell us whether our subsequent theories of its nature address the topic we were concerned with when our theorizing began.[6]

What applies in metaphysics generally applies to the metaphysics of truth. This suggests a simple answer to our question. A theory is about truth as opposed to something else if it incorporates most of what I will call the "core truisms" about truth—the nominal essence of truth. So what are these? Well, one obvious contender is the truism celebrated by correspondence theories of truth: the idea that truth is objective. To speak truly is to "say of what is, that it is," as Aristotle said.[7] And since what we say, at least when we are sincere, is an expression of what we believe or judge, a parallel truism holds about true propositions we believe. That is,

> *Objectivity*: True propositions are those that when we believe them, things are as we believe them to be.[8]

Two more obvious contenders are platitudes celebrated by epistemic theories of truth such as classical pragmatist theories:

> *End of Inquiry*: True propositions are those we should aim to believe when engaging in inquiry.

> *Norm of Belief*: True propositions are those that are correct to believe.

There are doubtless many other obvious and fundamental platitudes about truth, but the historical importance of these three suggests they are among the most central. They connect truth to inquiry, belief, and objective being—how things are. It is difficult to deny that truth has these relations in the platitudinous sense identified by the truisms. We would find it puzzling, to say the least, if someone claimed to believe truly that roses are red but denied that this is how things are. We would ask for an explanation, and if none was forthcoming, we would suspect that that they mean something different by "believing truly" than what we mean. Likewise, with *End of Inquiry*: if you don't think that truth is, other things being equal, what we are trying to get at when asking questions, then you are probably using "truth" to talk about something other than what the rest of us use that word to talk about.

Call such truisms "core truisms." Core truisms about truth cannot be denied without significant theoretical consequence and loss of plausibility. If you do deny any one of them, you must be prepared to explain how this can be so in the face of intuitive opposition. And denying *many or all* would mean that, at the very least, other users of the concept would be justified in taking you to be changing the subject.[9]

Two points to allay misunderstanding. First, in saying that these principles are truisms, I don't mean that they are consciously endorsed by all the folk. They are the sorts of principles we believe tacitly. And what someone tacitly believes is more often revealed in action than in verbal reports. So the fact that, for example, many college freshmen would appear to deny *Objectivity* by saying that "what is true for me might not be true for you" doesn't mean that they think that believing makes it so. Most freshmen, I think, are not going to *act* consistently with the idea that belief is sufficient for truth. Second, the fact that there is disagreement among experts about which are the *core* truisms doesn't imply that there are no such truisms, or that we don't tacitly believe some rather than others. Nobody ever said it would be easy to specify the content of our tacit beliefs about matters as complicated as truth.

On the view I am suggesting, then, what makes a theory about truth rather than something else is that it incorporates the core truisms, in the sense of either including them among the principles of the theory or including principles that directly entail them. And we'll count it as a *theory* of truth (as opposed to just a chat about it, say) just when it *explains* those truisms. And an obvious way to do that is to show why they are true by pointing to some property or properties that all true propositions have that results in those propositions satisfying the truisms. Such a property will have the features described by the core truisms. Features of this sort could obviously be called core features. But in the present case we might as well call them the "truish features."

3   A Functional Analysis

Our first question for a pluralist theory of truth was: how do we identify the properties in virtue of which propositions are true? We now have an answer. A property determines that a proposition is true when it has the truish features. That is:

Truish: A property determines that propositions are true just when it is such that propositions that have it are objective, correct to believe, and those we should aim to believe in inquiry.

The truish features are relational; they specify that truth has a role in a structure of interrelated properties, revealed by the folk truisms—what we called its nominal essence. There may be other features that are part of truth's nominal essence, of course, features that—while possibly going beyond the core—also help to demarcate truth in a structure of relations. These include relations to assertion, negation, and logical consequence. But at its heart, that structure connects truth with belief, inquiry, and objective being.

This, in effect, is the basic insight and starting point of what I've elsewhere called the functionalist theory of truth. The guiding idea of that view is that we think of the core truisms as revealing what truth does—its functional role. That is,

$(F)(\forall x)$ x is true if, and only if, x has a property that plays the truth-role.

In effect, our discussion above tells us what constitutes playing the truth-role. A property plays the truth-role when it has the truish features. Moreover, this idea—the idea that true propositions have a property that has the truish features (or we can now say: "plays the truth-role")—is a consequence of what it takes for a theory to *even count* as a theory of truth. These features tell us what a property *must* be like to play the truth-role.[10] Thus while we initially appealed to the truish features only to help *identify* that property or properties that plays the truth-role, it seems warranted to go further and take those truish features as defining that role. This means treating the truish features as features of truth's nominal essence that are conceptually essential—essential by way of the very concept of truth.[11]

Understood in this way, our functional understanding of truth is presupposed in our grasp of the concept.[12] Not surprisingly, then, the major metaphysical theories of truth's nature are perfectly consistent with it. Take a standard monist theory such as the correspondence theory of truth. Understood from a functional perspective, this is the view that there is only one property that has the truish features and that therefore plays the truth-role: the correspondence property. Even deflationist theories can be understood in this way. Indeed, deflationists are obviously functionalists: they tell us that truth's nature is exhausted by its function, which by their account is quite thin: truth functions as an expressive device, and that is all. Consequently, on their view, truth does have a functional role, and that role, insofar as it is played by any property at all, is played by the property of being an expressive device.

So the functionalist theory itself is not a metaphysical theory of the nature of truth. It doesn't tell us what truth is. But it does give us a way of answering a question that any metaphysics of truth must answer, and a question that is particularly important for pluralism. It tells us how to identify the properties that make judgments true. They are the properties that they play the truth-role or have the truish features.

Indeed, it is difficult to see what other sort of answer a pluralist *can* give to our question. Pluralism is the view that there is more than one property, $F_1, \ldots, F_n$, in virtue of which propositions are true. Either $F_1, \ldots, F_n$ possess the truish features or they do not. If they do, then they all have something in common: they all satisfy the truisms—which is to say that they all fall under the same (functional) description. If they do not, then, for reasons adduced above, we should not regard the position as a theory of *truth* at all. It is the view, instead, that the word "true" picks out various properties, none of which have anything truish in common. This would, in effect, be a form of eliminativism about truth, not pluralism.

A similar dilemma confronts anyone who takes "true" to be straightforwardly ambiguous like the word "bank"—that is, as a word with more than one meaning and referent. Either the properties referred to by the predicate bear the nominal essence of truth in common, or they don't. If they do, then why not take that shared nominal essence as the common meaning of "true"? If they don't, then it is misleading to say that "there is more than one way to be true." There is not more than one way to be a bank. Riverbanks and the Bank of America are not two ways of being the same thing. There are simply different meanings to the word. Analogously with an ambiguity view about "true." What we believed was in common between the different uses has, on this view, been eliminated.[13]

So we now have a way for the pluralist to identify those properties in virtue of which propositions are true. But we still need address our second question: to say what truth is—and how it is related to those properties that determine it. Here the functionalist faces some options.

4 The Nature of Truth: Four Initial Options

If the above remarks are right, pluralists must be functionalists about the concept of truth, or at least about how we identify the referent(s) of that concept. But that still leaves open our second question, which is how to relate the various properties pluralists are pluralists about to the property of truth itself. Here are four options for the pluralist cum functionalist:

Truth is the realizer property. On this view, there is a single functional concept of truth, but it picks out different properties when ascribed to different kinds of propositions.[14] This is the version of pluralism defended by Crispin Wright (2001). The concept acts as a nonrigid definite description. In this way, "true" is like "the color of the sky at noon." The latter phrase expresses a single uniform concept, but it denotes different properties in different environmental contexts. Analogously, "true" expresses a single description (as given by *Truish* above) but that description applies (or can apply) to distinct properties. Hence on this view, we might say that truth *just is* whatever property plays the truth-role for a given kind of proposition.

Realizer functionalism is reductive in nature, and thus akin to other reductive functionalisms, such as those championed by Lewis (1980) and Kim (1998) with regard to psychological properties. On this sort of view, there is no fact about whether, for example, x is in pain over and above whether x has some physical property P, and so "there is no need to think of [pain] itself as a property in its own right" (Kim 1998, 104). Realizer functionalism is parallel: there is no fact of the matter whether a proposition is true over and above whether it has some lower-level property like superwarrant or correspondence. Consequently, "truth" does not name a property shared by all truths.

Realizer functionalism has its attractions, but it faces some by-now familiar problems. One of the most discussed concerns the truth of "mixed" compound propositions.[15] Consider the proposition

(*Water*) Waterboarding is painful and waterboarding is wrong.

Intuitively, the conjuncts of this proposition are of distinct kinds. One is normative, the other not. So according to realizer functionalism, the truth concept expresses one property when ascribed to one conjunct (some correspondence property, say) and another property (superwarrant, say) when ascribed to the other. But if so, what property does it pick out when ascribed to (*Water*) as a whole?

This is a significant problem, and not just for realizer functionalism, as we'll see below. But it is particularly damning for any view, like realizer functionalism, which denies that there is a "global" truth property—a property expressed by the truth concept that applies across the board to propositions of every type. Indeed, as a number of authors have argued, it seems that any satisfactory resolution of the problem will require just such a property (Tappolet 1997; Lynch 2006; Cotnoir 2009; Pedersen 2010).

A second problem for realizer functionalism is that it undermines one of the motivations for adopting pluralism in the first place. As we just noted, the analogous position in the philosophy of mind implies that pain is not a real psychological kind. There is nothing in common, in other words, between the states we describe as pain states in dogs and the states we describe as pain states in humans. Consequently, the view gives up the ability to appeal to pain as such in general psychological explanation. And this is a loss. For we do find it useful and informative to talk about pain as such in order to explain other things of psychological interest, such as fear or anger. A similar loss occurs with realizer functionalism about truth. It implies that true propositions do not form a real kind. The only property shared by all and only true propositions is one that is not, by the lights of the theory itself, ascribed by our use of "true" or denoted by "truth." Consequently, there is no property we ascribe by "true" that can be appealed to in order to explain certain general facts. One such general fact, for example, we might wish to explain is:

Unity: beliefs with radically distinct kinds of content are equally apt for one kind of normative assessment.

We might put this by saying that they are open to being assessed as correct or incorrect in the same sort of way. What explains this? The simple explanation is that beliefs are correct when they have the property *truth*. Of course, to those who already believe that truth as such has no general explanatory role to play—who believe that it does not figure in explaining anything else of interest such as belief, or content, or meaning— this will not be troubling. But then they will not have needed realizer functionalism to reach that conclusion. But to those who see truth as at least a potentially valuable explanatory resource, realizer functionalism remains dissatisfying.

Truth is the role property. This view (Lynch 2001, 2004c, 2006) attempts to avoid the above problems by identifying truth with what is sometimes called the "role" property: or the property of having a property that plays the truth-role. This allows one to say that there is a single property of truth. Hence there is no barrier to *Unity*: any proposition is correct just when true—that is, just when it has the property of having a property that plays the truth-role.

But this position is ultimately unsatisfying. First, like its cousin "realizer functionalism," it says nothing about mixed conjunctions other than they are true when they have the property of having a property that plays the truth-role. But it doesn't tell us what property a mixed conjunction has that plays the truth-role.

Second, the property of having a property that plays the truth-role does not obviously have the truish features that define truth's functional role. Is the property of having a property that plays the truth-role the property that we aim our beliefs to have in inquiry? It doesn't look like it.

Truth is a disjunctive property. A third option is to take the functional concept of truth to denote a single disjunctive property.[16] Suppose, for simplicity's sake, that some propositions are true when superwarranted and all other propositions are true when they represent things as they are. If so, then we might say that our functional description of truth just picks out a property defined like this:

> A proposition is true$_D$ just when it is either superwarranted or represents things are they are.

If we can accept that a proposition is correct just when it is true$_D$—when it is either superwarranted or representing—this view allows us to grant the simple explanation of *Unity*. But it too seems to founder on mixed conjunctions like *Water* above. For again the question is what makes the conjunction *itself true*. And the conjunction itself is surely not true because it has the property of, say, being either superwarranted or representing the facts. For that to be the case, *Water* must have one of the disjunct properties; but it is not clear what property that would be. The proposition that water-boarding is painful might represent some fact (or object/property pair). It is far from clear that the proposition that waterboarding is painful and waterboarding is wrong itself represents any fact.

Truth is a disquotational property. A final possibility is that truth itself is a merely disquotational property: that is, the property of being an expressive device.[17] This would be the result if we took it that the function of truth was as thin as the deflationists typically take it to be. On this view, the concept of truth would be the concept of the property whose only feature is that it is *a device for generalization via disquotation.* There is nothing else to say about truth itself other than that.

The problem with this view becomes apparent once we remember it is to be combined with the metaphysics of pluralism. The combined view is odd, to say the least: truth itself is a disquotational property. If a proposition p has that property, you can infer p, and if p, you can infer it has that property. But whether a proposition has that property is determined by whether it has some more substantive property, like correspondence. But *why* would a proposition's having the disquotational property depend on its having some other, presumably non-disquotational, property? Moreover, the view would rule out appealing to truth itself to explain phenomena like *Unity* above. So like the realizer view, it is not clear that it would have virtues over and above those of deflationism simpliciter.

5   Truth as Immanent

Recall where we are: I've said that pluralists should be—indeed, have to be—functionalists. The properties in virtue of which propositions are true are those that play the truth-role. What constitutes a property playing that role is its having the truish features. But our second question is still outstanding: what do these properties have to do with truth?

In order to answer this question, the pluralist cum functionalist needs two things. She needs an account of what functionalists sometimes call "realization" and she needs an account of the property truth itself.

I think we can meet both demands at once. Start with the thought that properties can have their features essentially or accidentally. A functional property is defined by its functional role, which, I've suggested, is best seen as the sum of those relational features implicit in the nominal essence of the property. Those features can therefore be thought to be essential to it. Thus, for the functionalist, the natural suggestion is to *equate* the property of truth with the property *that has the truish features essentially* or that plays the truth-role *as such.* It is the property that is, necessarily, possessed by believed contents just when things are as they are believed to be; possessed by propositions believed at the end of inquiry and that makes propositions correct to believe.

This gives us a straightforward account of what truth is. Yet once we understand truth this way, we can go on to say that the property can be *immanent* in other properties.[18] An immanent property is a property that can be manifested by other properties. M manifests an immanent property F just when it is a priori that F's conceptually essential features are a subset of M's features. Again, a conceptually essential feature of F is an essential feature of F that (a) is part of the nominal essence of F; (b) holds as a matter of conceptual necessity; and so, (c) helps to distinguish F from other properties. Since every property's conceptually essential features are a subset of its own features, every property manifests itself. So immanence, like identity, is reflexive. But unlike identity, it is nonsymmetric. Where M and F are distinct—individuated by nonidentical sets of conceptually essential features and relations—and F is immanent in M, M is not immanent in F. Intuitively put, where F is immanent in M, it will be the case that *part of being M is being F.*

Applied to truth, the initial thought is this: for some propositions, truth is manifested by, or immanent in, their correspondence to various bits of reality. Part of what it is for those propositions to correspond is for them to be true. Just as the psychological functionalist will claim that which physical property *realizes* pain in a given organism is determined by facts about the organism, the alethic functionalist will claim that which property *manifests* truth for a particular proposition will depend on facts about that proposition. Two kinds of facts are clearly relevant. The first is what the proposition is about. The second is the proposition's logical structure.

This second point is not surprising. That a proposition's logical structure should help to determine how it is true is familiar from traditional correspondence views, according to which the only sort of propositions that correspond to facts are atomic. Similarly, which property manifests truth for a proposition depends on whether it is atomic or not. How we understand this, however, depends on how we understand the first sort of fact.

In *TOM*, I suggested that pluralists hold that truth for atomics is always manifested relative to what I called a domain of inquiry. As I defined it, a propositional domain is a subject-matter: mathematics and ethics are two examples. How do we know whether a proposition is about one subject rather than another? How else? By looking at the objects and properties that the concepts that compose that proposition are about.

I still take this to be fairly straightforward. Almost any philosopher will think that there are different kinds of content and will take it for granted that we believe all sorts of propositions: propositions about ethics, about mathematics, about the sundries of everyday life. No one, presumably, will deny that these propositions concern not just different subjects, but *fundamentally* different subjects. And *any* philosopher who wishes to claim that we should treat propositions about these subject matters differently—for example, by saying that they aren't representational, or are all false—must have a way of distinguishing propositions of different kinds from one another. Nothing about pluralism distinguishes it in this regard.

Nonetheless, talk of "domains," does suggest, if it does not imply, that subject matters come in natural kinds, and that as a result, we can sort them into these kinds with little difficulty. That is implausible. We can admit, as is obvious, that beliefs have different kinds of content, but we needn't say that the propositions that are those contents divide into natural or rigid kinds.

So why the use of the term "domain"? One reason was this. There are doubtless propositions that correspond but are not superwarranted. For example, consider

(*Star*) At this very moment, the number of stars in the universe is odd.

Presumably, either this proposition or its negation is true. But neither is superwarranted. No matter how many stages of inquiry we go through, we are never going to possess warrant for or against *Star*. Yet presumably there either are or are not an odd number of stars in the universe at this moment.

If both correspondence and superwarrant manifest truth—play the truth-role—for *Star* then we have a problem. Assume that falsity is truth of negation. Assume that *Star* is not superwarranted, but that it does correspond with reality. Conclusion: it is both true and false. In *TOM*, I solved this by drawing a page from the philosophy of mind. Just as a given neural property only realizes pain relative for a given organism, so a given semantic property like correspondence only realizes truth for a domain. But this was more theory than I needed. All I really needed to say was this: properties like correspondence manifest truth for some propositions and not others, *and* only one property of a proposition manifests truth for that proposition.[19]

Let's unpack this. We can say that where M is a property distinct from truth,

> If p is an atomic proposition, then: p is true if and only if it has the property M that manifests truth for p.

And

> If p is atomic and p is M, then: M manifests truth for p, if and only if it is a priori that the truish features are *a proper subset* of M's features.

So an atomic proposition is true when it has the distinct *further* property that manifests truth *for* p.[20] Not being true consists in lacking that property, either because there is no property that manifests truth, in which case the content in question is neither true nor false, or because there is such a property, but the proposition in question fails to have it, in which case it is false.

But if it is not the facts about the domain to which a proposition belongs that determine which property manifests truth for a proposition, what does? The very same facts as before. Think about it this way. No matter what your theory of truth might be, the question of what makes a particular proposition true (or even truth-apt) will depend on the facts about that proposition. What is it about? What concepts does it employ and so on? These are the questions we will ask when confronting this issue. It would be curious if our answers didn't sort themselves into groups, since, as I've already noted, it is obvious that propositions do come in at least rough kinds—kinds that are individuated by differences in the sorts of properties and objects that the various sorts of propositions are about.

If this is right, there is no need for the pluralist to sort (atomic) propositions into strict domains. She takes each proposition as it comes, finding that, in fact, they come in groups, in bunches, in mobs.[21]

6   Plain Truth

Our third question concerns what determines which property manifests truth for any given proposition. We have an answer now for atomic propositions. But what about logically complex propositions? In particular, if more than one property plays the truth-role, then what plays it for compound propositions like two and two is four and murder is wrong? A significant benefit of understanding truth as an immanent property is that that answer drops right out of the metaphysics. The functionalist can say that compounds, mixed or not, are *plainly* true. Nothing manifests their truth other than truth; so nothing plays the truth-role other than truth.

The picture here is familiar from older correspondence theories of truth, according to which atomic propositions like grass is green were thought to correspond to the facts, and the truth of compounds was understood as derivative. Likewise, in *TOM*, I suggested that the truth of compounds is grounded in atomics in a certain sense: "there can be no change in the truth-value of a compound proposition without change in the truth-value of at least *some* atomic propositions" (Lynch 2009a, 90). I called this the weak grounding principle. It is weak for two reasons: it doesn't require that propositions in question depend for their truth-value only on atomics, and it doesn't require that the atomics they depend on (in the case of compounds) are those that directly compose them. But it does reflect a general intuition, and one that Stewart Shapiro (2011) has challenged in a recent article: that plain truths/falsehoods will always depend on some unplain truth/falsehood.[22]

Shapiro's question is whether there might be some plain truths that don't supervene on any unplain truth. One example he considers is truth attributions such as

(1) The proposition that grass is green is true.

This is an atomic proposition. It ascribes a property—truth—to an object, a proposition. In virtue of what is it true? There are various answers available to the functionalist; sorting them clearly reveals their relative merits.

One possibility is the *inheritance view*: Truth attributions are true in the same way as the proposition to which truth is ascribed. Thus (1), for example, is true however

(2) Grass is green

is true. So if (2) is true because it corresponds to reality (however that is cashed out) then so is (1). Truth attributions *inherit* the property that manifests their truth from the proposition to which they attribute truth. Thus (1) will be correspondence true, and so will any proposition that attributes truth to *it* and so on up the ladder of semantic ascent.

There are two reasons the functionalist should not hold this view. First, it implies that truth attributions are true in different ways. But that means that it is in tension with the idea that which property manifests truth for a proposition depends on the subject matter it is about. There would be no tension if and (2) are the same proposition. But they are not.

The second problem is that the inheritance view is hopeless in the generalizations like

(3) Everything Stewart says is true.

The inheritance view says that a truth attributer inherits the way it is true from the truth attributee. But obviously Stewart may say all sorts of propositions, about all sorts of things. Given functionalism, they might have their truth manifested in distinct ways; (3)'s truth would inherit too many manifestations of truth.

Another possibility is *a levels or hierarchy view*.[23] The idea here is to hold that every level of truth attribution is made in a different domain, and hence that every truth attribution is true in a different way than the one preceding it on the semantic ladder. For reasons having to do with the paradoxes, you might add that no domain has the resources to make truth attributions about itself. As Shapiro (2011, 40) notes, the shade of Tarski is close. But this position also faces significant problems. Here are three. First, *why* think that (1) and an attribution of truth to (1) manifest truth differently? Second, given that we can continue to attribute truth to the truth attribution to (1) and so on, this seems to imply that there are an indefinite number of different properties that manifest truth. And finally, note that the levels view implies that (1) and an attribution of truth to (1) are not cognitively equivalent. As with an inheritance view, this may or may not be a bad thing, depending on one's view about how to read the T-schema.

Given these considerations, I favor the *plain truth view*. Truth attributions are plainly true. This seems particularly sensible in the case of a proposition like (1). For it is intuitive that (1) is true because (2) is true. While (1) and (2) are both atomic, (1) is clearly true *because* of (2), and (2)'s truth will be manifested by correspondence. The plain truth of (1) is founded on the unplain truth of (2). This is clearly consistent with the general picture I defend in *TOM*.

So far so good, admits Shapiro. But what about (3)? Again, it seems that this too is an excellent candidate for plain truth. Shapiro is not so sure. One issue he raises is complexity:

> The problem is that there is no limit to how complex these propositions can be … as we chase down the various propositions that [(3)] depends on, we [may] end up considering more and more complex propositions, with no upper limit. (2011, 42)

Fair enough. The truth-value of (3) depends on what Stewart says. But I don't see the problem. The weak grounding principle only requires that there be some unplain truth-values (such as the truth-values of some atomics) that the plain truth-value of (3) depends on. Given that (3) is a universal generalization, if Stewart utters any unplain truth, then this constraint is satisfied. Whatever else he utters is irrelevant as far as the principle goes.

I think a similar response is merited to another example Shapiro considers, a truth-attribution to a generalization of the T-schema, or:

TS': It is true that for every proposition p, p is true if and only if p.

Here too, I am inclined to say that the truth of TS' is plainly true. But, says Shapiro, one of the proposition TS' generalizes over is TS' itself. We are caught in a loop, and so "it is simply not true that the truth-status of any given proposition depends *solely* on the truth-status of atomic propositions" (2011, 43). Granted. But again, that does not violate the weak grounding principle: for it does not claim that the truth-value of compounds supervenes on only atomics. It claims that their subvening base must include at least some atomics. And the truth-value of TS' certainly does.

But Shapiro may insist that there is still a problem. Thus Stewart, in our version of the example,

> might have said that most of what his [disciples] say is true, and one of those [disciples] (or all of them) may have said that [(3)], that everything [Stewart] says is true. So, the process of unpacking the various pronouncements, to figure out which truth-realizers are invoked, goes on forever. (2011, 42)

Note the epistemic language here and in the earlier quotation: the process of "figuring out" what properties play the truth-role never stops. Doubtless. But, of course, how difficult it is for us to *know* what plays the truth-role for a given proposition isn't the question. The issue is whether there *are* any unplain truths on which the truth-value of (3) depends. I don't see that Shapiro's actual example does the trick: if only one of the things that Stewart says is that what his disciples say is true, then the subvening class on which the truth of (3) depends may well include some unplain truths. But put that aside. Abstracting from the details, the fundamental question Shapiro is asking still stands: might there not be some propositions whose plain truth (value) doesn't depend on any unplain truth (value)? The question is whether the functionalist can allow for this possibility.[24]

I submit that the functionalist can grant two points. Some atomic propositions are plainly true. That much, as I have already noted, is completely consistent with what was said in *TOM*, which applied the weak grounding principle to compounds while leaving it open that some atomic propositions might also be plainly true. The other point is perhaps more interesting. There may, after all, be propositions that are plainly true but whose truth (value) does not depend on the truth-value of any unplain truth (value).

Indeed, there are reasons to consider this over and above those suggested by Shapiro's comments. Consider, for example, logically necessary truths, such as an instance of the propositional version of the T-schema, or even any instance of:

(4) If p, then p.

This is again not atomic. But its truth-value does not depend on the truth-value of its atomic components; p could have any truth-value and (4) would still be true. Indeed, it doesn't depend on the truth-value of any proposition in the actual world. For this reason it seems curious to say that it corresponds to reality either. What reality, exactly? And being a necessary truth, it seems less than plausible to say that its truth is somehow epistemically constrained and hence that its truth is manifested by its being super-warranted. It seems much more plausible to simply say that (4) is plainly true—but not because its truth depends on some other truth, but simply because its truth is basic and ungrounded on the actual truth-value of any proposition. Indeed, that very fact is what helps to explain what makes necessary truths a distinct kind of truth. Part of what makes the content of such propositions distinctive is that their truth, in a sense, needs no metaphysical explanation.

Here's the point I wish to emphasize in light of Shapiro's comments. The key move of functionalism is to allow that sometimes—that is, for certain types of propositions—a property other than truth can play the truth-role, and in so doing manifest or realize truth. It is not—at least it should not—be part of the view that every true proposition has its truth manifested by some property distinct from truth. Moreover, as I have already argued, I think that in a wide spectrum of cases—including truth attributions—plain truth is weakly grounded in unplain truth. But I am also perfectly happy to admit that in other cases—such as (3)—this might not be so. But whether it is or isn't really doesn't hang on whether the weak grounding principle is true. It hangs on the nature of the type of content in question, and what sort of theoretical apparatus is needed in order to explain that nature.

The functionalist will insist that for some kinds of beliefs and assertions, understanding their propositional content will require understanding that those contents are true in virtue of having some distinct property that manifests truth. For such contents, the property that plays the truth-role has explanatory value.

Compare identity. Suppose we think that some things, like necessarily existing objects, are just plainly identical across time. Their identity is not manifested by any other property. That hardly means that some things might not be identical in a particular way. Personal identity across time might well be manifested by psychological continuity. It all depends—not only on what we think we must say in order to account for personal identity, but more importantly, on what we think we must say about personal identity *in order to explain other phenomena of interest—such as personal responsibility and human rights.* The same holds in the case of truth. The reason I think that there is more to say about truth in some domains is the same reason other substantivist theorists of truth think this: we must say more about it in order to explain *other phenomena of interest: such as the differences in content between moral, mathematical, and physical-object propositions.*

So, for example, I have argued that if we want to understand the content of our moral judgments, then we need to understand the truth of those judgments as epistemically constrained (2009a). And we can do that only if we think there is more to say about moral truth than plain truth—if we think that it is an epistemically constrained property that manifests truth in the moral domain. Given that posit, we can say that what differentiates ethical judgments from other kinds of judgments is that they have a different kind of truth-condition, and hence a different kind of content. Likewise, even when there may *not* be more to say about what manifests truth for a given class of propositions—say logically necessary conceptual truths—that fact itself can, as we've seen, be informative. The very fact that there *isn't* more to say about their truth is part of what explains why those propositions are the kind of propositions they are. Thus the possibility of ungrounded plain truth, far from being a problem to be explained away, offers the possibility of new explanations.

But isn't plain truth just deflationary truth? No. Think again about what deflationism involves. Broadly speaking, deflationary views involve two commitments. First, the concept of truth is considered as an expressive device of generalization. Second, whatever property, if any, that concept denotes is itself metaphysically transparent. A property is metaphysically transparent just when all the essential facts about the property can be known via grasp of the ordinary folk concept alone. This makes, on the deflationist view, *being true* very unlike the property *being water*, say. We can't know all the essential facts about being water from grasping the ordinary concept of water. But we can grasp all the essential facts about truth, says the deflationist, from grasping the ordinary, expressive concept of truth.

Plain truth is not deflationary truth. The property of being true, I claim, is the property that has the truish features essentially. The truish features are those conceptually necessary features of truth described by our folk platitudes about truth. That is, the property of truth is the property propositions have when they are objective, correct to believe, and the sort of propositions we aim at in inquiry. These features go well beyond the mere expressive device imagined by deflationists. So truth is not just an expressive device on my view. Indeed, I'm not sure it is even essentially such a device. Moreover, truth is not metaphysically transparent either. While you can know the truish features of truth just by grasping the concept of truth, you can't know all the essential features of truth that way. Here is one essential feature of truth you can't know that way: that it is open to multiple manifestation.

Functionalists get to keep truth in their philosophical tool-kit. Not so the deflationist; if truth is a merely expressive device, then we better be able to explain everything we want to explain without appealing to any substantive facts about its nature. This is like hoping to solve all carpentry problems with a hammer. Some jobs call for complicated tools; sometimes you need complex notions like truth in order to get a grip on the nature of content or knowledge.

In sum, Shapiro is of course right that any truth theory must confront that which brings us to the edge of paradox—if only because what brings us to the edge can sometimes throw us over. But these phenomena don't raise special problems for the functionalist. Indeed, they suggest that functionalism has the resources to offer some new explanations for how certain truths are true.

7 Conclusion

We have put three questions to the pluralist. We now have three answers.

- How do we identify those properties by virtue of which propositions are true? Answer: By seeing which properties play the truth-role, and hence have the truish features.

- How are those properties related to truth? Answer: Truth as such is the property that has the truish features essentially. But truth can be immanent in distinct properties, properties that have the truish features accidentally.

- What determines which of these properties a given proposition must have in order to be true? Answer: Two things. First, the logical structure of the proposition and second, the subject matter of the proposition.

These are not the only three questions a pluralist must answer. Nor, perhaps, are these the only answers available. But if the pluralist wishes to make sense of her view, some such answers must be given. Avoiding them is not an option.[25]

Notes

1. Crispin Wright is the most important advocate of pluralism. His original statement is C. J. G. Wright (1992); some important revisions to his view were made in his 2001 essay: there, as here, the position is presented in terms of properties.

2. This notion is obviously derivative of Crispin Wright's notion of superassertibility. For a related epistemic notion of truth, see Putnam (1981).

3. By a "plausible" correspondence theory of truth I mean a correspondence theory that goes beyond simply affirming the correspondence, or Objectivity, platitude about truth and explains this platitude by appeal to a theory of correspondence, or what in contemporary terms is called "representation." See Russell ([1912] 2001) (chapter 1 of this volume) and Wittgenstein (1922). See also Lynch (2009a).

4. For explicit acknowledgments of this sort, see Horwich ([1990] 1998) and Williams (2001).

5. See Lynch (2009a) for just such an attempt.

6. The strategy is, of course, familiar. See Jackson (1998) and C. J. G. Wright (1992).

7. *Metaphysics* Γ. 7.27 (1993).

8. Together with some further and reasonably obvious assumptions, *Objectivity* underwrites further derivative principles which are typically highlighted by philosophers. One related principle is that when, for example, I believe that roses are red, things are as I believe them to be just when roses are red. That is,

> With respect to the belief that p, things are as they are believed to be if, and only if, p.

With this point in hand, we can derive, together with the idea that it is the proposition which is believed that is primarily true or false, instances of the equivalence schema

> *ES*: The proposition that p is true if, and only if, p.

9. For an earlier, and somewhat different, discussion of truisms, see the exchange between myself and C. D. Wright (Lynch 2005; C. D. Wright 2005).

10. As just noted, there will be other features, and possibly other core features, that will help us demarcate the truth-role. Specifying the extent and limits of these features of truth, and determining which are more centrally weighted than others, is an important further project for the alethic functionalist, just as it is for functionalists in the philosophy of mind. But however those questions are decided, the basic functionalist idea is that truth's conceptually essential features jointly define the truth-role. See Lynch (2009a, chap. 1) for more discussion.

11. Obviously, not every essential feature of a property is conceptually essential. Being identical to itself and being distinct from the number 1 are both features of truth, for example. But neither serves to identify truth (they don't distinguish truth from other properties) and certainly neither is a conceptual truth about *truth*. Compare David's remarks (2013).

12. In a recent article, C. D. Wright (2010) argues that functionalist views face a problem of epistemic circularity. Wright has in mind versions of the view that explicitly employ Ramsification techniques for making an implicit definition of truth (see Lynch 2001, 2004b). Such techniques are useful, but as our discussion illustrates, they are not necessary to make the functionalist's basic point. Nonetheless, Wright may suspect his worry is more general; he writes: "But any implicit definition proceeds on the basis of explicit decisions that the principles constitutive of [the relevant Ramsey sentence] are themselves true. Hence the circularity. In turn, making any explicit decisions that they are true requires already knowing in advance what truth is. Hence the epistemic circularity" (C. D. Wright 2010, 272). This is a general problem—but it is, I would suggest, too general to be just a problem for the pluralist. Any attempt to define—or even fix the reference of—"true" by appeal to what I've called "truisms" will face such a problem. But then the problem is one for any view.

13. For further problems with such a view, see Tappolet (1997); Pedersen (2006); and Lynch (2009a).

14. A lengthier discussion of Wright's position can be found in Lynch (2006).

15. A sampling of the literature, here, includes Williamson (1994); Tappolet (2000); Pedersen (2006); Edwards (2008, 2009); and Cotnoir (2009).

16. See Pedersen (2010) for discussion of versions of this alternative. In a forthcoming paper, he suggests that there are properties specific to the various compounds in virtue of which they can possess the disjunctive property. This leads, as he acknowledges, to a multiplication of truth determining properties.

17. A variant is tentatively suggested by Cotnoir (2009).

18. Why talk of manifestation and immanence rather than realization? To avoid confusion; "realization" is generally understood by philosophers of mind to be an a posteriori, nonrational relationship.

19. A number of commentators have suggested this point to me, including, most recently, David (2013).

20. David (2013) complains that I must relativize playing the truth-role, not manifestation. But playing the truth-role means having the truish features, and properties that have those features manifest truth. It is manifestation that is in the metaphysical driver's seat.

21. So does the pluralist believe that we always know what subject we are talking about? No. Are there interesting philosophical problems about when we are talking about ethics and when the law and, when we are talking about mathematics and when physics? Sure. But they aren't special to pluralists.

22. Shapiro is right to point out that in *TOM*, I only consider the plain truth of compounds. I say that if a compound's truth-value is weakly grounded then it is plainly true. That leaves open that some atomics might also be plainly true (see Lynch 2009a, 90).

23. Shapiro (2011) himself suggests a similar line; Cotnoir (2013) independently develops it in detail.

24. Consider: if what I assert is (3) and the only thing Stewart asserts is that everything Lynch says is true, then our mutual admiration society really does form a closed loop.

25. Sections of this paper were presented at the *Truth* Workshop at UConn in May 2009; at a conference honoring Crispin Wright at the Australian National University; at a meeting of the Society of Realist/Anti-realist Discussion; and at the 2010 Central APA. Thanks for helpful discussion to Aaron Cotnoir, Marian David, Patrick Greenough, Claire Horisk, Henry Jackman, Stewart Shapiro, Crispin Wright, and Jeremy Wyatt. A special thanks to Cory Wright and Nikolaj Pedersen for their helpful comments.

References

Aristotle. 1993. *Metaphysics*. Translated by C. Kirwan. Oxford: Oxford University Press.

Cotnoir, A. 2009. "Generic Truth and Mixed Conjunctions: Some Alternatives." *Analysis* 69: 473–479.

Cotnoir, A. 2013. "Pluralism and Paradox." In N. J. L. L. Pedersen and C. D. Wright, eds., *Truth and Pluralism: Current Debates*, 339–350. New York: Oxford University Press.

David, M. 2013. "Lynch's Functionalist Theory of Truth." In N. J. L. L. Pedersen and C. D. Wright, eds., *Truth and Pluralism: Current Debates*, 42–68. New York: Oxford University Press.

Edwards, D. 2008. "How to Solve the Problem of Mixed Conjunctions." *Analysis* 68: 143–149.

Edwards, D. 2009. "Truth Conditions and Truth: Resolving the Problem of Mixed Conjunctions." *Analysis* 69: 684–688.

Field, H. 2001. *Truth and the Absence of Fact*. Oxford: Oxford University Press.

Gupta, A. 1993. "A Critique of Deflationism." *Philosophical Topics* 21: 57–81.

Horwich, P. [1990] 1998. *Truth*. Oxford: Oxford University Press.

Jackson, F. 1998. *From Metaphysics to Ethics: A Defense of Conceptual Analysis*. Oxford: Oxford University Press.

Kim, J. 1998. *Mind in a Physical World*. Cambridge, MA: MIT Press.

Lewis, D. 1980. "Mad Pain and Martian Pain." In N. Block, ed., *Readings in the Philosophy of Psychology*, vol. 1, 216–222. Cambridge, MA: Harvard University Press.

Lynch, M. P. 1998. *Truth in Context*. Cambridge, MA: MIT Press.

Lynch, M. P., ed. 2001. "A Functionalist Theory of Truth." In *The Nature of Truth*, 723–749. Cambridge, MA: MIT Press.

Lynch, M. P. 2004a. "Minimalism and the Value of Truth." *Philosophical Quarterly* 54: 497–517.

Lynch, M. P. 2004b. *True to Life*. Cambridge, MA: MIT Press.

Lynch, M. P. 2004c. "Truth and Multiple Realizability." *Australasian Journal of Philosophy* 82: 384–408.

Lynch, M. P. 2005. "Alethic Functionalism and Our Folk Theory of Truth: A Reply to Cory Wright." *Synthese* 145: 29–43.

Lynch, M. P. 2006. "ReWrighting Pluralism." *Monist* 89: 63–84.

Lynch, M. P. 2009a. *Truth as One and Many*. Oxford: Oxford University Press.

Lynch, M. P. 2009b. "The Value of Truth and the Truth of Values." In A. Haddock, A. Millar, and D. Pritchard, eds., *Epistemic Value*, 225–242. Oxford: Oxford University Press.

Pedersen, N. J. L. L. 2006. "What Can the Problem of Mixed Inferences Teach Us about Alethic Pluralism?" *The Monist* 89: 103–117.

Pedersen, N. J. L. L. 2010. "Stabilizing Alethic Pluralism." *Philosophical Quarterly* 60: 92–108.

Putnam, H. 1981. *Reason, Truth, and History*. Cambridge: Cambridge University Press.

Russell, B. [1912] 2001. "Truth and Falsehood." In M. P. Lynch, ed., *The Nature of Truth*, 17–24. Cambridge, MA: MIT Press. (Reprinted as chapter 1 in this volume.)

Shapiro, S. 2011. "Truth, Function, and Paradox." *Analysis* 71: 38–44.

Tappolet, C. 1997. "Mixed Inferences: A Problem for Pluralism about Truth Predicates." *Analysis* 57: 209–211.

Tappolet, C. 2000. "Truth, Pluralism, and Many-Valued Logic: A Reply to Beall." *Philosophical Quarterly* 50: 382–385.

Williams, M. 2001. "On Some Critics of Deflationism." In R. Schantz, ed., *What Is Truth?*, 146–160. Berlin: Walter de Gruyter.

Williamson, T. 1994. "Critical Study of *Truth and Objectivity*." *International Journal of Philosophical Studies* 30: 130–144.

Wittgenstein, L. 1922. *Tractatus Logico-philosophicus*. Translated by C. K. Ogden. London: Kegan Paul.

Wright, C. D. 2005. "On the Functionalization of Pluralist Approaches to Truth." *Synthese* 145: 1–28.

Wright, C. D. 2010. "Truth, Ramsification, and the Pluralist's Revenge." *Australasian Journal of Philosophy* 88: 265–283.

Wright, C. J. G. 1992. *Truth and Objectivity*. Cambridge, MA: Harvard University Press.

Wright, C. J. G. 2001. "Minimalism, Deflationism, Pragmatism, Pluralism." In M. P. Lynch, ed., *The Nature of Truth*, 751–788. Cambridge, MA: MIT Press. (Reprinted as chapter 29 in this volume.)

31 Truth, Winning, and Simple Determination Pluralism

Douglas Edwards

There is good reason to think that there is a useful analogy between truth and winning.[1] When playing a game, the object of that game is to win, and this tells us something important about the practice of playing games. Likewise, when believing or asserting, the object is to believe or speak truly, and this tells us something important about the practice of believing or asserting.[2] It also, of course, tells us something important about truth, just as the observation about games tells us something about winning. In this chapter, I want to explore this analogy to demonstrate one way that we can arrive at an attractive formulation of *pluralism* about truth, which I call "simple determination pluralism."

1 Winning and Truth, Unity and Plurality

Where winning is typically the goal of playing a game, truth is typically the goal of asserting or believing. In a particular game, the players will typically be trying to win that game, and in asserting or believing, an assertor or believer typically aims to hit the truth.

Given the clear multiplicity of games, there is a strong sense of *pluralism* about winning: *what it takes to win* will change from one game to the next. It is also plausible to think that we have an understanding of winning that is *not* tied to any *particular* game, expressed by the thoughts that winning is the general aim when playing any game and that winning is desirable. These might be said to be general features of winning that transcend any particular features regarding what it takes to win any particular game. We also often ascribe a general property of winning, such as when we say on Sports Day "These are the winners" when gesturing toward the children holding sweets in their hands. There is a sense in which we would want to say that they share a property in common—*being winners*—which is distinct from the various ways in which they have become winners.

There is also a strong sense of *unity* with truth: truth is what all assertions and beliefs aim at and is the property that all true propositions have. Truth is a distinctive and unified norm of assertion or belief formation in the way that winning is a distinctive and unified norm of certain kinds of activity.[3] Moreover, if one takes seriously the project under discussion in this book—alethic pluralism—then there is also a strong sense of *plurality* to truth: even if we take it that truth is a single property, there may be very different things to say about how different kinds of propositions get to be true. This thought is supported by the idea that what there is to say about the truth of, say, mathematical propositions may be very different from what there is to say about the truth of propositions about the material world, which in turn is different from what there is to say about moral truths.

2 Winning: A Proposal

With these thoughts in mind, suppose we were to try to give a theory of winning. To satisfy the twin constraints of unity and plurality, I suggest that we need to make sense of the idea that there is a single property of winning, and that there are a number of different ways to get to have this property. I contend that the best way to think of this structure is to hold that, for each game, there will be a *winning-determining* property, the possession of which by a player will determine possession of the general winning property.

First of all, what can we say about the nature of the general winning property? We need not look far to answer this question as we can begin by describing winning as the property that one aims to achieve when playing a game. There may also be other features we can use to describe winning, such as that if one has the property of winning the game is over; the property of winning is a desirable property; if one has the property of winning, one has been engaged in some form of competitive activity; and winning is a form of success.

A full list of features like these should give us a complete specification of the *property* of winning: they are used as descriptions that characterize the nature of the winning property and are intended to do so exhaustively. Consequently, there will be no *reductive* account of the property of winning that attempts to identify winning with any other property or properties.

To establish what the *winning-determining* property is for a game, the natural place to look is at the rules of the game in question. For the kinds of games we are interested in, there must be some move that one makes or some achievement in the context of the game, which determines that one has won that game. For a game to have this kind of structure, it is imperative that rules of the game are specified, which establish the permissible and impermissible moves, numbers of players permitted, and, of course, the specifications for winning that game. When we have done this, we will find that a conditional can be constructed of the form:

> (*Cx*) When playing game *x*: if one possesses property F then one has won (has the property of winning).

Specific examples of conditionals of this form for chess and tennis, respectively, are plausibly:

(*Cc*) When playing chess: if one has the property of having checkmated one's opponent's king, then one has won.

(*Ct*) When playing tennis: if one has the property of amassing a majority of the allotted sets, then one has won.

The rules of each game thus specify a property the possession of which determines possession of the property of winning. On this view, we treat the game-specific property as the property that determines the possession of the separate property of winning, and the nature of the game-specific property will be established by the rules of the game in question. The key distinction, then, is between winning and *what it takes to win*, or between the property of winning and the properties that determine winning.

This account explains both the unity and the plurality involved in winning. We have a single property of winning, which is shared by all winners and is the property that one aims to achieve when playing a game. We also have an explanation of how this property is attained, which fits nicely with the intuitive thought that it is the *rules* of the game in question that establish the property that determines winning.

3 Truth: Simple Determination Pluralism

If one takes truth pluralism seriously, then truth, like winning, has claims to both unity and plurality. We can now consider how a pluralist theory of truth analogous to our account of winning might look, which I call "simple determination pluralism" about truth.

First, we would start by collecting a list of truth features, or truth "platitudes," and rewrite them so that they make reference to a property. What we would end up with would be a list of claims like the following:[4]

Truth is the property that is the goal of inquiry.[5]

Truth is a property that is distinct from justification.

Truth is a property that is distinct from warranted assertibility.

The proposition that p has the property of being true if and only if p.[6]

To have the property of being true is to tell it like it is.

To assert p is to present p as possessing the property of truth.

A full list of platitudes, or features, like this would give us a complete description of the nature of truth. There will be no reductive account of truth available: unlike some views (e.g., Wright 1992, 2003), the platitudes are not to be used to find another property that exhibits the truth features that will then be identified with truth.[7] All true propositions, then, will possess this "simple" truth property. *This* property is truth, and this ensures that the generality constraint is met: there is *one* property that is truth, and this property is possessed by all true propositions.[8]

We now need to address the question of how propositions get to have this truth property. To explain this, we are going to need to say some more about domains of discourse.

Take it that a domain of discourse is like a game in that there is a goal for those participating in that discourse: to hit the truth. The idea is that truth is attained in virtue of the possession of a *distinct* property that, in accordance with the nature of the domain, *determines* truth in that domain. To establish which property determines truth in a domain, we need to examine carefully the domain in question. What we will need to do is to examine the rules of a domain to generate conditionals analogous to (*Cx*). To do this, I suggest we will need to carefully examine at least the following two features.[9]

First, we will need to examine the nature of the domain itself and the nature of the subject-matter of that domain. The main purpose of this exercise is to establish what kind of content is in play, in particular, whether that domain can be said to deal in what we might call "genuinely representational" content. One way that we can do this is to develop a set of criteria by which to judge whether a domain deals in genuinely representational content. This is a project undertaken by Wright (1992) and developed by Fine (2001). I will not develop the precise criteria that we should use here, as it is clearly worthy of careful study independently, but I suggest that the establishment of the kind of content operational in a domain is the first step to establishing the required conditionals.

Once the first task has been completed—namely, when we have a grasp on how to establish in general the kind content in a domain, and when we have established of a particular domain what kind of content it deals in—we then need to look at the practices of assertion and belief-formation in that domain. In particular, we need to look at what *kind* of property would be required to determine truth in that domain, and whether this property is a property that is properly described in terms of a relation between linguistic and nonlinguistic entities (such as a correspondence property, for example), or a relation between linguistic entities (such as a coherence property), or a construction out of justification or warrant (such as superassertibility). Part of this job will have been done by the establishment of the content of a domain, in that if a domain is deemed to deal in genuinely representational content, it is likely that a property like correspondence will be the truth-determining property for that domain. However, the issue is not fully decided until we look at the standards for assertion and belief formation, and at whether the property in question is able to play the required role in those practices.[10]

Of course, these two tasks are big tasks, and any pluralist view should take seriously the size of the project ahead when it comes to establishing what the relevant properties are in individual domains of discourse. However, as we are dealing with framework issues in this chapter, we can bracket these concerns for the moment and finish the explanation of the structure of simple determination pluralism.

Suppose, then, that the two tasks I have outlined have been accomplished to a reasonable standard. If so, we should get conditionals of the form:

(*Cdx*) In domain of discourse *x*: if ⟨p⟩ has property F, then ⟨p⟩ is true (has the property of truth).[11]

Some examples of these might be:

(*Cmw*) In material world discourse: if ⟨p⟩ corresponds to the facts, then ⟨p⟩ is true.

(*Ca*) In arithmetical discourse: if ⟨p⟩ coheres with basic axioms, then ⟨p⟩ is true.

(*Cmo*) In moral discourse: if ⟨p⟩ is superassertible, then ⟨p⟩ is true.

On the supposition that that there is only one truth-determining property in a domain, these will form one direction of *biconditionals* of the form:[12]

(*Bdx*) In domain of discourse *x*: ⟨p⟩ is true (has the property of truth) iff ⟨p⟩ has property F.[13]

Using our examples, we can construct the following:

(*Bmw*) In material world discourse: ⟨p⟩ is true iff ⟨p⟩ corresponds to the facts.

(*Ba*) In arithmetical discourse: ⟨p⟩ is true iff ⟨p⟩ coheres with basic axioms. (*Bmo*) In moral discourse: ⟨p⟩ is true iff ⟨p⟩ is superassertible.

It is important to note that there will be an *order of determination* on these biconditionals from right to left that reflects the explanatory primacy of the original conditionals. In the material world domain, for example, it is *because* ⟨p⟩ corresponds to the facts that ⟨p⟩ is true, whereas it is not *because* ⟨p⟩ is true that ⟨p⟩ corresponds to the facts. The nature of each domain will thus specify a property the possession of which *determines* the possession of the separate truth property.

The structure of simple determination pluralism is thus as follows. Truth is given as the property that is exhaustively described by the truth platitudes. This property is the property possessed by all true propositions, regardless of domain. For each domain there will be a property that determines possession of the truth property, and these properties are held fully distinct from the truth property itself. The relationship between the truth-determining properties and truth is underwritten by the conditionals of the form (*Cdx*) above, which in turn ground the order of determination on the biconditionals of the form (*Bdx*).

4 Advantages of Simple Determination Pluralism

I have noted that the view presented accounts for the unity of truth by holding that there is a single property shared by all true propositions. While this feature alone may give the view an advantage over some pluralist theories, there are other positions that allow for a single truth property.[14] In the remaining space, I will briefly consider how simple determination pluralism measures up to these views.

4.1 Second-Order Functionalism and Disjunctivism

One proposal about the general truth property is given in the "second-order functional-ist" proposal of Lynch (2001, 2006) and discussed by C. D. Wright (2010). On this view, the truth platitudes carve out a functional role, and different properties (such as cor-respondence, coherence, and superassertibility) realize this role in different domains of discourse. Truth is then identified with the second-order property of having *one of* the domain-specific realizers. All true propositions thus share a property in common—the property of having one of the domain-specific realizers—even though they may not share *the same* domain-specific realizer.

A similar proposal is the "disjunctivist" view discussed by Pedersen (2010) and Ped-ersen and Wright (2013). On this view, the single truth property is again formed using the domain-specific realizer properties, but the property is not formed by existential generalization, but through disjunction: the disjunctivist holds that truth is the dis-junctive property of either corresponding or cohering or being superassertible. Again, all true propositions from all domains will possess this property, even though they may not all share the *same* disjunct.

Both of these views give us generality, but they both suffer from the same kind of concern. As Lynch (2009, 66–67) notes, it is part of the methodology of both of these kinds of views that a theory of truth is designed to give us a property that satisfies the truth platitudes: the platitudes describe *essential* features of truth, and any property that does not satisfy those platitudes cannot be identified with truth. The worry is that both of the properties identified by the second-order functionalist and the disjunctivist may fail to meet this constraint. Here is Lynch on second-order functionalism:

> Suppose the color red is a second-order property: being red is having the property of having a property with certain features, such as reflective variance. Does the property of having a prop-erty with a given reflective variance itself have that reflective variance? Not obviously; indeed, obviously not. (2009, 66)[15]

Carrying the argument over to the second-order truth property, we can ask: given that truth is the property of having a property with certain features, such as being the goal of inquiry, is the property of having a property that is the goal of inquiry the goal of inquiry? Answer (according to Lynch): No.[16]

The point, if good, would also seem to carry over to the disjunctive proposal: the individual disjuncts are identified by their ability to realize the truth role, which means that they must each exhibit the truth features, such as being the goal of inquiry. But is the disjunctive property of having either property 1 that is the goal of inquiry or prop-erty 2 that is the goal of inquiry or property 3 that is the goal of inquiry *itself* the goal of inquiry? Again, it seems not.

I do not wish to claim that these considerations are conclusive, but they do point to some problems for these approaches that are not shared by simple determination pluralism.[17] Because simple determination pluralism holds that truth is the property that is described entirely by the truth platitudes, there can be no question that this property will fail to exhibit any of the features laid out in those platitudes. These kinds of concerns about the veracity of the truth property on offer will thus not apply to simple determination pluralism, which is to its advantage.

4.2 Manifestation Functionalism

The other main competitor in this area is "manifestation functionalism" (Lynch 2009, 2013).[18] On this view, truth is identified with the property that exhibits the truth features essentially, and this property is immanent in, or manifested by, the domain-specific properties by virtue of those properties possessing the essential features of the truth property as a proper part. There is kinship between manifestation functionalism and simple determination pluralism in that both have a very similar account of the general truth property, which enables both views to avoid the concern raised above about second-order functionalism and disjunctivism.

However, there are also important differences. One is that manifestation functionalism wants to maintain an intimate connection between truth and the domain-specific properties by holding that truth is a *part of* these properties. Simple determination pluralism, on the other hand, holds that truth is entirely separate from the truth-determining properties, which get their status as truth-determining properties from facts gleaned about the nature of the domains in question.

Again, it is not my aim here to offer conclusive reasons to favor simple determination pluralism over manifestation functionalism, just to note some plausible advantages. For manifestation functionalism to succeed, it is crucial that the complex metaphysics of manifestation works. However, this is very questionable: Lynch's notion of manifestation is a new and controversial notion, and it has some serious problems.[19]

Simple determination pluralism, on the other hand, requires no complex and controversial metaphysics. It offers the same benefits as manifestation functionalism just through the establishment of the relevant biconditionals in each domain, which nail down the determination of truth in each domain. Thus, simple determination pluralism has an advantage over manifestation functionalism because it requires no complex metaphysics, and it has the added bonus of not being hostage to the success of the controversial manifestation relation.

5   Conclusion

Simple determination pluralism is thus worth taking seriously as a form of alethic pluralism. It meets the twin constraints of unity and plurality by holding that there is a single truth property with a plurality of truth-determining properties, and there are prima facie reasons to think that the view is structured in such a way that avoids some of the problems with other pluralist views on the table. By taking the analogy between truth and winning seriously, it also highlights the *normative* aspect of truth, namely that it is the goal of assertion or belief. Finally, it is worth noting that it presents a framework that has the potential to have application beyond truth to pluralist projects in general, offering a way of capturing unity and plurality that is different from the standard functionalist approaches.[20]

Notes

1. The classic statement of this idea is due to Dummett (1959). The analogy is also discussed in Glanzberg (2004) and briefly discussed in relation to alethic pluralism in Edwards (2011).

2. This is not to say that the aiming need be conscious in each case. Also, for the purposes of this chapter, I will bracket the issue of where other forms of cognitive achievement, such as justification and knowledge, fit as norms of assertion and belief.

3. For an argument for this claim, see Lynch (2006).

4. This list of platitudes takes inspiration from the list of C. J. G. Wright (2003, 271–272).

5. Sub-versions of this platitude would include aforementioned claims of the form approximating "truth is the property that is the goal of assertion" and "truth is the property that is the goal of belief."

6. For ease of use, I will use propositions as the chosen bearers of truth, with an assertion or belief being true insofar as *what* is asserted or believed (a proposition) is true.

7. This view of the truth property is similar to that advanced by Lynch (2009). The similarities and differences between simple determination pluralism and Lynch's view are discussed briefly below and in more detail in Edwards (2011).

8. This allows simple determination pluralism to respond to problems for views that do not allow for a single truth property. The problem of mixed inferences (Tappolet 1997; Pedersen 2006) can be solved as there is a single truth property preserved across valid inference. The problem of mixed compounds (Tappolet 2000) is more complex, but I have outlined a solution elsewhere (Edwards 2008, 2009) that is available to the simple determination pluralist; see also Cotnoir (2009) and Cook (2011) for discussion.

9. This issue is also discussed, approached in a slightly different way, in Edwards (2011).

10. For example, even in a genuinely representational discourse, there might still be issues about correspondence as a truth property if it could be shown—perhaps through arguments akin to Dummett's (1959) concerns—that such a property could have no governing impact on the practice of assertion or belief formation.

11. "⟨p⟩" abbreviates the words "the proposition that p."

12. Without thus supposition, there is a risk of contradiction, as, within a domain, one proposition may possess one truth-determining property and lack another.

13. Analogous biconditionals are more complicated in the games case due to circumstances like forfeiture.

14. See, for example, C. J. G. Wright (1992, 2003).

15. See also Kim (1998) and Horton and Poston (2012) for similar concerns about second-order properties.

16. This is not because of the exclusivity of "the" in *"the* goal of inquiry"—the argument would also run with *"a* goal of inquiry." I used the former to fit with the platitudes as stated above.

17. See C. J. G. Wright (2013) for some trepidation about the force of the concerns in the second-order case, and Pedersen and Edwards (2011); Edwards (2012); and Pedersen and Wright (2013) for some thoughts on the disjunctivist's response to this problem.

18. Lynch calls the view "alethic functionalism," but I use "manifestation functionalism" to clearly distinguish the view from second-order functionalism.

19. See, for example, Edwards (2011) and C. J. G. Wright (2013).

20. I would like to thank Nikolaj Pedersen and Cory Wright for inviting me to contribute to this volume (*Truth and Pluralism: Current Debates*, 2013), and Aaron Cotnoir, Michael Lynch, Aidan McGlynn, and Crispin Wright for helpful discussion and comments. This paper was written with the support of a postdoctoral award from the Irish Research Council for the Humanities and Social Sciences and a visiting research fellowship from the Northern Institute of Philosophy, Aberdeen, both of which I gratefully acknowledge. This research was supported by a Marie Curie Intra European Fellowship within the 7th European Community Framework Programme.

References

Cook, R. T. 2011. "Alethic Pluralism, Generic Truth, and Mixed Conjunctions." *Philosophical Quarterly* 61: 624–629.

Cotnoir, A. J. 2009. "Generic Truth and Mixed Conjunctions: Some Alternatives." *Analysis* 69: 473–479.

Dummett, M. 1959. "Truth." *Proceedings of the Aristotelian Society* 59: 141–162.

Edwards, D. 2008. "How to Solve the Problem of Mixed Conjunctions." *Analysis* 68: 143–149.

Edwards, D. 2009. "Truth-Conditions and the Nature of Truth." *Analysis* 69: 684–688.

Edwards, D. 2011. "Simplifying Alethic Pluralism." *Southern Journal of Philosophy* 49: 28–48.

Edwards, D. 2012. "On Alethic Disjunctivism." *Dialectica* 66: 200–214.

Fine, K. 2001. "The Question of Realism." *Philosophers' Imprint* 1: 1–30.

Glanzberg, M. 2004. "Against Truth-Value Gaps." In Jc Beall, ed., *Liars and Heaps: New Essays on Paradox*, 151–194. Oxford: Oxford University Press.

Horton, M., and Poston, T. 2012. "Functionalism about Truth and the Metaphysics of Reduction." *Acta Analytica* 27: 13–27.

Kim, J. 1998. *Mind in a Physical World: An Essay on the Mind-Body Problem and Mental Causation.* Cambridge, MA: MIT Press.

Lynch, M. P. 2001, ed. "A Functionalist Theory of Truth." In *The Nature of Truth*, 723–749. Cambridge, MA: MIT Press.

Lynch, M. P. 2006. "ReWrighting Pluralism." *The Monist* 89: 63–84.

Lynch, M. P. 2009. *Truth as One and Many.* Oxford: Oxford University Press.

Lynch, M. P. 2013. "Three Questions about Truth." In N. J. L. Pedersen and C. D. Wright, eds., *Truth and Pluralism: Current Debates*, 21–41. New York: Oxford University Press.

Pedersen, N. J. L. L. 2006. "What Can the Problem of Mixed Inferences Teach Us about Alethic Pluralism?" *The Monist* 89: 102–117.

Pedersen, N. J. L. L. 2010. "Stabilizing Alethic Pluralism." *Philosophical Quarterly* 60: 92–108.

Pedersen, N. J. L. L., and Edwards, D. 2011. "Truth as One(s) and Many: On Lynch's Alethic Functionalism." *Analytic Philosophy* 52: 213–230.

Pedersen, N. J. L. L., and Wright, C. D., eds. 2013. "Pluralism about Truth as Alethic Disjunctivism." In N. J. L. L. Pedersen and C. D. Wright, eds., *Truth and Pluralism: Current Debates*, 87–112. New York: Oxford University Press.

Tappolet, C. 1997. "Mixed Inferences: A Problem for Pluralism about Truth Predicates." *Analysis* 57: 209–210.

Tappolet, C. 2000. "Truth, Pluralism, and Many-Valued Logics." *Philosophical Quarterly* 50: 382–383.

Wright, C. D. 2010. "Truth, Ramsification, and the Pluralist's Revenge." *Australasian Journal of Philosophy* 88: 265–283.

Wright, C. J. G. 1992. *Truth and Objectivity.* Cambridge, MA: Harvard University Press.

Wright, C. J. G. 2003. "Truth: A Traditional Debate Reviewed." In *Saving the Differences: Essays on Themes from Truth and Objectivity*, 241–287. Cambridge, MA: Harvard University Press.

Wright, C. J. G. 2013. "A Plurality of Pluralisms?" In N. J. L. L. Pedersen and C. D. Wright, eds., *Truth and Pluralism: Current Debates*, 123–153. New York: Oxford University Press.

32   Austere Truth Pluralism

Filippo Ferrari, Sebastiano Moruzzi, and Nikolaj Jang Lee Linding Pedersen

1   Truth Pluralism: Strong versus Moderate

In its most generic formulation, truth pluralism is the thesis that there is a plurality of ways of being true. This contrasts with truth monism: there is just one way of being true. The most prominent incarnation of pluralism is *domain-based*: there are several ways of being true because different properties are truth-relevant for different domains. Thus, correspondence to reality might be the property relevant to the truth of <Mt. Everest is extended in space>, while coherence with the body of law might be the property relevant to the truth of <Martha Stewart's insider trading is illegal>.[1] This is the type of pluralism found in the work of prominent pluralists such as Crispin Wright and Michael P. Lynch.[2]

Strong pluralists reject the monist idea of a single truth property that applies across the board—a *generic* truth property. Rather, there is a plurality of properties $t_1, \ldots, t_n$ that reduce or constitute truth for less than all-encompassing ranges of propositions. Thus, the truth of <Mt. Everest is extended in space> reduces to its corresponding to reality, and the truth of <Martha Stewart's insider trading is illegal> reduces to its cohering with the body of law. However, no truth-reducing property—that is, none of $t_1, \ldots, t_n$—reduces truth for all propositions. Truth is many, not one.

By contrast, moderate pluralists seek to accommodate the key point of monism *and* the key point of pluralism. Put in a slogan: truth is both one and many. To achieve the combination of unity and diversity, moderate pluralists adopt a network analysis, characterizing a unique concept **truth** through a collection of core principles. These principles pin down truth's role within a larger network of concepts. Michael Lynch, the most prominent moderate pluralist, works with the following core principles:[3]

(O) For every proposition p, the belief that p is true if and only if, with respect to the belief that p, things are as they are believed to be. (*Objectivity*)

(NB) For every proposition p, the belief that p is correct if and only if p is true. (*Norm of Belief*)

(EI) For every proposition *p*, other things being equal, if *p* is true, then believing *p* is a worthy goal of inquiry. (*End of Inquiry*)

Being true, the property, is the property picked out by the concept **truth**. That is, truth is the property that necessarily has the *core features* (referring to the features captured by the core principles):

(t) The property of being true is the property that necessarily has the core features.[4]

The core principles provide unity at the conceptual level: there is a single, univocal truth concept. They also unify at the metaphysical level: correspondence, coherence, and other ways of being true (if any) all share the features marked by the core principles. Indeed, it is in virtue of this fact that they qualify as ways of being *true*. Crucially, the unique concept—**truth**—has a metaphysical mirror image: the property characterized by (t).

The property characterized by (t)—call it "T_G"—is a *generic truth property*. It applies across all truth-apt domains: any proposition, if true, is so in the sense of being T_G. Thus, <Mt. Everest is extended in space> is true in the sense of being T_G, and the same goes for <Martha Stewart's insider trading is illegal>, as well as any other true proposition. Truth is one. However, there is a plurality of truth-grounding properties. <Mt. Everest is extended in space> because it corresponds to reality, whereas <Martha Stewart's insider trading is illegal> is true because it coheres with the body of law. Truth is many.[5]

Between strong pluralism and moderate pluralism, the latter is the more dominant view. This chapter offers a push in the opposite direction. It does so in two ways. First, we argue that moderate pluralists need to think of their own view in a way that is much closer to strong pluralism than they typically acknowledge. Second, we present a novel version of strong pluralism. Section 2 highlights how moderate pluralists make very convenient use of the dual nature of their view: focusing on the plural nature of truth on some occasions but quickly pushing this aspect of their view in the background and focusing on generic truth on other occasions. Section 3 issues a note of caution: moderate pluralists should not and cannot ignore their distinctively pluralist commitments. Indeed, the plurality of truth-grounding properties plays an incliminable role in explaining the metaphysical *unity* of truth, a key feature of moderate pluralism—and a monist one at that. Section 4 introduces the basics of austere pluralism—a novel, radical form of strong pluralism. Section 5 presents responses to the problem of mixed compounds and the problem of mixed inferences, widely regarded as major challenges for strong pluralism. Section 6 argues that austere pluralism is entirely adequate for capturing the core of truth pluralism and discusses how the view fares with respect to different forms of parsimony (spoiler alert: much better than moderate pluralism). Section 7 concludes.

2   Convenient Truth: The One-Many Duality of Generic Truth

The most common pluralist move against monism is to invoke the so-called *scope problem*: no monist theory has a scope sufficiently wide to accommodate all truth-involving discourse. While correspondence might deliver a plausible account of truth for discourse concerning the empirical world (e.g., <Mt. Everest is extended in space>), it cannot plausibly be applied to legal discourse (e.g., <Martha Stewart's insider trading is illegal>). On the other hand, while coherence with the body of law might plausibly be applied to legal discourse, it cannot plausibly be applied to discourse about the empirical world. In general, for any monist theory there is some range of truths $p_1, ..., p_n$ that it cannot plausibly accommodate.[6]

Strong pluralists and moderate pluralists alike appeal to the scope problem. In doing so they draw on the distinctively *pluralist* aspect of their view: the commitment to a plurality of truth-relevant properties. Moderate pluralists are keen to emphasize this commitment in order to undermine monism and get pluralism off the ground. However, interestingly, sometimes moderate pluralists very quickly switch attention to generic truth—the *monist* aspect of their view—when confronted with challenges that take aim at the idea of truth's having a plural nature. Consider, for example, mixed inferences of the following sort:

(MIX)   (1) If Peter punched Bob in the face, then Peter is guilty of battery.

(2) Peter punched Bob in the face.

———————————————————————————

(3) Peter is guilty of battery.

This is a mixed inference since it cuts across domains. <Peter punched Bob in the face> pertains to the empirical domain while <Peter is guilty of battery> pertains to the legal domain.

(MIX) is a valid inference. Now, the standard definition of validity is in terms of necessary truth-preservation: an argument is valid if and only if, necessarily, if the premises are true, then so is the conclusion. But this seems to raise the following question for the pluralist: what truth property is applicable to both premises and the conclusion? Since <Peter punched Bob in the face> and <Peter is guilty of battery> are true in different ways (if true), there seems to be no common property that the pluralist can appeal to in order to account for the validity of the inference from (1) and (2) to (3). This is the *problem of mixed inferences*.[7]

Confronted with this problem, some moderate pluralists conveniently shift attention from their distinctively pluralist commitments to generic truth. This is meant to give them a straightforward way to deal with mixed inferences. What property is preserved in mixed inferences? Generic truth! Generic truth saves the day.[8]

3 Return of the Many: The Unity of Truth Grounded by the Plurality of Its Grounds

It may well be tempting for moderate pluralists to try to take advantage of the dual nature that truth enjoys on their view, conveniently switching back and forth between their pluralist and monist commitments depending on the issue under consideration. However, in this section we argue that moderate pluralists must always keep the pluralist aspect of their view in focus. For, the explanation of the unity of truth—the supposed monist aspect of their view—is inseparably tied to its plurality. Although this may sound like an oxymoron, in what follows we show that it is not. We do so by scrutinizing the unity of truth from a metaphysical perspective.

What does the unity of truth amount to from a metaphysical point of view? It amounts to all the properties that play the truth-role sharing the core features (i.e., the features captured by the core principles). Adopting Lynch's choice of core principles, this means that the unity of truth consists in the fact that all truth properties share the features marked by Objectivity, Norm of Belief, and End of Inquiry. From now on we will use the following convention: we say that a true proposition possesses the core features as a shorthand for the fact that the property playing the truth-role that is possessed by the proposition. These features unify all truths by making them enjoy a considerable degree of qualitative similarity. It is one thing to tell a story about what the unity of truth consists in; it is another to tell a story about how it is explained. *Explaining* the unity of truth cannot be done by pointing out that all true propositions possess the core features. Rather, it is explained by providing an account of *why* all true propositions possess the core features.

We turn to this task now. In executing it we help ourselves to some machinery from contemporary metaphysics: grounding. Grounding is characterized structurally, typically in terms of (strong) asymmetry, irreflexivity, and transitivity:

(SA) If $[p] \leftarrow [q]$, Γ then not: $[q] \leftarrow [p]$, Δ. (*Strong asymmetry*)

(SI) Not: $[p] \leftarrow [p]$, Γ. (*Strong irreflexivity*)

(ST) If $[p] \leftarrow [q]$, Γ and $[q] \leftarrow \Delta$, then $[p] \leftarrow \Gamma, \Delta$. (*Strong transitivity*)

"$[p]$" is read as *the fact that p* and "$\leftarrow$" as *grounds*. Upper-case Greek letters refer to (possibly empty) sets of facts. Strong asymmetry says that, if $[q]$ grounds $[p]$, then it is not the case that $[p]$ is among the grounds of $[q]$. According to strong irreflexivity, no fact can be among its own grounds. Strong transitivity says that if $[q]$, Γ grounds $[p]$ and Δ grounds $[q]$, then Γ, Δ ground $[p]$.[9]

Grounding is a metaphysical relation of asymmetric dependence meant to capture *because* and *in virtue of* talk. Relatedly, the idea that grounding provides *metaphysical explanations* has gained considerable currency in the literature in recent years. One prominent view on explanation takes explanations to be answers to why-questions.[10] If we consider the question "Why p?," an explanation has the form "p because q." Given the intimate link between grounding and "because" talk, one can thus regard instances of grounding as delivering explanations of why a given fact in terms of other facts.

The grounding-theoretic framework just introduced can be fruitfully applied to the task at hand—namely, explaining why true propositions possess the core features. According to the moderate pluralist's characterization of truth—that is, (t) above— truth is identified with the property that necessarily has the core features. Thus, the task of explaining why true propositions possess the core features amounts to the task of accounting for why those propositions instantiate (generic) truth. This is an issue concerning grounding.

Let us consider atomic propositions first. Suppose that p is a true atomic proposition. Why, according to the moderate pluralist, does p instantiate truth? Because it instantiates the truth-grounding property of its domain.[11] Bearing in mind the intimate link between truth and possession of the core features, for true atomics, possession of the core features is thus explained by their instantiating the truth-grounding property of their respective domains.

Let us consider truth-functional compounds. Consider a true conjunction $p \wedge q$, and suppose that p and q are both atomic. Why is $p \wedge q$ true? Because p is true, and q is true. Now, since both p and q are atomic, p is true because it possesses the truth-grounding property of its domain, and the same goes for q. By the transitivity of grounding, $p \wedge q$ is true because p possesses the truth-grounding property of its domain, and q possesses the truth-grounding property of its domain. Again, bearing in mind the intimate link between truth and possession of the core features, we get that $p \wedge q$ possesses the core features because p possesses the truth-grounding property of its domain, and q possesses the truth-grounding property of its domain. Suppose that we are dealing with a true disjunction $p \vee q$, and that p and q are both atomic. Why is $p \vee q$ true? Because p is true or because q is true. In turn, p is true because it instantiates the truth-grounding property of its domain, or q is true because *it* instantiates the truth-grounding property of its domain. By the transitivity of grounding, $p \vee q$ is true because p instantiates the truth-grounding property of its domain, or q instantiates the truth-grounding property of its domain. Switching to the core features: $p \vee q$ has the core features because p instantiates the truth-grounding property of its domain, or q instantiates the truth-grounding property of its domain.

To illustrate these points, let us consider a specific atomic proposition and a specific compound, <Mt. Everest is extended in space>, and <Mt. Everest is extended in space, and Martha Stewart's insider trading is illegal>. <Mt. Everest is extended in space> is true because it corresponds to reality. Now, being true and having the core features amount to the same thing, so <Mt. Everest is extended in space> has the core features because it corresponds to reality. How about the compound? The conjunction <Mt. Everest is

extended in space, and Martha Stewart's insider trading is illegal> is true because <Mt. Everest is extended in space> is true, and <Martha Stewart's insider trading is illegal> is true. As before, <Mt. Everest is extended in space> is true because it corresponds to reality, and <Martha Stewart's insider trading is illegal> is true because it coheres with the body of law. By the transitivity of grounding, <Mt. Everest is extended in space, and Martha Stewart's insider trading is illegal> is true because <Mt. Everest is extended in space> corresponds to reality, and <Martha Stewart's insider trading is illegal> coheres with the body of law. Since truth and possession of the core features come to the same thing, <Mt. Everest is extended in space, and Martha Stewart's insider trading is illegal> possesses the core features because <Mt. Everest is extended in space> corresponds to reality, and <Martha Stewart's insider trading is illegal> coheres with the body of law.

True conjunctions, true disjunctions, and other true compounds possess the core features due to the standing of their atomic constituents vis-à-vis the truth-grounding properties of their respective domains. By transitivity, the same point holds if one or more constituents of a compound are compound.[12]

Let us reflect on the significance that this result has in relation to the unity of truth. Recall that, from a metaphysical point of view, the unity of truth is given by all truths sharing the core features. These features unify all truths by making them enjoy a considerable degree of qualitative similarity. However, the take-home lesson from the considerations offered in this section is this: from a metaphysical point of view, the unity of truth must be understood in a fundamentally plural way. Instances of truth are ultimately grounded by facts about what truth-grounding properties are instantiated, meaning that instances of the core features are likewise ultimately grounded by facts about what truth-grounding properties are instantiated. Thus, the unity of truth is inseparably tied to its plurality. Truth is one because its grounds are many.

Prominent moderate pluralists are keen to stress that one of their main goals as truth theorists is to shed light on the *metaphysics* of truth.[13] Among their chief concerns is to spell out, support, and defend the idea that there is a generic truth property, and hence that truth is one and unified. In light of this, it is rather interesting that reflection on the metaphysics of moderate pluralism seems to lend support to the conclusion that a key characteristic of moderate pluralism—the unity of truth—must be radically revised. The unity of truth is explained by its plurality.

Moderate pluralists are keen to appeal to their distinctively pluralist commitments when pushing the scope problem against monism. However, these commitments tend quickly to slide into the background and are replaced by a focus on generic truth when challenges or problems for pluralism surface. One lesson that moderate pluralists should take away from this section is that they should not—and cannot—hide their pluralism behind their supposed monist commitment to the unity of truth. For, from a metaphysical point of view, the unity of truth must be understood in a fundamentally plural way.[14]

4   Austere Truth Pluralism

In the previous section we argued that moderate pluralists need to rethink the nature of their own view. They have to recognize that the plurality of truth-grounding properties plays an indispensable explanatory role, even in explaining the unity of truth—an aspect of their view that they take to line up with monism. In this section we drop the focus on moderate pluralism and zoom in on strong pluralism. We present the basics of a novel incarnation of the view: austere truth pluralism. A core commitment of austere pluralism is that logic is not representational: it is not a theory about the world. Several philosophers have endorsed nonrepresentationalism about logic. One recent example is Robert Brandom, who takes logic to be an expressive tool for articulating our reasons, pro and con, for atomic propositions expressed by our language.[15]

We embed logical nonrepresentationalism within a truth pluralist framework. For the purposes of this chapter, we merely give a bare-bones introduction of logical nonrepresentationalism. We do so in order to focus on certain other tasks: spelling out how nonrepresentationalism about logic works *when combined with strong truth pluralism* and showing how this combination of pluralism and nonrepresentationalism can be of help to strong pluralists.[16]

Let us use *logical representationalism* as a label for the view that complex sentences express complex propositions that are composed of atomic propositions and logical connectives. The way the propositional structure is produced for any arbitrary sentence is usually rendered by means of the compositional machinery of truth-conditional semantics. Of course, logical representationalism has not been the only game in town in the philosophy of language. Nominalists like Quine avoided commitments to propositions, preferring to give an alternative story about the semantics for natural language. For others, like Dummett, what was primary in the explanation of meaning was not truth, but justification. Still others, like Davidson, preferred to give an explanation of meaning just focusing on the truth conditions of sentences and not on propositions.

Logical nonrepresentationalism constitutes a radical alternative to all of these approaches. The central tenet of logical nonrepresentationalism is that logical vocabulary does not map onto propositional contents. The occurrence of logical vocabulary in logically complex sentences does not contribute to the expression of complex propositional contents. Rather, logical vocabulary is a linguistic tool for expressing our attitudes toward propositions not involving logical notions (i.e., atomic propositions).

Utterances of atomic sentences express atomic propositions—the smallest truth-apt semantic unit. Declarative use of an atomic sentence (e.g., an assertion) signals acceptance of an atomic proposition (i.e., the atomic proposition expressed by the asserted atomic sentence). Thus, for example, suppose "Sushi is delicious" expresses the atomic proposition that sushi is delicious. Assertion of "Sushi is delicious" signals acceptance of the atomic proposition that sushi is delicious.[17] However, crucially, the declarative use of complex sentences does not express complex propositions: rather, it expresses a certain complex arrangement of cognitive attitudes toward atomic propositions.

Consider negation. The declarative use of "Sushi is not delicious" expresses a certain attitude: the rejection of the atomic proposition that sushi is delicious. Here it is important to note that rejection of <sushi is delicious> is not to be equated with acceptance of the complex proposition <it is not the case that: sushi is delicious>. In fact, for the austere pluralist there is no such proposition!

Complex sentences involving dyadic logical operators involve arrangements of the attitudes of acceptance and rejection. Let's consider conjunction. The declarative use of the complex sentence "Sushi is delicious and it is expensive" does not express a complex proposition, but rather a *certain arrangement of attitudes* toward the atomic propositions involved. More precisely, it expresses the arrangement constituted by the acceptance of <sushi is delicious> and the acceptance of <sushi is expensive>. Again, to stress, this arrangement is not to be equated with acceptance of the complex proposition <Sushi is delicious and sushi is expensive>. For, according to the austere pluralist, this proposition does not exist! The thought is thus that conjunction, instead of contributing to the formation of a complex content, expresses a certain arrangement of attitudes of acceptance toward atomic propositions.

Let us try to spell these ideas out in a more detailed and rigorous way. In doing so we help ourselves to the framework developed by Thomas Brouwer.[18] Brouwer draws a distinction between first-order and higher-order attitudes. *First-order attitudes* are attitudes toward atomic propositions. As indicated above, we operate with two such attitudes: acceptance and rejection. *Patterns* are sets of attitudes (which can be either toward atomic propositions or toward patterns). *Higher-order attitudes* are attitudes toward patterns—that is, attitudes toward sets of attitudes toward propositions or patterns. Brouwer introduces two higher-order attitudes: ruling in and ruling out. These are both ways of being opinionated. Ruling in a pattern $\mathfrak{P}$ is a willingness to instantiate $\mathfrak{P}$, while ruling out $\mathfrak{P}$ is an unwillingness to instantiate the pattern.[19] Ruling in and ruling out are mutually exclusive. One cannot rationally both rule in and rule out a given pattern.[20]

We directly represent reality with first-order attitudes that always relate to atomic propositions. Higher-order attitudes induce attitudinal constraints or requirements that help to articulate which first-order attitudes are appropriate to have or to lack. Suppose that Sophie rules out the pattern {accept <p>, reject <q>}—where <p> and <q> are atomic propositions. Then Sophie's attitudes toward <p> and <q> are constrained in certain ways. For example, if she already accepts <p>, then ruling out {accept <p>, reject <q>}— that is, being unwilling to instantiate this particular pattern—means that she cannot rationally reject <q> but must accept it.[21] Suppose instead that Sophie already accepts <p> and rejects <q>. Then her ruling out {accept <p>, reject <q>} requires her to revise her attitudes. She should refrain from accepting <p> or refrain from rejecting <q>.

Consider now the other higher-order attitude, ruling in. Suppose that Sophie rules in the pattern {accept <*p*>, reject <*q*>}. The willingness to instantiate {accept <*p*>, reject <*q*>} constrains the correctness of Sophie's attitudes in a single way: accept <*p*> and reject <*q*>. Why? Because this is the only correct way to rationally instantiate {accept <*p*>, reject <*q*>}.

On this view, we, as human subjects, have simple or complex cognitive attitudes that articulate our stance on how we represent reality. Cognition consists not only in representing reality by means of the simple attitudes of accepting and rejecting atomic propositions but also in having complex attitudes regarding what to accept and reject. Following Brouwer (2013, 94), we can provide a recursive characterization of complex attitudes:

A *level-1 pattern* is a set of simple attitudes (of acceptance and rejection) toward atomic propositions. A *level-2 pattern* is a set of attitudes of acceptance and rejection toward atomic propositions *and/or* attitudes of ruling-in and ruling-out level-1 patterns. A *level-3 pattern* is a set of attitudes of acceptance and rejection toward atomic propositions *and/or* attitudes of ruling-in and ruling-out patterns of a level less than 3. And so on.

Cognitive agents aim to have the correct attitudes for representing reality. Attitudes have the following correctness conditions (Brouwer 2013, 161), starting with the simple attitudes of acceptance and rejection and moving on to attitudes toward patterns:

(COR$_A$)   Accepting an atomic proposition <*p*> is correct if and only if <*p*> is true.

(COR$_R$)   Rejecting an atomic proposition <*p*> is correct if and only if <*p*> is not true.

(COR$_{RIL1}$)   Ruling in a level-1 pattern is correct if and only if all of the attitudes in the pattern are correct.

(COR$_{ROL1}$)   Ruling out a level-1 pattern is correct if and only if some of the attitudes in the pattern are not correct.

(COR$_{RIL2}$)   Ruling in a level-2 pattern is correct if and only if all of the attitudes in the pattern are correct.

(COR$_{ROL2}$)   Ruling out a level-2 pattern is correct if and only if some of the attitudes in the pattern are not correct.

... and so on.

What these correctness conditions show is that the correctness condition of any cognitive attitude is determined *just* by atomic propositions. No complex propositions are needed.

Now turn to language. For the logical expressivist, there is a sharp divide between nonlogical vocabulary and logical vocabulary. Nonlogical expressions such as "Paris," "big," "sushi," "tasty," "right," and "wrong" have a minimal representational function in the following sense: they contribute to the determination of the truth conditions of atomic propositions that are expressed by the atomic sentences containing these expressions. The truth conditions of atomic sentences are explained by the truth conditions of the atomic propositions that are semantically expressed by them.[22] In contrast, logical vocabulary plays a different role. The point of a logical expression is to be a linguistic vehicle for the expression of attitudes of any complexity (Brouwer 2013, 201). Logically complex sentences express the ruling in or ruling out of some pattern of attitudes. We can articulate this view by means of the following semantic clauses:

(EXP_{ATOM}) If "p" is atomic, then "p" semantically expresses the atomic proposition $<p>$.

(EXP_{NEG}) "Not-p" semantically expresses ruling out {accept p}—that is, the unwillingness to accept p.

(EXP_{DISJ}) "p or q" semantically expresses ruling out {reject p, reject q}—that is, the unwillingness to reject p and reject q.

(EXP_{CONJ}) "p and q" semantically expresses ruling in {accept p, accept q}—that is, the willingness to accept p and accept q.

(EXP_{COND}) "If p then q" semantically expresses ruling out {accept p, reject q}—that is, the unwillingness to accept p and reject q.[23]

With the semantic clauses in place, we can define the truth conditions of atomic and complex sentences. Let us first consider the simple cases of atomic sentences and complex sentences with atomic sentences and propositional connectives as their only constituents:

(T_{ATOM}) If "p" is atomic, "p" is true if and only if the atomic proposition $<p>$ is true.

$(T_{NEG-ATOM})$ "Not-p" is true if and only if ruling out {accept p} is correct.

$(T_{DISJ-ATOM})$ "p or q" is true if and only if ruling out {reject p, reject q} is correct.

$(T_{CONJ-ATOM})$ "p and q" is true if and only if ruling in {accept p, accept q} is correct.

$(T_{COND-ATOM})$ "If p then q" is true if and only if ruling out {accept p, reject q} is correct.

On the proposed picture, truth-*properties* apply only to atomic propositions. The truth-predicate also applies. However, while the truth-*predicate* applies to complex sentences, there is no truth *property* that does so (for there are no complex propositions to match complex sentences). Whether the truth-predicate applies to a given complex sentence is determined by whether the relevant attitudes toward patterns of propositions are correct—and the attitudes themselves are not truth-apt, merely correct or incorrect (though their correctness conditions ultimately depend on the standing of the relevant atomic propositions vis-à-vis the truth-properties of their respective domains).

Let "negative attitude related to the pattern expressed by "'p'" refer to rejection if "p" expresses a level-1 pattern (i.e., a set of attitudes of acceptance or rejection of atomics) and ruling out if "p" expresses a higher-level pattern. Let "positive attitude related to the pattern expressed by "'p'" refer to acceptance if "p" expresses a level-1 pattern (i.e., a set of attitudes of acceptance or rejection of atomics) and ruling in if "p" expresses a higher-level pattern. We can then generalize (T$_{\text{NEG-ATOM}}$), (T$_{\text{DISJ-ATOM}}$), (T$_{\text{CONJ-ATOM}}$), and (T$_{\text{COND-ATOM}}$) to complex sentences of any logical complexity, as follows:

(T$_{\text{NEG}}$)   "Not-p" is true if and only if ruling out the pattern expressed by "p" is correct.

(T$_{\text{DISJ}}$)   "p or q" is true if and only if ruling out {the negative attitude related to the pattern expressed by "p," the negative attitude related to the pattern expressed by "q"} is correct.

(T$_{\text{CONJ}}$)   "p and q" is true if and only if ruling in {the positive attitude related to the pattern expressed by "p," the positive attitude related to the pattern expressed by "q"} is correct.

(T$_{\text{COND}}$)   "If p then q" is true if and only if ruling out {the positive attitude related to the pattern expressed by "p," the negative attitude related to the pattern expressed by "q"} is correct.

Reflecting on the framework presented in this section, we see that it is of a mixed sort. It is not purely expressivist, as atomic sentences semantically express (atomic) propositions. However, the framework is partly expressivist because complex sentences express (higher-order) attitudes rather than propositional contents.[24]

In the next section we use our framework to solve the problems of mixed compounds and mixed inferences, two major challenges confronting pluralists about truth.

5   Applying Austere Truth Pluralism: Mixed Compounds and Mixed Inferences

Let us explore how the proposed framework can be brought to bear on the problem of mixed compounds. If the challenge of mixed compounds is framed in terms of propositions, the impact of the separation of semantics and metaphysics is immediate: there is no such thing as the complex proposition <Mt. Everest is extended in space, and Martha Stewart's insider trading is illegal>, so there is no legitimate concern to be raised about which truth-property this proposition has. In general, since there are no compound propositions, a fortiori, it makes no sense to ask what truth-property mixed compound *propositions* have. Once general metaphysicalism is rejected, the problem of mixed compound propositions evaporates.

If the challenge of mixed compounds is framed in terms of sentences, it remains a legitimate question to ask which property the truth-predicate denotes when applied to complex sentences. However, it is a legitimate question that the austere pluralist is well equipped to answer. On the austere pluralist view, the mind has an explanatory priority over language when it comes to logically complex sentences: the application of the truth-predicate to these sentences is fully explained by which attitude toward the relevant atomic propositions is correct to take. This is reflected by the truth conditions of complex sentences: their semantic status—that is, their truth or falsity—is explained just in terms of the correctness conditions of patterns of attitudes, and in turn, these are ultimately completely determined by the truth conditions of *atomic propositions*. This point signals a radical departure from the standard pluralist frameworks. Both moderate and strong pluralists accept the principle that whenever a sentence is true there is (at least) a corresponding truth property that applies to content semantically expressed by the sentence. The austere pluralist rejects this principle for logically complex sentences. Thus, the austere pluralist does not need to commit to any truth-property beyond those that apply to atomic propositions in order to account for the truth of complex sentences. This point applies in the case of both pure and mixed compounds.

To illustrate, consider a conjunctive sentence "*p* and *q*," where both "*p*" and "*q*" are atomic. First, applying the truth condition for conjunctions with only atomic constituents, we get the following:

(A) "*p* and *q*" is true if and only if ruling in {accept *p*, accept *q*} is correct.

Since "*p*" and "*q*" express atomic propositions, {accept *p*, accept *q*} is a level-1 pattern. The correctness condition for ruling in level-1 patterns tells us that

(B) Ruling in {accept *p*, accept *q*} is correct if and only if accepting <*p*> is correct and accepting <*q*> is correct.

Now, the correctness condition for attitudes toward atomic propositions delivers:

(C) Accepting <*p*> is correct if and only if <*p*> is true, and accepting <*q*> is correct if and only if <*q*> is true.

Since austere pluralism is a form of strong pluralism, the truth of *p* and *q* should be accounted for in a reductionist way:

(D) <*p*> is true if and only if <*p*> has the truth-reducing property of its domain, and <*q*> is true if and only if <*q*> has the truth-reducing property of its domain.

Finally, by the transitivity of the biconditionals in (A)–(D), we get:

(E) "*p* and *q*" is true if and only if <*p*> has the truth-reducing property of its domain, and <*q*> has the truth-reducing property of its domain.

—where, again, both <*p*> and <*q*> are atomic propositions.

(E) shows how the truth of conjunctions featuring only atomic sentences is completely determined by the standing of the atomic propositions expressed by their constituent atomic sentences. This applies both in the case of pure and mixed conjunctive sentences. The only difference between pure and mixed conjunctions is the number of truth-reducing properties involved in their truth conditions. If "*p* and *q*" is a pure conjunction, then the truth-reducing property relevant to determining whether "*p* and *q*" is true is the same for <*p*> and <*q*>—so only one truth-reducing property is involved. However, if "*p* and *q*" is a mixed conjunction, the truth-reducing properties of <*p*> and <*q*>'s respective domains are different. Thus, while "2+2=4, and 9+3=12" is true if and only if <2+2=4> coheres with the axioms of arithmetic and <9+3=12> does so as well, "Mt. Everest is extended in space, and 9+3=12" is true if and only if <Mt. Everest is extended in space> corresponds to reality, and <9+3=12> coheres with the axioms of arithmetic.

The treatment of sentential truth for conjunctions with only atomic conjuncts can be generalized to conjunctions of arbitrary complexity, and similarly for other sentential compounds. In all cases the recipe is the same: apply the truth conditions for complex sentences, correctness conditions for attitudes (which subsume acceptance and rejection of atomic propositions as well as ruling in and ruling out patterns), and the strong pluralist's idea that different properties reduce truth for different domains. Given the availability of this sort of treatment, there is no pressure on the austere pluralist to endorse any distinct truth-property as the referent of "true" in order to account for the truth of complex sentences. Atomic propositions and their truth-reducing properties do all the work.

Let us now turn to mixed inferences. As in section 2, consider the following instance of modus ponens:

(MIX) (1) If Peter punched Bob in the face, then Peter is guilty of battery.

(2) Peter punched Bob in the face.

_____

(3) Peter is guilty of battery.

A standard account of validity ties validity to necessary truth-preservation:

(PRE) An argument is valid if and only if, necessarily, if the premises are true, then its conclusion is true.[25]

The problem for the pluralist is that in mixed inferences the conclusion and at least one of the premises are true in different ways. However, in that case what truth property can be applied to both the premises and the conclusion to account for the validity of mixed inferences such as (MIX)?

Our strategy for dealing with the problem of mixed inferences is to switch attention from the account of validity in terms of necessary truth-preservation to the following alternative account:

(IMP) An argument is valid if and only if it is impossible for all of the premises to be true and its conclusion false.

(IMP), like (PRE), is a standard account of validity. (IMP) defines validity in terms of *exclusion of a certain combination* of semantic standings—namely, the premises' being true and the conclusion false. We help ourselves to (IMP) and, given this account of validity, show that the austere pluralist has the resources to account for the validity of mixed inferences. We consider the propositional version of the problem first and then turn to the sentential version.[26]

As seen above, the propositional version of the problem of mixed compounds evaporates once the framework of austere pluralism is adopted. This is because mixed complex sentences do not express propositions, and hence there is no legitimate question to raise about what truth-property mixed complex *propositions* possess.

Mixed inferences are not validity-apt, with validity regarded as a feature that involves propositions and properties. In this sense the propositional version of the problem of mixed inferences does not arise. The explanation is the same as before. A presupposition of propositional-property validity-talk is that the premises and the conclusion all express propositions—which, in turn, can instantiate semantic properties. However, valid mixed inferences involve at least one compound sentence. Within the framework of austere pluralism such sentences do not express propositions. Hence, a presupposition of proposition-property validity-talk is not satisfied. The propositional problem of mixed inferences thus evaporates within the framework of austere pluralism, just like the propositional version of the problem of mixed compounds.

Turn now to the sentential version of the problem of mixed inferences. We show that it is impossible for the premises to be true and the conclusion to be false in (MIX). We do so by applying the truth conditions for sentences, correctness conditions for patterns, and the strong pluralist's idea that different properties reduce truth for different (base-level) domains.

The truth conditions of sentences (1), (2), and (3) in (MIX) are understood in terms of the correctness of the relevant attitudes:

(1-TC)   "If Peter punched Bob in the face, then Peter is guilty of battery" is true if and only if ruling out {accept <Peter punched Bob in the face>, reject <Peter is guilty of battery>} is correct.

(2-TC)   "Peter punched Bob in the face" is true if and only if accepting <Peter punched Bob in the face> is correct.

(3-TC)   "Peter is guilty of battery" is true if and only if accepting <Peter is guilty of battery> is correct.

(1-TC) involves a level-1 pattern—that is, attitudes toward atomic propositions. When applied to (1-TC), the correctness condition for ruling out level-1 patterns yields the following:

(1-TC*)   Ruling out {accept <Peter punched Bob in the face>, reject <Peter is guilty of battery>} is correct if and only if some attitude in the pattern is not correct—that is, accepting <Peter punched Bob in the face> is not correct or rejecting <Peter is guilty of battery> is not correct.

The respective correctness conditions for acceptance and rejection of atomic propositions tell us that accepting <Peter punched Bob in the face> is not correct if and only if <Peter punched Bob in the face> is not true, and rejecting <Peter is guilty of battery> is not correct if and only if <Peter is guilty of battery> is true. Applying these observations to (1-TC*), we obtain:

(1-TC**)　　Ruling out {accept <Peter punched Bob in the face>, reject <Peter is guilty of battery>} is correct if and only if <Peter punched Bob in the face> is not true, or <Peter is guilty of battery> is true.

Now, given the strong pluralist's truth-reduction thesis, (1-TC**) should be construed as follows:

(1-TC***)　　Ruling out {accept <Peter punched Bob in the face>, reject <Peter is guilty of battery>} is correct if and only if <Peter punched Bob in the face> is not T_1, or <Peter is guilty of battery> is T_2,

where T_1 and T_2 are the truth-reducing properties of, respectively, the empirical domain and the legal domain.

Finally, combining (1-TC) and (1-TC***), we get:

(1-TC****)　　"If Peter punched Bob in the face, then Peter is guilty of battery" is true if and only if <Peter punched Bob in the face> is not T_1, or <Peter is guilty of battery> is T_2.

(1-TC****) connects the truth of the conditional sentence in (1) and the semantic standing—conceived in terms of properties—of the propositions expressed by its atomic constituents. For (2-TC) and (3-TC), this connection is more straightforward to achieve, as they both involve atomic sentences.

Applying the correctness conditions for acceptance of atomic propositions to (2-TC) and (3-TC), we get:

(2-TC*)　　"Peter punched Bob in the face" is true if and only if accepting <Peter punched Bob in the face> is true.

(3-TC*)　　"Peter is guilty of battery" is true if and only if accepting <Peter is guilty of battery> is true.

Given the truth-reduction thesis, (2-TC*) and (3-TC*) must be understood along the following lines:

(2-TC**)　　"Peter punched Bob in the face" is true if and only if accepting <Peter punched Bob in the face> is T_1.

(3-TC**)　　"Peter is guilty of battery" is true if and only if accepting <Peter is guilty of battery> is T_2, where, as before, T_1 and T_2 are the truth-reducing properties of, respectively, the empirical domain and the legal domain.

Is it possible for sentences (1) and (2) to be true and (3) false? No, for that would require <Peter punched Bob in the face> not to be T_1 or <Peter is guilty of battery> to be T_2, <Peter punched Bob in the face> to be T_1, *and* <Peter is guilty of battery> not to be T_2. However, these requirements are incompatible—that is, the truth conditions of premises (1) and (2) and the falsity condition of the conclusion (3) are incompatible. Since it is impossible for the premises to be true and the conclusion false, (MIX) is valid.

The validity of (MIX) has been accounted for at the level of sentences. As in the case of mixed compounds, the account offered appeals to the truth conditions for complex sentences, correctness conditions for attitudes (which subsume acceptance and rejection of atomic propositions as well as ruling in and ruling out patterns), and the strong pluralist's idea that different properties reduce truth for different domains. What this shows is that sentential validity can be accounted for by appealing solely to our preferred austere metaphysics—that is, atomic propositions, their truth-reducing properties, and attitudes toward atomic propositions and patterns. We conclude that, contrary to claims made by monists and moderate pluralists, accounting for the validity of mixed inferences does not pose an insurmountable challenge to strong pluralism.

6   Austere Truth Pluralism: Further Reflections

In this penultimate section of the chapter, we do two things. First, we observe that austere pluralism offers an adequate framework for capturing the core idea behind truth pluralism: alethic variation across domains. Second, we offer a comprehensive discussion of austere pluralism and parsimony, a theoretical virtue that often carries significant weight in theory choice. We distinguish between two types of parsimony and consider each in isolation and also together. We argue that, compared to moderate pluralism, austere pluralism fares better in each case.

6.1   Capturing the Core Idea behind Truth Pluralism
The key idea behind pluralism is that truth exhibits a diverse nature across domains. This is transparent in the way that truth pluralism is usually presented, as reflected by two representative passages drawn from, respectively, Lynch and Edwards:

> One reason [to be a truth pluralist] concerns the sheer variety of the propositions one believes: that six is an even number; that Napoleon lost the battle of Waterloo, that Microsoft is a powerful corporation; that murder is wrong and thankfully illegal as well. The most basic motivation for a pluralist treatment of truth is that it isn't at all obvious that the truth of these propositions, ranging as they do over history, mathematics, ethics, and so on, must all be true in the exact same way. Pre-theoretically, it seems at least as plausible to think that the truth of, e.g., ethical claims consists in something quite different than the truth of assertions concerning the physical world. (Lynch 2004, 385)

> According to the alethic pluralist, there will be a robust property in virtue of which the propositions expressed by sentences in a particular domain of discourse will be true, but this property will change depending on the domain we are considering. In other words, although the notion of truth as correspondence to the facts might fit our domain of discourse about the material world, a different notion of truth—perhaps one with less metaphysical baggage, constructed out of coherence, or justification or warrant—may fit the domains in which the correspondence notion looks problematic. (Edwards 2011, 31–32)

The chief aim of truth pluralists is to capture alethic diversity across domains and to do so in a way that allows them to address the scope problem. This is what drives them toward pluralism.

Austere pluralism provides an adequate framework for achieving the aim of capturing alethic diversity, the key distinguishing feature of pluralism. The view attributes different truth-reducing properties (correspondence, coherence, superassertibility, etc.) to atomic propositions pertaining to different domains. Therein lies the diversity of truth and, in turn, this diversity gives the austere pluralist the resources to deal with the scope problem.

There is nothing about the idea of alethic diversity by itself that puts any theoretical pressure on pluralists to opt for moderate pluralism rather than strong pluralism. Indeed, that pressure derives from the idea of *alethic unity*—that is, an idea that stands in complete opposition to the idea of alethic diversity. And, again, it is worth emphasizing that alethic diversity—not unity—is the key distinguishing feature of pluralism. It is the alleged explanatory advantages of alethic unity—at the metaphysical level represented by the generic truth property—that are meant to count in favor of moderate pluralism and against strong pluralism. However, this does not in any way tell against austere pluralism's adequacy as a way to capture the idea of alethic diversity. (And, besides, the explanatory advantages of moderate pluralism are illusory—as argued in the case of mixed compounds and inferences in section 5.)

6.2   Ontological Parsimony

In this subsection we consider an important theoretical virtue: parsimony. We discuss two understandings of ontological parsimony and argue that, compared to moderate pluralism, austere pluralism does better with respect to each of them and does so, too, if they are taken to complement one another. Parsimony is widely regarded as an important abductive criterion for theory choice. If austere pluralism can account for the same range of alethic phenomena as moderate pluralism, then austere pluralism's better standing vis-à-vis ontological parsimony seems to rule in favor of the view.

In order to support their endorsement of a generic truth property, moderate pluralists argue that this kind of property is needed to explain a range of alethic phenomena—including the truth of mixed compounds and the validity of mixed inferences. This is a widely used move in discussions concerning existence. Meeting explanatory needs lends support to existence claims. However, this is only one-half of the story. The other half embodies an attitude of ontological parsimony: being explanatorily dispensable speaks against existence claims. Perhaps the most famous incarnation of this idea is Ockham's razor:

(OR) Do not multiply entities beyond necessity,

where the expression "beyond necessity" is tied to explanation. When it is said not to multiply entities beyond necessity, what this means is not to multiply entities beyond what is needed to explain some target range of facts, data, or phenomena.

Moderate pluralists argue that a generic truth property is needed to explain a target range of alethic phenomena, including the truth of mixed compounds and the validity of mixed inferences. If their case is compelling and meeting explanatory needs supports existence claims, there is a reason to endorse the existence of a generic truth property. How might the austere pluralist engage with this line of argument? Ockham's razor suggests the following strategy: show that the target range of alethic phenomena can be explained without appealing to a generic truth property. This, together with Ockham's razor, rules against the existence of a generic truth property.

One might think that there are grounds for optimism about this strategy for austere pluralists, especially given the account of mixed compounds and inferences provided in the previous section.[27] We would, of course, *like* this strategy to work. However, in order to assess whether the strategy might be successfully executed it is relevant to distinguish between two readings of Ockham's razor—one qualitative, another quantitative:

(OR*) Do not multiply types of entities beyond necessity.

(OR#) Do not multiply the number of entities beyond necessity.

For both the qualitative and the quantitative reading, the relation "being more ontologically parsimonious than" can be understood in terms of proper subsethood. For (OR*), given two ontologies O_i and O_j, say that O_i is qualitatively more ontologically parsimonious than O_j if and only if the set of *types* of entities in O_i is a proper subset of the set of *types* of entities in O_j. For (OR#), given two ontologies O_i and O_j, say that O_i is quantitatively more ontologically parsimonious than O_j if and only if the set of entities in O_i is a proper subset of the set of entities in O_j.

The qualitative reading of Ockham's razor has traditionally enjoyed a more prominent status than the quantitative reading. Recently, however, a considerable number of philosophers have investigated, advocated, or relied on the quantitative reading.[28]

Suppose that the quantitative reading is adopted. In that case the Ockham strategy holds considerable promise of being executed. In section 5 we presented a strongly pluralist account of both the truth of mixed compounds and the validity of mixed inferences that does not involve a generic truth property, countering moderate pluralists' claim to the effect that generic truth is needed to account for relevant alethic phenomena. Work is likewise being done by strong pluralists to address other alethic phenomena.[29]

Moderate pluralists endorse the existence of a plurality of properties whose instances ground instances of generic truth within different domains. Strong pluralists likewise endorse a plurality of properties intimately related to truth, although, unlike moderate pluralists, they take these properties to reduce rather than ground truth within specific domains. Moderate pluralists endorse one additional property: generic truth. This means that their preferred metaphysics of truth is less quantitatively parsimonious than the metaphysics of austere pluralism. Combine this observation with the explanatory dispensability of generic truth and apply Ockham's razor. Result: austere pluralism fares better than moderate pluralism.

Suppose instead that the qualitative reading of Ockham's razor is adopted. In that case assessing the relative merits of austere pluralism and moderate pluralism becomes a more delicate matter. Given this reading of the razor, in order for austere pluralism to fare better than moderate pluralism it must be shown that the inclusion of a generic truth property inflates the moderate pluralist's ontology *typewise*. As such the generic truth property must qualify as an entity of a type distinct from the ontological type of the truth-relevant properties endorsed by the austere pluralist (correspondence, coherence, and so on). Does it?

Generic truth and domain-specific truth-relevant properties are all properties. Hence, in order for the ontological type-parsimony strategy to be executable, the broad category of properties would have to include proper, distinct ontological types. It might be natural to think that distinctions between types are generally meant to track qualitatively significant differences. Thus, in particular, distinctions between ontological types within the broad category of properties should be based on such qualitative differences. Now, one might think that generic truth and nongeneric truth-relevant properties are *not* significantly different from a qualitative point of view. Why? Because generic truth and nongeneric, domain-specific truth-relevant properties all have the features captured by the core principles (see section 1). Both strong pluralism and moderate pluralism carry this commitment. This means that nongeneric, domain-specific truth-relevant properties share a significant qualitative similarity with generic truth. However, if distinctions between types track qualitatively significant differences, then perhaps generic truth and nongeneric, domain-specific truth-relevant properties are of the *same* type. In that case the property ontology of austere pluralism and moderate pluralism would be equally qualitatively parsimonious. Hence, the qualitative reading of Ockham's razor could not be invoked to lend support to austere pluralism over moderate pluralism.

This need not be the end of the story, however. For observe that generic truth and domain-specific properties' sharing some significant qualitative similarity does not rule out the possibility that there are significant qualitative differences between them. Indeed, there *must* be at least some qualitative differences pairwise between generic truth and each domain-specific property. Generic truth is a minimal property. It is characterized by the core principles. These principles are also characteristic of the domain-specific properties. However, while the core principles capture the essence of the generic truth property, the nature of the domain-specific properties (correspondence, coherence, superassertibility, and so on) goes beyond those principles. This point is widely acknowledged by pluralists.[30]

Every domain-specific property has some feature that is not domain-general and serves to characterize it. Less than domain-general features include realism-relevant features such as Epistemic Constraint, Cognitive Command, Width of Cosmological Role, and the Euthyphro Contrast:

Epistemic Constraint: for every p, if p is true, then p is feasibly warranted.

Cognitive Command: a given domain D exhibits Cognitive Command if and only if "it is a priori that differences of opinion arising within it can be satisfactorily explained only in terms of 'divergent input,' that is, the disputants' working on the basis of different information (and hence guilty of ignorance or error, depending on the status of that information), or 'unsuitable conditions' (resulting in inattention or distraction and so in inferential error, or oversight of data and so on), or 'malfunction' (for example, prejudicial assessment of data, upwards or downwards, or dogma, or failings in other categories already listed)." (Wright 1992, 92–93)

Width of Cosmological Role: a given domain D exhibits Wide Cosmological Role "just in case mention of the states of affairs of which it consists can feature in at least some kinds of explanation of contingencies which are not of that sort—explanations whose possibility is not guaranteed merely by the minimal truth aptitude of the associated discourse." (Wright 1992, 198)

Euthyphro Contrast: for a given domain D and a truth-relevant property F, the Euthyphro Contrast amounts to the following contrasting claims: *certain D-statements are F because they are true*, and *certain D-statements are true because they are F*. (Wright 1992, 80)[31]

To illustrate the point about less than domain-general features, consider superassertibility. This property is understood as follows: a statement P is superassertible if and only if it is—or can be—warranted, and warrant for P would survive any arbitrary extension and improvement of our information and arbitrarily close scrutiny of its pedigree (Wright 1992, 48).

Superassertibility is one of the candidate properties for reducing truth within specific domains, and it has the feature of being epistemically constrained. Every proposition whose truth reduces to superassertibility is feasibly warranted. This follows from the characterization of superassertibility. However, some truths are not epistemically constrained. For example, one of "The number of stars in the universe right now is even," and "The number of stars in the universe right now is odd" is true. However, if "The number of stars in the universe right now is even" is true, it is not feasibly warranted. It outruns our epistemic reach; similarly for "The number of stars in the universe right now is odd." Thus, some truths are not epistemically constrained, and hence, epistemic constraint is a less than domain-general feature.

Since Epistemic Constraint, Cognitive Command, Width of Cosmological Role, and the Euthyphro Contrast are not domain-general, the generic truth property cannot have them. For each less than domain-general feature, generic truth will be like certain domain-specific properties in the sense of lacking that feature. For example, generic truth and correspondence both fail to be epistemically constrained. However, the generic truth property is special because, unlike the domain-specific properties, it fails to have *all* less than domain-general features. Thus, while generic truth is like the domain-specific properties in virtue of satisfying the core principles, it would seem to be qualitatively distinct from them in this particular regard. This, we submit, is a significant qualitative difference between the generic truth property and the domain-specific properties.[32] It is a difference that enjoys explanatory power. Why do moderate pluralists and strong pluralists give different kinds of semantics? Because moderate pluralists endorse generic truth and strong pluralists do not. Generic truth is a different type of property than domain-specific properties.[33]

Thus, if types of properties are distinguished by significant qualitative differences, one might think that the generic truth property is of a different type than domain-specific properties. In that case, combined with the explanatory dispensability of generic truth, the qualitative reading of Ockham's razor *can* be used to favor austere pluralism over moderate pluralism.

Lastly, instead of taking the qualitative and quantitative readings to be in competition with one another, they can be taken to complement each other. Let us consider two ways they might do so. First, one can take the qualitative reading to be primary and the quantitative reading secondary in the following sense: first assess competing views using the qualitative reading of Ockham's razor. If the views under consideration do equally well with respect to qualitative parsimony, then move on to the quantitative reading. Here, again, austere pluralism will come out on top. If our argument in favor of generic truth's being typewise distinct from domain-specific properties is sound, austere pluralism will trump moderate pluralism in the first round. However, even if we suppose that the two views tie with respect to qualitative parsimony, austere pluralism will prevail in the second round because it is quantitatively more parsimonious than moderate pluralism. Alternatively, one might think that neither reading takes priority over the other. If so, there could be tough cases in which one view is more qualitatively parsimonious than another view, but for quantitative parsimony, it is the other way around. For present purposes, however, we do not need to worry about such cases. For, again, with respect to qualitative parsimony, austere pluralism does better than moderate pluralism, or, at worst, the two views do equally well. With respect to quantitative parsimony, austere pluralism does better. Overall, then, austere pluralism does better.

In sum, whether focus is restricted to either quantitative parsimony or qualitative parsimony or they are taken to complement each other, austere pluralism comes out as being more parsimonious than moderate pluralism. Combined with the explanatory dispensability of generic truth, Ockham's razor rules in favor of austere pluralism.[34]

7   Conclusion

As noted at the outset, moderate pluralism is the dominant view in the pluralism debate. It is our hope that we have managed to show that austere pluralism—a form of strong truth pluralism—should be taken seriously as a contender in the pluralist landscape. We have done three kinds of work to level the playing field. First, we have argued that moderate pluralists conveniently take advantage of the dual nature of their view, switching back and forth between their distinctively monist and distinctively pluralist commitments depending on the issue or task at hand (section 2). Crucially—and perhaps somewhat ironically—the plurality of truth-grounding properties plays an ineliminable role in explaining the metaphysical *unity* of truth, a key feature of moderate pluralism—and a monist one at that (section 3). Second, we have introduced and articulated austere pluralism, a novel form of strong pluralism (section 4), and shown that it is entirely adequate for capturing the core idea of truth pluralism (section 6.1) and can deal with the problem of mixed compounds and the problem of mixed inferences, two challenges usually regarded as stumbling blocks for strong pluralism (section 5). Third, we have argued that austere pluralism fares better than moderate pluralism with respect to ontological parsimony, an important theoretical virtue (section 6.2).

Notes

We are grateful to a number of people for discussions that have helped shape our thinking about truth pluralism, including Jc Beall, Elke Brendel, Colin Caret, Aaron Cotnoir, Douglas Edwards, Will Gamester, Jinho Kang, Nathan Kellen, Junyeol Kim, Michael P. Lynch, Erik Stei, Andrea Strollo, Elena Tassoni, Joe Ulatowski, Cory D. Wright, Crispin Wright, Andy Yu, Luca Zanetti, and Elia Zardini. We are especially grateful to Jeremy Wyatt for very extensive and helpful comments on an earlier version of this chapter.

1. Angle brackets are used to represent propositions.

2. Wright (1992, 1998, 2001, 2013); Lynch (2001, 2004, 2006, 2009, 2013, 2018). See also Pedersen (2006, 2010, 2012a, 2012b, 2014); Edwards (2011, 2012, 2013, 2018a, 2018b); Pedersen and Edwards (2011); Pedersen and Wright (2012, 2013a, 2013b); Cotnoir (2013b); Yu (2017); Kim and Pedersen (2018); Pedersen and Lynch (2018); Ferrari and Moruzzi (2019, 2020); Gamester (2019).

A different kind of truth pluralism, motivated by considerations on semantic paradox, has also attracted attention in the literature. See, e.g., Beall (2013); Cotnoir (2013a); Scharp (2013).

3. Lynch (2009, 2013).

4. Lynch (2009, 74; 2013, 31); Edwards (2011, 40; 2013a).

5. Strictly speaking: truth is one, and the *grounds* of truth are many. *Because*-talk is pervasive in the work of moderate pluralists. See, for example, Lynch (2009, 76); Edwards (2013, 118).

6. See, for example, Sher (1998); Lynch (2004, 2009). An important qualification is that the scope problem is invoked against *substantivist* or *inflationary* monist views—that is, views that take truth to be one and to have a substantive/explanatory nature. Pluralists launch other arguments to rule out deflationism as a viable candidate, typically concerning normativity (Wright 1992; Lynch 2009)—but see Ferrari (2018) and Ferrari and Moruzzi (2019) for some replies to these arguments.

7. Tappolet (1997).

8. Lynch (2004, 403); Edwards (2013, 116n8).

9. Rosen (2010).

10. van Fraassen (1980). Hempel (1965) is a prominent predecessor. Skow (2016) likewise focuses on answers to why questions but reframes the debate in terms of reasons why.

11. Again, see, for example, Lynch (2004, 403); Edwards (2013, 116n8).

12. Moderate pluralists use different terms for their favored one–many dependence relations. However, it is clear from their widespread use of "because" that, for atomics, both Lynch and Edwards can plausibly be fitted into the grounding-theoretic framework relied on here. Edwards likewise explicitly uses "because" talk in his treatment of compounds (e.g., 2008, 2009, 2011, 2013, 2018b). Lynch takes true compounds to be what he calls "plain truths." Unlike atomic propositions, the truth of compounds is not linked directly to instances of truth-grounding properties such as correspondence or coherence. However, Lynch still takes plain truths to satisfy a weak grounding principle (2009, 90). According to this principle, there is a relation of asymmetric supervenience between the status of compounds vis-à-vis truth and the status of atomic propositions vis-à-vis truth-grounding properties. For a more detailed account of the grounding-theoretic metaphysics presented here, see Pedersen (2020); Ferrari et al. (ms); Kim and Pedersen (ms).

13. Lynch (2009) and Edwards (2018), for example, are explicitly and repeatedly described as metaphysical projects.

14. Further critical works on moderate pluralism that are congenial to the argument of this section include Pedersen (2020, ms-a, ms-b); Ferrari et al. (ms); Kim and Pedersen (2018, ms).

15. Brandom labels his position *logical expressivism*. The logical expressivist, as described by Brandom, "thinks of logical vocabulary as introduced to let one say in the logically extended object-language what material relations of implication and incompatibility articulate the conceptual contents of logically atomic expressions" (Brandom 2018, 4). Another recent example is Thomas

Brouwer, who takes logical vocabulary to map onto attitudes rather than propositional contents (Brouwer 2013, 80).

16. Several recent expressivist approaches can be used to add further details to the bare-bones logical nonrepresentationalist account presented here. See Schroeder (2008); Brouwer (2013); Brandom (2018).

17. We assume, as a plausible starting point, a bilateralist approach toward acceptance and rejection (see Smiley 1996), according to which rejection is not defined in terms of acceptance and negation. While we take acceptance and rejection to be mutually exclusive, we do not commit to their being exhaustive: one might introduce suspension of judgment as a third primitive cognitive attitude.

18. Brouwer (2013).

19. Brouwer (2013, 89–90).

20. Brouwer (2013, 122).

21. Again, this is assuming that there are only two first-order attitudes, acceptance and rejection.

22. For ease of exposition, we set aside issues of context-dependence here.

23. These clauses capture the classical understanding of logical connectives. Nonclassical connectives express different constraints on complex attitudes.

24. This bifurcation might raise issues about how exactly to understand certain doxastic and semantic phenomena—disagreement being one example. For instance, if John utters "London is beautiful" while Sarah utters "London is not beautiful," the two are intuitively disagreeing. However, within the framework of austere pluralism this disagreement cannot be understood as John expressing a proposition—that London is beautiful—and Sarah expressing another, semantically incompatible proposition since, instead, she is expressing a complex attitude. Austere pluralists can, however, capture the disagreement intuition by pointing out that the truth conditions of the sentences uttered, respectively, by Sarah and John cannot be jointly satisfied.

25. Usually, it is also added that the argument has the feature of being necessarily truth-preserving *in virtue of its logical form*. This qualification is needed in order to rule out as logically valid certain types of arguments—for example, arguments with metaphysically or conceptually necessary truths as their conclusion.

26. While we use (IMP) for the purposes of our discussion here, see Gamester (2019) for a discussion of mixed inferences against the background of (PRE). Gamester offers several reasons for thinking that the common talk of truth-*preservation* cannot be taken literally.

27. Other accounts have been developed by strong pluralists. See Cotnoir (2013b) and Yu (2017) for mixed compounds and inferences. See also Pedersen and Lynch (2018) for an outline of a strongly pluralist account of mixed inferences (due to Pedersen). See Pedersen (2006) for mixed inferences, and Pedersen and Kim (2018) for mixed compounds. See Ferrari, Moruzzi, and Pedersen (ms) for extensive discussion of strongly pluralist accounts of mixed compounds and inferences and several criticisms of moderate pluralism.

28. See Nolan (1997); Baker (2003); Tallant (2013); Vanderburgh (2014); Schaffer (2015); Sober (2015); Jansson and Tallant (2017). For the sake of illustrating the difference between the two readings, consider two ontologies O_1 and O_2 with the same types of particles, $p_1, \ldots, p_n$ (where p_1 are electrons). Suppose that O_1 and O_2 have the same number of particles for each of $p_1, \ldots, p_n$, except p_1. O_1 has two more electrons than O_2. Adopting the quantitative reading of the razor, O_2 comes out as being more ontologically parsimonious than O_1, as O_2 has fewer entities (of whatever type) than O_1. Adopting the qualitative reading of the razor, O_1 and O_2 come out as being equally ontologically parsimonious, as they have the same *types* of entities. Those who advocate the qualitative reading will say that O_1 is not more ontologically parsimonious than O_2 in any interesting sense. On the other hand, suppose that O_3 is a dualist ontology with both mental and physical entities and O_4 is a materialist ontology with just physical entities. Advocates of the qualitative reading count this difference in terms of types of entities between O_3 and O_4 as more philosophically interesting than the difference in terms of the number of electrons in the case of O_1 and O_2.

29. See Ferrari, Moruzzi & Pedersen (ms).

30. See, e.g., Wright (1992, 78–79, 142–143; 2001, sec. 3); Lynch (2009, chaps. 2–4).

31. These features play a central role in Wright's work on truth (see especially Wright [1992]). Epistemic constraint is used generally in the pluralism literature (see, e.g., Lynch [2009]; Pedersen [2014]). The first part of the Euthyphro Contrast is meant to be realist in the sense that the "because" is supposed to indicate that truth is constitutively independent of F where F is some property tied to our cognitive capacities (e.g., superassertibility). The second part of the contrast reverses the because claim and thus rejects the idea of the constitutive F-independence of truth.

32. This rests on the assumption that the range of domain-specific properties does not include a deflationary property—that is, a property exhaustively characterized by the Equivalence Schema or Disquotational Schema. This assumption is justified in the engagement with representative moderate pluralists such as Edwards and Lynch, as they are *inflationary* pluralists. Both take the network analysis to include principles that inflate generic truth—and any domain-specific property—beyond anything acceptable to a deflationist. For an exploration of the possibility of a locally deflationary version of truth pluralism, see Ferrari and Moruzzi (2019). Their 2020 work is also relevant.

33. We here take a qualitative difference between two properties F_1 and F_2 to be significant if the fact that F_1 and F_2 exhibit this difference enjoys explanatory power. Thanks to Jeremy Wyatt for this suggestion.

34. We also note that austere pluralism is more parsimonious in two additional, quite specific ways. Austere pluralism is quantitatively parsimonious with respect to propositions. The view only accommodates atomic propositions and hence is much more lightweight than the swath of positions whose ontology of propositions likewise accommodates complex propositions. Relatedly, austere pluralism abandons the idea that reality includes a type of formal, abstract structure that exactly mirrors the structure or form of logical vocabulary.

References

Baker, A. 2003. "Quantitative Parsimony and Explanatory Power." *British Journal for the Philosophy of Science* 54: 245–259.

Beall, Jc. 2013. "Deflated Truth Pluralism." In Pedersen and Wright 2013b, 323–338.

Brandom, R. 2018. "From Logical Expressivism to Expressivist Logic: Sketch of a Program and Some Implementations." *Philosophical Issues* 28: 70–88.

Brouwer, T. 2013. "The Metaphysical Commitments of Logic." PhD thesis, University of Leeds.

Cotnoir, A. 2013a. "Pluralism and Paradox." In Pedersen and Wright 2013b, 339–350.

Cotnoir, A. 2013b. "Validity for Strong Pluralists." *Philosophy and Phenomenological Research* 83: 563–579.

Edwards, D. 2008. "How to Solve the Problem of Mixed Conjunctions." *Analysis* 68(298): 143–149.

Edwards, D. 2009. "Truth-Conditions and the Nature of Truth: Re-solving Mixed Conjunctions." *Analysis* 69(4): 684–688.

Edwards, D. 2011. "Simplifying Alethic Pluralism." *Southern Journal of Philosophy* 49(1): 28–48.

Edwards, D. 2012. "On Alethic Disjunctivism." *Dialectica* 66(1): 200–214.

Edwards, D. 2013. "Truth, Winning, and Simple Determination Pluralism." In Pedersen and Wright 2013b, 113–122.

Edwards, D. 2018a. "The Metaphysics of Domains." In J. Wyatt, N. J. L. L. Pedersen, and N. Kellen, eds., *Pluralisms in Truth and Logic*, 85–106. London: Palgrave Macmillan.

Edwards, D. 2018b. *The Metaphysics of Truth.* Oxford: Oxford University Press.

Ferrari, F. 2018. "The Value of Minimalist Truth." *Synthese* 195(3): 1103–1125.

Ferrari, F., and Moruzzi, S. 2019. "Ecumenical Alethic Pluralism." *Canadian Journal of Philosophy* 49(3): 368–393.

Ferrari, F., and Moruzzi, S. 2020. "Deflating Truth about Taste." *American Philosophical Quarterly* 57(4).

Ferrari, F., Moruzzi, S., and Pedersen, N. J. L. L. Ms. "True Pluralisms: The Ways of Truth." Unpublished manuscript.

Gamester, W. 2019. "Logic, Logical Form and the Disunity of Truth." *Analysis* 79: 34–43.

Hempel, C. 1965. "Aspects of Scientific Explanation." In *Aspects of Scientific Explanation and Other Essays in the Philosophy of Science*, 331–496. New York: Free Press.

Jansson, L., and Tallant, J. 2017. "Quantitative Parsimony: Probably for the Better." *British Journal for the Philosophy of Science* 68: 781–803.

Kim, S., and Pedersen, N. J. L. L. 2018. "Strong Truth Pluralism." In J. Wyatt, N. J. L. L. Pedersen, and N. Kellen, eds., *Pluralisms in Truth and Logic*, 113–130. London: Palgrave Macmillan.

Kim, S., and Pedersen, N. J. L. L. Ms. "Return of the Many: A Critical Appraisal of Moderate Truth Pluralism through the Metaphysics of Grounding." Unpublished manuscript.

Lynch, M. P. 2001. "A Functionalist Theory of Truth." In M. P. Lynch, ed., *The Nature of Truth: Classic and Contemporary Perspectives*, 723–749. Cambridge, MA: MIT Press.

Lynch, M. P. 2004. "Truth and Multiple Realizability." *Australasian Journal of Philosophy* 82: 384–408.

Lynch, M. P. 2006. "ReWrighting Pluralism." *The Monist* 89: 63–84.

Lynch, M. P. 2009. *Truth as One and Many*. Oxford: Oxford University Press.

Lynch, M. P. 2013."Three Questions for Truth Pluralism." In Pedersen and Wright 2013b, 21–41.

Lynch, M. P. 2018. "Truth Pluralism, Quasi-Realism, and the Problem of Double-Counting." In J. Wyatt, N. J. L. L. Pedersen, and Nathan Kellen, eds., *Pluralisms in Truth and Logic*, 63–84. London: Palgrave Macmillan.

Nolan, D. 1997. "Quantitative Parsimony." *British Journal for the Philosophy of Science* 48: 329–343.

Pedersen, N. J. L. L. 2006. "What Can the Problem of Mixed Inferences Teach Us about Alethic Pluralism?" *The Monist* 89: 103–117.

Pedersen, N. J. L. L. 2010. "Stabilizing Alethic Pluralism." *Philosophical Quarterly* 60: 92–108.

Pedersen, N. J. L. L. 2012a. "Recent Work on Alethic Pluralism." *Analysis* 72: 588–607.

Pedersen, N. J. L. L. 2012b. "True Alethic Functionalism?" *International Journal of Philosophical Studies* 20: 125–133.

Pedersen, N. J. L. L. 2014. "Pluralism×3: Truth, Logic, Metaphysics." *Erkenntnis* 79: 259–277.

Pedersen, N. J. L. L. 2020. "Moderate Truth Pluralism and the Structure of Doxastic Normativity." *American Philosophical Quarterly* 57(4).

Pedersen, N. J. L. L. Ms-a. "Determination Pluralism Grounded." Unpublished manuscript.

Pedersen, N. J. L. L. Ms-b. "Grounding Manifestation Pluralism." Unpublished manuscript.

Pedersen, N. J. L. L., and Edwards, D. 2011. "Truth as One(s) and Many: On Lynch's Alethic Functionalism." *Analytic Philosophy* 52: 213–230.

Pedersen, N. J. L. L., and Lynch, M. P. 2018. "Truth Pluralism." In M. Glanzberg, ed., *The Oxford Handbook of Truth*, 543–575. Oxford: Oxford University Press.

Pedersen, N. J. L. L., and Wright, C. D. 2012. "Pluralist Theories of Truth." *Stanford Encyclopedia of Philosophy*. https://plato.stanford.edu/entries/truth-pluralist/.

Pedersen, N. J. L. L., and Wright, C. D. 2013a. "Pluralism about Truth as Alethic Disjunctivism." In Pedersen and Wright 2013b, 87–112.

Pedersen, N. J. L. L., and Wright, C. D. 2013b. *Truth and Pluralism: Current Debates*. New York: Oxford University Press.

Rayo, A. 2013. *The Construction of Logical Space*. Oxford: Oxford University Press.

Rosen, G. 2010. "Metaphysical Dependence: Grounding and Reduction." In B. Hale and A. Hoffmann, eds., *Modality: Metaphysics, Logic, and Epistemology*, 109–136. Oxford: Oxford University Press.

Schaffer, J. 2015. "What Not to Multiply without Necessity." *Australasian Journal of Philosophy* 93: 644–664.

Scharp, K. 2013. *Replacing Truth*. Oxford: Oxford University Press.

Schroeder, M. 2008. *Being For: Evaluating the Semantic Program of Expressivism*. Oxford: Oxford University Press.

Sher, G. 1998. "On the Possibility of a Substantive Theory of Truth." *Synthese* 117: 133–172.

Skow, B. 2016. *Reasons Why*. Oxford: Oxford University Press.

Smiley, T. 1996. "Rejection." *Analysis* 56: 1–9.

Sober, E. 2015. *Ockham's Razors: A User's Manual*. Cambridge: Cambridge University Press.

Tallant, J. 2013. "Quantitative Parsimony and the Metaphysics of Time: Motivating Presentism." *Philosophy and Phenomenological Research* 87: 688–705.

Tappolet, C. 1997. "Mixed Inferences: A Problem for Pluralism about Truth Predicates." *Analysis* 57: 209–210.

Tappolet, C. 2000. "Truth Pluralism and Many-Valued Logic: A Reply to Beall." *Philosophical Quarterly* 50: 382–384.

Vanderburgh, W. 2014. "Quantitative Parsimony, Explanatory Power and Dark Matter." *Journal for General Philosophy of Science* 45: 317–327.

van Fraassen, B. 1980. *The Scientific Image*. Oxford: Clarendon Press.

Williamson, T. 1994. "A Critical Study of *Truth and Objectivity*." *International Journal of Philosophical Studies* 30: 130–144.

Wright, C. 1992. *Truth and Objectivity*. Cambridge, MA: Harvard University Press.

Wright, C. 1998. "Truth: A Traditional Debate Reviewed." *Canadian Journal of Philosophy* 28(S1): 38–74.

Wright, C. 2001. "Minimalism, Deflationism, Pragmatism, Pluralism." In M. P. Lynch, ed., *The Nature of Truth*, 751–789. Cambridge, MA: MIT Press.

Wright, C. 2013. "A Plurality of Pluralisms." In Pedersen and Wright 2013b, 123–153.

Yu, A. 2017. "Logic for Pluralists." *Journal of Philosophy* 114: 277–302.

33 Deflationism, Pluralism, Expressivism, Pragmatism

Simon Blackburn

> "Yes, but has nature nothing to say here?" Indeed she has—but she makes herself audible in another way.
> —Wittgenstein, *Zettel*, sec. 364

The four words of my title form a set of cardinal points in current debates about semantic theory and the shape it should take. I should guess that in the contemporary debates most combinations are found and probably as many denials that those combinations can be motivated, or coherent, or even consistent. Yet it seems to me that there are reasonable readings of all of them on which these questions become focused and even capable of fairly definitive answers. It is the purpose of this chapter to lay out the landscape, as I see it, and to invite others to use my marks in the jungle when plotting their own routes.

Deflationism

For the purpose of this chapter I am going to take deflationism in the theory of truth to consist of three theses:

(A) That there is complete cognitive equivalence between T*p* and *p*.

(B) That conforming to that equivalence is all that is required to manifest complete understanding of the truth predicate.

(C) That the utility of the predicate is therefore purely logical: it is a device for indirect reference and generalization.

I derive these from the seminal discussion in Paul Horwich's book *Truth* (1990), and I shall do no more than sketch some of their features.

The first is too familiar to need much introduction. Frege says, "It is really by using the form of an assertoric sentence that we assert truth, and to do this we do not need to use the word 'true'" (1897, 129). His view has been shared by many others, through

Ramsey, Ayer, Quine, Davidson, and Brandom. Whether these writers have all absorbed the full message of Frege's insight will shortly concern us. But if we call the thesis in (A) the transparency property of truth, then few can be found to object, and I shall certainly not be calling it into question here.

The second thesis is slightly more elusive, and we shall find it queried. It makes a strong claim, for we can see it as issuing a bold challenge to would-be falsifiers: find a context that I cannot explain by use of the transparency property. Only then will this thesis be called into question. Horwich and others have done much to make this challenge formidable. But to see how they have done this, we need first to visit the third and final claim.

By saying that "is true" is to be seen as a device of indirect reference and generalization, deflationists mean that there are many indirect methods of referring to what someone said and many ways of generalizing over actual and potential sayings. Again, there is widespread agreement that the truth predicate serves at least this logical function, and again, I shall take it for granted in what follows. It is more contentious whether it does more than serve this function, and this will occupy us in due course. But let me briefly indicate two thoughts that might seem inflationary, but that, clearly enough, the logical function enables the predicate to discharge.

The first is the place of truth in thoughts about explanation. We are successful, very often, because our beliefs are true. We would not be so successful were they not. This is undoubtedly so. But innumerable *individual* explanations of this form can be deflated. I was successful in seeing a nightingale because I believed they would be found here and my belief was true reduces, via the transparency property, to my being successful in seeing a nightingale because I believed they would be found here, and they are. We want to generalize the pattern, we have the device to hand, and this is what the generalization deploys. There is no *property* of truth intrinsic to the explanation, but only a vast array of explanatory stories of the identical form, none of which need use the predicate and none of which, therefore, requires the identification of any mysterious property or relation to which the predicate might be supposed to refer.

The second is the place of truth in thoughts about aims, goals, or normativity. "You must take care that what you say is true" is a schema for collecting individual pieces of advice: "you must take care that if you say that aardvarks amble, then it is true that aardvarks amble." Again, the truth predicate can be knocked out of these individual statements with no change, for the same norm or aim is put by saying "you must take care that if you say that aardvarks amble, then aardvarks amble," and again the generalization or schema of normative advice (or obligation or aspiration) introduces nothing more.

A Threatened Pluralism

These arguments for the adequacy of deflationism certainly make difficulties for any kind of pluralism that works in terms of different concepts of truth in different areas, or even, in Crispin Wright's preferred version (1992), different conceptions of one overarching concept of truth. If there is no property or relation in question and therefore no mode of presentation of a property or relation, how could there be room for different "conceptions" of such a thing? And looking at the diagnostics Wright offered for understanding which conception of truth is in play in different areas, the deflationist response is very apparent. Wright advances such markers as "width of cosmological role," involvement with our own potentially mutable responses ("Euthyphronic properties"), and the question of whether irresoluble disagreement implies a cognitive defect in one or another party ("cognitive command") as marking out the relevant distinctions. These might separate the conception of truth in play when we discuss scientifically heavyweight subject matter, such as the weight or shape of an object, from more lightweight matters, such as its color, or more contestable matters, such as its beauty.

The deflationist response is clearly that while these distinctions are no doubt very interesting and have a pedigree going back to seventeenth-century or even classical atomism, it is a kind of double counting to think that they strike at the conception of truth involved. They strike at the level of the proposition: they mark distinctions of subject matter and perhaps eventually distinctions of objectivity or the possibility of cognitively fault-free disagreement. But why add to a distinction of content, another, mirroring, distinction, one only applying to kinds of truth or conceptions of truth?

Frege's Reaction

This would certainly have been Frege's reaction. Frege discussed where his work had left the concept of truth particularly in the brief posthumous paper, "My Basic Logical Insights" (1915). Here Frege says roundly that "the sense of the word 'true' is such that it does not make any essential contribution to the thought" (251). He aligns the function of the term with the force of making an assertion, continuing:

> So the word "true" seems to make the impossible possible: it allows what corresponds to the assertoric force to assume the form of a contribution to the thought. And although this attempt miscarries, or rather, through the very fact that it miscarries, it indicates what is characteristic of logic.

Frege famously made a sharp distinction of force from content. The same content can be put forward or presented with very different force, notably as asserted or only as conjectured (or hypothesized), or in contexts that take away the seriousness of assertion, for example on the stage or in other contexts of pretense.

Frege was acutely aware of this distinction. I interpret his remark about "seeming to make the impossible possible" as indicating that at first appearance, the words "is true" might—per impossible—function as an indicator of assertoric force. Indeed, in ordinary speech, something of the kind certainly happens, as when you say something, are challenged with some version of "Surely you cannot be serious?" and reply along the lines: "It's true, I am telling you"—signifying that your original saying was a genuine assertion. But of course Frege well knows that no word in a sentence can ensure that the thought presented is also asserted. He seems to be wrestling with the problem of the truth predicate seeming to try to occupy this impossible role in the last paragraph of his note (1915, 252):

> Now the thing that indicates most clearly the essence of logic is the assertoric force with which a sentence is uttered. But no word, or part of a sentence, corresponds to this; the same series of words may be uttered with assertoric force at one time and not at another. In language assertoric force is bound up with the predicate.

This is not entirely clear, since the last sentence seems to indicate some version of the very doctrine that the first part denies, nominating the predicate as some kind of privileged bearer of force. Even if Frege meant to say that in language assertoric force is bound up with the act of predication, the issue is still left unclear, since in at least one perfectly good sense, in indirect and unserious contexts, predication still occurs, yet assertoric force is lacking.

Deflationism Compromised?

Thus far, I have laid out familiar defenses of deflationism and claimed the authority of Frege against a kind of pluralism that it seems to undercut. However, these familiar points do not mark the end of the story. To see why not, I shall present the argument as it is developed in a recent paper by Dorit Bar-On and Keith Simmons. They also take their cue from Frege. But, they claim:

> As we continue to reflect on or theorize about a language and its practitioners, we may turn to the speech act of assertion. We may say, following Frege, that to assert is to put forward as true. Here is the word "true" again, appearing in the language in which we theorize. In our mouth, the word "true" is not used as a disquotational or denominalizing or prosentential device. We are not even purporting to describe some sentence or thought. This is not a first-order use, and it cannot be disquoted away. (2007, 77)

This is taking the equation that to assert is to put forward as true in an inflationary spirit. The idea is that while first-order uses of the truth predicate are susceptible of deflationist theory, when we step back and reflect on the basic act of assertion, we need an equation in which the notion of truth plays an indisputable role, yet one that cannot be seen either as a disquotation or in terms of the logical activities of indirect reference and generalization that are the deflationist's meat and drink.

It is certainly undeniable that we would like to say something about the speech act of assertion. And we would not be saying anything interesting by deflating truth as it occurs in the equation that to assert is to present as true. In usual deflationist fashion, we would approach this via the schema that to assert that *p* is to present *p* as true; we would analyze this as a summary generalization over cases such as "to assert that aardvarks amble is to … what? … that aardvarks amble"—and the only term we could put in would be "assert" or a synonym, giving us that to assert is to assert. Bar-On and Simmons say roundly that in their mouths the word "true" is not susceptible of deflationist treatment. What we find instead is that it might be, but at the cost of the equation that to assert is to present as true reducing to the tautology that to assert is to assert.

It is clear, as well, that there is no other way of evading this collapse, if our resources begin with the presentation of a thought. As Bar-On and Simmons make very clear and as we can see from Frege again, to assert is not simply to present a thought, to imagine a state of affairs, or to do anything short of claiming truth. But are they right that this requires us to backtrack on all the deflationist insights that so far seem so promising? They themselves do not suggest that we take refuge in a thick or robust approach, ahead of which lie the impassable deserts in which correspondence, coherence, pragmatism and other landmarks prove to be nothing but mirages? There may be a different way out.

A Normative Approach

This way out would be to approach the nature of assertion in terms of the status and responsibilities accorded to one who asserts. The act is identified in terms of proprieties surrounding it and liabilities that are incurred when they are transgressed against. This is the approach championed by Robert Brandom (1994), and there is unquestionably something attractive about it. If you assert that *p* then you become liable to censures and reproaches if *not-p*, ranging from mild disappointment to utter ostracism, whereas if you had merely floated the thought that *p*, then you may escape the indictment (you may not entirely escape criticisms, for sometimes merely putting the thought into someone's head could constitute a malicious act. It was Iago's preferred modus operandi after all). Moreover, and centrally to Brandom's account, someone who asserts is making the kind of commitment that means he is liable to be asked for reasons but is also able to offer it in turn as a reason for other commitments. There are rules or norms, "social-deontic attitudes," governing both input and output.

Brandom presents his approach in terms of a generalized pragmatism, and it is part of a program of freeing our theorizing about language from some of the tyranny of ubiquitous semantic notions, such as truth and reference. But we have to move carefully here. Locating thinkers or speakers in a landscape in which we *only* answer to statuses accorded to us or denied to us by fellow thinkers and speakers risks distorting our positions. For we do not just answer to each other. We answer to each other because of what we get right or wrong *about* the things we are involved with—the things we are talking about. Substituting concern with each other for concern with the world is a mistake. If I am deciding whether an object is red or square or weighs five pounds, I am not primarily concerned with what other people will say in the case nor with predicting the penalties if I am out of step with them. To use an old analogy, it is not like tuning up with the orchestra, where my prime concern is to listen to whether my note is the same as the notes of other players.[1] We are not after democratic harmony but getting the judgment right. In the general case, I can make sense of the idea that most members of my community might themselves get the issue wrong, but when it is a case of simply being in step with others, this possibility does not arise: an individual may be out of step with others, but if the entire parade is marching the same way, there is nothing for them to be out of step with.

To see the importance of this point, consider a case not of assertion but of promising. We can use the same general normative terms about the act of promising. If I promise to meet you in Times Square at a given time, I take up a certain status: let us say I accord you the right to expect something of me or voluntarily put myself under a duty, and I am liable for social penalties if I fail or fail lacking sufficient excuse. All this is surely correct. But equally surely, it does not sideline or supersede the involvement of Times Square in the promise. It is not just any old actions that discharge my liability or show me failing to fulfill it. It is actions that result in my being or not being in Times Square. Similarly, if I make a bet with you I enter a "normative space" of privileges and liabilities, but those privileges and liabilities are only triggered by whether some event occurs: the event referred to in the content of the bet. Our attention must be directed on the race, just as the attention of the promisee must be directed on Times Square.

Of course, Brandom's concentration on reasons gives him what he regards as a sufficient account of these foci of attention, in terms of harvesting input and output reasons for the various judgments that would acknowledge the fulfillment or otherwise of the promise or settlement of the bet. This is the ambition of showing that his "social-deontic attitudes" give us an entrée into the theory of content, and he would need, it seems to me, to show how they relate to such things as observation and attention on the input side and action, success, and failure on the output side. This is a very tall order, but here I make no judgment on its success or prospects for success.

For we can acknowledge the undoubted importance of rules and statuses in describing the speech-act of assertion without supposing that they give us any particular line on theory of the *content* of judgments made, nor therefore on whether in order to isolate that content we need to introduce such notions as reference and representation. For this is not the game we were chasing. We simply wanted a notion of assertion wide enough to embrace all sorts of content. And for this purpose, the notion of shifting status is entirely appropriate, just as it would be if we essayed a general account of promising or betting.

Bar-On and Simmons suggest in their paper that by saying a great deal about assertion, in terms of "social-deontic attitudes," Brandom forfeits his claim to be deploying only a deflationist account of truth.[2] The idea is that if asserting is given a thick or robust story, then, since they are the same thing, so is "presenting as true" and hence truth itself is inflated as part of the inflated compound. But this seems to me to risk asking for unreasonably clean hands. The question was whether, given that "asserts" and "presents as true" are synonyms, we read the equation left to right, supposing that assertion explains presenting as true, or right to left, supposing that presenting as true explains asserting. By reading it left to right, we give an account of a context in which the word appears and which otherwise might have been taken to be inflationary, but we show that the appearance is harmless or in other words that ingredients that are common property and that can do nothing to incite correspondence and the rest are sufficient to explain it. As a comparison, suppose the argument was played out in terms of "doubting whether true" or the state of one who raises a doubt about truth. This is a particular state and could be given a fairly thick or robust treatment (there are norms for whether doubts are sensible, for instance). But since in any case doubting whether p is true is just doubting whether p, there is no reason to suppose that any thickness in the story is *derived* from the presence of a synonymous phrase with the word "true" in it. But that is what we would need to think in order to suppose that this is a strike against deflationism.

Deflationists do not, therefore, immediately succumb to Bar-On and Simmons's doubts. But it remains to be seen whether they can provide any useful theory of content without reinflating the notion of truth. Some of that emerges when we tackle our next topic, the prospects for pluralism.

A Different Pluralism

When everything is above board, a person making an assertion is giving voice to a commitment of his own and intends that the person receiving it shares the commitment: either is already or becomes of one mind about the topic. There is responsibility involved because commitments are, taking on board ideas present in the work of Alexander Bain, preparations for action.[3] Even commitments that are apparently remote from the here-and-now, the environment that provides the immediate context of action and that punishes or rewards action with successes and failures, lay a trail that may lead to these things. It may be less important whether you are right about the date of Henry VIII's accession to the throne than about whether there is a bus bearing down on you. But the habit of accuracy, like the habit of sincerity, is itself a precious possession, and disapproval rightly follows assertions that show that you have not got it.

So we might put the moral of the last section in a slogan by saying that we should be looking not for truth makers but for assertion licensers. For the norm-abiding asserter needs the warrant he can cite, and somebody accepting the assertion as intended, which means welcoming it within his own repertoire of potential sincere assertions, will need to suppose that such warrant exists. In straightforward cases, he will suppose that the very warrant the original asserter would cite exists, but in less straightforward cases he may "lay off," deploying his own resources rather than taking his informant's word for it. All this may suggest that we are moving toward something like a Dummettian "assertibility condition" semantics rather than a truth-conditional one. But that is not at all clear, and in the light of our Fregean explorations of deflationism neither is the difference. For there will be no general contrast between incorporating an assertion into one's own repertoire and supposing it true.

All this may make the prospects for either pluralism or expressivism as a distinct view of various fields seem rather bleak. Are we poised to put up with a blanket notion of assertion and acceptance and corresponding to those a blanket notion of belief, smothering any of the differences that expressivists believed themselves to have found? I think we can get a clue to why this is not the upshot by looking at the kind of consideration that has been in play throughout the history of the subject. Let me start with Berkeley, a regrettably unsung hero of insight into how to do things with words, certainly compared with the more glamorous Hume. Berkeley writes:

> Besides, the communicating of ideas marked by words is not the chief and only end of language, as is commonly supposed. There are other ends, as the raising of some passion, the exciting to or deterring from an action, the putting the mind in some particular disposition— to which the former is in many cases barely subservient, and sometimes entirely omitted, when these can be obtained without it, as I think does not unfrequently happen in the familiar use of language. (1710, 83–84)

Berkeley applies this idea in at least five areas of his philosophy. They are the nature of the self, the nature of agency and force, the nature of normative and evaluative language, at least some theological sayings, and finally at least some mathematical sayings. About force Berkeley is particularly explicit: "And if by considering this doctrine of force, men arrive at the knowledge of many inventions in mechanics, and are taught to frame Engines by means of which things difficult and otherwise impossible may be performed, and if the same doctrine which is so beneficial here below, serves also as a key to discover the nature of the celestial motions, shall we deny that it is of use, either in practice or speculation, because we have no distinct idea of force?" (1732, 503).

Hume shares Berkeley's view about force (under the topic of causation) and evaluative language and is not far away when it comes to the self and theological language. If we jump over two centuries, we come to Ramsey, who thinks the same about chance and probability, causation and evaluation, and then of course the later Wittgenstein, whose insistence that we pay attention to what is actually *done* with words infuses his discussions of necessity, mathematics, ethics, religious language, and psychological sayings. Wittgenstein also applies the doctrine to philosophical sayings themselves, in the doctrine that we should see them as injunctions or the laying down of grammatical rules.[4]

Now it is not presently my purpose to chart all the wrinkles in these different writers' treatments of these themes but to point to the surprising similarity of the lists. It is not too much to say that the shoe pinches in pretty much the same place across the generations. One suggestion, made by Hilary Putnam, is that an empiricist prejudice is at work, to the effect that if we cannot picture something then we cannot have a concept (or in the older terminology, an idea) of it. This might just about diagnose Berkeley and Hume, but it would be very difficult to see it as applying to Wittgenstein or for that matter to the many physicists from the time of Newton to that of Wittgenstein's idol Hertz, who found something especially problematic about the notion of force until eventually its eradication from a properly formed physics became a widely shared ideal. So is there a better principle explaining why the same suspects so constantly re-emerge?

Putnam himself criticizes the empiricists for not understanding the way in which scientific theorizing engenders an understanding of theoretical terms, even when our ability to picture referents for those terms deserts us. Where we have an explanation, there we have an understanding of whatever has its necessary place in the theory doing the explaining. This may well be true and a just enough criticism, although the passage I quoted from Berkeley about force suggests he is perfectly aware of the shape of scientific theory, while treating it in an instrumentalist spirit. But in any case Putnam's diagnosis immediately suggests a more charitable explanation. If we associate representation not with the ability to *picture* so much as with the ability to *explain*, then even on Putnam's grounds we should start to sympathize with the thought that something else than simple representation is at work in these areas when we become baffled at explaining in any such terms why we go in for such sayings. Do we go in for asserting causal connections because we are responsive to and understand them? Do we go in for asserting evaluative and normative statements because we are responsive to values and norms and understand what it is to which we are responsive? And the same question presses for necessities in general (we are not responsive to distributions of properties across possible worlds because they do not affect us), for abstracta, for chances, for theological realms, and so on.

Because we—some of us—cannot find a satisfactory theory of our receptivity to these facts, we need to cast around for something else. And this is what Berkeley, Hume, Ramsey, or Wittgenstein gives us. We do not need to see ourselves as receptive to or responsive to any enchanted realities in order to explain what we do when we deploy these terms. We only need to think of our responses to the everyday and our needs as we tell each other of the way to cope with it. Hence we get a plurality of little or local pragmatisms: theories of use that eschew using the apparent denizens of the relevant theories (selves, necessities, forces, values, abstracta) as part of any explanation of why we ourselves are talking in these terms.

One way of pursuing such an agenda, to be sure, would be simply to go for a reduction of content. But by now it is notorious that such programs fail with a crashing inevitability. And they turn their backs on the obvious resource that the tradition leaves us. We may be doing something distinctive as we talk in the relevant terms, even if we need postulate no distinctive part of the world that we are describing, just as I am doing something distinctive when I make a bet or a promise or order you to shut the window, without in any way describing any special ways in which things stand.

The concentration on explanation makes a kind of expressivism almost inevitable as soon as we give our functional story of the reason why we have these pronouncements and commitments in terms that do not include mention of what, superficially, they purport to describe. For in the absence of reductions, anything other than expressivism would mean a fracture between the explanation and the truth of the output, which must surely render our own satisfaction with such pronouncements extremely vulnerable. Thus suppose a theologian who becomes convinced that the true explanation of the prevalence of religious sayings is emotional or social. But suppose he also sets his face against an expressive or functional story of what we are doing as we talk of the Holy Ghost and its structure. Then surely the dissonance between what explains the pronouncement and what the pronouncement appears to be about would be bound to suggest skepticism or an error theory. The whole business would have been exploded. On the other hand, if he can steel himself to admit that the sayings are expressive in intent, so that the words of the creed are, as it were, continuous with the organ music that precedes them or the feelings of reverence toward the world, love of fellows, or for that matter hatred of outsiders that they inspire, then there is no blanket error in sight. There would, of course, remain room for particular emotions and attitudes and mental postures to raise eyebrows, in this area as in all others.

Beliefs and Their Mental and Social Neighbors

Above, I took issue with Wright's transportation of distinctions of content into distinctions of conceptions of truth. The same strictures might seem to apply directly to transporting distinctions of content into differences in the act of asserting. But I think that would be wrong, for it may be that it is differences in the acts of asserting and accepting that play a role in explaining the identity of particular families of content, or propositions.

Consider, for instance, the simple English indicative conditional. I accept the view of Gilbert Ryle that the conditional "if p then q" can best be explained by considering its cousin "p so q."[5] Putting this into public space, we assert p and we assert q, but it would be wrong to see us as having yet a third belief. Rather we also express allegiance to a movement of the mind from the one acceptance to the other. We issue, as Gilbert Ryle put it, an inference ticket, which others may decide to incorporate into their cognitive architecture or ways of dealing with the world, or may not. If we want to consider the merit of that ticket itself but without committing ourselves to p or q, we use the conditional form. Accepting the conditional is adopting a disposition to use the inference, or, on occasions when you want to speak your mind sincerely, to issue the ticket in one's own voice. We doubt the conditional if we have reservations about the movement in question or wish to hedge it or qualify it or contextualize it, or want to warn against being too confident in the consequent having accepted the antecedent.

This functional story stands at some distance from one conducted entirely in terms of belief: a story that would begin and end by saying that we believe various conditional facts to obtain. I believe it has advantages over any such story, both in its ability to explain the puzzling relation between conditionals and the corresponding truth function of material implication and in its metaphysical economy, but I shall not defend that here.

Consider instead other things, such as metaphor. Wittgenstein says:

> If we hold it a truism that people take pleasure in imagination, we should remember that this imagination is not like a painted picture or a three-dimensional model, but a complicated structure of heterogeneous elements: words and pictures. We shall then not think of operating with written or oral signs as something to be contrasted with the operation with "mental images" of the events. (1979, 7e)

Here is one way of interpreting him. Romeo says that Juliet is the sun; suppose Mercutio agrees. It is surely flat-footed to begin and end with describing Romeo as expressing a belief and Mercutio as believing the same. Rather, Romeo has issued a kind of invitation to search for features of Juliet in a state of mind guided, as Wittgenstein suggests, by the thought of the sun or image of the sun. Mercutio accepts his invitation although he might do so even if his exploration does not issue in anything Romeo intended, for instance if dwelling on the salient fact that the sun is hot, he comes to suppose that Juliet is sexually athletic or enthusiastic. Here the distance from belief is more obvious, since what Romeo intended is insulated from what would normally be implications licensed by the syntactic form of what he said. For example, having announced that Juliet is the sun, if later in the day he also asserts that the sun is 93 million miles away, he cannot be faulted for refusing to infer or to believe that Juliet is 93 million miles away.

This compartmentalization is one of the things Wittgenstein highlights as a way of doubting whether what Hume called the "somewhat unaccountable state of mind" of the religious adept fits easily into the category of belief.[6] Wittgenstein directs us to notice various ways in which the role of religious sayings is dissimilar in important ways from the role of other expressions of belief. Suppose the adept says, for example, "The Holy Ghost, proceeding from the Father and the Son, is of one substance, majesty, and glory, with the Father and the Son, very and eternal God," where this for him is a serious use of language. In his mind, what he says requires saying. But Wittgenstein thinks that something would be out of kilter if, for instance, the adept affirms this, and I reply "well I am not sure about that," treating it like other beliefs as a potential subject for discussion rather than an article of faith. More importantly, the adept is also apt to discourage questions about specifics as missing the point or even blasphemous: God sees everything, but it would be crass to ask about the color of his eyes or shape of his eyebrows. Full inferential power is also lost: that is, the syntactic form of the saying would suggest certain inferences, which are in fact not made. Thus we get the phenomenon of compartmentalization. The Roman Catholic physicist feels no need to consider the implications of his Sunday commitment to transubstantiation when he returns to the laboratory on Monday. Again, the consequence of dissent or doubt here is different from that of dissent or doubt in normal cases: it is generally not a sin to doubt whether particular things exist, but in this domain it can be. In other words, when we look at the *function* of the affirmation in our "stream of life," significant differences from more mundane cases of belief begin to show up.

We might add, as Wittgenstein does not, that the results intended by those who are professionally involved in transmitting the practice are somewhat different from those intended by those involved in teaching other beliefs. In the normal case, teachers want understanding, primarily shown by an independent ability to work through the implications of what is taught for what to expect and how to act. In the religious case, they cannot aim at that and are likely instead to want passivity or surrender. So long as the somewhat unaccountable state of mind issues in the right devotions, the right allegiances, or the right donations, that is enough. If it doesn't, then talk of heresy and sin raises its ugly head.

My final example, perhaps unsurprisingly, is that of evaluation. There is one fundamental thing to say about the proposition that X is good and its various embellished versions (X is as good as a … ; X is a good F; X is good for … ; X is good from such-and-such a point of view). This is that by asserting it, you express approval or endorsement of X (perhaps as a … or for … or as seen by the occupants of some point of view). By putting approval or endorsement into public space, as something to be accepted by others, you also put yourself into a "social-deontic" space as well. You will be expected to back your endorsement with reasons, that is, by pointing out features of X that are themselves good bases for the attitude. Your selection of those features itself becomes a candidate for acceptance or rejection. This is a different issue, of course, for someone may share your approval of X but not approve of your reasons for that approval and substitute his own. Your view of the implications of what you say is assessable in the same way, and "implication" here may include intention, choice, and action.

These thoughts, say expressivists, give us enough to explain the arrival of evaluative pronouncements in our repertoires and to explain what they do both when asserted directly and when occurring in indirect contexts. For since our own endorsements and approvals are among the things with good or bad inputs and good or bad outputs, they get into the domain of things to and from which inference tickets need issuing. Hence the appearance of the evaluative sentence in conditionals should not surprise us.

Truth Again

So is it wrong to talk of believing that if you drink too much you will impair your balance; that the Holy Ghost, proceeding from the Father and the Son, is of one substance, majesty, and glory with the Father and the Son, very and eternal God; that Juliet is the sun; or that health is a good thing? For most purposes, not at all. We can usually get by using "belief" and its associates, notably assertion and truth, as umbrella terms covering the acceptance of whatever is conveyed by indicative sentences. But that should not be thought to deny a finer grained taxonomy, one more adequate to the functional nuances and more adequate as well as the basis for an explanation of what we are doing. This finer grained taxonomy will distinguish beliefs from dispositions to make inferences, from being in the grip of a picture, from accepting or prompting invitations to see one thing in the light of another, or from attitudes such as endorsement and approval. This pluralism comes into its own when on its basis we can understand the behavior of the propositions believed or, if we like to put it this way, understand the role those propositions play in our mental and social economies.

It is natural to present this view, as I have done both here and in previous writings, in largely *contrastive* terms. One the one hand, there is belief, and here, on the other hand, there is, say, the issuing of an inference ticket. But we could maintain the pluralism while blurring, or in many cases disavowing, the contrast. Consider, for instance, everyday middle-sized dry goods. It is evident that believing that there is a chair here is partly constituted by a variety of inferential dispositions: it includes being prepared to suppose that I will not be able to occupy some space without displacing the chair; that had you tried to occupy that space you would have met resistance; that without force being applied there will continue to be a chair there, and so forth. "Belief" begins to look like a portmanteau including assent to inferences, counterfactuals, and other salient consequences or constituents of a world with a chair, there. The full truth would not be captured by a snapshot or single time-slice of reality.

I do not mind seeing such inferences not so much as contrasted with belief as partly constitutive of belief. The parallel in the case of evaluation would, I take it, be something like Hilary's Putnam's conception of Quine's world, which is grey with its blend of the white of analytic and the black of synthetic, as also pink with its blend of the red of evaluation and grey of fact. But just as the analytic chemist faced with a compound proceeds by analyzing out the constituent elements, so too, even if we too are faced with compounds, the path of progress may consist in finding in more detail what they are made of.

Notes

1. See also Blackburn (1984, 83–87).

2. See Brandom (1994, chap. 5).

3. See, for example, Bain (1875, 505, 595).

4. I shall not here rehearse the evidence for this strand in Wittgenstein. See Blackburn (1990) for details.

5. For details, see Ryle (1950).

6. Hume (1757, 451).

References

Bain, A. 1875. *The Emotions and the Will*. 3rd ed. London: Longmans, Green & Company.

Bar-On, D., and Simmons, K. 2007. "The Use of Force against Deflationism: Assertion and Truth." In D. Greimann and G. Siegwart, eds., *Truth and Speech Act: Studies in Philosophy of Language*, 61–89. London: Routledge.

Berkeley, G. 1710. *A Treatise Concerning the Principles of Human Knowledge*. Reprinted in Berkeley 1843, 70–147.

Berkeley, G. 1732. *Alciphron: Or, the Minute Philosopher: In Seven Dialogues Containing an Apology for the Christian Religion, against Those Who Are Called Free-Thinkers*. Reprinted in Berkeley 1843, 297–528.

Berkeley, G. 1843. *The Works of George Berkeley: Including His Letters to Thomas Prior, Dean Gervais, Mr. Pope, etc.: To Which Is Prefixed an Account of His Life*. Vol. 1. London: Thomas Tegg.

Blackburn, S. 1984. *Spreading the Word*. New York: Oxford University Press.

Blackburn, S. 1990. "Wittgenstein's Irrealism." In R. Haller and J. Brandl, eds., *Wittgenstein: Towards a Re-evaluation*, 13–26. Vienna: Verlag Hölder-Adler-Tempsky. Reprinted in S. Blackburn, *Practical Tortoise Raising*, 200–219. Oxford: Oxford University Press, 2010.

Brandom, R. 1994. *Making It Explicit*. Cambridge, MA: Harvard University Press.

Frege, G. 1897. "Logic." In Frege 1979, 126–151.

Frege, G. 1915. "My Basic Logical Insights." In Frege 1979, 251–252.

Frege, G. 1979. *Posthumous Writings*. Edited by H. Hermes, F. Kambartel, and F. Kaulbach. Oxford: Blackwell.

Horwich, P. 1990. *Truth*. Oxford: Blackwell.

Hume, D. 1757. *The Natural History of Religion*. Reprinted in Hume 1779, 401–469.

Hume, D. 1779. *Essays and Treatises on Several Subjects by David Hume*. Vol. 2. Dublin: J. Williams.

Ryle, G. 1950. "'If,' 'So,' and 'Because.'" In M. Black, ed., *Philosophical Analysis*, 302–318. Ithaca, NY: Cornell University Press.

Wittgenstein, L. 1979. *Remarks on Frazer's Golden Bough*. Edited by R. Rhees and translated by A. C. Miles. Atlantic Highlands, NJ: Humanities Press.

Wright, C. 1992. *Truth and Objectivity*. Cambridge, MA: Harvard University Press.

34 Conceptual Engineering and Replacements for Truth

Kevin Scharp

1 Conceptual Engineering

Conceptual engineering is an exciting new movement in analytic philosophy that focuses on how to evaluate our concepts and how to improve them. Philosophers have been doing this sort of thing for a long time, but the recent excitement is over thinking *explicitly* about how best to improve our concepts. Conceptual improvement has itself become a major topic in philosophy.

The idea that Western philosophers should be answering "what is" questions, like "What is knowledge?" and "What is virtue?" goes back to the ancient Greeks. Over 2,000 years later, *analytic* philosophy was founded on the idea that the best way to answer these kinds of questions is by providing conceptual analyses. A conceptual analysis of knowledge would be something like a definition of "knowledge" and similarly for "virtue." In addition to this dominant *descriptive* theme in Western philosophy, there have been those emphasizing the *prescriptive*—calling for changes in how we think or talk. However, it has only been in the last couple of decades that significant numbers of Western philosophers have turned their attention to conceptual engineering as an explicit philosophical methodology that is worthy of study in its own right.

Many conceptual engineers focus on meanings in addition to concepts, and there is considerable disagreement about the distinction between concepts and meanings. Some treat them more or less the same, while others are careful to distinguish them.[1] Usually, the term "conceptual engineering" is taken to cover both the projects focusing on concepts and those focusing on meanings. In what follows, I will take meanings to be semantic values studied by those doing natural language semantics, whereas concepts are discussed at length below. Because conceptual engineers are divided on whether it is acceptable to phrase their philosophical projects in terms of concepts, I intend to use the phrase "representational device" as a general term to cover concepts, meanings, words, or any other way of representing the world that might be affected by one of these proposals from conceptual engineers.

There are two major groups within contemporary philosophy that provide contrast with conceptual engineering: (i) the conservatives, who take proper philosophy to be purely descriptive, and (ii) those philosophers who think we ought to focus on finding better beliefs and theories. Examples of conservative stances are the ones Ludwig Wittgenstein and David Lewis take in the following passages:

> Philosophy may in no way interfere with the actual use of language, it can in the end only describe it. For it cannot give it any foundation either. It leaves everything as it is.[2]

> One comes to philosophy already endowed with a stock of opinions. It is not the business of philosophy either to undermine or to justify these preexisting opinions, to any great extent, but only to try to discover ways of expanding them into an orderly system.[3]

Philosophers have made few explicit statements to the effect that we ought to aim to find better beliefs about philosophical topics, but this view seems to be widespread. For example, it is natural to interpret philosophical debates as comprised of factions each arguing that their theory is right and the others are wrong. For example, epistemological internalists argue that everyone should adopt their beliefs about the conditions on knowledge, while epistemological externalists argue that everyone should adopt *their* beliefs about knowledge. Neither side in this dispute focuses on whether the concept of knowledge is a good concept, whether it has any internal defects, whether it ought to be replaced with one or more concepts that do its jobs better, and so on. It is these latter issues that conceptual engineers emphasize. Since concepts are usually assumed to be the constituents of beliefs and other thoughts, anyone who thinks our concepts need to be changed also thinks that at least some of the beliefs involving those concepts need to be changed as well. So conceptual engineers agree that we need new beliefs, but say that we first need better representational devices out of which better beliefs can be constructed.

In general, we have three major camps—(i) those who see proper philosophy as purely or mostly descriptive, (ii) those who see proper philosophy as primarily engaged in a search for the right beliefs (theories), and (iii) those who see proper philosophy as primarily focused on a search for the right representational devices. These three groups can be thought of as increasingly radical—the first camp (the conservatives) think our concepts and beliefs are mostly in order, the second camp (the moderates) think our concepts are in order, although we need better beliefs (i.e., theories), and the third camp (the conceptual engineers) think we need better concepts and better beliefs. Of course, these categories are intended for heuristic purposes—not all philosophers fit neatly into one camp, and there are varying degrees of overlap between the camps. Still, they are helpful for understanding the thrust of the conceptual engineering movement and what its proponents see as their opposition.

Conceptual engineers think that certain philosophical problems can be addressed by: (i) thinking about how to evaluate our concepts or meanings and (ii) if the evaluation is negative, thinking about how to make improvements. The potential improvements are a diverse lot. They include: no longer using some concept or meaning for some purpose, introducing a new concept or meaning for some purpose, altering an existing concept or meaning, and changing which concept is expressed or meaning is had by a certain word. In some of these cases, we can think of an individual concept or meaning being improved. This kind of change requires thinking of concepts or meanings as things that can keep their identities through changes. If meanings are just intensions or extensions, then this isn't a plausible assumption because intensions are just mathematical functions and extensions are mathematical sets. If one has a more exotic view of meanings, then perhaps they can retain their identities through changes. Since concepts are mental representations, they might be able to persist through changes as well, but on some views they cannot. Whatever one's views on these matters, we can call *revision* any process of changing an existent concept or meaning. In particular, *conceptual revision* is changing a concept and *semantic revision* is changing a meaning.

In contrast to revision, the process of introducing a new concept or meaning to do something we previously tasked with some old concept or meaning is called *replacement*. Again, we can distinguish conceptual replacement from semantic replacement, but it is important to recognize that neither one involves changing an existing meaning or concept. Instead, replacement is a change to our conceptual scheme or meaning repertoire as a whole.

I defend a replacement strategy for the concept of truth. We ought to replace our concept of truth, for certain purposes, with a team of two concepts as a way of addressing the problems caused by the liar and other paradoxes.[4] This might seem like a lot of work, but it turns out that by "we," I mean only those theorists engaged in doing semantics for expressively rich languages (like English) that have the resources to formulate the paradoxes. I am definitely not suggesting that anyone else do anything at all with respect to the concept of truth (unless perhaps they find themselves trying to solve the liar paradox or its relatives).

This replacement project involves multiple parts. There is an *evaluation of our concept of truth* as defective—the concept itself is the source of the paradoxes. There is a *characterization of the defect*—the concept of truth has certain constitutive principles and these are inconsistent. By following these inconsistent constitutive principles, one can reason to a contradiction in the liar paradox. There is also a *suggestion for replacement*—when doing semantics for natural language, one ought to use the two replacement concepts instead of the concept of truth.

In the rest of this chapter, I place this project in a more general context. The next two sections lay out a comprehensive case for the claim that the *concept* of truth is inconsistent and that there is no *property* of being true. I then look at some properties that are similar to what we thought the property of truth should have been like and say a bit about what these properties might be like. Finally, I close with a discussion of various strategies for replacing the concept of truth.

2   Two Traditions on Truth

Over the last decade or so, there has been a fruitful interaction between those working on the nature of truth and those working on the paradoxes that affect truth, like the liar paradox. The project of replacing truth, described above, is an application of conceptual engineering to the literature on the paradoxes affecting the concept of truth. The liar paradox is the most famous of these, and it is that by reflecting on sentences like "This very sentence is not true," it is easy and quick to derive a contradiction: the sentence is both true and not true.[5] There is a school of thought on the liar paradox that diagnoses all the paradoxes as defects in our very concept of truth. We can call this the *inconsistency approach.*

Inconsistency theorists claim that the principles essential to the concept of truth permit a competent reasoner to derive a contradiction (e.g., liar sentences are both true and not true). The inconsistency approach goes back to Alfred Tarski's pioneering work in the 1930s, but it has really taken off since 2002, when Matti Eklund published "On Inconsistent Languages."[6] Since then, much has been done to explore various options and provide details for what were once just suggestions. Because my own work falls in this tradition, I am especially interested in these exploratory endeavors. Much has been written about how concepts can be inconsistent, how inconsistent concepts can be possessed and used, and what sorts of logics and semantics go best with an inconsistency approach. However, there is little on the property of being true from this perspective.

On the other hand, there has been a tremendous amount of work within the "nature of truth" tradition on the *metaphysics of truth.* The central issue in the metaphysics of truth discussion is whether the property of being true is deflationary or substantive. Is being true more like a logical property (e.g., being necessary) or more like a scientific property (e.g., being a mammal)? Is the property of being true cut out to explain anything?[7] Almost all the work on the metaphysics of truth assumes without question that the concept of truth is just fine and that there is a unique property of being true.

Our unifying topic is: *What does the metaphysical landscape look like for the inconsistency theorist?* This particular bridge over the two broad traditions has yet to be investigated in much detail. Is there a property of being true? If so, what is its nature? Might there be more than one equally good candidate for this property? If so, what are these candidates? How exactly can there be a property of being true if the concept of truth is defective? And, most importantly, if there is no such property, then are there any properties that are somewhat similar to what we thought the property of truth would be like? For this last question, think about it in this way. We have lots of beliefs about the nature of the property of being true.[8] If there are no properties that satisfy these beliefs, then there still might be properties that come close enough to count as the property of being true. And even if there are no properties that come close enough, there will no doubt be properties that are somewhat similar in various ways to what we thought the property of truth would have to be like.

In order to have a term for talking about all these properties at once without pre-judging whether there is a unique property of being true, we can use "aletheic property" ("Aletheic" is just an adjective synonymous with "pertaining to truth.") Hence, an *aletheic property* is any property that is similar to what we think the property of truth would have to be like. With this terminology in hand, we can say: we are investigating the class of aletheic properties, and in particular we are investigating the aletheic properties from the point of view of an inconsistency approach.

According to the usage here, *the property of being true* is the property designated by *the English word "true,"* which expresses *the concept of truth*. When something is true, it has the property of being true, whether it is a sentence, story, song, proposition, theory, utterance, prediction, or whatever. Likewise, anything that has the property of being true is true. The property (being true), the word ("true"), and the concept (truth) are not to be confused.[9] Inconsistency theorists focus on the concept of truth and the word "true," while the metaphysics of truth is about the property of being true. We shall question whether there is a property of being true but *not* whether there is a word "true" or whether there is a concept of truth.

3 Truth Platitudes

Roughly, a *platitude* is a claim that seems obviously true, self-evident, or commonsensical. The platitudes for a given concept might be analytic (i.e., true in virtue of their meaning alone), but for our purposes, we do not need such a strong assumption. All the platitudes we care about are intuitively uncontroversial. We can say that all the platitudes we consider would be accepted by the vast majority of competent users of "true" as obvious. Moreover, they all count as *constitutive* of the concept of truth in a certain sense. Namely, if a person rejects one of these principles in a conversation, that is a pro tanto reason to think that the person's word "true" does not express the concept of truth. I have developed this notion of constitutive principles elsewhere, but it will not play a role in what follows.[10]

The point of assembling the platitudes is to find something in the world that does the best job of satisfying the platitudes. If the world cooperates, then the platitudes will be satisfied by a unique thing in the world. However, even if nothing perfectly fits the platitudes, something might fit them relatively well—well enough to say that it is what the term in question is ultimately about. In either of these cases, one might continue the investigation by considering whether the thing that fits the platitudes is fundamental or derivative and, if it is derivative, how it relates to the fundamental level of reality.

What are the platitudes for truth? There are so many to choose from, but we are going to focus on a very specific set of logical platitudes. *Logical platitudes* are those that involve truth and other logical expressions; for example, a conjunction is true if and only if both conjuncts are true. We focus on 12 specific platitudes because they are so central and they were the source of a very thorough investigation. My aim in discussing truth platitudes is to argue that there is no property of being true because no real property even comes close to satisfying most of the central logical platitudes for truth.

Harvey Friedman and Michael Sheard focused on 12 logical platitudes for truth. We call them the *Friedman-Sheard Criteria*:[11]

(T-In) If p, then ⟨p⟩ is true. [E.g., if snow is white, then "snow is white" is true.]

(T-Out) If ⟨p⟩ is true, then p. [E.g., if "snow is white" is true, then snow is white.]

(T-Enter) If it is provable that p, then it is provable that ⟨p⟩ is true. [E.g., any theory that has "snow is white" as a theorem also has "'snow is white' is true" as a theorem.]

(T-Exit) If it is provable that ⟨p⟩ is true, then it is provable that p. [E.g., any theory that has "'snow is white' is true" as a theorem also has "snow is white" as a theorem.]

(¬T-Enter) If ⟨p⟩'s negation is provable, then it is provable that ⟨p⟩ is not true. [E.g., any theory that has "snow is not white" as a theorem also has "'snow is white' is not true" as a theorem.]

(¬T-Exit) If it is provable that ⟨p⟩ is not true, then ⟨p⟩'s negation is provable. [E.g., any theory that has "'snow is white' is not true" as a theorem also has "snow is not white" as a theorem.]

(T-Rep) If ⟨p⟩ is true, then ⟨⟨p⟩ is true⟩ is true. [E.g., if "snow is white" is true, then "'snow is white' is true" is true.]

(T-Del) If ⟨⟨p⟩ is true⟩ is true, then ⟨p⟩ is true. [E.g., if "'snow is white' is true" is true, then "snow is white" is true.]

(T-Comp) Either ⟨p⟩ or ⟨p⟩'s negation is true. [E.g., either "snow is white" is true or "snow is not white" is true.]

(T-Cons) It is not the case that both ⟨p⟩ and ⟨p⟩'s negation are true. [E.g., it is not the case that both "snow is white" is true and "snow is not white" is true.]

(U-Imb) If every instance of a universal generalization is true, then the universal generalization is true. [E.g., if all the instances of "everything is white" are true, then "everything is white" is true.]

(E-Exc) If an existential generalization is true, then some instance of the existential generalization is true. [E.g., if "something is white" is true, then some instance of "something is white" is true.]

Friedman and Sheard worked meticulously to find every inconsistent subset of these principles, and they gave consistency proofs for each consistent subset. That means they found every single paradox hiding in these principles, and they figured out which groupings of principles are paradox-free. It turns out that a grand total of *27* (!) distinct paradoxes are lurking in these 12 logical platitudes for truth.

We have to be careful because Friedman and Sheard make several background assumptions in their reasoning:

(MP) If a conditional is true and its antecedent is true, then its consequent is true. [E.g., if "if snow is white, then something is white" is true and "snow is white" is true, then "something is white" is true.]

(Taut) All tautologies are true. [E.g., "if snow is white, then snow is white" is true.]

(PRE) All axioms of PRE are true, where PRE is a certain mathematical theory that contains specific mathematical equations. [E.g., "$0=0$" is true.]

Friedman and Sheard also assume Peano arithmetic, which is a popular axiomatic theory of arithmetic (e.g., a theory of the natural numbers, addition, multiplication, etc.).

In assuming (PRE) and Peano Arithmetic, Friedman and Sheard are following standard protocol in the literature on axiomatic theories of truth. They use numerals in their object language to refer to symbols, expressions, and sentences of the object language via a famous method called Gödel numbering. The truth predicate of their object language has only numbers in its extension, and these are intended to be interpreted as the Gödel numbers of the true sentences of the object language. Because Friedman and Sheard use Gödel numbers and arithmetic to prove various things about the sentences of their object language, they need some kind of mathematical theory for these proofs; Peano Arithmetic and PRE are the mathematical theories they use.[12]

Because we care about natural language, we are not concerned with any of these details beyond noting that we achieve the same sorts of aims by assuming various things about sentences of English (e.g., that liar sentences exist and that the liar is identical to the sentence "the liar is not true"). Given that (MP), (Taut), and (PRE) are assumed throughout their discussion, it makes sense for us to add them to the list of Friedman-Sheard Criteria. There is no reason to think that they are somehow more sacrosanct than any of the other platitudes. However, giving up (PRE) would not help much with the aletheic paradoxes in natural language because reliance on (PRE) is largely an artifact of the object language in Friedman and Sheard's treatment. When reasoning about natural language paradoxes, we use various assumptions about which words refer to which sentences instead.

Friedman and Sheard showed that there are exactly nine maximal consistent subsets of the Friedman-Sheard Criteria. These subsets are:

A. T-In, T-Enter, ¬T-Exit, T-Del, T-Rep, T-Comp, U-Imb, E-Exc.

B. T-Rep, T-Cons, T-Comp, U-Imb, E-Exc.

C. T-Del, T-Cons, T-Comp, U-Imb, E-Exc.

D. T-Enter, T-Exit, ¬T-Enter, ¬T-Exit, T-Cons, T-Comp, U-Imb, E-Exc.

E. T-Enter, T-Exit, ¬T-Enter, T-Del, T-Cons, U-Imb.

F. T-Enter, T-Exit, ¬T-Exit, T-Del, U-Imb.

G. T-Enter, T-Exit, ¬T-Exit, T-Rep, U-Imb.

H. T-Out, T-Exit, ¬T-Enter, T-Rep, T-Del, T-Cons, U-Imb.

I. T-Exit, ¬T-Exit, T-Rep, T-Del, U-Imb.

Every other subset of these principles that is not listed explicitly here or is not a subset of one of these listed is inconsistent. In figure 34.1, there is a table of the Friedman-Sheard Criteria on the left and the consistent subsets on the top, with "✓" indicating inclusion of the platitude on the left of that row in the subset listed at the top of that column.

Remember that the three additional platitudes that Friedman and Sheard used as background reasoning should be appended to each of the nine consistent subsets of Friedman-Sheard Criteria.

Some observations about the table deserve comment. First, Friedman and Sheard label the maximally consistent subsets in the order in which they prove them consistent, and they begin with the easiest cases first. Other than that there is nothing significant about the order.

Next, Universal Imbibe (U-Imb) is a member of every single consistent subset, which means that it is not involved in any of the paradoxes Friedman and Sheard find; none of the other Friedman-Sheard Criteria is like this. I shall use the term "innocuous" for this feature, and "destructive" for its converse. With this terminology, we can say that (U-Imb) is *the most innocuous* of the Friedman-Sheard Criteria, given their background assumptions.

Note how *destructive* (T-In) and (T-Out) are individually; that is, each one is inconsistent with lots of other subsets of the Friedman-Sheard Criteria. Each one shows up only one time among the consistent subsets of Friedman-Sheard Criteria; (T-In) is in subset A, and (T-Out) is in subset H. None of the other criteria are even close to being that destructive. Remember that (T-In) and (T-Out) are the two conditionals conjoined in the famous biconditional:

(Schema T) ⟨p⟩ is true if and only if p.[13]

So *each direction* of (Schema T), *all by itself*, is ridiculously destructive. No wonder they cause so much trouble together!

Only one subset contains (T-Enter), (T-Exit), (¬T-Enter), and (¬T-Exit) together. If one is looking for a more innocuous version of (Schema T) that is consistent, then this combination is one option.[14] Together these four rules say something like: a theory proves a sentence if and only if the theory proves the truth attribution to that sentence, and a theory proves a negated sentence if and only if the theory proves the negation of the truth attribution to that sentence. Again, these rules cannot be used in hypothetical reasoning—for example, when one argues using a reductio or conditional proof. Even

	A	B	C	D	E	F	G	H	I
(T-In) $P \to T\langle p \rangle$	✔								
(T-Out) $T\langle p \rangle \to P$								✔	
(T-Enter) $\vdash P \to \vdash T\langle p \rangle$	✔			✔	✔	✔	✔		
(T-Exit) $\vdash T\langle p \rangle \to \vdash p$				✔	✔	✔	✔	✔	✔
($\neg$T-Enter) $\vdash \neg p \to \vdash \neg T\langle p \rangle$				✔	✔			✔	
($\neg$T-Exit) $\vdash \neg T\langle p \rangle \to \vdash \neg p$	✔			✔		✔	✔		✔
(T-Comp) $T\langle p \rangle \lor T\langle \neg p \rangle$	✔	✔	✔	✔					
(T-Cons) $\neg (T\langle p \rangle \land T\langle \neg p \rangle)$		✔	✔	✔	✔			✔	
(T-Del) $T\langle T\langle p \rangle \rangle \to T\langle p \rangle$	✔		✔		✔	✔		✔	✔
(T-Rep) $T\langle p \rangle \to T\langle T\langle p \rangle \rangle$	✔	✔					✔	✔	✔
(U-Imb) $(\forall x)T\langle \phi(x) \rangle \to T\langle (\forall x)\phi(x) \rangle$	✔	✔	✔	✔	✔	✔	✔	✔	✔
(E-Exc) $T\langle (\exists x)\phi(x) \rangle \to (\exists x)T\langle \phi(x) \rangle$	✔	✔	✔	✔					

Figure 34.1

Maximal consistent subsets of Friedman-Sheard Criteria.

though this combination of the four derivation rules is considerably more innocuous than (Schema T), they are still *very* destructive together—they occur together only in subset D.

The most important thing to note is how *empty* the table is. Only 54 of the 108 squares are occupied. *Half!* Even if the table were only 75% occupied, that would be really bad—there would be lots of contradictions within those 12 Friedman-Sheard Criteria.

The Friedman-Sheard Criteria seem to give us *nine* aletheic properties—one property for each consistent subset of the Friedman-Sheard Criteria. We can call any property that satisfies the platitudes in subset A *the property of being FSAtrue*. We can call any property that satisfies the platitudes in subset B *the property of being FSBtrue*. And so on.

At last we have something to work with when thinking about which property is the property of being true.[15] And the results are grim. We are assuming for now that there is a property of being FSAtrue and a property of being FSBtrue and so on for each of our nine families. But which one of these is the property of being true? Of course, none of them satisfy all the Friedman-Sheard Criteria. But more damning is that none of them *even come close* to satisfying all the Friedman-Sheard Criteria. The best meet two-thirds of the criteria (subset A and subset D). Maybe you think that is close enough to count as the property of being true, but that view runs into another problem—there are two properties that satisfy 8 out of the 12 criteria. So even if the Friedman-Sheard Criteria were the only truth platitudes, no property comes close to satisfying all of them, and multiple distinct properties seem to do equally good jobs of satisfying some of them.

4   The Nightmare

There are 27 distinct paradoxes among the 12 Friedman-Sheard Criteria, and there are nine maximal consistent subsets of these criteria. The largest two maximal subsets have only eight members, but the average size of the maximal subsets is a mere six members. There are 495 distinct subsets of the Friedman-Sheard Criteria with eight members, but only *two* of these subsets are consistent! Let that sink in for a moment.

Moreover, if we were to weight the Friedman-Sheard Criteria, (T-In) and (T-Out) would easily get the highest weights because of how central they are to the functioning of "true." Recall that these are each direction of the celebrated (Schema T). But each of these central criteria shows up in only one of the maximal subsets.

However, the situation is actually much worse. For complex technical reasons, no aletheic properties satisfy three of these maximal subsets of platitudes—A, D, E. Hence, only Subsets B, C, F, G, H, and I are satisfied by properties at all.

In addition, Subset G and Subset H violate obvious conditions on theories of any kind—that is, that theories should be consistent and not self-refuting.[16] When we eliminate subsets A, D, E, G, and H, we are left with only *four* subsets of Friedman-Sheard critieria, and each of these subsets contains only *five* members. Five! Out of 12 criteria.

And none of these four subsets—B, C, F, and I—contain either of the most important criteria: (T-In) and (T-Out).

The number of ways in which one can derive contradictions from the logical platitudes about truth is simply mind-boggling. This is exactly the nightmare scenario that many theorists writing about the nature of truth pray never happens. All the candidate properties are so far from satisfying even minimal subsets of truth platitudes that there is no decent way to judge which one of the aletheic properties is *the* property of being true. They are so far from what we think of when we think of the concept of truth that it does not make sense to call any of them the property of being true. The result of this exercise is that there is no property of being true.[17]

If we place these results in the literature on the inconsistency approaches to the paradoxes, then the familiar perspective is changed dramatically. The *usual* point at which those of us who are inconsistency theorists about truth conclude our case is that (Schema T) is both central to the concept of truth *and* inconsistent in reasonable logics. Hence, the concept of truth is defective.[18] That is, the typical inconsistency theorist puts *all* the weight on a *single* logical platitude, (Schema T), and a *single* paradox, the version of the liar that shows (Schema T) is inconsistent. I want to be clear that I agree with this conclusion, but this standard argument for the inconsistency of truth, by itself, is not enough. It does not give us anything like a comprehensive picture of the defect in our concept of truth. *Inconsistency theorists have, so far, only seen the tip of the iceberg.* There are 27 distinct paradoxes in just the 12 most basic logical platitudes for truth. The concept of truth is far, far worse off than we have noticed.

5   If There Is No Property of Being True, Then What Is There?

Now that we have some sense of which aletheic properties exist and how they differ from what we intuitively take the property of being true to be like, we can turn to the question of what these aletheic properties are like. In particular, we can think about the question of whether deflationism is right about any of these aletheic properties.

Deflationism about truth has been influential in analytic philosophy for decades now, but there has been recent interest in what deflationists should say about the property of being true. First-generation deflationists tended to deny that there was any property denoted by "true," but the subsequent debate made it clear that most of them meant instead that there is no *substantive* property denoted by "true."[19] Even so, most of the attention was on what form a deflationary theory of truth should take and on what a deflationist should say about the role of truth predicates in our linguistic practice. However, the debate has now shifted to deflationary views on the property of being true, with the result being that earlier characterizations have been seen as inadequate. There is a new sense that the debate over deflationism about truth might well be adjudicated best by evaluating what deflationists say about the property of being true.

Jeremy Wyatt's 2016 paper, "The Many (Yet Few) Faces of Deflationism," catalogs five deflationary theses about the property of being true:

(Transparency) Being true is a metaphysically transparent property,

(Non-explanatory) Being true is a non-explanatory property,

(Unconstituted) Being true is not constituted by any other property,[20]

(Abundant) Being true is an abundant property, and

(Logical) Being true is a logical property.

These need not be accepted by every deflationist, but each has considerable support. A few clarificatory comments on these deflationary theses are in order.

First, being true is a *metaphysically transparent* property if and only if anyone who possesses the concept of truth is in a position to know all the essential facts about the property of being true. In other words, the property of being true does not have some hidden essence to be discovered by some investigation. Simply having the concept of truth is enough to be in a position to know everything important about the property of being true (but not, obviously, which things have that property).

Second, being true is a *non-explanatory* property iff there are no facts that are explained by facts about the property of being true.[21] It is important to stress that "true" might occur in a theory only in its expressive role as a device of generalization despite the fact that the theory in question is genuinely explanatory. The word "true" serves as a device of generalization when it changes a sentence position into a singular term position in a sentence. (Non-explanatory) entails that the word "true" does not (or should not) play any role in any explanatory theory other than this generalizing role.

Third, the property of being true is *not constituted* by any other property iff it is not the case that there is some property, being F, such that all and only things that have the property of being true have the property of being F, *and* anything that has the property of being true has it *because* it has the property of being F. For example, if truth is properly analyzed as correspondence with the facts, then true things have the property of being true *because* they have the property of corresponding with the facts. Deflationists deny that truth is constituted by correspondence or by anything else. We could say that, together, (Non-explanatory) and (Unconstituted) imply that the property of being true doesn't explain anything and nothing explains it.

A property is *abundant* iff it is to some extent unnatural, in Lewis's sense. Naturalness, for Lewis, is objective, and it explains objective similarities among things.[22] Natural properties "cut nature at its joints," in Plato's phrase. Most metaphysicians accept that there are degrees of naturalness, but it is not clear whether deflationists endorsing (Abundant) mean that being true is merely not perfectly natural or they mean that it is highly unnatural.[23]

A property is *logical* iff it is invariant under certain one-one transformations of the world onto itself.[24] There are other ways to define "logical," but Wyatt follows Tarski, who was inspired by Klein, and this invariance tradition is one of the most respected when it comes to defining what is logical. A one-one transformation of the world maps everything in the world to something in the world. For example, the identity transformation maps everything to itself. If the distribution of a property is unaffected by any such transformation, then the property is logical.

What are we to make of these deflationary theses? We already know that there is no property of being true, so deflationist theses about truth in particular are false. Nevertheless, there are aletheic properties, and these are somewhat like what we expected the property of being true to be like. It makes sense to investigate whether any of the aletheic properties count as deflationary in any of these ways. That is our focus in the rest of this section.

Do the aletheic properties satisfy (Transparency)?[25] For example, is the property of being FSAtrue metaphysically transparent? Is anyone who possesses the concept of FSAtruth in a position to know all the essential facts about the property of being FSAtrue? This depends on what one takes to be *essential* to the property of being FSAtrue. If we assume that possessing the concept requires some kind of acceptance of the axioms in subset A of the Friedman-Sheard Criteria, then the answer is clearly *no*.[26] One might understand and accept these axioms without being able to figure out that there is only one model for this subset whose domain is the natural numbers and whose arithmetic vocabulary have their standard interpretations. And such a person might also not be in a position to figure out that everything is in the extension of "true" in this model. The fact that every sentence of the object language has the property of being FSAtrue seems essential to me, but people differ on what is essential even in obvious cases, much less on esoteric subjects like this one. This result is even *necessary* in some sense because it holds in all the relevant models. The same sort of thing can be said for the other aletheic concepts and properties. I doubt that any of them is transparent.

(Non-explanatory) should be treated as highly dubious. The concept of truth shows up in truth-conditional semantic theories, which are among the most widely accepted theories for doing natural language semantics in the science of linguistics.[27] Denying that these theories have explanatory power would be like denying that Newton's theory of mechanics or Maxwell's theory of electrodynamics has explanatory power. It is an open question as to whether any of the aletheic properties (or their related concepts) have this explanatory power, but they might work in the same sorts of semantic theories just as well as we thought truth would.[28]

Although we now know that there is no property of being true, the verdict on the explanatory power of the genuine aletheic properties is complex. Truth-conditional semantic theories come in a dizzying variety, and they are often tailored to the specific linguistic expressions under consideration. Are any of the aletheic properties we canvassed up to the task? In the vast majority of cases, the clauses of a truth-conditional semantic theory could be added consistently to any of the axiomatic theories we have studied. The reason is that these semantic theories are not designed to apply to language fragments that contain truth predicates. Instead, semantic theories for epistemic modals, for example, apply to language fragments that contain epistemic modals, and semantic theories for conditionals apply to language fragments that contain conditionals. The problems in which we are interested crop up only for a truth-conditional semantic theory when they are interpreted as applying to sentences in which truth predicates occur. Hence, in this sense, any of our aletheic properties would be up to the task of satisfying the principles of most truth-conditional semantic theories.

But there is a catch. If we ask ourselves whether any of the aletheic properties studied so far could satisfy *all* the principles of a truth-conditional semantic theory when it is interpreted as applying to a language with a truth predicate and the resources to construct liar sentences, then the answer is *no*. There are plenty of paradoxes hiding among these principles, and so no aletheic property is going to satisfy all of them (for a detailed argument, see Scharp [2013]). Therefore, any of the aletheic properties could serve an explanatory role in almost any truth-conditional semantic theory, but when it comes to a truth-conditional semantic theory *for a truth predicate*, none of them are up to the task. Never fear, because there is a way to fix this problem, which is a topic of the next section.

Are any of the aletheic properties *unconstituted*? This is hard to say because it is not obvious how to individuate properties, and it isn't clear what kind of dependence is invoked with the claim that the property of being true is *constituted* by some other property. If something like a reductive explanation is given as the reading of "constituted," then the answer is probably going to be *no* because uncontroversial reductive explanations (think thermodynamics and statistical mechanics) are rare in philosophy. If the standard for successful reduction is somewhat relaxed, say, to a weak supervenience claim, then perhaps the odds are a bit better, but probably not by much. What kind of explanatorily powerful property is going to explain any one of these aletheic properties? They are each hopelessly gerrymandered—their extensions zigzagging around to avoid the plethora of impossibility results. Hence, it looks like all of the aletheic properties are unconstituted.

One might protest this conclusion: but we already have such properties! Correspondence to the facts or coherence, or superwarrant maybe.[29] My reply: none of the classic analyses of truth are remotely plausible in light of the results in sections 3 and 4. First of all, there is no property of being true. That result is inconsistent with every purported constitution theory for the property of being true. Second, even if one denies this conclusion, it is hard to see that the property of corresponding to the facts could constitute any one of the aletheic properties. Consider the property of being FSFtrue (i.e., satisfying subset F of the Friedman-Sheard Criteria). This property fails to obey (¬T-Enter). Hence, even if one can prove a theorem from subset F of form ¬p, one cannot conclude that ¬Tp. For example, it would be like proving "snow is not white" but failing to prove "'snow is white' is not true." Does the property of corresponding to the facts behave just like this? Highly doubtful. And the same goes for the other familiar analyses of truth.

What about *abundance*? All of the aletheic properties are highly unnatural in one sense. Naturalness is supposed to explain the objective similarities between things. If we intuitively think of all the truths as having some kind of objective similarity, then every aletheic property is going to violate this in myriad ways. And it is hard to believe that anyone thinks that all the FSFtruths or all the FSCtruths have objective similarity. Hence, all the aletheic properties are deflationary in this sense.

Finally, what about the logicality of the aletheic properties? Wyatt argues that no deflationist should accept this thesis because it is easily refuted.[30] His argument is that some transformations will map some true proposition onto a false proposition, so truth is not preserved under all transformations. But Wyatt assumes that propositions are things in a particular world, whereas it is much more common to assume that propositions are sets of possible worlds, and so not members of any particular possible world. If that is right, then propositions are not among the things in a world, and so Wyatt's argument fails.

Certainly, some aletheic properties count as logical: when the predicates that denote them get their own clauses in the semantic theory for languages in which they occur, just like negation and the rest of the logical vocabulary. If that is the case, then the interpretation of the predicate is by definition invariant across all models.[31] So at least some aletheic properties count as logical properties.

We can summarize the results in this section:

(i) No aletheic properties are transparent.

(ii) No aletheic properties are non-explanatory.

(iii) All aletheic properties are unconstituted.

(iv) All aletheic properties are abundant.

(v) At least some aletheic properties are logical (depending on how one understands logical expressions and how one formulates a semantic theory for a language with expressions that denote these properties).

It deserves to be emphasized that deflationist theories of truth have multiple aspects or parts, some of which pertain to the property of being true, some to the concept of truth, some to the word "true," and some to the structure of any acceptable theory of truth. Moreover, there is no property of being true, so any theory, deflationist or not, that entails that there is such a property is false. At present, we are evaluating only *deflationist views of aletheic properties*, not deflationist views as a whole. As such, even those versions of deflationism that come out as acceptable on the present inquiry might be false for some other reason (e.g., because deflationist theories are typically taken to consist of all and only the nonparadoxical instances of (Schema T), but it is difficult or impossible to specify in advance which instances these will be).

6 New Aletheic Concepts

There is a meaningful English word, "true," and there is a concept of truth expressed by that word, but the concept of truth is defective in the sense that its platitudes are inconsistent. Moreover, they are *seriously* inconsistent—the average size of the nine maximally consistent subsets of 12 Friedman-Sheard Criteria is only six, and the average size of the somewhat reasonable ones is only five. As such, there is no property of being true. Still, there are plenty of properties that are somewhat like what we think the property of being true should have been like. These are the *aletheic properties*, and there is one for each consistent subset of platitudes for the concept of truth.

Instead of ending our inquiry in this bleak place, we have decided to see whether we can improve our situation by adding new aletheic *concepts* to our conceptual scheme. Our guide to the world of new aletheic concepts is the realm of aletheic properties. In other words, for each aletheic property, there is a new aletheic concept, distinct from the concept of truth. There are, of course, lots of other concepts that are similar to but distinct from the concept of truth, but the ones based on aletheic properties come with a guarantee: *I am not inconsistent.*[32] Each new aletheic concept has, as its constitutive principles, all the platitudes in the theory it satisfies—for example, the concept of FSFtruth has as its platitudes all the axioms of Subset F of the Friedman-Sheard Criteria, which is satisfied by the property of being FSFtrue.

One significant issue for choosing between new aletheic concepts is whether the aletheic properties they denote are deflationary or substantive, and in what sense. We saw five ways of drawing the deflationary/substantive distinction for the aletheic properties from Wyatt and conducted a preliminary investigation into which aletheic properties have these features. Against the background of a conceptual engineering project, the question becomes: what do we want our replacement concepts to be?[33] What are the considerations for and against various features—explanatory power, expressive power, naturalness? And which ones do we want, given what we are interested in doing with our replacement concepts?

There is good reason to think that no single new aletheic concept is up to the whole job because no single aletheic concept can do everything we expect the concept of truth to do. For example, it is widely accepted that we use "true" to endorse propositions that we cannot assert directly. We can capture this role by saying that a truth predicate functions as a *device of endorsement* (i.e., an attribution of truth to a sentence entails that sentence). The flip side of this role is *a device of rejection*. In order to serve as a device of endorsement, the truth predicate must obey (T-Out), and in order to serve as a device of rejection, the truth predicate must obey (T-In). Of course, we already know that in a classical setting no single concept obeys these two principles; thus, no concept can serve as both a device of endorsement and rejection given classical logic and the expressive resources to construct liar sentences. However, if we replace truth with two concepts, we can split the workload, allowing one to serve as a device of endorsement and the other to serve as a device of rejection.[34]

Another aspect of the same problem—that no single aletheic concept can perform truth's explanatory role—pertains to truth-conditional semantics in both philosophy and linguistics. Recall that *any* of the aletheic properties could serve the explanatory role required by the vast majority of semantic theories in the truth-conditional tradition. The reason is that few of these theories are intended to apply to fragments of natural language that include a truth predicate. However, none of them can be used to formulate a successful truth-conditional semantic theory that applies to the fragments of a natural language containing a truth predicate and minimal expressive resources (e.g., names of sentences). This should be obvious: the aletheic properties differ substantially from what we thought the property of being true should be like, so the aletheic properties deliver nothing like what we think of as truth conditions.

However, if we adopt the concepts I suggest as replacements for truth—ascending truth and descending truth—into our conceptual scheme, then we can formulate a successful semantic theory using them. Ascending truth obeys something like (T-In), and descending truth obeys something like (T-Out). The semantic theory that uses these replacement concepts specifies *ascending* truth conditions and *descending* truth conditions for all the sentences in a fragment of natural language that contains a truth predicate, an ascending truth predicate, and a descending truth predicate. Moreover, for safe sentences—roughly, the nonparadoxical ones—the ascending truth conditions are identical to the descending truth conditions, which are identical to the truth conditions. Thus, *ascending and descending truth-conditional semantics* reduces to *truth-conditional semantics* in all the familiar cases where the distinction between ascending truth and descending truth is negligible. That is similar to the situation in physics—relativistic mechanics reduces to Newtonian mechanics in all the familiar cases where the distinction between relativistic mass and proper mass is negligible. All this with classical logic and no revenge paradoxes; for details, see Scharp (2013).

Whether my suggested replacements for the concept of truth can actually do all the things we think truth should be able to do is still an open question. Truth's expressive role is complex and truth's explanatory role is vast. Here I have focused only on the expressive roles of acceptance, rejection, and generalization and the explanatory role in contemporary natural-language semantics. As such, we have just scratched the surface of the conceptual engineering project for truth.

What we desperately need is a catalogue of all the inconsistencies among all the central logical platitudes for truth listed in section 2 and a catalogue of all the maximal consistent subsets of these criteria. John Burgess has already suggested doing something like this, so we can reiterate his call to arms.[35] We can call it the *aletheic platitudes project* (APP). When complete, APP would be a gold mine for the study of aletheic properties. Moreover, APP would finally allow us to complete the conceptual engineering project of finding the best team of new aletheic concepts to replace our defective concept of truth. I think the community of mathematically minded philosophers and logicians can work together to make APP a real success.

Notes

1. See Scharp (2013) and Cappelen (2018) for those that distinguish them.

2. Wittgenstein (1953, sec. 124).

3. Lewis (1973, 88).

4. See Scharp (2013).

5. See Künne (2003) for an overview of the *nature of truth tradition*, and see Field (2008) for an overview of the *paradox tradition*.

6. Tarski (1933); Eklund (2002). See also Burgess (2006); Scharp (2013).

7. See Beall and Armour-Garb (2005) for a helpful summary and classic papers on deflationism. See Wyatt (2016) for an overview of the discussion about whether the property of being true is deflationary.

8. I am not going to be precise about this matter yet. I use phrases like "beliefs about what truth should be like" and "beliefs about what truth must be like" and "beliefs about what is essential to truth" interchangeably. See section 3 for further discussion of this topic and the nature of the platitudes for truth.

9. See Bar-On and Simmons (2007) and Asay (2013, chap. 1) for good examples of clarity on this.

10. See Scharp (2013); see also Lynch (2009, 13) for a similar view.

11. Friedman and Sheard (1987). See also Friedman and Sheard (1988); Leigh and Rathjen (2010); Leigh (2015). In the remainder, "p" is a sentential variable, which means the instances of the schema have a sentence in place of "p," and the angle brackets are a naming device associated with sentential variables. That is, in the instances of the schema, the name of the sentence replaces the angle bracket expression. Quotation marks are used to form names of the expressions occurring inside them.

12. Friedman and Sheard also use (PRE) in results about the proof-theoretic strength of various theories, but this topic is independent of ours.

13. In each instance of Schema (T), the letter "p" is filled in with a sentence, and "<p>" is filled in with a name of that sentence.

14. See Greenough (2001) for a philosophical motivation for this combination.

15. An alternative approach would investigate properties that satisfy *many but not all* instances of certain truth platitudes, rather than properties that satisfy *all* the truth platitudes in some maximal consistent set of platitudes. For example, Horwich (1998) makes a suggestion like this

for just (Schema T). Evaluating this alternative is beyond the scope of this chapter. See McGee (1992); Horwich (1998); and Schindler (2015) for discussion.

16. See Scharp (2020) for more details.

17. If I *had* to pick, I would follow Jeremy Wyatt who (personal communication) suggested Subset F as the closest to what the property of being true would be like because it alone among the survivors has both directions of some kind of disquotational platitude: (T-Enter) and (T-Exit)—as well as (¬T-Exit). Also, note that some deflationists (e.g., expressivist views like those described in Schroeder [2010]) might welcome the conclusion that there is no property of being true. Still, disquotationalists and minimalists, which make up the overwhelming majority of deflationists, do accept that there is a property of being true, just not a substantive property. See more on this in section 5.

18. Eklund (2002); A. Burgess (2006); and my own presentation in Scharp (2013).

19. See Armour-Garb and Beall (2005) for a survey.

20. Wyatt claims that (Unconstituted) should not count because Horwich rejects it, but I include it because it is prominent in the literature and adds to the discussion.

21. Wyatt formulates this condition in terms of facts about *the essence of* the property of being true. However, I am not clear on what this rules out. Regardless of how one formulates the condition, deflationists have long held that the property of being true can play no role in explaining meaning. As long as this result follows, nothing turns on the differences in formulation for (Non-explanatory).

22. See Lewis (1986); see also Sider (2011).

23. See Asay (2013) and Edwards (2013).

24. This is very rough; see MacFarlane (2000) for a detailed treatment.

25. Thank you to a referee who emphasized this question.

26. And I would say that the antecedent of this conditional is far too demanding for concept possession.

27. See Chierchia and McConnell-Ginet (1990).

28. Many deflationists have defended the immodest view that deflationism *is* incompatible with truth-conditional semantics, but there are attempts to reconcile deflationism with a reasonable modesty toward the sciences. For example, Michael Williams argues that the concept of truth plays only a generalizing role in truth-conditional semantic theories; see Williams (1999). See also A. Burgess (2011) and McGee (2016).

29. See Künne (2003) for detailed commentary on each of these attempts to analyze truth.

30. Wyatt (2016, 16–17).

31. See Scharp (2013), where this sort of formulation is given for ascending truth and descending truth.

32. And an even further guarantee against consistent but omega-inconsistent concepts. As far as I know, no one has considered omega-inconsistent concepts before.

33. See Haslanger (2000) for inspiration here.

34. See Scharp (2013) for a detailed argument.

35. J. Burgess (2011).

References

Armour-Garb, B., and Beall, Jc, eds. 2005. *Deflationary Truth*. New York: Open Court.

Asay, J. 2013. *The Primitivist Theory of Truth*. Cambridge: Cambridge University Press.

Bar-On, D., and Simmons, K. 2007. "The Use of Force against Deflationism." In D. Greimann and G. Siegwart, eds., *Truth and Speech Acts*, 61–89. New York: Routledge.

Beall, Jc. 2009. *Spandrels of Truth*. Oxford: Oxford University Press.

Burgess, A. 2006. "Identifying Fact and Fiction." PhD diss., Princeton University.

Burgess, J. 2011a. "Friedman and the Axiomatization of Kripke's Theory of Truth." In N. Tennant, ed., *Foundational Adventures: Essays in Honor of Harvey M. Friedman*, 125–148. London: Templeton Press/College.

Burgess, A. 2011b. "Mainstream Semantics+Deflationary Truth." *Linguistics and Philosophy* 34: 397–410.

Cappelen, H. 2018. *Fixing Language: Conceptual Engineering and the Limits of Revision*. Oxford: Oxford University Press.

Chierchia, G., and McConnell-Ginet, S. 1990. *Meaning and Grammar: An Introduction to Semantics*. Cambridge, MA: MIT Press.

Edwards, D. 2013. "Truth as a Substantive Property." *Australasian Journal of Philosophy* 91: 271–294.

Eklund, M. 2002. "Inconsistent Languages." *Philosophy and Phenomenological Research* 64: 251–275.

Field, H. 2008. *Saving Truth from Paradox*. Oxford: Oxford University Press.

Friedman, H., and Sheard, M. 1987. "An Axiomatic Approach to Self-referential Truth." *Annals of Pure and Applied Logic* 33: 1–21.

Friedman, H., and Sheard, M. 1988. "The Disjunction and Existence Properties for Axiomatic Systems of Truth." *Annals of Pure and Applied Logic* 40: 1–10.

Greenough, P. 2001. "Free Assumptions and the Liar Paradox." *American Philosophical Quarterly* 38: 115–135.

Haslanger, S. 2000. "Race and Gender: (What) Are They? (What) Do We Want Them to Be?" *Noûs* 34: 31–55.

Horwich, P. 1998. *Truth*. 2nd ed. Oxford: Clarendon Press.

Künne, W. 2003. *Conceptions of Truth*. Oxford: Clarendon Press.

Leigh, G., and Rathjen, M. 2010. "An Ordinal Analysis for Theories of Self-Referential Truth." *Archive for Mathematical Logic* 49: 213–247.

Leigh, G. E. 2015. "Some Weak Theories of Truth." In T. Achourioti, H. Galinon, J. M. Fernández, and K. Fujimoto, eds., *Unifying the Philosophy of Truth*, 281–292. New York: Springer.

Lewis, D. 1973. *Counterfactuals*. Oxford: Blackwell.

Lewis, D. 1986. "New Work for a Theory of Universals." *Australasian Journal of Philosophy* 61: 343–377.

Lynch, M. 2009. *Truth as One and Many*. Oxford: Oxford University Press.

MacFarlane, J. 2000. "What Does It Mean to Say That Logic Is Formal?" PhD diss., University of Pittsburgh.

McGee, V. 1992. "Maximal Consistent Sets of Instances of Tarski's Schema (T)." *Journal of Philosophical Logic* 21: 235–241.

McGee, V. 2016. "Thought, Thoughts, and Deflationism." *Philosophical Studies* 173: 3153–3168.

Priest, G. 2006. *In Contradiction*. 2nd ed. Oxford: Oxford University Press.

Scharp, K. 2013. *Replacing Truth*. Oxford: Oxford University Press.

Scharp, K. 2020. "Conceptual Engineering for Truth: Aletheic Properties and New Aletheic Concepts." *Synthese*. https://doi.org/10.1007/s11229-019-02491-4.

Schindler, T. 2015. "A Disquotational Theory of Truth as Strong as Z_2^-." *Journal of Philosophical Logic* 44: 395–410.

Schroeder, M. 2010. "How to Be an Expressivist about Truth." In C. D. Wright and N. J. L. L. Pedersen, eds., *New Waves in Truth*, 282–298. New York: Palgrave Macmillan.

Sider, T. 2011. *Writing the Book of the World*. Oxford: Oxford University Press.

Tarski, A. 1933. "The Concept of Truth in Formalized Languages." In J. Corcoran, ed., and J. H. Woodger, trans., *Logic, Semantics, Meta-Mathematics*, 152–278. Indianapolis: Hackett, 1983.

Williams, M. 1999. "Meaning and Deflationary Truth." *Journal of Philosophy* 96: 545–564.

Wittgenstein, L. 1953. *Philosophical Investigations*. Translated by G. E. M. Anscombe. Oxford: Basil Blackwell.

Wyatt, J. 2016. "The Many (Yet Few) Faces of Deflationism." *Philosophical Quarterly* 263: 362–382.

35 Keeping "True": A Case Study in Conceptual Ethics

Alexis Burgess

I Introduction

Our conceptual resources change with time. Public or personal, mental or linguistic, representation seems to be a fairly fluid phenomenon. There are good old questions here about analyticity and vagueness. Should we just construe "conceptual change" as a kind of belief revision? How might one draw a principled line between developing a given concept and simply replacing it with a new one? These are issues in the *metaphysics* of representation, if you will. Another nice set of questions—less celebrated, but equally significant, I would suggest—concerns the "ethics" of conceptual choices and changes.[1] Laboring under the legacy of the linguistic turn, we can still be pretty quick to lobby for revision or replacement when a term of interest strikes us as laden with some pernicious proto-theory or plagued by other defects, like imprecision, indeterminacy or incoherence. We are not, of course, quixotically trying to reform folk usage from on high; we are just trying to hone certain concepts for the purposes of mature philosophical theorizing.[2] Or so we might say. The present essay probes our motives for effecting conceptual change. Quite generally, the question is: Why should we revise?

Obviously the answer may well depend, in any given case, on the particular concepts and defects at issue, as well as the nature of the project in whose service revisions are proposed. But certain basic ideals about truth or the aim of inquiry might crop up time and again. "If we are trying to describe reality accurately, then our ideology had better take this shape ..." Those with noses for circularity may therefore be especially interested to see what such arguments look like when the allegedly defective concepts are *themselves* representational. Roughly following Tarski, for example, one could argue that the semantic paradoxes point up some sort of "inconsistency" in our ordinary notions of truth and reference.[3] But of course, these are the very notions we are wont to use in semantics, in describing the features/flaws of our conceptual schemes, and in arguing for specific revisions. So, one might like to know: if we accept some version of the so-called inconsistency theory of truth (for the sake of argument), what exactly should we *do* about it? Does inconsistency theory *justify* the revision/replacement of

our ordinary notion of truth? Thus begins the case study in conceptual ethics conducted in the pages below.[4]

The last decade or so saw a great resurgence of interest in this Tarskian thought, but
a consensus on its "practical" consequences has yet to emerge.[5] I ultimately argue that
something like Matti Eklund's version of the view, around which much of this literature has been organized, actually supports a kind of anti-revisionism or "retentionism"
about truth.[6]

The next two sections of the article are more negative; the final two, more positive. Section II details different kinds of inconsistency theory on the market, and criti-
cally canvasses four quite general arguments for revisionism they might be taken to
support: prudential, normative, metaphysical and semantic. Section III introduces
Eklund's brand of inconsistency theory, with its distinctive commitment to the idea
that the semantic values of inconsistent expressions are whatever "come closest" to
satisfying the principles constitutive of their meanings. Kevin Scharp, a fellow inconsistency theorist (and arch-revisionist), has understandably objected to Eklund's use
of our ordinary semantic concepts in articulating the view that *those very concepts* are
inconsistent. Attempting to adjudicate this dispute, I eventually come to the view that
the arguments on either side are simply inconclusive. The overarching moral of the
first half of the paper is therefore that we have yet to see any decisive reason to revise
or replace our ordinary notion of truth in light of inconsistency theory.

Section IV switches gears and begins to build a positive case for retaining truth, with
materials borrowed from Eklund. This argument makes use of our ordinary semantic
notions, and therefore invites a circularity objection similar to Scharp's. I respond to the
objection by drawing an analogy to a passage from David Lewis's anti-skeptical response
to Putnam's Paradox: "We may indeed have given a correct account of the constraint
that makes determinate reference possible, couched in a language that does indeed have
determinate reference in virtue of the very constraint that it describes!"[7] Finally, section
V reinforces the argument for retaining truth through a series of (somewhat) technical
observations, revealing an unexpected rhetorical use for a certain strand of mathematical
work on the paradoxes.

II Inconsistency and Revisionism

I will continue to elide the distinction between mental and linguistic representation, writing indifferently of our concept of truth and (the meaning of) the English
expression—often using the fudge-word "notion" to cover both. No doubt there are
subtle and significant issues about the relationships between inconsistency theories
at these two levels of representation; but the questions of interest in the present paper
arise equally in both cases, and it is not at all clear that the differences between mental
and linguistic representation should affect their answers. A more pertinent choice point

for our purposes has to do with the allocation of "blame" for the semantic paradoxes. I have been writing thus far as if all inconsistency theorists think our ordinary notion of truth is defective, but in fact Eklund and others are often more neutral, allowing that the logical concepts used to execute a given paradox might be to blame instead (or in addition). To simplify our case study, however, I propose that we continue to focus on inconsistency theories of *truth*, specifically. (As we shall see in the next section, Eklund's version of inconsistency theory can easily be tailored to fit this form.) I accordingly just take classical logic for granted throughout the article, sidelining the vexed question of logical revision in the interest of isolating the (hopefully) more tractable question whether to revise or retain truth in particular.

The inconsistency theory of truth (ITT) is offered in the first instance as part of a theory of the content of our ordinary notion of truth. It can be usefully compared to deflationism about truth, though the two views are logically independent. Like some versions of deflationism, ITT centrally involves the thought that Tarski's equivalence principle is "part and parcel" of our ordinary notion of truth. On the other hand, proponents of ITT need not accept the deflationary idea that this equivalence "exhausts" the concept. Moreover, and more importantly for our purposes, inconsistency theory is addressed in the first instance to the semantic paradoxes (rather than to the expressive functions of truth-talk). I say "addressed" because—unlike Kripke's fixed-point construction, for example[8]—inconsistency theory is not so much an attempt to *solve* the paradoxes, as an effort to explain why they arise (and survive traditional remedies, strengthened, to exact their revenge). Liar-style reasoning is compelling, according to ITT, because each step is sanctioned either by classical logic or by (an instance of) a principle somehow constitutive of the meaning of "true." On the assumption that classical logic is beyond reproach, the inconsistency theorist concludes that our ordinary semantic concepts are "responsible" for the paradoxes.[9] Of course, one does not have to be an inconsistency theorist in order to say that the Liar indicates a problem with the T scheme. What is distinctive of ITT, as I am developing it here, is that it blames the paradoxes on a principle simultaneously claimed to be in some sense *analytic*.

That said, only a few inconsistency theorists think Tarski's scheme is analytic in the traditional "truth in virtue of meaning alone" sense of the term. Most proponents of ITT want to avoid dialetheism and skirt the standard Quinean criticisms of alethic analyticity.[10] Different inconsistency theorists favor different positive conceptions of analyticity or "meaning constitution." One might suggest, for example, that using the truth predicate in *propria persona* brings with it a kind of discursive commitment to accept any instance or application of the T scheme (which the speaker recognizes as such). Or on an epistemic version of the view: our semantic competence with "true" might deliver defeasible, prima facie justification to believe any given instance of the T scheme—which justification could be defeated upon recognition that classical logic can be used to derive contradictions from that instance.

However exactly we flesh out ITT, the kind of inconsistency at issue will inevitably look like a fairly serious conceptual defect. And one might naturally presume that defective concepts ought to be revised, replaced or eliminated.[11] Suppose, for example, that some tribe spoke a language featuring Prior's "tonk." Deploying this expression could easily lead members of the tribe to unjustified and indeed disastrous beliefs. But then again, so could deploying a consistent concept like (let us suppose) *manifest destiny*, or *race*. Perhaps the use of inconsistent concepts is a more reliable recipe for disaster than the use of consistent concepts. On the other hand, we can safely bet that no bridge has ever fallen, no heart has ever been broken, no election has ever been compromised just because someone was led by Curry reasoning to an absurdity. The paradoxes rarely arise in ordinary conversation or deliberation; and if ever they do, we have better sense than to follow the arguments where they lead.

Now, these behavioral data are sometimes invoked to argue against inconsistency theory. With Crispin Wright, one might reasonably wonder how a relatively stable linguistic practice like truth-talk or vague discourse could possibly be governed by inconsistent rules.[12] Eklund calls this kind of consideration the problem of discipline. Various solutions have been proposed in the literature; but the important observation for our purposes is that—whatever the best response happens to be—the problem of discipline is argumentatively upstream from the question of revision pursued in the present paper. This is a simple but crucial dialectical point. Here we are just *assuming* that some version of ITT is right, and therefore that it underwrites replies to this challenge and others. However the inconsistency theorist accommodates the data of discipline, they are data; and one of the things they seem to establish is that ITT does not provide any purely *prudential* reason to revise or replace our ordinary notion of truth.

But perhaps it provides others. Let us briefly consider three additional, increasingly compelling arguments for revisionism in light of inconsistency theory: normative, metaphysical, and semantic, respectively.

Suppose we had a normative conception of meaning constitution, on which using an expression in one's thought or talk establishes some sort of obligation to reason in accordance with its meaning-constitutive principles. One could argue on this basis that deploying our ordinary notion of truth (or any other inconsistent concept) brings with it a commitment to accept contradictions—indeed: to accept anything and everything. Now, there is admittedly something unsavory about being committed to contradictions, but one wonders whether this feeling just amounts to a kind of intellectual vanity. Granted, we should try to honor our obligations to ourselves and others. But it is not at all obvious that this platitude applies to the relevant notion of dialectical/cognitive commitment; or for that matter, even if it does, whether the platitude outweighs the practical costs of effecting conceptual change. Given how complicated consistent surrogates for our ordinary notion of truth tend to be, we might reasonably prefer to

retain the concept as we find it and simply flout (or deny) the hypothesized commitments to follow paradoxical arguments where they lead.[13]

A different motive for revision has to do with the metaphysics of truth—the project
of limning the nature or essence of the property itself. One might grant that representations can be inconsistent, in something like the sense we gestured at above, but quite
reasonably insist that the world itself cannot. (Compare the popular, if not irresistible
claim that language can be vague, but the world is of necessity precise.) Perhaps it is
just metaphysically guaranteed that, for any given property, nothing simultaneously
instantiates and fails to instantiate the property. Call this the worldly consistency
principle, and consider the following instance of it:

(1) The strengthened liar sentence is *not* both true and not-true.

In a classical setting, the T sentence for the strengthened liar can be used to derive
a contradiction from (1). So, the metaphysical argument for revisionism continues,
we had better not accept the T sentence for the strengthened liar. Of course, if inconsistency theory is right, then all instances of the T scheme will be equally meaning-
constitutive. But the metaphysical project of determining what the property of truth is
"really like" will require giving up some of these instances, in accordance with worldly
consistency.

Note that the foregoing argument hinges on inflationary assumptions about truth.
These assumptions might be utterly uncontroversial in other cases of allegedly inconsistent concepts, like *personal identity* or Newtonian *mass*. But deflationists about truth will
be unimpressed by any metaphysical argument for revisionism. Of course, most deflationists are not inconsistency theorists. Brandom, Field, and Horwich all agree that we
need some *solution* to the paradoxes, in keeping with the spirit of the previous paragraph,
even though they would not couch their favorite solutions in excessively metaphysical terms. Sociology aside, however, the pertinent point is that combining deflationism
and ITT arguably diminishes this felt need. Once we have accepted that the paradoxes
arise because some suitably unrestricted version of the T scheme is analytic of our ordinary notion of truth, and dismissed the project of limning the nature of truth itself, it
becomes quite unclear why we should bother to try to solve the paradoxes.[14]

The most interesting arguments for revisionism, it seems to me, have to do with the
role of truth in the theory of meaning. As we are about to see, semantic considerations
are front and center in the debate between Eklund and Scharp. But there is a more
abstract argument in the vicinity worth registering first. The basic idea is that a rigorous
scientific enterprise like formal semantics requires some consistent surrogate for our
ordinary notion of truth. (Note that this motive for revision is not entirely unrelated
to the metaphysical motive, since it is often said that truth-conditional semantics is in
tension with deflationism.) Indeed, one could argue that philosophers and linguists

have already "decided" in favor of revision, using Tarskian truth predicates for Davidsonian semantics and the notion of truth-in-a-model for Montagovian semantics. These are well-defined, unparadoxical notions from applied mathematics, similar in many ways but arguably not identical to our ordinary notion of truth. Since these innovations have undoubtedly paid off, one might conclude that the question of revision is simply moot.

On the other hand, insofar as semantic theory is supposed to enjoy some measure of psychological plausibility, one could argue that it *has* to invoke our ordinary notion of truth. For the folk simply lack the conceptual and syntactic machinery of Tarski's hierarchy, one might think. Contrary to the semantic case for revision, then, the best way to understand truth-in-a-model might be: plain old truth, relative to the model's assignment of semantic values.[15] Moreover, even if we grant for the sake of argument that formal semantics does legitimately use surrogates for our ordinary notion of truth, it is hardly clear that the *consistency* of those surrogates has played an essential role in the progress of formal semantics. Maybe our ordinary notion of truth—or some more sophisticated, but still inconsistent successor concepts—would have served our theoretical purposes just as well.[16] But in order to argue from *inconsistency* to revision, along the lines described above, the consistency of our surrogates has to do some heavy lifting.

Much more could be said on these various scores. And if we abstract away from the particular defect of inconsistency, a host of additional arguments for revising a given concept could be mounted. Here I have simply been concerned to articulate and distinguish a few possible reasons a proponent of ITT might be tempted to revise or replace our ordinary notion of truth, and to offer some preliminary lines of resistance. The exercise is valuable in itself, since inconsistency theorists are rarely so explicit about the pros and cons of revisionism. More instrumentally, though, I offer these brief remarks mainly as warm-up and scene-setting for a close reading of a recent exchange between Eklund and Scharp. The motive to revise implicit in this exchange is intertwined with, yet separable from, those we have canvassed thus far. As I would put it, on Scharp's behalf: there seems to be something illicit about *using* the concept of truth to develop the view that it is inconsistent. Or more generally: it feels like there is something wrong with using defective concepts to characterize their defects. Let us see whether these feelings hold up under scrutiny.

III Eklund's Refrain and Scharp's Complaint

For our purposes, the crucial feature of Eklund's version of inconsistency theory is a claim that I call "Eklund's Refrain." Here is one characteristic formulation: "When the meaning-constitutive principles of a language, or a fragment thereof, are inconsistent, the semantic values of the expressions in the language-fragment are what come closest to making the meaning-constitutive principles true."[17] Eklund tells us that closeness is not merely a matter of how *many* principles a candidate semantic value vindicates.

Some meaning-constitutive principles (MCPs) may be more important than others insofar as they "are more *firmly entrenched*, or more *fundamental*" to the intuitive senses of the expressions in question.[18] This qualification about weighting becomes crucial when one starts to worry about the determinacy of the extension of an inconsistent expression—about whether "too many" candidate semantic values might be tied for closest.[19] But we have other things to worry about; so let us just construe closeness cardinally and simplify Eklund's Refrain to read: when the MCPs of an expression are inconsistent, the semantic value of that expression is what makes as many MCPs as possible come out true.

One might reasonably wonder why the world should be so kind as to sort out our conceptual blunders, providing consistent semantic values for our inconsistent expressions.[20] Eklund is careful not to rest the case for his Refrain on any dubious principle of self-interpretive charity. Instead he tries to justify it by appeal to the Ramsey/Lewis account of implicit definition, in cases where "nothing makes all theoretical claims in which a particular theoretical term occurs true."[21] But of course, proof by authority is only sound when the authorities have proof. Deflationists about truth, reference and other representational notions will take little comfort in this allusion to Lewis's metasemantics, or any other substantive story about word/world relationships. And inflationists wary of reference "magnetism" will want to know whether and how Lewis's account can be derived from more basic, naturalistic assumptions about intentionality. All of which is just to register the obvious point that Eklund's Refrain requires justification, over and above whatever evidence can be marshaled in favor of the bare-bones inconsistency theory from the previous section.[22]

There will be more to say about the metasemantic picture common to Eklund and Lewis later in the paper. For the moment, however, let us turn to look at how it impacts the debate over revisionism about truth. As we noted earlier, Eklund is inclined to lay blame for the sematic paradoxes evenhandedly, over the whole suite of MCPs for each and every concept deployed therein. Having set the logical constants aside, however, we can just focus on the MCPs for "true." In a sense, there is only one pertinent principle: the T scheme. But of course, schematic sentences are not the sorts of things that can be true or false. To avoid gratuitous complications concerning substitutional quantification, let us follow Eklund and take the relevant MCPs to be *instances* of the T scheme. In the case of interest, his Refrain will therefore read: the semantic value of "true" is just whatever makes as many T sentences as possible come out true. In fact, for our purposes, we can even dispense with the notion of semantic value, simplifying the proposal as follows:

(ER) As many T sentences as possible are true.

Now, Eklund has yet to endorse any particular, formal theory of truth as the best (or a best; or even just one reliable) instrument for determining whether a given English T sentence is true or false or neither. He assures us that the paradoxes are resolved in one way or another—or, what he thinks more likely, indeterminately over several different ways—since the constraint of possibility in ER ensures that the *true* MCPs for "true" cannot be used to derive a contradiction. But we are left largely in the dark about *which* MCPs these are. In a slogan (not his own): the paradoxes solve themselves.

So, modulo the qualifications about classical logic and closeness/cardinality, the upshot is just that Eklund endorses a version of ITT that includes ER. Since ER makes use of the notion of truth (in addition to mentioning it), Eklund effectively uses a notion he deems inconsistent to develop the very view that it is inconsistent. And as we have anticipated, one can easily get the feeling that there is something circular, self-undermining, or otherwise illicit about this gambit. Scharp admirably attempts to convert this feeling into an argument, as part of a larger case that his colleagues in inconsistency theory have underestimated the need for conceptual revision. It will be worth quoting him at some length:

> Let L be an inconsistent language and ML be the language in which Eklund's theory is formulated (L and ML might be the same language since, unlike traditional approaches to the liar, Eklund's theory does not require an expressively richer metalanguage). Both L and ML contain truth predicates, but it is the truth predicate of ML that is used by Eklund's theory (call it τ). We know that since τ is a truth predicate, it has certain constitutive principles. We also know that because τ expresses an inconsistent concept, not all of its constitutive principles are true (or valid). Eklund does not tell us which of truth's constitutive principles fail, but we know that some do. The question is: how can τ function properly in Eklund's theory, which is supposed to provide a semantics for L, if some of its constitutive principles fail? Monoaletheism (i.e., no sentence is both true and false) is an essential principle for a non-dialetheic semantics, and I do not see how a semantic theory could assign the right truth conditions to the sentences of L unless the truth predicate it employs obeys the ascending and descending truth rules (i.e., <p> follows from <<p> is true>, and <<p> is true> follows from <p>). However, these are the very principles that give rise to the liar paradox. Thus, some of them have to fail; otherwise, Eklund's theory would be inconsistent. In sum, Eklund's theory casts truth in a crucial explanatory role, and it implies that some of truth's constitutive principles are untrue; however, it seems that if some of truth's constitutive principles fail, then it is unsuited to play this explanatory role (I see this problem as an analog of a revenge paradox for Eklund's theory). At the very least, Eklund owes us an explanation of how truth can function properly in his semantic theory even though it is an inconsistent concept (and consequently, some of its constitutive principles fail).[23]

Let me first address a potential source of confusion. One might wonder why Scharp assumes that τ expresses an inconsistent concept. After all, he implicitly acknowledges at the outset that Eklund is free to distinguish object language and metalanguage.[24] So the inconsistency of the truth predicate in the object language does not immediately entail the inconsistency of the truth predicate in the metalanguage. The reason Scharp takes τ to be inconsistent, I would suggest, is that he is trying to mount an *argument* for revising truth. If his opponent already employs a consistent surrogate for truth (in his semantic metalanguage), the battle is over before it begins. Now, we have much more to say about revisionary reformulations of Eklund's view in section V. But for the time being, let us continue to assume that Eklund wants to use our ordinary, inconsistent notion of truth to articulate his version of ITT.

Scharp's argument goes beyond the abstract worries about the role of truth in semantics that we considered at the end of the previous section. He contends that ER in particular—not ITT in general—somehow jeopardizes truth-conditional semantics. (After all, Scharp is an inconsistency theorist himself.) Although Eklund's Refrain is never explicitly invoked (under this name or any other) in the passage excerpted above, it does make two crucial, tacit appearances. First, it underwrites Scharp's basic contention that ML contains a truth predicate. For ER is the only tenet of Eklund's theory that actually makes use of the notion of truth. Second, ER is implicitly at play in the claim that Eklund is committed to thinking that some of τ's constitutive principles fail. Together, these two observations help clarify Scharp's allusion to revenge paradoxes. He thinks something goes wrong when we apply ER to the notion of truth that figures in ER itself.

With this dialectical structure in view, we might reconstruct Scharp's argument as follows.[25] Mainstream semantics derives its sentential meaning specifications from T sentences. But Eklund thinks that not all T sentences are true. He is therefore faced with an embarrassing choice between untrue and "fragmentary" semantic theories. Take the T sentence for the strengthened liar. If Eklund refrains from accepting this T sentence (on pain of accepting its absurd classical consequences), then he is forced to sit mute on the semantics of the strengthened liar. The problem is not so much that Eklund cannot "assign the right truth conditions" to paradoxical sentences, as that he cannot consistently assign them truth conditions at all. Any semantics for an inconsistent language that incorporates ER will therefore be incomplete, in the pretheoretic sense that it will be silent on some of its avowed subject matter. Or so it seems to Scharp. Hence his request for an explanation of how truth can "function properly" in Eklund's version of ITT. Here are three answers Eklund might offer, in order of decreasing extremity. First, most radically, he could just renounce the truth-conditional semantic tradition, opting instead for some use-theoretic alternative. Merely invoking the notion of truth in ER obviously does not enjoin a wholesale commitment to truth-conditional semantics. Second, Eklund could take up Douglas Patterson's suggestion that the explanatory power of Davidsonian semantics, for example, does not actually hinge on speakers' *knowing* the theory, but merely on their believing or cognizing it, in something like Chomsky's sense.[26] The idea would be to grant that our semantic theory is inconsistent and therefore untrue (taking on the first horn of Scharp's dilemma), but maintain that it nevertheless captures the contents of the mental states that underwrite linguistic competence. Eklund has not, as it happens, taken up Patterson's proposal, but I think it merits further investigation. One issue worth pursuing is whether the proposal can be extended to non-Davidsonian semantic frameworks, like the model-theoretic framework of contemporary linguistic semantics, or the kindred framework of structured propositions dominant in the philosophy of language.

For present purposes, however, I just want to register that reifying meanings as structured propositions provides a third, independent answer to Scharp's challenge. In this semantic framework, the meanings of sentences are set-theoretic complexes built up from the semantic values of their significant parts. Nothing precludes the strengthened liar sentence from being meaningful in this sense. Suppose for the sake of illustration that the semantic values of predicates are ordered pairs of extensions and anti-extensions; that the values of singular terms are their referents; and that the values of logical constants are Boolean operations. The meaning of the strengthened liar sentence would then be a complex comprising (i) the extension and anti-extension of the truth predicate, (ii) the sentence itself, and (iii) the negation functor.

Eklund could therefore discharge Scharp's explanatory burden in a variety of ways. As it happens, however, Eklund is not so much opposed to revisionism as disinterested in the debate we have set out to adjudicate:

> I do not wish to take a stand myself on the issue Scharp focuses on, of whether the concept of truth should be replaced with another concept for theoretical purposes. Even if the inconsistent concept of truth should not be employed it can still meaningfully be asked which sentences are and are not true. (Compare perhaps: even if we ought not to use the word "Boche" when we speak of Germans, we can still meaningfully ask what "Boche" is and is not true of.)[27]

In other words: Eklund set out to execute a descriptive semantic project, and Scharp is harping on higher-order, normative issues in the philosophy of semantics.

Then again, if it does turn out that we ought to eschew our ordinary notion of truth for serious theoretical purposes, presumably one of the many things we should not do is ask "which sentences are and are not true." Scharp can grant that this question is intelligible enough for ordinary, practical purposes; but Eklund poses it in a philosophical context. Moreover, if we were to reformulate Eklund's question using some sanitized semantic notion(s), why should we expect that a similarly sanitized version of his Refrain would provide the right answer to it? There are countless possible surrogates for truth, some of which may vindicate the corresponding versions of ER, and some of which may vitiate them. So it is not at all clear that Eklund can reasonably expect his version of inconsistency theory to be unaffected by the outcome of our revision/retention dispute.[28]

These considerations lead me to suspect that Eklund might have some positive argument for retaining truth in mind. It should be said, however, that he never explicitly mounts anything resembling the argument developed below. More generally, the rest of the paper has much less to do with Scharp and Eklund themselves, as compared with our discussion in the present section. I continue to associate their names with revisionism and retentionism, respectively, in the interest of humanizing our debate; but this is largely just a dramatic liberty on my part, not an imputation.

IV   Retaining Truth: Circularity and Regress

Our main goal in the first half of the paper was to rebut various arguments for revisionism. Our goal in this second half of the paper is to mount a positive argument for the opposite policy: retaining our ordinary notion of truth despite its inconsistency. I want to stress that these are distinct projects. Even if the reader found our replies to the arguments for revisionism unsatisfying, she might still be interested to see whether we can argue for retentionism directly. Indeed, the case for retaining truth might ultimately outweigh the case for replacing it, even if the latter remains compelling when considered in isolation.

The positive argument I have in mind centrally involves Eklund's Refrain. Here is a first, very rough pass. Consider the body of nonsemantic sentences of English—those making no use of "true" or cognate expressions. Now consider the collection of T sentences generated from the members of this body. With Tarski's pioneering work in mind, we should expect that this second set is classically consistent. In which case, ER would seem to guarantee the truth of all its members. In particular, it would entail that "Snow is white" is true iff snow is white. Since snow is in fact white, and we are taking classical logic for granted, the sentence "Snow is white" will be true. Similarly, ER seems to ensure that a sentence like "Snow is black" will end up in the anti-extension of the truth predicate. So the semantic value of the truth predicate should settle any nonsemantic question we care to raise, whether in philosophy, biology or fundamental physics. What about semantic questions? Well, we can just repeat the foregoing line of reasoning with "Kripke" in place of "Tarski," and "grounded" in place of "nonsemantic." So, for example, ER should ensure that:

(2) "'Snow is white' is true" is true iff "Snow is white" is true.

Of course, nothing we have said thus far bears on the truth-value of the truth-teller, or paradoxical sentences featuring the notion of ungroundedness. But we have said enough to suggest that our ordinary notion of truth should suffice for the purposes of workaday linguistic semantics and other theoretical enterprises—not to mention ordinary conversation and deliberation. It is unclear what more we could hope for; or so the argument goes.

There are two immediate problems with this initial case for retaining truth, one more obvious than the other.[29] The obvious problem is that the argument seems circular, essentially using the ordinary notion of truth (in ER) to establish the legitimacy of continuing to use the ordinary notion of truth. The less obvious problem is that the argument slips tacitly, and without justification, from the claim that a given T sentence is true to the disquoted use of that T sentence. ER does not directly deliver the T sentence for "Snow is white." At best it tells us that this T sentence is *true*. But in order to establish that "Snow is white" is in the extension of the truth predicate, we needed to use the T sentence itself. Call this T sentence "TS." We can derive TS from the claim that TS is true, if we avail ourselves of the T sentence for TS. Unfortunately, even if we could argue that ER guarantees the truth of this second T sentence as well, we would need a third T sentence in order to use the second T sentence. Regress threatens. The aim of the present section is to develop a version of the foregoing argument for retaining truth against charges of circularity and regress. As we shall see, the two charges actually interact; but let us begin with regress.

There are at least three different ways one might try to treat our regress. A natural first thought would be to supplement ER with a metasemantic principle to the effect that candidate meanings for a given expression are more "eligible," other things being equal, to the extent that they vindicate more of our intuitive judgments involving that expression. Call this principle Common Sense (CS). CS goes well beyond ER, encompassing claims involving a given expression that are *not* among its MCPs. One might have hoped that this expansion in scope would allow the aspiring retentionist to circumvent the regress above and argue *directly* that the extension of the truth predicate settles a great many of our ordinary truth-attributions—indeed, settles them in our favor. Unfortunately, the relevant article of common sense (involving the notion of truth) is that "Snow is white" is true.[30] CS "vindicates" this claim in the same sense that ER vindicates T sentences: by counting them true. So all we are entitled to conclude is the left hand side of (2). In the absence of T sentences like (2), we cannot infer that the extension of the truth predicate settles any nonsemantic questions.[31]

A second, somewhat more promising strategy for dealing with the regress objection would be to construe the use of truth in ER disquotationally. We do not have to be card-carrying deflationists to suggest that "true" is merely playing an expressive role in Eklund's Refrain, effectively transforming quantification over MCPs into a logically complex content with MCPs as constituents. The idea would be that we can approximate the claim that "as many MCPs as possible are true" using a (possibly infinite) disjunction of (possibly infinite) conjunctions of MCPs—each one generated from a different maximal consistent set of MCPs. In the case of truth, this recipe would yield a disjunction of conjunctions of T sentences, one for each maximal consistent set of them. The regress never arises because ER, thus construed, delivers T sentences "predisquoted." We do not need additional T sentences to perform the disquotation.

Unfortunately, this response to the regress objection only amplifies the circularity problem. For the disjunctive, disquotational paraphrase of ER makes use of our ordinary notion of truth in each and every T sentence occurring within it. (Retreating to CS hardly helps, since it essentially involves semantic notions as well.) We can hone the present circularity worry by comparing it to Scharp's complaint from the previous section. Recall that Scharp was suspicious about using truth to *formulate* the view that truth is an inconsistent concept. Even if his objection to ER falls through—as I argued earlier—there might still be something problematic about using our ordinary notion of truth to *justify* its continued use. Indeed, our argument for retaining truth seems to violate a prima facie reasonable prohibition against "rule circular" justification: do not rely on an instance of a general principle when trying to justify that very principle. Here the principle might be something like: the concept of truth can be legitimately used for arbitrary theoretical purposes. In which case the instance presupposed by our argument for retentionism would be: the concept of truth can be legitimately used to formulate ER. Now, Scharp might not have given us good reason to doubt this instance. But it may still be viciously circular to rely on this instance in an argument for the general principle.

Viciousness is notoriously difficult to define in the abstract. I think we can make some headway adjudicating the present case by considering something David Lewis wrote in response to Putnam's model-theoretic argument for rampant referential indeterminacy. Recall that the crucial maneuver in that article was just to distinguish between (i) genuinely conforming to some constraint and (ii) merely "satisfying" a theory that purports to describe that constraint, in the technical, model-theoretic sense of satisfaction. In the following passage, Lewis anticipates and dismisses one reason for suspicion of the bruited distinction:

> The rules of disputation sometimes give the wrong side a winning strategy. In particular, they favour the sceptic. They favour the ordinary sceptic about empirical knowledge; they favour the logical sceptic, Carroll's tortoise or a present-day doubter of non-contradiction; and they favour the sceptic about determinate reference. It goes as follows. The Challenger asks how determinate reference is possible. The Respondent answers by giving an account of his favorite constraint. The Challenger says: "Unless the words of your answer had determinate reference, you have not answered me unequivocally. So I challenge you now to show how the words of your answer had determinate reference. If you cannot, I can only take you to have proposed an addition to total theory—*that* I can understand, but that is futile." If the Respondent answers just as before, he begs the question and loses. If he answers differently, he does not win, for he gets another challenge just like the one before. And so it goes. The Challenger is playing by the rules, and the Respondent cannot win. And yet the Respondent may indeed have given a correct account of the constraint that makes determinate reference possible, couched in a language that does indeed have determinate reference in virtue of the very constraint that it describes! ... Moral: truth is one thing, winning disputations is another.[32]

The analogous defense of our circular argument for retentionism would be: Eklund may indeed have given a correct account of the constraint (ER) that makes legitimate use of our ordinary notion of truth possible, couched in a language that is legitimate to use in virtue of the very constraint that it describes! Many of us have learned to live with this dogmatic reaction to epistemic and logical skepticism. Following Lewis, we have also gotten used to the idea that Putnam's "just more theory" response to reference-winnowing constraints might be dialectically insurmountable and yet wrong for all that. Perhaps we should just extend our dogmatism to the defense of retention-ism sketched above.

Perhaps; but I think we can do a bit better. Notice that there is an important disanalogy between Eklund vs. Scharp, on the one hand, and Lewis vs. Putnam, on the other. On pain of sitting mute, Lewis cannot help but express his favorite constraint on reference using some language or other; and that is all Putnam needs to remount his permutation argument. Someone in Eklund's position, on the other hand, could in principle attempt to defend the retention of truth without using any inconsistent concepts. In particular, we might try to develop something like the argument sketched at the start of the present section without deploying our ordinary semantic notions. Pursuing this strategy would of course require reformulating ER sans truth. Candidate reformulations will fall into one of two main classes: those that abjure the use of semantic notions altogether; and those that invoke consistent surrogates for our ordinary semantic notions.[33] At first blush, our disjunctive/disquotational paraphrase of ER might have looked like a promising reformulation of type one. As we noted, however, it makes infinite use of our ordinary notion of truth. In fact, I cannot see any way to make good on the first of these two strategies. But the second option is actually quite promising.

This should sound surprising, for the second option looks self-undermining. After all, the retentionist thinks there is no theoretical or practical need to revise our ordinary notion of truth. Admitting that we need to revise truth in order to establish retentionism therefore seems tantamount to abandoning retentionism. Now, there is certainly a nice irony here, but it is hardly a refutation. The retentionist can always just rest content with the qualified conclusion that we need not revise truth for any *further* theoretical or practical purposes—beyond the purpose of reformulating ER to *argue* for this qualified conclusion. Moreover, this special purpose only arises if we are gracious enough to address our imagined objector's dissatisfaction with the Lewisean gambit. We are trying to meet the objector half way and argue for retentionism on his own terms. If he insists that any such argument will inevitably undermine itself, we might reasonably decide to be less gracious. Indeed, should the argument of the next section successfully establish the qualified conclusion above, we might plausibly "kick away the ladder" of replacement concepts used therein, and embrace the simpler argument for retaining truth based on Eklund's original Refrain (or its disjunctive/disquotational partner).

However we finesse this dialectical involution, we have at least identified a research project that bears directly on the revision/retention dispute. The project has three parts, corresponding to the following three questions. First, are there any consistent surrogates for our ordinary notion of truth that vindicate their associated reformulations of

ER? If so, can any of these reformulations plausibly be used to execute a version of the argument for retaining truth sketched at the start of the present section? And, finally, even if both answers are positive, might there still be some reason to prefer a surrogate for truth that either vitiates its associated version of ER or otherwise fails to sustain the sketched argument? Most of the work in the next-and-final section speaks to the first two questions, but I have something to say about the third by way of conclusion. We should also keep an eye on the threat of regress addressed earlier. I said that there were three different ways to try to treat the problem, and thus far we have only met two: Common Sense and disquotation.[34]

V Constructing a Kickable Ladder

Let T* be a consistent "truth-like" predicate: consistent in the syntactic sense that no absurdity can be derived from its meaning-constitutive principles using classical rules of inference; and truth-like in the vague but intuitive sense that its MCPs are suitably similar to those for our ordinary notion of truth (modulo the replacement of T* for T). Formulated using T*, Eklund's Refrain would amount to the claim that, when the MCPs of an expression are inconsistent, the semantic value of that expression is what makes as many MCPs as possible come out T*.[35] Simplifying the case of interest as before, we arrive at:

(ER*) As many T sentences as possible are T*.

Now, in order to respect our dialectical prohibition against circular justification, we had better not allow any sentences making unquoted use of T to be MCPs for T*. Why? Well, since T* is consistent by design, we ought to be able to accept all of its MCPs. But an interlocutor with revisionist sympathies will cry foul if we start the argument for retaining our ordinary notion of truth by invoking a surrogate whose meaning guarantees anything involving unquoted use of that notion. This is a significant handicap. In particular, it prohibits us from saying that any instance of the T* scheme generated from a T sentence is an MCP for T*.[36] For the right-hand side of any such instance will be a T sentence, which makes unquoted use of T.

This restriction means that there will not be any obvious way to derive T sentences from the MCPs for T* together with ER*. But the argument for retentionism sketched at the start of the previous section made crucial use of T sentences, derived in an analogous way. How can we adapt the argument without violating our dialectical prohibition? Impressionistically, our strategy will be to reproduce the argument *within the scope of T*.* As we shall see, the strategy actually improves upon our original argument, rendering the allusion to Kripke's fixed-point construction superfluous, and smoothly blocking the regress objection.[37]

Our original argument essentially purported to show that bivalence holds for a large and interesting class of sentences: those that are grounded in something like Kripke's sense. Hence the claim that the semantic value of the truth predicate settles most any question we might care to raise in the course of ordinary, scientific or philosophical inquiry. Now, in the present setting, we could simply stipulate the analogue of bivalence for T*, without any restriction to grounded sentences. In other words, we could just take it to be an MCP for T* that:

(B) For all S, either S or its negation is T*.

Since the quantifier ranges over arbitrary sentences involving our ordinary notion of truth, B effectively ensures that T* will "take a stand" on any ordinary truth attribution. In and of itself, however, B does not guarantee that the stand will be sensible. In particular, B does not tell us anything about the relationship between the T*-statuses of truth ascriptions and the sentences *to which* they ascribe truth. For all we have said thus far, "Snow is white" and "'Snow is white' is not true" might both be T*.

Enter ER*, to assure us that "many" T sentences will be T*.[38] So long as we can coherently stipulate that *modus ponens* preserves T*—a crucial point, to which we return shortly—we can conclude that the T*-statuses of "many" sentences and the corresponding truth ascriptions will be sensibly coordinated. More prosaically: if the T sentence for a sentence S is T*, and S itself is T* (and the extension of T* is closed under *modus ponens*), then the ascription of truth to S must also be T*. So, the argument continues, whatever virtues accrue to a sentence when it is counted T* will be straightforwardly inherited (in many cases, as per ER*) by the corresponding, ordinary truth ascription. Say for example our revisionary opponent were prepared to grant that some such T* is a reasonable aim of assertion and belief. We could then conclude that many categorical truth ascriptions meet that aim, to the same extent that it is met by the sentences to which truth is ascribed.

Note that the foregoing argument does not hinge on any question-begging derivation of claims involving our ordinary notion of truth; for that notion is always quarantined within quotation marks, safely within the scope of T*. Moreover, precisely *because* we never have to disquote, the regress objection from the previous section simply does not arise. The new argument "uses" T sentences exclusively within the scope of T*. It need not, and cannot (on pain of violating our dialectical strictures), use MCPs for T* to derive those T sentences. But there are, of course, several other concerns that need to be considered.

One pressing question is: how many is "many"? By our argument's lights, the extent to which we can reasonably use our ordinary notion of truth will largely depend on how many T sentences are T*. (Though not on how many instances of the T* scheme are MCPs.) Suppose we were to say, in the hope of maximizing the argument's scope, that *every* T sentence is T*. The suggestion is not obviously incoherent. After all, the inconsistency of the set of T sentences does not entail the inconsistency of the set of ascriptions of T* to T sentences. The ascription of T* to the T sentence for the standard, strengthened liar, for example, cannot be used to derive a contradiction in the absence of the T* sentence for that T sentence.[39] And remember, we said at the outset that no T* sentences generated from sentences involving our ordinary notion of truth will be among the MCPs for T*.

One might naturally object that "possible" in ER was clearly meant to modify "T sentences," and therefore that any surrogate built to the foregoing specifications will inevitably have "too many" T sentences come out T*. After all, the T sentence for the strengthened liar is a logical impossibility. The point is well taken, but it merely serves to clarify a crucial contrast between ER and ER*, and the roles they play in the respective arguments for retaining truth. Eklund's original Refrain was a substantive, controversial principle borrowed from Lewisean metasemantics. And of course the objector is exactly right about its intended interpretation. ER*, on the other hand, can just be taken as an MCP for T*. It is stipulative. So we can read it however we like. In particular, we can read it in such a way that the relevant possibility is the consistency of T* ascriptions (rather than the consistency of the T sentences to which T* is ascribed). If we are revising truth, we can revise ER as well. Indeed, for our argumentative purposes, we might as well forget about ER and just take the claim that every T sentence is T* to be an MCP for T*.

Here is a related, but better, objection. Our argument for retaining truth made crucial use of the assumption that *modus ponens* preserves T*. Following the precedent just set, we could gloss this assumption as yet another MCP for the T* we have been building. But if we are also assuming that every T sentence is T*, Curry reasoning would threaten to establish that *every* sentence of the object language is T*. For Curry's paradox can be run using little more than *modus ponens*.[40] Now, this result would not be paradoxical in itself—absent appropriate T* sentences facilitating the derivation of disquoted absurdities. It would, however, go to show that T* is a rather useless and uninteresting concept. Semantic virtues should be discriminating, not universal. More to the point: if T* applied to everything, it would presumably be "trumped" by other consistent surrogates for truth. Those sympathetic to revisionism, and unimpressed with the appeal to Lewis in the previous section, would naturally request that our argument be mounted using some more plausible replacement concept. So, in order to make good on the present version of the argument, we will need some way of blocking Curry without abandoning *modus ponens* or the T scheme (and using a single conditional to express both).

Fortunately, there is already a cottage industry building formal systems to these specifications.[41] This is the "unexpected rhetorical use" for mathematical work on the paradoxes foreshadowed in section I. Now, contributions to this literature are usually described as nonclassical logics, but we can easily redescribe them as candidate revisions to our ordinary notion of truth. The idea would simply be to interpret T* as what is preserved by the "valid" inferences in some such system. More precisely: given a consequence relation characterizing some suitable deviant logic, we can generate MCPs for T* by transforming "logical truths" into T* ascriptions, and validities into material

conditionals bridging T* ascriptions. (Then we can add as many T* sentences as our dialectical strictures permit.) This gambit has all the virtues of theft over honest toil—and
then some. For our external logic can be classical even if our internal logic is deviant.

We posed three questions at the end of the last section, and we are now in a position to answer two of them. Yes, there are consistent surrogates for our ordinary notion
of truth that vindicate their associated ER*'s.[42] And yes, some such ER* can be used to
execute a version of the argument for retaining truth. Our third question, however, is
still at large. Might there be independent reason to prefer a T* that happens to undermine our argument?

VI Coda

There are countless possible surrogates for truth, many of which will vitiate the corresponding versions of ER*; and we have no uncontroversial metric for deciding between
replacement concepts from these two classes.[43] It is a deep and difficult question how,
more generally, to choose among candidate replacements for a given concept. (Note
the irony here; we might have expected at the outset that a retentionist could avoid this
arduous work.) Now, at a high level of abstraction, the guiding norm has probably got
to be something like: excise the motivating defect with minimal violence to our original concept. But there are many kinds of conceptual violence: mismatches in extension,
intension, conventional implicature, syntactic or mathematical complexity, etc. The
scorecards for two surrogates might well be incommensurable. Indeed, with respect to our
concept of truth, the historical progression of formal theories illustrates that degrees of
complexity and extensional match can be inversely related. Worse still, when the defective concepts at issue are representational (or logical, or otherwise basic to our conceptual
schemes), the content of our "guiding norm" will depend on which surrogate concepts
we use to interpret it.

In the absence of an answer to our third question, let me just conclude by considering how a surrogate put forward by *one* real-life revisionist might bear on our discussion.
Somewhat surprisingly, Scharp himself develops a consistent truth-like predicate that
vindicates its associated version of Eklund's Refrain. In fact, we can actually prove that he
is implicitly committed to the claim that this surrogate applies to every instance of the T
scheme—just like the T* described above. Scharp's version of revisionism is therefore self-
undermining, if everything we said in the previous section was correct. Let me explain.

Scharp begins by observing that every truth-theoretic paradox uses both directions
of the T scheme, which suggests the possibility of segregating the two directions, taking each to be constitutive of the meaning of a different truth-like predicate.[44] What
he calls ascending truth (A) is stipulated to satisfy T-introduction, while descending
truth (D) it taken to satisfy T-elimination. He then provides axiomatic theories of both
A and D, in a classical background logic, on which they turn out to be dual notions:

~Ap iff D~p. Now, in the current dialectical setting, Scharp should not accept the version of ER formulated using D, since that would immediately entrain commitment to sentences involving our ordinary notion of truth. Since A and D duals, he also cannot reject—that is, accept the negation of—the ascription of A to any sentence featuring our ordinary notion of truth. For such a denial would commit him (by D-elimination) to the negation of the sentence at issue, which equally features truth. Since his background logic is classical, excluded middle holds for A ascriptions; so he must accept every ascription of A to sentences featuring the ordinary notion of truth. In particular, Scharp is committed to the ascending truth of every instance of the T scheme.[45]

Of course, this *ad hominem* point does not undermine revisionism *tout court*. It just goes to show that the aspiring revisionist must be careful not to give his retentionist opponent the tools to mount the kind of argument we developed in the previous section. What is more, the revisionist owes us a positive argument for preferring his surrogate over one that sustains ER*. Mathematical work on the paradoxes will be central in settling this debate, even if the retentionist ultimately wins the day. The means of (suppressing) a revolution need not be consistent with its ends. Nor is it clear that our original argument for retaining truth, from section IV, is viciously circular. Lewis may have already given us enough artillery to suppress revisionism. In any event, we have at least shifted the burden of proof. The arguments of sections II and III established that there is no quick route from inconsistency theory to the need for conceptual change— at least in the case of our ordinary notion of truth. Other case studies in conceptual ethics should proceed with similar sensitivity to the idiosyncrasies of their target notions. But in broad strokes, conservative metasemantic principles like those in Eklund and Lewis should tend to support retentionism. At the very least, I hope the present essay has illustrated the significance of various undertheorized practical questions about conceptual activity and suggested some fruitful methods for approaching them.

Notes

This essay grew out of a presentation at the 7th Barcelona Workshop on Paradoxes of Truth and Denotation, where I received very helpful feedback from Bradley Armour-Garb, David Braun, Hartry Field, Michael Glanzberg, Anil Gupta, David Ripley, James Woodbridge, and many others. Thanks as well to an anonymous referee. And especially to Matti Eklund and Kevin Scharp, for invaluable exchanges on these topics spanning several years now.

1. I use "ethics" expansively, for normative and evaluative theorizing about a given topic. Conceptual ethics is accordingly the business of figuring out which concepts we should or ought to use. For a survey of the field, see Burgess and Plunkett, "Conceptual Ethics I & II"; and for related discussion, Chalmers, "Verbal Disputes."

2. "There are, however, philosophers who overdo this line of thought, treating ordinary language as sacrosanct. They exalt ordinary language to the exclusion of one of its own traits: its

disposition to keep on evolving. Scientific neologism is itself just linguistic evolution gone self-conscious, as science is self-conscious common sense." Quine, *Word and Object*, 3.

3. Actually, Tarski claimed that natural languages *tout court* are inconsistent, owing to their "universality." But the relevant dimension of universality has to do with which instances of the T scheme we allow, making it possible to blame the truth-theoretic paradoxes on the concept of truth itself. More on this choice point to follow.

4. Readers who reject the Tarskian idea should at least be able to see parallel issues for (i) other possible defects in our representational concepts, (ii) inconsistency theories of other topics, like vagueness and personal identity, or (iii) revisionism about very basic notions—logical, mereological, set-theoretic—on which we tend to rely in philosophical debate generally, and metasemantic debate about revisionism in particular. I will try to flag some of these additional questions as they arise, but our primary aim is simply to execute the case study carefully.

5. See, for example: Armour-Garb, "Consistent Inconsistency Theories"; Azzouni, "Strengthened Liar"; Bave, "On Using Inconsistent Expressions"; Burgess and Burgess, *Truth*; Eklund, "Inconsistent Languages," "Deep Inconsistency," and Meaning-Constitutivity"; Patterson, "Inconsistency Theories"; Scharp, "Truth and Aletheic Paradox," "Replacing Truth," and *Replacing Truth*. Concerning practical upshot specifically: Patterson argues that Davidsonian semantics does not actually require a coherent truth predicate, whereas Scharp thinks inconsistent concepts should be banned from mature theorizing about any subject matter whatsoever.

6. On its face, this position would seem to have profound implications for the philosophical interpretation of technical work on the paradoxes. For, if retaining truth in the face of inconsistency turned out to be the right policy, consistent formal models for truth-talk would not only be descriptively inadequate—as per inconsistency theory itself—they would be unnecessary even as revisionary proposals. Or so it might seem. Countervailing considerations from Eklund and elsewhere arise in the course of our investigation.

7. Lewis, "Putnam's Paradox," 226.

8. Kripke, "Outline of a Theory of Truth."

9. I do not mean to suggest that these are the only two options open to the truth theorist. Instead of blaming logic or blaming truth, one might target the mechanisms of self-reference and/or quantifier domain restriction (at least for propositional versions of the paradoxes). The point of these preliminary remarks is just to convey a rough sense of ITT's content and motivations. Readers interested in seeing a larger menu of possibilities can consult Feferman, "Toward Useful Type-Free Theories I," or Leitgeb, "What Theories of Truth."

10. Dialetheism is the view that logical contradictions can be true. One notable exception to the trend mentioned above is Azzouni, who not only grants that some contradictions are true, but actually accepts the classical consequence that *everything* expressible in an inconsistent language is true. Just to be clear: dialetheists characteristically reject "explosion," enforcing a distinction between the truth of an isolated contradiction and the "trivializing" inconsistency that Azzouni embraces. Azzouni, "Strengthened Liar."

11. For a defense of eliminativism, and some additional criticism of Eklund, see Bave, "On Using Inconsistent Expressions."

12. Wright, "On the Coherence of Vague Predicates."

13. For a classic discussion of mathematical complexity and cognitive heuristics, see Cherniak, "Computational Complexity." Perhaps the normative argument for revisionism could be bolstered by developing a conception of the relevant "acceptance" attitude on which it is not even *possible* to accept contradictions (or at least, those we recognize as such), and then appealing to the plausible general principle that we should not commit ourselves to do what cannot be done. For present purposes, however, let us just rest content with the observation that the normative motive to revise truth hinges on substantive, controversial assumptions about meaning constitution, practical reason and (on this second telling) *modal* psychology.

14. This response to the metaphysical argument obviously does not speak to inflationary inconsistency theorists. In *Truth*, John Burgess and I argued that deflationism and ITT make particularly good bedfellows; but even we would allow that ITT can be coherently combined with some version of correspondence theory, say. For present purposes, then, let us just rest content with the observation that the metaphysical motive to revise hinges on the outcome of an ongoing and long-standing debate between deflationists and their opponents. Hopefully we can all agree that it is at least worth looking to see whether there are any other, nonmetaphysical arguments for revisionism available. If there are, we might be able to settle the question of revision without resolving the deflationism debates. If there are not, we can at least conclude that the project of the present paper is crucially connected to those debates. Moreover, as I argue in sections IV and V, one can actually make a positive case for *retaining* our ordinary notion of truth, quite independently of any contentious metaphysical assumptions. Of course, this independence guarantees that the case for retentionism does not directly undermine the metaphysical argument for revisionism. But one might still outweigh the other in our final accounting. Burgess and Burgess, *Truth*.

15. Now, the claim that semantics employs our ordinary notion of truth could be construed as evidence against ITT, in parallel to Wright on the data of discipline above. Again, however, if we hypothetically accept inconsistency theory and imagine these challenges answered in one way or another, then the progress of truth-conditional semantics would appear to support retention rather than revision. Patterson argues that the adequacy of Davidsonian semantics does not require its consistency—merely that it be cognized, in something like Chomsky's sense, by users of the language at issue. Patterson, "Inconsistency Theories."

16. To put the point in stark relief: for all we know, set theory itself could turn out to be inconsistent. After all, we can only prove the consistency of ZFC relative to other theories.

17. Eklund, "Deep Inconsistency," 322.

18. Ibid. (emphasis in original).

19. For example, Vann McGee proves that for *every* nontautological instance of the T scheme for the language of Robinson's arithmetic (supplemented with a truth predicate), there is *some* maximal consistent set of T sentences that excludes it. McGee, "Maximal Consistent Sets."

20. And if indeed we are so lucky, one's grip on the sense in which our words are inconsistent might well begin to slip. Bradley Armour-Garb develops a version of this objection: "Even assuming that there need not be a *single*, determinate consistent maximisation, if we grant, with Eklund, the (mere) *presence* of consistent maximalisations [*sic*], we will be forced to conclude that liar-revealing inconsistency is merely an appearance. If this is right, are we not forced to conclude that Eklund does not, after all, hold an inconsistency view?" I do not mean to suggest that this objection ultimately succeeds; just that it might naturally be leveled. Armour-Garb, "Consistent Inconsistency Theories," 643 (emphasis in original).

21. Eklund, "Deep Inconsistency," 322; Lewis, "How to Define Theoretical Terms."

22. One simple alternative would be to concede that *no* instances of the T scheme are true (or, for that matter, false). When the MCPs for some expression are mutually unsatisfiable, perhaps we should just say that they are all unsatisfied—that the expression simply lacks a semantic value. Scharp originally took this line, though he later changed his mind. One might fear that this addendum to inconsistency theory would make a mystery of the familiar and predictable patterns exhibited by our use of the truth predicate. But every version of ITT maintains that the T scheme is somehow built into the meaning of "true." However the building metaphor is unpacked, it will presumably account for our tendency to rely on T equivalences in ordinary reasoning. Scharp, "Truth and Aletheic Paradox."

23. Scharp, "Replacing Truth," 613.

24. What he says explicitly (if parenthetically) is that Eklund's theory does not *require* an expressively richer metalanguage. In other words: it permits the identification of object language and metalanguage. And this in turn seems to imply (albeit only pragmatically) that Eklund's theory also permits distinguishing them. Perhaps Scharp means to cancel this implication with his presumption that τ is inconsistent. But the fact remains that nothing in Eklund precludes distinguishing object language and metalanguage. I labor this interpretive point just to buttress the dialectical hypothesis offered above.

25. I must admit that the proffered reading does not make perfect sense of absolutely everything Scharp says, but I cannot see a single, uniform reading that does substantially better in this regard. At any rate, we can at least construe my "reconstruction" as an argument against Eklund in the general spirit of Scharp's remarks.

26. Patterson, "Inconsistency Theories."

27. Eklund, "Meaning-Constitutivity," 570.

28. Perhaps Eklund could remain neutral on the revision/retention dispute by more closely following the form of his own analogy to slurs, where the target notion is quarantined inside quotation marks. That is to say, maybe Eklund's question should really be read as: What is in the extension of "true"? Unfortunately, if the ordinary notion of truth is unfit for serious theorizing, then so too is the notion of extension. After all, the extension of a term is just the set of everything to which it applies, and the notion of application is just as paradoxical as the notion of truth. Witness the antinomy of heterological terms, or the conceptual connection between

"applies to" and "is true of." Arguments for ITT should therefore carry over without remainder to support inconsistency theories of application and extension. Similarly, one would expect that arguments from inconsistency theory to revisionism should be largely insensitive to the differences between these various semantic notions. So, semantic ascent hardly absolves Eklund of the obligation to answer Scharp.

29. A third, unobvious problem stems from the fact that there may be distinct, denumerable, classically consistent sets of T sentences. See note 19 in this connection. Luckily, the version of the argument above developed in the next section sidesteps this particular peril.

30. That *snow is white* is also an article of common sense, but not one involving the notion of truth.

31. Moreover, Common Sense offers no help with contentious truth-attributions; or for that matter, those drawn from more specialized enterprises like natural science or philosophy. And of course it requires justification over and above whatever we might say in favor of ER.

32. Lewis, "Putnam's Paradox," 225–226.

33. The vagueness of "semantic" gives rise to borderline cases. How should we classify a version of ER that invokes the notion of warranted assertability, for example? Eklund briefly entertains this variation, in the context of a response to Patterson. For present purposes, however, suffice it to say that the second strategy, above, can be fruitfully pursued without complicating our discussion by the introduction of epistemic notions like warrant or justification. Eklund, "Meaning-Constitutivity," 571.

34. A note on generality before we zoom further in. Our case study in the rationale for effecting conceptual change has focused on one particular kind of conceptual defect—inconsistency—and one particular kind of concept—the semantic. If one thought our ordinary semantic concepts exhibited other defects, many of the same questions and answers we have been considering would naturally arise. But some of them will not arise for nonsemantic concepts. As we noted in opening, the sort of circularity we have been exploring is obviously due to the fact that the defective concepts at issue are the very concepts we are wont to use in characterizing conceptual defects. That said, we have been helping ourselves to a lot of concepts besides truth and satisfaction to conduct the case study. Any concepts that are especially central to our thought and talk about the world in general—logical, mereological, set-theoretic—will inevitably crop up in our semantic and metasemantic theorizing in particular. Not only are we adrift on Neurath's raft, there are certain basic tools we will need to make repairs. Now, many of these tools may not be at all defective. And even if some are, whether or not we ought to toss them overboard will depend on the details of the case. Eklund's Refrain is not meant to be a panacea. Even when the defect at issue is inconsistency, we should be wary of hasty generalization. Our argument for retaining truth crucially depended—and will continue to depend, throughout its refinement—on the fact that the principles constitutive of the meaning of "true" include instances of the T scheme in particular.

35. I continue to take liberties with use/mention for ease of writing/reading, disambiguating only when the difference makes a crucial difference.

36. This is perfectly compatible with ER*, since a T sentence can be T* without the T* sentence for that T sentence being an MCP.

37. Nor does it require an "expressively richer" metalanguage. We must, of course, *distinguish* our inconsistent object language (e.g. English) from the consistent metalanguage in which our revisionary semantics is given. But the latter will be expressively poorer, I suppose, for the absence of our ordinary, inconsistent semantic concepts. Informally, we can think of the metalanguage as what results from replacing each of these concepts with a consistent surrogate. We shall be a bit more rigorous in due course.

38. In the absence of B, ER* would not tell us much of anything about our ordinary notion of truth. If "Snow is white" is not T*, the mere fact that its T sentence is T* will not get us to the conclusion that "'Snow is white' is true" is T*. It might be that *no* categorical truth ascription is T*, as far as ER* is concerned. B is basically playing the role that excluded middle (tacitly) played in our original formulation of the argument—just getting sentences in the game, so to speak. Of course, as we have said, B is also analogous to bivalence. But the *role* that B is playing in the present argument is more closely analogous to the role previously played by LEM. After all, bivalence was the conclusion of the old argument, whereas B is just an enabling condition for the new argument.

39. The point does not depend on a hierarchical conception of the relationship between T and T*. Even instances of the T scheme for sentences featuring T* may be T*. Consider for example the claim that the T sentence for the T* strengthened liar (i.e. $\lambda^* = \lambda^*$ is not T*) is itself T*. Even granting the T* sentence for this T sentence, we cannot derive a contradiction; for there is nothing paradoxical about the claim that $T(\lambda^*)$ iff λ^*.

40. One also typically uses substitution, the equivalence of p and p&p, and something like "pseudo" *modus ponens*: if p & (if p then q), then q.

41. For an overview and additional references, see Beall, "Curry's Paradox," sec. 3.

42. Or something near enough: that every T sentence is T*. This does entail that *at least* as many T sentences as possible come out T*. Of course, it sounds strange to say that *more* than as many T sentences as possible come out T*. But once we have noted the scope ambiguity viz. "possible," the strangeness should dissipate. There is nothing odd, paradoxical or otherwise illicit about an artificial predicate applying to inconsistent sentences. Indeed, the ordinary predicate "is a sentence" applies to inconsistent sentences. If there is something wrong with a surrogate for truth, in particular, having this feature, it remains to be seen.

43. Two potential complaints against a surrogate that applies to all T sentences are that it cannot be used to explain (i) the sense in which our ordinary notion of truth is defective, or (ii) why classical logic is in good order. In response, we might rest content with the explanation of (i) couched in terms of our syntactic notion of consistency. And Achilles considerations suggest that there may not be any good account of (ii). But a proper defense of this second thought is well beyond the scope of the present paper.

44. Scharp, "Truth and Aletheic Paradox," "Replacing Truth," and *Replacing Truth*.

45. Actually, this brisk argument demonstrates that Scharp has inconsistent commitments. He takes it to be axiomatic that contradictions are never A, but of course the conjunction of any truth ascription and its negation will be A according to the foregoing reasoning. How might

Scharp resolve this tension? One option (floated in personal communication) would be to revise his axiomatization so that A and D are no longer duals. A simpler, but more radical move would be to purge the ordinary notion of truth from the object language, effectively abandoning hope of providing a semantic theory for inconsistent expressions. A third option would be to accept that some sentences featuring our ordinary notion of truth are D. In fact, according to the theory developed in his recent book, so long as a sentence is "safe"—a technical notion for Scharp, which we can approximate as "unparadoxical"—either it or its negation will be both D and A. But this concession gives the whole game away. Scharp now admits the legitimate use of our ordinary notion of truth, which is precisely the issue we have been grappling with. This in itself is no mark against Scharp. It just goes to show that his present time-slice is not the interlocutor we have been pitting against the retentionist in the pages above. If there is any objection in the vicinity, it would simply be that Scharp has not fully appreciated the impact of his concession on the motivation for his revisionary project.

References

Armour-Garb, B. "Consistent Inconsistency Theories." *Inquiry* 50 (2007): 639–654.

Azzouni, J. "The Strengthened Liar, the Expressive Strength of Natural Languages and Regimentation." *Philosophical Forum* 34 (2003): 329–350.

Bave, A. "On Using Inconsistent Expressions." *Erkenntnis* 77 (2012): 133–148.

Beall, Jc. "Curry's Paradox." *Stanford Encyclopedia of Philosophy*. Spring 2013. http:// plato.stanford .edu/archives/spr2013/entries/curry-paradox/.

Burgess, A., and Burgess, J. *Truth*. Princeton, NJ: Princeton University Press, 2011.

Burgess, A., and Plunkett, D. "Conceptual Ethics I & II." *Philosophy Compass* 8(12) (2013): 1091–1110.

Chalmers, D. "Verbal Disputes." *Philosophical Review* 120 (2011): 515–566.

Cherniak, C. "Computational Complexity and the Universal Acceptance of Logic." *Journal of Philosophy* 81 (1984): 739–758.

Eklund, M. "Deep Inconsistency." *Australasian Journal of Philosophy* 80 (2002): 321–331.

Eklund, M. "Inconsistent Languages." *Philosophy and Phenomenological Research* 64 (2002): 251–275.

Eklund, M. "Meaning-Constitutivity." *Inquiry* 50 (2007): 559–574.

Feferman, S. "Toward Useful Type-Free Theories I." *Journal of Symbolic Logic* 49 (1984): 75–111.

Kripke, S. "Outline of a Theory of Truth." *Journal of Philosophy* 72 (1975): 690–716.

Leitgeb, H. "What Theories of Truth Should Be Like (but Cannot Be)." *Philosophy Compass* 2 (2007): 276–290.

Lewis, D. "How to Define Theoretical Terms." *Journal of Philosophy* 67 (1970): 427–446.

Lewis, D. "Putnam's Paradox." *Australasian Journal of Philosophy* 62 (1984): 221–236.

McGee, V. "Maximal Consistent Sets of Instances of Tarski's Schema (T)." *Journal of Philosophical Logic* 21 (1992): 235–241.

Patterson, D. "Inconsistency Theories of Semantic Paradox." *Philosophy and Phenomenological Research* 79 (2009): 387–422.

Quine, W. V. O. *Word and Object*. Cambridge, MA: MIT Press, 1960.

Scharp, K. "Replacing Truth." *Inquiry* 50 (2007): 606–621.

Scharp, K. *Replacing Truth*. New York: Oxford University Press, 2013.

Scharp, K. "Truth and Aletheic Paradox." PhD diss., University of Pittsburgh, 2005.

Wright, C. "On the Coherence of Vague Predicates." *Synthese* 30 (1975): 325–365.

Contributors

William P. Alston was Professor of Philosophy at the University of Michigan and Syracuse University, among others.

Bradley Armour-Garb is Professor of Philosophy at the University of Albany–SUNY and a Fellow of Wolfson College, University of Oxford.

Jamin Asay is Associate Professor of Philosophy at the University of Hong Kong.

J. L. Austin was the White's Professor of Moral Philosophy at Oxford University and one of the founding figures of ordinary language philosophy.

Dorit Bar-On is Professor of Philosophy at the University of Connecticut.

Jc Beall is the O'Neill Family Chair of Philosophy at the University of Notre Dame.

Simon Blackburn is a Fellow of Trinity College, Cambridge, Distinguished Research Professor at the University of North Carolina at Chapel Hill, and Visiting Professor of Philosophy at New College of the Humanities.

Brand Blanshard was Professor of Philosophy at Swarthmore College and the Sterling Professor of Philosophy at Yale University.

Alexis Burgess is an independent philosopher based in Los Angeles.

Donald Davidson was the Willis S. and Marion Slusser Professor of Philosophy at the University of California, Berkeley, among others.

Michael Dummett was the Wykeham Professor of Logic at Oxford University.

Douglas Edwards is Assistant Professor of Philosophy at Utica College.

Filippo Ferrari is Research Fellow in Philosophy at the University of Padua.

Hartry Field is the Silver Professor of Philosophy and University Professor at New York University.

Dorothy Grover was Professor of Philosophy at the University of Illinois at Chicago.

Christopher Hill is the William Herbert Perry Faunce Professor of Philosophy at Brown University.

Jennifer Hornsby is Professor of Philosophy at Birkbeck, University of London.

Paul Horwich is Professor of Philosophy at New York University.

William James was a founding figure of pragmatism and academic psychology, as well as Professor of Philosophy at Harvard University.

Nathan Kellen is an instructor at Owensboro Community and Technical College.

Junyeol Kim is Visiting Assistant Professor of Philosophy at the University of Connecticut.

Michael P. Lynch is Board of Trustees Distinguished Professor of Philosophy at the University of Connecticut.

Ruth Garrett Millikan is Board of Trustees Distinguished Professor Emerita at the University of Connecticut.

Cheryl Misak is University Professor and Professor of Philosophy at the University of Toronto.

Sebastiano Moruzzi is Associate Professor in the Department of Philosophy and Communication Studies at the University of Bologna.

Nikolaj Jang Lee Linding Pedersen is Professor of Philosophy at Underwood International College, Yonsei University.

Charles Sanders Peirce was the founder of American pragmatism.

Hilary Putnam was the Cogan University Professor Emeritus at Harvard University.

W. V. O. Quine was the Edgar Pierce Professor Emeritus at Harvard University.

Frank Plumpton Ramsey was a Fellow in Mathematics at King's College and an influential figure in philosophy, mathematics, and economics.

Richard Rorty was Professor of Philosophy at Princeton University, the Kenan Professor of the Humanities at the University of Virginia, and Professor of Comparative Literature at Stanford University.

Bertrand Russell was a winner of the Nobel Prize in Literature and one of the founders of the analytic approach to philosophy.

Kevin Scharp is Reader in Philosophy at the University of St. Andrews.

Gila Sher is Professor of Philosophy at the University of California, San Diego.

Keith Simmons is Professor of Philosophy at the University of Connecticut.

P. F. Strawson was the Waynflete Professor of Metaphysical Philosophy at Oxford University.

Alfred Tarski was Professor of Mathematics at the University of California, Berkeley.

Ralph C. S. Walker is Emeritus Fellow of Philosophy at Magdalen College, University of Oxford.

James Woodbridge is Associate Professor of Philosophy at the University of Nevada, Las Vegas.

Crispin Wright is Global Professor of Philosophy at New York University and Professor of Philosophy at the University of Stirling.

Jeremy Wyatt is Lecturer in Philosophy at the University of Waikato.

Index

Note: page numbers followed by *f* and *t* indicate figures and tables.